the battered child

Fourth Edition, Revised and Expanded

Edited by
Ray E. Helfer, M.D., and
Ruth S. Kempe, M.D.

The University of Chicago Press

Chicago and London

The University of Chicago Press, Chicago 60637
The University of Chicago Press, Ltd., London

© 1968, 1974, 1980, 1987 by The University of Chicago
All rights reserved
Published 1968. Fourth Edition 1987
Paperback edition 1988
Printed in the United States of America

04 03 02 01 00 99 98 97 96 95   7 8 9 10 11

Library of Congress Cataloging-in-Publication Data

The battered child.

   Includes bibliographies and index.
   1. Child abuse—United States.   2. Child abuse—
United States—Prevention.   I. Helfer, Ray E.
II. Kempe, Ruth S.   [DNLM: 1. Child Abuse.
WA 320B3346]
HV6626.5.B38   1987   362.7′1   86-19342
ISBN 0-226-32631-4
ISBN 0-226-32632-2 (pbk.)

⊗ The paper used in this publication meets the minimum
requirements of the American National Standard for Information
Sciences—Permanence of Paper for Printed Library Materials,
ANSI Z39.48–1984.

This fourth edition
is dedicated to C. Henry Kempe

This fourth edition
is dedicated to C. Henry Kempe

Contents

vii

Part IV   Prevention   423

Editors' Note

What better individual could we have share with us his final thoughts on the problems of child abuse than C. Henry Kempe? During his life he inspired thousands of professionals and helped millions of families who struggled with the consequences of abuse and neglect. Since he first coined the phrase "the battered child syndrome" twenty-five years ago, over fifty thousand children have been killed by the very parents charged with their safety and at least twenty-five million more have been abused, neglected, or sexually exploited.

Shortly before his death in March 1984, Henry Kempe wrote about his remaining concerns and his hopes for the future of child protection. These remarks are reprinted here as a fitting foreword to the fourth edition of the book he wanted to share with all those committed to helping these unfortunate children and their families.

Foreword

C. Henry Kempe

I thought I might express to you some concern I have had and still have. I am deeply troubled by malpractice lawsuits against social workers dealing in child abuse cases. They are, in part, our own fault. Nobody can predict human behavior, although all of us try to do so; and all of us do make serious mistakes, generally on the side of undue optimism for the child's future in his home.

The most common reasons are clear: Just as our clients become dependent on the good therapist (transference is the word we use), we, as therapists for the family, usually the mother, do not sufficiently analyze the effect that this needy and dependent person has on us. We may be too deeply involved in pity and unrealistic expectations to be objective. A psychologist, caring for a very sick mother, recently said in court, "This woman needs this child to make her better!" Is it the child's job to "cure" his mother? Certainly not. Unless we are able to think of the child's needs as equally important, we will continue to be in this bind. I made it a rule to take the primary child protection worker of any hospitalized child abuse case to the ward and show him the bandaged, burned child or the child in a cast with fractures, or the serious bruising of his face and the X-rays of his skull, which is a tough way to get the child actually "seen"; it often worked well.

I mentioned to one of our lawmakers that while a parent's death caused by his child is called murder and taken very seriously, a child's death caused by his parent usually results in lesser charges. He said, half in jest, "They (parents) are adults like me, and children don't vote; furthermore, they (children) are not very vocal before my committee!"

There are now thousands of interdisciplinary teams all over the world. As opposed to some in Europe, in our country many of these teams are advisory only. It is tragic, but not surprising that there are too few multidisciplinary teams within the agencies responsible for child protection. Social work schools and protective service supervisors hammer away at the notion, even now, that because social workers alone are mandated by law to provide

Remarks prepared by Dr. C. Henry Kempe to be read at The Kempe National Center's Thirteenth Annual Child Abuse and Neglect Symposium, Keystone, Colorado, May 24, 1984. Reprinted from *Child Abuse and Neglect, The International Journal* 9 (1985): 155–57, by permission of Pergamon Publishers.

child protective services, they, and they alone, have to carry the ball. This leads to lawsuits.

If, for purposes of a given troubled family being evaluated, the team including the protective service workers and their supervisor were all included in making the recommendation to the family court as a matter of routine, all of us would carry responsibility together. I might add that I feel that all supervisors should, as a matter of professional pride, carry a caseload of at least two families at all times; only in this way will they know how the front line feels, and they will both earn the front line's respect and maintain their own skills.

Burnout is in large part due to the loneliness of having to be the identified person. Many protective service workers hope that the ball drops after he is no longer in the picture. Chances of this occurring are pretty good. In fact, within a year or so a frontline worker may move up to supervisor or return for more education (a favorite way to handle burnout). This is a grave situation and a terrible waste of human resources and abilities. No business could ever afford the staff turnover that occurs among frontline protective service workers.

A hospital-based advisory team cannot function in a vacuum. The members at times need to go to court, where on occasion they may openly and professionally disagree with a social service department's recommendation. Few teams do that. It did not make me popular when I did this in the early days in Denver, but it surely gets the attention of the department and the courts as they hear other options and opinions presented.

Far better than involuntary legal termination of parental rights is voluntary relinquishment. I know this is often very hard to bring about among abusive parents, but it must be tried first. Within twenty-five years, I expect that it will be much more socially acceptable. I do not worry about the recent Supreme Court ruling that requires that legal termination of parental rights be based on "clear and convincing evidence." We have always felt and acted that way. It is sad that many departments have simply stopped trying because of what they now consider a big new roadblock to termination. It isn't! Does it take the child's death to effectively terminate rights? I think not. We all know that torture, life-threatening neglect, long desertion, and other conditions can be shown to be "clear and convincing evidence." Many of our judges are far ahead of protective services when termination is first mentioned, often very late in a hopeless situation.

The professional's guilt feelings about termination is related to the fact that this demonstrates failure of our own treatment, and no one feels right about giving up. The reality is that we must not tattoo on our chests the motto: I CAN HELP ANYONE! We may be able to help most involved in this situation, but children are on a schedule of development and the biological clock ticks away. By all means, continue to treat the troubled family, but give the children their fair chance for reasonable lives. Their rights are by now, I hope, equal to adults' rights. If not, it is high time to get to that point in a civilized society.

Finally, on a happier note, credit must be given when work is done well, rather than just giving the heat when things go wrong. An "open" system has been tried by some child protective departments and it does work. Community boards can review the good work done as well as the bad, much like the weekly "complication and death" conferences held in all hospitals to learn from our mistakes. One should never try to bury one's mistakes; somebody finds out in time in any case, and it is better to be up-front from the first. All that can be guaranteed is to do the best we can and get the best data base available. That is what a team can do best. *Nobody, but nobody, can do it all alone.*

Currently, at least 25% or more fatal cases of child abuse are in the active file of our protective service departments and others are in the "closed" files. I hate closed files, because they are seen by city councils and county commissioners as examples of "successes." There is pressure to close files. We all know that families need contact for many, many years, even if only by phone from time to time, to find out how things are going. I realize that many clients move off and are gone from our care. But others are just a few blocks away, and we should try to stay in touch. Here a visiting nurse can be of help to find them and help prevent trouble.

We have to work with what we have. Primary prevention is not a luxury many departments enjoy, but secondary prevention is! The close care, often by good visiting nurses and lay friends, for the young mother and the isolated family that is started when the child is born, can provide all with extra services. Giving extra care labels no one as a potential child abuser, as is often said; it just means that we quietly do a bit more for those who may need more. If only one-fourth of these families actually need this help, it is still money well spent. This has been shown in study after study in England, in Holland, in Scandinavia, and in Denver.

Happily, the Kempe National Center's Annual Child Abuse and Neglect Symposium is a lively exchange between all of us. The faculty learns from all the participants. The fact that many of you wish to share your own work with us greatly adds to our own skills. It is a joy to be together for the common goal to do the best job for families we serve. After all, we chose this work, and we all need to recharge our batteries by hearing praise and by knowing that everybody else has problems, many of which are bigger than our own.

Finally, the Kempe Center is always there as a resource for you in your work. I still get some calls, generally after work hours, from worried workers. I make suggestions when I can and reassure when that seems right. Most of the time, I suggest trying to get to know more. The more facts one has, the better the decision making.

Preface to the Fourth Edition

The seven years that have lapsed since the publication of the third edition of *The Battered Child* have seen some significant progress in several, but not all, areas within this complex field. On the positive side, considerable experience has been gained in understanding family assessment, treatment, and the physical and developmental effects of abuse and neglect. A literal explosion of information and interest has occurred in the area of sexual abuse. These gains are depicted in this edition. On the negative side, there have been considerable setbacks in the national commitment to the problems faced by these children and their families. This has resulted in the domino effect of less research, fewer protective service workers, retreat into the isolation of the past by many departments of social services, fewer cases substantiated after a report has been received, and an overall decrease in available services for those caught up in the cycle. Were these adversities not sufficient, we lost a friend and advocate when Henry Kempe died early in 1984. I have appreciated the continued support, encouragement, and help of Ruth Kempe as we have worked together on this edition.

In this atmosphere of gains and losses, the fourth edition presents some new and exciting approaches, information, ideas, and suggestions.

The editors have kept the standard format which has stood the test of time. Part I, Context, establishes the foundations upon which these abnormal rearing practices are laid by presenting the historical, cultural, epidemiological, developmental, and psychological bases for child abuse, neglect, and sexual exploitation. Each of these five chapters are revised or rewritten, except Dr. Steele's classic monograph on the psychodynamic factors. This has not been changed, a tribute to the insight of this remarkable man.

Part II, Assessment, has been expanded significantly. Six of the eleven chapters are new, four have undergone major revision, and two remain unchanged. Every component of the multidisciplinary team assessment is covered in depth. This section provides all disciplines with detailed discussions of their roles in carrying out comprehensive assessments of the members of the family.

Part III, Intervention and Treatment, has been broadened by the addition of three new chapters on treatment, a new chapter on the role of law enforcement, and a greatly expanded discussion of the law and lawyers.

The least amount of progress has occurred in the area of prevention. This is discussed in Part IV in an overview, a revision of the parent-infant relationship chapter, and a new look at our national priorities. Prevention approaches are difficult to undertake until our skills, knowledge, national commitment, and public readiness are in the right combination, as yet not realized on a large scale. The potential is still great.

This edition ends with some final thoughts and eight recommendations for future directions.

The editors are encouraged by the enormous grass roots concern that has emerged during the past seven years. These special people will make a difference.

R.E.H.

Preface to the Third Edition

Nineteen eighty marks the twentieth year since the phrase "the battered child" was coined in the attempt to bring to the attention of the country and the world the plight of abused and neglected children. This goal has clearly been achieved. Programs have been developed, laws passed, insight gained, and yet the problem persists. One and one-half percent of the children in the United States are reported annually to protective service units as victims of suspected abuse and neglect. The important word in the previous sentence is *annually.* Every year another one and one-half percent is added to the toll.

Twelve years have passed since the publication of the first edition of *The Battered Child.* Finding sufficient material to fill that edition was difficult. The opposite is true for the third edition: we found it difficult to limit the contributions.

Considerable discussion was held over the question of the title. Is it appropriate to preserve the title *The Battered Child* when the field has expanded far beyond the severely physically battered child? This book seems to be well entrenched as a primary source of current knowledge on the subject. Rather than change the title and start anew, the editors and publisher decided to maintain the title and expand the concept to include the vast array of manifestations of abuse and neglect of children. The material covered in this third edition is not, therefore, limited to physical abuse.

Part I reviews the background material, an understanding of which is necessary to put the problem of abuse and neglect into perspective. This section has been completely rewritten, and new authors have been added. Basic concepts are discussed, the historical and cross-cultural aspects reviewed, the way stress and crises (including parental alcohol and heroin addiction) affect and influence parent-child interactions is analyzed, and the devastating influences abuse has on the child's development are summarized. Dr. Steele has completely rewritten and updated his chapter on psychodynamics, a piece of work that truly is another classic.

In Part II the issues of assessment are discussed, both for the child and the family. This section contains many practical suggestions for all professionals confronted with the awesome obligation of evaluating a suspected case of child abuse. In addition to discussions of radiological assessment and pathology, six new contributions review interviewing techniques, physical findings, failure to thrive, child neglect, sexual abuse, and abuse by burning.

Part III includes seven chapters, all of which deal with current methods of intervention and treatment, both short- and long-term. Protective services, child therapy, law enforcement, and foster placement—all these difficult subjects are reviewed. Discussions of the community consortium, the roles of the lawyer, and the consequences of abuse round out this section on intervention.

Part IV is included with great hope and expectation—at last, a section on prevention. This has been a long time coming, too long indeed. Preventive programs are beginning to yield results. The future looks bright. Some states are implementing these preventive concepts as part of the routine services to new parents and their babies. We await the long overdue involvement of the school system in this endeavor. Its contribution could be most significant.

In the mid-1970s Vice-President Mondale pioneered federal legislation for the benefit of children. The results have been gratifying. How desperately do our children need a political advocate in the 1980s.

The editors are committed to improving the plight of every abused and neglected child. Our society cannot afford to do anything less. We are indebted to the contributors for their work. Together we are turning the corner and moving toward prevention.

R.E.H.   C.H.K.

Preface to the Second Edition

There are fifteen women in a house of correction just outside one of our larger cities. All of them are there for the same reason: they have been convicted of crimes against children—cruelty or manslaughter. Geraldine is one of these women. Still young, she was reared in a traumatic, motherless atmosphere, ran away from home as a teenager, became pregnant, married an emotionally ill college graduate, and began to have more children after placing her first child up for adoption. Her second child died in its first year of life from the effects of severe physical abuse. The third was born in prison.

The "justice" achieved by the criminal court after sentencing her to from two to four years in prison is exemplified by the sentencing judge's response to a request for early parole. No one knew who killed the baby—the mother, the father, or both—but a confession had been obtained from the mother, so she was tried and convicted; the father, remaining at home and now on welfare, cares for the prison-born child. An attempt was made to have Geraldine released so that a program of social and psychiatric treatment could be initiated. The judge, emotional and removed from the reality of the situation, chided proponents of the therapeutic program and suggested that he would approve early parole only if the mother submitted to sterilization.

Geraldine is still in prison, but in another year she will be freed and reunited with her emotionally disturbed husband and her new baby, with (no doubt) more babies to come; the process of criminal rehabilitation has again been flouted. And in the same institution there are fourteen other women convicted of similar offenses.

In spite of the Geraldines, there is evidence of slow but definite progress. Since *The Battered Child* was published in 1968, understanding has deepened, many more people have become involved, some courts have improved, treatment programs are being developed all over the country, and abuse and neglect are generally recognized at a much earlier point in the child's life. For example, in 1972 almost ten thousand cases of suspected abuse and neglect were reported in New York City alone. This fact is encouraging to many, since the feeling is that the lid is now off and solutions must and will be found.

A second book, *Helping the Battered Child and His Family* (Lippincott, 1972), has been published; the mass media have shown increasing interest and willingness to be helpful; and a few foundations have expressed interest in funding service and research projects. The biggest lack remains the apathy of federal agencies in the field of child welfare. Time is even changing this.

In the second edition of *The Battered Child,* the editors have deleted material no longer applicable, updated other contributions, and added more recent information. A chapter on the New York experience has been added. The section on the reporting laws, pathology, and X-ray has been extensively revised. Certain discussions, covered in greater detail in *Helping the Battered Child and His Family,* have been removed and duplication avoided. The classic chapters by Steele and Pollock and by Davoren, however, have been left untouched.

Adequate demographic data which provide up-to-date evidence of the true incidence of significant child abuse in the United States are not available. Comparing current reporting of child abuse under state laws, we find that many communities are running a rate of 375 reports of suspected abuse per million population per year. No one has tried to compare the reported rate of suspected child abuse to the actual incidence—only a house-to-house, block-to-block intensive study can give us this information. Even so, such a ratio would only be valid in the community studied, because the number of reports compared to the true incidence depends on many variables, including physicians' interest and education, community attitudes, receptivity of the public agencies—especially the child-protective services—and, of course, the police and the juvenile courts.

In the absence of detailed information on incidence, it is still possible to assess the experience of a large metropolitan area such as New York City through the report of the Select Committee on Child Abuse authorized by the New York State Assembly. It provides information which can be used quite readily by other metropolitan areas and is a valuable contribution to the study of a difficult problem in a major center.[1]

The editors are convinced that recognition and treatment of battered children will accelerate during the seventies. The involvement and interest of both professionals and lay workers are encouraging. Geraldine, her husband, and her family see it differently, however. They will continue to withdraw, and their children will run the risk of repeated injury, until many more devoted and informed individuals proliferate into every nook and cranny of our service agencies, police, hospitals, courts, schools, and, above all, our communities.

R.E.H.   C.H.K.

---

[1] The New York City data are confusing in that the state requires the reporting of both abuse and neglect. There is no specific way of separating the New York City report into these two categories of the abnormal rearing problem. In 1972, therefore, the New York City rate for *both* entities was 1,200 per million population.

Preface to the First Edition

Tens of thousands of children were severely battered or killed in the United States in 1967. This book is written about and for these children. Who are they, where do they come from, why were they beaten, and—most important—what can we do to prevent it?

Presented herein is a multidisciplinary approach to the problem. There is both agreement and controversy among the contributors, but each has one goal in mind—to provide the reader with all of the available information which can hopefully be utilized to change the fate of these children and their parents.

We would like to express our sincere appreciation to all of the contributors and their staffs for sharing with us their experiences and research in the field of child abuse. We are also greatly indebted to Miss Katherine Oettinger and Dr. Arthur Lesser and their staff at the Children's Bureau for their continued help and support. Miss Jean Rubin, a former member of the Children's Bureau, was most helpful during a critical period in our study.

Each of our patients has provided us with a unique learning experience. We would like to express our appreciation not only to these children but also to their parents, who for the most part have been cooperative and helpful in making this work possible.

R.E.H.   C.H.K.

PART

Context

Violence has become an integral part of life for a large percentage of the families throughout the world. It erodes the very foundations upon which they are built and creeps into the next generation, unnoticed until its effects have undermined these young families as well.

The authors who have contributed to Part I discuss, in considerable detail, the dynamics of this family violence in our history, our cultures, the development of our children and future parents, and our day-to-day crises.

Some day, maybe, there will exist a well-informed, well-considered, and yet fervent public conviction that the most deadly of all possible sins is the mutilation of a child's spirit; for such mutilation undercuts the life principle of trust, without which every human act, may it feel ever so good and seem ever so right, is prone to perversion by destructive forms of conscientiousness.

ERIK ERIKSON
J. Am. Med. Assoc. (1972)

1 Children in a World of Violence: A History of Child Abuse

Samuel X Radbill

> Moral ideas do not necessarily unfold with the flow of time. They
> have a tendency to cling to what is old and thereby hallowed.
> OWSEI TEMKIN, *Respect for Life*

Violence against children has been manifested in every conceivable manner: physically, emotionally, through neglect, by sexual exploitation, and by child labor. In 1895, the Society for the Prevention of Cruelty to Children summarized many of the ways London children were battered: by boots, crockery, pans, shovels, straps, ropes, thongs, pokers, fire, and boiling water. They described neglected children who were miserable, vermin infested, filthy, shivering, ragged, nigh naked, pale, puny, limp, feeble, faint, dizzy, famished, and dying. Children were put out to beggary by those responsible for their pallor, emaciation, and cough; children were held in the clutches of idle drunkards and vagrants; little girls were victims of sexual abuse. Children were little slaves of injurious employment in circuses, were displayed as monstrosities in traveling shows, and were exploited in diverse other modes (1, p. 875).

Even now abuse takes bizarre forms. One mother recently baffled seven physicians for two years while a young girl suffered repeated severe infections requiring hospitalization in at least seven hospitals. Her mother continually injected the child with fecal bacteria and then withheld the antibiotic treatment ordered, because she had a weird desire to be part of the glamor of the hospital—a sort of Munchausen syndrome by proxy (2, p. 3).

Intentional poisoning of children (3, p. 719) has received more attention since Dr. C. Henry Kempe and his associates reported it as one of many evidences of child abuse. Epidermal bite marks as well as oral lacerations, dental neglect, and injuries to jaws and teeth are also accompaniments of the battered child syndrome (4, p. 75). Cases have been unearthed from medicolegal papers as early as the eighteenth century (5, p. 198).

The Right to Live

In ancient times, when might was right, the infant had no rights until the right to live was ritually bestowed. Until then, the infant was a nonentity and could be disposed of with as

Samuel X Radbill, M.D., is retired from the Graduate School of Medicine, University of Pennsylvania, Philadelphia.

Figure 1.1

Anton Wiertz (1806–65), *Faime, Folie, Crime*. This Flemish realistic artist tended toward the gruesome in some of his work; here he depicted a crazed mother with grinning mien, swinging a knife, and holding in her lap her dead child wrapped in rags, while to her right is seen the left leg of the child stewing in a cauldron over the fire. Brussels Museum.

little compunction as for an aborted fetus. The newborn had to be acknowledged by the father; what the father produced was his to do with as he wished. Proclaiming the child as his own not only assured life and welfare, but also inheritance rights (6, p. 61). Children's rights were always a prerogative of parenthood. As head of the family the father had the ultimate authority; even the mother was subordinate.

With some, the child was not really of this world until she had partaken of some earthly nourishment. A drop of milk or honey or even water could ensure life to the newborn. An eighth-century story tells of a grandmother who, outraged by her daughter-in-law's numerous brood of daughters, ordered the next daughter to be slain. Her servants kidnapped the baby as soon as she was born, before she could be put to the mother's breast, and tried to drown her in a bucket of water. A merciful neighbor, however, rescued the infant and put a little honey in its mouth, which it promptly swallowed. The child was thus protected and its right to live assured. In British New Guinea traditionally an infant was taken to the banks of a stream and its lips moistened with water. The baby was thrown away if the water was not accepted by the baby.

To determine fitness to live, the Germans would plunge the newborn into an icy river. This was done not only to toughen the child, but to test its hardiness. Some North American Indians threw the newborn into a pool of water and saved it only if it rose to the surface and cried. Elsewhere there were other ordeals for survival.

In the Society Islands, a parent could not kill with impunity a child who had survived for a day; in some places the child was safe even after a half hour of survival.

The child was a nonperson in some societies until it received a name. This identified the individual. The Christian child did not get heavenly recognition until he was christened, at which time a name was assigned. The soul of a child that died before baptism was believed not to go to heaven, but to be condemned to everlasting limbo. The body of such a child could not be buried in hallowed ground, but instead was disposed of in the same manner as that of a dead dog or cat (7, p. 39).

Illegitimate children have long been outlawed and especially liable to abuse. Born in sin, they were without benefit of clergy or inheritance. As William Blake lamented in the eighteenth century, "the youthful Harlot's curse / Blasts the new-born Infant's tear." Earlier, in the Middle Ages, only the children of priests and bishops were permitted to marry, for money could buy a papal dispensation of legitimacy (8, p. 27). Illegitimate children were unwelcome, ostracized, often abandoned or killed by their despondent mothers. If they survived they were subject to degradation and abuse. Lack of family unity was a serious impediment to normal development. The church offered protective institutions that hid the mothers' identity, hoping to encourage compromised mothers to spare their infants. A study in 1917 indicated that of the four to five thousand illegitimate children born in Chicago every year one thousand disappeared completely. In 1915, Norway adopted a law which conferred rights upon such children including the right to a father's name, to parental support, and to inheritance equal with that of siblings born in wedlock (9, pp. 172–73). Only within recent years has some alleviation from the stigma of illegitimacy been granted in the United States.

Exposure and Infanticide

Exposure and infanticide have been universal forms of lethal child abuse throughout the years. There was usually the hope that exposed children would be saved, but almost invariably exposure resulted in death. Infanticide was not only condoned, sometimes it was compulsory. A weak, premature, or deformed infant was likely to be strangled when the mother was not looking. Diodorus Siculus, Greek historian during the late first century B.C., said the Ceylonese put to death the weak or infirm children and also discarded those that had no courage or could not endure hardship. Egyptians, on the other hand, sentenced parents who killed their child to hug the corpse continuously for seventy-two hours, thinking that it was not fit for those who gave life to the child to die, but that they should be punished in such a way as to create repentance and deter them from further such attempts (10, pp. 40, 83).

The Greeks did not want any cripples to grow up, believing their defects would pass to their offspring, and so allowed only healthy newborns to be kept alive. Plato accepted this, and Aristotle recommended a law prohibiting crippled children to be reared. Even Soranus, a second century Greek physician, instructed midwives to examine each child at birth and get rid of any not fit to be raised. The image of the newborn was hardly better than that of a pet animal. This freedom for parents to kill anomalous births persisted among some European country folk into the nineteenth century (11, p. 173). Girls were especially at risk. They never had rights equal with their brothers and were far more likely to be killed, sold, or exposed. Under the influence of Christian missionaries, in 1654 the Chinese interdicted drowning little girls (12, p. 56). But legal punishment throughout the centuries never stamped out infanticide, exposure, or the sale of children.

The mentally retarded child also had a hard lot. The deranged instilled the fear of the devil into people. Idiots were changelings whose souls were possessed by Satan, and many a simpleton had the devil knocked out of him.

Castration, to produce eunuchs for harems in the Orient and to preserve effeminate bodies and retain boys' good singing voices in the West, was a form of mutilation which was outlawed in the seventeenth century by China. Although the early Roman emperors frowned at gelding boys, this abuse persisted in the West until Pope Clement XIV (1769–74) prohibited castrates from singing in churches.

The old English coroner's records, as far back as 1194, and the Bills of Mortality, as early as 1519, provide inklings of various manners in which children were abused. Among 9,535 burials in London, the Bill of 1623 lists "seven overlaid and starved at nurse," obviously infants. The ages of those burned, scalded, or drowned were not given. In the records from 1788 to 1829, babies were listed as drowned in pits full of water, cisterns, wells, ponds, and even pans of water. These are choice contrivances for disposing of unwanted kittens, puppies, and unwanted babies. Privies were another favored disposal place (13, p. 7).

Child Labor

Child labor, under the apprenticeship system, in workhouses, in orphanages, as well as in industry, also brutalized children, leading to sporadic outbursts of anguish (14, 1:122). When the English evangelist George Whitefield established the Bethesda Orphan House in Georgia in 1738, he preached: "Lord, do Thou teach and excite them to labor." But the cruel punishment inflicted on the children there raised such an outcry on the part of the community that such strict discipline had to be ameliorated (15). Johann Peter Frank (1745–1821), the German physician who founded the science of public health, was shocked by the agrarian child labor used in Continental viticulture, which resulted in youngsters becoming deformed and misshapen. He advocated laws in the eighteenth century to provide age limits for specific kinds of work and to prohibit forcing weak children to do the heavy work of artisans and half-grown boys to do the labor of men. But such laws had to wait another century before they were to be enacted. In America Horatio Alger spoke up for the Italian "Ragazzos," children brought here in the late nineteenth and early twentieth centuries and indentured into factories.

The guilds of the Middle Ages regulated the work of children, not out of compassion, but to prevent competitive cheap labor. The statute of artificers in 1562 gave the government regulating control over apprentices, binding children to their masters by indenture for seven years, a system of enslavement that endured until 1815. In the seventeenth century six-year-old children toiled in the clothing industries; and the great demand for chil-

Figure 1.2.

Child being beaten in an English woolen mill around 1850. Courtesy of Bettman Archive.

dren in the factories after the industrial revolution burst forth, early in the eighteenth century, led to further excruciating exploitation. "Pity those little creatures," Josiah Quincy wrote in 1801, when child labor was viewed as beneficial not only to society but to the child as well. He found children from four to ten years old employed in cotton mills "with a dull dejection" in their countenances. They were battered both physically and psychologically (14, 1:174). A ghastly machine, jocularly called "Sherrington's Daughter," was used to punish idle children. It bent their heads down between their knees so that blood flowed from nose and ears.

There was no protection in the mills for children when they were mercilessly beaten and overworked, until the child labor laws initiated reforms during the nineteenth century. Children were transported to the American colonies in droves to be apprenticed until the age of twenty-four. Pauper children were sold by the almshouses into apprenticeship and treated atrociously. Colonial newspapers constantly advertised for runaway children. As late as 1866 a Massachusetts legislative report hailed child labor as a boon to society. Writing on child labor laws in 1891, Abraham Jacobi, the father of American pediatrics, cried out against the employment of mere babies in the mines and as chimney sweeps. He deplored inexpensive child labor supplied to greedy industry by the poorhouses. The working child was even more abused in rural areas (16, p. 97).

Chimney sweeps were a particularly sad lot. William Blake called them England's disgrace, "little black things among the snow crying 'weep!' 'weep!' in notes of woe." These waifs were purposefully kept small and thin so that they could clamber up narrow, soot-

Figure 1.3.
William Hogarth (1697–1764), *Gin Lane*

clogged flues. Auenbrugger, famous in medical history for his book on thoracic percussion, wrote a libretto in 1781 for the Chimney Sweep Opera in Vienna and three years later was ennobled for his humanitarian work on behalf of the poor (17, p. 9).

Alcohol

Alcohol not only harms the unborn child but also the child nurtured by an alcoholic mother. When the British National Society for the Prevention of Cruelty to Children sought out the victims of neglect, about 90% were found to be neglected because of excessive drinking by one or both parents. The worst cases were found where the mother was a habitual drunkard. Such mothers lost all sense of parenthood; their houses were rarely clean, their children rarely washed, and these children quickly swelled the infant mortality rate. The English Poor Law Act of 1899 allowed provisional adoption by the Board of Guardians of such neglected children (18, pp. 72–73).

Overlaying

The English Bills of Mortality for 1629–36 and 1694–1703 listed 529 infants "overlaid and starved." Of 217 deaths in one London parish, 46 were those of infants who were overlaid (13, p. 41). Overlaying (lying upon) a child was more frequent on Saturday nights for obvious reasons. In the English daily papers almost every week inquests were reported of infants overlaid or suffocated in bed by one of the parents; at least half of the victims were under a month old. In 1920 there were no less than twenty deaths from this so-called carelessness in the city of Birmingham, where an act of 1909 made death by overlaying a criminal offense (18, p. 84).

Sexual Abuse

Concern about the battered child proceeded to an interest in sexually abused children. Historically, sexual offenses against children were common. A variety of defloration rites at puberty or in preparation for marriage could be painfully abusive; yet these rites were not just indulged, they were often publicly enforced (19, p. 347). The most enlightened, civilized human beings sometimes lapse into such rude instincts of savagery.

Child marriage, especially for girls, was widely prevalent in the past. Johann Peter Frank thought sixteen was the ideal age for women to marry and advocated premarital sex education for the prospective bride and groom. In New England, Anne Bradstreet was married at fifteen and John Winthrop at seventeen. Some Hindus considered it disgraceful for a girl to remain unmarried by the time menstruation was established; premenstrual copulation was extensively practiced under cover of marriage. About 20% of these marriages involved girls of twelve or thirteen. Deaths of these children during their first sexual act were not rare, but they were usually concealed (20).

In some cultures daughters, as well as wives, were loaned to guests as an act of hospitality. We find this in Irish heroic tales, in French medieval literature, and among the Eskimos and primitive tribes of North America. Neither was it always a disgrace to hire out girls for sexual use; the child was a marketable commodity. Physically developed, alluring youngsters of ten or twelve were apt to become prostitutes. Unemployed young girls, especially if sexually developed, frequently and willingly submitted to sexual acts for a reward; on occasion parents exhorted them to do it. The London Society for the Protection of Young Females recorded children no older than eleven entrapped in houses of prostitution; they were not permitted to leave until they were "broken in." Very few left once they were indoctrinated. Ambroise Tardieu, in a study of sixty cases in which sex offenses were repeated on the same child, found that twenty-nine of the girls were under eleven and that all sixty were remarkably well developed. Albert Moll found a child of eight copulating regularly and becoming pregnant at nine, and another child pregnant at eight. He stressed that spontaneous awakening of sexual drive in the young favored intercourse and that premature intercourse awakened sexual libido (21, p. 197).

The medical literature relating to precocious impregnation is full of astonishing instances: Savonarola mentioned it in 1497 in a child of nine, Mandelso in 1658 quoted a case at six, several at eight and nine, and even more at ten and older. He hinted, in three very precocious pregnancies, of sexual abuse in that one of the children was of very humble parents, one born in an almshouse, and the third raised in a house of prostitution. Many ancient authors also reported pregnancy before the onset of menstruation (22, p. 38). There was a report of a girl in 1658 who began to menstruate at the age of two and became pregnant at six. More such cases were reported in the eighteenth century (23).

In 1897 there were 3,085 convictions in Germany for sex offenses against children, and in 1904 there were 4,378 (21, p. 229).

The Children's Home of Leytonstone in England was founded in 1865 following a great outcry about little girls under twelve years of age, some only six, "who had been so grievously dragged into terrible sins that they could no longer be kept in village schools or orphan homes intended for the training of comparatively pure Christian children." The home endeavored to improve the lot of these children by instituting a family life-style for them with work and play (24).

In the days before bacterial diagnosis was available, leukorrhea in children caused considerable concern. Some thought that "no impure connection" occurred in the great majority of cases and advised that the suspicion should be dispelled from the minds of parents as it gave rise frequently to unfounded charges; but it was acceded that in a few cases there could be no doubt that a criminal assault was the source of the disease. No diagnosis could be made that a gonorrheal discharge was due to sexual intercourse unless there was evidence of violence and spermatozoa could be detected in the vagina (25, pp. 878–79). An earlier textbook of pediatric surgery (26, p. 125) cited a curious case in which a woman communicated gonorrhea to two girls by washing them with her own sponge. This type of infection was again recently (1979) reasserted in a pediatric journal. The Commissioners of Public Charities and Correction of New York City in 1869 stated that there were thirty thousand children in the city streets, their only occupation being beggary and pilferage; the girls were prostitutes by the age of fifteen, the brevity of their lives, shortened by syphilitic disease, the only check upon the increase of their numbers. To break up this career of crime, children in the streets were arrested and sent to the Juvenile Retreat on Randall's Island; the Children's Aid Society then secured reputable homes for them (27, p. 91).

Because boys as young as twelve or fourteen frequented the brothels, the town of Ulm in 1527 ordered brothel keepers to keep them out (28). In 1839, a Parisian police commissioner devoted a full chapter of his annual report to sexual abuse of children (29). Children in France were legally prohibited from appearing on theatre stages in 1848 because of moral as well as physical iniquities.

Pederasty

Jean Jacques Rousseau described a homosexual experience as a youth and called pederasts "chevaliers de la manchette" (knights of the cuff) (30, pp. 67–69). Pederasty, literally *boy loving*, refers to sexual perversion with a boy. In the early part of this century Dr. Moll was astounded to learn how many homosexuals formed affinities with schoolboys. This depravity was so common in ancient Rome that the poet Martial declaimed against the vice, applauding the emperor's law protecting children from the pander's art in one of his epigrams: "The pander seized our cradles for his prey / and forced young babies to earn a shameful pay / until Rome's great father, wrathful at the sight, / saved the poor children from their monstrous plight" (31, p. 265). In Greece pederasty inspired disgust and was punished, but the Romans continued it in spite of interdicting laws. This was particularly scandalously true during the reign of the licentious, insane emperor, Caligula (32, p. 128).

Sexual mishandling frequently led to venereal disease in children. There was a superstition that venereal disease could be cured by transference through sexual intercourse with children. The consequences are not hard to imagine. Many times sexual abuse came to light only after gonorrhea or syphilis was discovered in the child. Perverted sexual behavior among vagabond waifs and school children caused consternation when disclosed. Sometimes these children infected each other.

Masturbation

Nurses were wont to stroke an irritable child's genitals to soothe it. More often they did this to stimulate their own lust. S. A. Tissot, whose book on onanism influenced medical thought in the nineteenth century and terrified a wide public readership, warned parents about domestics who secretly instructed children in lesbianism (33, pp. 29–30). "In this kind of cultivation there are gardeners of both sexes," he warned. Men who were impotent, or feared they might be, were sometimes tempted to test their sexual prowess on children. Frequently they substituted improper contacts with girls for actual coitus. Masturbation, onanism, self-abuse, or self-pollution was considered unclean and vile and blamed for every disease imaginable.

Sexual Violence

Rape was common in the unbridled days of the past, especially during wartime. It occurs in the Bible as well as in Greek and Roman history and played a prominent part in the drama of historic violence. Hercules violated the fifty daughters of Thestius, and Helen of Troy was deflowered by Theseus at the age of seven, according to one story, and according to another at the age of twelve.

Flagellation was a common form of sexual abuse. One sadistic little girl of six abused a boy of seven, who bore his martyrdom with dull resentment, but liked his beatings because the pain gave him a thrill of bitter delight (21, p. 137). Voluptuous sensations could lead seductive youngsters to instigate beatings purposely.

In nineteenth-century newspapers appeared lurid accounts of children battered in devious ways for the satisfaction of the sexual lust of sadists. These sex torturers placed ads in the papers to obtain children, using code words which were understood by the initiates. German law finally put a stop to advertisements for immoral purposes. When sexual relations with a person under fourteen became statutory rape, complications arose if both parties were underage, willing partners.

Incest

Incest differs from rape in that rape implies violence. The incidence of incest is impossible to calculate, because incest always happens in secret. Figures vary from 1 to 5,000 per million population (34, p. 300). A study of 530 female college students revealed 45 (8.5%) had experienced sexual activity with a family member, yet very few incestuous relationships ever became known (35, p. 406). The American Humane Society in 1969 estimated between 200,000 and 300,000 female children are molested in the United States annually, with at least 5,000 instances of father-daughter incest (36, p. 22). Concealment was the hallmark of the endogamous family; incest surfaced outside the family chiefly as a result of physical maltreatment, pregnancy, or venereal disease.

Anthropologically and historically sexual unions between father and daughter, mother and son, or brother and sister were not infrequent, but it was usually abhorred. In Bologna a cobbler who thus abused his own daughter in 1305 was dragged through the streets, quartered, and burned alive. The laws of Justinian did not require parents to nourish children conceived incestuously.

Incest was especially devastating to the child because it was a taboo. The taboo often extended to adoption, fosterage, milk-brotherhood (i.e., those who were nursed by the same woman), and other intimate relationships similar to blood kinship. When it extended to housemates in general, children were prudishly separated at home and in schools. Between five and ten years of age, some primitives terminated association of boys with their mothers and sisters. Even where sexual freedom among children of the same household existed, illicit marriage was strictly forbidden. Father-son incest was doubly taboo.

Many reasons have been discussed by anthropologists as to why incest was taboo. While the taboo was primarily ethical and religious, exogamy tended to preserve family unity and to maintain better intrafamily and community relationships. A moral code imposed psychologic restraint and seemed to have certain genetic advantages, in line with the general belief that family inbreeding intensified hereditary traits. Because incestuous mothers were so young, there was an increased morbidity and mortality among the offspring. Never was there a claim that it was healthful.

Advancement of Children's Rights

Esteem for the child was slow to appear. Until the Middle Ages, childhood was over almost as soon as the child was weaned. Among the Israelites, weaning took place at the age of three; then the little boy could enter the house of God along with the men; at thirteen, the age of puberty, he was counted among the men. Medieval children were sent away from home by the age of seven for upbringing; this custom eventuated in the apprentice system. The Italians thought the custom showed a lack of affection toward children by the English (8, p. 315). In the thirteenth century, children began to appear in art, portrayed with various childhood attractions. By the sixteenth century, the moral philosophy of men like Erasmus, himself a wronged illegitimate orphan, and Montaigne, raised by an indulgent father, stirred the hearts of many to adopt nonviolent methods of rearing children and wakened compassionate solicitude for the oppressed and the handicapped child. Their ethics carried over to the seventeenth century and after, influencing men like Rousseau, a libertine who had fathered at least six illegitimate children who vanished before he turned humanitarian, who wrote, "Speak less of the duties of children and more of their rights."

In the seventeenth century there was a shift from communal to family groups, and society was thrilling more deeply to the charms of children. The child gradually achieved a place of honor in the family, and the family attained an independent status (7, p. 42). Step by step, the child was increasingly idolized. In the eighteenth century, Richardson's novel, *Pamela,* spoke out against child abuse, as did Scott's *The Heart of Midlothian* in the nineteenth century. Victor Hugo's Cosette, the foster child who was abused as a household

drudge in *Les Misérables,* and the many young characters in nearly all of Dickens's senti-
mental Victorian novels stirred up ferment for humane treatment of children.

By 1871 the New York State Medical Society could rightly say, in a resolution supporting foundling asylums, that humanity recognized the right of every newborn to be protected and supported. This was the same year of the oft told story of Mary Ellen, the
battered child for whom protective services could only be invoked through the Society for
the Prevention of Cruelty to Animals (37, p. 142). By the beginning of the nineteenth
century, the public conscience had been aroused on behalf of the oppressed, the neglected,
and the handicapped. Schools sprang up for the blind, the deaf, and the mentally retarded,
so that exceptional children were no longer jettisoned. By the end of the century, Abraham
Jacobi exclaimed that the greatest improvement in public morals consisted in acknowledgment that protection of the feeble is among the inalienable rights of all such beings. Point-
ing at the large numbers of abandoned children devoid of the care and protection of the
family circle, whose parents were in hospitals, in prisons, or dead, he declared these all
had a claim on the aid of the community (38, p. 217).

Protective Services for Children

Child welfare began in Mesopotamia six thousand years ago, when orphans had a patron
goddess to look after them (39), The *Rigveda* also mentions another deity among the ancient Hindus who rescued the exposed child and endowed him with legal rights (40,
p. 34). The gods reflected a mirror image of mankind, affording a picture of what went on
among the people.

The Bible commands, "Do not sin against the child" (Genesis 42:22). The laws of
Solon, 600 B.C., required the commander of an army to protect and raise, at government
expense, children of citizens killed in battle; and the wives of the Roman emperors extended child welfare. Then there was jolly old St. Nicholas Thaumaturgos, wonder worker
of the third century, who was patron saint of children and protector of the feebleminded.

In the main, protective services have always consisted of placing children in institutions
or under foster care. In spite of good intentions, children suffered physical and psychological damage under this system. However, without such intervention, they were even
more apt to be maimed and killed.

Institutional Care

At a very early period, Athens and Rome had orphan homes; *brephotrophia* were mentioned in 529 in the laws of Justinian. With the rise of Christianity, the church provided for
foundlings and every village had a *xenodochium,* a hospice for pilgrims and the poor,
which embraced children (41). By the sixth century the *brephotrophium* at Trier had a
marble receptacle in which a child could be safely deposited secretly. Similar institutions
throughout France in the seventh century were the antecedents of the welfare system in the
nineteenth century.

The first foundling hospital was established by Datheus, the archpriest of Milan, in 787.
Others blossomed forth in rapid succession. In Naples, with a population of about
400,000 and 15,000 births a year in the nineteenth century, there were over 2,000 found-

Figure 1.4.
The Foundling, 1835. Reproduced from Adele Schreiber, *Mutterschaft*
(Munich: Albert Langen, 1912), 467.

lings in the asylum. The foundling hospital of St. Petersburg was the most magnificent in Europe. The Russians were very proud of it and endowed it munificently. Upwards of 25,000 children were enrolled regularly upon its books. About one in four died, and the foundling hospitals did not prevent exposure or infanticide (42, p. 275).

British law, which also applied to the American colonies, initiated early involvement of government in public welfare. The main reliance was on almshouses, where, to offset expense and save children from the sin of idleness, they were forced to work.

Children fared badly under the dismal routine of institutions. They suffered from deprivation and starvation, with little consideration for their recreational needs. A visitor to a foundling asylum was dejected by the sight of children sitting all day long bound to potty chairs (43, p. 188). Few survived. Those who did, were starved, overworked, cuffed, degraded, despised, and unpitied. In Paris, a street beggar could buy an infant at the Hotel Dieu for twenty sous to be maimed so that it would attract pity and more liberal alms; or a wet nurse could buy a replacement for an infant entrusted to her care that died (43, p. 198). To add to their misery, almshouses made children, as young as five or six, toil in the workhouses.

Foundling homes, orphanages, almshouses offered little surcease from death. Protestant countries were convinced that they encouraged immorality; in addition, they objected to the cost and believed foster care was cheaper. To avoid the failings of institutional life, children were farmed out to foster care as soon as possible.

Figure 1.5
New York Foundling Asylum, Randall's Island

Foster Care

Foster care was also mentioned in antiquity. Removal to private homes often subjected children to maltreatment and neglect, but gave them a sporting chance of survival. Even so, 80% of illegitimate children put out to nurse in London during the nineteenth century perished. As a matter of fact, some nurses had a reputation as skilled baby killers. The Germans called them "angel makers." These harpies commanded extra fees to take charge of unwanted babies and even profited from insurance benefits on the dead infants. Foster care could be a sordid business.

A German report of 1881 stated that 31% of illegitimate children died under foster care, allegedly from natural causes, but really from freezing, starvation, or deliberate destruction. A favorite method of doing away with infants was to give them nothing but pacifiers soaked in brandy. Seldom were foster parents called to account. In spite of such gross irregularities, foundlings made out better under foster care than in foundling institutions.

The Pennsylvania Society to Protect Children from Cruelty estimated in 1882 that about seven hundred infants perished annually in Philadelphia from abuse and neglect, and urged the establishment of special children's asylums combined with a system for placement in foster homes based upon those current in Europe (44).

When children spent their entire childhoods in a succession of foster homes, the lack of the security of a permanent home life marred their emotional development and sowed the seeds of unhappy consequences in later life. Tansillo's poem *La Balia* (The Nurse) decried the eighteenth-century fashion of surrogate care under some wretch of vulgar birth and frail conduct, just out of jail, or some strumpet. In England, Jonas Hanway (1712–86), reporting that only one out of seventy children entrusted to parish care grew up, only to be crippled and sent out into the streets to beg, steal, or fall into prostitution, brought about parliamentary reform that required all young foster children to be registered. The *British Medical Journal* in 1903 chided the system of baby farming and urged the licensing of foster parents and inspectors to see that the children were properly cared for (45, p. 154).

In the United States, Charles Loring Brace, founder of the Children's Aid Society in 1853, heeded Horace Greeley's cry of "Go West, young man! Go West!" He believed the only salvation for older, unwanted children, many vagrant, was to relocate them with farmers' families where their food and costs were well repaid by their profitable labor on the farms. Between 1853 and 1890 the Children's Aid Society transplanted ninety thousand urban vagrants, averaging about nine years of age, to foster homes in the West (46). Those under thirteen fared better than the older ones. An investigative study in 1884 reported that 78% of the younger group were doing well as compared to 65% of the others, of whom 30% had apparently disappeared (14, 2:308).

The pros and cons of institutional care versus foster care were long debated. Advanced in favor of the latter were less cost and the blessings of family life, while supporters of institutions argued the cost would be insignificant with proper economy and that surrogate parents gave little service for the pittance they received, from which they still expected to profit.

Hundreds of thousands of children and their families have been helped by the wise use of foster care. Contact with the child by one or both parents, when possible, not only aids the child's mental development, but also boosts the morale of the foster parents and their respect for the child. The Child Welfare League studied foster care in 1965, and the Columbia School of Social Work has undertaken to determine what happens to children as a result of placement under foster care. Believing that foster children are prime candidates for emotional and physical distress, a bill is before the Pennsylvania legislature to set up a panel to review the matter periodically. There is still an uneasy feeling that the thousands of children adrift in the foster care system have to be rescued (47).

Child Protective Laws

Traditionally, the father's authority, like the royal prerogative, could be asserted without question, but through the years it has been increasingly limited by statutes and changing public opinion. The father's authority was modified in Rome in 450 B.C. and again in A.D. 4. The Christian church fathers in the fourth century, in line with the Judaic commandment, "Thou shalt not kill," equated infanticide with murder. This was a landmark in the history of children's rights. A succession of imperial edicts after that guaranteed the child's right to life.

The grave injustice possible from a false accusation of sexual abuse of children created a perplexing problem for experienced physicians (25, pp. 878–79). According to Dr. Moll, an innocent defendent was seldom exonerated when accused by a little girl or her parents (21, pp. 227–28).

The church, the courts, and public opinion were often apt to be lenient toward a guilty mother in cases of infanticide. The vagaries of the law in this respect were brought out by a seventeenth-century English practitioner. One "comely, well-favored servant" the jury did not find guilty, because she was so pretty and beloved of soldiers, who "pitied her misfortune." The foreman of the jury saw "no reason why a woman should be hanged for a mistaken harsh word or two in the statutes." A less-fortunate woman who buried her child in secret in 1670 was executed. So, too, a feebleminded girl who could not distinguish between labor pains and a bowel movement and aborted in a ditch, "though the whole bench saw she was a foole," was hanged. The penalty for disposing of a child in secret was hanging; if a mother took back her abandoned child she was exonerated (48, pp. 31–34, 274–75).

In medieval times the church governed birth, marriage, and death, making the rules for law and medicine. A penance was set for overlaying (lying upon) a child. In the twelfth century, penance was also incurred when infants died of scalding. Refusing to nurse and death of a child by the mother's hand likewise brought church censure. The Bishop of Bamberg in the twelfth century, because killing girl babies was such a widespread sin in his domain, forbade it; but a thirteenth-century German law permitted a man distressed by poverty to exterminate or sell his children, provided he did not sell them to pagans or, in the case of girls, into prostitution.

The secular courts steadily increased their jurisdiction over infanticide. In 1224 overlaying was so prevalent that the statutes of Winchester penalized women just for keeping infants in bed with them. Church admonitions were repeated so often, many people's eyes must have been shut to reality. The royal courts of Henry I assumed authority when a child was killed by anyone other than the parent. When Henry VIII broke off from the church of Rome, secular authorities took complete jurisdiction. The laws became more stringent, although many modifications were made through the years. Rapid urbanization made concealment more difficult, and society began to reevaluate the worth of the child (49, pp. 1–14).

In spite of shocking evidence to the contrary, numerous inquests of battered children returned a verdict of natural death. In his inimitable fashion, Dickens, in *Oliver Twist* (1839), describes the ordinary inquest:

> Occasionally, when there was some more than usually interesting inquest upon a parish child who had been overlooked in turning up a bedstead, or inadvertently scalded to death when there happened to be a washing . . . the jury would take it into their heads to ask troublesome questions, or the parishioners would rebelliously affix their signatures to a remonstrance. But, the impertinencies were speedily checked by the evidence of the surgeon, and the testimony of the beadle; the former of whom had always opened the body and found nothing inside (which was very probable indeed), and the latter of whom invariably swore whatever the Parish wished.

Oscar Wilde, in a letter to the *Daily Chronicle,* 27 May 1897, from personal experience in the Reading jail, wrote an impassioned plea for prison reform especially regarding children incarcerated even before adjudication. "The cruelty that is practiced by day and night on children in English prisons," he said, "is incredible. . . . Every child is confined to its cell for 23 hours out of 24. . . . If an individual, parent or guardian, did this to a child he would be severely punished. The Society for the Prevention of Cruelty to Children would take the matter up at once. . . . But our society does worse. . . . Inhuman treatment of a child is always inhuman by whomsoever it is inflicted." Tiny children were fed horribly revolting food which he described in detail. They were terrorized by the prison system. "No child under fourteen years of age should be sent to prison at all," he declared (50, pp. 109–20).

When young children were imported for sexual misuse, the Society for the Prevention of Cruelty to Children became involved with the white slave question and was instrumental in passing protective laws against this kind of child abuse. The Mann Act, more recently, also particularly protects girls. The Lindbergh Law against kidnapping was another step in the progress of child protective laws. The progression of child labor laws has already been discussed.

A significant step was separation of minors from adult criminals and the institution of juvenile courts about seventy-five years ago. A juvenile court was established in Chicago at the turn of this century, and in 1907 the Los Angeles Police Department began to specialize in juvenile affairs, creating in 1910 a separate juvenile bureau. This police department in 1970 set up a desk for abused children and in 1974 established the first battered child unit to handle physical and sexual abuse of children.

Prior to 1964, there were no effectual child abuse reporting laws. The 1962 conference chaired by Dr. Kempe engendered the model child-abuse law that, within the remarkably short space of five years, was adopted by every state. Experience and increased insight into the psychodynamics of the abusive parent led to revisions. First the laws were aimed at case finding and deterrent punishment, but soon it was apparent that the entire family was often involved in the battered child syndrome.

Child Abuse As a Pediatric Problem

Except for medical care of the injured child, the problems of the battered child in the past ordinarily were not the concern of physicians. Their mission was to heal the sick, not to deal with social problems. The cross the child had to bear was the responsibility of society. The physicians of yore were implicated, not in the course of practice, but rather in company with other compassionate citizens as a moral obligation. They did not handle social, psychological, cultural, religious, or economic afflictions, shunned politics, left morals to theologians, and scrupulously avoided any controversial police activity that might conflict with the sacred Hippocratic principle of confidentiality. They divulged privileged communications only when the public health required it, as during the plague. Child abuse, like child labor, juvenile delinquency, and similar social questions historically were ethical and moral problems, not strictly medical. Only of late have such matters been attached to pediatrics.

Nevertheless, the medical profession was not unmindful. Abraham Jacobi, when he was president of the New York State Medical Society in 1882, formed a committee to cooperate with the Society for the Prevention of Cruelty to Children in formulating legislation to improve child labor laws.

Medicine was oblivious to child abuse until concern about child abuse grew out of Dr. John Caffey's perturbation of mind about curious X-ray manifestations in the bones of some children. Radiology appeared just at the dawn of the twentieth century. Caffey was one of the first to devote special pediatric attention to it when in 1925 he took charge of the Babies Hospital X-ray department in New York. Radiologists, like pathologists, were essentially "back-room boys" and rarely went to the bedside. Caffey, however, was trained as a pediatrician, and, even as a radiologist, he was very much involved with children, their parents, and their concerns. As an adept pediatrician he was able to relate these unexplained X-ray findings to clinical pictures. While he soon recognized that multiple fractures were due to trauma, he was unable to convince his colleagues that parents might be the instrument of this trauma. In 1946 Caffey published a paper entitled "Multiple Fractures in the Long Bones of Infants Suffering from Chronic Subdural Hematoma"

(51). This attracted the attention of pediatricians to the ramifications of child abuse. This issue then smoldered for several years.

Multiple long-bone fractures had been confused with rickets, scurvy, and osteogenesis imperfecta; and even though Paré and Vesalius in the sixteenth century knew about traumatic subdural hemorrhage, Virchow in the nineteenth, decided the subdural hematomas he saw at the autopsy table were inflammatory reactions of obscure origin. Caffey and his neurosurgical colleagues were aware, as were some of his pediatrician friends, that subdural hematomas were traumatic (52). In 1946, he made the point in his report that trauma had to be seriously considered as a cause of long-bone fractures, since it was already recognized as the cause of subdural hematoma.

Dr. Frederic N. Silverman, another radiologist, extended Caffey's convictions, emphasizing in 1951 the intentional infliction of these injuries (53). Finally, when Wooley and Evans blasted the medical profession in 1955 for its reluctance to concede that the multiple injuries to children were committed willfully, the profession began to pay attention. Dr. Kempe and his staff studied all the different features of child abuse from 1951 to 1958 and linked child abuse to pediatrics. Kempe was a member of the program committee of the American Academy of Pediatrics and, when he became chairman in 1961, organized a multidisciplinary conference with the emotive title of the "Battered-Child Syndrome" (54). This conference, and its provocative title, set ablaze an impassioned outburst on behalf of abused children. A bandwagon effect was generated. The Children's Bureau climbed aboard with generous grants for study of the subject, and the American Humane Society carried out surveys, issued pertinent publications, and convened national symposia considering many different angles. A "child abuse" heading first appeared in the *Quarterly Cumulative Index Medicus* in 1965, under which about forty published articles were listed. Centers were set up to look into the basic causes of abnormal rearing processes that generate child abuse and to initiate new methods of dealing with them.

In Great Britain a 1966 study by the National Society for the Prevention of Cruelty to Children revealed that more than half of abused children were less than a year old, battered by their own mothers. The rest were battered by fathers, stepfathers, or boyfriends of the mothers. Almost all required hospitalization, nearly half of them repeatedly. The Society set up centers with programs in corrective mothering, patterned after those set in motion by the Denver group, and named the London center "Denver House" to honor the pioneering efforts of Dr. Kempe's group.

In Sweden, child abuse was first recognized as a pediatric problem in 1957. The Swedish National Bureau of Health then issued regulations, offered counseling services, and set up a research institute for the study of child abuse (55).

Prevention and Treatment

In the past, social problems were relegated to private benevolent societies and the law. When people were chagrined that the Society for Prevention of Cruelty to Animals founded in 1866 preceded the Society for the Prevention of Cruelty to Children, other child protective groups were organized. Their principal achievements consisted in reforming child labor and in separating abused children from further harm and finding shelter for them. The Society for the Prevention of Cruelty to Children was founded in 1874, and by the end of the nineteenth century there were such child protection agencies in England, France, Germany, Italy, the United States, and just about every other civilized country in the world.

The approach to child protection has shifted from the punitive to the therapeutic (56, 57). Slowly, but steadily, emphasis upon rescuing children and prosecuting offending parents gave way to treatment and rehabilitation. The child protective laws are now oriented toward nonpunitive protection of children, helping families in crisis, preserving good standards of parental behavior, and providing basic needs for optimum care of children in a harmonious family relationship. To cure is the voice of the past, to prevent the divine whisper of today (45, p. 155).

Until Kempe issued his clarion call for the "Battered-Child Syndrome" conference, protective services comprised separation of the victim from, and punishment of, the evildoer. Now a new tack is taken: early recognition of children at risk and rehabilitation of troubled families, aiming to preserve the natural development of the child in his normal domestic habitat. With the acceptance of child abuse as a pediatric responsibility, new life was instilled into the campaign for children's rights.

References

1. Burdett, Henry C. 1895. *Burdett's Hospital and Charities Annual*. New York: Scribner.
2. *American Medical News,* 4 May 1979, pp. 1–21.
3. Saulsbury, Frank T., et al. 1984. Child Abuse: Parental Hydrocarbon Administration. *Pediatrics* 73:719.
4. Furness, J. 1974. *Police Surgeon* 6:75–87.
5. Sognnaes, R. D. 1976. Forensic Stomatology. *New England J. Med.* 296:198–200.
6. Harper, Robert F. 1904. *The Code of Hammurabi, King of Babylon about 2000 B.C.* 2d ed. Chicago: University of Chicago Press.
7. Ariès, Philippe. 1962. *Centuries of Childhood: A Social History of Family Life,* trans. Robert Baldick. New York: Knopf.
8. Tuchman, B. W. 1978. *A Distant Mirror: The Calamitous 14th Century.* New York: Knopf.
9. Slinger, W. H. 1919. *Child Placing in Families.* New York: Russell Sage Foundation.
10. Booth, G. 1721. *Historical Library of Diodorus the Sicilian.* London.
11. Ploss, H. H. 1876. *Das Kind im Brauch und Sitte der Volker.* Vol. 2. Stuttgart.
12. Payne, G. H. 1928. *The Child in Human Progress.* New York: Sears.
13. Forbes, T. R. 1978. Crowner's Quest. *Trans. Am. Philos. Soc.* 68:7–41.
14. Bremner, Robert H. 1970. *Children and Youth in America.* 3 vols. Cambridge, Mass.: Harvard University Press.
15. Radbill, S. X. 1976. Reared in Adversity: Institutional Care of Children in the 18th Century. *Am. J. Diseases in Children* 130:751–56.
16. Tillman, E. B. 1958. *Rights of Childhood.* Ph.D. diss., University of Wisconsin.
17. Willius, F. A. 1950. Historical Comments. In *Diagnosis and Treatment of Cardiovascular Disease.* 4th ed., W. D. Stroud, vol. 1. Philadelphia: F. A. Davis.

18. Ashby, H. T. 1922. *Infant Mortality.* 2d ed. Cambridge: Cambridge University Press.

19. Crawley, Ernest. 1902. *The Mystic Rose: A Study of Primitive Marriage.* New York: Macmillan.

20. Editorial. *Indian Medical Gazette,* September 1890.

21. Moll, Albert. 1913. *Sexual Life of the Child,* trans. Eden Paul. New York: Macmillan.

22. Gould, George M., and Pyle, Walter L. 1890. *Anomalies and Curiosities of Medicine.* Philadelphia: Saunders.

23. Hoffman, J. W. 1981. Precocious Motherhood. *Pediatric Annals* 10:165–69.

24. [Cotton, Agnes.] 1873. *Woman's Work: The Children's Home, Leytonstone,* ed. W. C. Cotton. Chester: Philipson and Golden.

25. Holmes, Timothy. 1882. *System of Surgery,* ed. John H. Packard Vol. 3. Philadelphia.

26. Foster, C. 1860. *Surgical Diseases of Children.* London: Parker.

27. *Harper's Weekly* 13 (1869): 91.

28. Boesch, Hans. 1900. *Kinderleben in der deutschen Vergangenheit.* Leipzig: Eugen Diederichs.

29. Beraud, J. B. 1839. *Les Filles publiques de Paris.* Paris.

30. Rousseau, Jean Jacques. 1945. *Confessions.* New York: Modern Library.

31. Pott, J. A., and Wright, F. A. n.d. *Martial.* New York: Macmillan.

32. Rosenbaum, Julius. 1839. *Die Lustseuche im Altertum.* Halle: Lippert.

33. Tissot, S. A. A. D. 1832. *Treatise on Diseases Produced by Onanism.* New York: Collins & Hanway.

34. Nakashima, I. I., and Zakas, M. S. W. 1979. Incestuous Families. *Pediatric Annals* 8:300.

35. Rosenfeld, A. A. 1979. Endogamous Incest. *Am. J. Diseases in Children* 133:406–10.

36. Pennsylvania Coalition Against Rape. 1979. *A Special Report: The Sexual Victimization of Children.* 12 March.

37. Riis, Jacob. 1892. Little Mary Ellen's Legacy. In *The Children of the Poor.* London: Sampson, Low, Marston.

38. Robinson, W. J. 1909. *Collectanea Jacobi,* vol. 6. New York: Critic & Guide.

39. Radbill, S. X. 1973. Mesopotamian Pediatrics. *Episteme* 7:283.

40. Pinkham, M. W. 1941. *Woman in the Sacred Scriptures of Hinduism.* New York: Columbia University Press.

41. Radbill, S. X. 1955. History of Children's Hospitals. *Am. J. Diseases in Children* 90:411–16.

42. Sanger, William W. 1898. *History of Prostitution.* New York: Medical Publishing Co.

43. Peiper, Albrecht. 1965. *Chronik der Kinderheilkunde.* 4th ed. Leipzig.

44. Crew, J. J. *Care of Deserted Infants.*

45. *British Med. J.,* 17 January 1903, p. 154–55.

46. English, Peter C. 1984. Pediatrics and the Unwanted Child in History. *Pediatrics* 73:699–711.

47. Editorial. *Philadelphia Inquirer,* 16 April 1979.

48. Willughby, Percival. 1972. *Observations in Midwifery.* Wakefield, England: S. & R. Publishers.

49. Damme, Catherine. 1978. The Worth of an Infant under Law. *Medical History* 22:1–24.

50. Wilde, Oscar. 1931. The Case of Warder Martin. In *The Writings of Oscar Wilde*. Vol. 4. New York: Wise & Co.

51. Caffey, John. 1946. Multiple Fractures in the Long Bones of Infants Suffering from Chronic Subdural Hematoma. *Am. J. Roentgenology* 56 (2): 163–73.

52. Reinhart, J. B. 1979. Personal communication.

53. Silverman, Frederic. 1953. The Roentgen Manifestations of Unrecognized Skeletal Trauma. *Am. J. Roentgenology Radium Ther. Nucl. Med.* 69:413–27.

54. Kempe, C. H.; Silverman, F. N.; Steele, B. F.; Droegemueller, W.; and Silver, H. K. 1962. The Battered-Child Syndrome. *JAMA* 181:17–24.

55. Lagerberg, D. 1978. Child Abuse: A Literature Review. *Acta Paediatrica Scandinavica* 67:683–90.

56. Chesser, E. 1952. *Cruelty to Children*. New York: Philosophical Library.

57. Clayton, Janet E. 1920. *The Child Welfare Movement*. London.

2 Child Abuse and Neglect: The Cultural Context

Jill E. Korbin

A basic premise of society is that human nature compels parents to rear their young with solicitousness and concern, good intentions, and tender loving care. Evidence to the contrary, that parents harm or fail to adequately care for their offspring, forces the recognition that child abuse and neglect are well within the repertoire of human behavior. Child abuse emerged from a relatively obscure radiological diagnosis (1, 2) to a matter of public and professional concern in the United States in the early 1960s (3–7). Questions inevitably arose as to whether the problem was universal or unique to the United States. Attention was focused first on societies most like the United States; other Western nations experienced similar transformations from initial denial that child abuse existed to a recognition of its multiple manifestations (8). This repeated experience of nations first denying the existence of child abuse only to "discover" it later promoted a skepticism that child abuse and neglect could be absent anywhere and stimulated interest in the broader cross-cultural record.

This chapter considers what a cross-cultural perspective contributes to the understanding of child abuse and neglect. If behavior is to be understood, a wider range of human cultural adaptation than that afforded by Western industrialized nations must be encompassed. A cross-cultural perspective on child maltreatment challenges complacency about what is good or bad for children and forces a re-examination of commonly held definitions and causal explanations for child maltreatment. At the time of the publication of the third edition of *The Battered Child* in 1980, knowledge about child abuse and neglect was based almost entirely on research and clinical experience in Western nations (9). Since that time, the literature on culture and child maltreatment has expanded considerably. Nevertheless, cross-cultural research on child abuse and neglect is only in its initial stages and many questions remain.

The term *cross-cultural* refers to the perspective afforded from a consideration of diverse societies around the world. These societies may be in places such as New Guinea,

Jill E. Korbin, Ph.D., is assistant professor of anthropology at Case Western Reserve University, Cleveland.

East Africa, Asia, or South America and may appear exotic and far removed from relevance to the problems faced by Euro-American child protection workers. *Cross-cultural* also refers to ethnic or multicultural diversity that is of more immediate impact on child protection work. There are close parallels between the kinds of knowledge and principles that can be generated by examining distant cultures and those cultures living in proximity to one another in multicultural nations. An ability to transcend cultural boundaries, what may be called "cultural translation" (10) or "ethnic competence" (11) is equally important when conducting anthropological fieldwork in remote areas of Oceania or when providing services in ethnic communities in Los Angeles, Honolulu, or London.

The cross-cultural literature specifically concerned with child abuse and neglect has arisen from two primary, and often overlapping, sources. The first includes child advocates and professionals such as social workers, health care providers, researchers, and educators in diverse nations who have sought to demonstrate the existence of child maltreatment in their own nations as a first step in combating the problem (12–50). The spectrum of child maltreatment is addressed in this growing literature, including physical abuse and neglect, sexual molestation, nutritional deprivation, psychological abuse, and institutional abuse. Causal factors, when suggested, most often echo the medical model upon which the first work on child abuse was based in the United States and European nations. This literature is particularly useful in establishing that a breadth of child maltreatment issues are recognized in diverse nations that are by no means unique to Euro-American societies. The second primary source of literature encompasses social and medical researchers, primarily from the United States, who have sought to delineate the parameters and assess the patterns of child abuse across diverse cultural and ethnic groups (51–67). While this literature is limited by definitional and methodological problems, it nevertheless underlines the importance of a cultural perspective in practice and theory.

Cross-cultural information on child abuse and neglect is limited. Anthropological research has tended to focus on normative cultural behavior, rather than deviance from culturally accepted standards (68). Attention to child maltreatment has been sparse, but represents a growing research interest (59, 61, 63, 64, 69–77). Since child maltreatment is a low base-rate behavior, it may not be observed in smaller scale societies during the traditional yearlong period of anthropological fieldwork, or cases may be so few that they are difficult to interpret. Observed cases of the "battered child" among Inuit peoples, for example, were rare and in seeming contradiction to a commonly held picture of indulgent and warm Inuit parenting. Similarly, cases of child maltreatment among Hawaiian-Polynesians seemed rare exceptions to the dominant cultural pattern of warmth and indulgence (71). These cases, then, however few within any culture, do not find their way into the literature and thus do not contribute to the understanding of patterns within and across cultural contexts. At this point in the state of the knowledge, a lack of published cases in the cross-cultural literature does not necessarily mean an absence of the problem. Literature on child maltreatment in one nation may simply mean that international networking has alerted professionals in that nation to the problem. Reports of child prostitution in Sri Lanka or The Netherlands, for example, do not necessarily mean that the problem is absent in neighboring countries. The global distribution of child abuse and neglect is a pressing question that demands careful research.

Culture and the Definition of Child Abuse and Neglect

Definitional ambiguity is a major impediment to cross-cultural child abuse and neglect research and professional practice. Questions of prevalence and causation necessarily hinge on how the problem is defined. The first task, then, is to decipher cultural definitions of child abuse and neglect. The classically battered, burned, or starved child looks sadly similar regardless of nationality, racial classification, or ethnicity. The majority of cases of child maltreatment, however, fall into a grey area and require an appreciation of the cultural context in which acts of omission or commission result in harm to the child (see chap. 22).

Cross-cultural variability in child rearing beliefs and behaviors makes it evident that there is not a universal standard for good child care nor for child abuse and neglect. This presents a dilemma. Failure to allow for a cultural perspective in defining child abuse and neglect promotes an ethnocentric position in which one's own set of cultural beliefs and practices are presumed to be preferable, and indeed superior, to all others. Nevertheless, a stance of extreme cultural relativism, in which all judgments of humane treatment of children are suspended in the name of culture, may justify a lesser standard of care for some children. To address this dilemma, definitional issues must be structured into a coherent framework so that child abuse and neglect can be appropriately identified within and across cultural contexts.

Culturally appropriate definitions of child abuse and neglect require attention to both the viewpoint of the culture in question, termed the *emic* perspective, and the viewpoint of an outsider, or the *etic* perspective. These terms derive from linguistics (78), in which *emic* utterances (e.g., phonemes) refer to meanings as they are understood by the participants in the conversation. *Etic* utterances (e.g., phonetics) can be described by independent observers, regardless of their meanings. Consideration of the *emic* perspective has been central in anthropology's efforts to organize and explain the diversity of human behavior that has been documented cross-culturally. However, an *etic* frame of reference allows interpretation of the behavior from a wider perspective on human cultural adaptation. An understanding of both *emic* and *etic* perspectives is necessary to sort out the impact of the cultural context in which behavior, including child abuse and neglect, takes on meaning.

Identification of child abuse and neglect relies on a complex interaction of: (a) harm to the child; (b) caretaker behaviors that produced or contributed to that harm; and (c) societal assignment of culpability or responsibility (see chap. 4). Child abuse and neglect statistics in Euro-American nations reflect harm to a child that resulted in an official report. Straus, Gelles, and Steinmetz, in contrast, suggest that concern should be placed with aggressive and assaultive behaviors rather than whether such behaviors actually result in harm (79). Whether child abuse and neglect are defined as caretaker behaviors or child outcomes, the cultural context cannot be ignored. With respect to acts by caretakers, the same behavior may have varying meanings and interpretations in different cultural contexts. Constant physical contact with an infant, for example, taking an *etic* perspective, can be described in the same way across cultures. However, it may carry an *emic* meaning of indulgence in societies with low infant mortality while signaling a concern for physical survival in societies with high infant mortality (80, 81). Similarly, physical harm is inadequate in itself as the critical defining element of child maltreatment. It is not meaningful in terms of advancing knowledge to equate bruises inflicted on a child by an angry parent in the United States with bruises inflicted during the Vietnamese curing practice of "coin rubbing" (82). The intent of the adults, the interpretation by the child, and cultural meanings must be considered.

Three levels of distinction are necessary for culturally appropriate definitions of child maltreatment: (1) cultural differences in child rearing practices; (2) idiosyncratic departure from one's cultural continuum of acceptable behavior; and (3) societal harm to children (9, 61). The first level encompasses practices that are viewed as acceptable in the culture in which they occur, but as abusive or neglectful by outsiders. Cultural conflict in the definition of child abuse and neglect is most likely at this level. At the second level, idiosyncratic abuse or neglect signals a departure from the continuum of culturally acceptable behavior. While cultures differ in their definitions of child maltreatment, all societies have criteria for behaviors that fall outside the realm of acceptability. It is at this level that child abuse and neglect is most legitimately identified across cultural contexts. And, at the third level, societal conditions such as poverty, inadequate housing, poor health care, and lack of nutritional resources either contribute powerfully to child maltreatment or are considered in and of themselves as abuse and neglect. While there can be no doubt that these conditions seriously compromise the survival and well-being of children, they are beyond individual parental control.

Definitional confusion in the cross-cultural literature on child maltreatment has arisen from confounding these three levels. An extensive anthropological literature on cultural diversity demands these levels of distinction. Literature from developing nations also differentiates traditional cultural practices that involve pain and suffering from idiosyncratic forms of abuse and neglect that more recently have been identified in urban centers (e.g., 41).

In the absence of an adequate data base for systematic comparisons, the cross-cultural literature on child maltreatment largely has been limited to a listing of the harms to which children come in different cultural contexts. What most often ensues is a cataloging of practices at the first definitional level, those that appear abusive when viewed from outside the cultural context (the *etic* perspective), but not as such when viewed from within (the *emic* perspective).

Cultural Differences in Definitions of Child Abuse and Neglect

When cultures come into contact, the situation is ripe for conflict on a range of issues, including child care patterns (9, 61). Disparities between *emic* (insider) and *etic* (outsider) perspectives can occur both on an international level and among ethnic groups within any nation. Initiation rites that occur in many parts of the world provide a dramatic example of this type of cultural conflict. During such rites, preadolescent and adolescent boys and girls undergo a range of ordeals that may include genital operations such as circumcision, clitoridectomy or infibulation, facial and body scarification, beatings, hazings, and deprivation of food and sleep. Euro-American peoples tend to deplore these rites and have sought to eradicate them through colonial prohibitions or international pressure.

It is equally instructive to consider Euro-American child care practices through the eyes of other cultures. Middle-class white American parents, for example, tend to follow pediatric advice that it is developmentally important for young children to sleep independently from others, particularly their parents. Hawaiian-American women, in contrast, were incredulous at the verification of a "rumor" that *haole* (literally meaning outsider, but most commonly used to refer to whites) parents put infants and young children in a separate bed, and further in a separate room for the entire night. While this seems like a benign example, many cultures believe that isolating children for the night is not only detrimental to social development but also potentially dangerous. Child care practices reflect larger cultural values and socialization goals. In traditional Japanese culture, two generation cosleeping is preferable and expected throughout most of the life cycle (83). Traditional Japanese and Hawaiian-Polynesians place a high value on interdependnece among family members in contrast to the independence inculcated at an early age by middle-class white American parents. Similarly, letting an infant "cry itself to sleep" lest it become "spoiled" is difficult to comprehend in a highland New Guinea society where it is believed that a crying infant's spirit can escape through the open fontanelle causing death (84).

Anthropologists, missionaries, and others who have lived in diverse cultures with their children have come into direct contact with different perceptions of what is abusive or neglectful. Emelie Olson, who conducted anthropological research in Turkey, was accompanied by her eighteen-month-old daughter. Olson worried that Turkish infants were uncomfortable and would suffer ill effects as she watched them sweat profusely under multiple layers of heavy wool clothing in even the warmest weather. The Turkish women, however, predicted doom when Olson let her daughter play outside in a tub of water on a hot day, in direct violation of their belief that small children get chilled very easily and that this can result in death (85).

Conflict in definitions of child abuse is not limited to that between industrialized and developing, Western and non-Western, or colonial and subjugated peoples. Conflict also ensues among smaller scale societies living in proximity to one another. The 'Mbuti (formerly referred to as Pygmies) did not practice initiation rites. They regarded the rites of their nearby Bantu neighbors as unduly harsh and abusive. The Bantu rites included circumcision without anesthesia, deprivation of food and sleep, and frequent beatings and hazings. The Bantu villagers, at the same time, regarded the 'Mbuti as exceedingly neglectful of their children's welfare. Without rites of initiation, in the Bantu's view, boys were forever doomed to the status of children. They could never marry, have children, own land, or be a full participant in the culture. With increasing contact and economic dependence on the Bantu, the 'Mbuti reluctantly agreed to have their sons initiated alongside the Bantu boys. Nevertheless, the 'Mbuti continued to regard the Bantu rites as excessively harsh and interfered in the rites by bringing their boys food and blankets and trying to shield them from pain. This type of interference was strictly forbidden. It constituted further proof for the Bantu that the 'Mbuti were inadequate parents who coddled their sons through the rites rather than allowing them to achieve legitimate manhood (86). This conflict between 'Mbuti and Bantu is just as meaningful as conflict between larger nation-states or within multicultural societies about inappropriate child treatment and the definition of abuse.

If the cultural context, or *emic* meaning, of a behavior is not well understood, ethnocentrism may dictate that the dominant culture will tolerate the behavior or attempt to eradicate it either through punishment or education. Two examples illustrate this:

In the first case, a woman in London cut the faces of her two young sons with a razor blade and rubbed charcoal into the lacerations. The woman was arrested for child abuse. However, an investigation quickly indicated that the woman and her children belonged to an East African tribal group that traditionally practiced facial scarification. Her actions were an attempt to protect the cultural identity of her sons. Without such markings, they would be unable to participate as adults in the culture of their birth (87). If this mother failed to assure her children of appropriate adult status with scarification, she would have been viewed abusive or neglectful within the context of her tribe. The woman was released and her children returned to her custody. She was warned, however, that she could not engage in such behavior in the future while living under English law.

In the second case, members of a highland New Guinea group were concerned that the American anthropologists living in their midst allowed their newborn infant to cry without immediately picking him up. At that point in time, these American parents were adhering to their own folk belief that picking up a baby each time it cries will "spoil" the child. In contrast, the New Guinea group believed that it is exceedingly dangerous for a child to be allowed to cry unattended. In addition to being detrimental to the child's immediate well-being and comfort, it was believed that if an infant cries too long, its spirit escapes through the still open fontanelle causing death. The Americans tried to impart their folk knowledge that letting the child cry was preferable to spoiling it. Unable to tolerate this danger, however, the villagers picked up the baby when it cried—perhaps their form of protective custody (88).

Principles applicable in dealing with cultural differences in more remote cultures can be applied to diverse groups within multicultural nations where proximity and power differentials make cultural conflict a pressing matter. In the United States, misinterpretation of physical injury as possible abuse has arisen between Western health care providers and immigrant groups. The Vietnamese practice of *cao gao* (coin rubbing) is a well-known example. The practice, in which heated metal coins are pressed forcefully on the child's body, leaving bruises, is believed to reduce fever, chills, and headaches (82). While the bruises are indeed inflicted, parental intent is to cure. With an understanding of the context, one would be hard pressed to define the practice as abuse. Similar issues have arisen with respect to cupping (89, 90) and moxibustion (91).

Traditional practices taken to excess may sometimes result in harm. Some Hispanic groups attribute listlessness, diarrhea, and vomiting to *mollera caida* (fallen fontanelle). Traditional curing includes holding the child upside down, often with the top of the head in water, and shaking the child to return the fontanelle to its proper position (92). If this remedy is applied too vigorously, it may result in retinal hemorrhages that resemble inflicted physical abuse (93). Nevertheless, it is firmly based on traditional healing practices and as such must be differentiated from idiosyncratically inflicted abuse.

Again, it is instructive to view middle-class white child rearing practices in the United States through the eyes of diverse cultures. Colicky infants and small children would arouse suspicion of bad child care practices or inflicted trauma among Hawaiian-Polynesians. They believe that tossing or jiggling infants and small children will cause *opu huli,* a turned or displaced stomach. *Opu huli* may occur at all ages, but young children are believed to be particularly susceptible. Symptoms include indigestion, fussiness, and general discomfort. Should a small child exhibit symptoms of *opu huli,* diagnostic measures confirm the problem and specific healing massages must be applied. Since *haoles* do not subscribe to this medical belief, in the eyes of Hawaiians they take undue risks with the health and well-being of their children by jiggling them to evoke a smile or quiet their crying (70; see chap. 10).

While it is critical to argue for an understanding of the cultural context, it is equally important to avoid blind acceptance of harm to children couched in justifications of traditional practices. Too little attention has been directed toward normative child-rearing practices that function "to selectively reduce the probability of survival" (73). In Sierra Leone, the Temne bathed infants in cold streams and dried them in the open air despite a relatively high rate of infant mortality due to pneumonia (94). In Ecuador, mothers believe that males must be breast fed longer than females, which compromises the development and survival of daughters (73). Female genital operations of clitoridectomy and infibulation, in addition to their painfulness, carry a significant risk of infection, sterility, and later death during childbirth (95). Initiation rites without doubt are painful, frightening experiences for young boys that may serve as a culturally acceptable release of hostility toward the young (84, 96).

Child care practices also may be adaptive in one setting but potentially harmful or dangerous in another. For example, Polynesians believe that sibling caretaking is important for the social development of children (97–99). In traditional rural settings, sibling caretaking occurred in an environment relatively free of physical hazards, embedded in multi-age groups of children, and usually with adults nearby to call upon in an emergency. As Maoris in New Zealand and other Polynesians moved to urban areas, sibling caretaking put both the young caretakers and their charges in potentially dangerous situations. Substandard urban housing increased the risk of accidents, and isolation of families decreased the likelihood that there would be others to call upon for assistance (99).

Cultural patterns of child care persist through the force of custom and because parents believe that adherence to the dictates of their cultural tradition will enhance their children's, and their own, well-being. The cultural context of a behavior must be viewed holistically. No single element of a cultural pattern can be removed from its context and judged in isolation from other integrated aspects of that culture. As Erikson has noted, "[a] system of child care can be said to be a factor making for trust, even when certain items of that tradition taken singly may seem unnecessarily cruel" (100). Nevertheless, any practice, whether collective or individual, that compromises children's development and survival must be critically considered. Practices that inflict potential physical or psychic pain and harm on all children, or all children in particular categories, must be subjected to empirical tests of harm and not judged on an implicit or explicit ethnocentric basis. The changing nature of child-rearing advice in Euro-American societies stands as a caution against too facile determinations of what is good and bad for children. "Best" child care advice has varied from one generation to the next as to breast versus bottle or schedule versus demand feeding, for example. Further, the causal tie between traditional practices believed to be beneficial and increased morbidity and mortality is often difficult to demonstrate in environments of high infant mortality due to poverty and disease (73, 80).

The definition of child abuse and neglect will, by necessity, retain a large measure of relativity at this first level of culturally accepted practices. A hallmark of anthropological inquiry is to search for the meaning and explanation of any practice and its place within the cultural context. Explanation and understanding, however, do not preclude recognizing the attendant suffering of children or taking a position (96). *Emic* and *etic* perspectives must be reconciled. How is the line drawn between circumcision at adolescence and circumcision at birth? How would Euro-Americans convince traditional peoples in highland New Guinea that circumcision is more painful for an adolescent than an infant? How would traditional highland New Guinea peoples convince Euro-Americans that circumcision has no meaning to an infant who does not understand the deep cultural significance of the rites and further, that infancy is a time when the child should be spared all discomfort? How is the line drawn between scarification and orthodontia? Both are painful experiences for the child, but they are intended to enhance the child's attractiveness. What is thought of the middle-class American parent who spares the child physical pain by not correcting an exaggerated overbite so that the child is ridiculed throughout the school years? How is a traditional Yoruba parent regarded for refusal to have scarification performed because of the pain? These marks are not only cosmetic, but signify important cultural and religious meaning. The child may be spared pain in childhood but will never be accepted as an adult in traditional culture.

Idiosyncratic Child Abuse and Neglect

Once cultural variability in child-rearing practices and therefore in definitions of child abuse and neglect is acknowledged, assessments of what is abusive and what is culturally acceptable behavior must be made. Such distinctions are a legitimate and often pressing concern for child protection workers.

All cultures have continua for acceptable parenting. The most indulgent of cultures, in which children are rarely subjected to any sanctions, and the most punitive of cultures, in which children may be severely beaten for misbehavior, have concepts of child maltreatment. Polynesia as a culture area is noted for its indulgence of children. In one Polynesian society, children could be pinched lightly on the mouth for misbehavior. More severe punishments were prohibited. In administering this punishment, one man left a scratch on the lip of his grandchild. From the *etic* perspective of United States child protection workers, this would hardly be cause for alarm. However, this deviation from culturally accepted practices resulted in the grandfather being soundly berated by his cultural peers for the abuse by *emic* standards (101). At the other end of the spectrum stand the Ik of East Africa. Relocated from their traditional lands to an area that provided only marginal subsistence, the Ik considered it foolhardy to share food or shelter with their children past the age of three. A mother who behaved in a contrary fashion, feeding and sheltering her daughter, was considered neglectful in that the child would not learn to fend for herself. And indeed, when her mother could no longer care for her, the girl perished, "proof" of the error of the mother's ways (102).

The line that separates acceptable child-rearing practices from unacceptable is a fine one and requires a clear understanding of the cultural context. Despite Sweden's law banning physical punishment, Swedes do not necessarily agree on where the line should be drawn between *aga* (beating) and acceptable discipline (103).

Difficulties in differentiating culturally acceptable child-rearing practices from idiosyncratic abuse are exacerbated by the nature of service provision. In general, service providers are restricted in their community contacts to problematic individuals and families rather than to the continuum of acceptable and unacceptable behaviors. Providers tend not to see the countless times that belts are picked up in threat or the times that a child is hit, but not harmed or pained, if there is a consensus by parent, child, and community that the action was within acceptable bounds. Instead, the cases in which belts are used and children are left with buckle marks, bruises, welts, and injuries are more commonly seen by professionals working with child abuse. Cultural acceptance of physical discipline cannot be equated with explanations obtained in clinical experience with abusive parents. The refrain, "This is how we do things in our culture or community," deceptively resonates to the refrain from abusive parents, "This is how I was raised and this is how I will raise my children." The complex relationship between "proper" child-rearing practices and the larger cultural context is illustrated in the words of an urban United States black woman concerned with the rise in juvenile delinquency:

> Children is not like they was. You never had no juvenile, nothin' like that. . . . And there's a law you can't whup your children, and if you can't whup your children, you look for all this to happen. Everybody should know how to whup 'em without beatin' 'em and bruisin' 'em up. (104)

To gain the support of diverse ethnic and cultural groups for the prevention and treatment of child abuse, it is more fruitful to capitalize on the standard in virtually all cultures that children may not be damaged rather than attempting to eradicate deep-seated cultural practices that have not been demonstrated conclusively to be harmful.

Societal Level Abuse and Neglect

With respect to the third definitional level, children subjected to the deleterious effects of poverty, malnutrition, or international strife also may be labeled "abused" or "neglected," particularly in popular literature. These conditions, that affect adults and children alike, are difficult to define strictly as abuse and neglect for which caretakers are accountable. Societal and idiosyncratic abuse and neglect of children also may overlap. In poor countries, not all children leave their homes to engage in street begging or prostitution. It is important to explore both the societal conditions and the family dynamics that permit some children and not others to be exploited.

The Cultural Context of Child Abuse and Neglect

The most potentially valuable contribution of a cross-cultural perspective is clarification of the conditions under which child abuse and neglect are likely to occur. In the third edition of *The Battered Child* (9), characteristics of Western industrialized nations were discussed as leading to a comparatively high rate of child maltreatment. At that time, knowledge about child abuse and neglect was based almost entirely on the United States and other Western nations. With the growing international literature on child abuse and neglect, it is clear that child abuse is not restricted to European and North American nations. It is also clear that child maltreatment seems more likely to occur under some circumstances than others, regardless of national boundaries. At this point in the state of the knowledge, it is more fruitful to examine the cross-cultural record for factors implicated across cultural contexts than to attempt to compare incidence and prevalence rates. For the purposes of this chapter, a brief discussion of social supports, cultural sanctioning of physical discipline, and categories of vulnerable children will illustrate the utility of the cross-cultural record.

Social Supports

The presence or absence of social support networks has been importantly related to child abuse and neglect in the United States (105). The cross-cultural literature lends strong credence to social supports being a critical deterrent to abuse and neglect (55, 61). The consequences of parental inadequacy or aggression are potentially less serious when child rearing is embedded in a larger network of individuals than two biological parents. Embeddedness of child rearing in larger kin and community networks provides assistance to parents and also helps to ensure that child care behaviors will be open to scrutiny and community standards maintained.

Cross-culturally, mothers who are isolated in child care tasks with little or no periodic relief are harsher and more rejecting toward their children (64, 106). Children whose social networks are inadequate or have broken down are particularly vulnerable to maltreatment. Among the Gusii of East Africa, children from broken homes or out-of-wedlock unions accounted for only 2.5% of the population, but 25% of the malnourished children (107). Among another East African group, children from intertribal marriages were at increased risk of neglect. If the intertribal marriage floundered, or the parents provided inadequate care, neither the kin group of the mother nor that of the father felt that the child fell under their protection (69). In China, stepchildren and orphans are thought to require special protection under the law from maltreatment (108). Abusive Hawaiian-Polynesian families are less likely to be actively involved in the '*ohana*, the extended kinship network (52). Hawaiian-Polynesian children are explicit in their strategy of screaming more loudly than a spanking warrants in order to draw in the help of nearby kin (71). In contrast to the privacy of American households, in most of the world's societies neighbors and kin need not hesitate to intervene in overly harsh parental action.

Cultural Sanctioning of Physical Discipline

Cultural sanctioning of physical discipline has also been posited as a necessary condition for child abuse (105, 109). Physical aggression within the family occurs with sufficient frequency in the United States that it cannot be neatly labeled deviant (79). Further, physical discipline of children is instituted early. Despite the fact that mothers attending routine, well-child clinic visits believed that children should not be spanked until one year of age, one-fourth spanked infants younger than six months of age, and one-third spanked infants younger than one year of age (110). Incidents of child abuse are frequently explained by parents as discipline out of control (111).

The cross-cultural literature provides mixed evidence on the relationship between cultural sanctioning of physical discipline and child abuse. Dubanoski and Snyder (53), in examining patterns of child abuse reports in Hawaii, found that cultural factors including attitudes toward the use of physical punishment had a significant effect on proportions of child abuse in the population. Samoans, who believe that children should be physically disciplined to ensure proper behavior, had higher rates of physical abuse than would be expected. Japanese parents, in contrast, who do not hold a similarly high regard for the value of physical discipline, were lower than expected for physical child maltreatment.

On the other hand, the cross-cultural record indicates that in many societies physical discipline is swiftly and unself-consciously administered, but children with inflicted injuries are rare (61). Physical discipline may be more dangerous for children when it is negatively sanctioned (112). If physical discipline is a measure of last resort, following negotiation, threats, and pleas, by the time it is actually administered parental anger and frustration may be more likely to exceed acceptable boundaries. Cultural groups may be more adamant about their right to discipline than actually is translated into action.

While cultures vary considerably in their acceptance of physical discipline of children, convergence is likely in judgments of abusive incidents (57). Cultural sanctioning of physical discipline, under the right circumstances, undoubtedly can spill over into idiosyncratic abuse. What requires further examination is whether the causal argument works in the other direction, that cultural beliefs in physical discipline set the stage and provide a necessary condition for child maltreatment. An important question that must be resolved, and to which the cross-cultural evidence can contribute, is whether child abuse is most appropriately seen as parental *discipline* out of control or parental *rage* out of control.

Vulnerable Children

Research in Euro-American nations has focused more on the characteristics of abusive and neglectful adults than on their children. The cross-cultural literature, however, provides better information on categories of children who are vulnerable to abuse and neglect. Overall, the cross-cultural literature indicates that child abuse and neglect are less likely in cultures in which children are highly valued for their economic utility, as bearers of cultural or religious continuity, or as sources of emotional satisfaction. Nevertheless, even in societies that place a high value on children, some children are less valued than others. Characteristics of children at risk of abuse and neglect may be culture bound, *emically* defined, or tangible and evident from an outside, *etic,* point of view.

Virtually all societies have values concerning preferred and disvalued characteristics in their members, including children. Among the Bariba of West Africa, infants born in certain positions, such as face down, or with the appearance of teeth are thought to be witches and treated accordingly (113). Cultural criteria vary such that a trait that is esteemed by one society may be abhorred by another. An aggressive male child would be highly valued, and even encouraged in his aggressiveness, among the Yanomamo of South America (114) where "fierce" warriors are exemplars of their culture. Among the Machiguenga, also of South America, an aggressive child would fare less well since anger is highly disvalued (115). These categories of children, based on cultural preferences and beliefs, are difficult to delineate without a thorough knowledge of the cultural context.

Ethnographic literature and demographic analyses (77, 116) suggest that some categories of children are vulnerable to maltreatment across cultures. This does not mean, of course, that all children in these categories are maltreated, just that they are at increased risk. Deformed or handicapped children may receive a lower standard of care because they are regarded as a burden, as an ill omen or as nonhuman. Multiple births in some cultures are considered propitious while in others they signal bad luck or are thought to resemble animal litters rather than human births. One or both of a set of twins may be destroyed at birth or maltreated during childhood (72). Children whose births are difficult may be considered dangerous or malevolent and thus be vulnerable to maltreatment. In developed and developing countries, children born out of wedlock may be subject to stigmatization by the community and ill-treatment by their parents. Illegitimate children were abandoned in great numbers on the streets of New York and London, thereby stimulating the establishment of foundling homes. Illegitimate children in Sepik societies were sometimes sold to neighboring tribes whose young boys required a homicide victim in order to enter manhood (117).

Gender preferences may also have serious consequences for children. In cultures where a strong preference for a son exists, such as India and China, deliberate female infanticide may occur or the girl child may receive a lower standard of food and medical attention than her brothers, resulting in increased female morbidity and mortality (74). While adopted daughters in Taiwan are legally protected, they may be treated as slaves or sold into prostitution if their adoptive parents so wish (118, 119).

Children living in situations of rapid socioeconomic and sociocultural change are also at increased risk of maltreatment. Even a modest environmental change can significantly alter child care practices. Some Native American groups, for example, became more harsh in their toilet training practices not only because of contact with whites who demanded early toileting compliance, but also because of a change from dirt floors that were easily cleaned to wooden floors that required more care (120). Immigrant and urbanizing families face unique problems that can create situations ripe for intrafamilial conflict and abuse. Children, through formal schooling, obtain better knowledge of their new environment and society than their parents. They become less obedient and compliant as parental superiority in knowledge decreases (121). Mothers who move to urbanizing areas and come into situations of culture contact have been found to be less confident in their efficacy in child rearing than they were in their traditional living circumstances (122). Their difficulties are compounded by findings that children in urbanizing areas tend to be more disruptive in their behavior (123). These conditions, coupled with the stress of substandard housing, unemployment, and poverty, can escalate into situations at risk for abuse.

Maltreatment of vulnerable children may take a multitude of forms. Children may be deliberately killed, sexually misused, sold for economic gain, or neglected. What has been termed passive infanticide, underinvestment, or selective neglect may be more frequent cross-culturally than physical assault (77, 116, 124–127). These parental behaviors are defined as "any combination of medical, nutritional, physical, or emotional neglect of an infant or young child in comparison to other children in the family or to children of families in similar socioeconomic and educational circumstances" (126). If parents regard a child as unlikely to survive or to become capable of economic self-sufficiency in adulthood, or to be unsatisfactory in some other way, they may be less willing to invest emotional and material resources in that child to the detriment of competing offspring.

Conclusion

Child abuse and neglect transcend national and cultural boundaries. The problem has been officially recognized in the United States for slightly more than twenty years. European and Western national have, in most cases, followed a similar pattern of initial denial that child abuse and neglect exist within their boundaries to a recognition of multiple types of child abuse and neglect. In developing nations, child abuse and neglect have rightfully been of lesser concern than infant and child morbidity and mortality due to disease and malnutrition. Nevertheless, developing nations are increasingly recognizing that maltreatment of their children is an issue demanding attention. Cultural competence challenges ethnocentric beliefs about what is good for children or what is abusive and neglectful. It also furthers knowledge of the circumstances under which child abuse and neglect are most likely to occur, and, in turn, most likely to be prevented.

References

1. Caffey, J. 1946. Multiple Fractures in the Long Bones of Infants Suffering from Chronic Subdural Hematoma. *Am. J. Roentgenology* 56(2): 163–73.
2. Caffey, J. 1957. Some Traumatic Lesions in Growing Bones Other Than Fractures and Dislocation—Clinical and Radiological Features. *British J. Radiology* 30: 225–38.
3. Adelson, L. 1961. Slaughter of the Innocents. A Study of Forty-Six Homicides in Which the Victims Were Children. *New England J. Med.* 264: 1345–49.
4. Elmer, E. 1960. Abused Young Children Seen in Hospitals. *Social Work* 5(4): 98–102.
5. Kempe, C. H.; Silverman, F. N.; Steele, B. F.; Droegemueller, W.; and Silver, H. K. 1962. The Battered-Child Syndrome. *JAMA* 181: 17–24.
6. Nelson. B. 1984. *Making an Issue of Child Abuse. Political Agenda Setting for Social Problems.* Chicago: University of Chicago Press.
7. Pfofl, S. J. 1977. The "Discovery" of Child Abuse. *Social Problems* 24(3): 310–23.
8. Kempe, C. H. 1978. Recent Developments in the Field of Child Abuse. *Child Abuse and Neglect: International J.* 2(4): 261–67.
9. Korbin, J. E. 1980. The Cross-Cultural Context of Child Abuse and Neglect. In *The Battered Child.* 3d ed., ed. C. H. Kempe and R. E. Helfer, 21–35.
10. Spradley, J. P. 1979. *The Ethnographic Interview.* New York: Holt, Rinehart and Winston.
11. Green, J. W. 1978. The Role of Cultural Anthropology in the Education of Social Service Personnel. *J. Sociology and Social Welfare* 5(2): 214–29.
12. Agathonos, H. 1983. Institutional Child Abuse in Greece: Some Preliminary Findings. *Child Abuse and Neglect: International J.* 7(1): 71–74.
13. Agathonos, H.; Stathacoupoulou, N.; Adam, H.; and Nakou, S. 1982. Child Abuse and Neglect in Greece: Sociomedical Aspects. *Child Abuse and Neglect: International J.* 6(3): 307–11.
14. Arnold, E. 1982. The Use of Corporal Punishment in Child Rearing in the West Indies. *Child Abuse and Neglect: International J.* 6(2): 141–45.

15. Bhattacharyya, A. K. 1979. Child Abuse in India and the Nutritionally Battered Child. *Child Abuse and Neglect: International J.* 3(2): 607–14.

16. Bhattacharyya, A. K. 1981. Nutritional Deprivation and Related Emotional Aspects in Calcutta Children. *Child Abuse and Neglect: International J.* 5(4): 467–74.

17. Caffo, E.; Guaraldi, G. P.; Magnani, G.; and Tass, R. 1982. Prevention of Child Abuse and Neglect Through Early Diagnosis of Serious Disturbances in the Mother-Child Relationship in Italy. *Child Abuse and Neglect: International J.* 6(4): 453–63.

18. de Silva, W. 1981. Some Cultural and Economic Factors Leading to Neglect, Abuse and Violence in Respect of Children within the Family in Sri Lanka. *Child Abuse and Neglect: International J.* 5(4): 391–405.

19. Fergusson, D. M.; Flemming, J.; and O'Neill, D. P. 1972. *Child Abuse in New Zealand*. Wellington: Government Press.

20. Gaddini, R. 1983. Incest As a Developmental Failure. *Child Abuse and Neglect: International J.* 7(3): 357–58.

21. Gaddini, R. 1984. On the Origins of the Battered Child Syndrome. Abuse as Acting Out of Preverbal Events. *Child Abuse and Neglect: International J.* 8(1): 41–45.

22. Haditono, S. R. 1981. Prevention and Treatment of Child Abuse and Neglect among Children under Five Years of Age in Indonesia. *Child Abuse and Neglect: International J.* 5(2): 97–101.

23. Ikeda, Y. 1982. A Short Introduction to Child Abuse in Japan. *Child Abuse and Neglect: International J.* 6(4): 487–90.

24. Izuora, G. I., and Ebigbo, P. 1983. Emotional Reactions of Adult Africans to Children with Severe Kwashiorkor. *Child Abuse and Neglect: International J.* 7(3): 351–56.

25. Jacobson, R. S., and Straker, G. 1979. A Research Project on Abusing Parents and Their Spouses. *Child Abuse and Neglect: International J.* 3(1): 381–90.

26. Jinadu, M. 1980. The Role of Neglect in the Aetiology of Protein-Energy Malnutrition in Urban Communities of Nigeria. *Child Abuse and Neglect: International J.* 4(4): 233–45.

27. Jinadu, M. K.; Daramola, S. O.; and Ikpatt, S. F. 1982. Some Factors Affecting Mother-Child Relationships Following Low Birthweight Delivery in a Nigerian Sociocultural Environment. *Child Abuse and Neglect: International J.* 6(1): 57–62.

28. Kellerman, F. J. S. 1979. *Child Battering*. Department of Social Welfare and Pensions. Pretoria: Republic of South Africa.

29. Loening, W. 1981. Child Abuse among the Zulus: A People in Transition. *Child Abuse and Neglect: International J.* 5(1): 3–7.

30. Maroulis, H. 1979. Child Abuse: The Greek Scene. *Child Abuse and Neglect: International J.* 3(1): 185–90.

31. Martinez-Roig, A.; Domingo-Salvany, F.; Ibenez-Cacho, J.; and Llorens-Terol, J. 1983. Psychologic Implications of the Maltreated-Child Syndrome. *Child Abuse and Neglect: International J.* 7(3): 261–63.

32. Mehra, B. K. 1982. Highlights on Abuse in Education: A View from India. *Child Abuse and Neglect: International J.* 6(2): 225–28.

33. Mehta, J.; Lokeshwar, M.; Bhatt, S.; Athavale, V.; and Kulkarni, B. 1979. "Rape" in Children. *Child Abuse and Neglect: International J.* 3(3/4): 671–77.

34. Mehta, M. N. 1982. Physical Abuse of Abandoned Children in India. *Child Abuse and Neglect: International J.* 6(2): 171–75.

35. Mehta, M. N.; Prabhu, S. V.; and Mistry, H. 1985. Child Labor in Bombay. *Child Abuse and Neglect: International J.* 9(1): 107–11.

36. Mumba, J. F. 1981. Adoption in Zambia. *Child Abuse and Neglect: International J.* 5(2): 197–99.

37. Nakou, S.; Adam, H.; Stathacopoulou, N.; and Agathonos, H. 1982. Health Status of Abused and Neglected Children and Their Siblings. *Child Abuse and Neglect: International J.* 6(3): 279–84.

38. Nathan, L., and Hwang, W. T. 1981. Child Abuse in an Urban Centre in Malaysia. *Child Abuse and Neglect: International J.* 5(3): 241–48.

39. Nwako, F. A. 1974. The Child Abuse Syndrome in Nigeria. *International Surgery* 59:613–16.

40. Ojofeitimi, E. O., and Odusote, A. O. 1982. Assessment of Marginal Nutrition and Means of Preventing Communicable Diseases in Twins. An Implication for Intensive Follow-Up. *Child Abuse and Neglect: International J.* 6(3): 295–97.

41. Okeahialam, T. C. 1984. Child Abuse in Nigeria. *Child Abuse and Neglect: International J.* 8(1): 69–73.

42. Oyemade, A. 1980. Child Care Practices in Nigeria—An Urgent Plea for Social Workers. *Child Abuse and Neglect: International J.* 4(2): 101–3.

43. Robertson, B. A., and Juritz, J. M. 1979. Characteristics of the Families of Abused Children. *Child Abuse and Neglect: International J.* 3(3/4): 857–62.

44. Semiawan, C. 1981. An Invitational Environment to Treat and Prevent Emotional Deprivation: A Meaningful Approach to Increase Psychological Development. *Child Abuse and Neglect: International J.* 5(4): 481–86.

45. Sereewat, S. 1983. The Work of the Foundation for Children in Thailand. *Child Abuse and Neglect: International J.* 7(3): 359–61.

46. Tauber, E. E.; Meda, C.; and Vitro, V. 1977. Child Ill-Treatment as Considered by the Italian Criminal and Civil Codes. *Child Abuse and Neglect: International J.* 1(1): 149–52.

47. Tevoedjre, I. 1981. Violence and the Child in the Adult World in Africa. *Child Abuse and Neglect: International J.* 5(4): 495–98.

48. Tsiantis, J.; Kokkevi, A.; and Agathaonos-Marouli, E. 1981. Parents of Abused Children in Greece: Psychiatric and Psychological Characteristics. *Child Abuse and Neglect: International J.* 5(3): 281–85.

49. Van Staden, J. 1979. The Mental Development of Abused Children in South Africa. *Child Abuse and Neglect: International J.* 3(3/4): 997–1000.

50. Zimrin, H. 1983. Building Up a New Service for the Abused Child. *Child Abuse and Neglect: International J.* 7(1): 55–60.

51. Cohn, A. H. 1982. Stopping Abuse before It Occurs: Different Solutions for Different Population Groups. *Child Abuse and Neglect: International J.* 6(4): 473–83.

52. Dubanoski, R. 1981. Child Maltreatment in European- and Hawaiian-Americans. *Child Abuse and Neglect: International J.* 5(4): 457–66.

53. Dubanoski, R., and Snyder, K. 1980. Patterns of Child Abuse and Neglect in Japanese- and Samoan-Americans. *Child Abuse and Neglect: International J.* 4(4): 217–25.

54. Eisenberg, L. 1981. Cross-Cultural and Historic Perspectives on Child Abuse and Neglect. *Child Abuse and Neglect: International J.* 5(3): 299–308.

55. Garbarino, J., and Ebata, A. 1983. The Significance of Cultural and Ethnic Factors in Child Maltreatment. *J. Marriage and the Family* 45(4): 773–83.

56. Gelles, R., and Pedrick-Cornell, C. 1983. *International Perspectives on Family Violence.* Lexington, Mass.: Lexington Books.

57. Giovannoni, J., and Becerra, R. 1979. *Defining Child Abuse.* New York: Free Press.

58. Kammerman, S. 1975. Eight Countries Cross-National Perspectives on Child Abuse and Neglect. *Children Today* 4:34–37.

59. Korbin, J. E. 1977. Anthropological Contributions to the Study of Child Abuse. *Child Abuse and Neglect: International J.* 1(1): 7–24.

60. Korbin, J. E. 1979. A Cross-Cultural Perspective on the Role of the Community in Child Abuse and Neglect. *Child Abuse and Neglect: International J.* 3(1): 9–18.

61. Korbin, J. E., ed. 1981. *Child Abuse and Neglect: Cross-Cultural Perspectives.* Berkeley: University of California Press.

62. Lauderdale, M.; Valiunas, A.; and Anderson, R. 1980. Race, Ethnicity, and Child Maltreatment: An Empirical Analysis. *Child Abuse and Neglect: International J.* 4(3): 163–69.

63. Levinson, D. 1981. Physical Punishment of Children and Wife Beating in Cross-Cultural Perspective. *Child Abuse and Neglect: International J.* 5(2): 193–95.

64. Rohner, R. 1975. *They Love Me, They Love Me Not: A Worldwide Study of the Effects of Parental Acceptance and Rejection.* New Haven, Conn.: Human Relations Area Files Press.

65. Spearly, J. L., and Lauderdale, M. 1983. Community Characteristics and Ethnicity in the Prediction of Child Maltreatment Rates. *Child Abuse and Neglect: International J.* 7(1): 91–105.

66. Straus, M. 1983. Societal Morphogenesis and Intrafamily Violence in Cross-Cultural Perspective. In *International Perspectives on Family Violence,* ed. R. Gelles and C. Pedrick-Cornell, 27–43. Lexington, Mass.: Lexington Books.

67. Taylor, L., and Newberger, E. 1979. Child Abuse in the International Year of the Child. *New England J. Med.* 301:1215–12.

68. Edgerton, R. B. 1976. *Deviance: A Cross-Cultural Perspective.* Menlo Park, Calif.: Cummings.

69. Fraser, G., and Kilbride, P. 1980. Child Abuse and Neglect—Rare but Perhaps Increasing Phenomena among the Samia of Kenya. *Child Abuse and Neglect: International J.* 4(4): 227–32.

70. Green, J. 1978. The Role of Cultural Anthropology in the Education of Social Service Personnel. *J. Sociology and Social Welfare* 5:214–29.

71. Korbin, J. E. 1984. Deviance in Child Rearing: Cross-Cultural Issues in Child Abuse and Neglect. Paper presented at the Annual Meeting of the American Anthropological Association, Denver.

72. Levy, J. 1964. The Fate of Navajo Twins. *Am. Anthropologist* 66:883–87.

73. McKee, L. 1984. Sex Differentials in Survivorship and Customary Treatment of Infants and Children. *Med. Anthropology* 8(2): 91–108.

74. Miller, B. 1981. *The Endangered Sex: Neglect of Female Children in Rural North India.* Ithaca, N.Y.: Cornell University Press.

75. Minturn, L. 1984. Changes in the Differential Treatment of Rajput Girls in Khalapur: 1955–1975. *Med. Anthropology* 8(2): 127–32.

76. Scheper-Hughes, N. 1984. Infant Mortality and Infant Care: Cultural and Economic Constraints on Nurturing in Northeast Brazil. *Social Science and Medicine* 5: 535–46.

77. Scrimshaw, S. 1984. Infanticide in Human Populations: Societal and Individual Concerns. In *Infanticide: Comparative and Evolutionary Perspectives*, ed. G. Hausfater and S. Hrdy, 439–62. New York: Aldine.

78. Pike, K. 1954. *Language in Relation to a Unified Theory of the Structure of Human Behavior*. Vol. 1. Glendale, Calif.: Summer Institute of Linguistics.

79. Straus, M.; Gelles R.; and Steinmetz, S. 1980. *Behind Closed Doors. Violence in the American Family*. New York: Anchor.

80. LeVine, R. 1977. Child Rearing as Cultural Adaptation. In *Culture and Infancy: Variations in the Human Experience*, ed. P. H. Leiderman, S. Tulkin, and A. Rosenfeld, 15–27. New York: Academic Press.

81. Super, C. 1984. Sex Differences in Infant Care and Vulnerability. *Med. Anthropology* 8(2): 84–90.

82. Yeatman, G. W.; Shaw, C.; Barlow, M. J.; and Bartlett, G. 1976. Pseudobattering in Vietnamese Children. *Pediatrics* 58:616.

83. Caudill, W., and Plath, D. 1966. Who Sleeps by Whom? Parent-Child Involvement in Urban Japanese Families. *Psychiatry* 29:344–66.

84. Langness, L. L. 1981. Child Abuse and Cultural Values: The Case of New Guinea. In *Child Abuse and Neglect: Cross-Cultural Perspectives*, ed. J. Korbin, 13–34. Berkeley: University of California Press.

85. Olson, E. 1981. Socioeconomic and Psychocultural Contexts of Child Abuse and Neglect in Turkey. In *Child Abuse and Neglect: Cross-Cultural Perspectives*, ed. J. Korbin, 96–119. Berkeley: University of California Press.

86. Turnbull, C. 1961. *The Forest People. A Study of the Pygmies of the Congo*. New York: Simon and Schuster.

87. Royal Anthropological Institute. 1974. The Case of Mrs. Adesanya. *Royal Anthropological Institute News* 4:2.

88. Langness, L. L. 1979. Personal communication.

89. Asnes, R. S., and Wisotsky, D. H. 1981. Cupping Lesions Simulating Child Abuse. *J. Pediatrics* 99:267–68.

90. Sandler, A. P., and Haynes, V. C. 1978. Nonaccidental Trauma and Medical Folk Belief. A Case of Cupping. *Pediatrics* 61:921–22.

91. Feldman, K. W. 1984. Pseudoabusive Burns in Asian Refugees. *Am. J. Diseases in Children* 138:768–69.

92. Clark, M. 1959. *Health in the Mexican-American Culture*. Berkeley: University of California Press.

93. Guarnaschelli, J.; Lee, J.; and Pitts, F. 1972. "Fallen Fontanelle" (Caidade Mollera): A Variant of the Battered Child Syndrome. *JAMA* 222:1545.

94. Dorjan, V. Rural-Urban Differences in Infant and Child Mortality among the Temne of Kolifa. *J. Anthropological Research* 32:1.

95. Hosken, F. 1979. *The Hosken Report. Genital and Sexual Mutilation of Females*. Lexington, Mass.: Women's International Network.

96. Keesing, R. 1982. Introduction. In *Rituals of Manhood. Male Initiation in Papua New Guinea,* ed. G. Herdt. Berkeley: University of California Press.

97. Gallimore, R.; Boggs, J.; and Jordan, C. 1974. *Culture, Behavior and Education. A Study of Hawaiian-Americans.* Beverly Hills, Calif.: Sage.

98. Korbin, J. 1978. *Caretaking Patterns in a Rural Hawaiian Community: Congruence of Child and Observer Reports.* Ph.D. diss., University of California, Los Angeles.

99. Ritchie, J., and Ritchie, J. 1981. Child Rearing and Child Abuse: The Polynesian Context. In *Child Abuse and Neglect: Cross-Cultural Perspectives,* ed. J. Korbin, 186–204. Berkeley: University of California Press.

100. Erikson, E. 1963. *Childhood and Society.* 2d ed. New York: Norton.

101. Firth, R. 1970. Education in Tikopia. In *From Child to Adult: Studies in the Anthropology of Education,* ed. J. Middleton. New York: Natural History Press.

102. Turnbull, C. 1972. *The Mountain People.* New York: Simon and Schuster.

103. Haeuser, A. 1982. Sweden's Law Prohibiting Physical Punishment of Children. Milwaukee, Wisc.: Region V Resource Center on Child Abuse and Neglect.

104. Snow, L. 1977. Popular Medicine in a Black Neighborhood. In *Ethnic Medicine in the Southwest,* ed. E. H. Spicer. Tucson: University of Arizona Press.

105. Garbarino, J. The Human Ecology of Child Maltreatment: A Conceptual Model for Research. *J. Marriage and the Family* 39:721–35.

106. Minturn, L., and Lambert, W. 1964. *Mothers of Six Cultures. Antecedents of Child Rearing.* New York: John Wiley and Sons.

107. LeVine, S., and LeVine, R. 1981. Child Abuse and Neglect in Sub-Saharan Africa. In *Child Abuse and Neglect: Cross-Cultural Perspectives,* ed. J. Korbin, 35–55. Berkeley: University of California Press.

108. Korbin, J. 1981. "Very Few Cases": Child Abuse and Neglect in the People's Republic of China. In *Child Abuse and Neglect: Cross-Cultural Perspectives,* ed. J. Korbin, 166–85. Berkeley: University of California Press.

109. Gil, D. 1970. *Violence against Children, Physical Child Abuse in the United States.* Cambridge: Harvard University Press.

110. Korsh, B.; Christian, J.; Gozzi, E.; and Carlson, P. 1965. Infant Care and Punishment: A Pilot Study. *Am. J. Public Health* 55(12): 1880–88.

111. Kadushin, A., and Martin, J. 1981. *Child Abuse. An Interactional Event.* New York: Columbia University Press.

112. Parke, R., and Collmer, C. 1975. *Child Abuse: An Interdisciplinary Analysis.* Chicago: University of Chicago Press.

113. Sargent, C. 1984. Born to Die. The Fate of Extraordinary Children in Bariba Culture. Paper presented at the Annual Meeting of the American Anthropological Association, Denver.

114. Chagnon, N. 1968. *Yanomamo: The Fierce People.* New York: Holt, Rinehart and Winston.

115. Johnson, O. 1981. The Socioeconomic Context of Child Abuse and Neglect in Native South America. In *Child Abuse and Neglect: Cross-Cultural Perspectives,* ed. J. Korbin, 56–70. Berkeley: University of California Press.

116. Scrimshaw, S. 1978. Infant Mortality and Behavior in the Regulation of Family Size. *Population and Development Review* 4(3): 383–403.

117. Gewertz, D. 1977. From Sago Suppliers to Entrepreneurs: Marketing and Migration in the Middle Sepik. *Oceania* 48(2): 126–40.
118. Wolf, A. 1974. Marriage and Adoption in Northern Taiwan. In *Social Organization and the Applications of Anthropology,* ed. R. Smith, 128–60. Ithaca: Cornell University Press.
119. Wu, D. Y. H. Child Abuse in Taiwan. In *Child Abuse and Neglect: Cross-Cultural Perspectives,* ed. J. Korbin, 139–65. Berkeley: University of California Press.
120. Honigman, J. 1967. *Personality in Culture.* New York: Harper and Row.
121. LeVine, S., and Levine, R. 1985. Age, Gender and the Demographic Transition: The Life Course in Agrarian Societies. In *Gender and the Life Course,* ed. A. Rossi, 29–42. New York: Aldine.
122. Graves, N. 1972. City, Country, and Child Rearing: A Tri-Cultural Study of Mother-Child Relationships in Varying Environments. Ph.D. Diss., University of Colorado.
123. Weisner, T. 1979. Urban-Rural Differences in Sociable and Disruptive Behavior of Kenya Children. *Ethnology* 18(2): 153–72.
124. Johansson, S. 1984. Deferred Infanticide: Excess Female Mortality during Childhood. In *Infanticide: Comparative and Evolutionary Perspectives,* ed. G. Hausfater and S. Hrdy, 463–86. New York: Aldine.
125. McKee, L. 1984. Sex Differentials in Survivorship and Customary Treatment of Infants and Children. *Med. Anthropology* 8(2): 91–108.
126. Scrimshaw, S. 1983. Infanticide as Deliberate Fertility Regulation. In *Determinants of Fertility in Developing Countries: A Summary of Knowledge,* ed. R. Lee and R. Bulatao, 714–31. New York: Academic Press.
127. Sheper-Hughes, N. 1984. Infant Mortality and Infant Care: Cultural and Economic Constraints on Nurturing in Northeast Brazil. *Social Science and Medicine* 5: 535–46.

3 Stress and Child Abuse

Murray A. Straus and Glenda Kaufman Kantor

Life is full of paradoxes, and perhaps even more so in the family than elsewhere. Two of these ironic or paradoxical aspects of the family concern the high level of stress and the high level of violence that is characteristic of American family life.

In the case of violence, the paradox is that the family is, at one and the same time, the most physically violent group or institution that a typical citizen is likely to encounter (1–5) and also the group to which most people look for love, support, and gentleness. So the hallmarks of family life are both love and violence.

Much of the work of the Family Violence Research Program at the University of New Hampshire has been designed to unravel that paradox. We are a long way from a full explanation. However, some progress has been made. This chapter examines one of the several factors which go into that explanation: the link between stress and violence.

Another irony of family life is the fact that although the family is a place where one can find respite from the tensions of the world, the family is at the same time a group with its own inherently high level of conflict and stress. The theoretical case for this view is detailed elsewhere (6, 7). In this chapter we will illustrate but two stress-producing aspects of the family.

One source of family stress is the fact that, in addition to the normal differences and

Murray A. Straus, Ph.D., is professor of sociology and Glenda Kaufman Kantor, Ph.D., is a postdoctoral research fellow at the University of New Hampshire.

This chapter is one in a series of publications of the Family Violence Research Program at the University of New Hampshire. The program is supported by the University of New Hampshire and by NIMH grants MH27557 and T32 MH15161. A program bibliography and list of available publications will be sent on request.

It is a pleasure to acknowledge the many helpful criticisms and suggestions by the members of the Family Violence Research Program seminar: Joanne Benn, Diane Coleman, Ursula Dibble, David Finkelhor, Jean Giles-Sims, Cathy Greenblat, Suzanne Smart, and Kersti Yllo, the computer analysis by Shari Hagar, and the typing of this chapter by Sieglinde Fizz.

The theoretical and methodological sections of this chapter are the same as those in a parallel paper on "Stress and Assault in a National Sample of American Families" (45), but the sample and data differ. The sample for this chapter consists of only those families with at least one child at home, and the data for this chapter focus on child abuse rather than on assaults by the spouses on each other.

conflicts between two or more people, the family has built into its basic structure both the so-called battle of the sexes and the generation gap. A second source of stress is inherent in what is expected of families. For example, families are expected to provide adequate food, clothing, and shelter in a society which does not always give families the resources necessary to do this. Another example is the expectation that families bring up healthy, well-adjusted, law-abiding, and intelligent children who can "get ahead in the world." The stress occurs because these traits, and the opportunity to "get ahead," are all factors which are to a greater or lesser extent beyond the control of any given family.

The basic argument of the chapter is probably clear by what has just been said: that a major cause of the high rate of child abuse is the stress and conflict which tends to characterize families. Of course, this is only a plausible argument. Brenner (8), for example, has shown a clear relationship between stress as indexed by the unemployment rate and the rate of assault and homicide in the United States, Canada, and Great Britain. But is it that people are assaulted or murdered by unemployed members of their own families? This needs to be demonstrated with empirical data. Consequently, a major part of this chapter is devoted to such an empirical study.

The Theoretical Model

Although the empirical findings will start with the relationship between the level of stress in families and the level of child abuse, it is not argued that stress *directly* causes child abuse. Violence is only one of many possible responses to stress. Among the alternatives are passivity, resignation, or just leaving. University departments, for example, are also stressful environments, but the rate of physical violence within such departments is close to zero.

The absence of any necessary link between stress and violence is shown in Brenner's data on the correlates of unemployment (8). Unemployment is highly correlated not only with assault and homocide, but also with annual rates of hypertension, deaths from heart attacks, mental hospital admissions, and alcoholism. Similarly, Brown and Harris (9) studied a random sample of women in London using highly reliable and valid data on life stresses. The interesting point is that they demonstrated a clear tendency for these women to respond to stress by *depression* rather than violence. In a few instances, case control studies or lower socioeconomic clinical samples suggest either an ambiguous or negligible relationship between stress and child abuse (10–12).

On the other hand, others argue for theoretical formulations such as the multifactorial model of Gil (13) and the ecological model of Garbarino (14) based on Bronfenbrenner's work (15). Both Gil and Garbarino categorize stress largely in socioeconomic terms, while other investigators have gone beyond the chronic nature of stress-related poverty to a consideration of the acute nature of stressful life changes. For example, the prospective study of Egeland and his associates (16) found that stressful life events, along with particular maternal-infant interaction patterns and infant characteristics, were major predictors of child abuse. Similar findings have been reported by other researchers (17–20), although these authors point to the importance of stress as mediated by other variables such as social support, intergenerational family violence, and youthful parents. In par-

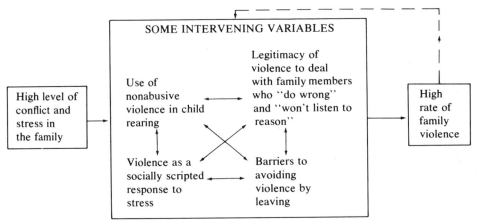

Figure 3.1

Partial model of relationship between stress and family violence. This diagram is labeled as a "partial" model for two main reasons: First, it includes only a sampling of the intervening variables which could be included in the center box. Second, it omits negative feedback loops (i.e., deviation dampening processes) which must be present. Without them the violence would escalate to the point where the system would self-destruct—as it sometimes, but not typically, does. See Straus (1) for a systems model of family violence which includes negative feedback processes and other elements of a cybernetic system.

ticular, Justice, Calvert, and Justice (19) utilized multiple measures for their controlled clinical sample and concluded that both recent life changes and a violent social script significantly differentiated abusive from nonabusive parents.

Mediating Variables

The above suggests that other factors must be present for stress to result in violence. The central box in figure 3.1 illustrates some of the other variables. For example, people are unlikely to respond to stress by violence unless this is part of the socially scripted method of dealing with stress and frustration—as it is in our society. So, an important part of the model is the existence of norms or images of behavior which depict striking out at others when under stress as part of human nature.

However, these are very general behavioral scripts. They cannot explain *family* violence, because they are part of the society's image of basic nature in *all* types of situations. They may be part of the explanation, but they are not sufficient. To find the additional variables which will lead to a sufficient explanation, one has to look at the nature of the family itself.

Normative Legitimacy of Family Violence

One very simple but nonetheless important factor is that the family has different rules about violence than other groups. In an office or a factory, the basic rule is that no one can hit anyone else, no matter what they do wrong. A person can be a pest, an intolerable bore, negligent, incompetent, selfish, or unwilling to listen to reason. But that still does not give anyone the right to hit such a person. In the family the situation is different. There the basic rule is that if someone does wrong and "won't listen to reason," then violence is permissible and sometimes even required.

This is clearly the case with respect to the rights and obligations of parents, but it also applies to spouses. As one husband said about an incident in which his wife threw a coffee pot at him, "I was running around with other women—I deserved it." Statements like that are made by many husbands and wives. In fact, the evidence suggests that a marriage license is also a hitting license (2, 21). Still, that does not explain why or how such a norm arose or why it persists. Here again there are a number of factors, one of which is shown in figure 3.1: the "nonabusive" use of violence in child rearing, that is, physical punishment.

Family Socialization in Violence

Physical punishment provides the society's basic training in violence, but, of course, training which applies most directly to behavior in the family. At least some use of physical punishment is just about universal in American society, typically beginning in infancy (22). What are the reasons for saying that learning about violence starts with physical punishment?

When physical punishment is used, several things can be expected to occur. Most obviously, the infant or child learns to do or not to do whatever the punishment is intended to teach, for example, not to pick up things from the ground and put them in his or her mouth. Less obvious, but equally or more important, are four other lessons which are so deeply learned that they become an integral part of one's personality and world view.

The first of these unintended consequences is the association of love with violence. Mommy and daddy are the first, and usually the only ones, to hit an infant. For most children this continues throughout childhood (23). The child therefore learns that the primary love objects are also those who hit.

Second, since physical punishment is used to train the child or to teach about dangerous things to be avoided, it establishes the moral rightness of hitting other family members.

The third unintended consequence is the "Johnny, I've told you ten times" principle—that when something is really important, it justifies the use of physical force.

Fourth is the idea that when one is under stress, is tense, or angry, hitting—although wrong—is understandable, that is, to a certain extent legitimate.

Involuntary Nature of Family Membership

The last of the mediating variables we will discuss is the simple fact that the family is only a semivoluntary institution. This is most obvious in the case of children. They cannot leave, nor can parents throw them out until a legally set age. So leaving—which is probably the most widely used and effective method of avoiding violence—is not available as an alternative in the parent-child relationship.

A number of other factors should be included in figure 3.1 and in this discussion. Those which have been discussed, however, should be sufficient to illustrate the theory which guided the analysis in this chapter.

By way of summary, the theory underlying this chapter rejects the idea that humans have an innate drive toward aggression or an innate tendency to respond to stress by aggression. Rather, a link between stress and aggression occurs only (a) if the individual has learned an "aggressive" response to stress, (b) if such a response is a culturally recognized script for behavior under stress, and (c) if the situation seems to be one which will produce rewards for aggression.

Sample

The data used to examine this theory were obtained in January and February of 1976. Interviews were conducted with a national-area probability sample of 1,146 persons with at least one child age three through seventeen living at home. Each respondent had to be between eighteen and seventy years of age and living with a member of the opposite sex as a couple. However, the couple did not have to be formally married. A random half of the respondents were female and half were male. Interviews lasted approximately one hour, were completely anonymous, and interviewers were of the racial or language group which was predominant in the sampling area for which they were responsible (4).

Definition and Measures of Stress

There has been considerable debate about the concept of stress (24–31). Is the stress caused by illness, unemployment, family conflict, getting married, or being promoted to a new job a property of the situation? For some people, a new set of job responsibilities is experienced as stress, whereas for others, *lack* of such new responsibilities is a stress.

The definition used here treats stress as a function of the interaction of the subjectively defined demands of a situation and the capacity of an individual or group to respond to these demands. Stress exists when the subjectively experienced demands are inconsistent with response capabilities. This can be demands in excess of capabilities or a low level of demand relative to response capabilities. A more adequate formulation of the concept of stress includes a number of other elements. For example, Farrington (6) has identified six components which need to be taken into account in research on stress: the stressor stimulus, objective demands, subjective demands, response capabilities, choice of response, and stress level. Important as these six components are, they will be ignored in this chapter because there is no way to investigate them with the data available.

There is a gap between the definition of stress given above and data actually reported here. This is because the methodology of this chapter *assumes* (a) that some *life event,* such as moving or the illness of a child, produces a certain, but unknown, degree of demand on parents, (b) that on the average this is subjectively experienced as a demand, (c) that the capabilities of parents to respond to these demands will not always be sufficient, and (d) that the result is a certain level of stress. On the basis of these assumptions, it is possible to investigate the relationship between such stressful life events and the level of violence in the family. Obviously, this leaves a large agenda for other investigators to develop a more adequate measure of stress.

As indicated above, the aspect of stress which is measured in this study is limited to

TABLE 3.1   **Percentage Experiencing Life Stresses during Previous Year**

Stressful Event	Male (N=519)	Female (N=616)	Total (N=1135)
1. Troubles with the boss	28.3	9.6	18.2
2. Troubles with other people at work	35.6	9.4	21.4
3. Layoff or job loss	9.8	5.9	7.7
4. Arrest or conviction for serious crime	1.9	0.5	1.2
5. Death of someone close	39.8	34.7	37.0
6. Foreclosure of a mortgage or loan	1.5	1.5	1.5
7. Pregnancy or birth of a child	8.4	15.1	12.0
8. Serious sickness or injury	15.0	15.8	15.4
9. Serious problem with health or behavior of a family member	19.6	29.6	25.0
10. Sexual difficulties	9.8	12.5	11.3
11. In-law troubles	12.7	13.7	13.2
12. New, serious financial problems	15.2	12.5	13.7
13. Separation or divorce	3.3	2.3	2.9
14. Big increase in arguments with spouse/partner	8.5	11.1	9.9
15. Big increase in hours worked or job responsibilities	33.3	17.8	24.9
16. Move to different neighborhood or town	15.8	13.6	14.6
17. Suspension or expulsion of child from school	2.3	2.6	2.5
18. Apprehension of child in illegal act	3.9	4.4	4.2

what are called *stressor stimuli*. These data were obtained by a modified version of the Holmes and Rahe stressful life events scale (32). Because of limited interview time, the scale used here was restricted to the eighteen items listed in table 3.1.[1] The scores on this scale ranged from 0 to 13, with a mean of 2.4 and a standard deviation of 2.0.

Sex Differences

The 519 fathers in this sample experienced a somewhat higher number of stressors during the year (2.7) than did the 616 mothers (2.1). Despite this fact, table 3.1 shows that for the most part the experiences reported by the fathers and mothers are quite similar. The exceptions are events to which men and women have different exposure. For example, fewer women have paid employment, so it is not surprising that two to four times as many

[1] See Thoits (46) for a comprehensive analysis of the "life events" methodology. The stress index used in this study actually departs in other ways than length from the Holmes and Rahe scale. (a) One of the criteria used to select items from the larger original set was to eliminate stresses which have a *positive cathexis*. This was done on the basis of methodological studies which show that it is the *negative* items which account for most of the relationship between scores on the stress index and other variables (47, 48). We modified some items and added some which are not in the Holmes and Rahe scale to secure a set of stressors which seemed best for the purpose of this research. (c) The Holmes and Rahe weights were not used in computing the index score for each respondent. This was based on research which found that weighting makes little difference in the validity of scales of this type (49) and of the Holmes and Rahe scale specifically (50).

An important limitation which this stress index shares with the Holmes and Rahe index is that one does not know the time distribution of the stressful events. At one extreme, a person who experienced four of the stressors during the year could have had them spread out over the year, or at the other extreme, all four could have occurred at roughly the same time.

men as women experienced an occupationally related stress, such as trouble with a boss or job loss.[2]

There are a few other interesting sex differences. First, item 4 shows that four times as many men were arrested or convicted of a serious crime. An interesting sidelight is that there is such a high rate of arrest or conviction (2 per 100 men).

The only other item with a nontrivial difference is item 7, experiencing a pregnancy or having a child. This difference is probably due to men misunderstanding the question. It was meant to apply not only to the women but also to the men in the sample whose wives became pregnant or had a child in the last year.

Frequency of Different Stressors

The most frequently occurring stress among the eighteen items on the list is the death of someone close to the respondent (item 5). This happened to 37% of our respondents during the year we asked about. The next most frequent stress is closely related: a serious problem with the health or behavior of someone in the family (item 9). This occurred in the lives of 25%. For men, however, occupational stresses occurred more frequently. Over 28% had a difficulty with their bosses (item 2), and, at the positive end, over 33% had a large increase in their work responsibilities (item 15).

Definition and Measure of Child Abuse

Measuring child abuse also poses many difficulties (33). The technique used in this study is known as the Conflict Tactics Scale (34). It consists of a checklist of acts of physical violence. The respondent is asked about difficulties with other family members in the past year and then is asked if, in the course of such difficulties and conflicts in the past year, he or she did any of the items on the list. The list starts with nonviolent tactics, such as talking things over, and then proceeds on to verbally aggressive tactics, and finally to physical aggression, that is, violent acts.

Child Abuse

The list of violent acts in turn was designed to represent a measure of the severity, as well as the frequency, of family violence. The list starts out with pushing, slapping, shoving, and throwing things. These are what can be called the "ordinary" or "normal" violence of family life. It then goes on to kicking, biting, punching, hitting with an object, beating up, and using a knife or gun. This latter group of items was used to compute a measure of "severe violence" which is the measure of child abuse in this chapter, because it consists of acts that put the child at risk of serious injury.

---

[2] See Straus (21) for a discussion of the reasons for the higher rate of child abuse by mothers. In respect to the difference in the relationship between stress and child abuse for mothers and fathers, it is interesting that this reverses when the dependent variable is spouse abuse. When the dependent variable is violence against a spouse (either ordinary violence or severe assaults), it is violence by *wives* which is most closely correlated with stress (see Straus [45] and p. 00).

TABLE 3.2 **Violent Acts and Child Abuse Index Rates by Age of Child (per hundred children)**

Conflict Tactics and Child Abuse Index	Age				
	3–4 (N=179)	5–9 (N=347)	10–14 (N=365)	15–17 (N=238)	Total (N=1129)
Kicked, bit, punched	6.1	3.2	2.2	2.5	3.3
Hit with an object	19.6	19.7	9.6	4.2	15.4
"Beat up" child	1.1	0.9	1.1	1.7	1.2
Used a knife or gun	0.0	0.0	0.3	0.0	0.1
Child Abuse Index	19.8	20.9	10.2	5.6	14.0

Incidence of Child Abuse

The rates of child abuse revealed by this method are truly astounding. Each year, 14 out of every 100 American children, age three through seventeen, experienced an assault that was serious enough to be included in our Child Abuse Index (see table 3.2). This means that of the 46 million children of this age group in the United States who live with both parents, approximately 6.5 million are abused each year.

It might be objected that this index uses too liberal a definition of child abuse, because one of the items is "hitting with an object." For some parents, that could be the traditional strap, cane, or paddle, rather than an out-of-control assault. So, we recomputed the index, leaving out the data on hitting with objects. The rates drop sharply to "only" 3 or 4 out of every 100 parents and to an estimate of 1.7 million children per year.

The data just presented might overstate the amount of child abuse, because a family is included if even one isolated incident of abusive violence occurred during that year. On the other hand, these rates may understate the extent to which children are severely assaulted by their parents, because the figures do not take into account how often such assaults occurred. The answer to this question is that if one assault occurred, several were likely. In fact, in only 6% of the child abuse cases was there a single incident. The mean number of assaults per year was 10.5 and the median 4.5.

It is obvious that the incidence of child abuse obtained by this method is many times that estimated by the American Association for Protecting Children (AAPC). AAPC has published figures indicating approximately a million children per year are abused. However, that includes neglect, sexual abuse, and psychological abuse. The physical abuse figure they report is approximately 480,000. What accounts for the difference between that half million and our minimum figure of almost 2 million? There are two main reasons:

1. The AAPC figures are based on incidents which come to official attention. This leaves out the vast number of cases in which physical abuse is suspected and not reportedly, as well as the equally vast number of cases in which a child is nonaccidentally injured, but there is no suspicion of abuse.

2. Probably the most important reason why our rates are so much higher is that our data are based on violent acts carried out, rather than on injuries produced. Fortunately,

children are resilient. Many are the children who have been thrown against walls and who simply bounced off with, at most, a bruise. Only the relatively rare instances in which immediate and obvious injury occurs stand much chance of being suspected as parental abuse.

Why These Figures Are Underestimates

For reasons described elsewhere (4), the sample did not include children in the high-risk-of-abuse first two years of life. This is one of several factors which make even our very high rates of child abuse an underestimate. The second such factor is that these are self-reports by parents to a stranger doing a survey. Not every parent who has punched or kicked a child is going to admit that in such an interview. Third, the Conflict Tactics Scale includes only a limited list of all the possible abusive acts. For example, we omitted burning a child, wiping out the child's mouth with noxious substances, and sexual abuse. Fourth, we interviewed either the father or the mother and have data only on that person's abuse of the child. But most children have two parents and therefore twice the risk—or at least a higher risk—of being abused than our figures show. A fifth factor making these underestimates is that our data are based on children living with two parents. The two parents need not be the child's natural parents. However, the omission of children living in one-parent households may lead to underestimating because child abuse may be greater under the strain of trying to raise children without the aid of a partner.

Stressful Life Events and Child Abuse

The data plotted in figure 3.2 show that the higher the stress score, the higher the rate of child abuse. However, the relationship between stress and child abuse is minimal for mothers. Perhaps this is because, even under low-stress conditions the rate of child abuse by mothers is high (see n. 2). But for fathers, there is a clear increase in abuse as the number of stressors experienced during the year increases.

An analysis identical to that in figure 3.2 was done, except that the dependent variable was not limited to severely violent acts. That is, the measure included pushing, slapping, shoving, and throwing things. Except for the fact that the rates are much higher, the results are similar.

The importance of this similarity is that it helps establish a connection which is extremely important for understanding child abuse. Over and over in our research, we find a clear connection between the "ordinary" violence of family life, such as spanking children or pushing or slapping a spouse, and serious violence such as child abuse and wife beating. Actually, the connection goes deeper. *Verbal* aggression is also part of this pattern of relationships. People who hurt another family member verbally are also the ones most likely to hurt them physically (35). Moreover, the same set of causal factors applies to both the milder forms of violence and to acts of violence that are serious enough to be considered child abuse or spouse abuse. The similarity of the relationship between stress and the overall violence indexes with the relationship between stress and child abuse is but one of many such examples found for this sample (4).

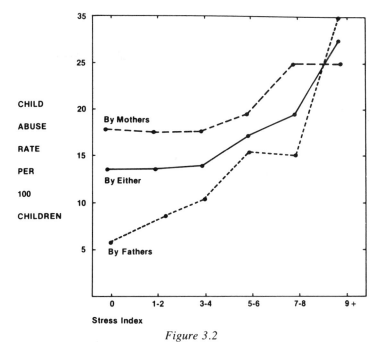

Figure 3.2

Child abuse rate by stress index score. The number of fathers and mothers on which each of the rates is based is: 0 = 73 fathers and 123 mothers; 1–2 = 198 fathers and 273 mothers; 3–4 = 147 fathers and 141 mothers; 5–6 = 59 fathers and 45 mothers; 7–8 = 19 fathers and 16 mothers; 9+ = 6 fathers and 4 mothers.

Factors Linking Stress and Child Abuse

Interesting as these findings are, they do not reflect the theoretical model sketched at the beginning of this chapter in figure 3.1. One might even say that the data just presented distort the situation because the graph tends to draw attention away from a very important fact: most of the parents in this sample who experienced a high degree of stress did *not* abuse a child.

A critical question is brought to light by this fact. Why do some people respond to stress by violence, whereas others do not? Part of the answer was suggested in the center box of figure 3.1 and the accompanying explanation. It will be recalled that this theory asserts that stress will result in aggressive acts (such as child abuse) only if certain mediating variables are also present. The balance of this chapter will be devoted to an empirical test of this theory.[3]

[3] Figure 3.1 is intended to illustrate the general nature of the theory rather than to list all the variables which need to be taken into account. There are also two aspects of the model which are included simply to alert readers to their importance, but which will not figure in the empirical analysis. First, this chapter will not deal with feedback processes. Second, within the center box illustrating some of the intervening variables, the arrows show that each of these variables is related to the others. They are a mutually supportive system, and interaction effects are no doubt also present. However, in this chapter these and other intervening variables will be dealt with one by one.

The first step in the analysis designed to take these mediating or intervening variables into account was to distinguish between parents in the sample who experienced none of the stressful events in the past year (N = 149). These two groups were then further divided into those who were in the high quarter of each mediating variable versus those in the low quarter. This enables us to see if the mediating variable was, as specified in the theoretical model, necessary for life stresses to result in violence.

If the theory outlined in figure 3.1 is correct, the parents who had the combination of both high stress and the presence of a mediating variable will have a high rate of child abuse, whereas parents who also experienced high stress, but without the presence of a mediating variable, will not be more violent than the sample as a whole, despite the fact that they were under stress during the year.

Socialization for Violence

In the first section of table 3.3, the first line runs directly contrary to the theory being examined. It shows that parents who were physically punished the most by their *mothers* when they were teenagers were *less* abusive under stress than the parents who were not hit at this age by their mothers. On the other hand, the second line of tble 3.3 shows that parents whose *fathers* hit them as teenagers have a child abuse rate which is 33% higher than parents who were under equally high stress that year, but who did not experience this much violence directed against them as teenagers. The difference between the effect of having been hit by one's mother versus by one's father suggests that violence by the father against a teenage child is a more influential role model for violent behavior which the child will later display under stress.

The next two lines of table 3.3 refer to violence *between the parents* of the parents in this sample. The child abuse rate by parents whose own fathers had hit their mothers was 44% higher than the rate for parents whose fathers never hit their mothers (22.7 per 100 versus 15.8). Surprisingly, there is only a small difference (and in the opposite direction) for parents who had grown up in families where their *mothers* had hit their fathers.

Legitimacy of Family Violence

The second section of table 3.3 reports *semantic differential* scores (36) in response to questions about slapping a child and slapping one's husband or wife. Each score is made up by combining the ratings for how "necessary," "normal," and "good" the respondent rated slapping.

The first line of the second section shows that parents who approved of slapping a child had a slightly greater rate of child abuse than did the parents with a score of zero on this index. When it comes to approval of slapping *a spouse*, there is a 72% difference in the predicted direction. These findings are consistent with the theoretical model asserting that the relation between stress and child abuse is a process that is mediated by social norms rather than a direct biologically determined relationship. However, since these are cross-sectional data, the findings do not prove the correctness of the model. It is also quite plausible to interpret the greater child abuse rate by parents who approve of violence as an after-the-fact justification. Except for a few variables which clearly occurred at a previous

TABLE 3.3   **Effect of Intervening Variables on Incidence of Child Abuse by Parents Experiencing High Stress (per hundred children)**

Intervening Variable	Indicator of Intervening Variable		Child Abuse Rate When Intervening Variable is:	
	Absent	Present	Absent	Present
Childhood Experience with Violence:				
Physical punishment after age 12 by mother	None	4+ per yr.	20.8	15.6
Physical punishment after age 12 by father	None	4+ per yr.	14.0	18.6
Respondent's father hit mother	None	1+ per yr.	15.8	22.7
Respondent's mother hit father	None	1+ per yr.	17.1	15.4
Legitimacy of Family Violence:				
Approval of parents slapping a 12 yr. old	None	High ¼	15.8	17.0
Approval of slapping a spouse	None	Any approval	13.5	23.2
Marital Satisfaction, Importance of Marriage, and Violence:				
Marital Satisfaction Index	High ¼	Low ¼	11.1	21.3
Marriage less important to husband than to wife	No	Yes	15.4	22.2
Violence between the parents	None	Any in past year	16.7	21.6
Socioeconomic Status:				
Education	High ¼	Low ¼	12.1	13.8
Husband's occupation	White collar	Blue collar	17.6	18.5
Income	>$22,000	<$9,000	14.3	25.0
SES Index for family	High ¼	Low ¼	10.0	20.0
Marital Power:				
Power Norm Index	Equal	Husb. *should* have final say	8.3	19.6
Decision Power Index	Equal	Husb. *has* final say	13.3	15.0
Social Integration:				
Organizational Participation Index	11+	None	16.7	25.4
Religious service attendance	Weekly	0–1 per yr.	12.0	27.9
Relatives living near	13+	0–2 per yr.	25.0	16.2

NOTE: The N's vary because, even though the intent was for the high and low groups to be the upper and lower quarters, this was not always possible. In the case of occupational class, for example, the comparison is between a dichotomous nominal variable. In the case of continuous variables, we sometimes wanted to preserve the intrinsic meaning of a score category, such as those with a score of zero, even though this might be more or less one-quarter of the sample. Another factor causing the N's to vary is that the division into quarters was based on the distribution for the entire sample of 2,143, rather than just the subgroup of high-stress parents analyzed in this table.

time, such as the ones on violence experienced as a child, this caution applies to most of the findings to be reported.

Marital Satisfaction, Importance of Marriage, and Violence

The first line of the third section compares parents who were low in marital satisfaction with parents in the high quarter. The low quarter parents had an 87% higher rate of child abuse. A similar difference is shown by comparing couples in which the husband rated the marriage as a less important part of his life than the marriage played in the life of his wife. Finally, the third line of the third section shows that child abuse occurs at a 30% higher rate in families in which there was an incidence of physical violence between the parents during the year.

Of course, as noted above, these differences, like a number of others reported in this chapter, could reflect the effect of family violence rather than being a cause. Only a longitudinal study can adequately sort out this critical issue. On the basis of this study, it can only be said that the findings are not contrary to the idea that parents under stress are more likely to be violent if they do not find the marriage a rewarding and important part of their lives.

Socioeconomic Status

Four aspects of socioeconomic status (SES) are examined in the fourth section of table 3.3. The first of these, the educational level of the couple, shows findings which many will find surprising. Parents in the high quarter of education were only slightly less violent than those in the low quarter. This is inconsistent with the widely held view that less-educated people are more violent. Actually, a careful review of the available studies fails to support this widespread idea (37). A number of studies (including an analysis of this sample by Finkelhor [38]) suggest there is little or no difference in aggression and violence according to education.

The husband's occupational class also makes little difference for child abuse (second line of the fourth section). On the other hand, if the combined income of the couple was $9,000 or less, the rate of child abuse was 75% higher than in families with a more adequate income (25.0 per 100 versus 14.3 per 100).

The last line of the fourth section attempts to take into account the several aspects of family socioeconomic status. We computed an index which combined the occupational levels, educations, and incomes of both the husband and the wife. The combination of these factors turns out to be very important. Parents in the low quartile on the SES index had a child abuse rate that is double that of parents in the top quarter of the SES distribution.

Marital Power

One of the most important factors accounting for the high rate of *marital* violence is the use of force by men as the "ultimate resource" to back up their position as "head" of their families (2, 3, 37, 39, 40). Perhaps similar processes are at work in respect to child abuse.

The first line of the fifth section of table 3.3 shows that the assault rate of parents who subscribe to the norm of male dominance in family decisions is 136% higher than it is for couples who are not committed to such male dominance norms. However, the second line suggests that in respect to the actual decision power, the difference is minimal. Perhaps the closer association between male dominance norms and child abuse than between actual male dominance in family decisions and child abuse is because many of the male dominant marriages are male dominant by mutual agreement or at least by acquiescence.

Social Integration

The last set of mediating factors included in this chapter explores the theory that child abuse will be higher in the absence of a network of personal ties. Such ties can provide help in dealing with the stresses of life and perhaps intervention when disputes within the family become violent. In particular, Garbarino and Gilliam (41) have equated both the cultural legitimacy of violence against children and social isolation as conditions central to the existence of child abuse. The finding that social support mediates the stress/child-abuse relationship is confirmed by a number of empirical studies (16, 17, 19, 42–44).

The first line of the sixth section of table 3.3 shows that parents who belonged to no organizations (such as clubs, lodges, business or professional organizations, or unions) had a substantially higher rate of child abuse than did the parents who participated in many such organizations. The same applies to parents who attended religious services as compared to those who rarely or never did.

The third line of the sixth section, however, shows opposite results. Parents who had many relatives living within an hour's travel time had a *higher* rate fo child abuse than did those with few relatives nearby. This finding is not necessarily inconsistent with social network theory. The usual formulation of that theory *assumes* that the network will be *prosocial*. Usually that is a reasonable assumption. However, a social network can also support *antisocial* behavior. A juvenile gang is an example. That is the essence of the *differential association* theory of criminal behavior. In the present case, the assumption that the kin network will be opposed to violence is not necessarily correct. Many parents experiencing difficulty managing their children are advised by their own parents to give the child a "sound thrashing."[4]

Summary and Conclusions

This chapter was designed to determine the extent to which stressful life experiences are associated with child abuse and to explore the reasons for such an association. The data used to answer these questions come from a nationally representative sample of 1,146

[4]However, an alternative interpretation of the effects of relatives' proximity needs to be considered. Family proximity may in fact be more characteristic of the kinship network of lower socioeconomic groups; lower socioeconomic status has already been shown to be strongly associated with higher abuse rates. An analysis detailed elsewhere (51) examined network embeddedness and family violence. This analysis, controlling for race and class differences, revealed that structural measures of social integration (number of years in the neighborhood, number of non-nuclear family adults living at home, and number of husband-wife relatives living nearby) are associated with lower rates of child abuse.

parents. Stress was measured by an instrument patterned after the Holmes and Rahe scale. It consisted of a list of eighteen stressful events which could have occurred during the year covered by the survey. Child abuse was measured by the severe violence index of the family Conflict Tactics Scale. This consists of whether during the past year the parent had punched, kicked, bit, hit the child with an object, beat up the child, or attacked the child with a knife or gun.

The findings show that parents who experienced none of the eighteen stresses in the index had the lowest rate of child abuse. As the number of stressors experienced during the year increased, so did the rate of child abuse. This was most clear in the case of the fathers.

The second part of the analysis was designed to test the theory that stress by itself does not necessarily lead to child abuse. Rather, it was assumed that other factors must also be present. Several such factors were examined by focusing on parents who were in the top quarter in stresses experienced during the year. These parents were divided into low and high groups on the basis of variables which might account for the correlation between stress and child abuse. It was assumed that, if the theory is correct, the parents who were high in the presumed intervening variable should have a high rate of child abuse, whereas the parents in the low category of these variables should not be more assaultive than the sample as a whole, despite the fact that they were under as much stress during the year as was the other high-stress subgroup of parents.

The results were generally consistent with this theory. They suggest the following conclusions: (a) Physical punishment by the fathers of the parents in this sample and observing their own fathers hit their mothers trained parents to respond to stress by violence. (b) Parents who believe that physical punishment of children and slapping a spouse are appropriate behaviors have higher rates of child abuse. However, a longitudinal study is needed to establish whether this is actually the causal direction. (c) Parents under stress are more likely to abuse a child if marriage is not an important and rewarding part of their lives and if they engage in physical fights with each other. (d) Education by itself does not affect the link between stress and child abuse. However, the combination of low income, education, and occupation does. (e) Parents who believe that husbands should be the dominant person in a marriage, and to a lesser extent husbands who have actually achieved such a position of power, had higher child abuse rates than parents in more equalitarian marriages who were also under stress. (f) Parents who were socially isolated (in the sense of not participating in clubs, unions, or other organizations) had higher rates of child abuse, whereas those who were involved in supportive networks of this type, did not have higher then average rates of abuse, despite being under high stress. However, the opposite was found comparing those with many versus few relatives living nearby.

Although consistent with the data, the interpretation presented here was not proved by the data. Many of the findings are open to other equally plausible intrpretations, particularly as to causal direction. The question of causal direction can only be adequately dealt with by a longitudinal study. In the absence of such prospective data, the following conclusions must be regarded only as what the study suggests about the etiology of child abuse.

We assume that human beings have an inherent *capacity* for violence, just as they have an inherent capacity for doing algebra. This capacity is translated into actually solving an equation, or actually abusing a child, *if* one has learned to respond to scientific or technical problems by using mathematics, or learned to respond to stress and family problems by using violence. Even with such training, violence is not an automatic response to stress, nor algebra to a scientific problem. One also has to believe that the problem is amenable to a mathematical solution or to a violent solution. The findings presented in this chapter show that violence tends to be high when these conditions are present: for example among those whose childhood experiences taught them the use of violence and whose present beliefs justify the appropriateness of hitting other family members. If conditions such as these are present, stress is related to child abuse. If these conditions are not present, the relation between stress and child abuse is absent or minimal.

References

1. Straus, Murray A. 1973. A General Systems Theory Approach to a Theory of Violence between Family Members. *Social Science Information* 12:105–25.
2. Straus, Murray A. 1976. Sexual Inequality, Cultural Norms, and Wife-Beating. *Victimology* 1:54–76.
3. Straus, Murray A. 1977. Wife-Beating: How Common and Why? *Victimology* 2:443–58.
4. Straus, Murray A.; Gelles, Richard J.; and Steinmetz, Suzanne K. 1980. *Behind Closed Doors: Violence in the American Family.* New York: Doubleday.
5. Straus, Murray A., and Hotaling, Gerald T., eds. 1980. *The Social Causes of Husband-Wife Violence.* Minneapolis: University of Minnesota Press.
6. Farrington, Keith. 1980. Stress and Family Violence. In *The Social Causes of Husband-Wife Violence,* ed. M. A. Straus and G. T. Hotaling. Minneapolis: University of Minnesota Press.
7. Gelles, Richard J., and Straus, Murray A. 1979. Determinants of Violence in the Family: Toward a Theoretical Integration. In *Contemporary Theories about the Family,* ed. W. R. Burr, R. Hill, F. I. Nye, and I. L. Reiss. New York: Free Press.
8. Brenner, Harvey M. 1979. The Impact of Social and Industrial Changes on Psychopathology: A View of Stress from the Standpoint of Macrosocietal Trends. In *Society, Stress, and Disease,* ed. L. Levi. London: Oxford University Press.
9. Brown, George W., and Tirril, Harris. 1978. *Social Origins of Depression: A Study of Psychiatric Disorder in Women.* London: Tavistock Publications.
10. Gaines, Richard; Sandgrund, Alice; Green, Arthur H.; and Power, Ernest. 1978. Etiological Factors in Child Maltreatment: A Multivariate Study of Abusing, Neglecting, and Normal Mothers. *J. Abnormal Psychology* 87:531–40.
11. LeTourneau, Charlene. 1981. Empathy and Stress: How They Affect Parental Aggression. *Social Work* 26:383–89.
12. Starr, Raymond H., Jr. 1982. A Research-Based Approach to the Prediction of Child Abuse. In *Child Abuse Prediction,* ed. R. H. Starr. Cambridge, Mass.: Ballinger.
13. Gil, David. 1977. Child Abuse: Levels of Manifestation, Causal Dimensions and Primary Prevention. *Victimology* 2:186–94.
14. Garbarino, James. 1976. A Preliminary Study of Some Ecological Correlates of

Child Abuse: The Impact of Socioeconomic Stress on Mothers. *Child Development* 47:178–85.

15. Bronfenbrenner, Urie. 1974. Developmental Research, Public Policy, and the Ecology of Childhood. *Child Development* 45:1–5.

16. Egeland, Byron; Breitenbucher, Mary; and Rosenberg, Deborah. 1980. Prospective Study of the Significance of Life Stress in the Etiology of Child Abuse. *J. Consulting and Clinical Psychology* 48:195–205.

17. Gaudin, James M., and Pollane, Leonard. 1983. Social Networks, Stress and Child Abuse. *Children and Youth Services Review* 5:91–102.

18. Herrenkohl, Ellen C., and Herrenkohl, Roy C. 1981. Explanations of Child Maltreatment: A Preliminary Appraisal. Paper presented at the National Conference for Family Violence Researchers. University of New Hampshire, Durham.

19. Justice, Blair; Calvert, Anita; and Justice, Rita. 1985. Factors Mediating Child Abuse as a Response to Stress. *Child Abuse and Neglect: International J.* 9:359–63.

20. Newberger, Eli H., and Marx, Thomas J. 1982. Ecological Reformulation of Pediatric Social Illness. Paper presented at the Annual Meeting of the Society for Pediatric Research, 13 May 1982, Washington, D.C.

21. Straus, Murray A. 1979. Family Patterns and Child Abuse in a Nationally Representative American Sample. *Child Abuse and Neglect: International J.* 3:213–25.

22. Steinmetz, Suzanne K., and Straus, Murray A., eds. 1974. *Violence in the Family.* New York: Harper and Row.

23. Straus, Murray A. 1971. Some Social Antecedents of Physical Punishment: A Linkage Theory Interpretation. *J. Marriage and the Family* 33:658–63.

24. Dohrenwend, Barbara Snell, and Dohrenwend, Bruce P. 1980. What Is a Stressful Life Event? In *Selye's Guide to Stress Research,* ed. Hans Selye, vol. 1. New York: Van Nostrand Reinhold.

25. Howze, Dorothy C., and Kotch, Jonathan B. 1984. Disentangling Life Events, Stress and Social Support: Implications for the Primary Prevention of Child Abuse and Neglect. *Child Abuse and Neglect: International J.* 8:401–9.

26. Lazarus, Richard S. 1966. *Psychological Stress and the Coping Process.* New York: McGraw-Hill.

27. Levine, Sol, and Scotch, Norman A. 1967. Toward the Development of Theoretical Models: II. *Milbank Memorial Fund Quarterly* 45:163–74.

28. McGrath, Joseph E. 1970. A Conceptual Formulation for Research on Stress. In *Social and Psychological Factors in Stress,* ed. J. E. McGrath. New York: Holt, Rinehart and Winston.

29. Mechanic, David. 1962. *Students under Stress: A Study in the Social Psychology of Adaptation.* New York: Free Press.

30. Scott, Robert, and Howard, Alan. 1970. Models of Stress. In *Social Stress,* ed. S. Levine and N. A. Scotch. Chicago: Aldine.

31. Selye, Hans. 1966. *The Stress of Life.* New York: McGraw-Hill.

32. Holmes, Thomas H., and Rahe, Richard H. 1967. The Social Readjustment Rating Scale. *J. Psychosomatic Research* 11:213–18.

33. Gelles, Richard J. 1975. The Social Construction of Child Abuse. *Am. J. Orthopsychiatry* 44:363–71.

34. Straus, Murray A. 1979. Measuring Intrafamily Conflict and Violence: The Conflict Tactics (CT) Scales. *J. Marriage and the Family* 41:75–88.

35. Straus, Murray A. 1974. Leveling, Civility, and Violence in the Family. *J. Marriage and the Family* 36:13–29 (addendum in August 1974 issue, 36:442–45).

36. Osgood, C.; Suci, G.; and Tannenbaum, P. 1957. *The Measurement of Meaning.* Urbana, Ill.: University of Illinois Press.

37. Straus, Murray A. 1980. Socioeconomic Status, Aggression, and Violence. Unpublished paper.

38. Finkelhor, David. 1977. Education and Marital Violence. Mimeo.

39. Allen, Craig, and Straus, Murray A. 1980. Resources, Power, and Husband-Wife Violence. In *The Social Causes of Husband-Wife Violence,* ed. M. A. Straus and G. T. Hotaling. Minneapolis: University of Minnesota Press.

40. Goode, William J. 1971. Force and Violence in the Family. *J. Marriage and the Family* 33:624–36.

41. Garbarino, James, and Gilliam, Gwen. 1980. *Understanding Abusive Families.* Lexington, Mass.: Lexington Books.

42. Justice, Blair, and Duncan, David F. 1976. Life Crisis As a Precursor to Child Abuse. *Public Health Reports* 91:110–15.

43. Salzinger, S.; Kaplan, S.; and Artemyeff, C. 1983. Mother's Personal Social Networks and Child Maltreatment. *J. Abnormal Psychology* 92:68–76.

44. Turner, R. Jay. 1983. Direct, Indirect and Moderating Effects of Social Support on Psychological Distress and Associated Conditions. In *Psychosocial Stress,* ed. H. B. Kaplan. New York: Academic Press.

45. Straus, Murray A. 1978. Stress and Assault in a National Sample of American Families. Paper presented at the Colloquium on Stress and Crime, National Institute of Law Enforcement and Criminal Justice—MITRE Corporation, 5 December 1978, Washington, D.C.

46. Thoits, Peggy A. 1983. Dimensions of Life Events That Influence Psychological Distress: An Evaluation and Synthesis of the Literature. In *Psychosocial Stress,* ed. H. B. Kaplan. New York: Academic Press.

47. Gersten, J. C.; Langner, T. S.; Eisenberg, J. G.; and Orzek, L. 1974. Child Behavior and Life Events: Undesirable Change or Change Per Se. In *Stressful Life Events: Their Nature and Effects,* ed. B. S. Dohrenwend and B. P. Dohrenwend. New York: Wiley.

48. Paykel, E. S. 1974. Life Stress and Psychiatric Disorder: Applications of the Clinical Approach. In *Stressful Life Events: Their Nature and Effects,* ed. B. S. Dohrenwend and B. P. Dohrenwend. New York: Wiley.

49. Straus, Murray A., and Kumagai, Fumie. 1980. An Empirical Comparison of Eleven Methods of Index Construction. Mimeo.

50. Hotaling, Gerald T.; Atwell, Saundra G.; and Linsky, Arnold S. 1978. Adolescent Life Changes and Illness: A Comparison of Three Models. *J. Youth and Adolescence* 7:393–403.

51. Cazenave, Noel A., and Straus, Murray A. 1979. Race, Class, Network Embeddedness and Family Violence: A Search for Potent Support Systems. *J. Comparative Family Studies* 10:280–99.

4 The Developmental Basis of Child Abuse and Neglect: An Epidemiological Approach

Ray E. Helfer

The purpose of this chapter is to build a foundation for understanding the short-term and long-term effects of child abuse and neglect on the normal developmental processes of children. The cornerstone of this foundation is the epidemiology of this malady of our society. This approach not only enhances one's understanding of the manner in which the problems of abuse and neglect are transmitted from generation to generation but also creates the framework for building effective and efficient treatment and for providing preventive interventions.

The Epidemiological Approach to Abuse and Neglect

When an epidemiologic approach to a given problem is considered, one thinks of "patterns of disease occurrence in human populations and the factors that influence these patterns" (1). Lilienfeld and Lilienfeld state that the general purposes of epidemiologic studies are:

1. To elucidate the etiology . . .
2. To evaluate the consistency of epidemiologic data with etiologic hypothesis . . .
3. To provide the basis for developing and evaluating preventive procedures and public health practices.

As these principles are applied to direct clinical observations, in a large number of cases the science of clinical epidemiology can be applied (2). This approach deals with analysis of group data, probability, past experience, and the evaluation of systematic errors by sound scientific principles. The ultimate goal is to use these principles to develop treatment and preventive approaches.

Applying the concepts of clinical epidemiology to the problems of child abuse and ne-

Ray E. Helfer, M.D., is professor in the Department of Pediatrics and Human Development, College of Human Medicine, Michigan State University, East Lansing.

The epidemiological section of this chapter has been modified from Ray E. Helfer, "The Epidemiology of Child Abuse and Neglect," *Pediatric Annals* 13(1984):747–51 and is reprinted here with permission.

glect makes good sense. This should not imply, however, that this malady of our society is a *disease* in the common use of that word. Even though abuse and neglect are more global constructs than a single disease entity, epidemiology can facilitate the understanding of this complex interactional breakdown.

A few articles have been published in recent years that attempt to apply some concept of epidemiology to child abuse and neglect (3–8). For the most part, these authors have used a very limited definition of epidemiology. Rather than the total scientific approach, they report only demographics and/or incidence data. The intent of this review goes further by utilizing clinical epidemiology to clarify our understanding of the complex problems of abuse and neglect.

Definition

The working definition of this complex family problem resulting in a breakdown in the interpersonal interactions within the family unit is:
Any interaction or lack of interaction between family members which results in non-accidental harm to the individual's physical and/or developmental states (see chap. 22).
Key words and phrases within this definition are:

Interaction   —in contrast to a unilateral process
Family member—individuals who are personally very close to each other
Non-accidental —in contrast to intentional
Harm   —in contrast to injury
Developmental —to broaden beyond physical harm only

Twenty-five years ago the phrase, "the battered-child syndrome" was coined by Dr. C. Henry Kempe (9). This was done to draw attention to the physical aspects of "non-accidental harm." A much broader definition is now used to describe our understanding of these problems, problems which are subsumed under the overall umbrealla of "breakdown in the interaction within the family."

Etiology

Caution must be used when the term "etiology" is applied to child abuse and neglect. A similar degree of caution is necessary when this term is used in discussing cancer and other complex maladies. Approximately twelve years ago the "etiology" of child abuse and neglect was proposed as a series of interacting entities, a process or sequence of events (10, 11). These interacting variables are still applicable as one considers the etiological concepts of abuse. Overt abuse and/or neglect is likely to occur when the following are in place:

The Potential to Abuse within the Parent or Guardian	+	The Special Person	+	The Stress or Crisis(es)

When these interacting factors occur in sequence and in the proper "amount," the outcome is often abuse and/or neglect, although the abuse may well be manifested in many different forms. The etiology of child abuse and neglect must be seen as a complex series

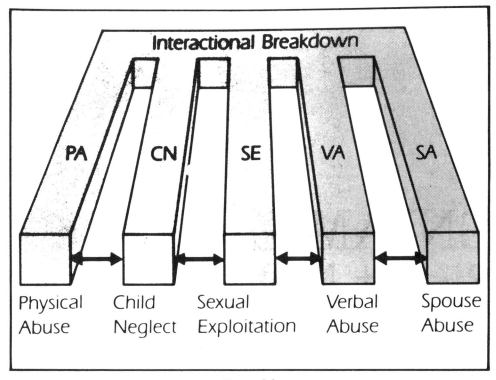

Figure 4.1

Classification of interactional breakdown within the family structure: *Parental actions or inactions*

of circumstances beginning with early rearing experiences and the way these circumstances effect a parent's learned ability to develop and maintain close personal relationships.

Classification and Terminology

This interactional definition must be expanded into a working classification which is best understood by sequential diagrams (see figs. 4.1 and 4.2).

In figure 4.1 the five major methods by which an interactional breakdown occurs between parents and their children are depicted: child abuse, child neglect, sexual exploitation, verbal abuse, and spouse abuse. Figure 4.2 demonstrates *some* of the many *physical* states that can result in the child from this nonaccidental harm. They range from no visible harm to death. The horizontal arrows indicate that these manifestations of interactional breakdown within the family can appear in several forms. The developmental component to this classification system are discussed later.

Special mention should be made of three specific manifestations of parent-child interactional breakdown: emotional abuse, failure to thrive, and sexual exploitation. These phrases are used and misused so commonly in the literature and daily discussions that an attempt must be made to clarify them.

The phrase "emotional abuse" should be eliminated from any classification as a *pri-*

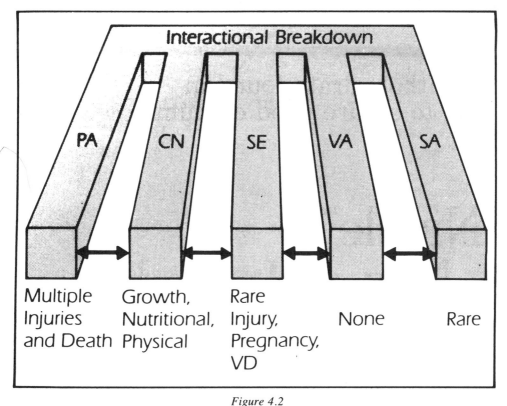

Figure 4.2

Classification of interactional breakdown within the family structure: *Manifestations in the child*

mary entity. The abuse of one's emotions raises vague, almost indefinable constructs, often different for each individual. All five forms of parent-child interactional breakdown lead to emotional distress within a family, often causing the child or children to exhibit emotional unrest. Verbal abuse more accurately describes the belittling and other attacks upon the child's self-worth. The phrase "emotional abuse" should be abandoned and "verbal abuse" substituted to describe this pathological behavior by the caregiver.

In like manner, the phrase "failure to thrive" is greatly misused by professionals. It means different things to different people. Failure to thrive is the failure to grow and develop, over time, as compared to predetermined standards. This term should be limited to infants less than two years of age. In recent years the phrase "non-organic failure to thrive" has found its way into the literature. To many, especially nonmedical professionals, this may imply something very erroneous, even mystical, that some infants do not grow for some non-organic reason. This is nonsense. The adjective "non-organic" as a modifier of failure to thrive should be erased from our memory and literature. Infants who fail to thrive do not grow adequately because they do not get enough calories (12). The reason they do not get enough calories may be due to disease or feeding methods. Using the adjective "non-organic" is most misleading and very difficult to explain to protective service workers, parents, judges, and others.

The phrase "sexual exploitation" is used rather than "sexual abuse" for two reasons: first, to be all-encompassing to include the variety of interactions that adults use to take advantage of vulnerable children in a sexual manner, varying from inappropriate fondling to incest and pornography. Rape and sexual misconduct by strangers are not included in this family dysfunction classification. Second, sexual abuse as a term may be misleading since *physical* injury often is absent in these children. The phrase sexual exploitation more accurately describes this problem.

Frequency

With few exceptions, studies seeking to define the incidence (numbers of new cases within a specific population over a given period of time) and prevalence (total number of cases in a population in a certain period) of child abuse and neglect are fraught with innumerable complexities. If all the money and time spent, and being spent, in trying to define these numbers were directed toward prevention programs . . . (little is gained by completing this fantasy).

The best incidence data available come from the annual report of the American Humane Association (13). Thirty-four states volunteered to share their reporting data for tabulation. The limitations of these data are significant in that the states are not all represented, the criteria for reporting vary, the criteria for subsatantiating a case once it is reported varies greatly from county to county and worker to worker, and the amount of public awareness from place to place is different.

What can be said from such limited information is this: in any given year approximately 1.25% to 1.5% of ur children throughout the United States are reported to the designated social agency as *suspected* of being physically abused, neglected, or sexually exploited. These data come directly from the calls and written reports received by agencies in compliance with the reporting laws in each state. If the cut-off for reporting is considered to be eighteen years of age, between 900,000 and million children are reported annually; approximately 30% are repeats and 70% new cases. Twenty-five percent are reports of physical abuse, 55% of neglect, 10% of sexual exploitation, and 10% unknown.[1]

Prevalence data are a bit firmer and are derived from what young adults report about their own childhood. One must keep in mind that this information comes from an adult reporting on his/her *perception,* either in a direct interview (14) or on a questionnaire (15). Prevalence also depends heavily on the sample that is asked to reflect on their childhood experiences and the type of the adverse interaction reported.

When 2,500 young women were asked to complete a standardized questionnaire at the time of hospital confinement for delivery of their baby, the overall rate of severe physical punishment used in these women's childhood was about 20%. The variation was great, from slightly less than 20% in a medium-sized New England town to over 60% in a large city ghetto (15). College students in six New England institutions reported sexual exploitation in their childhood to have occurred 19% of the time for the females and 8% for the males (16). The percentages in another female population was 16% (17).

---

[1]These are estimates because no good national data exist. They should hold up over time, however.

TABLE 4.1   Demographic Highlights From AHA Annual Report, 1981*

A. **Type of Maltreatment**
   Physical   —27% (Major 4%)
   Neglect   —59%
   Sexual   — 7%

B. **Source of Report**
   Non-Professionals —41%
   School   —13%
   Medical   —11%

C. **Caretaker Composition**
   Male/Female   —50%
   Female Only   —43% (vs. 14% nationwide)
   Male Only   — 5%

D. **Stress Factor**
   Family Interaction —73%
   Poverty   —44% (vs. 13% nationwide)
   Health   —40%

E. **Race**
   White   —68%
   Black   —22%
   Hispanic — 8%

F. **Age**
   Average age 7.2 years for total reports
   Average age 3.3 years for fatality groups
   Children are vulnerable at *all* ages for *all* forms of maltreatment.

G. **Public Assistance (PA)**
   Families receiving PA at time of report—43% (11% nationwide)

H. **Relationship of Perpetrator**
   95% "parental"

I. **Action Taken on Report**
   Case not opened —48%
   Case opened   —44%
   In process   — 5%
   Court Action   —18% (of those opened)

---

*Since these are highlights only, the subtotals will not add up to 100%.

Finally, the permanent physical morbidity and mortality rates from abuse and child neglect are not known. Even the numbers of deaths are hidden by the failure of many medical examiners to report abuse and neglect and by the subtleties of certain forms of death, such as asphyxiation from abuse in an infant presented as a sudden infant death syndrome (SIDS).

Demographic Features

The American Humane Association (AHA) maintains the most accurate compendium of data relating to child abuse and neglect reporting laws (13). While their totals are taken from all 50 states plus Puerto Rico and the Virgin Islands, the breakdown information is derived from case reports from only 34 states. In 1981 there were 850,980 total reports; the 34 states reported 420,216 (40% of total). This 40% is not a true sampling of the total since these 34 states voluntarily supply their data.[2] In addition, each state has slightly different criteria for reporting and certainly has different criteria for determining indicated or substantiated cases. The reporting timetable results in a two-year delay in publishing the report. Even with all these limitations, the AHA data are all that are available. From this information the valuable statistics presented in table 4.1 have been gleaned.

Mode of Transmission

The epidemiologic approach to understanding abuse and neglect requires that serious consideration be given to how this problem passes from one generation to another. The adverse effects of abuse and neglect of children are transmitted by way of developmental deficits learned during childhood (18). A child who, over time, watches his mother being beaten by his father or her boyfriend not only experiences the fear that accompanies the witnessing of this act but also learns how two people who mean a great deal to each other resolve their interpersonal conflicts. A young girl who, over time, must assume the role of sexual partner for her older brother, father, and/or stepfather is not experiencing the developmental growth in her own sexuality which is necessary to permit her to sort out these roles during later childhood, adolescence, and adulthood. Both these children emerge from adolescence into young adulthood with very limited skills in developing and maintaining close personal relationships with significant others and ultimately with their own children.

Figure 4.3 demonstrates that developmental insults affect the parents and the child(ren) in varying degrees in each of the five major pathological interactions (or lack of interactions). Figure 4.3 also depicts the "developmental bottom line or outcome," that is, the limited or deficient skills in the ability to develop and maintain close personal relationships (see chap. 18).

Through these many developmental deficits, the transmission of this form of pathological interaction is carried from one generation to another. Does every abused or neglected child run the risk of transmitting the problem to their families? If not, why not? These are questions yet to be answered, and key answers they will be. To date, those young adults who seem to have emerged from adverse childhood experiences less affected are those who have experienced a positive mentor relationship during their abuse and/or neglect. Someone, an aunt, uncle, teacher, and/or coach, said, "You're okay," during these dreadful years and/or, "When you're with me, you're safe." This observation is supported only by clinical vignettes. Serious research must test the mentor hypothesis further.[3]

---

[2] The federal government could easily require states to pool their data in order to receive federal funding.

[3] If this hypothesis can be supported, the concept may open new avenues for therapeutic and preventive approaches.

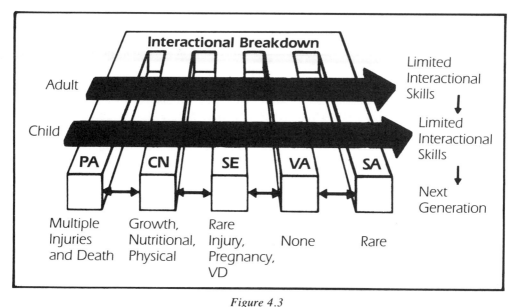

Figure 4.3

Transmission of interactional breakdown to future generations: *Developmental Consequences*

Treatment and Prevention

The primary justification for taking this epidemiological approach is to develop a basis for understanding the problem and for developing logical treatment and prevention programs.

Treatment endeavors, if they are to be based upon our epidemiologic understanding, must attack the basic erosion of the abused child's developmental process or sequence. These approaches can assist in the reconstruction of these developmental deficits. Merely understanding the deficits is not sufficient. The retraining of one's skills in interpersonal interaction, which were supposed to be learned in childhood, is crucial. The most discouraging aspects of treatment is that these approaches are rarely generalizable, that is, they are not able to be implemented on a large scale, from county to county or state to state. Unlike the building of water treatment plants and adding fluoride to the water supply or immunizing thousands against polio, transmitting a working multidisciplinary treatment program from one municipality to another, from one law enforcement agency or mental health center to another, from one county social service agency to another requires a rediscovery and reconstruction of the "wheel." This is most inefficient.

The epidemiological approach to the *prevention* of abuse and neglect teaches us certain basic lessons. In public health, we have known for years that the prevention of something negative occurs with the production of something positive. One prevents cholera and dysentery by cleaning our sewer and water systems. Polio is prevented by enhancing the production of antibodies by the immune system. Polio is not prevented by making more braces and iron lungs, although these are most important if one has the malady.

While this is readily apparent to some, many departments of social services have not learned this approach and do not have any administrative methodology to implement it when they do understand.

If the epidemiological approach to understanding child abuse and neglect is going to be justified, it must provide information and concepts that lead to new or revised treatment and preventive approaches. It must stimulate thought, ideas, visions, fantasies.

This review gives emphasis to the interactional construct, that is, when there is a breakdown in the interpersonal interactions of two or more people who mean a great deal to each other, the risk for abuse and/or neglect is present. The potential to abuse is flamed by stress and crisis. How the problem is manifest will vary from time to time, child to child. Even though the demographic data have significant limitations, one glaring conclusion is evident. Single, poor women of all races with young children are most vulnerable.

The frequency data, both incidence and prevalence, reveal the problem to be enormous. Since the basic mode of transmission from generation to generation is via the developmental deficits within the parents, and since these developmental scars "heal" much more poorly than do physical injuries to the body, the prevalence rate is alarming. Generation after generation are affected by the limited skills of developing and maintaining long-term close personal relationships.

The Developmental Process

One should perceive an individual, as he proceeds from infancy through adolescence and into adulthood, as moving through dynamic and ever-changing periods. What happens during this day-to-day process has a most critical effect on functioning capabilities later in life. Many things are *supposed* to happen during childhood which permit a child to formulate and practice the skills necessary to function as a young adult. Those who interact with the child during these critical years have a great impact on a significant portion of this process. Some of the skills a child learns, like walking, running, and toilet training, seem to be rather "automatic," being influenced for the most part solely by time and growth. However, other developmental achievements must be carefully nurtured and modeled throughout the childhood years for the child to become a reasonably functional young adult. These include interpersonal skills, that is, the ability to get along with others and to function in an acceptable and constructive manner during the interpersonal process (see chap. 18).

Imagine that the developmental process of a child moving from infancy through adolescence is like a missile and its payload moving through a trajectory from the launching pad to its celestial goal. The launching pad is birth, and the celestial goal is adulthood. Anything that happens to modify the trajectory will have an influence on the ultimate landing site of the payload. Those who guide the path of the missile toward the celestial body must be readily available and well trained to modify any unexpected and serious deviations in the process. To complete this analogy, the actual trajectory is child development, and the parents, family members, teachers, and others who interact with the child during these critical years are those who have the responsibility for the guidance system.

Consider, for example, an infant who is separated temporarily from her mother immediately after birth because of the illness of the mother. This is a serious developmental insult in the child's life, and every means must be used to correct the negative effect if a permanent "scarring" of the developmental process is to be prevented. Consider also a three-year-old child who, because of serious illness, is placed in a hospital and undergoes surgery and a variety of other painful and difficult procedures, during which time she may well be separated from those who have the most impact on her "developmental guidance." If this insult continues for a period of three or four weeks, there may be a slowing down of growth, and there certainly will be negative effects upon the developmental process occurring during this critical period. In most situations in which the child has experienced a normal childhood prior to entering the hospital and lives in an environment where modifications can be made in order to overcome the insult to her "developmental trajectory," the effects of these insults may not be permanent. On the other hand, a child with an environment that adds little more than one insult after another to this developmental process (for example, a child reared in an environment of never-ending violence as the solution to interpersonal problems) may well have her developmental process further scarred by the hospital experience.

In the discussion that follows, emphasis will be given to those developmental traits which seem to be most deficient in young adults reared in an abusive and neglectful environment. Additional emphasis is also given to those developmental deficiencies which affect interaction between child and parents. These, of course, are the developmental skills which demonstrate the most serious deficiencies in those reared in an abusive environment.

The Developmental Deficits: Growing Up to Be "Out of Control"

The Senses

Understanding the importance of serious developmental deficiencies of the senses experienced by those who have been reared in an abusive environment requires knowledge of the normal development of the senses (see Dr. Ann Wilson's review of the subject in chap. 23). Dr. Wilson points out that an infant has a highly sophisticated system of touch, taste, smell, vision, and hearing. She also reviews the importance of the new baby's vestibular system. There are six senses, rather than five, if one considers the significance of the sense of movement. One must not lose sight of the fact that the newborn infant is not only very capable in these six sensory areas, but also very dependent upon them for the establishment of a communication system with the world about him (18).

Now consider the environment which suppresses the development of this sensory system. An infant or young child is supposed to learn that use of the senses results in positive feedback, a nice feeling. Crying brings someone to hold, rock, and comfort the infant; looking into mother's eyes makes the child feel loved and wanted; being touched is nice, most of the time; the smells of mother's house remind the child of positive feelings, and so on. On balance, the senses should be conditioned positively. Only on occasion is it necessary to have negative reactions to certain tastes, smells, etc. (19, 20).

Consider what happens when touching hurts, *most of the time;* smells about the house bring on very negative feelings, *most of the time;* mom's eyes show the threat of a swat; when the child listens to mom and dad talk, he becomes afraid, since the messages he hears are threats, screams, and anger. Over and over, day after day, the child is bombarded with negative sensory messages, messages that truly force the senses to "shut down" (see Dr. Wilson's discussion on habituation, chap. 23). The child learns that it is far safer not to listen, not to look, and not to be touched, for when these senses are used, he hurts much more or receives no feedback whatsoever.

As a result, the child's senses become "muted," used only when absolutely necessary. This does not mean that if an individual reared in this manner were to have his hearing or vision tested, the results would indicate abnormalities. What is meant is that those reared to mute their senses have learned, very early in childhood, that their lives are less confused and hurt less when people do not look them in the eye, listen to what they say, touch them, or get too close.

The significance of these deficiencies in the senses is great. The ability to communicate with those about you and with the environment in general is severely limited. Holding loved ones very close and looking into their eyes carries messages that few can express with words. When one enters the home in which one was reared, the overall reaction to the unique smells and visual and auditory stimuli should be positive and comforting, rather than, "My God, this hurts!"

Children and adults reared in abuse have had their senses trained in such a way that to use them for receiving or transmitting positive messages is not part of their communication systems. While this makes it difficult for these young people to communicate with their peers, think of the results when someone with muted senses tries to establish a communication system with a newborn infant. Recall that new babies are *dependent* upon their six senses for communication (22). Little wonder young adults, reared in abuse, find interaction with their new babies so difficult. The result is a mother-baby or father-baby interaction that breaks down all too early in their relationship.

The World of Abnormal Rearing (W.A.R.)

The senses are not the only tools for learning how to interact with our environment or those about us. Many other skills must be learned in childhood, skills which enhance the young adult's ability to interact and feel that "I'm a very special person."

A few years ago the concept of the "world of abnormal rearing" (W.A.R.) was proposed (22). This was devised in order to better understand what occurs when one's childhood does not provide a very favorable environment in which to learn basic interpersonal skills. Adults who are victims of the W.A.R. truly have "missed out on childhood," that is, missed learning many of those basic skills necessary to interact with others. Being aware of the W.A.R. cycle and the implications it has for the developing child and the adult will help prepare for the relearning phase. Understanding and then overcoming many of these basic developmental deficits require a knowledge of their origin.

A very special note must be made at this point. Referring to W.A.R. children or adults from the W.A.R., does *not* imply that all, or even most, were physically beaten. For every adult who was actually beaten as a child, there are probably scores who look back at their childhoods and say, "I wasn't beaten, but it was really a bad experience." Some W.A.R. children are beaten, some are sexually molested, others are ignored, some are belittled, some find themselves so controlled that they cannot function outside of their own homes,

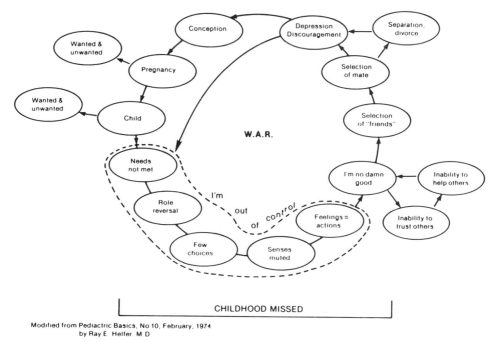

Modified from Pediatric Basics, No 10, February, 1974
by Ray E. Helfer, M.D.

Figure 4.4

World-of-abnormal-rearing cycle. Modified from Helfer (22)

and so on. This W.A.R. is hell, no matter how it manifests itself. Specific intervention programs are intended to help those adults who are trying to break out of the cycle.

Before discussing the relearning aspect of treatment which will help in breaking loose from the holds that the W.A.R. has on those who lived through it, the various segments of this cycle must be reviewed. Understanding these concepts is essential to learning ways of breaking out. This W.A.R. is a never-ending cycle, passing from one generation to another. Unless a gallant effort to escape is made, and escape is possible for most, the future will most likely be a copy of the past. The "world of abnormal rearing" is diagrammed in figure 4.4.

Needs Met and Delayed Gratification

One of the most important skills that a child must learn during the brief years of childhood is how to get his or her needs met in an acceptable manner and when the most appropriate time is to seek this fulfillment. What behaviors or actions are acceptable at home, at school, or in the play yard with friends? All people have needs, and we all must fall back on the foundations laid in childhood as we develop ways to have these needs met.

An infant is hungry, cold, and wet—his needs are very specific. He cries and hopes the cries bring a soft mother or father with food, a warm body, and dry clothes. As life progresses, crying is reserved for more extreme needs which often are stimulated by pain or fear. A two-year-old may not cry to get the desired ice cream; rather, he may resort to a temper tantrum. Many parents find this an undesirable behavior and work hard to teach the child to substitute for the hollering and kicking a "please" and "thank you."

> A young mother said to me, as she reflected on a recent disagreement she had had with her boyfriend, "Isn't it interesting that my boyfriend beats me just like my husband used to?" Yes, I admitted that I found that interesting, I needed to hear more; so I said, "You find that interesting? Tell me, when was the last time your boyfriend beat you?"
>
> "Oh, last weekend. We went out, and he got mad at me for flirting with another guy. When we got home, he beat me."
>
> "Didn't it hurt?" I asked.
>
> "Yeah, a bit. Not too much, though. Anyway, I know he likes me," she added.
>
> Now, that raised my interest; so I replied with, "How do you know that he likes you?"
>
> "Why would he get jealous and beat me if he didn't like me?" she responded with great logic.
>
> That statement troubled me. It certainly made sense, but I could not muster the strength to follow through just then. A pediatrician has a built-in escape from such stressful moments and can always say, "Well, I must get on to examining your child." This ploy is used by some at the outset of the visit to avoid even the slightest chance of discussing these touchy issues. The visit ended, and I found myself writing in big letters on the child's records a reminder to delve further into this issue on the next visit.
>
> Later, as this matter was discussed further with this woman, I learned more about the beatings her husband had given her and how she had interpreted them. Then I asked the key question, "How was it when you were little?"
>
> "Oh, not bad with mom," she commented.
>
> "How about your dad?"
>
> "Well, he was pretty quiet and didn't pay much attention to me."
>
> "Didn't that bother you?" I asked.
>
> "Yes, and I used to bug him a lot."
>
> "What did he do when you bugged him" I continued.
>
> "He'd hit me a lot," she said.
>
> "Why, then, did you bug him?"
>
> She lifted her head, looked directly at me, and for the first time our eyes met as she said very slowly, "Gettin' hit is better than being left alone."

This young woman learned very early in life that when she had a need for a man's attention she had to "bug" him so much that he would eventually show her that he was aware of her presence by beating her. She was willing to put up with the hurt to have her needs met.

All children struggle with this critical component of development. If a child's environment is reasonably stable and secure and the parents have a good understanding of what the child's needs are and what the child must do and learn to have these needs met, then the outcome will be a child who learns acceptable skills for meeting these needs and when the best time is to use them.

The development of the ability and willingness to delay one's gratification is a slow but steady process which progresses throughout the child-developmental "trajectory." If you ask a three-year-old if he wants a stick of gum now or a whole pack on Sunday, he'll more than likely take the stick now. Postponing the need until Sunday requires considerably more developmental skills than are present in most three-year-old children. He first must know what Sunday is, that Sunday will happen, that a pack of gum is bigger than a stick, and that he can trust you enough to be around on Sunday and to follow through with your promise. Eventually the child learns these concepts and, depending on his needs and the nature of the immediate offer, the satisfying of this need may, indeed, be postponed. Delaying gratification is a very high-level skill, one which requires considerable training and modeling during childhood to learn.

Children who are abused are not so fortunate. "Why wait? Tomorrow is never better than today." For them tomorrow never comes; it is always today! These children find themselves in a world of unrealistic expectations. Their parents have little understanding of childhood and make demands that are far in excess of a child's capabilities. Babies shouldn't cry much, should eat well, smile early, and remind mom or dad of someone the parent likes; two-year-olds should shape up, not explore the cupboards and pull out the pots, not spill anything, and eat well. "Look after *me*," the child is told by the parent. "To hell with your needs," he hears in a variety of ways. One of the greatest struggles of the W.A.R. is the constant striving to meet the parents' *unrealistic* expectations, which they have set for the child. From success at school, to caring for mom and dad, the demands are *extreme*.

A child who struggles with these issues day after day learns, as the years of childhood wear on, that his needs are not being met; even worse, he is not learning the necessary skills to get these needs met. He is much too busy looking after the needs of his parents and other adults around him. If this weren't bad enough, the behaviors that are learned to meet the bare, essential needs are often extreme, inappropriate, and maladaptive.

Role Reversal and Responsibility

A child must learn during the brief years of childhood that *he* or *she* is responsible for his or her own actions. This is a concept that is acquired very gradually. It is tested by reality during adolescence, as the parents must accept less and less responsibility for a child's behavior and the adolescent begins to accept more and more. This can be an exciting and frustrating time. As the teenage years move on, one can see this maturing occur. For example, "It's your responsibility to decide," is constantly heard around our house these days. Our ten-year-old dughter wanted to watch a special on television on a school night. Thus began the checklist: homework done, pajamas on, teeth brushed, reading done? "Yes" was the reply to all. "OK, sounds like a good special to watch," I commented. The responsibility she took for getting ready to watch the special could now be rewarded. We've also heard comments like, "I don't want to get up and peddle my papers"; "I don't want to mow the neighbor's lawn"; "I don't want to take grandmother to church"; yet all were commitments which had been made previously. Responsibility and follow-through are very difficult lessons that must be learnt in childhood.

Children reared in the W.A.R. find themselves in late adolescence ill prepared to accept responsibility for their own actions. There seem to be two extremes—either they aren't required to accept any responsibility for what they have done, having been protected or "bailed out" all their lives, or they are forced to accept the responsibility for the inadequacies of their parents. This latter is so common and so confusing that it requires further explanation.

Some call this turnabout "role reversal." The child accepts the role of parents, and the parent takes on the role of the child. Role reversal is easy to understand when one sees a three-year-old soothing her crying mother, and later the same mother ignoring her crying child. The constant need to reverse roles, which often ends in failure and frustration, may well result in "learned helplessness" for this child.

All children at varying ages of their development want to please and care for "mommy" or "daddy." This is especially true in times of stress of crisis. "Thank God for children when the chips are down," for they really come through and help out. However, the extreme, the constant, the unrealistic expectations are most devastating to the developing child. Children have needs of their own that also must be met.

The aspect of role reversal demonstrated by the child taking care of the parent is relatively easy to understand. More subtle and more difficult to comprehend is when this role reversal requires and trains the child to assume the responsibility for the parents' errors. This feeling is embedded into the child's mind from a very early age in a variety of ways, encouraged by remarks such as these:

"If it weren't for you . . ."

"If you hadn't spilled that, I wouldn't have gotten mad."

"I hit you because you were bad."

"Your father would still be around if you . . ."

"I could have gone back to work if you hadn't . . ."

And so on and on. This child slowly begins "the guilt trip" which accompanies true role reversal. He becomes convinced that he is to blame for the parents' inability to handle crises, finances, etc. This guilt lasts into adulthood and manifests itself in a variety of ways. The ability to separate one's own responsibility from that of another is a learned function that develops in all children who are reared more normally. This is a gradually learned concept. A three-year-old finds the separation of his wishes from what happens very difficult, in fact almost impossible. "My mommy is mean; she won't buy me the ice cream. I wish mommy would go away forever." Ten minutes later the mother rushes out to a movie, leaves the child with a sitter, and the child believes his wish came true.

Our eleven-year-old daughter was pouring milk from a gallon jug into a glass one day. There was great shaking and grunting, but she finally succeeded. Her fifteen-year-old brother picked up the jug and mimicked his sister's every action, making fun of her. I made it very clear that I didn't find his behavior at all humorous, indicating my displeasure over what he did. Ten minutes later, the eleven-year-old said, "I got John in trouble."

"No, Betty," I replied, "John got John in trouble."

"But if I hadn't of shook, he wouldn't have gotten into trouble."

"John got into trouble for what *he* did, not what you did," I replied—a very difficult concept to comprehend, but one of major importance. Learning that one is responsible for one's own actions and not the actions of another is *not* built into the abusive environment. In fact, it teaches the opposite.

Decision Making and Problem Solving

A child must learn the skill of making decisions during the protected years of childhood, when a "goof up" or bad decision won't be all that harmful. Options must be identified and weighed, priorities set, and a plan or solution agreed upon. One of our teenagers lamented the other day, "Decisions are too tough; you decide for me." Our seven-year-old is constantly asking, "What do you think I should do?" Sometimes we fall into the trap of making the decision for them. It often is much quicker and less painful. But a trap it is.

> A young seventeen-year-old mother once called me and said, "I must see you; I'm going crazy."
> When she arrived sixty minutes later, I asked, "Why do you think you are going crazy?"
> "I have all these things in my head, and I don't know what to do."
> "What things?" I asked. I thought she was going to tell me about some delusion or psychotic fantasy. Nothing of the sort occurred.
> "Well," she said, "I'm bleeding, and my aunt is trying to get my baby; my boyfriend calls me collect, I can't say no; my rent is due; I don't know what to do with my check; my food is gone . . ." and on and on.
> "Betty," I said, "stop! Tell me the last time you made a decision."
> She thought for a full two or three minutes and finally said, "I don't think I ever made one." Later she did recall she made the decision to stop her birth control pills at sixteen so that she could become pregnant. She also had decided who the father was going to be.

Children must learn, at two and four and eight and sixteen, how to make decisions. Choices, choices! This is the key. "Do you want vanilla or chocolate ice cream?" "Do you want a cookie or a piece of cake?" "Do you want to go to bed *with* or *without* a treat?" "I don't want to go to bed," is the reply. "The choice is the treat, not the bed," the parent responds.

For years I used to struggle with two- and three-year-old children each time I wanted to look in their ears. The problem was clear. I used to say, "Can I look in your ears?"

"No!" he replied.

"Hold him down," I'd say to the mother, as I proceeded to look in the ears. The child screamed and hollered, vomited and peed all over me.

Now I say, "Which ear should I look in first?" With this I give him a choice. As the little hand moves toward one ear, I say, "That's going to be the one, isn't it?" His head nods slowly, and I exclaim with great excitement, "How did you know that was the ear I wanted to look in first?" Now I go home with little vomit and pee on my clothes and feel much less exhausted.

Choices lead to priority setting and decision making. But one ought not to give children choices when there are none.

"Do you want to shovel the driveway?" I ask my son.

"No," he says.

"Shovel the driveway," I command.

"Why did you ask me if I didn't have a choice?"

"Good point," I respond, "I'll figure out the answer while you're shoveling the driveway." A clear "goof" on my part.

Children who find themselves trapped in the W.A.R. rarely are given choices and rarely are allowed to make decisions. They are just told what to do or given no directions whatsoever. Even worse, they are often encouraged to decide and then are told what a stupid decision they made.

Day after day, young adults demonstrate how ill prepared they are in decision making. What are their options and how can the priorities be established? Without early experiences with trial and error in childhood, these decisions become major obstacles.

One seventeen-year-old mother related her story to me. "At nine, the sex started; by twelve I was enjoying it; by sixteen I hated it, and finally I hated myself." Then she added, "Do you know what one of the worse parts was? He never asked me if I wanted it." This woman not only had the insult of incest, but she had lost all control over her life. She had no choice.

Trusting Others

As development continues, it enters the realm of interrelating with others. Children must learn during their early childhood and have it reinforced throughout adolescence that there are some people who truly can be trusted and others who cannot. A two-year-old falls off his tricycle and hurts his knee; he runs, crying, to his mother or father, is picked up and consoled. "That really hurts," he hears. Two minutes later his knee is a bit better, and he returns to his play, having learned that knees get better and people are helpful, especially moms and dads.

Today I stayed home to work on this book. Everything was arranged for the house to be empty all day. Just as I was making progress, noontime arrived, and my seven-year-old barged in and said, "What's for lunch?"

"You were supposed to stay at school for lunch today," I said.

"I was?" he replied. As I found the cheese to make us both a grilled sandwich, the boy said, "Who goofed, you or me?"

"I guess I did," I replied; "I forgot to remind you to stay at school." After the sandwiches were eaten and we had chatted a bit, I said, "I'm glad you came home to keep me company when I ate my lunch."

"You are?" he exclaimed with obvious delight.

Look at these two incidents. What did the two-year-old and the seven-year-old learn? "It is rather nice being around people who like you. When I am in trouble and hurt or just when I want to chat, there usually is someone around." Suppose the two-year-old had heard, as his knee was hurting, "You clumsy kid, you fell of your trike again. If it weren't for you I could have some peace around here." Suppose the seven-year-old had heard, as he rushed in from school, "Oh God, are you home? You knew you were supposed to stay at school today. How do you expect me to get anything done with you around here?"

Trust is learned very gradually as a child moves from infancy through adolescence. Trust is built. Children not only learn whom to trust, but what these people can and cannot be expected to do. By the time an adolescent wants the car, a firm foundation of trust and realistic expectations should already have been laid.

W.A.R. children find themselves without such a foundation, or a very weak one at best. Instead of learning as a young child that people can be trusted, they learn that people hurt or disappoint.

"Don't come to me with your problems. I have enough of my own."

"You dumb idiot, you screwed up again."

"I brought you five hundred miles to play tennis in this tournament and you really blew it."

Over and over the W.A.R. child learns that when you go to others and seek help, you usually end up wishing you hadn't asked. This is especially devastating when the other person is mom or dad. If you cannot trust them when you are five or ten or fifteen years old, whom can you trust?

I asked an eight-year-old girl, reared in wealth but also abused, "What do you do when you have a problem?"

Her immediate reply was, "It's best if I deal with those myself." She had learned in her brief eight years that asking others for help led to trouble.

One of the basic bail-out methods which adults have when crises arise or a problem develops is to ask someone whom they can depend upon for assistance. When one's childhood fails to teach the basic skills of how and whom to trust, this bail-out process, so critical to adults and children, is in serious jeopardy. The result—retreat, withdraw, be alone!

"Isn't it tough to be alone all the time," I asked an attractive, young, divorced mother of two children.

"Not really," she responded.

I said nothing for a full minute, and then she continued in a very soft voice directed at the floor, "No man can hurt me when I'm alone." She knew, from some very bitter experiences as a child and young adult, that being alone with a man was very risky and often led to pain. Her solution, to isolate herself from the world, was safer.

The true defense when one does not trust others is to keep people out of one's life. Keep in mind the discussion above about touching and looking. "If I don't look at you, maybe you cannot hurt me so much." If all this weren't hard enough, many have the added burden of the never-ending guilt of role reversal: "If I don't take care of mom or dad, I feel awful."

One seventeen-year-old mother was having problems telling her social worker some of her personal concerns. I asked why. She said, " 'Cause if I tell the social worker about these things, then I have to tell my boyfriend."

"Tell your boyfriend?" I asked.

"Sure, that way he knows he can trust me."

Telling all was her way of gaining trust. The exact opposite is true of healthier, trusting relationships: "I trust you so much that you don't have to tell me everything." Child abuse and neglect truly distort the concept of trust.

Feelings and Actions

A child must learn on his developmental "trajectory" toward adulthood that how he feels and what he does are separate but related issues. This is such a critical point for an adult to understand that it must be emphasized over and over. Some will pick up this concept immediately; others will be most confused. The following examples may help explain.

Two of our sons, when aged ten and twelve, were playing hockey on opposite teams. The younger boy skated better than the older one and rather regularly passed him by as the scores piled up. On one of these passes, the older became furious, couldn't handle his anger any longer and tripped his younger brother. The younger of the two got mad and hit his bigger brother with his hockey stick. They both came home angry and crying. Finally the story came out—a golden opportunity to separate feelings from actions. After they both had settled down and I had a chance to plan a course of action, I said to the older boy, "I don't blame you for getting mad at your brother for skating around you all the time. I'd get mad too. *But* that doesn't give you the right to trip him."

"I don't blame you," I said as I turned to the smaller boy, "for getting mad at your brother for tripping you, but that doesn't give you the right to hit him with your stick."

Had I imposed a penalty of no hockey playing the next day without separating how they felt from what they did, they might have thought that they were being penalized for their feelings as well as their actions. The message they should hear is, "How you felt is understandable. What you did about it was inappropriate. For the *doing* you're being penalized."

Throughout childhood, this message must be delivered over and over:

"You *like* Susie, give her a *call*."

"You're *mad* at Jimmy, *tell* him how you feel."

"You feel *sad, crying* may help."

"You are *excited* about the game, *tell* me about it."

As these children grow into adolescents, they gradually begin to learn that they have *control* over what they *do;* they can control their actions. Even though feelings are hard to control, some satisfaction comes from knowing that what you do about them is your decision, your responsibility, and under your control.

Adults who have been brought up in an abusive environment find this concept very difficult to understand. One mother said, "I get so mad that I scream and holler and say awful things to my kids, and then I feel awful too." Another said, "I got angry at my baby and hit her."

To both of their comments I replied, "Do you realize you are talking about two things?" Their faces revealed confusion, and both replies were almost identical: "What do you mean, two things?"

This inability to separate feelings from actions manifests itself in many ways. W.A.R. children and W.A.R. adults frequently find themselves in serious difficulty because of this deficit. Anger leads to lashing out for some and complete withdrawal and guilt for others. The extremes of actions are often used.

"How can I tell my boyfriend I like him?" one young woman asked me.

"What do you do to show a man you like him?" I replied.

"Go to bed with him," she said.

"Right away?" I asked.

"What else can I do?"

This young girl found that she had no trouble finding a man to go to bed with her, but somehow it always turned out poorly. In her childhood she had missed out on learning the little inuendos of expressing her feelings. She didn't know how to touch his hand, look into his eyes, say "I like you," or smile at the right time. She replaced all of this with only one action for her feelings of liking—sex.

The major message is that how one feels and what one does are separate but related issues. One can control much of one's actions. A child must learn he or she has this degree of control. When abused children and adults are taught that feeling and action are the same, they mistakenly believe that they have little, if any, control over their lives.

Feelings of guilt are constant sources of confusion. "Is that an OK feeling?" is a frequent question. "Certainly," I respond, "but you have to decide how to handle, how to act on, that feeling." This concept is rarely appreciated by those reared in the W.A.R.

And On and On It Goes

The abused child continues, around and around, learning fewer and fewer skills of interaction. He is "out of touch" with the world about him; control over his life is lost, actually never gained. What better way to train a child to become a nonentity, functioning in the extremes, than to:

Mute his senses.
Fail to teach him how to get his needs met.
Teach him he is responsible for the actions of others.
Give him little practice in problem solving.
Convince him he cannot trust others.
Show him day after day that feelings and actions are one and the same.

The results! The results are contained in this book. The W.A.R. has convinced its victims that they are "no damn good," unable to help others, have minimal skills for finding and keeping real, close friends, much less a suitable mate, and are easily discouraged and depressed (see Fig. 4.4).

At that point in their young adult lives, they may enter the "I think I'll have a family" route as a solution to their loneliness. Some bypass this option and go on to work or school, trying to cope as best as they can, using what few skills they learned in their childhood. Some make it, many do not.

Considerable work can be done to facilitate their breaking out of this cycle (see chaps. 22, 23). Even more can be achieved if the cycle is interrupted before its damage has been too severe. Both of these issues are examined in this book.

References

1. Lilienfeld, A. M., and Lilienfeld, D. H. 1980. *The Foundations of Epidemiology,* 2d ed. New York: Oxford University Press.
2. Fletcher, R. N.; Fletcher, S. W.; and Wagner, E. H. 1982. *Clinical Epidemiology—The Essentials,* pp. 2–4. Baltimore: Williams and Wilkins.
3. Baldwin, J. A., and Oliver, J. E. 1975. Epidemiology and Family Characteristics of Severely Abused Children. *British J. Preventive Social Medicine* 29:205–21.
4. Christoffel, K. K.; Liu, K.; and Stamler, J. 1981. Epidemiology of Fatal Child Abuse: International Mortality Data. *J. Chronic Diseases* 34:57–64.
5. DeJong, A. R.; Hemada, A. R.; and Gary, A. 1983. Epidemiologic Variations in Childhood Sexual Abuse. *Child Abuse and Neglect: International J.* 7:155–62.
6. Gonzalez, P., and Thomas, M. 1977. Child Abuse and Neglect: Epidemiology in Kansas. *J. Kansas Med. Soc.* 78:65–69.
7. Greenberg, N. H. 1979. The Epidemiology of Childhood Sexual Abuse. *Pediatric Annals* 8:289–99.

8. Newberger, E. H., and Daniel, J. H. 1976. Knowledge and Epidemiology of Child Abuse: A Critical Review of Concepts. *Pediatric Annals* 5:15–25.

9. Kempe, C. H.; Silverman, F. N.; Steele, B. F.; Droegemueller, W.; and Silver, H. K. 1962. The Battered Child Syndrome. *JAMA* 181:17–24.

10. Kempe, C. H., and Helfer, R. E., eds. 1972. *Helping the Battered Child and His Family,* pp. xiv–xv. Philadelphia: Lippincott.

11. Helfer, R. 1973. The Etiology of Child Abuse. *Pediatrics* 51:777–79.

12. Goldbloom, R. B. 1982. Failure to Thrive. *Pediatric Clinics of North America* 29:151–66.

13. *Highlights of Official Child Abuse and Neglect Reporting, Annual Report.* Denver: American Humane Association, 1981.

14. Altemeier, W. A.; Vietze, P. M.; and Sherrod, K. B. 1979. Prediction of Child Maltreatment during Pregnancy. *J. Am. Acad. Child Psychiatry* 18:205.

15. Schneider, C.; Helfer, R. E.; and Hoffmeister, J. K. 1980. Screening for the Potential to Abuse: A Review. In *The Battered Child,* 3d ed., ed. C. H. Kempe and R. E. Helfer, pp. 420–30. Chicago: University of Chicago Press.

16. Finkelhor, D. 1979. *Sexual Victimization of Children.* New York: Free Press.

17. Russell, D. E. H. 1983. The Incidence and Prevalence of Intrafamilial and Extrafamilial Sexual Abuse of Female Children. *Child Abuse and Neglect: International J.* 7:133–46.

18. Helfer, R. E. 1984. *Childhood Comes First: A Crash Course in Childhood for Adults,* 2d ed. East Lansing, Mich.: Helfer Publications.

19. Stern, Daniel. 1971. Mother and Infant at Play: The Dyadic Interaction Involving Facial, Vocal, and Gaze Behaviors. In *The Effect of the Infant on Its Caregiver,* ed. M. Lewis and L. Rosenblum. New York: Wiley.

20. Montague, Ashley. 1971. *Touching.* New York: Columbia University Press.

21. *The Amazing Newborn,* a film distributed by Ross Company, Columbus, Ohio.

22. Helfer, R. E. 1974. Presidential Address, Ambulatory Pediatrics Association, *Pediatrics Basics,* no. 10, February, pp. 4–7.

5   Psychodynamic Factors in Child Abuse

Brandt Steele

Since our previous reports (1–3) of abusive parents, we have continued to study the behaviors, life histories, and psychological functioning of those parents and other persons who abuse the infants and children for whom they are providing care. Although our original work began in relation to the seriously injured children described under the title "the battered-child syndrome," we soon began including children who were less severely physically injured, those who were diagnosed as failing to thrive as a result of maternal deprivation, or those suffering from other forms of neglect. We have also seen those who were primarily suffering from emotional abuse and, particularly during the last few years, older children who have been sexually abused. We have evaluated and treated their caretakers. Thus, over the past two decades, we have covered a wide range of forms of maltreatment of children and studied a great variety of those parents or other caretakers who carry out their tasks in less than desirable or adequate ways.

The term *child abuse* will be used in this chapter to cover this whole spectrum of maltreatment of children. It is an extremely complex group of human behaviors characterized by maladaptive interactions between infants and children of all ages and their caretakers. We speak of it as a maladaptive in the direct biological sense. After ensuring his or her own survival, the prime task of any individual is to take part in the production of the next generation of individuals in a condition most likely to ensure survival of the species. Child abuse is therefore maladaptive in the sense that, to a greater or lesser degree, it damages immature members of our species in such a way as to interfere with their optimum development and to impair their adaptive survival abilities. Abuse involves children of all ages, from infancy through adolescence, and caretakers of both sexes, all ages, and with various kinds of relationships to the child. The caretakers who abuse are most often biological parents, but they may also be stepparents, adoptive parents, foster parents, grandparents, siblings, other relatives, babysitters, parental paramours, or other nonrelated persons such as teachers, either in or out of the household, who are involved in the child-caring tasks. Exceptions to this usual pattern of the caretakers being the abusers are the cases of infanticide and of serious injuries inflected upon children by psychotic or

Brandt Steele, M.D., is with the Department of Psychiatry, University of Colorado Medical Center, Denver.

81

seriously mentally disturbed strangers and the sexual abuse of children perpetrated by strangers, often with the use of force.

Common Characteristics of Abusive Behavior

In the face of such a variety of interactions and participants, it would seem difficult to find any common factors in abusive behavior. Yet it is possible, through careful study of the life histories and behaviors of the many kinds of abusers, to discern common themes and recurrent patterns of psychic function. In our work with abusive caretakers over the past two decades, we have never seen two who were exactly alike. Despite all their differences, however, they share a number of characteristics which they exhibit in varying degrees. These characteristics will be discussed in some detail below.

Child abuse is an extremely complex problem and, in addition to the impact it has on both its victims and perpetrators, it has many ramifications in the fields of medicine, social work, law, psychology, child development, psychiatry, and anthropology. All of these disciplines have something valuable to contribute to the elucidation and comprehension of child abuse phenomena. Our own personal bias is to understand the problem within the framework of human psychology and, more specifically, according to psychoanalytic concepts of human development and mental functioning. While we thus follow what is essentially a psychiatric approach to the problem of child abuse, we do not mean to imply by this that the child abuse syndrome is a mental illness in the usual sense of that term, nor can it be easily subsumed under any of the commonly accepted psychiatric nosological entities. Some caretakers who abuse children may also show characteristic symptoms of schizophrenia or depression or any of the various kinds of neuroses and character disorders. These occur with approximately the same frequency as they do in the general population, and the abuse is not necessarily a part of such psychic states. Many abusers have emotional problems which are also commonly seen in what are called "narcissistic character disorders" or "borderline states." Yet child abuse is not necessarily associated with either of these two entities. In general, it seems to be useful to consider child abusive behavior as a group of abnormal patterns of caretaker-child interactions related to psychological characteristics which can exist concurrently, but quite independently, of any psychiatric disorder or even in otherwise relatively healthy personalities. Abusive, neglecting behavior is not considered to be purely haphazard or impulsive, but rather to be understood as a particular constellation of emotional states and specific adaptive responses which have their roots in the earliest months of life.

By describing the intrapsychic state as the most necessary and basic matrix of abusive behavior, we do not mean to disregard the importance of other factors. Depending upon what particular population of abusers is studied or sampled, it can be shown with statistical significance that abusive, neglecting behavior can be precipitated or escalated by such things as poverty, bad housing, unemployment, marital strife, alcoholism, drug abuse, difficult pregnancies and deliveries, lack of education, lack of knowledge of child development, prematurity and illness of infants, deaths in the family, and a host of other things. Any of these can become a critical stress, precipitating a crisis, ending in abuse or neglect. An excellent review of social factors in abuse is that by Straus (4). In every case, such factors warrant our most intense concern and all our efforts toward alleviation. At the same time, we must realize that awareness of the importance of such social factors in situations of abuse does not answer what we consider more basic questions: Why, under circumstances of stress, do some persons respond with abusive behaviors, while others do not? Why do the majority of people in a low socioeconomic group treat their offspring with adequate kindness, consideration, and love without abuse, even in critical times? And, conversely, why do some people with adequate housing and wealth seriously harm their infants? We feel, in our efforts to answer these and similar questions, that it is necessary to turn to a deeper, more subtle psychological understanding of these individuals. As noted above, no two abusers are exactly alike, but we commonly find among them a certain constellation of emotional states and patterns of reaction which we consider to be essential, basic ingredients in the usual syndromes of abuse and neglect.

History of Abuse in Early Life

As reported in previous studies (1–3), it is common for abusive or neglectful caretakers to give a history of having experienced some significant degree of neglect, with or without accompanying physical abuse. In our experience it is quite rare to see an abuser who does not relate this history if questioned appropriately. This finding has been confirmed by other investigators (5–9), but it has also been questioned by other workers who have not obtained the history of early life neglect or abuse with as much frequency as we did. We have noted some things which may account for at least a certain number of those who do not claim a history of physical abuse in early life. We have seen several persons who, during evaluation for maltreatment of their children, stoutly denied having been mistreated themselves as children. Upon further questioning as to who did the disciplining in the family and what disciplinary measures were used, they freely described being whipped or beaten to the point of lacerations or bruising, but in no way did they consider this abuse, because the discipline was "appropriate punishment for misbehavior." Others will, for some time, maintain a denial of having been abused because of a persistent fear that, even though they are now adults, their parents might again attack them if they complain or criticize parental actions. Others hesitate to give a true history, lest the family be brought into some sort of difficulty or be disgraced in the community. More rarely, there is a genuine amnesia for the unpleasant events of childhood as a result of unusually strong repression. For example:

> Jack S., aged twenty-five, freely admitted bruising and breaking the arm of his two-year-old daughter during a hassle over an error in toilet training. Although he recalled his father whipping him once when he was an early teenager for joyriding on an illegally "borrowed" motorcycle, he firmly denied any possibility of abuse early in life. Later, he reported talking to his sister about his "crazy psychiatrist" who kept wondering if he had been abused as a child and seemed to doubt his denials. His sister responded by saying, "Jack, do you mean to tell me you've forgotten how father used to take you down to the coal bin in the basement and whip you until you were black and blue and mother was afraid he would kill you?" (Note that the mother, although concerned, was not described as intervening.) Following this revelation, Jack's amnesia gradually lifted, and he recalled many other events of his early life.

There are others who, although they actually remember maltreatment, find it too painful to deal with and comfort themselves by maintaining a fantasy that their parents really were good to them. Such fantasies, of course, can gain a good deal of support from the fact that the parents were, in reality, "good enough," at least part of the time, and the uncomfortable side of the ambivalence can be disregarded.

We have often found it more difficult to establish evidence of neglect in early life than to uncover the history of physical abuse, because it is much harder for people to describe how much love and care were not there than to recall how often they were hit. The common expressions we hear from abusive parents, both men and women, are variations on such themes as, "I never felt my mother ever really loved me or cared about me," or, "My parents never listened to me or paid any attention to what I felt or what was important to me," or, "I was the black sheep of the family, always left out," or very commonly, "I never in my life felt close to either mother or father," or, "It was never safe to ask for anything; I just did what I was told or what was wanted of me, but nobody ever really appreciated what I did or thought it was good enough." Another common source of feeling uncared for was the failure of one parent to interfere or protect the child while he was being beaten by the other parent. The child felt that neither one really cared about him. Similarly, girls, when trying to complain to their mothers about being sexually abused by males in the family, were often told they were lying or else "making it up" to cause trouble, or that it was all their fault anyway. And their mothers did nothing about the problem. This left the girls feeling hopeless and uncared for. Other, more obvious deprivations are often glossed over as just some of the "misfortunes of life" without recognition of the serious emotional impact which such things have on the growing child. We ascribe such events to a profound depression in the mother, an absence of the mother as a result of sickness or death, placements of the child with unsympathetic relatives or in unloving foster homes, absence of a father, an overburdened mother without enough time for any of her children, or multiple sicknesses with hospitalization in infancy and childhood. These and other similar experiences in early life can leave long-lasting feelings of deprivation and loneliness, even though they may be intellectually understood and accepted.

Lack of Empathy for Child

The history of neglect and abuse in the early years of the life of the abusive caretaker has been stressed because we believe that therein lies the source of the caretaker's later inability to provide empathic care for infants and children. By empathy we mean a caretaker's sensitive awareness of a child's state and needs and the ability to instigate appropriate responses thereto. Abuse and neglect are the outward behavioral evidences of a caretaker's inadequate empathy for the child. We believe such inadequate empathy is the tragic deficit present in the caretaker in all situations of abuse and neglect. Excessive punitive expression of aggression or neglectful disregard of a child's basic needs could not occur if normal, adequate empathy existed in the caretaker. As a corollary to this lack of empathic awareness of the child and appropriate responses to it, we find that in times of stress or crisis the caretaker gives priority to his or her own needs and ideas, while the child's needs are given only secondary consideration or are completely disregarded. This phenomenon is seen with striking clarity in cases of sexual abuse of small children. The child is exploited by being drawn into sexual activity which is primarily oriented toward the satisfaction of the adult caretaker, while, at the same time, little or no attention is paid to the child's age-appropriate needs and abilities. The child's obedient, submissive cooperation with the adult in the sexual activity and the pleasure which some children seem to derive from it have led many observers to minimize or disregard this nonempathic exploitation of the child.

Excessively High Expectations

It is quite common in situations of abuse and neglect to find the caretakers expecting their infants and small children to behave and perform tasks with unusual efficiency much too early in the child's life, while, at the same time, disregarding the child's own feelings and wants. This phenomenon has been well described by Morris and Gould (10) as *role reversal*. The child is treated as if he were an adult while the caretaker expects satisfactions of his or her own desires to be cared for.

> An example is Mrs. G., a young woman whose one-year-old baby girl had been severely burned by scalding water in the bathtub. She also had a boy two-and-a-half years old, and when asked about him she responded, "Oh, Buddy is very active. He's on the go all the time. He acts older than he is. He cleans the house, cleans my room, sweeps the floor in his room. He wants to help cook, but I think he's too young for that. Sometimes he's too helpful. He's never been with kids his own age, but it is helpful with him like that. It's not boring. Other kids his age just sit in the corner. He does watch kiddy shows, but he's up 'til two or three in the morning often helping me, and then he's up again at seven-thirty or eight. He only takes a nap once every two or three days. If I tell him to do something, he will do it. He makes his bed if I tell him to do it. If he doesn't, I bribe him. I'll send him to his room if he has a fit." When asked if Buddy was considerate of her moods, she replied, "Yeah, if I'm on the couch he gets a blanket and pillow, and brings me some water. He thinks that he made me sick and says, 'I sorry.' He even helps others too." When asked if he helped her take care of the baby, she said, "Oh, yeah, he bathes her, puts powder on her. He hunts for a bottle when she cries. Once there was no bottle. He took a whole half-gallon of milk out of the refrigerator and took it to her. He pushes her in her swing. He's very protective of her. He tells other kids that she's sleeping because he's afraid that they might hurt her, and he slaps kids if he thinks they will. He brings me clean diapers and throws the old ones out. He changed her once, but he did a goofy job of it. He wants to drive a car now." This mother also spoke of how she thought her stepparents were rather cruel to Buddy and said that, as a result, she found it hard to "holler at him." However, she added, "I did give him a licking last night. He knows by the tone of my voice if I'm mad. All I have to do is show him a belt lying around and he shapes up immediately." She claimed that while she was gone to a neighbor's, leaving Buddy to bathe himself, he got out of the tub and put his baby sister in water which was too hot.

It is obvious in this brief vignette that this mother gained satisfaction from the precocious pursuit of adult behavior she expected from her two-year-old boy. It is obvious that she was critical and punitive toward him if he did not meet expectations, that his own needs to live like a normal two-year-old boy were not considered. It is also significant to note how energetically this small boy devoted all his efforts toward trying to please his mother. Despite the fact that she loved her children and, in general, took very good care of them, this mother demonstrates a pervasive lack of empathy. She showed no real spontaneous, intuitive, sensitive feelings toward her infants. In talking about her boy, she uses no warm, loving words and says essentially nothing about what kind of human being he really is. She describes only what he does that is related to his usefulness to her and the household. Leaving her one-year-old daughter in the precarious care of the two-year-old brother, while she goes visiting, indicates a very disturbing lack of awareness of her children's needs and behavior and their need for guidance and protection.

It is very common for physical abuse to occur as a "justified" action or "appropriate disciplinary punishment" when children fail to meet excessively high caretaker expectations. It is also possible to see significant neglect occur as a result of a child's failure to perform well enough to satisfy caretaker expectations. An infant who fails to respond to mother's inept or inappropriately timed feedings or other caretaking procedures is perceived as being defective, negativistic, generally unfit or no good and is then deemed not worth caring for, resulting in "failure to thrive" or other forms of neglect. Thus, although both abusive and neglectful parents have the same pattern of high expectations of the child, their responses to the child's failure to meet expectations are quite different. In the one case, the child is perceived as failing to follow through to his full capabilities and therefore is punished to make him "shape up" and do better. In the other case, the child is seen as incapable of proper response, as worthless, and therefore is given only cursory, inadequate care or almost totally disregarded.

> Another young mother, Holly, was similar to Mrs. G., but showed even more significant misperceptions of her children. She had a twenty-two-month-old boy, whom she described as a great help around the household, although not so efficient as Buddy. While in the office with me, she frequently slapped little Sammy on his rear and would alternately tell him, "Stop doing that, come here," and, "Stop bothering me, go away." In the midst of this, he emptied my ashtray, wiped it with Kleenex, and replaced it on the desk. When I remarked on this behavior, his mother was obviously pleased and proud of his accomplishments. However, she had not allowed him to have any pleasure or freedom during this visit. She also had a five-and-a-half-month-old boy in the hospital with a fractured skull and fractured pelvis inflicted during punishment for being stubborn and lazy. She told of how he had been a very good baby at first but had gradually become very unsatisfactory. He would "do nothing for himself," would get sick deliberately to frustrate her, and would look at her with great anger in his eyes. This intelligent young woman was not completely unaware of normal child development, but this did not counteract her misperceptions. The punishment had occurred when she was under more than average stress due to marital difficulties and feeling very much alone and uncared for and, therefore, especially needy of compliant, helpful behavior from her two boys. Some understanding of her behavior could be gained from her statement, "My mother never cared about me, never listened to me or what I wanted. I was never anything but a servant in her house." Her inadequate empathy was documented on another occasion when she described how important it was not to spoil children by giving into them too much or by picking them up when they cried. Then she added, "But I know children need to be loved, too, so I've always made it a practice to pick my little babies up and hold them for ten minutes twice a day." She at other times also alluded to rather severe physical punishment during her early years.

It is obvious that Holly is severely deficient in empathy for her two children, and that her behavior as a parent has been profoundly influenced by her own early life experience, especially by her relationship to her mother.

Impaired Parent-Child Attachment

Not all abusive parents show the high expectations, lack of empathy, and punitive attitude toward failure with the unusual clarity demonstrated in the two cases above. But they do expect simple, obedient, correct, appreciative responses from their infants and small children during the ordinary tasks of feeding, bathing, toilet training, diapering, and taking naps, all according to parental desires of the moment, and they have other misperceptions of the child's abilities and intentions. The child's failure to please or obey is met by physical attack or verbal criticism or subsequent neglect. Indications of this disordered pattern of parental behavior can be observed at the time of the birth of the baby or in the immediate postpartum period. Gray and her colleagues (11), have clearly demonstrated that a most reliable sign of possible future difficulty in parenting is the evidence of poor attachment seen in the perinatal period. It is seen especially clearly in the mother's behavior toward her newborn baby immediately after delivery and during the first few feedings. It is possible to observe poor attachment by the father as well. Poor attachment is soon evidenced by the unempathic manner in which the parent performs the caretaking tasks. Caretaking is done mechanically, largely according to the caretaker's convenience and without any warm, sensitive interaction oriented toward satisfying the infant's needs and without proper responses according to the infant's state. In some ways the abusive syndrome can be considered a disorder of attachment with all its subsequent repercussions. Recent research (12–18) has amply illustrated the importance of mother-infant attachment in parent-child bonding and its effect on subsequent parent-child interactions and child development. Two processes are involved. One is the attachment of the infant to the caretaker, and the other is that of the caretaker to the infant. Disturbances can occur in either part of the process, and the factors which interfere with the infant's ability to attach well to the caretaker will be discussed later in this chapter. It is our strong belief, however, that it is the impairment of parent-to-child attachment that is most important in situations of abuse and neglect.

The propensity and ability of humans to attach to infants is not uniform or simple. In its most uncomplicated form, it has been best understood as the more or less automatic or instinctual response of a mother to her newborn infant during the first hour after delivery, during the infant's quiet-alert state, and in the subsequent interactions between them during feeding and general care. This is true as far as it goes and is undoubtedly the most characteristic, biologically appropriate time for a mother and infant to establish a bond of relationship between them. However, this paradigm of attachment in no way accounts for the equally strong, although subtly different, attachments that occur with those who have not been involved with the actual processes of pregnancy and delivery. We refer here to the strong attachment that can occur between father and infant, between adoptive parents and infant, as well as others. It is our firm conviction that those persons who have had a good early childhood experience themselves have the empathic ability to attach well to their infants in later years and that those who have suffered from abuse and neglect in early years have poor empathy and are unable to attach well. We thus see some of the dynamics which are so basic in the abuse and neglect cycle: caretakers who have been subject to unempathic care in their earliest years cannot attach well or be empathic to their own offspring and, hence, do not attach well and do not provide empathic care, thus providing the basic matrix for the next generation of abuse and neglect (2, 19). Obviously, this cannot be a completely rigid, inescapably determined process of repetition. Other factors can and do enter in to enhance or dimish the likelihood and severity of the cyclic recurrence. It is characteristic of human development that good and bad experiences in later childhood and after can influence, for better or for worse, psychological and behavioral trends established in the earliest years.

It is of interest to understand the mode of transmission and ramifications of the poor attachment and lack of empathy which we consider to be the basic core of the maladaptive, abusive, neglectful behavior of caretakers. Inasmuch as we see abusive care-takers repeating in their parental behavior the ways in which they themselves were treated as children, plus the fact that we see poor attachment immediately after the birth of the infant, it seems that the basic rudiments of the behavior are acquired at the very beginning of life. Benedek (20) has described how the experience of becoming a parent activates two sets of memories which are largely unconscious. One is the memory of how one was parented and the other is what it was like to be a small child. These two deeply embedded psychic representations provide the templates to guide caretaking behavior. The caretaker is identified with his own parents, and the new baby is endowed, through reverse identification, with the attributes of the caretaker himself as a small child. These very early, primitive identifications are intensified by the day-to-day interactions between caretaker and infant during the ensuing months and early years. We feel that the basic pattern which can appear later in the adult as abusive, neglectful behavior is firmly established by the third year, although it can also be further modified by ensuing experiences of the child with the same or other caretakers. This acquisition of behavioral patterns by the child, which are similar to those of his caretaker, can also be appropriately understood in the frameworks of social learning theory and role modeling. Yet, we believe the more basic determinants of caretaking behavior are established during the affect-laden identification experience of the first few months before the development of more truly cognitive learning can exert an influence. This process is, in itself, not deviant. It is a normal mode of establishing the basic ingredients of caretaking behavior for all persons. Those who have had a very good experience in the first months of being cared for empathically are quite likely to attach well and to have adequate empathy in their own, later, caretaking activities. Those who have not had such a good experience of positive attachment and empathic care in their beginning lives are severely hampered in their later caretaking ability because of the identification resulting from poor attachment and deficient empathy. This early origin of the adult's ability to be empathic with children has also been noted by Olden (21, 22), Josselyn (23), and others. It accounts for the fact that sensitive, empathic mothering is not something confined to biological mothers, but can exist in persons of both sexes, of all ages, as a behavioral expression determined by their own early life experience with either biological parents or other caretakers.

Deficits in the empathic care which all infants need for optimal growth and development are followed by specific psychological effects. In the normal, healthy, caretaker-infant dyad, there is a mutually rewarding, symbiotic relationship in which the caretaker sensitively becomes aware of appropriate responses to the infant's state and needs. As a result, the growing infant develops a feeling of what Benedek called "confidence" and Erikson described as "basic trust," a sense that the world and the people in it will be adequately good to one. In situations where there is lack of empathic care and experience of abuse and neglect, the symbiotic phase is highly distorted. Care is oriented much more toward the whims and convenience of the caretakers, with less appropriate response to the child. In this situation, it is impossible for the child to develop any sense that the world or the people in it in any way reliably respond to his own needs. Hence, he cannot develop basic trust, but, on the other hand, will view the world with some degree of doubt and suspicion. Later, facing impossible expectations from caretakers with inevitable failure followed by punishment, criticism, and disregard, he will have learned to pay little attention to his own inner feelings, because they are of diminished value in his dealings with surroundings. Constantly under primary control of the caretaker and plagued with the necessity to deny the self and adapt to caretakers, there will be marked difficulty in the separation and individuation phases of development. It is not surprising, therefore, that as a result of these experiences in chlidhood, we see adults who are somewhat socially isolated and have a great deal of difficulty in reaching out to others for help and assistance. They have no basic trust and have some fear that the very people to whom they will look for help will be the ones most likely to attack. They also feel their own deepest needs have never been and never will be fully satisfied. There is a low sense of self-esteem and some degree of chronic, low-grade, depressive feeling. Under these circumstances, it is not surprising that we find very commonly in descriptions of adult, abusive, neglectful caretakers characterizations of these people as dependent, immature, and having a poor sense of identity, low self-esteem, a pseudoparanoid attitude of fear of being attacked, a reluctance to form lifelines or seek help in family and community, and having a very suspicious attitude toward authority and a wish to avoid it. These characteristics of maltreating caretakers are all direct residuals of childhood experiences and are transferences to the present-day milieu of the feelings and attitudes which were appropriate toward the original caretakers of early years. It is important to understand the early origin and development of many of these characteristics, because it will help us understand the abusive, neglectful behavior of the caretakers and what strategies of management or therapy would be the most useful in helping them improve their child-caring abilities. It also points a way toward the use of helpful interventions in the perinatal period as a most effective time to help a family and to prevent the recurrence of abuse and neglect and the transmission of the pattern to still another generation.

Circumstances of Attack

Physical abuse is usually not a constant or daily occurrence. There are often many days, weeks, or even months between attacks. To be sure, there may be almost daily emotional abuse in the form of yelling and verbal castigation, belittlement, and criticism, as well as disregard and lack of attention. But it is the physical attacks occurring intermittently in discrete episodes which give us the clearest picture of the abusive phenomenon. There are four conditions which seem necessary for abuse to occur:

1. A caretaker who has the predisposition for abuse related to the psychological residues of neglect or abuse in his or her own early life.

2. A crisis of some sort placing extra stress on the caretaker.

3. Lack of lifelines or sources of help for the caretaker, because either he or she is unable to reach out or the facilities are not available.

4. A child who is perceived as being in some way unsatisfactory.

These four factors interact in a mutually reinforcing way. Abusive parents live in a state of precarious balance between emotional supply and demand. They are more needy because of their low self-esteem, but less able to reach out for pleasure and support, and so turn with increased need to those who are least able to provide full satisfaction, their infants. Any crisis, even a small one such as a broken washing machine, becomes unmanageable because of the parent's poor coping techniques and inability or reluctance to seek help. Financial and housing crises are very upsetting, but most devastating are emotional crises related to loss or abandonment by important persons or the emotional desertion of a spouse after marital conflict. It is the infant's disturbing behavior during ordinary care-taking, excessive crying, or his errors during toilet training which are the common stimuli to parental turmoil that culminates in the abusive act. The following discussion drawn from our previous study (2) presents our understanding of the circumstances of abusive attacks.

The parent approaches each task of infant care with three incongruous attitudes: first, a healthy desire to do something good for the infant; second, a deep, hidden yearning for the infant to respond in such a way as to fill the emptiness in the parent's life and bolster his or her low self-esteem; and third, a harsh, authoritative demand for the infant's correct response, supported by a sense of parental rightness. If the caring task goes reasonably well and the infant's response is reasonably adequate, no attack occurs and no harm is done except for the stimulation of aggression and accompanying strict superego development in the infant. But, if anything interferes with the success of the parental care or enhances the parent's feelings of being unloved and inferior, the harsh, authoritative attitude surges up, and an attack is likely to occur. The infant's part in this disturbance is accomplished by persistent, unassuaged crying, by failing to respond physically or emotionally in accordance with parental needs, or by actively interfering through obstructive physical activity. At times the parent may be feeling especially inferior, unloved, needy, and angry, and, therefore, unusually vulnerable because some important figure such as the spouse or a relative has just criticized or deserted him or her or because some other facet of life has become unmanageable.

On a deeper psychological level, the events begin with the parent's identification of the cared-for infant as a need-gratifying object equivalent to a parent who will replace the lacks in the abusive parent's own being-parented experience. Since the parent's past tells him that those to whom he looked for love were also the ones who attacked him, the infant is also perceived as a critical parental figure. Quite often abusing parents tell us, "When the baby cries like that it sounds just like mother (or father) yelling at me, and I can't stand it." The perception of being criticized stirs up the parent's feelings of being inferior. It also increases the frustration of his need for love, and anger mounts. At this time there seems to be a strong sense of guilt, a feeling of helplessness and panic becomes overwhelming, and the haziness is most marked. Suddenly a shift in identifications occurs. The superego identification with the parent's own punitive parent takes over. The infant is perceived as the parent's own bad childhood itself. The built-up aggression is redirected outward, and the infant is hit with full superego approval.

This sudden shift in identifications is admittedly difficult to document. Our patients cannot clearly describe all that happened in the midst of such intense emotional turmoil. We interpret it as regression under severe stress to an early period of superego development when identification with the aggressor established a strict, punitive superego with more effective strength than the gentler ego ideal. In such a regressive state the stronger, punitive superego inevitably comes to the fore.

Following the attack, some parents may maintain a strict, righteous attitude, express no sense of guilt about the aggression, insist they have done nothing wrong, and may be very resentful toward anyone who tries to interfere with their affairs. On the other hand, some parents are filled with remorse, weep, and quickly seek medical help if the child has been seriously hurt.

It has not been possible to obtain a clear story from all patients of what they actually did to the child at the time a serious injury occurred, even though abuse is admitted. They insist they did nothing differently than usual. In some cases this may be a defensive forgetting. In others we think it is probably a true statement. They have been hitting or yanking the child routinely and are not aware of the extra force used at the time of fracture.

The following condensed case histories, when added to the fragments already quoted, will illustrate the mainstreams of the patient's lives related to the ultimate abusive behavior.

Amy, twenty-six, is the wife of a successful junior executive engineer. She requested help for feelings of depression, fear she was ruining her marriage, and worry over being angry and unloving with her baby boy. She was born and raised in a well-to-do family in a large city on the West Coast. Her parents were brilliant, active intellectuals who apparently had minimal involvement in the earliest years of their children's lives. She and her younger sister and brother were cared for by governesses, about whom Amy has vague, fragmentary memories. One was very warm, kind, and loving. She recalls another who was demanding, stern, and mean and who roughly washed Amy's long hair as a punishment and held her nose to make her eat. We suspect, without adequate documentation, that the governesses raised the infants as much to meet the high behavior standards of the parents as to meet the variable needs and whims of their charges.

As a child Amy had more interaction with her mother, but she could not feel close or really understood by either parent. Both parents had compulsive traits of wanting everything in perfect order and tasks done "at once." Her father was quite aloof, uninterested in children because they could not talk to him on any worthwhile level. When Amy was about thirteen, both mother and father had psychotherapy. Since then, her father has been warmer and has some liking for small children, but he still maintains a pattern of wanting to be the center of the stage and have people pay attention primarily to him, not only in the family, but in all social situations. In recent years Amy has felt closer to her mother and has felt that they could talk more frankly and openly with each other. During her childhood, Amy felt inept, awkward, ugly, unable to be liked by other people, and somewhat dull intellectually. Even though she made good grades in school, they never seemed good enough to gain approval. (Her I.Q. is in the upper normal range.)

Although not physically punished or overtly severely criticized, Amy felt great lack of approval and developed a deep sense of inferiority, inability to please, and worthlessness; she thought of herself as almost "retarded." In college she was capable, but not outstanding, and after graduation she worked for a while, gaining a significant amount of self-respect and self-assurance. She had become a quite attractive, adequately popular girl and had made a good marriage. She and her husband are well-liked, active members of their social set.

Of her first-born child, Lisa, now age two and a half and doing well, Amy says, "I did not like her too well at first and didn't feel close to her until she was several months old and more responsive." By the time Lisa was a year old, with much maternal encouragement, she was talking and beginning to talk and Amy began to think much more highly of her, and for the most part, they get along well with each other. However, if Lisa has tantrums or does not behave well, whines or cries too much, Amy occasionally still shakes her and spanks her rather violently. Their second child, Billy, was born not quite a year and a half after Lisa. He was delivered by cesarean section, one month premature. He did not suck well at first and feeding was a problem. Also, Amy was sick for a while after delivery. She never felt warm or close or really loved him and had even less patience with him than with Lisa. His "whining" drove her "crazy" and made her hate him. Because of his crying and lack of adequate response, she would grow impatient with him and leave him or punish him roughly. She spent little time cuddling or playing with him, and he became, as a result, somewhat less responsive and did not thrive as well as he might have. When he was seven months old, during a routine checkup, the pediatrician unfortunately said to Amy,

"Maybe you have a retarded child here." Amy immediately felt intense aversion to Billy, hated the sight of him, couldn't pick him up or feed him easily, and began more serious physical abuse that evening. She felt depressed, angry, and irritable. Billy also seemed to stop progressing. However, when checked by another pediatrician, he was said to be quite normal. Amy felt reassured, but not convinced. She became aware that Billy was responsive and alert if she felt all right and loving toward him, but he acted "stupid" if she were depressed or angry at him. This awareness of her influence on him served only to enhance her feelings of worthlessness and guilt. At times when he was unresponsive or seemed to be behaving in a "retarded" way, and especially if he cried too much or whined, she roughed him up, shook him, spanked him very severely, and choked him violently. No bones had been broken, but there were bruises. Amy described alternating between feelings of anger at Billy because he was "retarded" and feeling very guilty because she had "squashed him" by her own attitudes and behavior.

Amy described being inadequately prepared for and overwhelmed by the tasks of motherhood. This was enhanced by her feeling that she was trying to accomplish the mothering tasks without the help that her mother had had in bringing up her children. Further difficulty arose because her husband, although overtly quite sympathetic with her difficulties and expressing wishes of helping her, would also withdraw from her in times of crisis and imply a good deal of criticism of the way she dealt with the children. She also felt that there had been no one to whom she could really turn to air her troubles and get comfort and help without too much admonition and criticism. Further, Amy had a cousin who was retarded, and she felt devastated by fantasies of the burden of bringing up a retarded child.

This case shows the identification of the abusive parent with her own parents' attitudes toward children, the premature, high expectation and need for the infant to perform responsively, and the inability to cope with the lack of good response. Most clearly, it shows the parental misperception of the infant as the embodiment of those bad behavioral traits (being "retarded") for which the parent herself was criticized as a young child. During treatment Amy's depressive feelings and sense of worthlessness were ameliorated. She began to interact more happily with her children, and they responded well to her change in behavior. Billy, particularly, began to thrive, grew rapidly, and became a happier, more rewarding baby. Amy and her husband began to communicate a little more effectively, and her aggressive behavior toward her children almost completely disappeared. After six months, treatment had to be terminated because of her husband's transfer to another city. We had the good fortune to see her and the children four years later. Amy was doing very well and the two children were active, happy, bright youngsters. Wisely, we believe, they have had no more children. The improvement that occurred in this situation is partly due to our therapeutic intervention, but we would guess that it is also due to the passage of time which enabled the children to grow up and inevitably become more behaviorally and conversationally rewarding to their mother.

Larry, age twenty-seven is a quiet, shy, unassuming, little man who works as a welder's assistant. Since childhood, he has been plagued by a deep sense of inferiority, unworthiness, and unsureness of himself in his work and in all human relations. There is also a deep resentment, usually very restrained, against a world which he feels is unfair.

He was brought up on a dairy farm, the third of five children. The oldest, a sister, is ten years his senior. He has never been able to find out the truth about her from his parents or other relatives but thinks all the evidence indicates she is a half-sister and an illegitimate child of his mother's before her marriage. Some resentment against his mother is based on this situation. His two younger sisters he felt were bothersome and annoying during their childhood. His brother, two years older, took advantage of him, and his parents always took the brother's side, allowing him to do many things for which Larry was criticized or punished. This brother was quite wild, and while on leave from the navy, he was in a serious auto accident. Larry said, "Too bad he wasn't killed," but then found out his brother had been killed. Overwhelmed by guilt and grief, Larry took leave from the army to take his brother's body home for burial.

Larry's parents were deeply religious. He imagined his mother became fanatically so following her illegitimate pregnancy. She was against cigarettes, alcohol, coffee, tea, and most of the usual forms of amusement. Even after his marriage, his mother told his wife not to make coffee for him. Larry felt she was always much more strict with him than with his siblings. She forced him to attend Sunday school and frequent church services, much against his will. She berated him for minor misdeeds, and constantly nagged and criticized him to the point where he felt everything he did was wrong and that he could never do right in her eyes. He occasionally rebelled by smoking or drinking. Larry's father drank moderately but became a teetotaler after his son's death. He often had outbursts of temper and once beat Larry with a piece of two-by-four lumber for a minor misdeed. Larry does not recall either mother or father spanking as a routine, but there were constant verbal attacks and criticism. He felt that neither of his parents, particularly his mother, really listened to him or understood his unhappiness and his need for comfort and consideration.

While he was in the army, Larry and Becky planned to marry. She was to come to where he was stationed, and they were to be married at Christmas time. He waited all day at the bus station, but she never appeared. Sad and hopeless, he got drunk. Months later, a buddy told him she had married somebody else the first of January. He saw her again a year later when home on leave. She had been divorced; so they made up and got married. She had a child, Jimmy, by her first marriage.

Larry has been dependent on Becky and fears losing her. Seeing Jimmy reminds him of her previous desertion. He feels she favors Jimmy; he is critical of Jimmy and occasionally spanks him. Becky has threatened to leave Larry over his aversion to Jimmy. During their five years of marriage they have been in financial straits, and at such times Becky and Larry have gone to their respective family homes for help until he could find a new job. Becky resented these episodes and criticized Larry for being an inadequately capable and providing husband.

They have had three more children of their own. Mary, age four, is liked very much by both parents, although Larry is more irritated by her than by their next child, David, age two and a half. David is "a very fine, active, alert, well-mannered little boy." He is quite responsive, and both parents like him and are good with him. Maggie, four-and-a-half months old, was thought by both parents to be "a bit different" from birth. She seemed to look bluer and cried less strongly than their other babies and was also rather fussy. Becky is fond of Maggie and gives her good mothering. Larry is irritated by her, much as he is by Mary, and more than by David, but he does not dislike her as much as he does Jimmy.

Maggie was admitted to the hospital with symptoms and signs of bilateral subdural hematoma. She had been alone with her father when he noticed a sudden limpness, unconsciousness, and lack of breathing. He gave mouth-to-mouth respiration, and she was brought to the hospital by ambulance. There was a history of a similar episode a month before when Maggie was three-and-a-half months old; when alone with her father she had become limp, followed by vomiting. Medical care was not sought until a week later. Following this, there was a question of increasing head size. No fractures of skull or long bones were revealed by X-ray. Two craniotomies were done for the relief of Maggie's subdural hematomas. During the month she was in hospital, we had frequent interviews with the parents. We were impressed by Becky's warmth, responsiveness, and concern over Maggie's welfare. Larry, however, maintained a more uneasy, aloof, evasive attitude, although he was superficially cooperative. What had happened to Maggie was not clearly established, but it seemed obvious she was the victim of trauma. We thought Larry was likely to have been the abuser, despite his maintenance of silence and innocence. We felt we had adequate, although meager, rapport with Larry and Becky and allowed them to take Maggie home with the adamant provision that she never be left alone with Larry.

A week later Larry called urgently for an appointment. Filled with shame, guilt, and anxiety he poured out his story. President Kennedy had been assassinated two days before. Larry was shocked, then flooded with feelings of sympathy for Kennedy and his family, anger at the assassin, grief over the unfair, unnecessary loss of an admired figure, and a sense of communal guilt. In this emotional turmoil he had a few beers at a tavern, went home and confessed to Becky what he had done to Maggie, and then phoned us. The circumstances of the attack were as follows: Larry's boss told him that his job was over. The construction contract had been suddenly canceled and there was no more work. Feeling discouraged, hopeless, and ignored, Larry went home, shamefacedly told Becky he had lost his job, and asked her if she wanted to go with the children to her family. Saying nothing, Becky walked out of the house leaving Larry alone with Maggie. The baby began to cry. Larry tried to comfort her, but she kept on crying; so he looked for her bottle. He could not find the bottle anywhere; the persistent crying and his feelings of frustration, helplessness, and ineffectuality became overwhelming. In a semiconfused "blurry" state he shook Maggie severely and then hit her on the head. Suddenly aware of what he had done, he started mouth-to-mouth resuscitation; then Becky came home and Maggie was brought to the hospital.

Recurrent in Larry's life are the themes of feeling disregarded and deserted and of being helplessly ineffectual in his attempts to meet expectations. These concepts of himself as worthless and incapable express the incorporation into his superego of the attitudes of his parents toward him during childhood; they have been enhanced by his later reality experiences of failure. He has further strong identifications with the aggressive parental attitudes of criticizing and attacking the weak, the helpless, and the maimed.

The attack on Maggie occurred when several of Larry's vulnerabilities were activated at the same time. He had experienced a lack of being considered and a feeling of failure in losing his job, his wife "deserted" him again with implications of criticism, he felt helpless to cope with the crying demands of the baby, and his own deep yearnings for love and care could not be spoken. Frustration and anger mounted, and the baby was struck. Larry said that in the "blurry" state he had a fleeting, queer feeling that he had hit himself.

Later we found similar circumstances were present when Maggie had been less severely injured a month before. Becky had started working evenings to supplement Larry's inadequate income. She would depart soon after he came home from his job, leaving him alone to fix supper, wash the dishes, and put the children to bed. He found the tasks difficult and was upset by the children's crying, particularly Maggie's. One evening, feeling overwhelmed, helpless, and unable to seek help, he attacked.

Larry's relationship to Becky was highly influenced by his unconscious tendency to identify her with his mother. This transference was facilitated by the reality that Becky had a child by a previous liaison, urged Larry to be more involved with the church, took Jimmy's side while disregarding Larry, frequently criticized Larry for failure to meet her expectations, and had several times deserted him, both emotionally and physically. Most basic and potent was Larry's urgent, dependent need to find in Becky the motherliness he had never known. Constantly, despite disappointments, he yearningly looked to her to satisfy the unmet needs of all his yesterdays. When she failed him, there were only the children to look to for responses which would make him feel better.

The preceding case material depicts the four cardinal features of abuse—the psychological set of the parent, the presence of a crisis, the misperception of a child, and the unavailability of help. It also illustrates another factor. Even in cases where one parent is the sole abuser, the spouse is invariably, albeit often unconsciously, instigating, approving, condoning, or passively not interfering with the abuse. This connivance is not surprising, as it is a common observation that persons who have the potential for abuse tend to marry those with similar backgrounds and potential, a process of assortative mating.

Young parents have told us they grew tired of following pediatric advice which was spoiling the baby and had decided to "bring it up the way we were brought up," following which the baby was punished and injured. Such marriages seem held together more by desperate, dependent neediness than by shared respect and love. Both partners have low self-esteem which leads them to believe they could never find anything better and they must cling to whatever they have. We believe that in marriages where only one partner has the abusive potential there is little likelihood of abuse or, if there is abuse, that it will be promptly discovered and treated.

Failure to Thrive

Among all the forms of child neglect, including failure to provide cleanliness, medical care, clothing, and emotional stimulation, the most clearcut clinical syndrome is that of the "failure to thrive due to maternal deprivation." (See chapter 16 for a full discussion of this condition.) The term "maternal deprivation" should not be understood as applying only to biological mothers, but rather as a descriptive term referring to the lack of empathic, sensitive awareness and response to an infant by its primary caretaker, whether it be mother, father, nurse, or other person (24). In some ways the condition is quite similar to "hospitalism," described by Spitz (25, 26), and it also resembles the state of infants in institutions reported by Provence and Lipton (27). The parents of infants who fail to thrive are essentially not much different from parents who abuse their offspring. Although the mother is predominantly involved with the infant, the father tends to be indifferent to the child's condition and is either uninterested or unable to intervene on the child's behalf. The mother shows the characteristics noted before in abusive mothers and, in fact, may often abuse the child physically concurrently with neglectful behavior producing failure to thrive, or she may abuse the child at other times when the other needs of the child are being met. Koel has reported on failure to thrive and fatal injury as a continuum (28), and we, too, have seen many children with evidences of both malnutrition and physical injuries.

We have found no consistent, significant, across-the-board, qualitative, difference between mothers whose infants are injured and those who fail to thrive. There is a tendency, however, for failure-to-thrive mothers to show a higher degree of depression, a lower self-esteem, and poorer coping ability in general. Not rarely do they take very poor care of themselves physically and neglect their personal appearance. They also seem to have more suppressed anger, which is not so righteously directed against the environment, as it is in many cases of physical abuse, but rather is internalized with much self-depreciation and an enhancement of a sense of worthlessness. This sense of worthlessness and ineptitude is deep and has been embedded in their character structure since early years. It seems to have been instigated by the recurring criticisms for failure to meet excessive parental demands and has been many times reinforced by the real failures of adult life which are inevitable because of the person's diminished ability to cope, to learn from experience, to ask for help. Each failure has led to more unsureness, depression, and apathy, thereby paving the way for even more failures in the future. These mothers tend to see their children more negatively, as being somehow defective, inefficient, recalcitrant, or somehow subtly deviant. Even in organically handicapped infants, they seem to exaggerate the deficits and cope with them poorly. Curiously, they may at the same time fail to see or respond to the obvious facts that the infant is significantly underweight, pale, wan, and apathetic. Their response to the infant is that the situation is hopeless, that the baby is not really worth caring for and is, therefore, significantly neglected and underfed. This misperception of the infant is related unconsciously to the mother's own perception of herself as a worthless human being. These behavioral patterns and characterological states, as well as the almost universal history of emotional deprivation or physical abuse in early childhood, have been reported by others (29–33).

It has sometimes been assumed that lack of knowledge of child development and inexperience in child care can account for cases of failure to thrive. While this may be true in some very young mothers and some culturally deprived persons, it is certainly not routine and is belied by the fact that many mothers of failure-to-thrive children have been able to take care of other babies without difficulty and that many such mothers are quite intelligent and well educated and competent in other areas of their lives. The problem lies in the mother's lack of empathic ability rather than in a cognitive deficit. We believe the programs for enhancing parental skills which can be quite successful are so largely because of the emotional support and approval provided rather than solely because of the technical knowledge gained. For instance, a young mother who was a physician and has had some experience in pediatrics, delivered a normal infant which she breast-fed and of which she was happily quite proud. However, after six weeks, it was evident the baby had gained practically no weight and was beginning to look seriously malnourished and apathetic. She seemed oblivious of her baby's poor condition, and her husband hesitated to intervene lest she would feel criticized. On further investigation, it became evident she was unconsciously extremely unsure of her ability to be a mother, a concept related to her own poor experience of being mothered as a small child, and she was fearful of being discovered as ineffectual. It was surprising and gratifying to her and to the staff that she responded quickly to support from her pediatrician and to loving encouragement from husband and friends. Soon the baby was plump, happy, and developing normally.

In failure-to-thrive cases, more often than in physical abuse, there is a history of the mother having had difficulties during pregnancy or delivery, or there is some abnormality of the baby or prematurity. These extra stresses in the prenatal and perinatal periods, added to the already existing poor psychological set of the mother and her much diminished ability to cope, make it difficult for the mother to attach and to be adequately motherly, and failure to thrive can easily ensue. The following case report illustrates the complex interaction of residuals of childhood deprivation, depression, current emotional difficulties, problems in pregnancy, and misperceptions of the infant.

A very well-educated, generally capable young woman consulted us because of depression, embarrassment over her failure to take good care of her baby, and anxiety over punitive behavior toward the child. She had never had a close empathic relationship with her own mother and had a lifelong feeling of being uncared for. After marriage, she lived in another city, and her pregnancy went well until the last few weeks when she returned to the city where her mother lived. She then became anxious and depressed; her relations with her husband were cold (he was absent, working on a new job), and her mother was either unconcerned or intrusive and inconsiderate. She developed mild preeclampsia and had a cesarean section. The baby was slightly small for gestational age and had mild, temporary, respiratory difficulty. Because of the baby's slight abnormalities, but more because of her own medical problems, the mother had little contact with her new infant and did not establish a good attachment. In the ensuing weeks, she did not regain full physical health, remained depressed, had difficulty feeding her baby, and would often lose patience with him, sometimes shaking and choking him with the production of minor bruises. She saw her baby as somehow inadequate, vaguely defective, and as stubbornly refusing to cooperate with her efforts to care for him. On a home visit, we observed the interaction during feeding. Mother very nicely picked up her baby boy, cuddled him in her arms, and put a spoonful of cereal in his mouth, which he eagerly accepted. However, before he had a chance to really mouth his food and swallow it, she had another spoonful of cereal, trying to push it between his closed lips. He turned his head away and refused the proffered food. Mother looked at him angrily, got up, and said, "See, he won't eat," and threw him angrily down in his crib. It is not surprising that this baby looked wan, apathetic, significantly underweight, and was behind in his development. Fortunately, the mother responded quite well to treatment. The baby quickly improved. She later had another child under better circumstances, attached well, and was a very good mother.

As noted above, failure-to-thrive parents, particularly mothers, have a very poor self-image and are particularly dubious about their abilities to be good parents. This sense of being inadequate or ineffectual can be greatly enhanced by delivering a baby with some abnormality or having a child who is sickly or unresponsive. Glaser and Bentovim (34) have reported that handicapped or chronically ill infants are more likely to be maltreated in the form of omission of care, and that within this group the neglect was worse with increase of social and emotional disturbance of the caretakers and family. They also found that nonhandicapped children were more likely to be physically abused. These observations seem to be in agreement with our idea that defective or ill children are perceived as more worthless and less deserving of care, while physically normal children are assumed to be able to perform well and deserve punishment if they do not do so.

Role of the Child in Abuse and Neglect

High-Risk Children

A great deal of information has been gained in recent years concerning the different kinds of infants and children who are at risk or who are most likely to be abused and neglected (18, 35–38). Included are essentially normal infants who are the product of a difficult pregnancy or delivery, born at an inconvenient time from an unplanned pregnancy, illegitimate, of the wrong sex, too active, too passive, the child of an unloved father, or born during a period of severe family stress and crisis. Other infants at risk are those who for some reason are more or less "abnormal." Included are infants both with significant prematurity, those who are small for gestational age, those who have various congenital deficiencies, abnormalities, and perinatal illnesses, particularly those which require hospitalization, and those who have later chronic or recurrent illness, again, especially if there is hospitalization. There is a third group of children who can be either essentially normal physically or show very mild deficiencies, but who are described as being "difficult," or "different." They are hyperactive, fussy, difficult to feed, hard to cuddle, have abnormal sleep patterns, cry excessively, and are seen as generally being inadequately responsive to caretaking efforts. Adopted children seem to be at some risk, as there is a higher incidence of adoptive children in the population of abused and neglected infants than is warranted by their incidence in the general population. Finally, there are children, usually somewhat older, described as deliberately provoking or "asking for abuse" when in foster care, just as they did in their own homes.

It is true that all the children enumerated above are at high risk for abuse and neglect. Valid statistics indicate that they are overrepresented in the observed populations of abused and neglected children, but it must also be noted that only a minor percentage of all the premature, congenitally defective, sickly, and difficult children are abused or neglected and, also, that only a small proportion of the total population of abused and neglected children come from this group of excessively high-risk infants. It is our experience that a majority of abused and neglected children had originally been quite normal and that many of the emotional difficulties, evidences of retardation, and behavioral problems are the results of previous abuse and neglect rather than "causes" of it.

It has been distressing to note that some investigators have subtly implied that the observed abuse and neglect of these high-risk infants cannot only be understood, but almost forgiven, inasmuch as the infant's fault explains the parental action. We are quite aware that some of these children are extremely difficult and place an enormous burden on their caretakers. Sometimes the experienced nurses on our wards who are accustomed to and expert in taking care of extremely difficult cases find that some of these children try their patience to the breaking point. But abuse and neglect can never be considered a permissible or appropriate response in such situations. To us, it is obvious that punishment or neglect of an infant can never, in any circumstance, be considered correct response to a fussy, premature baby or to the feeding problems resulting from a cleft palate. All of these high-risk circumstances are ones which call for much more attention and careful monitoring of the parent-infant dyad and the provision of extra services to the caretakers who are faced with coping with enormous extra burdens.

How then can we account for the fact that some caretakers abuse some infants who, through no fault of their own, have "conditions which place them at high risk"? One of the basic tenets of the abusive parent is the conviction or belief that a child's primary role is to behave and respond in such a way as to please and satisfy parents. Thus, we see the very early and excessive expectation of performance which was noted above. It is also the parental belief that children who fail to perform adequately well are therefore unsatisfactory and are either worthless or need to be punished to make them "shape up." Added to this is the significantly increased amount of care and special attention which they require. For the abusive caretaker, who is plagued with lifelong feelings of being unloved and ineffectual, this creates an unbearable situation and maltreatment is more likely to occur. In our estimation this is no different than other cases of abuse and neglect, except that there are more real reasons for considering the child to be unsatisfactory and, therefore, more stressful to the vulnerable parent who in other less serious circumstances with a more rewarding baby might not be so abusive.

While it is perfectly true that some children are extremely difficult and, by their behavior, push their caretakers beyond their ability to cope, we deplore any tendency to accent the provocative behavior of the child at the expense of disregarding the parents' own deficiencies in caretaking abilities. It is quite similar to the frequently noted tendency of maltreating parents themselves to blame everything on the child. This is not a new phenomenon, as indicated by the following story which has been handed down from the fifth century B.C. in China (39).

Tseng Tzu was one of the most famous disciples of Confucius. He was extremely dutiful to-ward his parents and became one of the twenty-four celebrated examples of filial piety. A story about him tells that once when he was hoeing melons for his father, he accidentally cut the root of one, and his father, becoming enraged, beat him so severely that he lost consciousness. Tseng Tzu submitted to this beating without complaint and upon reviving played his lute and sang as usual. It is said that when Confucius heard of this he told his disciples that it would have been filial for Tseng Tzu to have submitted to a light thrashing, but he should have avoided such a severe beating because, by not doing so, he was involving his father in an unrighteous act which does not become a filial son.

Attachment

The infants and children described above are not at risk simply because of immaturity, physical defects, or emotional aberrancy. There is also a marked diminution or complete lack of parental attachment to such infants. These difficulties in attachment are most likely to occur with parents who have had difficult childhoods themselves and are hence already deficient in empathy. Such predispositions for poor attachment are markedly in-creased, especially in mothers, by troubles during pregnancy, complicated deliveries, pre-maturity, cesarean sections, or illness of the infant or mother that necessitates the sepa-ration of the mother and child for a significant time in the postnatal period. It can be extremely difficult for even the best-prepared parents to attach to a child if, in the post-natal period, they cannot, because of medical conditions, pick up, hold, feed, or other-wise care for the new baby. In this latter case, however, it is possible for such parents to develop fully normal attachments when the medical crisis is over and they assume the normal tasks of parenting.

Attachment behavior is also profoundly influenced by the kind of fantasies parents have during the pregnancy. This is to some extent true of fathers, but is especially true of moth-ers, because the fetus is inside her and part of her, as well as a separate entity. Normally such fantasies are of having a fine baby, possibly with some preference for sex, which will be a pleasurable addition to the family. Such essentially pleasant fantasies are not counter-acted by the common anxieties concerning whether or not the baby will be normal and everything else all right. Parents at high risk for poor attachment and caretaking diffi-culties are, because of their own past lives, likely to have much more distressing fantasies during the prenatal period. One young mother described this clearly when she said early in pregnancy, "If it's a girl, it will be a mess. She will hate me as I hated my mother, and I will hate her like mother hated me." Another young mother, who could not be relieved of her anxiety that her baby might be born without arms or legs or might have defects in his back or head, delivered a normal baby, but she had seriously injured it several times be-fore it was a year old. Often fantasies are of the baby *in utero* developing into the same kind of child which the mother was. And this, of course, is a bad omen if the mother remembers herself as an extremely difficult, bad child, who often had to be punished. More seriously psychologically disturbed mothers may have fantasies of the fetus being some kind of parasitic invader who is destructively eating her up from the inside. If car-ried to term, such a baby, even though apparently normal, is likely to be maltreated and thought of as some kind of "monster." It must be remembered that not only can various organic difficulties during pregnancy give rise to negative fantasies on the part of the mother, but also that negative daydreams, fantasies, and night dreams can be evidence of psychological states which can, in turn, have profoundly disturbing effects on the pregnancy itself. Unrealistic expectations of the baby can be expressed in prenatal fantasy also. One young mother expressed the conviction that she would have a beautiful little girl who would help her overcome her emotional difficulties in life, and she looked forward with happy anticipation to birth. She delivered a boy, to whom she did not attach, as it was the wrong sex, and she could not mother him well. Other parents, including fathers, may have fantasies of the child growing up to be a disruptive influence in the family, making trouble between the parents, and causing serious conflicts with siblings. Such prenatal fantasies bear a very direct relationship to the parent's own childhood and certainly do not bode well either for full attachment or subsequent attitudes toward the infant by the caretaker.

The attachment of parents or other caretakers to their new infants is thus seen not as a simple, automatic process, but one that is highly influenced for better or worse by many other factors, particularly those which have their roots in the parents' own earliest childhood experiences and how well they were lovingly, sensitively cared for with adequate empathy. Probably nearly all parents have, to some degree, the expectation that having a child will somehow be a rewarding, fulfilling experience which will make their lives happier and more complete. This is true for the majority of parents, and the rewards of parenthood outweigh the trials and tribulations. But it is likely that if caretakers have problems and discontents of any significant degree, having a child will not solve such problems, but probably will make them worse. We believe this is one factor which leads to the somewhat higher instance of maltreatment of adopted children. The adoptive procedure itself, in almost all instances, is undertaken to solve a parental problem, particularly the deficit of infertility and the inability to have natural children. Fortunately, most adoptive parents have inner strength and past experience and empathy enough to manage their caretaking skills quite well. A number of them, however, seem to have problems in low self-esteem, incompetence, and a sense of being defective that are too deep to be solved by the adoption of a child. Hence, the adopted child is unconsciously seen as failing to solve the parental problem, is therefore an unsatisfactory child, and is at high risk for maltreatment. The fact that so many adoptive mothers attach so effectively to their infants and become perfectly adequate mothers indicates attachment is not a purely biological phenomenon which has to be accomplished in a critical period during the first few hours postpartum, although that period when the infant is in a quiet-alert state and the mother awake is possibly the most ideal time for attachment (40).

This discussion of attachment has primarily been concerned with the presence or absence of attachment, but there has also been the implication that in some instances there is not only a lack of positive attachment, but what might be called antagonism or antipathy toward the infant which is quite the opposite of positive attachment. Such "negative attachments" are often related to misperceptions of the child associated with fantasies of abnormality occurring during the prenatal period, or with excessive identifications of the child with the parent's own, bad, childhood self. They may also be related to the baby being unwanted, because it is a product of rape, incest, or, more commonly, the child of a now discarded lover or a deserting, divorced spouse. The baby may also be unwanted because of being unplanned or coming at a time of extreme inconvenience to the family because of financial problems, geographic moves, or family tragedies. If attention is not paid to such replacement of attachment by negative attitudes, serious difficulties in the caretaker-infant relationship resulting in maltreatment may well occur. We have often seen children seriously injured, neglected, even killed by parents who loathed their child, wanted to get rid of the child and give him or her up for adoption, but who were cajoled or shamed into keeping the child by relatives or health professionals. Negative attachments need special care. While it is sometimes true in cases where mothers and fathers are unhappy about a child that they will "learn to love it in time," such loving is far from automatic, and the negative feelings warrant serious attention if tragedy is to be avoided.

Atypical Abuse and Infanticide

There are some abusers, nearly all of them men in our experience, who repeatedly and cruelly injure the children with whom they are involved. They maltreat their charges much like other abusers, but do not confine themelves to the usual patterns of attacking a child because of some specific error or unacceptable behavior. They also indiscriminately attack for no more apparent reason than that the child is there as a handy person upon whom to release aggression. They may pinch, slap, or punch a baby each time they see it or go by its crib, extinguish cigarettes by stubbing them out on a child's foot or arm, or routinely kick a child playing on the floor. They have been described as "torturing" their offspring. Often they also abuse their wives or mistresses, get into fights, pass bad checks, and have frequent brushes with the law because of numerous traffic offenses and minor crimes. They may also be clever liars and manipulative "con men." Abuse of alcohol and drugs is common. Their personal relationships are shallow and exploitative. Such persons, who constitute possibly some 5%–10% of the abusive population, can best be described as sociopaths. They are characterized by their free, unconflicted discharge of aggression, their self-centered, narcissistic demands, and especially by their extreme lack of empathic caring for other human beings and disregard of others' welfare. In childhood, they had very little love, warmth, or consistency from their caretakers and were exposed to excessive and frequent violence in their homes. They are quite similar in these respects to men who murder without apparent motive as described by Satten et al. (41).

Not rarely, a child will die as a result of such persistent maltreatment by its sociopathic caretaker. Typically, the abuser shows little or no guilt or remorse, denies any possibility that his own actions might have contributed to the death, blames the death on his wife or other people, even including emergency room personnel, or assumes that the child had some previously unrecognized illness or defect. We consider it important to recognize such individuals as early as possible, since we have found it extremely difficult, if not impossible, to rehabilitate them to the point of being safe caretakers. Their abuse is repetitive and is easily transferred to other children in the family.

Mental illness may significantly interfere with parental abilities, either through disregard of the child or misperceptions of him. Severe depressive or schizophrenic psychosis may seriously compromise a caretaker's ability to perceive a child's needs and respond appropriately to them. Preoccupation with obsessive thoughts, delusions, and hallucinations or withdrawal into hopeless immobility results in profound neglect of the child, leading to delayed development, starvation, illness, and sometimes death. In other instances, the child is woven into the caretaker's delusional system and becomes a target of paranoid attacks. This is not unrelated to the severe beatings, sometimes fatal, administered by fanatic religious groups in order to "drive the devil out" of infants perceived as "evil." Toxic psychoses and delirious states induced by various hallucinogenic drugs such as LSD or by alcohol may also lead to severe neglect, abuse, and occasionally killing of infants; in such cases there is usually a history of significant preexisting emotional disturbance or mental illness.

The direct murder of children is predominantly the act of a psychotic or seriously mentally disturbed member of the family or a stranger (42). But infanticide, in general, which has existed throughout history and is still present all over the world, has much in common with the other forms of maltreatment (43, 44). It is essentially a human behavior which disregards the life and welfare of an infant and satisfies the needs and purposes of adults. The child is sacrificed for religious, military, or political purposes or for population control because of superstitions, parental convenience, or avoidance of shame and ostracism. Although legally considered as infanticide, there is a somewhat different kind of infant death which is the result of maltreatment (45) and death from prolonged failure to thrive. In the latter, there is less of an open, direct wish or attempt to kill the child, than of a pervasive indifference and disregard for the child and subsequent failure to provide life maintenance. In the more frequent cases of death resulting from repeated physical abuse, parents, as a rule, do not intend to kill the child, but on the contrary have an investment in a living child who must be punished to become more obedient and satisfying. Death is an unexpected, undesired, incidental result of the abuse. The abuser may be quite frightened by what has happened, may or may not seek immediate help, and may not understand that he has done something which would kill the child. He subsequently tends to feel guilt and great remorse, being quite opposite in this respect from the sociopath described above. There are also deaths which occur to children who are only occasionally mildly abused which are, in a sense, "quite accidental." For example, a small child may be forcefully hit on the back, causing him to stumble against a sharp corner of a coffee table, resulting in abdominal injury with ruptured liver and later death. The parent in such a case is likely to feel extremely guilty and be overwhelmed with grief, finding it quite difficult to understand why he is put in jail and treated like a common murderer.

Sexual Abuse

Although sexual abuse of children has been recognized for as long as any other form of maltreatment, it has been more concealed, less reported, and has attracted relatively little concern. Most attention has been directed toward statutory rape and toward the less serious problems of exhibitionism and pedophilia. A taboo of dealing with the common phenomenon of incest seems to have been as strong or stronger than the taboo of incest itself. However, with increasing public awareness and concern over the enormous number of cases of physical abuse and neglect and the courage given by the women's rights movement, sexual abuse has also become a matter of public concern. Cases, especially of incest of all varieties, are now increasingly reported in numbers approaching those of other kinds of abuse (46–51).

In view of the great variety of forms of sexual abuse—heterosexual, homosexual, children of all ages, sexual acts of all kinds—it is impossible to give a simple description which covers all cases. There are significant, different, psychodynamic factors in, for instance, those men who abuse only very young girls, those men who confine their acts to early adolescent boys, and women who selectively seduce either sons or daughters. Such specific preferential sexual behaviors can be best understood in terms of the distortions of psychosexual development commonly seen in cases of perversion and neurosis and are well described in the psychiatric literature. But the basic abusive pattern is not dissimilar from that seen in other kinds of maltreatment, physical abuse, neglect and failure to thrive, and emotional abuse. Physical and sexual abuse often coexist; a caretaker may sometimes physically abuse and at other times sexually abuse the same child. Or the sexual abuse itself may be accompanied by physical violence and trauma. In very young children especially, sexual abuse is often belatedly discovered only during investigation or treatment of the more obvious physical abuse which has been reported and which called attention to the case. Older children, from latency to adolescence, are more likely to be sexually abused by their caretakers without accompanying physical abuse, although there may have been physical abuse in earlier years.

Sexual abuse of children of all ages is not an isolated phenomenon occurring in an otherwise healthy life situation. It is the obvious, overt, symptomatic expresson of seriously disturbed family relationships and has always been preceded by more or less emotional neglect or mistreatment. Parents or other caretakers involved in sexual abuse are, in most ways, quite similar to those who are only physically abusive and neglectful and, as noted above, may at different times express any of these destructive behaviors. They suffer from the same severe lack of self-esteem, have a poorly integrated sense of identity, tend to be somewhat socially isolated, and have a history of emotional deprivation, physical abuse, and often very chaotic family lives in their early years. As in physical abuse there is often a history of generational repetition of sexual abuse, especially incest in various forms. Langsley, Schwartz, and Fairbairn (52) report a case of father-son incest in which the father was repeating his seduction by adult males experienced in his own childhood. Raybin (53) reported homosexual incest involving three generations, and Raphling, Carpenter, and Davis (54) described multiple incestuous relationships existing in a family for over three generations. Gebhard et al. (55) noted that men imprisoned for sexually molesting children had often been the subjects of sexual molestation themselves as children. Lukianowicz (47) and Yorokoglu and Kemph (56) also report sexual mistreatment of children by persons who had been sexually abused themselves. In addition to the obvious learning from role modeling which must occur in such family settings, there is also a deeper and compelling identification with the sexually abusive adults known in early childhood. This often gives incest a sort of moral approval in the subculture of some families and is clearly evident when we see some fathers say with some degree of righteous indignation, "My father had sex with all my sisters, so why should I not sleep with my daughters?" Mothers also, in identification with their own mothers, seem unable to protect daughters from sexual abuse and, in many instances, condone or actually promote the incestuous relationship between husband and daughter. Both fathers and mothers may righteously justify their incestuous activities by the rationalization that it is best for the child to learn about sex from a loving family member than from "no-good" peers.

The family backgrounds of those caretakers involved in sexual abuse of children are similar, in many respects, to the backgrounds of parents and others who have been involved in physical maltreatment and neglect. Several authors have accented the role of poverty (55, 57–59). There are also descriptions of the absence of reliable parental figures in early life, particularly fathers, and often the child was moved from one foster placement to another, either in or out of the family. The caretakers of early life are also described as punitive or uncaring (58, 60–63). Some sexual abusers describe extremely chaotic living conditions during their earliest years, with multiple changes of caretaking figures and exposure to extremely atypical, flamboyant sexual activities. For instance, one man said, "My father was a drunk and my mother was a whore. There were always other men and women coming into the house, and very free sexual activity of all kinds, both heterosexual and homosexual." We have, on the other hand, known sexual abusers who were brought up in extremely rigid, highly religious, but emotionally cold families, in which sex was a forbidden subject, even for education, and the children would become involved in aberrant sexual activity through seeking knowledge elsewhere. The common denominator in all these situations seems to be the absence of warm, loving, sexual relationships as a model for the child to emulate, lack of appropriate sexual education, and, most importantly for all, lack of empathic, sensitive care during the early impressionable, developmental years. Although we have no firm data, it is our impression that the more chaotic the sexual abuser's life has been in early childhood, the more likely he is to be sexually abusive to younger children, to be more aggressive in his abuse, and to show more perverse behavior and much less consideration for the victim. The more nearly the early life experience approached "normal," the more likely the abuser was to become involved with much older children and do so only under periods of unusual stress or when drunk. Substance abuse, including alcohol, is certainly a fairly common precipitating factor to acts of sexual abuse of children. There seems to be a difference, however, between the chronic alcoholic who has been a frequent sexual abuser and the person who has indulged in sexual acts with children, either within or outside the family, only on very rare occasions when drinking as part of his futile attempts to solve the anxiety and loneliness resulting from marital conflict or the stress of other problems.

As in other forms of abuse, in sexual abuse the child victim is often considered to be the one at fault or at least guilty of "contributory negligence," particularly if she gives any evidence of having had any pleasure in the activity. In cases of incest, the daughter is often said to have been quite seductive and not only willing to participate, but ready to instigate the incestuous behavior with her father. Such concepts are given further support by the observations of girls as young as three and four who have been placed in foster care because of sexual abuse in their homes, but who continue to approach all males very seductively and attempt to play with their genitals. There is no question about the accuracy of such observations. The question is how to interpret them. We believe, with very rare exceptions, that it is impossible for a young child to have such strong sexual drives and such seductive abilities that he or she can overcome a healthy adult's concepts of what is appropriate interaction between a caretaker and a child. It must also be kept in mind that little girls are often encouraged to be cute and seductive and are admired for it. For a "normal," healthy adult to be unable to resist erotic advances of a child is patently ridiculous. The essential ingredient for sexually abusive behavior is the lack of empathic consideration by the adult for the child's stage of development and abilities, plus the adult's placing the satisfaction of his own needs above those of the child. In this, we see the essence of sexual abuse of children, the exploitation of the child for the purpose of satisfying the adult. It is the recognition of having been exploited and uncared for as an individual human being that leads to the long-lasting residual damages of sexual abuse in development, rather than the actual physical sexual act itself. As in physical abuse, it is not the bodily damage or hurt itself that is most traumatic, but the fact that one was uncared for and misused by the ones to whom one must look for comfort, care, and protection. The resulting ambivalence, lack of trust, and difficulty in human relationships are inevitable and severe.

Although relationships between fathers and daughters and stepfathers and stepdaughters are by far the most commonly reported forms of incest, it is quite likely that sexual activities between brothers and sisters are even more common, ranging from simple visual inspection of each other to intercourse. It would seem useful to describe two different patterns of brother-sister interactions. The first is the fairly common effort of children to find out something about themselves and their functions by comparing themselves with the opposite sex and understanding the differences. This can happen either within the family with siblings or with other children and may progress to various attempts to explore and to imitate the sexual behavior of adults, about which they have either heard or seen examples. Such exploratory "educational" activities between brothers and sisters are usually engaged in by mutual consent and are mutually rewarding, and, even though they may, in some instances, progress to actual intercourse in older children, they are of short duration and provide channels for expanding relationships into other heterosexual contacts with peers and are not ordinarily productive of long-lasting, psychosexual difficulties. Although children involved in such activities may have some awareness that they are being "naughty," they do not develop a serious sense of guilt or disturbance of their sexual relationships unless the disapproval and punishment by authorities who discover the activity is unusually severe. There is another group of brother-sister relationships which, although superficially like the preceding, are not only motivated by normal sexual curiosity and search for identity but, in addition, a search for love, care, and acceptance from somebody. This seems to occur most frequently with siblings who, for one reason or another, feel emotionally deprived, neglected, or misunderstood by both parents and who do not feel free in any way to discuss their problems of any kind, including sexual, with the caretaking figures. Such relationships between brother and sister, expressed in the sexual sphere, become endowed with very intense needs for love and affection and are then extremely vulnerable to betrayal and exploitation, as well as abandonment. In such instances, the incestuous behavior can become traumatic and a source of much difficulty later.

Homosexual incest, like father-daughter incest, is often related to the emotional, sexual, or geographical absence or the death of the mother. The father (or stepfather), preferring out of his own insecurity to keep his sexual activity within the family, turns to the son to satisfy his sexual urges; the son submits to the sexual advances hoping to find some of the love and acceptance he has not received from the mother, along with the satisfaction of some sexual needs. We believe the boy's gender identity has usually been at least partially compromised before the homosexual seduction occurs because of long-lasting disturbances in family relationships. Certainly the father's homosexual tendencies existed in either open or covert form for many years.

The rarest type of incest is between mother and son; it seems to arouse more horror in people and has been the object of the most stringent taboo. In some ways it is similar to other forms of incest occurring in families with preexisting problems of many kinds, including disturbed sexual relations of the parents. The father may be emotionally or physically absent, and the mother turns to the son for love and attention, while the father is indifferent or turns to a daughter. After a father's death a teenage son may be told he is "now the man of the house and must take his father's place," and the advice is followed literally by both mother and son. Yet it seems doubtful if such social pseudoapproval would be followed if there were not preexisting excessively intimate interactions between them. In a half-dozen mother-son incest cases with which we have been involved (one of which proceeded to full intercourse) and in most of the few cases reported in the literature, there is evidence of significant neurosis, intermittent psychosis, or a severe borderline state in the mother (47, 54, 64). She has had previous difficulty in allowing separation and individuation to occur and has in other ways exploited the mother-son relationship.

We have been accenting the role of object relationships in the genesis of sexual abuse of children, and we believe this is the most important element in such behavior. It is also useful to consider the psychodynamic consequences of the Oedipus complex experienced by the victims of abuse. In the first place, it seems unlikely in view of the great extent of pregenital difficulty that there was ever the development of the fully, erotically tinged, oedipal complex as it is classically understood. At the oedipal period, these boys and girls were still too involved with the yearning for basic, empathic love, care, and consideration, and in the struggle to develop individual identity to be able to look to the parent of the opposite sex with strong, erotic yearning and a sense of concern over the reaction of the parent of the same sex. Most of them were still looking for basic care and protection in a nutritive framework. Both boys and girls turned to fathers or male figures for basic love and empathy, which they had not received in adequate quantities from their mothers. Boys thus tended to have homosexual tendencies, and girls turned toward their fathers, yearning for love and prematurely placing it in a heterosexual erotic context. The turning of girls to their fathers was not complicated by fears of loss of mother's love, because mother's love had not been there to lose. Boys could not turn to their mothers with strong erotic feelings, because they were still looking for the basic love and acceptance which was not there. Instead, they were afraid of their mothers; she was felt to be an engulfing, castrating figure, and we believe this accounts in some degree for the relative rarity of mother-son incest compared to the great frequency of father-daughter incest.

In some families, the oedipal configuration may have definite bearing on the later pattern of abuse, although it would not be a complete determinant of it. For instance, a young man who sexually and physically abused his two-year-old stepdaughter had grown up in a family in which he was severely physically abused by his father and mildly so by his mother. The father favored an older sister for whom he bought more clothes than he did for the mother and with whom he had an incestuous relationship. He also beat up this girl when, as an unmarried teenager, she became pregnant. The son repressed his anger at his mother for not protecting and caring enough for him and became much closer to her, with her encouragement. He also competed with his father by buying nightgowns and robes for his mother and trying in other ways to please and gain her favor. Later he became involved with women who were critical of his inability to satisfy their needs, materially or sexually, and once severely abused his wife who indicated she might be pregnant by another man. The abuse of the stepdaughter occurred under the influence of alcohol when the mother complained about the ineffectiveness of his efforts to care for her. It seemed to be a revengeful discharge of anger at females who would not be satisfied or let him love them— mother, wife, and baby. It was also a discharge of aggression in identification with the father who was incestuous and aggressive toward females and with whom he was competitive in his distorted oedipal struggles.

In most cases of sexual abuse of children the problem is an extremely complex one, and no simple etiology will explain any one case. There is nearly always a clear history of deficient "mothering" or other neglect in early years, plus the added factors of distorted sexual behavior in the family, leading to the inability to be empathic with children and to the sexual exploitation of them.

The Clinical Picture

The following condensed case history pictures with unusual clarity many of the commonly seen elements of physical and sexual abuse.

> Laura G. was an attractive young woman, age twenty-six, poised, friendly, and verbal. She was the wife of a noncommissioned career officer in the armed forces. Her reasons for coming to us were anxiety over marital problems, depression, and worry over abuse of her elder son.
>
> Laura was the elder of two children of parents living in very marginal economic circumstances on the outskirts of a small, rural town. Her father was mildly alcoholic; her mother more severely so. Her parents frequently argued and occasionally fought rather violently. Laura had never felt her mother was interested in her and had seemed far away and inattentive when Laura tried to talk to her. She recalled that even as a little child she worked very hard to do things to please her mother but never seemed able to do so and was often the subject of much criticism. She felt deprived, rejected, and hopeless. The younger brother, Joe, was her mother's favorite, the one to whom she gave all her love. Laura's relationship to Joe was always ambivalent—some love and companionship mixed with envy and hatred.
>
> Laura was deeply attached to her father from her earliest years. She felt very close to him and believed he returned her warmth, cared for her, and listened to her. Father, however, was not always kind. He often beat her with his hands or a belt until she was black and blue, and his favorite saying was, "I'll knock you through the wall." Sometimes he made her hold two bare electric wires in her hands while he turned on a current to give her a shock (he was an electrician by trade). He explained to her that he gave her these shocks to remind her that he was the boss and she must obey him. Despite such abuse, she felt close to him and liked to be around him and do things which pleased him. He would often praise her and give her credit for things she did well when she tried to help him. She spent much more time with him than she did with her mother, and by age four father had begun to extend his affectionate cuddling into some degree of genital fondling. She remembers him asking, "You want me to make it feel good down there?" and her answering, "Yes." By the time Laura was seven, the father was having regular sex play with her, and this soon progressed to intercourse which continued for several years. Laura enjoyed the closeness and pleasure of the sexual activity, but also felt it was somehow wrong, because her father admonished her not to tell other people. She was puzzled about just what was "wrong," as father seemed to gain pleasure from the activity and had asked her to do it, and she had always been taught to obey him. In addition, her mother did not seem to disapprove, even though she was aware of what was happening between Laura and her husband.
>
> The mother and father were rarely affectionate with each other and were often in open conflict. The mother rejected the father sexually and repeatedly told him to leave her alone. They usually

slept in different rooms. There was no doubt that mother was aware of the incest, because some-times after an argument with the father, she would encourage Laura to go and sleep with him. Sometimes she had asked Laura to get money from the father after she slept with him and bring it back to her so that she could buy a bottle of liquor.

When Laura was thirteen, her father became depressed, as far as she knew, because of his endless difficulties in trying to make a living. He committed suicide in the bedroom of their home using a shotgun to blow off part of his face and the top of his head, while Laura was helping her mother cook dinner. She was utterly devastated as well as shocked. Three days later, after the funeral, on a cold, gray, rainy day, Laura and her mother came back home and went into the bedroom. It smelled badly, and she opened the shutters and the windows to let in light and air, and she recalls, "I looked around the room, and there I saw bits of flesh and hair on the wall and the ceiling, all that was left of my father. He was the only one I ever loved, and the only person who ever loved me."

The next year, when she was fourteen, Laura acquired a steady boyfriend. He was friendly and affectionate to her and spoke in a way when they were alone that made her feel very beautiful and fine. She began having intercourse with him frequently and enjoyed it. In public, however, he fought with her and treated her as "something to wipe his feet on." She could not stand the mistreatment and broke up with him. Years later, she still dreamed about him and fantasized about him, even though she realized life with him would not have been good.

At fifteen, she began dating cadets at an air force base. She loved being treated "like a lady" by these somewhat older young men. Frequently the relationships became sexual affairs, but they did not seem meaningful to her and did not last very long. She became more promiscuous, and between ages eighteen and twenty-one she describes having affairs with thirty-two different men and had, at times, "carried on" with as many as three men in one day. At twenty-two she met and married a man who was very kind, patient, and considerate of her. He listened to her, tried to do things to please her and to make her happy. In spite of what seemed to her an ideal marriage, she continued periodically to have affairs and, at times, found her husband physically repulsive. By the time we knew her, she felt, by her behavior, that she had "ruined" him and changed him from a kindly person to an angry, punitive one. She avoided sex with him and was often very critical of him, despite all his efforts. Although it was not really necessary, Laura often worked part-time in order to "get money to help the family finances," thus reducing the financial burden on her hus-band, and also to get away from the house. At these jobs she often met the men with whom she would become involved.

Toward Jimmy, the older of her two sons, Laura had been extremely ambivalent. At times she had felt love for him and, in general, had taken good physical care of him. Yet, she was more likely to be filled with feelings of disgust and hatred, and had often wished that she could get rid of him or that he would die. She expected him to be quite capable and obedient, and for various misbehaviors she would beat him with her fists or whip him with a belt or board. She seemed to be aware that fundamentally Jimmy was a rather normal little boy, but she said, "He has all my faults, and I have tried to beat all his phobias and other problems out of him. I know it's not sensible, but I can't control myself. I think he must be me, and I'm a combination of my mother and my father. My mother would never pay any attention to me, and my father would beat me. I say to Jimmy, 'I'll knock you through the wall,' just like daddy used to say to me." Laura had a curious mixture of feeling guilty over her mistreatment of the boy, and yet, at the same time, feeling justifiably angry at him because of his deficits and failures. She also considered that she had brainwashed her husband into following her pattern of screaming and yelling at this boy, to whom he had previously been very good. Laura felt she had ruined both her husband and her son, but her guilty responsibility could not eliminate her anger. She would say, "I want to get rid of them both. I want them both to die. But I've thought of suicide myself because I've been ruining them." Although Laura did not drink regularly or excessively, after a social evening with a few drinks she was more likely to get into quarrels with her husband and have more trouble with Jimmy, with the likelihood of abuse.

With her younger son, Benny, Laura had a completely different relationship. She loved him dearly and had for him a warmth and affection she had not previously known she was capable of feeling. She surmised that he was like her younger brother, Joe, to whom her mother had given all her love and affection, and she was imitating her own mother in this. Laura was bewildered by these very intense and yet discrepant feelings. She was quite puzzled about her own identity, which she expressed at various times in such thoughts as, "I think Jimmy must be me, and I'm a combination of my mother and father. When I would talk to my mother, she would be far away and not answer. I do the same thing with Jimmy. It was father who used to beat me; now it seems Jimmy is me, and I'm beating him the way father beat me. Little Benny is my brother, Joe. Mother gave all her love and protection to Joe, and I am very kind and loving to him." Another time she said, "I don't know yet who I really am. I am beginning to think I am somebody and I know a little bit about who I am, but I'm having trouble becoming it and being something. I don't know whether I am my mother or my father or my brother, Joe, or a combination of all of them or whether I am my children."

After her marriage, Laura periodically made an attempt to establish some sort of friendly relationship with her mother, and there were occasional visits. But they never did reach any true emotional rapport nor could they discuss the events of Laura's earlier life. With her brother Joe she had a distant, hostile relationship. While there was no evidence of overt incestuous activity between Joe and his mother, she seemed to have exploitatively tried to keep him close to her and had hampered his separation and individuation. He eventually became seriously disturbed, and once, when he threatened to kill their mother, Laura offered her sanctuary and protection. At that time there was some feeling of closeness which was soon ruptured by her mother's inconsiderate disregard of her daughter's feelings and criticisms of her behavior.

Superficially, Laura appeared to be a popular, attractive, young married woman with two children, similar to many other young women who lived with their armed-service-career husbands around a military base. Yet she was seriously troubled, behaviorally and psychologically, both in her marriage and in her child-caring functions. In this tragic history are the themes of economic difficulty, alcoholism, social isolation, parental conflict, maternal deprivation, sibling rivalry, physical abuse, incest, and father-loss by suicide. As an adult, she shows many of the characteristics commonly met with in parents who maltreat children. She has a mild, chronic depression, very low self-esteem, inability to have pleasure or find satisfaction for her long-lasting emptiness and need for love and attention, lack of a coherent, consistent sense of identity, and misperceptions of her children. The striking split between good and bad objects, uncoordinated ego functions, and unintegrated components of identity are similar to those described as characteristic of "borderline states." These psychological difficulties seem to be clearly related to the experiences she had with the caretakers of her early life and the necessity for her to adapt somehow to them. She has identified with the several parts of the inconsistent caretaking behaviors of both mother and father and also maintains a self-concept closely related to herself as a child. She transfers and attributes to adults in her present environment and to her own children the attitudes and feelings she had toward the important figures of her early life. Her sexual behavior seems to be a frantic, desperate, compulsive search for a man to love and be loved by and is at least partly due to unresolved grief over the death of her father by suicide. She over-idealized her father, clinging especially to the loving side of her ambivalence toward him, has never fully relinquished her attachment to him, and has been unable to find an adequate replacement for the warm closeness she had with him, including the incest. Her promiscuity is undoubtedly related to the sexualization of this early love relationship with the father. Yet the desperateness of her search also suggests it has deep roots in an effort to find a substitute for the lack of basic, empathic love from her mother in her early life. Her inability to gain full satisfaction or pleasure from sexual activity stems partly from the fact that in itself sexual activity cannot replace this lack of a deep, early sense of being empathetically loved and cared for. It is also partly due to residual guilt in relationship to her father, which is not so much a feeling of having done something wrong sexually with him, but rather that she had not been able, even in her most warm and loving sexual surrender to him, to make him happy enough to prevent the suicide. Laura was aware that her sexual behavior was not really acceptable in society. Yet this was not totally a feeling of guilt over sexuality, but more a sense that she was ineffectual and never good enough for other people. It was not a strong, inner sense of having done something wrong for which she deserved punishment, nor did she give evidence of guilt over sexual behavior in relation to having displaced her mother in her father's affections. In fact, her earliest, powerful, superego identifications are with the mother who encouraged the sexual relationship with the father and with a father who instigated and appreciated the sexual relationship. Because she is still unconsciously fixated to the loving, sexual father of her childhood, who was also abusive, she has had the recurrent tendency to attach herself to men who not only love her, but who are also cruel to her, fight with her, or attack her physically. By criticizing and frustrating her husband who was originally quite affectionate and considerate to her, she managed to change him into a person who is mean to her and maltreats their child, thus recreating the father of her childhood.

Laura relives another part of the childhood drama in her ambivalent behavior toward her older son, Jimmy, whom she misperceives as almost a reincarnation of her own childhood self. In identification with her father, she loves Jimmy at times, but she also abuses him, hitting him, using a belt on him, and repeating to him the same words her father used, "I'll knock you through the wall." At other times, she repeats the behavior of her mother toward herself and is unresponsive, inattentive, and unempathic toward Jimmy. With her younger son, Benny, she repeats the kind, preferential care which her mother gave to her younger brother, Joe, and she also lavishes on Benny the love which she wishes she had had as a little girl, gaining some vicarious pleasure from this. In view of Laura's disturbing experiences in early life and the multiple, inconsistent identifications with her parents, it is not surprising that she is significantly hampered in her child-caring activities and has become what we call an abusive parent. Her tendency to repeat the past and get herself involved in unhappy experiences is an example of moral masochism in the sense described by Berliner as "self-defeating or destructive behavior" due to attachment to a sadistic love object. Difficulties in having pleasure or enjoying life generally, as well as constantly recurring patterns of getting into difficulty, are characteristic of most of the maltreating caretakers we have known. This masochistic tendency makes such persons increasingly vulnerable and unable to cope with the troublesome crises and difficulties that inevitably occur in all people's lives, especially in the care of children.

The process of responding to the parents of earliest years, the identification with them, and the persistence of these identifications into adult life is not in any way abnormal. It is a normal part of the psychic development of all children. As noted before, the problem lies in the kind of parent available for the identification process. Laura identified with both the punitive and loving aspects of her father and with the aloof, rejecting, uncaring aspects of her mother, as well as with her mother's loving care of a boy. In her social interactions, Laura maintained superficially close sexualized relationships with men and more distant, often antagonistic, relations with women. In therapy she established positive relationships with three successive male therapists whom she felt "understood" her, but remained suspicious and cool toward female clinic personnel.

Summary

Parents and others who maltreat the infants and children under their care are not haphazardly discharging destructive impulses in the form of abuse and neglect. They are following understandable and predictable patterns of parent-child interactions which have been basically determined by the way they themselves were cared for in infancy. Beginning with poor attachment in the perinatal period, followed in ensuing months and years by unempathic care, unrealistic demands, and excessive criticism, and punishment for failure, they developed poor self-esteem, poor basic trust, and fragmented identities. Deeply embedded identifications with their parents and their behaviors, which will surface most strongly in times of stress, lead to repetitions of the patterns in their own child-care behaviors. During the earliest, most impressionable period of life, while a child is under the exclusive care of its own family before contact is made with the wider culture, the patterns are transmitted from caretaker to child, and the potentials for physical abuse, neglect, and sexual exploitation are recreated for yet another generation.

References

1. Kempe, C. H.; Silverman, F. N.; Steele, B. F.; Droegemueller, W.; and Silver, H. K. 1962. The Battered-Child Syndrome. *JAMA* 181:17–24.
2. Steele, B., and Pollock, C. 1968. A Psychiatric Study of Parents Who Abuse Infants and Small Children. In *The Battered Child.* R. Helfer and C. H. Kempe. Chicago: University of Chicago Press.
3. Steele, B. F. 1970. Parental Abuse of Infants and Small Children. In *Parenthood: Its Psychology and Psychopathology,* ed. E. J. Anthony and T. Benedek. Boston: Little, Brown & Co.
4. Straus, M. A. 1979. Family Patterns and Child Abuse in a Nationally Representative American Sample. *Child Abuse and Neglect: International J.* 3:213–25.
5. Curtis, G. 1963. Violence Breeds Violence—Perhaps? *Am. J. Psychiatry* 120:386–87.
6. Fontana, V., and Besharov, D. 1977. *The Maltreated Child.* Springfield, Ill.: Charles C. Thomas.
7. Oliver, J. E., and Taylor, Audrey. 1971. Five Generations of Ill-treated Children in One Family Pedigree. *British J. Psychiatry* 119:552.
8. Silver, L. B.; Dublin, C. C.; and Lourie, R. S. 1969. Does Violence Breed Violence? Contributions from a Study of the Child Abuse Syndrome. *Am. J. Psychiatry* 126:404–7.
9. Spinetta, J. J., and Rigler, D. 1972. The Child-Abusing Parent: A Psychological Review. *Psychology Bull.* 77:296–304.

10. Morris, M. G., and Gould, R. W. 1963. Role Reversal: A Concept in Dealing with the Neglected/Battered Child Syndrome. In *The Neglected-Battered Child Syndrome.* New York: Child Welfare League of America.

11. Gray, J. D.; Cutler, C. A.; Dean, J. G.; and Kempe, C. H. 1977. Prediction and Prevention of Child Abuse and Neglect. *Child Abuse and Neglect: International J.* 1:45–58.

12. Ainsworth, M. 1973. Development of Infant-Mother Attachment. In *Child Development and Social Policy. Review of Child Development Research,* ed. B. Caldwell and H. N. Ricciuti, vol. 3. Chicago: University of Chicago Press.

13. Bowlby, J. 1969. *Attachment.* New York: Basic Books.

14. Brazelton, T. B.; Kozlowski, B.; and Main, M. 1974. The Origins of Reciprocity: The Early Mother-Infant Interaction. In *The Effect of the Infant on Its Caregiver,* ed. M. Lewis and L. Rosenblum. New York: Wiley.

15. Kennell, J. H., et al. 1972. Maternal Behavior One Year after Early and Extended Post-Partum Contact. *Developmental Medicine and Child Neurology* 16:172–79.

16. Klaus, M., and Kennell, J. 1976. *Maternal-Infant Bonding.* St. Louis: C. V. Mosby.

17. Lynch, M., and Roberts, J. 1977. Predicting Child Abuse: Signs of Bonding Failure in the Maternity Hospital. *British Med. J.* 1:624–26.

18. Ounsted, C.; Oppenheimer, R.; and Lindsay, J. 1974. Aspects of Bonding Failure: The Psychopathology and Psychotherapeutic Treatment of Families of Battered Children. *Developmental Medicine and Child Neurology* 16:447–52.

19. Melnick, B., and Hurley, J. R. 1969. Distinctive Personality Attributes of Child Abusing Mothers. *J. Consulting and Clinical Psychology* 33:746–49.

20. Benedek, T. 1959. Parenthood as a Developmental Phase: A Contribution to the Libido Theory. *J. Am. Psychoanalytic Assn.* 7:389–417.

21. Olden, C. 1953. On Adult Empathy with Children. *Psychoanalytic Study of the Child* 8:111–26.

22. Olden, C. 1958. Notes on the Development of Empathy. *Psychoanalytic Study of the Child* 13:505–18.

23. Josselyn, I. 1956. Cultural Forces, Motherliness and Fatherliness. *Am. J. Orthopsychiatry* 26:264–71.

24. Bullard, D.; Glaser, H.; Heagarty, M.; and Pivchik, E. 1967. Failure to Thrive in the Neglected Child. *Am. J. Orthopsychiatry* 37:680–90.

25. Spitz, R. 1945. Hospitalism. *Psychoanalytic Study of the Child* 1:53–74.

26. Spitz, R. 1946. Hospitalism: A Follow-up Report. *Psychoanalytic Study of the Child* 2:113–17.

27. Provence, S., and Lipton, R. 1962. *Infants in Institutions.* New York: International Universities Press.

28. Koel, B. S. 1969. Failure to Thrive and Fatal Injury as a Continuum. *Am. J. Diseases of Children* 118:565–67.

29. Barbero, G.; Morris, M.; and Reford, M. 1963. Malidentification of Mother-Baby-Father Relationships Expressed in Infant Failure to Thrive. *Child Welfare* 42:13.

30. Barbero, G., and Shaheen, E. 1967. Environmental Failure to Thrive. *J. Pediatrics* 71:639.

31. Elmer, E. 1960. Failure to Thrive: Role of the Mother. *Pediatrics* 25:717.

32. Fischoff, J.; Whitten, C.; and Pettit, M. 1971. A Psychiatric Study of Mothers of Infants with Growth Failure, Secondary to Maternal Deprivation. *J. Pediatrics* 79:209–15.

33. Leonard, M. F.; Rhymes, J. P.; and Solnit, A. J. 1966. Failure to Thrive in Infants. *Am. J. Diseases of Children* 111:600–612.

34. Glaser, D., and Bentovim, A. 1979. Abuse and Risk to Handicapped and Chronically Ill Children. *Child Abuse and Neglect: International J.* 3:565–75.

35. deLissovoy, Vladimer. 1979. Toward the Definition of "Abuse Provoking Child." *Child Abuse and Neglect: International J.* 3:341–50.

36. Friedrich, W. N., and Boriskin, J. A. 1976. The Role of the Child in Abuse: A Review of the Literature. *Am. J. Orthopsychiatry* 46:580–90.

37. Johnson, B., and Morse, H. A. 1968. Injured Children and Their Parents. *Children* 15:147–52.

38. Milowe, J. D., and Lourie, R. S. 1964. The Child's Role in the Battered Child Syndrome. *J. Pediatrics* 65:1079–81.

39. Creel, H. G., ed. 1948. *Literary Chinese by the Inductive Method.* Chicago: University of Chicago Press.

40. deChateau, P., and Wiberg, B. 1977. Long-term Effect on Mother-Infant Behavior of Extra Contact during the First Hour Post-partum. *Acta Pediatrica Scandinavica* 66:137–51.

41. Satten, J.; Menninger, K.; Rosen, I.; and Mayman, M. 1960. Murder without Apparent Motive: A Study in Personality Disorganization. *Am. J. Psychiatry* 117:48–53.

42. Adelson, L. 1961. Slaughter of the Innocents. *New England J. Med.* 264:1345–49.

43. Piers, M. W. 1978. *Infanticide: Past and Present.* New York: Norton.

44. Resnick, P. J. 1969. Child Murder by Parents: A Psychiatric Review of Filicide. *Am. J. Psychiatry* 126:325–34.

45. Steele, B. 1978. Psychology of Infanticide Resulting from Maltreatment. In *Infanticide and the Value of Life,* ed. M. Kohl. Buffalo: Prometheus Books.

46. Greenberg, N. H. 1979. The Epidemiology of Childhood Sexual Abuse. *Pediatrics Annals* 8:289–99.

47. Lukianowicz, N. 1972. Incest. *British J. Psychiatry* 120:301–13.

48. Meiselman, Karin C. 1978. *Incest: A Psychological Study of Causes and Effects with Treatment Recommendations.* San Francisco: Jossey-Bass.

49. Nakashima, I., and Zakus, G. 1977. Incest: Review and Clinical Experience. *Pediatrics* 60:696–700.

50. Summit, R., and Kryso, J. 1978. Sexual Abuse of Children: A Clinical Spectrum. *Am. J. Orthopsychiatry* 48:237–51.

51. Westermeyer, J. 1978. Incest in Psychiatric Practice: A Description of Patients and Incestuous Relationships. *J. Clinical Psychiatry* 39:643–48.

52. Langsley, D. G.; Schwartz, M. N.; and Fairbairn, R. H. 1968. Father-Son Incest. *Comprehensive Psychiatry* 9:218–26.

53. Raybin, J. B. 1969. Homosexual Incest. *J. Nervous and Mental Disorders* 148:105–10.

54. Raphling, D. L.; Carpenter, B. L.; and Davis, A. 1967. Incest: A Genealogical Study. *Archives of General Psychiatry* 16:505–11.

55. Gebhard, P. H., et al. 1965. *Sex Offenders: An Analysis of Types.* New York: Harper and Row.

56. Yorokoglu, A., and Kemph, J. P. 1966. Children Not Severely Damaged by Incest with Parent. *J. Am. Acad. Child Psychiatry* 51:111–24.

57. Kaufman, I.; Peck, A. L.; and Tagiuri, C. K. 1954. Family Constellation and Overt Incestuous Relations between Father and Daughter. *Am. J. Orthopsychiatry* 24: 266–77.

58. Reimer, S. 1940. A Research Note on Incest. *Am. J. Sociology* 45:566–75.

59. Weiss, J., et al. 1955. A Study of Girl Sex Victims. *Psychiatric Q.* 29:1–27.

60. Hartogs, R. 1951–52. Discipline in the Early Life of Sex-Delinquents and Sex-Criminals. *The Nervous Child* 9:167–73.

61. Lustig, N., et al. 1966. Incest: A Family Group Survival Pattern. *Archives of General Psychiatry* 14:31–40.

62. Weiner, I. B. 1962. Father-Daughter Incest: A Clinical Report. *Psychiatric Q.* 36:607–32.

63. Weiner, I. B. 1964. On Incest: A Survey. *Excerpt. Criminology* 4:137–55.

64. Wahl, C. W. 1960. The Psychodynamics of Consummated Maternal Incest. *Archives of General Psychiatry* 3:188–93.

PART

Assessment

Every case of suspected child abuse and neglect must be thoroughly evaluated. With over one and one-half percent of our nation's children being reported *each year* to the children's divisions of state or local social service agencies, this becomes an enormous task. Approximately eighty to eighty-five percent of these reports can be assessed very adequately by an experienced social worker from protective service, but the remainder are so severe or complex that a thorough assessment requires the input of professionals from several different disciplines. One should keep in mind that this does not mean sitting around a table and discussing a case or family that has been seen by only one member of a team. On the contrary, these difficult families must actually be *seen* and *evaluated* by different professionals, i.e., a psychologist or psychiatrist, a pediatrician, a social worker, and a public health nurse.

The contributors to this section have provided the necessary details for this comprehensive assessment to take place. These details should be considered with care. Reference should also be made to Friedman, Cardiff, Sandler, and Friedman, "Coping with the Dilemma of Child Abuse and Neglect," *Working for Children: Ethical Issues beyond Professional Guidelines,* ed. Judith Mearig (San Francisco: Jossey-Bass, 1978).

6 Communicating in the Therapeutic Relationship: Concepts, Strategies, and Skills

Mary Edna Helfer

Since the health provider/patient relationship is a transaction between human beings, the success of that transaction depends almost entirely on how well they understand each other, i.e., how well they communicate.

MICHELE TOLELA (1)

Communication is our most important medium for social contact and personal development. It is also our most prolific behavior; most of our daily activities involve communication. The average American spends about seventy percent of his or her active hours communicating—listening, speaking, reading, and writing (2). Communicating with others is so central to our existence that even in our attempts not to communicate, we still "say" something. Interacting with others is as vital to our survival in the social environment as the exchange of oxygen and carbon dioxide is to our physical environment.

Consider how helpless one becomes when unable to communicate. Even newborns are required to communicate from the moment of birth to maintain their very existence (see chap. 23). Our self-identity is a product of our communication efforts (3), and our behavior is adopted and adapted in response to the communication we receive and the messages we transmit to others. Communication is the tool utilized to alter our environment. At times, one's livelihood is dependent on the ability to influence the actions of others through communication. One's basic needs and, ultimately, species survival are dependent upon mastery of an intricate set of communication rules and behaviors.

Although all persons communicate, the ability to do so skillfully and with purpose rarely occurs as a natural gift. Knowledge, practice, and experience are required to develop precise, predictable, effective, and satisfying techniques of interaction.

Communication in the Therapeutic Relationship

Communication in the therapeutic relationship can be defined as a transactional process which involves a message exchange between participants through a common system of symbols, signs, or behaviors. The messages or signs fall into constellations of expressive behaviors (4). The three main signal systems are the lexical, kinesic, and somatic. The

Mary Edna Helfer, R.N., M.A., is director of Continuing Medical Education, College of Human Medicine, Michigan State University, East Lansing.

lexical system includes all speech activities, kinesic includes all body movements, and somatic incorporates the observable manifestations of the autonomic nervous system.

A formal language system enables us to express very complex or abstract ideas to another person. Speech is the verbal medium used by the patient to inform the health provider of symptoms and concerns, and it is used, in turn, by the provider to respond to the patient's needs (5). The manner in which the content of speech is expressed provides information which is as important as the words themselves. The volume, rate, pitch, inflection, intensity, and continuity all convey cues to the emotional state of the patient and are sometimes referred to as *paralanguage* (6). Paralanguage may communicate a message which will cause the interviewer to question how literally he or she can accept the overt message transmitted by the spoken word alone. Active listening is required to hear both components of speech.

The unspoken dialogue or pattern of nonverbal communication is equally important (7). It is the medium most frequently used to communicate emotion and subtleties of meaning which could not be conveyed if we were restricted to a single mode of communication. While research in the area of nonverbal communication is still limited, some estimates indicate that as much as ninety percent of our messages concerning feelings are communicated nonverbally (8). Kinesics, derived from the Greek word for movement, is the system which includes the way patients walk, their posture, gestures, and facial expression. Birdwhistell, a primary scholar in the area of kinesics, recognizes several regions of meaningful activity: total head; face and neck; trunk and shoulders; shoulders, arms, and wrists; hands and fingers; hips, upper legs, lower legs, and ankles; and feet. These areas have the capacity of combining, resulting in an astonishing number and variety of cues. These combinations may be thought of as a "vocabulary" of the unspoken dialogue.

The face is the most expressive part of the body (9). Ekman and Friesen conducted cross-cultural research on the recognition of facial expression, with the hypothesis that certain situations would evoke recognizable expressons of emotions among the five cultures studied. There was a high degree of similarity noted across cultures (10).

Somatic cues or signals are usually not under the patient's conscious control and may be viewed as reliable signs of affect. Breathing patterns, muscle tension, pupil dilation, skin color, tearing, and body perspiration are observable somatic signs.

The triad of the lexical, kinesic, and somatic combine to give a constellation of cues with specific meanings. Sadness, for example, is mirrored in the face of a depressed patient, who may also exhibit a downturned mouth, a low, slow, monotonous voice, downcast eyes, slumped shoulders, sighing respiratory movements, and a general decrease in body movement. An angry patient may present clenched teeth and fixed jaw, increased rate and volume of speech, increased muscle tension, flushed face, and increased perspiration to the observer.

The interviewer must avoid making judgments based on isolated signals from any given system. Communication may be very clear when all systems agree. However, as interviewers we usually must learn to actively listen and observe all three systems, determine the degree of congruence between them, and, when there are discrepancies, help the patient clarify the true meaning of his or her communication.

Understanding Anger and Depression during the Interview

The potential for a productive interview will be enhanced if the interview is conducted in a professional and nurturing manner. The interviewer can give the patient or client support and a sense of being understood, as well as providing an opportunity to "tell his story." A nurturing and supportive attitude is critical, for without a sense of being understood the parent may withhold or distort information that is critical for an accurate assessment of the child's injuries. Developing appropriate treatment strategies will also be compromised by inaccurate or incomplete data.

In order for an abusive parent to feel understood, the *provider* must identify or acknowledge the emotions the parent brings to the interview. Two of the more difficult emotional states to handle are anger and depression. Anger exhibited by patients can be particularly troublesome. It frequently provokes rejection by members of the service team and sends the patient on a shopping expedition for another doctor, social worker, or emergency room, wasting valuable time and causing duplication of efforts.

Anger may be expressed in a readily recognized form of direct confrontation and criticism or in a disguised indirect form. Bowden and Burstein describe several types of anger which are frequently encountered in dealing with patients (11). Parents may be characteristically angry; they may be angry as a result of a temporary process of assimilation within themselves; they may displace their anger by venting at one time feelings generated at a different time in another context; or they may be voicing a legitimate complaint about a given situation.

In dealing with situational anger one should listen and assess the complaint in an accepting and nonjudgmental manner. Usually the anger is temporary and, if given the opportunity for full expression, it may lead to an improvement in the openness and frankness with which the patient can talk with the physician or other provider.

Displaced anger is carried over from a previous setting or interaction. This may be an unconscious adaptive mechanism which permits the patient to vent feelings of anger while maintaining a positive image with the service team members on whom he or she feels most dependent for care of the child. All team members need to recognize and learn to deal with displaced anger, as most of them will have opportunities to be the recipients of such anger. The quality and depth of the client's feelings should be acknowledged. This may provide some dissipation of the anger and shift the focus to the more legitimate source of anger. Displaced anger is basically transitory and, if permitted open expression, may clear the way for improved communication.

Anger as a reaction to an internal process is not a reflection of the current interpersonal transactions, but a reflection of the patient assimilating the knowledge of his or her situation. It is seen in people who have suffered an acute reduction in their sense of adequacy and competence.

Dealing with characterologically angry patients is most difficult. Their critical early childhood experiences with help givers have convinced them in many pervasive and preverbal ways that help givers, such as physicians, teachers, and parents, are more likely to take advantage of them than to help them. They frequently are very rigid in their beliefs and attitudes, appear hyperalert during the interview, and seem unable to accept emotional support from team members. They rely heavily on projection as an adaptive mechanism. They often give a history of growing up in a hostile, nonnurturing environment, describing their parents as persons who always overpowered or degraded them. Their past experiences have convinced them that helpers are in reality punishers and are potentially dangerous people who cannot be trusted.

When working with individuals whose basic characters are built on anger, the help giver must be open and candid while communicating with them. Ambiguity is viewed as a threat. A consistent and authoritative posture may prove beneficial in working with these patients. Their anger is likely to erupt if the provider seems inconsistent or vacillates in making decisions. They despise weakness in themselves and others. Their areas of strength and competence should be maximized during interaction with them, thereby enhancing their self-esteem and reducing conflict. In extreme cases, these patients may act or appear paranoid or sociopathic and often require psychotherapeutic intervention.

Bowden and Burstein also describe a variety of depressive states and discuss some of the basic mechanisms underlying various stages of depression (11). The awareness of the several stages that are frequently encountered while interacting with highly stressed patients is obligatory.

Mourning is viewed as a healthy, normal reaction to loss and it usually follows a predictable series of responses as the person works through a problem and resolves the stress. The parent or caretaker of an injured child, for example, may appear very sad, as exhibited by their crying or other nonverbal behavior. They may have decreased interest in their other routine activities and responsibilities. In other cases, denial may be their first psychological response. Very little emotion may be exhibited as the parent tries to block out the event by saying, "This can't be really happening to me." This stage usually progresses to one of displaced anger—someone or something else is responsible for the problems.

The sense of loss, which will facilitate their moving to the grief stage, should be recognized. Grieving is a vital component, if one is to move on to reintegration and reinvolvement in trying to cope with their loss or failure. What is actually being grieved over may not be readily apparent to the interviewer, for what is important and internal for one person may have little meaning to another. On occasion, one is confronted with an individual who has every apparent reason to go through the grieving process but does not exhibit appropriate verbal or nonverbal behavior. These individuals must undergo additional assessment and possibly psychiatric care.

Secondary or reactive depression is usually exhibited in parents as a sense of worthlessness, guilt, or hopelessness about their situation and environment. Bowden and Burstein describe three causes of secondary depression. A common psychological pattern appears which may be very applicable in understanding the emotional state of many parents. There is a gap between the way these parents want to function or feel they should function, and the way they are able to function. Bowden and Burstein state:

> The childhood experiences of patients with secondary depression predispose to this reaction pattern in response to stress. Such children were often treated as inadequate and incompetent by their overly critical parents. Memories of statements such as, "You can't do anything right," are common. In addition, as children, these persons harbored much anger toward their parents but

felt guilty and afraid of expressing it, and they developed the pattern of turning the anger and self-reproach inward. (11)

Guidelines for Facilitating the Interview

An important component of eliciting history from a parent is for the parent to have a cognitive understanding of why some questions are being asked. The need to understand the total environment and the family dynamics pertaining to a particular child may not be obvious to the parent. Without a clear explanation the patient may not provide the necessary information for a "comprehensive overview" of the current living situation, family interaction patterns, and any crisis that may have contributed to the parental neglect or abuse. The process of verbalizing their situation may act as a stimulus for them to participate in thinking about alternative solutions to help resolve the problems that contributed to the abuse.

Several specific suggestions can be made to facilitate an interaction, especially one whose purpose is to establish rapport as well as gather certain factual information. Each of these suggestions requires considerable practice to implement. The concepts will not be difficult to grasp; setting them in action will be another matter. Some find that the skill of interviewing comes very naturally; others struggle with each new (and old) interaction. Consideration of these guidelines will be helpful in both situations.

The open-ended question. Many use this technique effectively. It can help one gather the most accurate and unbiased information and determine the ability of the patients to organize their thoughts and tell their own stories. The open-ended question can be used to gain both cognitive and affective information: "Describe the nature of your pain." "Tell me how you felt about your father's death." One must use this technique skillfully or the interview may get out of control. If the open-ended question leads to unproductive rambling, one can move to more specific, direct closed-ended questions.

The closed-ended question. Most providers are skilled in utilizing this form of questioning; so skilled, in fact, that some use nothing but closed-ended questions to gain information. "Do you have a cough?" "When did your father die?" This type of question is usually easy to answer and usually brings forth specific information. When used judiciously, it is most helpful. When used exclusively, it can destroy rapport. Questions should proceed from open-ended to closed-ended as the information needed becomes more specific.

Labeling. This is the most useful tool for building a positive relationship with the patient. The timely use of labeling can often break through the most resistant barriers. In order to learn the skill of labeling one must first recognize what should be labeled. One can hardly say, "That last question must have really upset you," unless there was recognition that the person was disturbed by the last question. A more appropriate response is, "It must be difficult for you to talk to me." The interviewer's feelings may also be labeled: "I'm feeling very frustrated; I keep getting mixed messages." "It is easier for me to talk to you when you smile." "I really had a bad week." *Never* say, "I know how you feel," unless you really have experienced *exactly* the same situation and are willing to talk about it in some detail. A better statement is, "If that had happened to me I might have felt just as you did." Well-timed and appropriate labels can turn a difficult interview into one that is both informative and productive for both individuals. Rapport follows. Keep in mind that labels are placed on both the patient's and the interviewer's feelings and reactions. Labeling enhances a positive interaction.

Confrontation. This technique allows the interviewer to confront the patient with any discrepancies between the verbal or logical component of his or her message and the nonverbal or kinesic cues he or she exhibits. Such confrontation is always based on specific observations with no inference made regarding motive. For example, "You say you had a good relationship with your mother, but you always look away from me when you talk about her." "You say things are going well at home, but you look very sad when you talk about Johnny's father." Confrontation may help the patient elaborate on these conflicting cues and help the patient get in touch with his or her feelings. Confrontation is one of the more difficult skills to acquire because it entails "listening on all channels" and is not part of our repertoire of routine social behaviors. Confrontation is risky to the interaction and is best used after some degree of rapport has been built.

Silence. The thought of sitting quietly, waiting for the other person to say something, makes some individuals most uncomfortable. Even a short five-to-ten-second pause may seem endless. This technique often allows both individuals to gather their thoughts and gain the courage to speak them. The use of silence can be self-defeating, however, if tensions rise to such a peak that thoughts and speech vanish. Silence must be used judiciously.

Feedback gestures and synchrony. Talking with someone who does not use feedback gestures and does not "get into sync" with you is most difficult. At times we may not realize synchronization has not occurred, and yet we come away from the interaction feeling very strange indeed. Often this "strangeness" is a result of receiving no feedback. We have no way of knowing if what was said was really heard. Many people get into "sync" automatically. A newborn baby can get into synchrony with his or her mother's voice, for example, if she varies the pitch sufficiently. When two adults communicate well, this synchrony is both verbal and nonverbal. The head nod, the body posture, expressions like "I see" and "really," eye contact, and the like are all ways of enhancing synchrony. Without synchrony the interaction is sterile, cold, and short-term. There is no rapport.

The Structure and Setting of the Interview

Careful consideration must be given to the structure and setting of the interview if one is going to get the most from any interaction with a patient. Doctors and social workers often pay little attention to these matters and then wonder why an interview went poorly. Sometimes psychologists and psychiatrists pay so much attention to these issues that the patient falls asleep because he or she is so comfortable. There must be a happy medium between psychologists' overstuffed chairs and the hallway conversations between doctors and their patients.

Comfort and privacy are crucial. Both individuals should be at the same eye level. This is especially important when interacting with a child. A doctor standing by a bedside, hovering over a patient who is lying in bed, does not meet the criteria for a good interactional situation. There should not be an awesome and formidable desk in between the two who are trying to establish rapport and share information. One should not be undressed and the other fully clothed with a white coat. How inappropriate for a physician to say, "Go into room two, put on the gown with the opening in the back, and I'll be right in to talk to you." Departments of social services are notorious for unbelievable settings in which personal discussions are supposed to occur: cubicles with open-top walls, no doors, busy hallways—none of these lend themselves to data gathering and rapport building.

Equally important to the setting of the interview is the sequence of the interview. The inexperienced student is often so intent upon gathering all the data that a rigid order of questions is followed, regardless of the answers. One student was observed in the following conversation:

"How are things going in school?"

"Not too well," was the reply.

"Tell me about your cough."

The ability to move back and forth from one area to another is a unique skill, not easily learned. One problem resulting from being too flexible is, of course, that one may never finish obtaining the information one set out to gather. It's important to develop the ability to identify certain issues for future discussion.

"How are things going in school?"

"Not too well."

"That sounds like something we should talk about as soon as you start feeling better."

A note is made in the record as a reminder to put this on the agenda; the next question is now more reasonable.

"Now tell me about your cough."

Starting the interview with an open-ended, nonthreatening question is usually best. "Tell me why you came to see me." Adding a label or two soon thereafter will be most helpful: "You must have been feeling pretty lousy all week." Once the opening barriers are broken down, a few closed-ended questions will help gather critically important information: "Do you have any money left for food?" or "Does your cough interfere with your breathing?"

During the course of the interview the interviewer must intersperse some key techniques that help facilitate both rapport building and data gathering. Using each of the skills described earlier will facilitate these two goals immensely. Considerable practice is required to become comfortable with these skills. They must become automatic, much like one's reactions when one's car hits a piece of ice and skids. This practice is best done under observation, preferably using videotape. This enables one to obtain immediate feedback.

Closure to the interview is of major importance. One must not close abruptly, say thanks, and leave. The patient's final impression and feeling of satisfaction will depend, in large part, on how the final minutes of the interview are handled. If the interview is complete, with no expectations for another meeting, then summary statements and questions are in order: "Let me review what I've heard," or, "Let's summarize a few major issues once again." If another meeting is anticipated, then the agenda and timetable should be set: "When we meet again we need to talk about . . . ," or, "I want to finish up with

. . . ," or, "That issue is pretty hard for you to talk about; we can discuss that next time." A time and place must be set for the next discussion. In either situation, final or temporary closure, the patient must be given the opportunity to bring up points or issues: "Is there anything else we should discuss before we close?"

Finally, no discussion on the structure and setting of an interview would be complete without mentioning a few additional cues or suggestions to help achieve the goals of rapport building and data gathering.

1. Incorporate the more personal issues within less-personal matters. It is quite easy for a physician to flow from less personal to personal, e.g., in inquiring about the health of the patient's parents, asking questions about how the interaction between parents and children went when the patient was a child is very natural and nonthreatening. In inquiring about symptoms in the genitourinary system (pain, discharge, urinary frequency, etc.) seeking additional information about sexual problems and activity is an easy transition.

2. Use discretion in taking notes during an interview. Writing constantly is distracting. Not writing anything may indicate disinterest; a happy medium is necessary.

3. The concept of "tracking/nontracking" is important to understand, for one will wish to use this technique during an interview. Some do it automatically, others find it most difficult. Tracking is following through for more details, e.g., "My mother and I look a lot alike." Your tracking response might be, "In what way?" Nontracking is to come to closure on a given issue by switching to another topic or question. Both can facilitate an interview when used skillfully.

4. One's dress and posture can say a great deal to the patient or client.

5. Opinion and judgmental statements present difficult issues. Giving your opinion during the interview, when done with care, can facilitate the discussion. If, however, these are felt to be judgmental, the patient may well clam up, rapport being lost momentarily.

There are many ways to improve one's interviewing techniques. The most important thing to keep in mind is that interviewing is a skill; and skills can be learned and improved with practice.

Special Considerations Relating to Child Abuse

Communicating with abusive or neglectful parents presents some very special problems and requires very special skills. This is probably one of the most difficult, if not the most difficult, interpersonal relationship to establish. There are very few clinical situations which generate such strong feelings of anger, hostility, and frustration in health care providers as dealing with parents who have abused their children. It may be very difficult for the emergency room nurses, physicians, or social workers to feel any empathy for the parents after caring for the child. Focusing on how the parents feel at the present time, faced with the consequences of their actions, is helpful. One need not condone or accept the parents' behavior, but rather try to understand their feelings. These complexities are discussed more fully in other chapters in this book.

One must first identify who the patient is. Some professionals may feel it is the child, others the mother or father, or possibly the siblings and grandparents. Approaching an interview with a predetermined notion that any one of these individuals is the only true patient will be most confusing. Child abuse and neglect is the symptom seen when a family's interactional system has broken down. The whole family must be perceived as the patient and approached and handled accordingly.

Unique, often strong, emotional ties bind the various members of a family together. At times, these are not easily understood, especially when a wife returns to her husband who beats her or a little girl runs to her father who sexually abuses her. These complex ties must be appreciated and considered when trying to establish a communication system with this family. Using all the skills at one's disposal, pulling out all the interpersonal and interactional stops, will be necessary.

Any time a parent is being interviewed about a child there is a conflict of interest that must be appreciated. The parent is very emotionally tied to the child and feels responsible for what happens, or has happened, to the child. If the child has pneumonia, for example, and the doctors asks, "Did he take his medicine?" or, even worse, "Did you give him his medicine?" there is an immediate conflict set up with the parent. Consider how a parent of a suspected abused child reacts when asked, "Who hurt your child?" or, even worse, "Did *you* hit your child?"

When one knows, with a reasonable degree of certainty, that something of a very negative nature has happened to a child, the rule is, *do not ask*. Stating the problem, as you see it, is always preferable. For example, "Your child has been hurt; tell me about it" is much preferable to, "Who hurt your child?" or even, "How did your child get hurt?" The parent is much less defensive with the former approach, and the conflict of interest, while still present, is less an interference.

Abusive parents have considerable difficulty using nonverbal communication skills. Even the few skills they do have are misread by most inexperienced professionals. Abusive parents often do not look at you eye to eye, they may rarely cry or have other facial movements, they may sit slumped in a chair, and they may be very aggressive or very passive. Most of the skills learned in graduate or medical schools to establish rapport may be of little use as one tries desperately to communicate with these sensory-muted parents (see chap. 4). Sometimes an interviewer feels as though he or she is trying to establish rapport with a robot.

Verbal skills may be equally guarded. Since young adults who were abused as children are trained not to trust others and to believe that all people hurt others, they are not likely to verbally respond to someone who says, "I'm here to help you," or, "I'm here to ask you a few questions." A much more appropriate opening is the label, "You must have had a rough week," or, "You look tired," or, "You're probably really concerned about your child."

Abusive parents are not reared to demonstrate motivation. Why be motivated? Tomorrow is no better than today; today is tomorrow. Professionals find it very difficult to establish a communication system with someone they view as unmotivated. When parents do not show up, follow directions, call, say thanks, ask questions, smile, etc., we are turned off. And yet, there *is* motivation there, shown in a variety of subtle ways. They may peek through the window, hoping you will come back; show up late, hoping you will still be there; bring their abused child to school, hoping someone will recognize their cry for help.

The bottom line is that abusive parents are not easy to like. Few of us were trained to communicate with someone we inherently dislike. We struggle, often very clumsily, using interactional techniques that are not helping us achieve our goals of rapport building and data gathering. Two key factors involved in learning to overcome this problem are: first, to understand these people in as much depth as possible—to know them, the childhood they came from, and how they arrived where they are; second, to work hard to separate their feelings from their actions (see chap. 4). You do not like what they are doing, or have done, to their child, but you can, in fact you must, accept how they are feeling and develop a communication system with them as people. This will not be an easy task, but when the shell is broken through one finds real, feeling people in desperate need of help, but they are rarely able or willing to ask for it.

Michele Tolela (1) gives an excellent summary of the communication process necessary for delivering services in situations of child abuse and neglect.

> Communication is a complex process—it is not a discrete phenomenon beginning with the first word spoken between two people and ending when the last word has been heard. Communication has a history in the past and pitfalls for the future. We should look at communication as a complex process that has to be learned, that can be learned.

References

1. Tolela, M. 1967. Communication: A Three Part Series. *Pennsylvania Med. J.* 70: 76–78, 84–85, 91–92.
2. Berlo, D. K. 1960. *The Process of Communication*. New York: Holt, Rinehart, and Winston, p. 1.
3. Miller, G., and Steinberg, M. 1975. *Between People: A New Analysis of Interpersonal Communication*. Chicago: Science Research Association.
4. Mayerson, E. W. 1976. *Putting the Ill at Ease*. New York: Harper and Row.
5. Cassell, E. J., and Skopek, L. 1977. Language As a Tool in Medicine: Methodology and Theoretical Framework. *J. Med. Education* 77:197–203.
6. Mehrabian, A., and Ferris, S. R. 1967. Inferences of Attitudes from Nonverbal Communication in Two Channels. *J. Consulting and Clinical Psychology* 31:248–52.
7. Burgoon, J., and Saine, T. 1978. *The Unspoken Dialogue: An Introduction to Nonverbal Communication*. Boston: Houghton Mifflin.
8. Birdwhistell, R. L. 1970. *Kinesics and Context*. Philadelphia: University of Pennsylvania Press.
9. Ekman, P.; Friesen, W. V.; and Ellsworth, P. 1972. *Emotion in the Human Face*. New York: Pergamon Press.
10. Ekman, P., and Friesen, W. V. 1971. Constants across Cultures in the Face and Emotion. *J. Personality and Social Psychology* 17:124–29.
11. Bowden, C. L., and Burstein, A. G. 1979. *Psychological Basis of Medical Practice: An Introduction to Human Behavior*. 2d ed. Baltimore: Williams and Wilkins.

7 The Assessment Process of a Child Protection Team

Richard Krugman

The child protection team at the University of Colorado University Hospital has met weekly since 1958 to review cases of suspected or known child abuse and neglect that have been identified in the in-patient or out-patient services of the hospital. This multidisciplinary group has had a diagnostic rather than a monitoring function, that is, it discusses only those cases that are either complex or the focus of disagreement among professionals (about 10% of the hospital's cases involving abuse and neglect). It provides recommendations concerning these cases to the county department of social services.[1]

The University Hospital child protection team was organized because the complexity of abuse cases often demand data from multiple sources in order to make an accurate assessment of whether a child is in fact a victim of abuse and, if so, what therapeutic interventions are necessary.

This chapter reviews the composition and organization of the University Hospital child protection team, the reasons for having such a team, and the process used to gather data and make assessments. This is only one example of a child protection team; you are encouraged to take what has been successful in our hands and adapt it to your own situation.

Richard Krugman, M.D., is Associate Professor, the Department of Pediatrics, University Hospital, University of Colorado, Denver.

Part of this chapter has been adapted from R. D. Krugman, "The Multidisciplinary Treatment of Abusive and Neglectful Families," *Pediatric Annals* 13 (1984): 761–64, by permission of the publisher.

EDITORS' NOTE: Chapter 8, which describes the function of protective services, and chapter 9, which describes the child psychologist's role in family assessment, amplify the material of chapter 7 by addressing many aspects common to the roles of other members of the child protection team.

A child protection team will vary in composition from one community to another, depending upon availability, special expertise, and interest within each profession. The function of the psychologist and the psychiatrist (child or adult) within the team may often be the same, although clearly each has different training and different but somewhat overlapping areas of expertise. Rather than describing in detail the assessment roles of each member of the team, it may be assumed that parts of chapters 7, 8, and 9 will apply to all members of the team and that the functions described for the psychologist in some communities will be served by a psychiatrist in others.

[1] The team is *not* the child protection team mandated under Colorado statute for Denver County. Each county in Colorado that reports fifty or more cases of abuse per year must have a multidisciplinary team to assist the county department of social services in making decisions on each case.

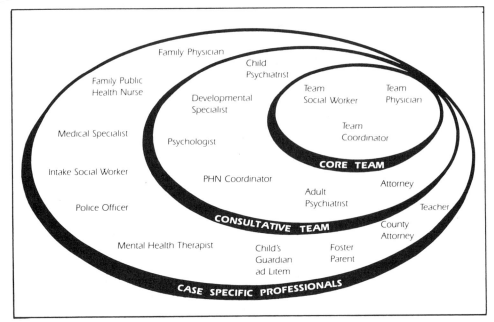

Figure 7.1

Child Protection Team Composition (provided by Joan Senzek Solheim).

A more in-depth analysis of child protection teams, their development and functions, is provided by Schmitt (1).

Composition and Organization of Team

Figure 7.1 schematically illustrates the organization of the University Hospital child protection team.

The members of the core team (social worker, physician, and coordinator) are the individuals who commonly see all of the hospital's child abuse and neglect cases. The team social worker evaluates the safety of the homes and recommends treatment strategies for the families. The team physician acts as the team's primary diagnostician and is also the contact person for other physicians in the hospital and the community who need another opinion on whether given patterns of injuries are accidental or non-accidental. The team coordinator is the case manager and functions as the contact person for the county agencies, police, physicians, families, and hospital professionals dealing with the cases. This function could be shared by the team physician and team social worker if the quantity of cases seen by the team is not sufficient to justify this additional position.

The members of the consultative team attend the weekly child protection team meetings and have broad experience in the area of abuse and neglect, but they are not necessarily involved in seeing each and every case. The psychiatrist and/or psychologist is primarily used in a diagnostic role, helping to sort out the small percentage of individuals who are psychotic, severely depressed, or sociopathic and assessing treatability. Having an attorney attend weekly meetings may seem to be a luxury, but numerous legal questions arise on both the civil and criminal side of each case. The presence of an attorney, whether from the hospital or from the community, adds greatly to the team's ability to make decisions. The child psychiatrist and/or developmental specialist assesses the child's emotional status and helps plan the ongoing mental health treatment for the child. The public health nurse coordinator is the link between the hospital nursing staff's observations and care plans and the community health nurse's ongoing health care plans.

Each case also has a varying number of case-specific professionals. Police officers often have valuable information to add based on their investigations. They can also let the team know if criminal charges are being pressed, a step which may decrease voluntary cooperation with a mental health treatment plan. Other professionals who have been involved with the child or the family before may also be a part of the team—teachers, family physician or other health care provider, and other attorneys. Certainly an assigned county social worker should be a part of the team as well as a guardian *ad litem,* if one has been assigned (see chap. 21).

Why Have a Child Protection Team?

The following case summary illustrates the need for child protection teams.

S.R., a twenty-seven-month-old boy, was brought to the University Hospital Emergency Room by his mother. She said that he had been complaining of abdominal pain for approximately one hour. She had returned home from work in the late afternoon and found S.R. lying on the floor in the living room, doubled over and crying in pain. Her boyfriend stated that S.R. had fallen off his Big Wheel earlier that afternoon and "hadn't been the same since." His mother noted that S.R. had wet his pants (he had been toilet trained at twenty-three months), and when he didn't seem to be getting better during the first half-hour she was home, she brought him to University Hospital. His past medical history was unremarkable, although his mother stated that he tended to "bruise easily" over the last three months. Social history revealed that she had moved to Denver from Wyoming four months ago and had met J.B., the boyfriend she was now living with, two weeks after her arrival. She worked from 7:00 A.M. until 3:00 P.M. He was a truck driver who worked 4:00 P.M. until midnight. There were no other siblings.

A medical examination, on admission to the Emergency Room, revealed a pale, shocky boy in acute distress. His blood pressure was 50/0, his pulse 140, and his temperature 36.5 C. He had multiple bruises about his face, oval grab marks on his arms, and multiple bruises over his back, his buttocks, and his legs that were of varying ages. His abdomen was rigid and a paracentesis revealed grossly bloody fluid. His venous hematocrit was 17%. He had no urine output.

He was taken to the operating room immediately and underwent an exploratory laparotomy. At surgery he was found to have a ruptured mesenteric artery, a contused liver, a contused pancreas, a duodenal hematoma, and retro-peritoneal bleeding around his kidneys. He received five units of whole blood during the surgery and was returned to the Intensive Care Unit in critical, but stable, condition.

What kind of help does S.R. need now? Who will give that help? The purpose of a multidisciplinary team becomes apparent from the perspective of this particular case.

Medical care clearly comes first. The child was fortunate that he arrived at the Emergency Room when he did. The surgeons attended to his abdominal injuries, stopped the bleeding, and saved his life. The pediatrician working with the surgeon was able to point out that the history offered for this particular injury (falling off his Big Wheel) was not consistent with the degree of abdominal injury the child had suffered. The recognition of a discrepant history introduces the possibility of abuse being the cause of his injuries.

The next critical step in protecting S.R. from further injury is consulting the core child protection team and ultimately reporting the case to the county department of social services (see chap. 10).

With the medical situation under control, the team social worker interviews the mother and her boyfriend to evaluate their functioning, to check the safety of the home, to see whether there are other children in danger, and to decide on an initial treatment plan (see chap. 8).

The adult psychiatrist or clinical psychologist needs to be available to assess the status of the mother's and her boyfriend's mental health, whether the boyfriend is dangerous to others, whether the mother is able to protect her child, and whether either is treatable.

The child psychiatrist and/or development specialist needs to assess the mental health treatment needs for S.R. (see chap. 9).

A public health nurse needs to begin planning for S.R.'s rehabilitation and medical needs at home.

The team coordinator needs to find out if the police are investigating the case and if they intend to press criminal charges against the boyfriend.

Finally, an attorney should be appointed to represent the child's best interests, since the mother, the boyfriend, and the county department of social services are all likely to have their own attorneys.

With so many people involved with this case, a team coordinator is needed to bring all the various pieces of information together so the team can assess the situation in a professional and competent manner.

Without all of these individuals, S.R. might recover from his physical injuries and be returned home only to suffer more abuse. The next time he might not survive.

Schmitt (1, p. 8) has outlined ten diagnostic purposes for child protection teams and ten treatment purposes. The diagnostic purposes are:

1. To insure a comprehensive evaluation and data base.
2. To establish the team as the hospital's investigatory and accusatory body.
3. Review cases for errors.
4. Review cases to evaluate the safety of the home.
5. Review cases to reach a consensus on diagnosis and treatment.
6. Formulate final recommendations for initial treatment.
7. Formulate tentative recommendations for long-term treatment.
8. Provide telephone consultation services regarding diagnostic questions for physicians and other professionals in the community.
9. Provide a referral mechanism for primary practitioners.
10. Improve communication between disciplines and agencies.

The treatment purposes Schmitt describes are:

1. Periodically review and evaluate cases for therapeutic progress and setbacks.
2. Revise treatment programs to suit the changing needs of the cases.
3. Utilize all community resources effectively and appropriately.
4. Prevent premature return of a child to an unsafe home.
5. Attempt to prevent repeated abuse with its concomitant high risk of death or disability.
6. Focus on family rehabilitation.

7. Provide telephone consultation services regarding treatment questions.
8. Coordinate and improve the emergency services for child abuse within the community.
9. Reduce interagency power struggles.
10. Insure a day in court for any child who needs it.

How Assessments Are Made

In any physical abuse and neglect case,[2] the initial assessment requires a decision as to whether the injury to the child is accidental or non-accidental. With the exception of certain obvious bruises or burns, the decision will rely on whether certain features are present in the case (2).

Discrepant history. This may be a history clearly impossible medically (e.g., S.R.'s injuries could not have occurred from simply falling off a Big Wheel). There may be changing histories over time, or there may be absolutely no history given to explain the injury.

Delay in seeking care. A delay may mean as long as days or weeks in cases of children who have burns, fractures, or other forms of trauma, or it may mean as short as a few minutes in the case of a baby who has been shaken violently and then put to bed, only to develop seizures or respiratory arrest a few moments later.

Crisis. This means a crisis in the eyes of the abuser. It may be major, such as unemployment or other financial pressures, or it may be minor, such as the washing machine breaking down.

Triggering behavior of the child. In infants (under a year old) the most common trigger is inconsolable crying. In older children, the most common trigger in severe abuse cases is loss of bowel or bladder control (3).

Prior history of abuse in the abuser's childhood. If the abusive adult is available for extensive history taking, one almost inevitably finds a prior history of inadequate nurturing in that individual's childhood, and most often, they have been abused in the same way they abuse their children.

Unrealistic expectations of parent. Abusive adults have unrealistic expectations for their children. They will expect a two-month-old infant to be able to bring a marriage together, or they will expect a ten-month-old infant to be perfectly toilet trained.

Isolation of family. Abusive parents are often isolated socially. They have few friends they can turn to for help when crises develop in their lives.

Pattern of increased severity of injury. Without intervention, cases of abuse often show a pattern of increased severity of injury. A child may have a bruise, then a fracture, then subdural hematomas, and finally death.

Visits to multiple hospitals and clinics. The child is often taken to different hospitals and clinics so that the health care providers are not able to detect the pattern of abuse evolving.

Table 7.1 provides a summary of the nine features just discussed and indicates the different professionals who are most likely to have the training, skills, and access to gather some, but not all, of the information needed to differentiate accidental from non-accidental injury.

[2] Sexual abuse assessment is discussed in chapter 14.

TABLE 7.1   Differentiation of Accidental and Non-Accidental Injury

Information Needed	Professional Primarily Involved in Obtaining Information
Discrepant history	Physician, nurse
Delay	Physician, police
Crisis	Social worker, police
Trigger	Physician, social worker, police
Prior history of abuse	Social worker, police
Unrealistic expectations	Physician, nurse, social worker, police
Isolation	Social worker, police
Pattern of increased severity	Physician
Multiple hospitals	Social worker, police, physician

If the determination is made that a child's injuries are clearly accidental, no child protection team involvement is necessary. However, if the physician or most professional care givers suspect abuse, under the laws of all states in the United States, they are required to report that suspicion to the county or state authorities. In practice, there are many cases that give physicians cause for worry (a "worry" is just short of "suspicion"). In these cases a consultation with a child protection team physician is useful. The team physician at University of Colorado University Hospital has 500 such contacts each year, in addition to the cases that are formally seen. These consults are generally to "look at a burn" or "check out a fracture." Many of these injuries are judged to be accidental; many more are suspicious and are reported. (These formed part of the 426 reported cases at University Hospital last year.) The basic principle is: When in doubt, report. There is no mortality and very little morbidity from a county social work evaluation.

Once a referral comes to the child protection team, the core team does its initial evaluation. The team physician reviews the medical history and examines the child, reviewing the findings with the child's primary physician and resident. Additional evaluation may be suggested, including a coagulation screen (PT,PTT, bleeding time platelet count) and/or a skeletal survey.

The team social worker interviews the family, paying particular attention to the current emotional, marital, employment, and financial status of the family, in order to assess their stresses, and their support systems (or lack of them). A history of the parents' childhoods is obtained to search for signs of abuse within their own childhood. Developing a family tree and a residence history is particularly useful, especially if there have been many moves. Information is also gathered on each of the individuals living in the child's environment (other siblings, grandparents, friends, etc.).

The team coordinator then brings this material together in a problem-oriented format (1, pp. 175–85) and presents it at the consultative team meeting. Other professionals involved with this child or family are members of this team. They review all the data gathered, add or deplete information as appropriate, and make recommendations to the county for the disposition of the case.

This process of data gathering and assessment takes time. This is emphasized to the physicians and nurses at our hospital to avoid last minute consultations. (E.g., "We have ruled out organic factors for this baby who is ready to go home today. Would you let us know if it is abuse?") Early involvement of the team in any potential case of abuse or neglect will expedite and improve the process of assessment.

Advantages of the Multidisciplinary Approach

The following case summary illustrates some of the advantages of multidisciplinary assessment.

> D.P., a three-month-old male infant, was admitted to University Hospital for an evaluation of poor weight gain. He was transferred from another hospital where he had stayed two days. Mrs. P. was being treated for a dental abscess at the dental clinic of the other hospital. When the dental receptionist noticed D.P. in his infant seat, she told Mrs. P., "Your baby looks awful," and insisted that he be taken to the pediatric clinic, where he was found to be 100 grams over his birth weight of 3140 grams. Mr. and Mrs. P. said he took five ounces of formula every three to four hours, and that he had had a cold for one to two weeks, but was otherwise well. They were unaware of his failure to gain weight, as he had not seen a physician since they had left the hospital in Kansas, where he had been born. D.P. was admitted to the hospital and was fed four to five ounces of formula every three to four hours. He gained 150 grams in two days. The staff was about to report the P. family to the county, since it was clear that D.P. had non-organic failure-to-thrive, but the parents bitterly complained about "the uncaring nurses and doctors" and "filthy conditions" at that hospital, so he was transferred to University Hospital for further care. A report was filed with the county.
>
> On arrival at University Hospital, the physical examination was remarkable because of D.P.'s wasted buttocks, legs, and cheeks. He was, however, alert and smiled responsively. The nurses noted that he was extremely hungry. During his four days at University Hospital he gained an additional 280 grams. His CBC (complete blood count), urinalysis, BUN (blood-urea nitrogen), and electrolytes were normal. A skeletal survey was negative. No further workup was done. The case was presented to our team for recommendations to the county for disposition and treatment.
>
> The pediatric ward resident's diagnosis was "non-organic failure-to-thrive." They didn't know whether the baby should go home or to foster care, but they did want D.P. out of his $900-a-day hospital bed. The nursing staff was divided as to whether D.P. should go home. Some had noted "good attachment" and "appropriate behavior" by Mrs. P. in her visits to the hospital when she cared for D.P. Others noted that she "seemed distant" and "misinterpreted his cries and smiles." One said "when he smiled at her, she called him 'rambunctious'".
>
> The social worker provided the information that the two-year-old sibling of D.P. "ran into my arms and, in fact, anyone's arms on the ward, and seemed to say 'yes' to everything." The family was living in a motel and their income was "marginal." Mrs. P. was twenty-nine years old; her husband was twenty-three. It was his first marriage; her third. The consensus of the hospital social services group was that home placement with follow-up in the failure-to-thrive clinic, twice weekly public health nurse visits, parenting classes, and registration for the Women, Infants, and Children Program would be a reasonable treatment plan.
>
> At that point, the consultant psychiatrist to the team asked if these two children were this mother's only children. The ward physicians and nurses said they thought so. He stated that he would be surprised if a mother with a baby with such a severe case of failure-to-thrive and an apparently severely neglected two-year-old had waited until she was twenty-seven years of age to have her first child.
>
> The county social worker added the information that a check of the Child Abuse Registry in three other states revealed that D.P. was actually Mrs. P.'s eighth child. The first three had been removed for physical abuse in Ohio, two were in foster care in Texas, and one was thought to

have been illegally sold in Kansas. The police officer confirmed that a child had been illegally sold and, in fact, provided the information that a warrant was pending for the arrest of both Mr. and Mrs. P. for this sale. A police investigation of their motel room the day before had turned up two contracts for the sale of D.P. and his two-year-old sister which were to be finalized the day after he was admitted to the hospital.

With this additional information, the physicians, nurses, and social services staff agreed that home placement was not in D.P.'s best interests. He and his sister were placed in foster care. The parents disappeared and, six months later, D.P. and his sister were adopted following termination of parental rights because of abandonment.

This case clearly shows the importance of many different people being involved and gathering information on a case. If it were not for the alert, persistent dental clinic receptionist who noticed D.P. and insisted on his being taken to a pediatric clinic, and the team psychiatrist whose experience was that an older mother who severely neglected her children was likely to have a long history of childhood abuse, early marriages, and many children, the outcome of this case would have been very different.

What are some of the specific advantages to the multidisciplinary child protection team?

1. The incidence of repeated abuse, serious injury, and death decreases. The team is able to bring together information from a variety of disciplines, information that any single discipline alone would not be likely to obtain on the basis of that discipline's training and experience. With a team, physicians will not be as likely to send children home prematurely. Fewer errors in decision making occur when more people obtain and review the available data.

2. As the team works together reviewing cases over months and years, each team member is educated in the basic approach of the various disciplines represented on the team. Even if the team attorney or consulting psychiatrist is not present for a given meeting, the team social worker, physician and coordinator will be able to add their perspectives based on the team's experience to the deliberations on a given case.

3. The hospital will more consistently fulfill its obligation, mandated by state laws, to report suspected abuse and neglect cases. An increasing number of lawsuits have been filed against professionals for failure to report. The presence of a functioning team decreases a hospital's risk of liability in this area.

4. The presence of a team that deals with abuse cases increases the case finding and reporting within the hospital and the community. Since many physicians in private practice seem reluctant to report families with suspected abuse, many will refer these cases to the team physician for evaluation. The team physician can act as a consultant, expedite the reporting process, and help the referring physician with written reports and court testimony. As previously discussed, the team physician, who sees many more abused children because of this referral pattern than physicians in private practice, can also help sort out the accidental from the non-accidental injuries. Of course, if the team physician has a question on these cases, he or she can bring that question to the team for review.

5. An important feature of the team meetings is the development of appropriate treatment plans for the child and for the family. State laws and child protection service practice require that all attempts be made to treat the family and return the child to the biologic home whenever possible. In the first case report given in this chapter, many questions need to be answered before the decision is made to return S.R. to his home environment.

Will the boyfriend who beat him because he wet his pants be there, or are the police going to arrest him and put him in jail? If the boyfriend *is* there, is S.R.'s mother going to be protective of S.R. or of the boyfriend? Is the boyfriend likely to respond to treatment, or is he not? Is the mother treatable? If neither will voluntarily seek treatment, will the county ask the court to order an evaluation and treatment? If none of these questions can be answered before S.R. is ready to go home, will the county place the child in foster care? In either case, is there someone available to treat S.R.? The pressures on county child protective services intake workers are so great that not all of these diagnostic and therapeutic questions are answerable, and often the team can expedite consultations with consultant professionals to help bring the treatment plan to fruition.

6. The preparation of expert witnesses and other testimony for court hearings improves, as does interagency cooperation. Furthermore, when the system fails, the team is likely to be the first group that recognizes that failure and can often take steps to try to improve the situation.

7. The weekly team meetings become a source of continuing education for each of the professionals who attend them regularly.

Of course there are also some disadvantages to this multidisciplinary team approach to the process of data gathering and assessment. It is difficult to get professionals in each of the many disciplines involved to volunteer their time to work together on behalf of abused children and their families. At the University Hospital, funding is provided by the hospital for the core team. The members of the consultative team and the case-specific professionals volunteer their time (approximately one hour per week). For those who are not convinced of the necessity for a multidisciplinary approach, or for those who are not personally or professionally interested in dealing with cases that involve abuse and neglect, this lack of funding becomes a convenient excuse for not being involved. If, for example, child psychiatrists insist that they are not available to assess adults when there are no adult psychiatrists or psychologists available to the team, or vice versa, the whole process may bog down.

The more individuals brought together into a group, the more likely it is that there will be interpersonal squabbles. Meetings may also degenerate into "Can you top this?" sessions, where individual after individual presents anecdotal information that is repetitive and does not substantively add to the process of assessment.

Finally, as Kovitz, Dougan, Russ, and Brummit (4) have pointed out, interdisciplinary composition alone is not enough to ensure that the team will function. Planning and ongoing review and evaluation are essential.

These drawbacks can easily be overcome by strong team leadership and by precise agendas that outline the diagnostic and treatment questions that are being asked. As long as the prime mission of the child protection team is to gather information and help with the assessment of a given abused child and his or her family, the interdisciplinary squabbles tend to diminish. This focus is the easiest to maintain.

What to Do if There Is No Team

While this chapter describes a typical multidisciplinary team found at many hospitals and in many counties, it is clear that there are many individual professionals who stand alone, unsupported and isolated in their efforts to protect children and assess and treat families.

Whether one is part of a large team or alone, the need for all available data remains. Therefore, the individual practitioner will either have to gather medical, social, law enforcement, and mental health data or find another "warm body" to help! Crucial to the success of an individual handling these cases effectively are:

1. Specialized training which is available from many continuing education programs in the field.

2. Linkage to an experienced multidisciplinary team or experienced professionals in a larger community who can provide consultation.

Just as we do not expect family physicians working in small rural towns to do open-heart surgery, we should not expect a solo practitioner to have all the skills needed to handle all abuse cases. A practical solution would be the development of a state, regional, and national network of professionals experienced in dealing with abuse cases. As long as there is access to a telephone, support is available.

References

1. Schmitt, B. D., ed. 1978. *The Child Protection Team Handbook: A Multidisciplinary Approach to Managing Child Abuse and Neglect.* New York: Garland Press.
2. Krugman, R. D. 1984. Child Abuse and Neglect: The Primary Care Physician's Role in Recognition, Treatment, and Prevention. *Primary Care* 11:527–34.
3. Krugman, R. D. 1985. Fatal Child Abuse: An Analysis of 24 Cases. *Pediatrician* (Basel) 12:68–72.
4. Kovitz, K. E.; Dougan, P.; Russ, R.; and Brummitt, J. R. 1984. Multidisciplinary Team Functioning: Fact or Fiction? *Child Abuse and Neglect: International J.* 8: 353–60.

8 The Function of Protective Services in Child Abuse and Neglect

Claudia A. Carroll and Carol C. Haase

Much of what is either effective or ineffective child abuse intervention in a community depends upon the posture taken by the local department of social services. (Throughout this chapter the department of social services or social service department will be mentioned; however, in different localities different names are used, such as the department of public welfare, the department of human resources, the department of human services, the social welfare department, etc.) In most states, the department of social services is the agency in the community legally responsible for the provision of child protective services. There are 3,300 such county departments of social services in the United States, most of which have either specific social workers or units to investigate, treat, and/or coordinate services to children and their parents.

The range of levels of responsiveness from social service departments to the mandate of providing protective services is enormous. Despite formidable obstacles, many departments of social services are doing a commendable job. These departments could be characterized as having "open systems," that is, as being responsive to the needs of referred families, progressive in program planning, and open to interagency coordination and cooperation in the community.

The opposite of these are described as "closed systems." These departments characteristically minimize the problems of child abuse and neglect in the community, provide little leadership in providing services to families, and diligently set up barriers within their system both to families and to other community agencies. It is estimated that 62 percent of all child abuse referrals are valid; a department reporting a number significantly lower than that may indicate that it is a department of social services that "screens out" rather than "screens in" families in need of treatment services.

Unfortunately, the frontline social worker often receives the brunt of the public's criticism, as it is he or she with whom it most frequently comes in contact. The public may tend to identify its frustrations over specific family situations with the social worker. In

Claudia A. Carroll, M.S.W., Psy.D., is a psychologist in private practice, and Carol C. Haase, B.A., is program coordinator with Child Help Diagnostic and Treatment at The C. Henry Kempe National Center for the Prevention and Treatment of Child Abuse and Neglect, Denver.

many of these situations, the social worker should be lauded for "hanging in there" when no one else will. Rather than the individual social worker, it is the administration of the department that must be questioned regarding agency policies, attitudes, and stance regarding protective services to children and their families. This is not to say incompetent social work should be excused under the rubric of poor administration of an agency— these are two separate issues.

It is important that the death of a child in a community is not misconstrued as evidence that the local departments of social services represents a poor or closed system. Even in the best of social service departments and with the best of services, children, most tragically, will die. In this field of protective services, human judgments are being made; and being human, mistakes are inevitable. The important factor here is to look at the mistakes and ascertain whether the child died or was injured because of a lack of responsiveness by the entire protective services system, including a closed social service department, or whether the death was a result of an incorrect human judgment. (The safest action would be to place all children referred to the department as a result of concern for abuse and neglect in foster care. Yet this course would be disastrous to countless numbers of children, and irreparable emotional damage would be done. Foster care is no panacea. It should be used, but judiciously.)

Determining whether the local department of social services is a closed or open system of protective services must be part of the diagnosis leading to change in each community. Enormous strides have been made in the past several years, even though we are still struggling today toward open, comprehensive, protective service systems. Considering that it was only about twenty-five years ago when Drs. Kempe and Steele began their pioneer work in child abuse and neglect, and that it was as recently as 1962 that the article "The Battered Child Syndrome" was published, progress has been made. This does not mean we can be complacent—far from it. The problem faced today in this work is one of urgency for the children of today, the parents of tomorrow. Many children of our nation are waiting unnecessarily for their rights for a safe and benevolent environment in which to grow and thrive to be adequately recognized and honored. This is not too much to ask for our children, nor for them to ask from us.

The field of protective services for children seems to have come full circle now as to the situations in which it will intervene. In the recent past, only the most serious physical abuse cases were those in which we felt justified to intervene and protect the child. To give testimony in a court case, the pediatrician went to court fully prepared with X-rays in hand, which the court enthusiastically embraced (1). Such explicit evidence of physical harm is no longer as necessary, because the definition of child abuse has been enlarged to include such areas as child neglect, sexual abuse, failure to thrive, emotional abuse, and threatened harm. Two recent trends have caused a compelling increase in the number of referrals to protective service agencies. Of these new referrals, the largest percentage have been cases of sexual abuse, a newer area of concern to all of us in the field and one we are learning more about each year. Another trend is the recognition of emotional abuse as being just as damaging to one's development as physical abuse, and even more so in some situations. There have been recent court cases in which termination of parental rights occurred on the basis of emotional abuse alone (2). This never would have happened ten years ago.

This enlarged understanding of child abuse and neglect is absolutely necessary if th field is going to move forward and meaningfully address the enormous problem of child abuse. Yet, what has happened is that an already overburdened system, the social service department, has been asked to take on an even greater caseload.

One way to avoid the problem of one agency (usually the department of social services) being asked to take on all this additional responsibility is to view child abuse as the community's problem. As such, a community response to child abuse is mandated. The social service department and all the other child-and-family-related agencies must work together to ameliorate the problems within families. Thus, the social service department becomes only one of at least fifteen potential components of a comprehensive protective services system (3). All fifteen components, cooperating in an interdisciplinary interagency effort, are necessary to do the job of protective services well. They are:

Legal services
Schools
Public health services
Child protection teams
Public and private hospitals and clinics
Law enforcement
Lay and community individuals and organizations
State social services department
County social services departments
Juvenile, civil, and criminal courts
Mental health private practitioners
Mental health public agencies
Private social services agencies
Parental consumer groups
Private physicians

Criteria of Good Child Protective Services in the Department of Social Services

As a major and central component of a comprehensive, interagency system of child protective services, the characteristics of a good social service department include the following:

1. There must be a commitment to making child protection services a priority of the whole department.

2. There must be a realistic budget that reflects both current and future needs based on sound statistical data collected within the department (e.g., the rate of intakes this year; the anticipated rate next year based on previous years' patterns and the population at risk). This makes long-range planning mandatory. Each social service department, with community input, should take an inventory of the services now provided and list priorities for the future.

3. Good working relationships with other community agencies must be maintained. Written agreements with other agencies are helpful.

4. There must be a functioning, active child protection team with a multidisciplinary and multiagency representation (see chap. 7).

5. A reasonable workload standard should be established for the protective services social workers. Quality service cannot be accomplished without this. Some states, such as Massachusetts, have passed legislation regarding caseload size (see appendix for one example of possible legislation). The recommended *maximum* workload for acceptable treatment services to occur under average circumstances is 20–22 families per social worker (4, 5). This number should not be viewed as an inflexible law "written in stone." At various times individual cases will be more time-consuming and stressful than the average case. This is especially true for complicated sexual abuse cases.

6. Consultative supervision must be provided for experienced, competent social workers, and teaching supervision for new protective service social workers. The supervisors should be well trained in the principles and practices of psychotherapy, and they should have firsthand experience with the realities of such stressful work by being the caseworker for at least one family. Knowledge of resources and a positive relationship with community agencies are also essential elements in supervision. Six social workers per supervisor is the maximum recommended.

7. Adequate medical, psychiatric, and psychological case consultation should be available to protective services staff (see chaps. 9–11).

8. There should be written department policy guidelines for such important decisions as court filings, placement, a child's returning home, case closures, and so on.

9. A broad variety of treatment services should be provided (see chaps. 17–19).

10. Skilled and trained social workers should perform child protective services work by choice, not chance. Too frequently, in order to meet ever-increasing workloads, entire units originally designed for other functions are converted precipitously into protective services units. If this must be done, adequate training, supervision, and education should be provided to the social workers. Anyone uninterested in doing this type of work should be reassigned to a different unit.

11. There should be an ongoing staff development program.

12. A responsive intake system should be available seven days a week, twenty-four hours a day. An answering machine referring the family elsewhere is not acceptable. A social worker needs to be on call to respond personally to cases as needed.

13. An active community education program should be geared to making the public aware of the problem of child abuse and neglect.

14. An adequate and responsive legal staff should be available to the protective services units. One full-time attorney is needed per 100,000 population in the community (4, p. 302; also see chap. 21).

15. The staff should be committed to serving families with potential as well as actual situations of child abuse and neglect.

16. State and national programs and legislation on child abuse should be developed with the help of protective service professionals.

17. A positive attitude should be maintained by the department of social services toward public scrutiny of the child protection system and department involvement in the community system. This can be accomplished through active lay involvement in the department (e.g., volunteer programs such as Foster Grandparents, Big Brothers, Lay Therapy), regular communication with the news media and legislature (e.g., inviting legislators to accompany a protective services social worker on home visits one day a year),

and encouraging and supporting self-help groups (e.g., Parents Anonymous, Parents United, and a child protection council).

Child Protection Council: A Community System

A child protection council can be one of the most effective groups in a community for providing community-wide education, coordination, and planning to help deal with the problems of child abuse and neglect.

Since the issues of child abuse and neglect are so complex, numerous procedures, professionals, agencies, and systems are involved with the abused child and family during resolution of the abusive situation. As many as thirty professionals may have contact with the child and family through the following stages: 1) child protective investigation, 2) criminal investigation, 3) juvenile court proceedings, 4) criminal court proceedings, 5) treatment, 6) disposition. Indeed, the abused child may be further victimized by the numerous systems and procedures activated during the course of the investigation (6).

The development of a child protection council provides multiagency reciprocity. Because the council is not attached to any one agency or system, the traditional problems of "turfism" can be transcended and people can participate out of genuine interest. Community agencies from all fifteen components of the child protective system might serve as professional participants. The list of lay groups interested in this could be quite extensive: PTA, Junior League, Welfare Rights, League of Women Voters, Foster Parents Association, Kiwanis, La Leche, Council of Jewish Women, Legal Aid, a guardian *ad litem,* a local legislator, and a member of the media. Such a group would provide a vehicle for community involvement, not specific case planning.

This council can: 1) serve as a forum for discussion and support of child abuse legislation, 2) enhance public awareness, 3) encourage needed community treatment programs, 4) address problems within the systems, 5) decrease duplication of procedures, 6) create change and ultimately develop interagency cooperation and communication.

It is important to tap people's interest in child abuse by providing ways in which they can become meaningfully involved. Forming working committees is an important step to keeping the council alive and growing. These committees might include: an educational and speakers' bureau to sponsor educational workshops and foster community awareness; a legislative committee to work for improved legislation and to interpret current legislation to the public; a task force on standards to define each component of a comprehensive protective services system and the community's expectations of each; a task force with the state department of social services to help in presenting pertinent data to the legislature, as well as to provide credibility for the budget requests; a public relations committee; and a membership committee to generate more participation (7).

The Current Dilemma of Protective Services

Society has charged social service departments with the tremendous obligation to protect children at risk. Yet protective services are struggling with ever-increasing workloads, strikingly low budgets, and a rapid turnover of well-trained and skilled social workers (the average tenure is two years), who are leaving the field because of these conditions and the inherent emotional pressures of such work.

This all speaks to the low priority, nationally and locally, given to children and children's rights. Children do not vote. They, therefore, have little impact on our legislatures and their decisions about funding for the needs of children.

The problem is twofold. On the one hand, children's programs are too frequently viewed as unimportant by those in power. On the other hand, social service departments have been reluctant to request adequate funding and have often merely requested what they thought the legislature would approve. The obligation of the professional protection services worker is to tell society what the true needs and costs are. Continuing to budget on a piecemeal basis will only continue our failure to adequately serve abused children and their families.

The true cost of good protective services programs, as well as the true cost of *not* funding protective services, needs to be proclaimed. For example, an institutionalized child who is brain-damaged as a result of child abuse costs the state approximately $700,000 during his lifetime (8). Further, studies across the United States show a high correlation between families who report abuse or neglect problems and those who report later delinquency by the children. If we were to look at the relationship between adult criminal offenders and their experiences of abuse or neglect as children, that correlation, too, would be startling.

Fortunately, in a few states the problem of child abuse is slowly making an impact on the legislatures and communities. The media have played a significant role in expanding public awareness of child abuse and neglect. Tragically, this has often happened as a result of news media coverage of severe cases involving the death or serious injury of a child. Some community media campaigns have focused on the availability or lack of various resources and services, the existing or proposed civil and criminal statutes pertaining to child abuse, and the roles of the professional protective services workers and agencies. However, few people in an average community have any idea what the protective service worker actually does. Typically, they are viewed suspiciously as "child snatchers" on the one hand, or as "ineffectual do-gooders" who return children to dangerous homes on the other. There must be a concerted effort to present the public with an accurate image of child protection services that is consistent with the facts and the complex nature of the work. Only then will the public support a reasonable allocation of funds for protection services.

The Organization of Protective Services

Organizationally, local departments of social services are responsible to the state social service department and ultimately to the federal Department of Health and Human Services. In some states the local departments are county administered, and they are responsible to either the county commissioners or the city council and the local advisory board. Many protective services programs within departments of social services are funded with 80 percent federal dollars and 20 percent state funds.

Some of the confusion over what a department of social services does results from its

TABLE 8.1   Department of Social Services

Financial Assistance Division	Social Services Division
Aid to Dependent Children	Adoption Services
Aid to the Needy Disabled	Adolescent Services
Food Stamps	Child Protective Services
Aid to the Blind	Supportive Services (homemakers, day care)
Old-Age Assistance	Foster Care Services
Medicaid	Adult Protective Services
Child Support and Enforcement	Work Incentive Programs (employment services)

dual role of providing both financial assistance and social services. These very different functions are housed under one roof, but in separate divisions (see table 8.1).

This distinction should be kept in mind in order to understand where protective services fit into the department of social services and how they work within the system. A large metropolitan social service department can be an amorphous, confusing system to outsiders and even to those within the agency. A family could be under the care of an Aid to Dependent Children technician who is totally unconnected with the protective services division. When wanting to make a referral or to speak with a family's social worker, it is important to be sure that the person you are speaking to is, in fact, from the social service division of the department.

Functions of Protective Services

Protective services can logically be divided into four services: intake or assessment of referred families, provision of treatment services, case coordination with other agencies in the community, and preventive services. Philosophically, each of these services requires that we keep in mind the potential positive or negative impact our very presence, let alone our efforts at intervention, may have on the abused child and the family. Intervention without long-term treatment, or with treatment available only months later, can potentially do more harm than the original incident of abuse or neglect. Whatever we do with a family, we must continually ask ourselves: Why are we doing this? What are the goals? To whom do we wish the child to become attached—the foster parents or the natural parents? Does the system have something better to offer the child and the parents than their current situation? For whom is this rule designed—the child, the parents, or the agency? These questions are necessary. We are involved in people's lives; intervention is a difficult and delicate process that should never be entered casually.

Intake

Intake is the initial phase of assessment during which immediate responsiveness is required from the protective services division. Referrals originate from a variety of sources—school, hospital, police, private citizen, relative, or the parent. An intake social worker is assigned to gather as much information as possible about the alleged incident as quickly as possible. This may take only a few hours or as long as thirty days.

The purpose of the intake investigation is to determine whether something has happened to the child. If so, what is the present risk to the child? If nothing has yet happened, many states' statutes allow an investigation to take place on the basis of potential harm or circumstances which might result in child abuse or neglect.

Treatment of the abusive family begins with the first contact by the intake social worker. The tone established between the intake social worker and the family will often influence that family's response to any services or treatments that follow. It is therefore essential that the intake worker be respectful, honest, and predictable with the parents (see chap. 6).

Upon completion of the intake investigation, a decision is made as to whether the family requires ongoing protective services. If so, the case is usually assigned to an ongoing protective services unit social worker. This brings us to one of the major problems in the organization of protective services programs. The continuity of a worker's involvement with the family is frequently lost when a family is transferred from one unit to another. The family often builds up a strong alliance with the worker with whom they have had initial contact, and it is not unusual for considerable time to be lost before the family has contact with a caseworker from the new unit. Possible alternatives to this system include assigning an intake worker to each ongoing protective services unit. This person would function as a member of the unit, and families could then be moved expeditiously within that unit. A foster-care placement worker could also be assigned to each ongoing protective services unit. Each placement worker would be responsible for a number of foster homes and would likely have a better sense of the type of children an individual foster family works with best. Further, this would minimize the number of placement workers the foster families have to work with.

Another alternative would be to have the child abuse and neglect intake workers rotate among all protective services units. Theoretically, it is much more logical for a family to see only one social worker. The person they talk with at the point of crisis has a much better opportunity to assess and develop a treatment plan before the family's defenses are up again in full force. While there are a few situations in which a family becomes so angry at the intake worker that they are unable to work together, this resistance usually can be worked through.

Regardless of how the units are organized, certain logical steps can facilitate the transfer of a family from one worker or unit to another. These include a face-to-face introduction of the family by the intake worker to their ongoing worker, the staffing of each case at the time of transfer so important information does not get lost, and establishing a procedure for conflict resolution when a consensus cannot be reached.

A useful intake organizational model to consider involves using two people during the initial investigation: a public health nurse or a nurse employed by the department of social services and an intake protective services social worker. The nurse might appear less threatening to the family, and he or she may be able to incite the cooperation of the family. A medical person can help assess the medical needs of the child and determine the degree of seriousness of any injuries. Also, the combination of two people in any serious intake situation can relieve some of the anxiety a single worker would naturally feel if assessing the situation alone.

It is important for the intake social worker to compile data from a variety of sources, including the child, the parents, school records, medical records, and the local child abuse registry. When we have made mistakes as a team at the University of Colorado Health Sciences Center, they have usually stemmed from lack of data or taking a shortcut where one should not be taken, such as sending a baby home from the hospital without the trauma-series X-rays because "the parents look good."

Multidisciplinary teams have been established in many areas of the country to review the action taken on new cases. In some localities the multidisciplinary team is located in the department of social services; in others, it is in another community agency. Actually, the location is of little importance as long as the department supports and is involved with the review team.

Treatment

Departments of social services should be among the primary providers of treatment services to troubled families (see chaps. 17–19). Among the services they should be providing are:

1. Therapy and counseling for children and parents (individual, marital, family, and group) or referral for treatment outside of the department. In instances when treatment is not directly provided by the department, the protective services units then function as monitoring programs rather than treatment programs because of the volume of referrals and cases assigned to them. Additional funding should be allocated to these units for contractual services for treatment of the abused child and family by professionals within the community. This is not the plan of choice, but of necessity, when protective services units are hampered by inadequate staffing.

2. Therapeutic foster care and crisis nursery placements.

3. Lay therapy.

4. Volunteer programs (Big Brother, Big Sister, transportation, Foster Grandparent).

5. Day-care resources and therapeutic day care for children with special needs.

6. Homemaker services.

7. Education in parenting.

8. Concrete emergency assistance, such as grocery orders.

Treatment involves the difficult task of helping parents grow up psychologically. Treatment for the children is equally important so that they will not become developmentally arrested but will have the opportunity for fulfilled, happy lives. One can be optimistic about the helping professions' abilities to work with families successfully, given the variety of treatment services available, a cooperative approach of agencies working together, and a reasonable prognosis for the parents' ability to make positive change.

The treatment needs of the child and the parents in each case are enormous. The following ideas are first steps toward more specific treatment goals.

1. Take the developmental needs of the child and the parents into account when considering the decisions to be made on a case. What is the *developmental diagnosis* of each?

Where are these parents stuck developmentally and how might they move forward? How might foster care affect a developmentally delayed, thirteen-month-old infant? How resilient is a child at that age to separation and loss?

2. How can we reduce the number of different workers assigned to a family? If the unfortunate reality is that they will have several workers before their case is closed, help them develop a relationship with the agency as a whole to mitigate their sense of abandonment and loss with each worker's departure.

3. Treat the parents respectfully, always.

4. Involve the parents in establishing their treatment plan. It will only work if they feel they have something invested in it in some way.

5. Protect the child from unnecessary interrogation and testimony. There is no need for a child to be repeatedly interviewed. If the intake worker takes a thorough written history with verbatim statements from the child, this should suffice in any court. We must be sure that we do not allow the system to heap more abuse on the child.

6. Consider all decisions through the eyes of the child. To whom is this child attached? Fortunately, more agencies are taking this question into account during such decisions as foster care and adoption. In the not-too-recent past, adoption by foster parents was considered suspect at best, despite the fact that the child may have thrived in the care of the foster parents and may have been in their care since infancy.

A good psychiatric evaluation in the early stages of a case can be instrumental in sorting out which cases are treatable and those few which are not. In the past departments of social services have sometimes felt too responsible and have exerted heroic efforts on behalf of everyone. A reasonable and fair treatment plan should be set up in the beginning stages of a case, and if after a year or so significant progress has not been made, termination of parental rights should take place and permanent planning for the child should occur.

Treatment review teams could be established within social service departments to review treatment plans and progress or lack of progress. They could be an adjunct to the multidisciplinary child protection team, which in practice focuses mainly on intake cases. (The multidisciplinary child protection team need not focus solely on new cases, but most existing teams have done this as a result of the sheer volume of cases.) Such treatment teams can also review ongoing family situations, decisions about whether a child may safely return home, and case closures. Seemingly, some of our gravest mistakes in protective services have been made after a case has been open for a period of time and children were returned home precipitously, or after an aspect of the treatment plan was changed unilaterally by one person without team consensus. A further extension of this concept would be a foster care review team which would monitor those children placed in foster care and review regularly the planning for them so they will not grow up in the limbo of foster care. We recently found in Colorado, for instance, that if a child remained in foster care for two months, he or she would most likely be there for two years.

Both the treatment review team and the foster care review team could be staffed by people within the department (e.g., staff social workers, the protective service supervisors, staff psychiatric/psychological consultants) and by people outside (e.g., public health nurse, mental health center representative, etc.)

With the increased knowledge of how to treat cases of child abuse, there has been a movement within all agencies toward increased specialization of treatment teams, such as sexual abuse treatment units. While this is generally providing better and more sophisticated intervention to more families, one word of caution is necessary for the families which may "fall through the cracks" of the specialization units. In other words, if the family doesn't quite fit into a unit's criteria, don't just close the case.

This brings us to those cases which are mistakenly screened out rather than assigned to agencies for preventive services (see chap. 22). With the high caseloads nationwide, it is understandable that departments seek to keep caseloads down by using certain criteria to screen out cases. However, we urge agencies to carefully screen the mild and moderate neglect cases. These are often cases in which short-term involvement and supervision could preclude more serious neglect later. Too often mild-moderate neglect cases are red flags warning of worse things to come. Further, the effects of neglect can be just as damaging, or in some cases more damaging, to the child's development as mild to moderate abuse. Another category of cases in which the department of social services should remain involved in some instances is "third party perpetrators." If the perpetrator is involved in the child's life in any way whether he or she lives in the home or not, that involvement warrants protective services involvement. Sometimes these out-of-home perpetrators are still highly involved with the child's life (or other children's lives) and these cases need more than just police referral. Criteria for screening cases need to be established on a state level with input from the local departments of social services and child protection teams. Broadening the criteria of cases in which the department will intervene, of course, will lead to higher caseloads and the necessity of an adequately staffed protective service division.

Case Coordination

In some areas of the country the protective services worker is strictly a case coordinator or case manager and the services to the family are provided by other agencies or professionals. In other areas, the protective services worker has a mixed responsibility of doing intake evaluations, treatment, and case coordination; this is preferable. Transferring all of the motivated clients to other agencies leaves the protective services social worker with just the hopeless situations. Case coordination is an important function of protective services, yet it should not be done to the exclusion of intake and treatment responsibilities.

Given the need in every child abuse and neglect situation for many agencies to be involved, someone needs to be identified as the case coordinator. This individual can make sure that all aspects of the family situation are considered and can keep agency representatives from tripping over each other in their efforts to help the family. We want to help, not overwhelm.

One of the dilemmas which case coordinators often face is that of becoming a passive onlooker rather than an active participant in the decision-making process regarding the child and the parents. However, the case coordinator, should be a decisive and moving influence in case planning.

Prevention

When the protective services staff hear someone ask what the department of social services is doing in the area of prevention, the response is usually from two very opposite ends of the continuum. Intellectually they agree that protective services should be involved in preventive work; emotionally they think, "This person is crazy! We can't even deal with all of the current families referred to the social service department."

The busiest department can have a role in prevention by being willing to accept and work with those high-risk cases where no physical injury has yet occurred but undoubtedly will without intervention. A newborn infant with actively psychotic parents should not, for example, have to suffer a skull fracture before something can be done. Foster care placement from the hospital or juvenile court action should be alternatives in such a potentially dangerous situation.

Other community agencies should carry primary responsibility for other types of prevention. Schools should provide parenting curriculum and experiential opportunities for youngsters to learn about the problems of being a parent. Hospitals can develop lay health visitor programs. Health and mental health agencies can provide parenting support groups. The social service departments should encourage good working relationships with these other agencies so that together they can develop new ideas for prevention (see chaps. 22–24).

Community Inventory

Having discussed the four major areas of protective services, one might wonder about the possibility of developing a list of priorities of services. All the services seem equally important!

The first step in planning a protective services program in a community is to take an inventory of the currently available services and resources. Only then can a list of priorities, unique to each community, be developed. A good beginning place is the list of seventeen suggested criteria for good protective services discussed earlier in this chapter. This list could be coupled with the list of eight types of treatment services also discussed earlier.

People sometimes become overwhelmed and discouraged, feeling that there is so much to do and yet not knowing where to begin. Begin with a goal that is attainable in the next year. You will not need a lot of resources to implement many good ideas. A child protection team can be two interested, committed people. Starting with three or four priorities provides a foundation on which to build. If we had to choose among all the ideas for services, the four priorities we would choose are: 1) a workload standard for protective service workers, 2) a strong lay therapy program, 3) extensive utilization of good day care, 4) available medical expertise.

Making Protective Services Social Work Manageable

Throughout this book possible ways of making the job of the protective services social worker more manageable, thus reducing the tremendous turnover of workers, are discussed. Right now it is unusual for a family to have the same social worker from the beginning to the end of their treatment. The repercussions of this situation are many. A family may be involved unnecessarily long with community agencies; poor decisions might be made because of lack of continuity; families may get lost, so to speak, between social workers in terms of their needs and priorities, and so on.

Other ways in which this work can be made more manageable include, but are not limited to, the following:

1. A variety of protective services experiences should be available to social workers so they do not become burned out in one area of responsibility. This could vary from some responsibilities for ongoing treatment with families, to supervision of lay therapists, to involvement with community activities, such as public speaking or being a co-leader of a parents' group. This approach ameliorates feelings of frustration, failure, and incompletion that often result if any one of these is the worker's exclusive task.

2. Agency policies should be flexible and reasonable, including compensatory time, flexible work hours, accessible ways of obtaining concrete services for a family, etc.

3. The juvenile court system should work with the social service department and view the social workers as competent professionals.

4. Skilled, available supervision and consultation as well as ongoing continuing education should be available to all protective service workers.

5. The philosophy of being "a member of a team" within the agency, that is, supported by supervisor and agency administration as well as outside agencies, should be put into practice. Being alone in this work is impossible.

Legal Role of Protective Services

Underlying each of the services discussed thus far (intake, treatment, case coordination, and prevention) is the legal role inherent in the department of social services. As the agency with the ultimate responsibility for the protection of the rights of children, the protective services division is faced with the concomitant responsibility of initiating civil juvenile court action in those cases that are sufficiently serious. One wonders if it is possible to be both the provider of treatment services and the initiator of court actions. Skilled protective services workers are able to juggle these seemingly disparate areas if they have established a relationship with the parents that is characterized by trust and straightforwardness. While there is a small percentage of cases where these roles are not compatible, in the vast majority of cases they are.

The state statute or juvenile code provides the state definition of child abuse and neglect which indicates when juvenile court action is appropriate. These codes are in turn interpreted by the local juvenile court judges. Thus, what will be adjudicated in one county, circuit, or district jurisdiction may not be heard in the next jurisdiction a few blocks or courtrooms away. The department of social services must be aggressive in continuing to bring to the attention of their juvenile court (even if they lose these cases at first) all those situations in which children's emotional or physical well-being is at risk. By bringing a case to the court's attention, the department has done everything within its power. Slowly, progress will be made, but only if departments of social services have the courage to persevere in bringing all serious cases to the attention of their courts, not just the ones they think the judge will decide in their favor.

On the whole, the juvenile court's increased sophistication in understanding failure to thrive, emotional abuse, sexual abuse, and developmental lags, is impressive. If given enough data by all of us in the field, juvenile courts will increasingly make decisions to protect children's rights.

As in other areas of this work, it is useful to have a checks-and-balances system to review which cases should or should not go before the court. Coupled with the professionals involved in a case, an overworked attorney handling juvenile cases would probably welcome the recommendations of the multidisciplinary team in making such difficult decisions.

Conclusion

In the past two decades, we have seen a major expansion of knowledge about child abuse and neglect and an upsurge of community awareness. With this has come a concomitant upsurge in families being reported to protective services. Although protective services are hard pressed at this point, there seems to be an increased willingness on the part of other agencies in local communities to become involved in this difficult business. Child abuse is now being defined as a community problem, not as solely the concern of one agency, the department of social services. We are beginning to think of a larger protective services system whereby one agency is an extension of another—encompassing the legal system, schools, health departments, child protection teams, public and private hospitals, law enforcement agencies, lay and community groups, parent-consumer groups, medical private practitioners, county and state social service departments, juvenile and criminal courts, public and private mental health resources, and private social service agencies.

Within this larger protective services system, the department of social services plays a key role, setting the stage for cooperation among agencies and providing leadership. Together we may all be able to offer quality intervention and treatment services to abused children and their families. It is the only way any of us will succeed.

Appendix

CITATION: *Lynch v. King*, 550 F.Supp. 325 (D. Mass. 1982), aff'd sub nom. *Lynch v. Dukakis*, 719 F.2d 504 (1st Cir. 1983).

"The decision reached by the Appellate Court was that . . . "In order to receive federal funds under Title IV-E of the Social Security Act (42 U.S.C. §§ 671 *et seq.*) the Department of Social Services of the Commonwealth of Massachusetts. ("DSS") must comply with the following requirements . . . I., . . .

    C. DSS may not assign to its social workers a number of cases that is greater than the number of cases that workers are able to carry and simultaneously fulfill their obligations, as outlined in A. and B. above, to provide case plans and periodic review. In determining DSS's compliance with this requirement, the court will use the following guidelines:

(1) DSS's establishment and maintenance of an average ratio, in each DSS area, of twenty "generic" or "mixed" cases per caseworker will be taken as a rebuttable presumption that DSS is assigning to its social workers only the number of cases that workers are able to carry consistently with fulfilling their obligations, as outlined in A. and B. above, to provide case plans periodic review.

(2) Only Social Workers I and II may be counted in computing the 1:20 ratio established in (1) above.

D. DSS, within 24 hours of receipt of a case by DSS, shall assign it to a Social Worker I or II— or to a supervisory Social Worker III who chooses to act as a direct service social worker in such cases and can do so consistently with performing his or her obligations, as outlined in A. and B. above, to provide case plans and periodic review. A case shall not be considered "assigned" until any existing case record has been delivered to the assigned social worker."

References

1. Kempe, C. Henry. 1964. Personal communication.
2. *People in the Interest of D.A.K.*, 198 Colo. 11, 596 P.2d 747 (1979), appeal dismissed sub nom. *J.K.S. v. Colorado* 100 S.Ct. 515, 444 U.S. 987, 62 L.Ed.2d 416 (1980).
3. Carroll, C., ed. 1979. *Standards for a Model Protective Services System.* Denver: University of Colorado Health Sciences Center.
4. Kawamura, G., and Carroll, C. A. 1976. Managerial and Financial Aspects of Social Service Programs. In *Child Abuse and Neglect: The Family and the Community,* ed. R. Helfer and C. Kempe. Cambridge, Mass.: Ballinger.
5. *Lynch v. King,* 550 F.Supp. 325 (D. Mass. 1982), aff'd sub nom. *Lynch v. Dukakis,* 719 F.2d 504 (1st Cir. 1983)
6. Egan, B., and Haase, C. 1983. A Multidisciplinary Approach to Child Abuse. In *In the Interest of Children: Quality Child Advocacy,* ed. E. I. Hoffenberg. Denver: National Association of Councils for Children, part 3, pp. 20–33.
7. Carroll, C. A., and Schmitt, B. 1978. Improving Community Treatment. In *The Child Protection Team Handbook: A Multidisciplinary Approach to Managing Child Abuse and Neglect,* ed. B. D. Schmitt. New York: Garland Press, pp. 33–34.
8. Kempe, C. H. 1976. Approaches to Preventing Child Abuse: The Health Visitor Concept. *Am. J. Diseases in Children* 130:941–47.

9 The Child Psychologist's Role in Family Assessment

Elizabeth A. W. Seagull

To function most effectively in assessing families referred because of possible child abuse or neglect, the child psychologist must be a member of a multidisciplinary team. The team concept has been discussed elsewhere (see chaps. 7, 8), but it bears repeating that complicated cases of child maltreatment are too multifaceted for any one discipline to handle competently alone. Severely dysfunctional families typically present several types of pathology, both physical and psychological, have problems in dealing with many systems in society, and cause a great deal of personal stress to the professionals involved. As Polansky et al. has pointed out, "Twenty years ago, the term for families very like those now thought of as maltreating was 'multi-problem'" (1, p. 19).

A family referred by a protective services worker to a multidisciplinary team may, for example, include a depressed mother with chronic back problems, a belligerent father with a history of fighting in bars who cannot keep a job, an oldest child who has been picked up by the police for truancy and vandalism, a preschool child already receiving special education for delayed speech and poor fine motor coordination, a listless toddler with asthma, and a baby who is not growing well. They may live in a house whose yard is littered with rusting parts of old cars from which they are about to be evicted for non-payment of rent. Frequently such families elicit anger, blame, and a sense of helplessness or hopelessness from those who try to help them. Often they are uncannily successful in getting the "helpers" to fight with each other.

Because of these typical characteristics of maltreating families, the initial task of the psychologist is to offer support, understanding, and acceptance of the other assessment team members. Often the psychologist is able to facilitate the team's functioning by remaining aware of the group process among the professionals involved and intervening as needed to help the team work well together. Noticing that a team which usually works well together is becoming divided and upset over a family tells us something about the family. It signals that the discussion should be temporarily turned away from the family and to-

Elizabeth A. W. Seagull, Ph.D., is with the Department of Pediatrics and Human Development, Michigan State University, East Lansing.

ward the team's response to it. How do we feel when we are in the same room with this family? What about them is making us feel so frustrated? How can an analysis of our own responses help us understand the problems outlined by the referring professional? At its best, the team should not only offer competent professional help to the referring person and the family, it should also serve as a haven of trusted friends and colleagues amidst the emotionally draining demands of work with abusive families.

The viewpoint discussed in this chapter developed in the context of seven years of intensive work as a member of such a caring and competent outpatient multidisciplinary assessment team. (This work resulted, in part, in a research study on foster care placement [2].) The mission of such a team is to develop recommendations for intervention which will have the highest likelihood of success with a particular family. The assessment is most successful when it is the beginning of a therapeutic process. This increases the probability that the family will participate cooperatively in the recommended treatment. In some cases, of course, families do not improve. Sometimes the team is unsuccessful in establishing a sufficiently therapeutic relationship with families, and they do not follow through on recommended interventions. Other families are unable to change in spite of following recommended treatment plans because their problems are so intractable. If this occurs, termination of parental rights to the children will, at some point, be considered as an alternative.

Termination of parental rights is an extremely serious step. The lay public, faced with sensationalized news accounts, vacillates between impatience with "the system" which allows abuse to occur and fear that legal terminations of parental rights can be accomplished too easily because of prejudice or disapproval of a family's llfe-style. No one wants to live in a society where it is easy for the relationship between parents and children to be permanently, legally severed.

The assessment team's secondary function in the community demands not only professional competence, but sensitivity to the delicate balance between parents' rights and childrens' needs. In cases where interventions have failed, the team must ask, "Did this family receive appropriate interventions?" If not, another treatment plan must be developed. If, on the other hand, the community has offered help to the family which was appropriate in quality and quantity, and if serious maltreatment of the children continues, professionals have a responsibility to make clear recommendations to the court about termination of parental rights. If the best available treatment has been attempted and has failed, nothing further can be gained by postponing a decision which will give the children a permanent home (3, pp. 40–49).

In a few cases, after time and therapeutic work, parents decide that the interests of their children are best served by voluntarily relinquishing them for adoption when their relationship has been too destructive and their ability to change has been too slow to meet the children's developmental needs. The following excerpt from a letter written by a mother to the child psychologist on a multidisciplinary team illustrates the team's role in the evolution of her decision to give up her children:

> I have been through a lot since I last saw you and I have done a lot of honest thinking and not as much running from facing the truth. I don't hate you no more, in my heart you are my friend now. I have reread the [team's report] again and I now know what I must do just for my own survival. I'm letting go of the kids and I am going to go on with life. [The children] are humans with

feelings too. I was just being selfish with wanting the kids with me no matter what the consequences were. I love my kids more than that. I'm just so sorry I didn't face this decision sooner.

The child psychologist who serves as a member of a multidisciplinary family assessment team must have specialized training in clinical work with children. Because there are so many different kinds of psychologists, and the terminology used to describe them may be somewhat confusing, the question, "What is a child psychologist?" will be addressed briefly here. Brief discussions of ethical issues and the characteristics of a successful multidisciplinary team are followed by a description of the process of psychological assessment of children, parents, and family interaction. Finally, the use of psychodiagnostic tests, the role of the psychologist who must work alone, working with trainees, and the psychologist's role in research are briefly discussed.

What Is a Child Psychologist?

The three major types of psychologists who work with children are: developmental psychologists, school and counseling psychologists, and clinical child psychologists.

The developmental psychologist has a Ph.D. degree. At first, developmental psychology focused exclusively on the development of children and adolescents, but it now incorporates the development of adults and the process of aging. These psychologists are primarily researchers rather than clinicians.

School and counseling psychologists generally have an M.A. degree, though some have a Ph.D. or Ed.D. They serve as consultants to teachers and other educators. They also provide direct counseling services to children, including the psychological evaluation of children who may need special educational services. They have a strong background in both education and psychology; many are former teachers.

Clinical psychologists usually have a Ph.D. or Psy.D. degree. They are trained in both research and applied clinical practice with adults and children. Clinical experience under the close supervision of fully trained and experienced clinical psychologists is an integral part of this training. Those who have had specialized training to work with children are called clinical child psychologists. (Some clinical psychologists have an M.A. degree and are licensed to practice only under the close supervision of a doctor of psychology, usually in agencies or in private group practices.)

This chapter discusses the role of clinical child psychologists in the assessment of families referred to them because of possible child abuse or neglect.

Ethical Issues of Family Assessment

Psychologists, like other professionals, have a well-defined code of professional ethics and an established system for handling reported violations. Two of the foremost ethical principles of psychologists are the patient's right to give informed consent before participating in either research or clinical activity, and the patient's right to confidentiality (4). Given the often adversarial circumstances surrounding the requests for family assessments because of suspected child abuse or neglect, questions arise as to how to handle the issues of informed consent and confidentiality. Helping to resolve such ethical issues is one of the crucial roles of the child psychologist in the multidisciplinary family assessment team.

Professionals without experience in working with abusive and neglectful families often imagine that it must be very difficult to obtain the cooperation of families for the assessment while remaining within the ethical guidelines. Actually, obtaining informed consent for the assessment rarely presents a problem among families who actually appear for the assessment. Families who refuse consent do so by simply not showing up. If a family keeps the initial appointment, they usually cooperate with the assessment process and, within the limits of their capabilities, even keep return appointments. The ethical treatment of families is the key to this success.

Ethical practices should be a standard feature of the team's operating routine. This will insure that they are not inadvertently overlooked. For example, the referring person can be asked to come with the family to the first appointment. The team, the referring professional, and the entire family can then meet together to go over the purpose of the assessment, what the family can expect of the team, what the team expects from the family, how the assessment will be paid for, and with whom findings will be shared. The family must be explicitly told that the findings of the team are *not* confidential, but that they will be shared in a report, as well as vocally, with the referring person and, in some circumstances, with attorneys, the court, and other professionals.

Family members should be encouraged to ask questions and to raise issues of concern to them. For example, if the parents believe that one of their children is "hyper" and impossible to control without harsh physical discipline, the team may decide to include an evaluation of the child's hyperactivity in the assessment. This kind of exchange helps families feel that the assessment is going to meet their needs and promotes their sense of ownership of the process.

Occasionally, families are unsure about the legal ramifications of the assessment process. If this issue is raised, they should be encouraged to contact their attorney for advice before proceeding with the assessment. At the family's request, team members can speak with the family's attorney to explain the assessment process. (Most attorneys advise families to participate.) Openness with the families conveys the team's respect for them and their needs, and it will enable at least some families to feel a sense of control and participation in the decisions made.

At the conclusion of the assessment, the team members, the referring person, and any other professionals involved with the family meet to discuss the case. Collected data are shared and potential recommendations discussed. The goal of this meeting is to develop a consensus of all the professionals working with the family as to what interventions are most appropriate. The family should be informed beforehand that such a meeting will take place, and their written consent should be sought if written documentation is exchanged between professionals. Although written informed consent is not strictly legally necessary in cases of suspected child maltreatment, asking the parents to give this consent is respectful of rights as parents. Parents almost always give such consent quite willingly once the need for interprofessional communication has been explained to them.

The final step in the assessment process is the interpretive session. Team members, together with the referring person, if possible, meet with the family once again and present their findings and recommendations. Although these interpretive sessions are often stressful for the staff as well as for the families, they represent the most ethical way to conclude the assessment process. The family has a right to hear the team's conclusions directly from team members rather than through a third party.

Interpretive sessions allow families to vent their anger, to cry, to ask questions, to challenge findings, or to agree with the team's conclusions and begin to move toward treatment. Although we worked with a violence-prone population, our team never had a violent incident occur as a result of an interpretive session. This strengthens the conviction that such direct feedback to families not only is ethically necessary, but also is likely to reduce violent reactions to painful feedback when the families can express their feelings to people who understand.

Characteristics of a Successful Child Protection Team

Mutual Respect and Support among Team Members

Team members must recognize the limits of their own competence and respect the areas of expertise of others on the team. If there is genuine respect for one another's competence, then asking for help, expressing puzzlement and confusion, laughing together, being angry together, and presenting work openly are natural consequences. In such an atmosphere, the expertise of the entire group is strengthened by the spontaneous teaching that takes place (5, pp. 276–77).

Respect for the expertise of other team members also facilitates open discussion of overlapping roles. Some teams, for example, may have members from several mental health disciplines. If the team has a psychologist, a psychiatrist, and a social worker, who should do what? The answer to this question should be negotiated between the team members. If the social worker has considerable experience in interviewing children and the psychologist and psychiatrist are adult oriented, then the social worker should have a primary role in assessing the children. If the psychiatrist is very good at conducting marital interviews, then these should be done by the psychiatrist. Furthermore, each team member should seek to learn some of the skills of the other members. As membership in the team changes with changing career demands, a particular colleague's expertise may not always be available. Roles will have to be renegotiated as new members join the team.

Acceptance of the Families

To speak of acceptance in the context of child abuse and neglect may seem strange, since the main function of the assessment team is to pass judgment on the family. Professionals working in child protection make a clear and explicit value judgment that the protection of children is more important than family privacy or the right to rear one's children according to one's own philosophy. How can judgment be reconciled with acceptance?

Distinguishing between feelings and actions is the key which allows team members to accept parents even though they may have treated their children in ways which provoke feelings of outrage, depression, or disgust. This is what abusive parents are asked to do in treatment: to learn to accept their feelings and to change their actions (6, pp. 94–96; 7, pp. 54–58). To ask this of them and not of ourselves would be hypocritical. Professionals must learn to accept the imperfect adult as a person who, although troubled, is a valuable human being with potential for change (8, pp. 65–69). This is possible even when the potential for change is slight. Polansky et al.'s concept of "damaged parents," human beings severely damaged by their own childhood experiences (1), is helpful in enabling professionals to accept parents who mistreat their children as valuable persons, in spite of strong negative feelings about their actions.

Flexibility

Families who are referred for assessment often lead chaotic lives. The family members scheduled for a given appointment may not appear, but others may appear in their place. For example, on a day when the father is scheduled to be interviewed, the mother may arrive with grandmother or a neighbor in tow. Rather than focusing on their irritation over the missing person, team members will find it more useful to consider any deviation from the agreed-upon plan as simply more data from which to draw conclusions. They should interview whoever comes and ask to see missing people at the next appointment. If certain key family members persistently miss appointments, they should be interviewed by phone or through the referring person. Whatever is learned as a result of these efforts to reach the person can be included in the report. All behavior has meaning and provides useful information in assessing families (9). If a family finds it too difficult to go to the team's usual meeting place, it can be useful to arrange a meeting at their home. As social workers have long known, seeing people in their home environment is especially revealing and will add greatly to the team's understanding of their everyday lives.

Psychological Assessment of the Children

While the pediatrician on the team assesses the child's physical development, the child psychologist may assess the child's social, emotional, cognitive, and language development. Child psychologists are familiar with a myriad of psychological tests from which to choose, based upon the child's age and the questions which the assessment is trying to answer. More importantly, their training makes them keen observers of children's behavior as well as sensitive interviewers of children. Their familiarity with the environmental conditions which promote or hinder optimal child development enables them to generate and test hypotheses during the course of the assessment about the circumstances of the child's life which are affecting the observed development and behavior. No two assessments are ever exactly alike. Each is geared to answer questions about the particular child and family being evaluated.

Together with other team members, psychologists obtain an overview of the reasons for the referral and participate in the introductory family interview. This enables them to formulate initial hypotheses about the problems the children may have that require further assessment. At the conclusion of the opening interview, the team may find it convenient to separate family members and carry out several parts of the assessment simultaneously. The clinical social worker, for example, may interview the parents about their marital and family history; the pediatrician or pediatric nurse may begin physical examinations of the children, while the psychologist meets with one or more of the children for observation and interviewing.

Assessing Developmental Level

Since both abuse and neglect are associated with deficits in development (10), all children who have suffered some form of maltreatment should have an assessment made of their development level. For infants and young children, the Denver Developmental Screening Test (DDST) is a useful tool for documenting the child's developmental level (11). This is a screening instrument, not a psychological test, and can be performed by the pediatrician or pediatric nurse. If results indicate that further assessment is needed, the psychologist can follow up with more detailed testing, such as the Bayley Scales of Infant Development (12), the McCarthy Scales of Children's Abilities (13), or the Stanford-Binet Intelligence Scale (14), depending on the child's age and whether the identified deficits are primarily in cognitive, language, and fine motor development, or whether gross motor development is also delayed. The DDST may also be used to document and supplement clinical observations of the child's behavior in a play setting. Deficits in language development are particularly characteristic of children from abusive and neglectful environments and should be carefully documented (15–18).

School-age children are often interviewed through the use of drawing materials. In the course of the interview the child is allowed to draw while being asked about school, family, and friends. The psychologist also asks for a sample of his or her writing. In addition to being a rich source of data regarding affective issues, the child's drawings and writing, combined with parental report and direct observation of the child's conversational level, allow the child psychologist to make an initial determination of the child's developmental level. A decision can then be made as to the need for a more formal assessment with testing. If there is a question about intelligence, a quickly administered screening test, such as the Peabody Picture Vocabulary Test (19), may be used with individuals ranging in age from three to eighteen to determine whether further testing is necessary.

As a part of the assessment of a school-age child, the school should be contacted because it is an important source of information about peer relationships and relationships to authority figures, as well as academic performance. An easily overlooked but quite helpful item of information from the school is the child's attendance record. Failure to send children to school on a consistent basis is a common feature of disorganized, neglectful families (20–22). Abuse is sometimes another reason for poor school attendance. Some families hold a child out of school following physical abuse which has left noticeable marks, because they know the school will question the cause of unusual bruises or burns.

Adolescents are usually quite comfortable telling the psychologist about their feelings toward their school and their performance in school. The school is also an important source of information about an adolescent's cognitive and social development. Since sexual abuse is perhaps the most common form of abuse suffered by adolescents, their social and emotional development is most likely to be impaired (23–27). In addition, they may show progressive school failure or truancy which may be based upon recent problems in motivation or concentration. School failure may also be the result of cumulative cognitive delays, particularly for those children who have suffered and still suffer from severe or ongoing neglect and abuse. A good interview is often a more powerful tool than a formal test for assessing an adolescent. Once teenagers feel safe, they usually find it a relief to talk with a sympathetic, skilled interviewer. When assessing teenagers who find it too difficult to talk directly with the interviewer, the Thematic Apperception Test (TAT) is useful for identifying major areas of concern in interpersonal relationships, affective themes, and positive and negative fantasies (28). Of special importance in the assessment of abuse is whether any interpersonal relationships are seen as positive and nonexploitative (adult meets the child's needs rather than vice versa), and whether the adolescent's stories show an understanding of effective strategies for solving interpersonal problems.

Issues Unique in the Assessment of Abused or Neglected Children

Every clinical child psychologist has been trained to assess children's development. As a member of a child protection team, however, the psychologist must know what to specifically look for in children who have been neglected or physically, sexually, or emotionally abused.

To be effective in this role, the child psychologist must become familiar with the professional literature on child maltreatment and must collaborate closely with colleagues from other disciplines. Close teamwork facilitates putting all the various pieces of the family assessment together to create a coherent picture, even though the assessment has been made by different individuals.

In every assessment the psychologist keeps in mind that any and all types of maltreatment may be present, even though the referral may only have indicated one type. If a child is neglected, for example, she may also be physically or sexually abused. The same principle applies to siblings. Although one child is sometimes singled out as the "family scapegoat" (29–31), if one child is mistreated usually all are mistreated in some way. This is especially true of neglectful families because the standard of living for the entire family is often quite low (1).

In the interview of a possibly maltreated child, answers to open-ended questions may give a general picture of the child's life and interests and may point toward other problem areas which need closer scrutiny. General questions also serve as a bridge to questions regarding the specific referral problem. Asking how a typical day is spent is a useful way to begin. With younger children, questions must be concrete: "Who puts you to bed?" "What did you eat for breakfast today?" These give important clues about the amount of supervision and care the child receives and the presence or absence of necessities for daily living. The child's answers, together with information from the parents, may indicate the nature and severity of neglect.

Children should be questioned about methods of discipline. Most physically abusive parents view their actions as physical discipline, a necessary part of proper child rearing (32). The psychologist should ask what the family's rules are which the children must obey and what chores they are expected to perform at home. This gives an idea of whether the household is chaotic (no rules, no routine) or whether expectations are unrealistic (e.g., a seven-year-old has complete charge of two younger siblings, including meal preparation, while her parents are away from home). A discussion of rules and routines leads naturally to the question of what happens when rules are broken or chores left undone. If the child does not mention physical punishment as a possible consequence, it should be asked about directly (e.g., "What about spanking?"). This can then be followed by an inquiry into the specifics of the method of spanking (what objects are used to hit the child, what body parts are hit, etc.). As the psychologist conveys an attitude of acceptance and understanding toward whatever the child says, most children are able to talk about abuse, even if they are initially reluctant because they fear the consequences of telling. It is important to understand the psychological importance to the child of even an abusive parent and to encourage the child to express positive feelings about the parent while owning negative feelings about the abuse (3, pp. 17–20).

Assessing Emotional Abuse

Neglect, family violence, and inappropriate sexual stimulation can all damage the child's emotional life. Assessment of the child's affective health is a very important part of the psychologist's task, but one which is more subtle than the assessment of development.

Attachment. A frequent finding is dysfunction in the quality of the parent-child attachment. There may be a failure of attachment on the part of the parent, commonly seen in cases of failure to thrive (see chap. 16), or there may be a distorted attachment in which the child symbolizes someone else to the parent (33, 34).

In assessing attachment from the child's point of view the following questions must be asked: To whom is this child attached? Is the child so needy that "instant attachments" are formed to any kind adult, such as the psychologist? Does the child view the parent as needing to be cared for by the child? Can the child identify both positive and negative aspects of his or her relationship to the parents? A child who has nothing negative to say about a parent is fearful of being truthful. Even very good parents are not perfect!

Questions about attachment are particularly salient when making recommendations for foster care or permanent termination of parental rights (3). Some children are firmly attached to a sibling, though unattached to a parent. Such children should not be separated from the sibling to whom they are attached. When a complete lack of attachment to parents is seen, it is usually in very young neglected children (age three and under) or in children who have spent very little time living with their parents, such as children who have spent most of their lives in foster homes or with relatives other than their parents. In rare instances, failure of attachment between a parent and an older child is so complete that the child flatly states, "I don't care if I never see her again." Problematic attachments are more common, and they offer some hope for the relationship. When some positive attachment exists, the family has a higher likelihood of success in treatment, as there is a foundation of caring to build upon. When parent-child relationships are characterized by complete lack of caring there is little hope that the family will ever be able to meet the child's needs. In such cases, swift and permanent termination of parental rights is in the child's best interests.

Both positive and negative emotions should be taken into consideration when assessing the child. Guilt, fear, anger, depression, and self-destructiveness are negative emotions commonly seen in maltreated children.

Guilt. Sexually abused children often feel guilty about having told the "family secret" of incest. Physically abused children often accept responsibility for their abuse. They have been taught that the abuse was their fault because of some childish misbehavior, or because of their failure to meet parental expectations, however unrealistic these may be. In children as young as four or five it is already possible to see the foundation being laid for the perpetuation of the cycle of abuse in the next generation: the automatic response of blaming the child for the abuse (35, see also chap. 4). Guilt in maltreated children may also serve as a defense against anxiety. Feeling responsible for the abuse at least gives the illusion of control in a rational environment. Guilt used as a defense against anxiety is commonly seen among rape victims and among persons with a catastrophic illness. Psychologically it seems to be more bearable to feel guilty than to face the terrifying reality that disaster is unpredictable and uncontrollable (36).

Fear. It is important to find out what the child is afraid of. Some children, for example, have been told by their parents that if they report the abuse, they will be taken away to a horrible foster home where they will be severely mistreated. Sexually abused children may have been threatened that telling will result in the father's suicide or the breakup of the family. Since many children have difficulty talking about this directly, the use of a few projective questions (e.g., What are some things that make you happy? What are some things that make you mad? What would you wish for if a fairy godmother gave you three wishes?) or items from an incomplete sentences test which are suitable for use with children (37) can help open the topic of negative emotions. These techniques are particularly useful with children six years of age or older. For children of school age, these items can be combined in a packet together with drawing tasks such as the House-Tree-Person (38), a drawing of the self (39), and a Kinetic Family Drawing (40). The child can work on these with a team member other than the psychologist or, if need be, alone. This enables the psychologist to accomplish more work during one visit, perhaps doing a play interview with dolls with a younger child while the older one works on the drawings and sentence completion test. The psychologist can then use these materials as the basis for a subsequent interview with the older child. Children generally enjoy working on such tasks and take pride in showing their work to the staff or to their parents.

Anger. This is generally considered to be a healthy response to abuse or neglect. However, anger may contain elements of identification with the aggressor if it is expressed by bullying younger children (35, 41). In adolescents anger often takes the form of antisocial behavior, such as the destruction of property. Therapeutically, it is perhaps the easiest negative emotion to work with in younger children, as the therapist can affirm the appropriateness of the angry feelings and then help the child to find acceptable channels for its expression. This process can begin during the assessment by helping the child to clarify what it is that makes him or her feel so angry and giving the child reassurance that the purpose of the assessment is to help the family so that these things will not happen again. In this context it is quite interesting to ask the children what they think should happen to "make things better in the family." Sometimes their responses are quite straightforward: "We shouldn't get hit for nothing." Or, "Dad should stop getting drunk."

Depression. The connections between abuse and depression are not fully understood, but it appears that depressed mothers are likely to be hostile to their children, and that abused children are often depressed (42, 43). One study of depressed children found that their parents were more likely to use corporal punishment and to hit them with objects than the parents of the control group of matched, nondepressed children (44). Other studies of depressed children describe the parents as hostile and rejecting in some cases, and as physically abusive in others (45–49). Among neglected children depression may be the outcome of the failure of primary attachment (34). Incest is frequently associated with depression in both mothers (as a causal factor) and daughters (as an outcome) (50). The evidence linking depression and maltreatment is increasingly compelling.

Assessing a child for depression is usually not difficult. A depressed child is withdrawn, has poor eye contact, flat or sad affect, and motor lethargy. Self-esteem is low, and somatic complaints without an identifiable medical cause are common (particularly abdominal pain, headache, and fatigue). Disturbances of eating and sleeping are not as common for a depressed child as they are for a depressed adult. The child often lacks friends and does more poorly in school than would be predicted by his or her intellectual capability (51). Among incest victims, a drop in school performance frequently corresponds to the onset of the incest. When these indicators are seen, it is important to evaluate the child for suicidal potential by asking directly whether the child has ever thought that life was just not worth living. An affirmative reply should be followed by questions to determine whether the child has ever considered acting upon this feeling, and if he or she has thought about how it might be done. The more detailed and realistic the child's plans are for suicide (in that the means described are actually available to the child), the higher the risk. Although suicide among young children continues to be rare, adolescent suicide has increased significantly in recent years, and it must be considered as a possibility in the depressed child and adolescent (52–54).

Child psychologists can sometimes obtain information from children which was only equivocally obtained by others. They may be asked to interview a child about a specific incident because of their understanding of the developmental aspects of the way the child tells the story of the abuse; for example, the child's sense of time, seeming irrelevancies that are quite relevant, and childish language in describing body parts. A psychologist may feel some conflict about doing this, knowing that repeated questioning about a specific incident may be traumatic for the child. However, if there is a special reason to go over ground already covered by the protective services worker or the police, the child's interests may ultimately be best served by the psychologist's assistance in conducting yet another interview. In such a case, the child should be told why the questions are necessary (e.g., to clarify a potentially important detail which the child told differently in two earlier accounts). If repeated clumsy interviewing or threats from adults have frightened the child, it may be impossible to successfully clarify the issue in one session. Repeated interviews may be needed before the child will trust the psychologist enough to reveal upsetting details about the abuse.

When the quality of the interview is likely to become a major issue in a case (e.g., when expert witness testimony from the psychologist may be needed), important aspects of the interview should be deferred until the psychologist has established rapport with the child and until a representative from the legal system can be present.

Psychological Assessment of the Parents

The findings resulting from the assessment of the parents is of singular importance in developing treatment recommendations. It is their ability to change, after all, that will be the key in protecting the children. Since the most straightforward cases are usually handled by protective services workers without referral to a multidisciplinary team, assessment of parents who are referred is likely to be difficult. It is therefore quite useful to involve team members from all disciplines in interviewing parents on different occasions, in different combinations. This accomplishes several objectives. First, close teamwork makes "splitting" the team unlikely. Families do not have much success in claiming that they have been given different messages by different professionals when the professionals are present at the same time. Second, conducting interviews jointly helps team members sharpen their skills of observation and judgment as team members can make comparisons of what they heard in the interview. Third, involving several team members in the interviews facilitates the development of a consensus about treatment recommendations.

The question of who conducts an interview is based on the professional's areas of expertise. The clinical social worker can conduct a marital interview with both parents during the first visit. During subsequent visits the pediatrician or pediatric nurse can obtain the adults' and childrens' health histories from the parents. This interview may be done jointly with the psychologist, psychiatrist, or social worker who then can obtain the personal history of each adult from birth to the time of the interview. Two interviewers then have the opportunity to observe each adult during an interview, with one conducting the interview and the other taking notes.

The child psychologist's goals in assessing the parents are: 1) To deal with here-and-now questions regarding the assessment, such as: How do the parents construe the process? What are their feelings and fantasies? 2) To obtain a detailed history of the adults' own childhood and family of origin. This enables the identification of areas of strength and vulnerability brought to the parenting role. 3) To obtain a history of the parents' adult development and life course with a focus on issues of problem solving and impulse control. 4) To determine the adults' view of their children and their relationship to them in terms of both nurturance and socialization. 5) To confirm or rule out disorders in the adults associated with extremely poor prognoses for adequate parenting. This last is, of course, based upon findings obtained throughout the assessment process. These five functions are discussed in more detail below.

That the child psychologist should be so involved in the assessment of adults may come as a surprise to some. However, assessment of adults in their role as parents is a standard function of child psychologists for which they have been thoroughly trained. Of course, in those cases in which the level of psychopathology of the parents outstrips the understanding and expertise of the child psychologist, an adult-oriented psychologist or psychiatrist should be used as a consultant to the team.

Reaction to assessment. The parents' reactions to the assessment process may be used to assess their functioning under stress and their ways of interacting with authority figures. Such responses are often the first indication that one is dealing with a borderline parent, so frequently encountered in abusive and neglectful families (55). How do they handle anger? Do they project blame onto others ("that bitch who reported me")? Or are they able to acknowledge their role in the abuse or neglect once their anger has been heard and accepted? Can they be realistic about what is likely to happen, or do they see either themselves or others as omnipotent? Do they have any friends or relatives whom they can use as support persons? One mother brought her pregnant fourteen-year-old cousin with her as the only significant support person who could be with her during a stressful interpretive interview. This spoke eloquently of the lack of caring people in her life who were available to help her with parenting.

Childhood history. Everyone who works in the area of child maltreatment knows the importance of obtaining the adult's own childhood history of abuse or neglect (see chaps. 17, 18). The work of Fraiberg and her colleagues suggests that the feelings the adults express when recalling mistreatment in childhood is equally important (34). Can they identify with that child-self who was hurt, or are those emotions completely split off, preventing them from empathizing with their own children? Was any adult in a positive relationship with them in their own childhood? If so, the chance of forming a positive transferential relationship to a therapist is much greater, a hopeful sign that the adult may be able to benefit from psychotherapy. A history of violence in the family of origin is significant, even though it may not have been directed at the individual being interviewed. Witnessing abuse of other family members seems to be as damaging to future parenting as having been the target of abuse (56).

In recent years professionals working in the field of abuse have become more sophisticated in routinely asking about sexual exploitation in the childhoods of all maltreating adults. As with physical abuse, the possibility of sexual abuse of siblings in the adult's childhood should be inquired about, as well as how the adult's parents handled their own sexuality in the family. Confining questions to whether the adult male offender was molested as a child often misses a history of precocious exposure to inappropriate sexuality in his childhood. We also need to find out if his father molested his sisters, if his grandfather molested his mother, or if either parent exposed him inappropriately to their sexual activities by having multiple lovers in the house or by having sex in front of the children. Asking adults about their sex education in childhood is a relatively nonthreatening way to begin this line of questioning.

Obtaining a history of neglect is more difficult than obtaining a history of abuse. As Polansky and his colleagues have pointed out, it is rare for an adult to cite this fact outright, both because people lack standards with which to compare their own childhoods and because of psychological defenses against remembering, for "who could bear to know he was being neglected?" (1, p. 7).

On the other hand, clues to neglect abound as the history unfolds. Tales of extreme poverty coupled with parental indifference are typical of the neglected. A history of juvenile delinquency either of the person being interviewed or of siblings is not uncommon. Some adults neglected in childhood experienced frequent or prolonged separations from their families as they were moved to relatives or removed by authorities to foster care in the days when foster parents were discouraged from forming attachments to their foster children. Parents with histories of multiple foster placements have good reason to have strong feelings about keeping their families together. The prognosis for change is more hopeful if the basis for these feelings is concern for the welfare of the child rather than the parent's need for the child as a "bulwark against loneliness" (1, p. 35).

Impulse control. Problems with impulse control in the adults are especially important in determining whether the children are safe in the home. Since maintaining the continuity of the parent-child relationship while the family is being helped is better for the child's emotional development if the child ultimately remains in the family, removal to foster care should not be recommended unless the child is judged to be unsafe in the home (2). Parents who have a history of impulsive behavior provide an environment for the child which is riskier than parents who have other problems. The impulsive parent, for example, may suddenly decide to leave the state or may seriously abuse the child in an outburst of rage. Less impulsive parents present less risk because they are more likely to use crisis intervention services while they are making gradual changes through treatment.

Impulsive behavior should be assessed in all areas of functioning, such as economic and sexual behaviors, and not confined to violent impulsive behavior. Questions about arrests for drunk driving and disciplinary offenses while in the military are especially revealing when interviewing men. Alcohol problems among impulsive adults are so common that alcohol and other substance abuse should be asked about routinely in these interviews. The association between alcohol and family violence is a strong one (57, pp. 111–18). As with other lines of questioning, the psychologist must recognize that refraining from showing disapproval is extremely important when asking about substance abuse if an accurate history is to be obtained. Questions must be framed so that people can admit their substance abuse without fear of reprisal. Subtle cues to drunken behavior must be followed up with appropriate questions. The professional's ability to get in touch with the sociopathic part of his or her own personality (58) enables her to grin as the parent brags about some antisocial escapade, and say, "I bet you were really drunk when you did that!"

Problem solving. Poor judgment in solving problems is commonly found among maltreating parents. In assessing this aspect of functioning such questions as how the adult conceptualizes problems, what solutions are considered, and how quickly decisions are translated into actions should be addressed. Does poor judgment stem from intellectual limitations (mental retardation), simple lack of knowledge, or problems in the social-emotional area of functioning? If the last of these is the case, is the difficulty due to neurotic, characterological, or psychotic processes? Each of these requires a different approach in intervention and each is associated with a different prognosis.

Relationship with children. The parents' view of their children and their relationship to them should be assessed both by history and by direct observation. For conceptual purposes, essential parenting functions can be thought of under one of two headings: nurturance and socialization. Nurturance includes physical caretaking, such as providing food, shelter, and protection from harm; emotional nurturance, such as providing appropriate physical closeness, eye contact, and expressions of pleasure in and approval of the child as a person; and nurturance of the child's intellectual development, such as talking to the child, encouraging the child's verbalizations, providing interesting sensory experiences, and allowing exploration of the environment in all sensory modalities while setting safe boundaries. In normal parenting these nurturing functions take place simultaneously, as when a mother participates in playful mutual babbling with her infant while giving him a bath.

In socialization, parents act as the agents of the larger society in taking primary responsibility for rearing children who will be able to meet cultural expectations for age-appropriate behavior. For younger children this primarily means self-care skills such as learning to feed themselves and to control their excretory habits. As children grow older, society demands more in the way of impulse control, such as not interrupting when others are talking, and expressing feelings in words rather than acting them out in tantrums. Eventually, parents are expected to convey to their children abstract values and attitudes which will govern their behavior in ways which promote the larger social good, such as altruism and respect for the feelings of others.

In normal development, attachments between parents and children formed and intensified in the context of nurturance provide the basis for socialization. This occurs first through modeling (children with positive attachments want to be like their parents), then through positive social reinforcement (children value their parents' approval, making it a powerful reinforcer), and, finally, through direct teaching (children gradually learn, through explanations, the basis of their parents' values, attitudes, and beliefs). From the parents' point of view, attachment to their children leads them to carry out this socialization function in the context of continued nurturance.

Maltreating parents neither nurture nor socialize their children sufficiently. As a result, severely neglected children often have a feral quality to their behavior. Neglectful parents are frequently oblivious to what the child's needs might be because of their own intellectual deficits or their preoccupation with self because of severe psychopathology. A schizophrenic mother of a young infant with deprivation failure to thrive, for example, explained that she did not feed him often because, "When I'm awake, he's asleep, and when he wakes up, I'm asleep." Asked if she did not hear the baby cry, she replied that she did, but since it was when she was sleeping, she saw no reason to get up. Of her son she said, "I guess we're just on different schedules."

Other neglectful parents may recognize some of their children's needs but simply be unable to meet them consistently because of overwhelming situational problems for which they lack the personal and social resources to cope. Chaotic families are frequently neglecting families. "Impermanence and unpredictability" (59, p. 193) is the phrase Minuchin and his colleagues used to describe such family environments. Although they studied the families of delinquents, most of the families in their study could also be classified as maltreating. Although the children's needs are sometimes met in such chaotic families, parental response is so inconsistent that the children cannot develop the cognitive, affective, and social skills necessary for competent functioning, thus perpetuating the cycle of neglect into the next generation.

When parental inability to function is not a major part of the picture, intervention in terms of increased resources—day care, nutritional supplementation, parent aide programs—is more likely to be of significant benefit to the children. In any case, such interventions must be tried in an attempt to improve the children's quality of life. Polansky et al. refer to such interventions as "parental prostheses" (1, pp. 221–37), a term which acknowledges that, while such interventions do not represent a "cure" for neglect, they may provide significant support.

Physically abusive parents are often quite neglectful of their children's emotional needs and, obviously, fail to provide adequately for their safety. In the area of socialization, the typical abusive parent may be overzealous, bent on socializing the child to expectations that society demands only of older children and oblivious of the high emotional and developmental costs of the methods employed. Both the goals and the means of socialization used are often inappropriate to the child's age. One mother of a four-year-old, for example, was observed giving her daughter a coin to put into the parking meter. She gave the child no instructions on using the elevator, finding the car, or properly working the meter, saying, instead, "Put this in the parking meter, and if I get a ticket it will be your fault, and you'll have to pay for it out of your own money!"

Abusive parents often misinterpret the meaning of their children's behavior, ascribing intention that is patently ridiculous. A three-month-old was brought to the pediatrician for a "well-baby visit." When his diaper was removed, his mother commented, "Look at how he wiggles his ass at the nurse. He's just like his father."

Sexually abusive parents typically distort their appropriate nurturant function, using physical closeness with the child to meet the adult's needs. The socialization function is also distorted, as incest violates a universal human taboo. Some parents involved in incest, like physically abusive parents, justify their actions as socialization. "I wanted her first sexual experience to be a good one. It was just sex education."

When sexual abuse has been intertwined with nurturance, the child will be quite confused about the difference between nurturance and sexuality. Furthermore, in some families the sexualized relationship will have been the child's only significant experience of emotional warmth. Replacing such experiences with healthy loving relationships in the family must be carefully considered in the treatment of the incestuous family. Simply removing the offender does not solve this problem.

Using the above framework for assessing parenting will enable each major area of parenting to be evaluated separately. When deficits are identified in specific areas of parenting, interventions suited to the deficits can be recommended. A useful way to begin this portion of the assessment is to obtain a history of the parents' attachment to each child (e.g., how the pregnancies came about, how they were viewed, whether the baby met parental expectations, etc.). The health history of each child is especially important in relation to the question of attachment. Some children may be protected from abuse because of their status as a "vulnerable child" (60). Other children are put at increased risk of abuse or failure to thrive because they are viewed as defective or difficult to care for (61, 62).

Parental values and beliefs regarding children's needs, behavior expectations, and appropriate disciplinary techniques should be elicited. This aspect of the history is usually quite easy to obtain. With the exception of some well-educated parents who are more sophisticated in their views of how they are likely to be judged, few parents try to conceal attitudes, values, and beliefs regarding their children which professionals would regard as quite damaging. This is consistent with Caldwell and Bradley's finding that, in general, "most mothers believe that what they do with and to their children is for the children's own good, and they often report with pride actions that you might expect them to try and conceal" (63, p. 90).

A formal test of attitudes toward parenting can be used to shorten interview time or for ease of documentation of attitudes (64–66). The parent's responses can then be followed up in the interview. Endorsement of extreme responses is particularly revealing. Such instruments must be used with the caution that authoritarian or neglectful attitudes do not, by themselves, constitute evidence of abuse or neglect. Unfortunately, unselected groups such as high school and college students and normal mothers have been shown to be deficient in parenting knowledge and surprisingly harsh in their endorsements of punishments (67–69).

In assessing incestuous families, the strength of the mother's emotional tie to her children versus her tie to her husband is of crucial importance in deciding whether it is safe to recommend allowing the child(ren) to remain in the home, while asking the abusing father to voluntarily move out for a period of time. If the mother's bond to the children is insufficiently strong, she cannot be counted on to protect her children by enforcing the exclusion of her husband from the household. When the team cannot be sure that his access to the children will be denied, temporary foster care for the children is the only safe alternative, though, sadly, this option is usually experienced by the children as a rejection and punishment for disclosure of the incest.

Possible Mental Disorders. By the time all of the above information is gathered by the team in its assessment of the parents, the psychologist will have a reasonably clear picture of the adult's functioning, especially with regard to the parenting role. Though the interviews need not follow the format of a standard psychiatric interview, the information gathered from them can be used to determine the presence of one of the five conditions associated with extremely poor prognosis for improved parenting: 1) antisocial personality disorder (formerly called sociopathic personality); 2) multiple personality; 3) uncontrolled psychosis; 4) mental retardation; and 5) religious fanaticism. When the presence of any of these disorders is suspected, the involvement of the adult-oriented psychologist or psychiatrist is particularly useful in making or confirming the diagnosis and indicating the prognosis.

Antisocial personality disorder is generally acknowledged to be virtually untreatable. Individuals with this disorder often spend significant portions of their lives in penal institutions (70).

For the other four conditions listed, the judgment that the prognosis for improved parenting is poor is made from the point of view of the child's sense of time (2). A mother with multiple personality, for example, is not untreatable, but all the best evidence we have indicates that successful treatment takes several years during which her functioning will be so unpredictable as to render her unable to parent adequately (71–73). Since the disorder is rather rare, many professionals have never seen a case, making it more likely that the diagnosis will be missed when it is present (74). The more dramatic presentations in which the individual "changes" before the eyes of the interviewer and insists that she is someone else, though infrequently seen, are so startling that under such circumstances the disorder is easily identified (75). A more subtle clue is a history of blackouts, time periods during which the individual can remember nothing, although others report that she continued to function. Sometimes these blank periods last as long as several years. Accompanying these spells of amnesia are experiences of waking up following a blackout, often in a strange situation, without the patient having any knowledge of how she came to be there. These experiences must be differentiated from blackouts due to alcohol or drug use. Suicide attempts, psychiatric hospitalizations, temporal lobe seizures, and conversion symptoms are common in the histories of individuals with multiple personality, as are early childhood experiences of sexual and physical abuse of unusual brutality. Almost all patients with the disorder are female (26, 76–82).

As noted in chapter 17, the psychotic adult is a poor risk as a parent if the psychotic process has continued over time. Although a history of a single psychotic episode, such as a postpartum psychosis, is not necessarily an indication that the individual will be unable to function as a parent, a history of repeated psychiatric hospitalizations and noncompliance with outpatient treatment is indicative of a poor prognosis for parenting. Schizophrenic, abusive parents pass on a legacy of double vulnerability to their children; genetic risk compounded by environmental insult (83).

In developing recommendations for families with parents who are severely psychiatrically impaired or mentally retarded, an important consideration is whether other adults are present in the household who can provide care and nurturance for the children and, if necessary, protect them from inappropriate actions of the impaired parent. Clinical experience suggests that some families with a severely impaired parent can care for their children at least marginally well without coming to the attention of protective services unless the higher functioning parent dies or otherwise leaves the inadequately functioning parent in sole charge of the children (84).

Religious fanaticism has received little attention in the child abuse literature, probably because of its relative rarity. When it is a factor in child maltreatment, however, it presents special problems because the basis for the maltreatment is defended as part of an elaborate belief system which usually has the support of a religious cult community. Even if the parents who are members of such groups might otherwise be open to change, group support for inappropriate actions toward the children effectively blocks outside attempts to help. Members of the larger community are defined as the outgroup, whose beliefs the "true believer" must resist if group membership is to be retained (85–87). Courts are often more reluctant to interfere with parental rights when parenting behavior is based on beliefs which are defended as religious, even when such behavior is otherwise unacceptable by community standards.

Psychological Assessment of Family Interaction

Even when the children and parents have been separately assessed, the team's assessment is not complete until the interaction *between* family members has been thoroughly evaluated. This is a particularly fruitful procedure with families who have been defensive in the interviews, but it is helpful in understanding all families. When compared with other families from the same social class, abusive and neglectful families have patterns of interaction in which there are fewer interactions between family members, and in which the interactions with the children tend to be negative (88).

Interaction between adults in the family can be observed initially during the joint interview of marital partners (or equivalent adults in the home). Access to a playroom is especially useful for observing the interactions between sibling groups of young children. With older children, siblings can be interviewed jointly without their parents present. Finally, the whole family should be observed in interaction.

In observations of siblings in the play setting, the strength of the children's bonds to each other should be noted, especially if there is a question as to whether the children should be placed together in foster care. Also important are whether the oldest child is punitive in responding to the younger children, perhaps modeling a long-standing pattern of parental caretaking behavior, and whether the children display age-appropriate social behavior in the interaction.

When parents and children are observed together, parents of young children should be asked to play with them. The child psychologist can then observe a sample of how the parents behave when they are on their "best behavior." Are the parents able to play with their children at all, or do they spend their time talking to other adults, or sitting numbly in a corner? Do the children approach their parents? If so, how do the parents respond? Do play activities in which parents and children engage together meet the adults' needs or the needs of the children? Can parents set appropriate limits, or are they overly harsh and restrictive, or, alternatively, completely laissez-faire? Do parents engage in any language stimulation or other simple "teaching" with their young children?

These observations are often the most powerful evidence of deficits in family interaction. It is heartrending to see a two-year-old, his broken leg in a cast, begin to cry because he has tripped and fallen down in play, only to hear his teenage mother react with, "Don't be a damn crybaby; I hate wimps!"

Observations of interaction in the family's own home are an even richer source of data for understanding the family.

The Use of Psychodiagnostic Tests

Psychodiagnostic tests are among the tools of the psychologist. Like the laboratory tests which physicians order, they must be used with understanding in connection with other clinical findings in order to be of value. Like the first year resident, the psychologist new to child maltreatment work will probably find it helpful to use several psychological tests in the assessment. With increasing experience, clinical judgment is sharpened, and psychologists will find that they need to use fewer psychodiagnostic tests, targeting them to specific purposes. Tests frequently used in the assessment of children have been mentioned in the section on child assessment.

When the nature of the adult's difficulty in adequately performing parenting functions is not clear after interviewing, psychodiagnostic testing may be needed to establish the diagnosis. Mental retardation, for example, is easily diagnosed through the administration of the Wechsler Adult Intelligence Scale—Revised (89). The Minnesota Multiphasic Personality Inventory (90) and the Thematic Apperception Test (28) are useful in identifying personality characteristics of adults. These tests are usually administered and interpreted by adult-oriented psychologists and can be extremely helpful in understanding the parent's personality in a relatively short period of time.

A note of caution is in order regarding the use of psychological test results as evidence when testifying in court. When a professional is qualified as an expert witness in court, he or she testifies on the basis of that expertise and knowledge of the case; the testimony does not rest on any one tool used in a particular assessment. Psychodiagnostic tests are tools, but they should never be the sole basis for assessing a family. Courts are not sophisticated in understanding psychodiagnostic tests, nor should they be expected to be. In view of this, testifying about concrete, readily observable aspects of parenting is far more useful than trying to turn the courtroom into a classroom by explaining recommendations in terms of psychological test findings.

For example: A mother had a measured full-scale IQ of 58. In court, the psychologist testified that the mother could not answer the simplest questions about how to feed her baby, had been unable to prevent other adults from stealing her benefit checks, and did not know how to ask for help when she became lost in the clinic building. This kind of testimony was completely understandable to judge and jury. Giving the IQ score might have resulted in becoming embroiled in a dispute with the defense attorney regarding the validity of intelligence testing.

The use of direct quotes is also effective in court. Rather than giving MMPI findings about an impulse-ridden father whose aggression is poorly controlled, a direct quote, such as, "If that sonofabitch judge tries to take my kid away, I'll come at him with a shotgun!" makes the point quite clearly.

When the Psychologist Works Alone

The model presented in this chapter is the child protection team model of outpatient assessment. However, not every psychologist who is asked to see maltreated children is a member of such a team. Under those circumstances, what should the psychologist do? First, if there is a well-functioning child protection team in the community, the referral should be sent on to them. Cases of maltreatment are so difficult to assess alone, that the team model is much preferred. If, as in most communities, no team exists, an ad hoc working team should be formed.

A children's protective services worker should be involved in every case of child maltreatment to provide social work skills. If the case has not yet been reported to the department of social services at the time the psychologist receives the referral, the psychologist should ask the referring person to make the report. If for some reason the psychologist's referral source does not do this, the psychologist must explain to the family the need to report the case, so that social work services, investigation, and case coordination can be provided by children's protective services. It is ethically necessary to explain this to every family before a report is made.

The child's family physician or pediatrician is a natural source of medical expertise for the ad hoc team. If the family has no identified physician, the protective services worker can arrange for the medical evaluation. The public health nurse would be a valuable team member if the family has been receiving public health services.

The final member of the ad hoc team should be a representative of the educational system, if this is appropriate in the circumstances. This may be a school teacher, principal, or counselor, or a representative from the Headstart or day care program attended by a younger child. If the children exhibit signs of developmental delay, physical handicap, learning disability, or emotional disturbance, they may qualify for free special educational services from birth on. In such cases, the school system should become involved once the problem has been identified, even though the child is not yet of school age.

Other disciplines can be added to the ad hoc team as needed. Although an ad hoc team is not usually able to provide the kind of emotional support for its members that an ongoing team furnishes, it can supply the needed professional expertise across disciplines that is typically needed to make a full assessment of the maltreating family. Forming an ad hoc team represents a lot of extra work in telephone calls and meetings, but it is a good opportunity to meet and learn from other professionals in the community while giving high quality service to the family.

Working with Trainees

No discussion of the role of child psychologists would be complete without some attention to providing training to students, the next generation of professionals. Along with clinical service and research, training is one of the three traditional functions of the clinical psychologist.

Depending upon the professions represented by the child protection team members, a team may have as trainees: pediatric residents, psychiatry residents, medical students, psychology interns, nursing students, and social work students. In general, trainees find child maltreatment work both fascinating and upsetting. In working with trainees sufficient time must be set aside for "debriefing" them after each of their first few clinic experiences. Since trainees in the mental health professions are usually allotted plenty of supervision time, debriefing is particularly important for medical students and pediatric residents who tend to be very tightly scheduled. Working with abusive, neglectful, and incestuous families calls forth many powerful feelings which professionals hardened to the work have learned to cope with in one way or another. The psychologist on the assessment team can be especially helpful in making the group meetings a place where the upset feelings of the trainee, together with those of the regular team members, can be recognized, discussed, understood, and accepted. If this can occur, the training experience will be far more valuable to trainees, perhaps enabling them to be more sensitive and empathic in their future interactions with abusive families. Modeling the use of the multidisciplinary team as a supportive environment for handling work-related stress can be one of the most important educational experiences offered to trainees.

The multidisciplinary team also gives trainees the opportunity to see professionals from other disciplines in the process of clinical work. Seeing other professionals in action enhances the trainees' understanding of what other professionals do and deepens their respect for their expertise. Training in a multidisciplinary setting provides many chances to discuss areas of common interest, to clarify misconceptions, and to ask questions about work in related fields. Professionals so trained are more likely to make appropriate referrals and to work cooperatively across disciplines once they are in practice.

A final consideration is the trainees' role in court testimony. Whenever possible, trainees involved in the assessment of abusive families should be protected from having to give testimony in court. A certain percentage of the families seen for assessment will end up involved in court actions for which testimony from the team will be required, but which families will be so involved is not always predictable. If observations made by trainees are always corroborated by permanent members of the team, the team members can provide all needed court testimony. There may be times when this is not possible. If a trainee is the only person able to testify to certain facts, the testimony should be limited to those specific findings with no opinions being given. It is important to make every effort to avoid putting trainees in the position of giving court testimony because: 1) trainees finish their training and leave, making it difficult to subpoena them; and 2) by definition, trainees are not experts. Families are entitled to have experts make the important recommendations that will permanently affect their lives.

Research

As a clinician, the child psychologist makes recommendations on the basis of the best available evidence. As a scientist, the psychologist keeps an open mind which questions everything. A very important role for the child psychologist in family assessment, then, is to develop and carry out research regarding questions which will, when answered, enable us to give better help to families in trouble and to more effectively prevent child abuse and neglect.

References

1. Polansky, N. A.; Chalmers, M. A.; Buttenwieser, E. W.; and Williams, D. P. 1981. *Damaged Parents: An Anatomy of Child Neglect.* Chicago: University of Chicago Press.
2. Scheurer, S. L., and Bailey, M. M. 1980. Guidelines for Placing a Child in Foster Care. In *The Battered Child,* 3d ed., ed. C. H. Kempe and R. E. Helfer, 297–305. Chicago: University of Chicago Press.
3. Goldstein, J.; Freud, A.; and Solnit, A. J. 1973. *Beyond the Best Interests of the Child.* New York: Macmillan.
4. American Psychological Association. 1981. Ethical Principles of Psychologists. *Am. Psychologist* 36:633–38.
5. Rogers, C. R. 1961. *On Becoming a Person.* Boston: Houghton Mifflin.
6. Ginott, H. G. 1965. *Between Parent and Child.* New York: Macmillan.
7. Helfer, R. E. 1978. *Childhood Comes First: A Crash Course in Childhood for Adults.* East Lansing, Mich.: Helfer Publications.
8. Ellis, A. 1967. *Reason and Emotion in Psychotherapy.* New York: Lyle Stuart.
9. Freud, S. 1951. *Psychopathology of Everyday Life.* New York: New American Library.
10. Martin, H. P. 1980. The Consequences of Being Abused and Neglected: How the Child Fares. In *The Battered Child,* 3d ed., ed. C. H. Kempe and R. E. Helfer, 347–65. Chicago: University of Chicago Press.
11. Frankenburg, W. K.; Dodds, J. B.; Fandal, A. W.; Kazuk, E.; and Cohrs, M. 1975. *Denver Developmental Screening Test: Reference Manual.* Denver: University of Colorado Medical Center.
12. Bayley, N. 1969. *Bayley Scales of Infant Development.* New York: The Psychological Corporation.
13. McCarthy, D. 1972. *McCarthy Scales of Children's Abilities.* New York: The Psychological Corporation.
14. Terman, L. M., and Merrill, M. A. 1972. *Stanford-Binet Intelligence Scale.* Boston: Houghton Mifflin.
15. Blager, F., and Martin, H. P. 1976. Speech and Language of Abused Children. In *The Abused Child: A Multidisciplinary Approach to Developmental Issues and Treatment,* ed. H. P. Martin, 83–92. Cambridge, Mass.: Ballinger.
16. Elmer, E. 1967. *Children in Jeopardy.* Pittsburgh: University of Pittsburgh Press.

17. Kent, J. T. 1976. A Follow-up Study of Abused Children. *J. Pediatric Psychology* 1:25–31.

18. Oates, R. K.; Peacock, A.; and Forrest, D. 1985. Long-Term Effects of Nonorganic Failure to Thrive. *Pediatrics* 75:39–40.

19. Dunn, L. M., and Dunn, L. M. 1981. *Peabody Picture Vocabulary Test—Revised.* Circle Pines, Minn.: American Guidance Service.

20. Farrington, D. 1980. Truancy, Delinquency, the Home, and the School. In *Out of School,* ed. L. Hersov and I. Berg, 49–63. New York: Wiley.

21. Galloway, D. 1982. A Study of Persistent Absentees and Their Families. *British J. Educational Psychology* 52:317–30.

22. Weitzman, M.; Klerman, L. V.; Lamb, G.; Menary, J.; and Alpert, J. J. 1982. School Absence: A Problem for the Pediatrician. *Pediatrics* 69:739–46.

23. deYoung, M. 1982. Self-Injurious Behavior in Incest Victims: A Research Note. *Child Welfare* 61:577–84.

24. James, J., and Meyerding, J. 1977. Early Sexual Experience and Prostitution. *Am. J. Psychiatry* 134:1381–85.

25. Rosenfeld, A. A. 1979. Incidence of a History of Incest among 18 Female Psychiatric Patients. *Am. J. Psychiatry* 136:791–95.

26. Saltman, V., and Solomon, R. S. 1982. Incest and the Multiple Personality. *Psychological Reports* 50:1127–41.

27. Silbert, M. H., and Pines, A. M. 1981. Sexual Child Abuse As an Antecedent to Prostitution. *Child Abuse and Neglect: International J.* 5:407–11.

28. Murray, H. A. 1937. Techniques for a Systematic Investigation of Fantasy. *J. Psychology* 3:115–43.

29. Bell, N., and Vogel, E. 1968. The Emotionally Disturbed Child as the Family Scapegoat. In *A Modern Introduction to the Family,* ed. N. Bell and E. Vogel, 382–97. New York: Free Press.

30. Friedrich, W. N., and Boriskin, J. A. 1976. The Role of the Child in Abuse: A Review of the Literature. *Am. J. Orthopsychiatry* 46:580–90.

31. Glaser, D., and Bentovim, A. 1979. Abuse and Risk to Handicapped and Chronically Ill Children. *Child Abuse and Neglect: International J.* 3:565–75.

32. Williams, G. J. 1980. Social Sanctions for Child Abuse and Neglect: Editor's Introduction. In *Traumatic Abuse and Neglect of Children at Home,* ed. G. J. Williams and J. Money, 9–13. Baltimore: Johns Hopkins University Press.

33. Cain, A. C., and Cain, B. S. 1964. On Replacing a Child. *J. Am. Acad. Child Psychiatry* 3:443–56.

34. Fraiberg, S.; Adelson, E.; and Shapiro, V. 1975. Ghosts in the Nursery. *J. Am. Acad. Child Psychiatry* 14:387–421.

35. Green, A. H. 1978. Psychopathology of Abused Children. *J. Am. Acad. Child Psychiatry* 17:92–103.

36. Gardner, R. A. 1970. The Use of Guilt As a Defense against Anxiety. *Psychoanalytic Review* 57:124–36.

37. Rohde, A. R. 1957. *The Sentence Completion Method.* New York: Ronald Press.

38. Buck, J. N. 1948. The H-T-P Technique, a Qualitative and Quantitative Scoring Method. *J. Clinical Psychology Monograph,* no. 5, pp. 1–120.

39. DiLeo, J. H. 1973. *Children's Drawings as Diagnostic Aids.* New York: Brunner/Mazel.
40. Burns, R. C., and Kaufman, S. H. 1970. *Kinetic Family Drawings (K-F-D): An Introduction to Understanding Children through Kinetic Drawings.* New York: Brunner/Mazel.
41. Reidy, T. 1977. The Aggressive Characteristics of Abused and Neglected Children. *J. Clinical Psychology* 33:1140–45.
42. Kinard, E. M. 1980. Emotional Development in Physically Abused Children. *Am. J. Orthopsychiatry* 50:686–96.
43. Kinard, E. M. 1982. Child Abuse and Depression: Cause or Consequence? *Child Welfare* 61:403–13.
44. Seagull, E. A. W., and Weinshank, A. B. 1984. Childhood Depression in a Selected Group of Low-Achieving Seventh-Graders. *J. Clinical Child Psychology* 13:134–40.
45. Petti, T. A.; Bornstein, M.; Delamater, A.; and Conners, C. K. 1980. Evaluation and Multimodality Treatment of a Depressed Prepubertal Girl. *J. Am. Acad. Child Psychiatry* 19:690–702.
46. Philips, I. 1979. Childhood Depression: Interpersonal Interactions and Depressive Phenomena. *Am. J. Psychiatry* 136:511–16.
47. Poznanski, E. O.; Krahenbuhl, V.; and Zrull, J. P. 1976. Childhood Depression: A Longitudinal Perspective. *J. Am. Acad. Child Psychiatry* 15:491–501.
48. Poznanski, E., and Zrull, J. P. 1970. Childhood Depression: Clinical Characteristics of Overtly Depressed Children. *Archives of General Psychiatry* 23:8–15.
49. Puig-Antich, J.; Blau, S.; Marx, N.; Greenhill, L. L.; and Chambers, W. 1978. Prepubertal Major Depressive Disorder: A Pilot Study. *J. Am. Acad. Child Psychiatry* 17:695–707.
50. Justice, B., and Justice, R. 1979. *The Broken Taboo: Sex in the Family.* New York: Human Sciences Press.
51. Poznanski, E. O. 1982. The Clinical Phenomenology of Childhood Depression. *Am. J. Orthopsychiatry* 52:308–13.
52. Green, A. 1978. Self-Destructive Behavior in Battered Children. *J. Am. Acad. Child Psychiatry* 17:92–103.
53. Massachusetts Medical Society. 1983. Violent Deaths among Persons 15–24 Years of Age—United States, 1970–1978. *Morbidity and Mortality Weekly Report* 32 (Sept. 9): 453–57.
54. Rosenn, D. W. 1982. Suicidal Behavior in Children and Adolescents. In *Lifelines,* ed. E. L. Bassuk, S. C. Schoonover, and A. D. Gill, 195–221. New York: Plenum Press.
55. Prodgers, A. 1984. Psychopathology of the Physically Abusing Parent: A Comparison with the Borderline Syndrome. *Child Abuse and Neglect: International J.* 89:411–24.
56. Strauss, M. A.; Gelles, R. J.; and Steinmetz, S. K. 1980. *Behind Closed Doors: Violence in the American Family.* Garden City, N.Y.: Anchor Books.
57. Gelles, R. J. 1972. *The Violent Home.* Beverly Hills, Cal.: Sage Publications.
58. Greenwald, H. 1967. Treatment of the Psychopath. In *Active Psychotherapy,* ed. H. Greenwald, 363–77. New York: Atherton Press.

59. Minuchin, S.; Montalvo, B.; Guerney, B. G., Jr.; Rosman, B. L.; and Schumer, F. 1967. *Families of the Slums*. New York: Basic Books.

60. Green, M., and Solnit, A. J. 1964. Reactions to the Threatened Loss of a Child: A Vulnerable Child Syndrome. *Pediatrics* 34:58–66.

61. Lynch, M. 1975. Ill Health and Child Abuse. *Lancet* 2:317–19.

62. Sherrod, K. B.; O'Connor, S.; Vietze, P. M.; and Altemeier, W. A. 1984. Child Health and Maltreatment. *Child Development* 55:1174–83.

63. Caldwell, B. M., and Bradley, R. H. 1984. *Home Observation for Measurement of the Environment*. *Rev. ed.* Little Rock: University of Arkansas. Unpublished manuscript.

64. Abidin, R. R. 1983. *Parenting Stress Index*. Charlottesville, Virg.: Pediatric Psychology Press.

65. Roth, R. M. 1980. *The Mother-Child Relationship Evaluation*. Los Angeles: Western Psychological Services.

66. Stollak, G. E. 1972. *Sensitivity to Children Questionnaire*. East Lansing, Mich.: Michigan State University. Unpublished manuscript.

67. Kallman, J. R., and Stollak, G. E. 1985. Child and Mother Perceptions of Maternal Behavior in Need-Arousing Situations. East Lansing, Mich.: Michigan State University. Unpublished manuscript.

68. Showers, J., and Johnson, C. F. 1984. Students' Knowledge of Child Health and Development: Effects on Approaches to Discipline. *J. School Health* 54:122–25.

69. Stollak, G. E.; Scholom, A.; Kallman, J.; and Saturansky, C. 1973. Insensitivity to Children: Responses of Undergraduates to Children in Problem Situations. *J. Abnormal Child Psychology* 1:169–80.

70. American Psychiatric Association. 1980. *Diagnostic and Statistical Manual of Mental Disorders*. 3d ed. Washington, D.C.: American Psychiatric Association.

71. Boor, M., and Coons, P. M. 1983. A Comprehensive Bibliography of Literature Pertaining to Multiple Personality. *Psychological Reports* 53:295–310.

72. Schreiber, F. R. 1973. *Sybil*. Chicago: Regnery.

73. Stoller, R. J. 1973. *Splitting: A Case of Female Masculinity*. New York: Quadrangle.

74. Rosenbaum, M. 1980. The Role of the Term Schizophrenia in the Decline of Diagnoses of Multiple Personality. *Archives of General Psychiatry* 37:1383–85.

75. Thigpen, C. H., and Cleckley, H. M. 1957. *The Three Faces of Eve*. New York: McGraw-Hill.

76. Bliss, E. L. 1980. Multiple personalities. *Archives of General Psychiatry* 37:1388–97.

77. Buck, O. D. 1983. Multiple Personality As a Borderline State. *J. Nervous and Mental Disease* 171:62–65.

78. Gruenewald, D. 1977. Multiple Personality and Splitting Phenomena: A Reconceptualization. *J. Nervous and Mental Disease* 164:385–93.

79. Rosenbaum, M., and Weaver, G. M. 1980. Dissociated State: Status of a Case after 38 Years. *J. Nervous and Mental Disease* 168:597–603.

80. Salama, A. A. 1980. Multiple Personality: A Case Study. *Canadian J. Psychiatry* 25:569–72.

81. Schenk, L., and Bear, D. 1981. Multiple Personality and Related Dissociative Phenomena in Patients with Temporal Lobe Epilepsy. *Am. J. Psychiatry* 138:1311–16.

82. Winer, D. 1978. Anger and Dissociation: A Case Study of Multiple Personality. *J. Abnormal Psychology* 87:368–72.

83. Anthony, E. J. 1978. From Birth to Breakdown: A Prospective Study of Vulnerability. In *The Child in His Family: Vulnerable Children,* ed. E. J. Anthony, C. Koupernik, and C. Chiland, 273–85. New York: Wiley.

84. Seagull, E. A. W., and Scheurer, S. L. 1984. Outcomes for Abused and Neglected Children of Mentally Retarded Parents. *Pediatric Research* 18:113A.

85. Brewer, M. B., and Campbell, D. T. 1976. *Ethnocentrism and Intergroup Attitudes.* Beverly Hills, Cal.: Sage Publications.

86. Hoffer, E. 1951. *The True Believer.* New York: Harper and Row.

87. Sherif, M., and Sherif, C. W. 1953. Groups in Harmony and Tension: An Integration of Studies of Intergroup Relations. New York: Harper.

88. Burgess, R. L., and Conger, R. D. 1978. Family Interaction in Abusive, Neglectful, and Normal Families. *Child Development* 49:1163–73.

89. Wechsler, D. 1981. *Wechsler Adult Intelligence Scale-Revised (WAIS-R).* New York: The Psychological Corporation.

90. Hathaway, S. R., and McKinley, J. C. 1970. *Minnesota Multiphasic Personality Inventory (MMPI).* New York: The Psychological Corporation.

10 The Child with Nonaccidental Trauma

Barton D. Schmitt

Physical abuse or nonaccidental trauma is one of the most common types of child mal-treatment seen by physicians. Each year in the United States approximately 1 percent of all children are documented as being abused. Substantiated new cases of physical abuse are 1,200 per million population per year (1). At least 4,000 children die each year from physical abuse. Approximately 10 percent of children under five years of age seen by emergency room physicians for trauma have injuries that were inflicted (2). Regardless of how many specialists are trained in this field, the recognition of inflicted injuries will continue to be the responsibility of primary care physicians and nurses (see chaps. 11–13).

Histories Offered for Inflicted Injuries

Although many child abuse diagnoses can be based on physical findings alone, the history of how the injury occurred becomes helpful when a child presents multiple, nondescript bruises. The assessment of the plausibility of the history is always a medical judgment. Professionals from other disciplines (e.g., social work, psychiatry, law enforcement, and the law) are not trained or expected to make this decision. The following histories are diagnostic or extremely suggestive of nonaccidental trauma (see table 10.1).

Eyewitness history. When a child readily states that a particular adult hurt him, the history is almost always true. When one parent accuses the other parent of hurting a child, the story is usually accurate, if the parents are not engaged in a custody dispute. Partial confessions by a parent are not uncommon and are as diagnostic as complete confessions

Barton D. Schmitt, M.D., is with the Department of Pediatrics, University of Colorado School of Medicine, Denver.

The author is deeply grateful to the following pediatricians for sharing photographs and experiences: Dr. Joan R. Hebeler provided figure 10.3; Dr. Richard D. Marble provided figures 10.6 and 10.9; and Dr. George W. Starbuck provided figures 10.10 and 10.12.

TABLE 10.1   Histories Offered for Inflicted Injuries

1. Eyewitness history
2. Unexplained history
3. Implausible history
4. Alleged self-inflicted injury
   (in young baby)
5. Alleged sibling-inflicted injury
6. Delay in seeking medical care

(e.g., a parent may admit that he caused one of the bruises, but not the others, or he may state that he felt like shaking or hitting the child prior to the injuries, but did not act on his impulse or cause any of the injuries).

Unexplained injury. Some parents deny knowing that their child had any of the bruises or burns discovered by the physician. Other parents have noticed the physical findings, but can offer no explanation as to how the injury happened. They may state, "I just found him that way," or, "He awoke that way." These parents would like us to believe that the injury was spontaneous. When pressed, they may become evasive or offer a vague explanation such as, "He might have fallen down." These explanations are self-incriminating. Most nonabusive parents know exactly how, where, and when their child was hurt. They also show a complete willingness to discuss the accident in detail. In these "unexplained" injuries, the exact perpetrator can often be identified by learning who was alone with the child when his discomfort and crying commenced.

Implausible history. Many parents offer an explanation for the injury, but one which is implausible and inconsistent with common sense and medical judgment. If the parents offer a blatantly phony history, the physician's job is rather easy. Occasionally, a minor accident is described, yet the injuries are major (e.g., a child reportedly has fallen onto a thick carpet, but has multiple body bruises). Another piece of strong evidence is when the behavior described which led to the accident is impossible for the child's level of development (e.g., a ten-month-old child who allegedly climbed into a tub and turned on scalding water). Some parents make their history implausible by repeatedly changing it.

Alleged self-inflicted injury. An alleged self-inflicted injury in a small baby is the most serious category. These children can be killed if they are sent home with the wrong diagnosis. In general, the child who is not crawling yet, is unable to cause an accident to himself. Fractures under this age are almost uniformly inflicted. Absurd stories such as, "The baby rolled over on his arm and broke it," or, "He got his head caught in the crib and bruised it," should be considered highly unlikely and acted upon accordingly. Histories implying that the child is masochistic should always raise questions (e.g., the child who hurts himself badly during a temper tantrum, gets subdural hematomas by hitting himself with a bottle, climbs up onto a hot radiator, or burns himself up to the elbows by immersing his arm in hot water). Children rarely deliberately injure themselves.

Alleged sibling-inflicted injury. When parents have difficulty coming up with an explanation, they commonly project the blame onto rough play with a sibling. They may state that the sibling dropped a toy on the injured child or threw a bottle at him. The number and

TABLE 10.2   Typical Sites for Inflicted Bruises

1. Buttocks and lower back (paddling)
2. Genitals and inner thighs
3. Cheek (slap marks)
4. Earlobe (pinch marks)
5. Upper lip and frenulum (forced feeding)
6. Neck (choke marks)

seriousness of the injuries usually contradict this explanation. In the small percentage of child abuse cases where the sibling is responsible, reporting is nonetheless mandatory to prevent recurrences.

Delay in seeking medical care. Most nonabusive parents come in immediately when their child is injured, by and large. In contrast, some abused children are not brought in for a considerable length of time, even when there is a major injury. In its extreme, they are not brought in until the child is nearly dead. During these delays parents are usually hoping that the event never occurred or that the injury will not require medical care. Another common behavior in the abusive situation is that the adult who was with the child at the time of the injury does not come to the hospital with the child.

Inflicted Bruises

Inflicted bruises occur at typical sites or fit recognizable patterns (e.g., human hand marks, human bite marks, strap marks, or bizarre shapes).

Typical sites. Inflicted bruises are so common at certain sites that finding them there is pathognomonic (table 10.2). Bruises that predominate on the buttocks, lower back, and lateral thighs are almost always related to punishment (i.e., paddling). Likewise, genital or inner-thigh bruises are usually inflicted for toileting mishaps (see figs. 10.1 and 10.2). Injuries to the penis may include pinch marks, cuts, abrasions, a deep groove from having it tied off with a rubber band, or amputation (3). Injuries to the genital area should raise the question of sexual abuse, especially when they are found in girls. Bruises on the cheek are usually secondary to being slapped (fig. 10.3). The outline of fingers may be evident within the bruise. Accidental falls rarely cause bruises to the soft tissues of the cheek, but instead involve the skin overlying bony prominences such as the forehead or cheekbone. Bruises on the earlobe are usually due to being cuffed. Children who are pinched or pulled by the earlobe usually have a matching bruise on each surface. Occasionally a child will suffer a ruptured eardrum from a blow to the ear. Bruises of the upper lip and labial frenulum are usually caused by impatient forced feedings or by jamming a pacifier or bottle into the child's mouth. Bruises in this area cannot be self-inflicted until the baby is old enough to sit up by himself and inadvertently fall forward. Bruises inside the lip may remain hidden unless the lip is carefully everted (fig. 10.4). The floor of the mouth may also be torn by similar actions (fig. 10.5). Usually a history of inconsolable crying can be obtained in these cases. Bruises or cuts on the neck are almost always due to being choked or strangled by a human hand, cord, dog collar, etc. (fig. 10.6). Other children receive neck marks from sudden traction on a shirt or bib. Accidents to this site are extremely rare

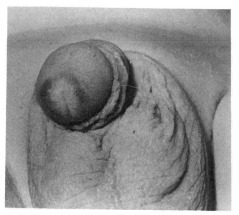

Figure 10.1

Pinch mark bruise of glans penis

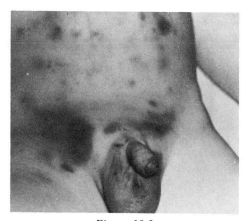

Figure 10.2

Multiple bruises and cuts of penis, scrotum, and abdomen

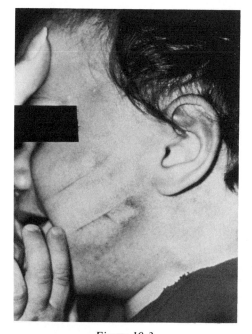

Figure 10.3

Slap mark of cheek. The outlines of three fingers are visible with a crease running through the lower one.

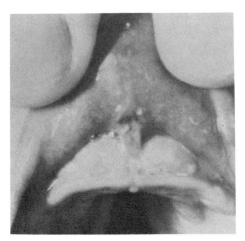

Figure 10.4

Torn upper labial frenulum in difficult-to-feed baby with cleft palate

Figure 10.5

Laceration of the floor of the mouth from jamming pacifier into the baby's mouth. Note friction burn of the nose.

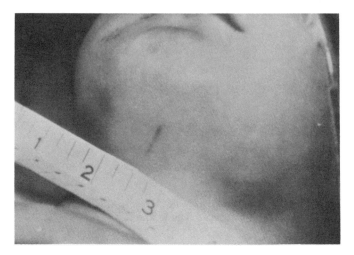

Figure 10.6

Two oval-shaped choke marks on the neck left by the human hand

TABLE 10.3　　**Human Hand Marks**

1. Grab marks or fingertip bruises
   (e.g., extremities or face)
2. Trunk encirclement bruises
3. Linear marks or finger-edge bruises
4. Slap marks
5. Hand print
6. Pinch marks
7. Poke marks

and should be looked upon with suspicion. Choke marks may be attributed to a resuscitation attempt, when in truth they are due to lifting a child off the ground by the neck while slapping him in the face or battering him against a wall. Resuscitative attempts do not leave bruises on the face or neck.

Human hand marks. The human hand can leave various types of pressure bruises (table 10.3). The most common types are grab marks or squeeze marks, oval-shaped bruises that resemble finger prints. Grab marks are usually due to being forcibly held during violent shaking. The most common site is the upper arm or shoulder (fig. 10.7). Grab marks of the lower extremities are also common until the child learns to walk. Grab-mark bruises can occur on the cheeks if an adult squeezes a child's face in an attempt to get food or medicine into her mouth. This action leaves a thumb-mark bruise on one cheek and two to four finger-mark bruises on the other cheek (fig. 10.8). Encirclement bruises occur when a child is grabbed about the chest or abdomen. This pattern (when complete) contains as many as eight finger-mark bruises on one side of the body and two thumb bruises on the other side. The examiner's fingers can fit easily into the configuration. Linear grab marks are caused by pressure from the entire finger (fig. 10.9). The outline of the entire hand print is sometimes seen on the back or at other sites. The human hand usually leaves outline bruises because mainly the capillaries at the edge of the injury are stretched enough to rupture. In slap marks to the cheek, two or three parallel linear bruises at finger-width spacing will be seen to run through a more diffuse bruise (fig. 10.3). The human hand can also leave pinch marks which give two crescent-shaped bruises facing each other (fig. 10.1). The shape of the bruise is primarily due to the fingernails. Poke marks from being jammed with the end of a straight finger leave small, circular bruises. Often three or four bruises are found in a cluster because the child has been karated with all the fingertips.

Human marks. Human bite marks leave distinctive, paired, crescent-shaped bruises that contain individual teeth marks (fig. 10.10). Sometimes the two crescents meet to form a complete ring of bruising. The most common dilemma facing the practitioner is to decide if a single bite on a child is from a playmate or from the parents. The point-to-point distance between the center of the canines (third tooth on each side) should be measured in centimeters. If the distance is greater than 3 cm., the child was bitten by an adult or someone, at least, with permanent teeth (i.e., over age eight). If the distance is less than 3 cm., the child was bitten by another young child with primary teeth (4). In serious injuries with several suspects, the exact perpetrator can be determined by having a dentist make wax impressions of each suspect's teeth and comparing them to photographs of the bite mark (5).

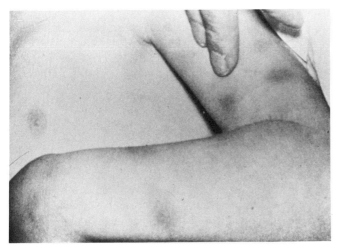

Figure 10.7

Grab marks (squeeze marks) on the upper and lower arm

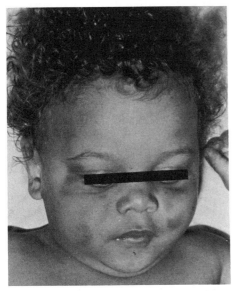

Figure 10.8

Squeeze marks on the face—one on the right cheek and two or three on the left.

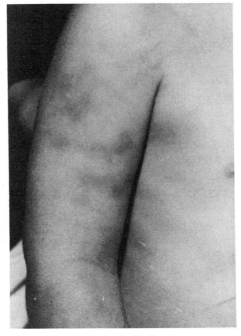

Figure 10.9

Linear finger-edge bruise on the upper arm

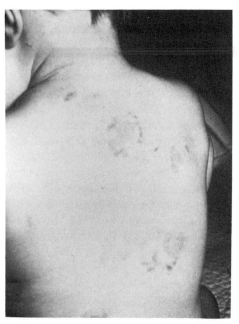

Figure 10.10

Multiple human bite marks (bitten by another child). Note the individual tooth marks.

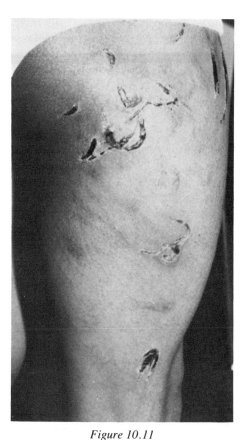

Figure 10.11

Loop mark bruises and abrasions (old and new) from beating with a doubled-over iron cord.

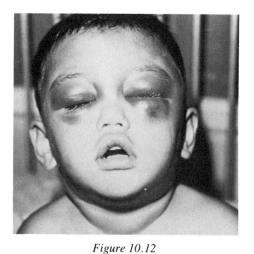

Figure 10.12

Bilateral severe swelling and bruising of the eyes from multiple blows to the upper face.

Strap marks. Strap marks are sharp-bordered, one- to two-inch wide rectangular bruises of various lengths, sometimes covering a curved body surface. These are almost always caused by a belt. Sometimes the eyelets or buckle of the belt can be discerned. Lash marks are narrow, straight-edged bruises or scratches caused by a thrashing with a tree branch or switch. Loop marks are secondary to being struck with a doubled-over lamp cord, rope, or fan belt (fig. 10.11). The distal end of the loop strikes with the most force, commonly breaks the skin, and may leave loop-shaped scars (6).

Bizarre marks. Bizarre-shaped bruises with sharp borders are always inflicted. When a blunt instrument (e.g., a toy or shoe) is used in punishment, the bruise or welt will resemble it in shape. A hairbrush leaves multiple punctate bruises. A comb leaves linear bruises or abrasions from being dragged across the skin. The wide assortment of instruments used to abuse children suggests that the caretaker who loses his temper grabs whatever object is handy (7). Children have been presented with tatoos inflicted with a sharp instrument such as a pin or razor. Numerous puncture wounds may be caused by a fork. Circumferential tie marks on the ankles or wrists can be caused when a child is tied up. If a narrow rope or cord is used, the child will be left with circumferential cuts. If a strap or piece of sheeting is used to restrain a child about the wrists or ankles, a friction burn or rope burn may result, usually presenting a large blister that encircles the extremity. The rope marks will not be circumferential if the child is tied directly to something. For example, rope burns have been seen about the thighs from tying the child to a potty seat. Gag marks may be seen as abrasions that run from the corner of the mouth. Children may be gagged because of too much screaming or yelling.

Accidental Bruises

A thorough knowledge of common and unusual accidents helps the physician recognize inflicted injuries. An understanding of unusual customs or practices that leave bruises is also helpful. Finally, the physician must remember that all bluish discolorations of the skin are not bruises.

Accidental bruises. Most children periodically acquire one or two bruises during falls or rough activity. Babies in the first few months of life commonly scratch themselves on the cheek, ear, nose, or even conjunctiva. This problem is due to long fingernails and disappears if the parent cuts them regularly. The most common site for multiple easily explained bruises in children of all ages is on the knee and shin. These bruises are due to normal falling down or bumping into objects while running. Bruises on the forehead are frequent at age two when the child decides he or she is an accomplished climber. While bruises from falling usually are circular with irregular borders so are grab marks, ring marks, or blows with a fist. Accidental bruises, however, usually occur on the skin overlying bony prominences (e.g., chin, elbow, forehead, spinous process, greater trochanter, etc.). Nondescript bruises become suspect as abuse when they occur on the soft parts of the body (e.g., cheek, fleshy part of the arm, buttocks, abdominal wall, etc.). Most falls produce one bruise on a single surface. Bruises on multiple body planes are usually inflicted, unless there is a history of tumbling accidents. True tumbling accidents also give bruises and abrasions over bony prominences. "Falling down a stairway" is often offered as a last-minute explanation for unexplained bruises in a child. A child who does tumble down the stairs ends up with very few bruises. Therefore, the number of bruises and the location of the bruises speak of an inflicted injury.

Unusual bruises. Some common practices can result in bruises that should not be confused with child abuse. The Vietnamese can induce symmetrical, linear bruises from coin rubbing (8). For symptoms of fever, chills, or headaches, the back and chest are covered with hot oil and then massaged in downward strokes with the edge of a coin (called *Cao Gio*). Some teenagers cause multiple petechiae on their chins by sucking on a cup until they create a vacuum and then sliding the cup onto their chins (9). A passionate and prolonged kiss can lead to an area of purpura commonly known as a "hicky." Vigorous sucking on hard candy can leave an area of purpura on the soft palate. On the other hand, purpura at this site has also been reported with fellatio. Multiple petechiae of the face and neck can occur following vigorous crying, retching, or coughing. This pattern is due to a sudden increase in superior vena cava pressure. Petechiae and purpura can even be seen in the conjunctiva or mouth from this mechanism. Obviously, tourniquets can also cause petechiae, especially in children who already have an erythematous rash.

Pseudobruises. Some skin conditions have been mistaken for bruises. The most common one is a Mongolian spot. This birthmark occurs in 95 percent of black babies, 81 percent of Orientals and American Indians, 70 percent of Chicanos, and 10 percent of whites (10). They are present at birth and last from two to three years. They are grayish blue, do not change color, and have clear-cut margins. Although they commonly occur on the buttocks and back, they can occur anywhere. They are a birthmark, not a bruise. Maculae cerulae are unexplained bluish spots on the skin that occur concomitantly with pubic lice. They resolve when the lice are treated. Localized brown splotches (phytophotodermatitis) can result from melanin production in areas inadvertently rubbed with lime, lemon, fig, celery, or parsnip (11). Children with allergic shiners may be referred for black eyes. Allergic shiners are due to long-standing venous congestion from allergic rhinitis and eye allergies. They are usually more brownish in color than blue, and the discoloration is mainly seen on the lower, medial eyelid. The presence of allergies and the duration of the finding points to the correct diagnosis. Hemophilus influenza can give a bluish cellulitis of the cheek. However, these children are sick, they have a fever, and the area is quite tender.

Inflicted Eye Injuries

Ocular damage in the battered child syndrome includes acute hyphema, dislocated lens, traumatic cataract, and detached retina (12). Over half of these result in permanent impairment of vision affecting one or both eyes. Retinal hemorrhages are also a clue to subdural hematomas in children with unexplained central nervous system findings. Retinal hemorrhage can also occur without clinically important intracranial hemorrhage in children with sudden compression of their chests. This finding is called Purtscher retinopathy (13). The differential diagnosis of retinal hemorrhages is direct head trauma, shaking injuries, increased intracranial pressure, hypertension, bleeding disorders, and gymnastic twirling on a horizontal bar. Retinal hemorrhages usually last ten to fourteen days.

Inflicted black eyes are more common than serious eye injuries. Children who have been hit about the eyes with an open or closed hand present massive swelling and bruising of both eyelids (fig. 10.12). Most black eyes caused by accidents only involve one side. The question that is frequently raised is whether a child can acquire two black eyes from a single accident, or more precisely, from striking a single object. The answer is yes. Bilateral black eyes can occur from blood seeping down from a large bruise on the forehead or from a basilar skull fracture. Blood moves with gravity. However, these children have minimal lid swelling and no lid tenderness. In addition, the onset of the black eye is delayed one or two days from the time of the injury. Therefore, these situations should not be confused with the child who has been beaten about the head and eyes.

Inflicted Head Injuries

Inflicted head injuries include subdural hematomas, subarachnoid hemorrhages, scalp bruises, traumatic alopecia, and subgaleal hematomas.

Subdural hematomas. Subdural hematoma is the most dangerous inflicted injury, often causing death or serious sequelae. Over 95 percent of serious intracranial injuries during the first year of life are the result of physical abuse (14). These children present irritability, vomiting, a decreased level of consciousness, breathing difficulty and apneic episodes, a bulging fontanel, and/or convulsions (15). The classic case of subdural hematoma is associated with skull fractures. These fractures are secondary to a direct blow from the caretaker's hand or from being hit against a wall or door. Numerous other bruises may also be present.

Inflicted subdural hematomas can also occur without skull fractures, scalp bruises, or scalp swelling. In fact, over one-half of the cases have no fracture (16). These findings used to be erroneously called "spontaneous subdural hematomas," but evidence clearly points to a violent, whiplash shaking mechanism (17). Rapid acceleration and deceleration of the head as it bobs about leads to tearing of the bridging cerebral veins with bleeding into the subdural space, usually bilaterally. Proof for this etiology comes from experimental studies done on animals and also the confessions of some of the parents. Most of these cases occur in babies under one year of age who are shaken to make them stop crying. Additional diagnostic evidence comes from the presence of retinal hemorrhages in these whiplash subdurals. X-rays of the long bones should also be obtained because they will reveal old or new fractures in 25 percent of the cases (16). Subarachnoid hemorrhages can result from the same mechanism and may be as common as shaking subdural hematomas. The concept of the "spontaneous subdural hematoma" in young infants must be discarded lest we send a child home to be reinjured or killed. Likewise, the diagnosis of "chronic subdural hematomas" secondary to birth trauma must be viewed with skepticism. Subdural hematomas due to birth injury will almost always produce acute signs and symptoms within twenty-four to forty-eight hours after delivery. (See chap. 12 for discussion of computed tomography in the diagnosis of subdural hematomas.)

Scalp bruises. Bruises of the scalp can occur with or without underlying skull fractures or brain injuries. These bruises are often difficult to see because they are deep in the scalp or they are hidden by the child's hair. Diagnosis of scalp bruises should be suspected by the finding of soft-tissue swelling on palpation or on skull films.

Traumatic alopecia and subgaleal hematomas. Some children are pulled or yanked by the hair. Sometimes the hair spirals at the broken end, probably secondary to stretching at

TABLE 10.4   Inflicted Abdominal Injuries (in order of frequency)

1. Ruptured liver or spleen
2. Intestinal perforation
3. Intramural hematoma of duodenum
   or proximal jejunum
4. Ruptured blood vessel
5. Pancreatic injury
6. Kidney or bladder injury
7. Chylous ascites from injured lymphatic system
8. Foreign bodies (swallowed or percutaneous)

this site prior to breakage. If the hair-pulling event is recent, the scalp may be tender and a few petechiae may be found at the hair roots. Unlike alopecia areata, there are no loose hairs at the periphery of the bald area. Unlike diseases that cause hair loss, there is no inflammation or scaling of the scalp. Violent and sudden lifting of a child by the hair can also cause a subgaleal hematoma, as evidenced by a diffuse, boggy swelling of the scalp. The aponeurosis which connects the occipital and frontalis muscles is lifted off the calvarium and the space rapidly fills with blood. This diagnosis is most likely if the child has braids at the site of the hematoma (18). Subgaleal hematoma can also be caused by shearing forces, but an unexplained one is probably inflicted.

Accidental head injuries from falls. Helfer, Slovis, and Black have reported the outcome of 246 young children who accidentally fell out of cribs or beds (19). In 80 percent of the children, there were no findings whatever of an injury. The other 20 percent had a single bruise, lump, or cut. Only 1 percent had skull fractures, and these were single and linear. Another 1 percent had a fresh fracture at another site, usually the clavicle or humerus. Important to us, none of the children had subdural hematomas, epidural hematomas, or any serious life-threatening injury.

Inflicted Abdominal Injuries

Intra-abdominal injuries are the second most common cause of death in battered children (20). Unlike the contents of the chest, the abdominal organs are not protected. Table 10.4 lists inflicted abdominal injuries in the approximate order of frequency. Most of the injuries are usually caused by a punch or kick that compresses the organ against the anterior spinal column.

The most common finding is a ruptured liver or spleen. These children present blood loss and shock. Second, blows to the abdomen can cause tears or rents in the small or large intestine. These children often present advanced peritonitis because of a delay in seeking medical care. An upright film of the abdomen will show free air under the diaphragm. Third, the most unique abdominal injury is an intramural hematoma of the duodenum or proximal jejunum (21). These children present projectile vomiting (bile stained if the obstruction is distal) and other signs of gastrointestinal obstruction. With supportive management, the hematoma usually resolves without surgery. Fourth, arteries or veins can be torn and these patients present in shock. Fifth, trauma is the most common cause of acute pancreatitis in children. Again, an anterior blow to the abdomen compresses the pancreas against the vertebral column. Sometimes the pancreas is transected. Children with acute traumatic pancreatitis have symptoms of abdominal tenderness, vomiting, and fever. Their serum and urine amylase levels will be markedly elevated. If the initial injury heals, it may progress to a pseudocyst of the pancreas (22). These children have persistent abdominal pain and vomiting. Their diagnosis is finally confirmed with the discovery of an abdominal mass on physical examination and the presence of a soft tissue mass on a lateral abdominal film displacing the stomach anteriorly. Sixth, kidney injuries usually result from blows to the back and present gross hematuria. The bladder may be ruptured by a blow to the lower abdomen. Two unusual presentations of child abuse are chylous ascites and a needle perforation of the liver (23, 24).

In all of these conditions, trauma to the abdomen is usually denied. Bruises of the abdominal wall (when present) help to establish the correct diagnosis. Unfortunately, there are no visible bruises or marks on the abdominal wall in over half of these cases. The abdominal wall is usually relaxed at the time of the injury, and the energy from the blow is mainly absorbed by the internal organs. The physician must consider child abuse in any abdominal crisis of undetermined etiology. (See chap. 12 for discussion of ultrasound in the diagnosis of abdominal injuries.)

Immediate Actions by the Physician

The detection of a child with suspected abuse demands some immediate actions by the physician. He must report all these cases to child protective services, hospitalize selected children, obtain a police hold on some children, and share his diagnosis and plans with the parents.

Report all suspected cases to child protective services. The physician is required to report these cases to the child protective service agency in the child's county of residence. The report should be made by phone immediately and in writing within forty-eight hours. This report should guarantee adequate evaluation, treatment, and follow-up, as well as fulfilling legal requirements.

Hospitalize any abused child needing protection during the initial evaluation period. The highest priority of initial management is to protect the child. Any child suspected of having been abused should be kept in a safe place until evaluations regarding the safety of the home are complete. All too often, a crying baby with a minor inflicted injury is sent home, only to return the next day with subdural hematomas or multiple fractures. The reason given to the parents for the hospitalization can be that "children with unusual injuries need to be hospitalized for a thorough evaluation." While the term "unexplained injuries" also may be used in the clinic setting, in general, the terms "inflicted injuries" or "abused child" should not. A psychosocial history or any incriminating questions usually can be delayed until the child is hospitalized. Also, discussion of the need to report the suspicious injuries to the proper authorities can be postponed. While the parents are never lied to, the best timing for telling them everything is usually after the child has been safely admitted to the ward. If the parents bring up the question of child abuse, the physician should honestly state that this is one of his concerns. If the parents refuse hospitalization, a police hold can be obtained.

TABLE 10.5   Medical Evaluation Checklist

1. History of injury
2. Physical examination of patient
3. Trauma X-ray survey on selected patients
4. Bleeding disorder screen on selected patients
5. Color photographs of selected patients
6. Physical examination of siblings
7. Official medical report in writing
8. Behavioral screening
9. Developmental screening

In many parts of the country, child protective service workers and emergency receiving homes are now available twenty-four hours a day. Unless the child's injuries require close medical observations, placement in an emergency receiving home is far less expensive than hospitalization. Approximately thirty minutes before the caseworker is expected to arrive, the physician should tell the parents that a caseworker has been called, that the caseworker is coming to the clinic to see them, and that his or her input is essential. If the delay is going to be prolonged (e.g., over one hour), less agitation is engendered if the parents initially feel they are waiting for lab results or X-ray results. Private physicians can usually be more open about these matters without running the risk that the parents will bolt from the medical facility.

Tell the parents the diagnosis. The physician (rather than someone else) should inform the parents that he has reported their child's injuries to protective services, since this report is based on medical findings. He should state that he is obligated by state law to report any unusual or unexplained injuries. He can reassure the parents that everyone involved will try to help them find better ways of dealing with their child. Maintaining a helping approach with these parents is often the hardest part of the therapy. Feeling angry with these parents is natural, but expressing this anger to the parents will jeopardize their cooperation (see chap. 6). The physician should keep in mind that the injury may have occurred in a moment of anger, that rarely was it deliberate, and that these parents already feel inadequate and unloved. The physician should encourage hospital visits by parents and be certain that the ward personnel treat them kindly. These parents need frequent, ongoing communication from the physician on their child's case or they may become unduly suspicious and angry.

The Medical Evaluation of Children with Physical Abuse

The following nine tasks represent the medical data base that must be collected in a comprehensive child abuse evaluation (see table 10.5).

1. *History of injury:* A complete history should be obtained as to how the injury allegedly happened, including the informant, date, time, place, sequence of events, height of fall, surface of impact, people present, time lag before medical attention was sought, and so forth. Unlike the psychosocial interview, which can be postponed, the detailed history of the injury should be elicited immediately before the parents have time to change it.

TABLE 10.6   Dating of Bruises

Age	Color
0–2 days	Swollen, tender
0–5 days	Red, blue, purple
5–7 days	Green
7–10 days	Yellow
10–14 days (or longer)	Brown
2–4 weeks	Cleared

If possible, the parents should be interviewed separately. The parents can be pressed for exact details when necessary. No other professional should have to repeat this detailed, probing interview. The physician must talk with the parents directly so that his or her history will not be considered as hearsay evidence in court. In rare situations, obtaining the history from the parents on the phone may suffice if they cannot come in. The physician commonly forgets to interview the child, which is often helpful if the child is over age three or four. This should be done in a private setting without the parents present.

2. *Physical examination of patient:* All bruises should be recorded as to size, shape, position, color, and age. If they resemble strap marks, grab marks, or marks from a blunt instrument, this should be recorded. The oral cavity, eardrums, and genitals should be closely examined for signs of occult trauma. All bones should be palpated for tenderness and the joints tested for full range of motion. In addition, special attention should be paid to the retina, for hemorrhages there may point to subdural hematomas from a shaking injury. The height and weight percentiles should be plotted, and if the child is underweight, the diet history should be explored. Physicians are commonly asked to date bruises. Table 10.6 condenses data from five studies on this subject (25). In general, if the bruises are swollen and tender, they are probably less than two days old. The initial color of bruises is red, blue, or purple. As hemoglobin is broken down, bruises undergo three additional color changes, beginning at the periphery of the bruise. The first color change to green occurs at a minimum of five days. Within a few days, the color changes to yellow, and eventually it progresses to brown. The brown color may persist from four days to four weeks before the bruise completely clears.

3. *Trauma X-ray survey:* Every suspected victim under two years of age should receive a radiologic bone survey. These films are of great diagnostic value, since the clinical findings of fracture often disappear in six or seven days even without orthopedic care. A child with multiple fractures may still move about and play normally. Between two and five years of age, most children also receive a bone survey unless the child has very minor injuries or is in a supervised setting (e.g., preschool). For children over age five, X-ray films need to be obtained only if any bone tenderness or limited range of motion is noted on physical examination. A recent study in routine skeletal surveys found that 11.5 percent had evidence of trauma (26). Of these, 21 percent were occult fractures (i.e., not suspected clinically). If films of a tender site are initially normal, they should be repeated in two weeks to pick up calcification of any subperiosteal bleeding or nondisplaced epiphyseal separations that may have been present (see chap. 12).

4. *Bleeding disorder screen:* A bleeding screen would include a platelet count, bleeding time, partial thromboplastin time, prothrombin time, fibrinogen level, and thrombin times. A normal bleeding panel strengthens the physician's court testimony that bruising could not have occurred spontaneously or as the result of a minor injury. On a practical level, bleeding tests are rarely indicated. Children with subtle bleeding tendencies demonstrate ongoing bruising in the school, office, hospital, and foster home. Screening is not needed for bruises confined to the buttocks, bruises resembling weapons, or hand-print bruises. It is also unnecessary when one parent or the child accuses a specific adult of hitting the child. The main indication for screening is nonspecific bruises which the parent denies inflicting or for which a history of alleged "easy bruisability" is given.

5. *Color photographs:* Color photographs are required by law in some states (27). A ruler and a tag with the date and child's name should be visible in each photograph. In most juvenile court cases, they are not essential to the primary physician's testimony. In cases where an expert witness who has not actually examined the child is to testify, they are mandatory. In cases where criminal court action is anticipated, they will usually be required and will be taken by the police photographer. Whether or not medical photography is available, the physician should carefully diagram the body-surface findings in the official medical chart and carefully date and sign the entry.

6. *Physical examination of siblings:* There is approximately a 20 percent risk that a sibling of a physically abused child has also been abused at the same time (28). Therefore, all siblings under the age of eighteen should be brought in for an inspection and palpation examination of the total body surface within twelve hours of uncovering an index case. If the parents say they cannot bring them in because of transportation problems, the protective service agency can accomplish this. If the parents refuse to have their other children seen, a court order can be obtained and the police sent out.

7. *Official medical report in writing:* The physician's findings should be recorded in a typed medical report. As it may be used in court, the accuracy and completeness of this report are very important. A copy of the admission workup to the hospital or the discharge summary will not suffice, because the evidence for the diagnosis of child abuse is often difficult for nonmedical people to locate in these highly technical documents. A well-written medical report often convinces the parents' lawyer that his clients' case is in great question, and he accepts ("stipulates to") the petition before the court and agrees to therapy for his clients. Therefore, a well-written medical report may keep the physician out of court and save time in the long run. The report should include: (a) a history—the alleged cause of the injury (with date, time, place, and so forth), (b) a physical exam—a detailed description of the injury using nontechnical terms whenever possible (e.g., "cheek," instead of "zygoma," "bruise," instead of "ecchymosis"), (c) results of lab tests and X-ray films, (d) a conclusion—a statement that this incident represents nonaccidental trauma, the reason behind this conclusion, a comment on the severity of the present injury (e.g., probable sequelae or estimated number of blows the child endured), and an estimate of the danger for serious reabuse. (See appendix for a sample medical report.)

8. *Behavioral screening:* The abused child inevitably has associated behavior problems (29). Some may be primary behaviors that make the child difficult to live with and hence prone to abuse (e.g., negativism and hyperactivity). Other behaviors may be secondary to abusive treatment (e.g., fearfulness and depression). Often the abused child's individual need for therapy will be overlooked unless these symptoms are uncovered. The child's be-

havior should be observed and discussed. Those children with major behavioral problems need referral for a complete assessment. The physician may provide counseling for minor problems.

9. *Developmental screening:* Abuse and neglect of the infant and preschool child can lead to developmental delays (30). These problems usually can be detected by routine use of the Denver Developmental Screening Test (DDST) or other developmental tests for this age group. Children with developmental problems need referral for more detailed testing. A school report may be helpful in the comprehensive assessment of the abused school-age child.

Appendix

PHYSICAL ABUSE—MEDICAL REPORT

DRL
BD: 2/12/81
CGH# 123456

This four-year-old boy was seen in the Colorado General Hospital Emergency Room at 3:20 P.M. on September 5, 1985. He was accompanied by Ms. Smith, the caseworker from Denver County, and the patient's mother.

HISTORY: The patient has many bruises, and his mother states that he commonly falls down. She denies that he has any unusual bleeding. In regard to the many bruises on his body, she admits to causing the ones on his face by squeezing it vigorously with her right hand to get his attention after misbehaving. She denies causing any of the other bruises and thinks that most of them occur through accidents which she did not witness. She claims that the bruise on his forehead and right ear were caused today when she suddenly returned to the room, opened the door, and hit him with the door. However, she denies that he fell down or was pinned against the wall. She claims that the numerous bruises on his buttocks are due to falling down the concrete basement stairs. She admits to disciplining him by occasionally slapping him on the mouth and also by spanking him on the buttocks. In interviewing the boy with the mother out of the room, he says that his mother hits him both with her hand and a belt. He says the bruises on his buttocks are due to being hit with a belt and that the bruises on one of his ears, at least, were due to her slapping him. He claims that his father does not spank him or hit him.

PHYSICAL EXAM: The boy is of average height and well nourished.
1. *Face.* The boy has a fresh, tender, swollen bruise about three-quarters of an inch in diameter on the right eyebrow. He has four bruises, all of which are circular, ranging in size from one-quarter inch to one-half inch, and yellowish blue in color. There are two on the left cheek, one on the chin, and one on the right cheek, just adjacent to the mouth. These are the bruises the mother admits to having caused.
2. *Ears.* The right earlobe is covered with large and small bruises on both surfaces. The left earlobe has approximately ten small, bleeding marks. The right eardrum has half a dozen hemorrhages on the surface. There is no bleeding apparent behind the eardrum.
3. *Scalp.* There is a one-inch-diameter tender swelling on the right parietal area. No bruise is apparent.

4. *Arms.* There are two one-half-inch circular bruises, close to each other, on the right upper arm on the outer surface. On the left mid-upper arm, there is an old, fading yellow bruise approximately one-half inch in diameter.

5. *Buttocks.* There are nine old bruises on the buttocks. These have a reddish yellow hue and are older than the mother's dating of his falling down the stairs two days ago. These range in size from two inches to one-half inch.

6. *Legs.* The right shin has three and the left shin has two old yellow red bruises, one-half inch or smaller in diameter. (These are normal.)

SKELETAL SURVEY: No bone injuries seen on X-ray.

CONCLUSION: This four-year-old boy has numerous bruises of different ages, covering many of his body surfaces. He has clearly been physically abused. The mother admits inflicting the squeeze marks on the face. The boy has obvious slap marks on both ears that could not have resulted from being hit accidentally by a door. The bruises on the buttocks also are clearly caused by spanking and substantiated by the patient himself. The bruises on the upper arms appear to be grab marks, but they are not conclusive. The bruises about the ears, the fact that the eardrum was injured on the right side, and the finding of an inflicted injury on the scalp, suggest a serious lack of restraint and the need for vigorous intervention.

JAMES L. ADAMS, M.D.

References

1. American Humane Association. 1981. National Study of the Incidence and Severity of Child Abuse and Neglect: May 1, 1979 to April 30, 1980. Denver: American Humane Association.

2. Holter, J. C., and Friedman, S. B. 1968. Child Abuse: Early Case Finding in the Emergency Department. *Pediatrics* 42:128.

3. Slosberg, E. J.; Ludwig, S.; Duckett, J.; and Mauro, A. E. 1978. Penile Trauma As a Sign of Child Abuse. *Am. J. Diseases in Children* 132:719–20.

4. Levine, L. J. 1984. Bite Marks in Child Abuse. In *Clinical Management of Child Abuse and Neglect: A Guide for the Dental Professional,* ed. R. G. Sanger and D. C. Bross, 53–59. Chicago: Quintessence Publishing.

5. Levine, L. J. 1973. The Solution of a Battered-Child Homicide by Dental Evidence: Report of Case. *JADA* 87:1234.

6. Sussman, S. J. 1968. Skin Manifestations of the Battered-Child Syndrome. *J. Pediatrics* 72:99.

7. Johnson, C. F., and Showers, J. 1985. Injury Variables in Child Abuse. *Child Abuse and Neglect: International J.* 9:207.

8. Yeatman, G. W.; Shaw, C.; Barlow, M. J.; and Bartlett, G. 1976. Pseudobattering in Vietnamese Children. *Pediatrics* 58:616–18.

9. Lovejoy, F. H.; Marcuse, E. K.; and Landrigan, P. J. 1971. Two Examples of Purpura Factitia. *Clinical Pediatrics* 11:183–84.

10. Jacobs, A. H., and Walton, R. G. 1976. Incidence of Birthmarks in the Neonate. *Pediatrics* 58:218–22.

11. Coffman, K.; Boyce, W. T.; and Hansen, R. C. 1985. Phytophotodermatitis Simulating Child Abuse. *Am. J. Diseases in Children* 139:239.

12. Gammon, J. A. 1981. Ophthalmic Manifestations of Child Abuse. In *Child Abuse and Neglect: A Medical Reference,* ed. N. S. Ellerstein, 121–39. New York: Wiley.

13. Tomasi, L. G. 1975. Purtscher Retinopathy in the Battered-Child Syndrome. *Am. J. Diseases in Children* 129:1335.

14. Billmire, M. E., and Myers, P. A. 1985. Serious Head Injury in Infants: Accident or Abuse? *Pediatrics* 75:340.

15. Merten, D. F., and Osborne, D. R. S. 1984. Craniocerebral Trauma in the Child Abuse Syndromes. *Pediatric Annals* 12:882.

16. Guthkelch, A. N. 1971. Infantile Subdural Hematoma and Its Relationship to Whiplash Injuries. *British Med. J.* 2:430.

17. Caffey, J. 1974. The Whiplash Shaken-Infant Syndrome. *Pediatrics* 54:396.

18. Hamlin, H. 1968. Subgaleal Hematoma Caused by Hair-Pull. *JAMA* 204:339.

19. Helfer, R. E.; Slovis, T. L.; and Black, M. 1977. Injuries Resulting When Small Children Fall out of Bed. *Pediatrics* 60:533–35.

20. Touloukian, R. J. 1968. Abdominal Visceral Injuries in Battered Children. *Pediatrics* 42:642.

21. Gornall, P., et al. 1972. Intra-Abdominal Injuries in the Battered-Baby Syndrome. *Archives of Diseases in Children* 47:211.

22. Penna, S. D. J., and Medovy, H. 1973. Child Abuse and Traumatic Pseudocyst of the Pancreas. *J. Pediatrics* 83:1026.

23. Boysen, B. E. 1975. Chylous Ascites. *Am. J. Diseases in Children* 129:1, 338.

24. Stone, R. K.; Harowitz, A.; San Filippo, J. A.; and Gromisch, D. S. 1976. Needle Perforation of the Liver in an Abused Child. *Clinical Pediatrics* 15:958.

25. Wilson, E. F. 1977. Estimation of the Age of Cutaneous Contusions in Child Abuse. *Pediatrics* 60:751–52.

26. Ellerstein, N. S., and Norris, K. J. 1984. Value of Radiologic Skeletal Survey in Assessment of Abused Children. *Pediatrics* 74:1075.

27. Ford, R. J., and Smistek, B. S. 1981. Photography of the Maltreated Child. In *Child Abuse and Neglect: A Medical Reference,* ed. N. S. Ellerstein, 315–26. New York: Wiley.

28. Lauer, B.; Ten Broeck, E., and Grossman, M. 1974. Battered-Child Syndrome: Review of 130 Patients with Controls. *Pediatrics* 54:67.

29. Morse, C. W.; Sahler, O. J.; and Friedman, S. B. 1970. A Three-Year Follow-up Study of Abused and Neglected Children. *Am. J. Diseases in Children* 120:439.

30. Martin, H. P., et al. 1974. The Development of Abused Children. *Advances in Pediatrics* 21:25.

11 Child Abuse by Burning

Kenneth W. Feldman

Burns are a feared, sometimes fatal injury. The pain of the treatment may equal that of the wounds. Even after lengthy and successful treatment, burn victims may be disabled and disfigured. These circumstances, singly or in combination, may cause prolonged psychological disability. When viewing a burned child, a health professional's attention is drawn to the problems of the treatment and consequences of burn injury. Although the incidence, causes, characteristics, and potential means of preventing burn injuries may attract less attention than immediate burn care, they often have immediate bearing on the treatment plan. The physician must assess the possibility of repeated injury, either accidental or abusive, and the probable quality of home care. Careful evaluation of the burn injury may lead to injury prevention for that child or other children.

Burns are the fourth most frequent cause of death in children under one year of age, and the third most frequent in children from one to fourteen years old (1, p. 8). Child abuse has frequently been the cause of burns. Studies have found that 4%–9% of children hospitalized for burns are the victims of abuse (2–4). Abuse rates in specific burn injuries can be even higher; abuse occurred in 28% of hospitalized tap-water burn victims (5). Burns have been the mode of injury in 6%–17% of children in institutional studies of abuse (3, 6, 7). Gil's 1967 nationwide survey of abused children found that 10% had burns (8, pp. 119, 122). Abuse should thus be a major diagnostic consideration in any case of a burned child. Most burns leave hallmarks suggesting agent, mode, direction, and time of injury. The physical findings of each burn should be studied with these questions in mind, and a hypothesis of injury should be formulated to compare with the caretaker's history.

General Characteristics of Burn Injury

Childhood burns, and accidents in general, often are related to environmental and psychiatric stress (9). In a 1944 study of burns in Edinburgh, Scotland (10), Wilkinson noted

Kenneth W. Feldman, M.D., is with the Odessa Brown Children's Clinic and the Ambulatory Division, Department of Pediatrics, University of Washington, Seattle.

197

that "bad accommodation is not so prominent a factor as the (poor) domestic habits of the family (11). Large, poor families in crowded accommodations in which child care was absent or the responsibility of slightly older siblings seemed predisposed to burn injury. Long and Cope found a high incidence (44%) of gross emotional disturbance within the family unit in a study of nineteen children on an inpatient burn unit (11). Holter and Friedman, studying families of thirteen children with greater than 15% body-surface-area burns, found that five children, eight mothers, and five fathers had serious preexisting emotional, psychiatric, or behavioral problems (12). Only three of the marriages were stable, while seven were "unhappy and unsatisfactory," and three were emotionally un-stable single-parent homes. Seven of the injuries appeared to be the direct consequences of family stress, carelessness, and poor child supervision. Three of the thirteen burns were frankly abusive. One-third of the burned children in Borland's study, and another family member in 29% of the families, had required medical attention for accidental in-jury within the previous year (13). Upsetting trigger events occurred in 25% of these fami-lies just prior to the child's burn injury.

The infant is most likely to become a burn victim. During infancy, children are physi-cally helpless, emotionally labile, and unreasonably demanding. Their curiosity far out-strips their caution. Normal infants frequently cry immediately, but fail to withdraw, when burned. Families of injured children tend to misunderstand the developmental status of their children and the child's ability to avoid hazards in the environment (9). In addition to normal childhood immaturity, further handicaps increase a child's burn proneness both by reducing the child's ability to sense or escape a burning situation and by increasing family stress. For example, meningomyelocele with paralysis and anesthesia, cerebral palsy, epi-lepsy, and psychiatric instability predispose to injury (14). Seventy-two percent of the burned children reported by Borland were less than five years old (13). Waller and Man-heimer, studying the well-defined population of a Kaiser prepaid health plan, found a burn injury rate of 29.3 per thousand per year in the first two years of life. The rate declined to a steady plateau of three to five cases per thousand per year from age three through child-hood (15). Likewise, abusive burns are concentrated among infants and toddlers with mean ages at injury of two to three (2, 4, 7).

Regional differences in life-style result in vastly different statistics on burn causation. In North Carolina, where open-flame gas heaters are the major mode of heating, clothing ignition burns are most common (16). In King County, Washington, where central or elec-tric baseboard heating is the rule, scalds are the predominant form of burn injury (17). As society and technology change, so will burn causation. The high energy costs of the 1970s led to increasing use of woodstoves for heating; woodstove burns of children followed as a natural consequence (18). Social class may also affect the accessibility to burn hazards. Poorer southeastern United States families are more likely to have open-flame gas heaters. Superimposed on such differences in environmental hazards are social and cultural differ-ences in the desirability and methods of child discipline. For example, Gil notes the fre-quent occurrence of abusive burning in Puerto Rican families as opposed to the more fre-quent abuse by the bare hands in white families (8).

Despite these regional and subcultural differences, 70%–90% of childhood burns occur in the home (13, 17, 19, 20). Burn injuries cluster in the more stressful hours of the day: the morning when children are arising from sleep and the "poison hours" of the late afternoon when presupper hunger, tiredness, and distracting activity are at their peak (10, 13, 21). Burn injuries are also most frequent in the winter months when crowding seems most oppressive and open sources of heat are in most frequent use (10, 13).

Although some studies have been biased by referral patterns to specific institutions, burn injuries seem to be overrepresented in the lower economic classes. Although only 9% of fathers in the Seattle area in 1950 were unskilled laborers, 24% of the inpatient burn victims were from this economic class (17). Most parents of burn-injured children in Missouri lack high school education, are poor, unskilled laborers, young, and have other children (13). Similarly, burns tend to occur in the English laboring classes (22). Because of inherent professional biases, actual diagnosis of abuse is more likely for the lower economic classes.

Although these comments are based on studies of burns in general, the reader should understand that abusive burns are likely to be underdiagnosed. The abusive burn is only a small, symptomatic segment of burn-prone children and their families. Nonabusive burns are frequently the result of neglectful episodes arising in families with social disruption that could have easily resulted in abuse. The high association of abusive burns, preexisting family stress, and psychiatric disability resulting from burn treatment and residual burn scarring has caused many burn units to routinely provide psychiatric and social work aid for burn victims. These units review all childhood burn incidents for possible abuse. Preventative intervention can then be initiated for abuse and potential abuse victims and their families.

Specific Patterns of Abusive Hot-Water Burns

Scald burns are the most frequent cause of thermal injury in children and of child abuse by burning (2, 7). Although tap water causes only a small part of all scald burns (7%–17%), Feldman et al. found them to be the most frequent cause of abusive scald burns (5).

In a 1978 survey of Seattle homes, 80% had water temperatures greater than 130°F and the average temperature of hot water was 142°F (5). This situation was largely determined by the then-current industry practice of presetting new electric heaters at 150°F and gas heaters at 140°F. Although a petition to the United States Consumer Protection Commission to limit the maximum setting on new home water heaters to 130°F was rejected, the publicity of that petition resulted in the industry voluntarily reducing the preset water heater temperatures. In 1980 the gas heater industry changed the preset temperature to "the minimum setting on the heater," which ranges between 120°F and 130°F. Since 1979 the electric heater industry has preset at a still unsafe 140°F. Both are required to use labels that warn of burn hazard. On a state level, Florida and Washington have passed laws limiting the preset temperatures on new home water heaters to 125°F and 120°F, respectively. The rapidity of scalding increases drastically above 127°F where one minute is required to cause full-thickness scalds of adult skin (fig. 11.1) (23). At 130°F such scald burns occur in thirty seconds, and at 150°F in two seconds. At temperatures above 140°F, where burn time is determined by the time required for heat to penetrate to the basal layers of the skin, children's thinner skin results in burns in about one-fourth of adult burn time (24).

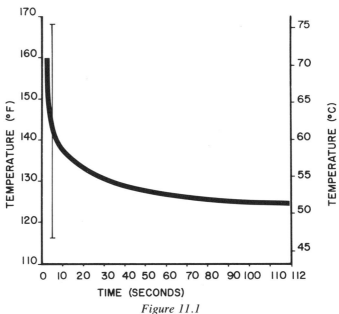

Figure 11.1

The mean ±2 standard deviations for Seattle-area home bathtub water temperatures are superimposed on the time versus temperature curve of hot water required to cause full-thickness scalds of adult skin. (Graph adapted from Moritz and Henriques [23].)

An unsafe situation is present in most United States homes where exposure to hot tap water is likely to result in severe burns. Abused children are often held under flowing hot water or immersed in tubs of drawn hot water. As opposed to coffee and tea spills, where a thin layer of hot water cools rapidly on exposure to the air, with tap water a large reservoir of heat energy remains in direct contact with the child. This results in large, deep scalds. The mean body-surface area receiving second-degree and third-degree burns in inpatient tap-water burns is 19% (5).

Twenty-eight percent of all inpatient tap-water scalds were found to be abusive. In 60% of the cases where history indicated that an adult drew the hot water, the burn was abusive. Likewise, when the history indicated that an adult was in the room at the time of injury, abuse was present 48% of the time. Abuse was more likely when an adult other than the caretaker at the time of injury brought the child to medical care (71%), and when care was delayed more than two hours after injury (70%). Hight et al. found delays greater than twenty-four hours in 25% of the abusive tap-water burns in their study (4).

Although boys were the victims of tap-water burns only slightly more often than girls, they accounted for 69% of the abusive tap-water burns (5).

Abusive tap-water burns were not significantly more extensive than accidental tap-water burns, and the age of abuse and nonabuse victims was not significantly different. Although the water temperature in Seattle homes was unrelated to the family's social class, tap-water scald burns, social stress, and abusive burns were all more frequent in the laboring and unemployed classes (5).

As in other forms of abuse, tap-water scalds often arise when a socially and emotionally isolated and stressed caretaker reacts to what is viewed as child misbehavior. He exposes the child to hot water as punishment or as an impulsive act to end fussiness. Such episodes are often related to stool and toilet training. Abusive tap-water-flow burns will appear similar to the coffee- and tea-spill burns described later, but they will involve the buttocks, perineum, and legs more frequently.

> The twenty-eight-month-old daughter of an unemployed logger on welfare soiled her diapers. He rinsed her buttocks under the running hot-water tap. She sustained 12% first- and second-degree burns of the buttocks, perineum, and left thigh.

Children may also be forcibly immersed in drawn hot water. When hot water has just been drawn, the bottom of the sink or tub remains at a lower temperature than the water it contains. If an infant's body is forcibly opposed to the bottom of the container, it may be spared burning. This creates an unburned central area—the hole in the doughnut effect. If a child is firmly held in a position of flexion, intertriginous areas and opposed areas of the limbs and trunk will be spared burning. An unrestrained child in a tub of hot water may be unable to extricate himself from the water, but will usually thrash about, creating splash burns, blurring of the waterline margin, and burning of flexion crease areas. When restrained, such splashing and blurring may be minimal, and clear margins of the burn allow one to reconstruct the child's position in the water.

In many cases the child's position will be physically and developmentally impossible for an unrestrained child to maintain. Immersion injuries involving the buttocks and perineum only, imply that the child was held in flexion and the buttocks dipped in drawn hot water. Splash marks and burns of the hands or feet would be present if the injury was accidental. Such hallmarks of immersion injury may allow medical personnel to discount fabricated histories of accidental injury. A hypothesis of forcible restraint may be made.

> A ten-month-old girl was brought to the emergency room two hours after her mother's companion was alleged to have spilled a pot of hot water on her. Forty percent full-thickness burns occurred in a pattern indicating that she had been immersed in hot water with her buttocks pressed against a cooler tub bottom. Sparing of flexion areas also implied forcible restraint. Old fractures of both radii were found on skeletal survey. Abuse was recognized because of the discrepancy between history and burn pattern (fig. 11.2) (6).

Stocking and glove injuries with sharp upper margins will be seen if a child's feet or hands are held in hot water.

> A three-month-old boy was being cared for by his sixteen-year-old father. The child sustained a second-degree stocking burn of his right leg. His father's history was that he had steadied the infant on top of the bathroom sink while he filled the sink, wet a wash cloth, and covered his face with it to soak a cold sore. When his father removed the wash cloth, he discovered the child's injury. The infant's mother called the child's pediatrician later in the day to express her concern about the possibility of abuse. The father had a history of emotional instability and easy frustration with the infant's fussing. After recovery, the child was discharged to the home with children's protective service supervision and counseling (fig. 11.3).

A child who is held in a tub of shallow water may "tripod," raise up on his hands and feet to protect his buttocks and perineum from burning. These children will present with stocking and glove burns of several limbs.

The rapidity of burning is inversely proportional to the thickness of the skin (23). Young

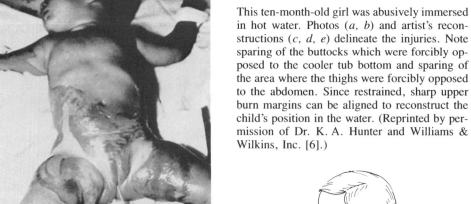

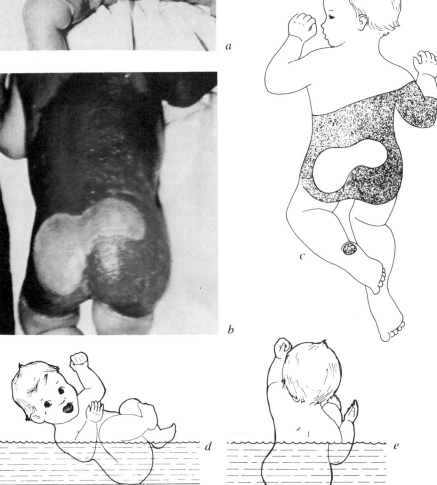

Figure 11.2

This ten-month-old girl was abusively immersed in hot water. Photos (*a, b*) and artist's reconstructions (*c, d, e*) delineate the injuries. Note sparing of the buttocks which were forcibly opposed to the cooler tub bottom and sparing of the area where the thighs were forcibly opposed to the abdomen. Since restrained, sharp upper burn margins can be aligned to reconstruct the child's position in the water. (Reprinted by permission of Dr. K. A. Hunter and Williams & Wilkins, Inc. [6].)

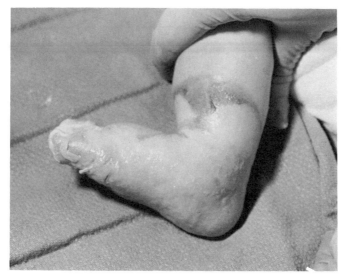

Figure 11.3

A three-month-old boy sustained a stocking burn of his right leg in the bathroom sink. The straight, sharp upper margin of the burn without splash burns implies restraint.

children's thin skin is likely to burn with less exposure time than an adult could tolerate and with cooler heat sources than an adult might expect to be damaging. When adults were surveyed to determine their awareness of hot-tap-water risk, no one knew what temperature would be hazardous (5). Adults may test the temperature of an infant's bath with their thick, heat-insensitive palmar skin. For reference, though most infants are comfortable bathing in 101°F water, hot tubs are seldom hotter than 108°F, usually 106°F. Normal adults sense that water is painfully hot at 109°F–113°F (25, pp. 1324–51). At the threshold temperature for burning, 113°F, six hours exposure is required to cause second-degree burns in both children and adults (24). Although a hurried caretaker may fail to recognize the risk of hot water, histories that the caretaker tested the bath water, found it comfortable, then put the infant in the tub should be suspect.

In most forms of child abuse, the instrument of injury (i.e., the hand or other object) is ever present. As such, the only means of preventive intervention is to recognize, treat, and support the potential abuser prior to the injury. Tap-water scalds are unique in that it is possible to modify the agent of injury to make it less destructive. Below 120°F, hot water is unlikely to inflict major injury. This is the lowest hot-water temperature attainable with many current water-heater thermostats. Some families will discover that their water heater cannot produce an adequate quantity of hot water at this temperature, but most homes can successfully function with a water-heater setting of 120°F–130°F. The risk of scalding is significantly greater at 130°F. The United States Consumer Product Safety Commission has already asked plumbing manufacturers to comply with a voluntary standard requiring mixing valves on new tubs and showers that would limit water temperature to 120°F or less. Unfortunately, these valves are expensive to install on existing tubs, and the frequent, abusive sink burns would not be prevented.

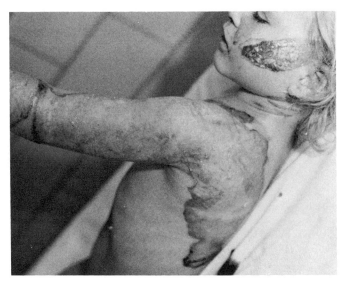

Figure 11.4

A three-and-a-half-year-old girl was said to have pulled a pot of hot water upon herself. The depth of the burn on her chest decreases in the pattern of thinning, cooling water. This downward flow pattern implies that she was upright at the time of injury. The direction of burning on her face and shoulder suggests that the water came from above and behind her left ear.

Until effective regulation is enacted, individual practitioners can recommend to their patients' families that they reset their water heaters to a safe level. Because of the energy-saving potential, many utility companies will reset the heater at the customer's request. In families with a recognized abuse potential, this might be a particularly helpful preventive measure.

A smaller percentage (6%) of scalds caused by liquids other than hot tap water are the result of child abuse (5). The agents are the usual causes of scalding which one sees in practice: coffee, tea, and cooking pots from the stove. The physical hallmarks of abuse in these injuries are more subtle, so that the general characteristics of abusive families and historical clues and inconsistencies must provide a greater part of the diagnosis. The child involved in an accidental scalding usually looks up and pulls a container of hot liquid down upon himself. The resulting burn (in face, arm, and upper trunk injuries) usually involves the under side of the chin and axilla on the injured side (26). Sparing of these areas may suggest that the hot liquid was poured or thrown upon the victim. The point of initial impact of hot fluid will be burned most deeply. From there, downward gravitational flow of cooling liquid will occur. Gradually, less severely burned areas will stream down from the most deeply burned site. The presence of a flow injury and position of the victim at the time of injury can be deduced from these patterns.

A three-and-a-half-year-old girl presented after having pulled a pot of hot water onto herself. She sustained 20% second- and third-degree burns. Flow patterns indicated that the burn occurred

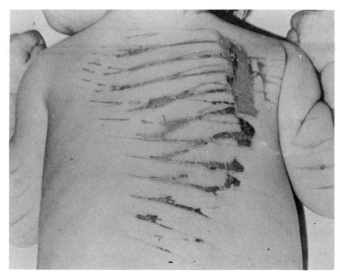

Figure 11.5

The back of this three-month-old was pressed twice against a hot wall-heating grate. The uniformity of depth of the burn, large clear imprint, and double imprint on a normally clothed body part make accidental burning unlikely. (Photograph courtesy of Dr. Barton Schmitt.)

while she was upright and that the fluid came from above and behind her left shoulder. The potential discrepancy between the burn pattern and history was not noted during her hospitalization (fig. 11.4).

Excessive splash burns above the site of primary impact suggest that fluid was thrown at the victim. Some scalds will occur on body parts where it is virtually impossible for the injury to have been accidental. In many cases, although one may be told that "he pulled a pot of hot coffee upon himself," the burns will be compatible only with immersion, and a presumptive diagnosis of inflicted tap-water injury can be made.

Specific Patterns of Other Burns

Contact burns are the second most frequent cause of abusive burns (2, 7). A majority involve contact with hot metal objects such as irons, stove burners, or heater grates. If such injuries occur by accident, brief, glancing contact of exposed body parts with a small portion of the hot surface is the rule. Abusive acts may result in prolonged, steady contact with a large portion of the hot surface. Symmetrical, deep imprints with crisp margins of the entire burning surface will suggest abuse, as opposed to small burn areas with slurred margins lacking a full imprint of the burning surface. Accidental contact burns are usually deeper and more intense on one edge of the burn. Burning of areas of the body where accidental brushing contact is unlikely, such as buttocks and perineum, suggests abuse (26). Multiple burned areas may also be noted.

The father of a three-month-old child pressed his back against a heating grate to stop the infant's fussiness. Second-degree burns healed without scarring and the child was safely returned to the home after family therapy (fig. 11.5).

Abusive contact burns also occur when small objects are heated and used to brand children. The top of metal cigarette lighters and knife blades are commonly used (26). Clear imprints of the burning object are often seen.

A separate group of contact burns is seen in our cigarette-smoking culture. Adults often have burning cigarettes on hand during times of frustration and may inflict deep, circular cigarette burns upon their children. These burns are often grouped and multiple, most often involving the hands and arms. Although accidental cigarette burns occur when a child brushes against a lighted cigarette that an adult is holding, these injuries are usually single, shallower, and not circular. Abuse should be suspected when cigarette burns are present on normally clothed body parts.

Two- and three-year-old siblings were brought to the emergency room with a total of about forty cigarette burns. They had been living with their heroin-addicted mother in a home of heroin addicts. The children were removed from the home and subsequently adopted (fig. 11.6).

Scars from therapeutic moxibustion may be found on the trunk and abdomen of Asian refugee children. Though they look like cigarette burn scars, history will reveal that they resulted from treatment by a folk medical practitioner (27).

In addition to infants, teenagers and young adults may also be the victims of inflicted

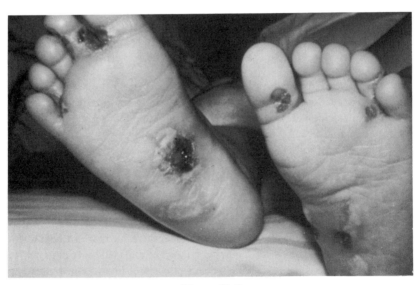

Figure 11.6

Multiple cigarette burns were present on the feet and other body parts of this two-year-old child and his three-year-old sibling. Deep and at times perfectly round burns the size of a cigarette tip are present on the sole of the foot. Multiple burns in this configuration and location rule out accidental injury. (Photograph courtesy of Dr. Barton Schmitt.)

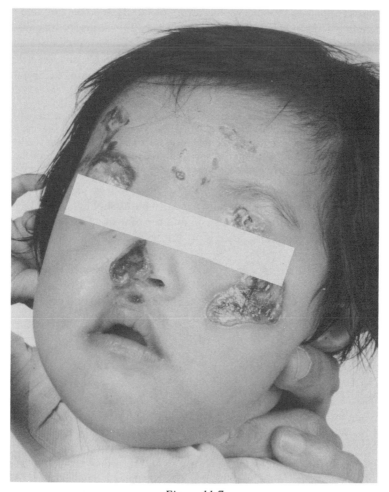

Figure 11.7

This 11-month-old girl was "found" in her crib with multiple electrical burns on her face. Visitation failed to reveal the source of the injuries.

burns. Some of the more violent segments of our society favor throwing caustic substances in the faces of their rivals. Fully 27% of all burns in the study of Crikelair et al. at the Harlem Hospital were the result of attacks (28). Fifteen of these thirty-three injuries were the result of lye or acid cocktails thrown in the face of a victim with the intent to blind and disfigure. The remaining attacks involved flames and flammable liquids (six), scalding water (eleven), and a hot knife used as a branding iron (one). Abusive clothing ignition, flammable liquid, and electrical burns will leave few physical clues of abuse, but the history and circumstances of the injury may point to the diagnosis. The victims of these injuries are often older children.

If infants are abusively burned in microwave ovens, characteristic burn patterns will result. Skin and deep muscle layers, with their greater water content, are preferentially burned, relatively sparing the intervening layers of fat. Tissue charring and microscopic nuclear streaming seen in electrical burns are absent (29). A parent may also attempt to incinerate an unwanted child (30).

Electric burns are deeply coagulative, necrosing injuries. Abusive electric burns may be multiple or occur at other locations than the angle of the mouth, the usual location of accidental injuries.

> The 11-month-old daughter of a Vietnamese refugee mother was brought to the emergency room with multiple electric burns of the face (fig. 11.7). Her mother stated that she and her twin sister had been well when put down together in their crib for a nap. An hour later she was discovered burned. History and public health nurse visitation failed to reveal a source of the burns in the vicinity of the crib. Three unrelated adult males resided in the home. The children were removed to protective custody.

Finally, the difference between wet burns and dry burns should be noted. The so-called wet burn, caused by a scalding liquid, has a number of characteristic features, including the splatter effect, sloughing and peeling of skin layers, and varying degrees of burn in close proximity.

The burn caused by a hot, dry instrument often has the absence of the findings noted above, plus certain characteristic features. Among these are delineated margin, often branding-type, scabbing of cutaneous edges about the burn, sometimes the odor of burnt skin, and the general dry nature about the burn site.

General Patterns of Abuse Involving Burns

Families who use burning to abuse their children exhibit many of the same characteristics of abusive families as noted elsewhere in this volume. Some points, however, deserve special comment. When treating a burned child, every effort should be made to acquire color photographs, including appropriate patient identification within the field of the photograph. Each person interacting with the family should record as accurately as possible the history of the mode and circumstances of injury. In these cases, the nurse, intern, resident, and attending physician should take and record independent histories from all available caretakers. Skeletal X-rays should be obtained where appropriate.

Abused children may be brought to medical care inappropriately late after their injuries, when infection or other burn complications have occurred. The status of the burn may imply that it is older than alleged. They may be brought to care by someone other than the caretaker at the time of injury. Medical attendants may receive several vague and conflicting histories of how the burn occurred. They may be told the child was "found burned," strong urine or soap "burned her bottom," or simply that there was no witness to the injury. Burns may be seen in children too young to have gotten in an injury situation as alleged. A six-month-old is unlikely to climb into the bathtub and turn on the hot water. Conversely, an older child may present with a burn that he should have been able to escape. A six-year-old is unlikely to sustain a perfect glove scald. An outreach worker should visit the home to reconstruct the injury situation, measure the water temperature and examine the bathroom where appropriate. Burn victims may present with histories unlikely to explain improbable distributions.

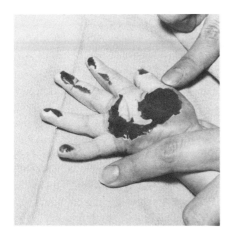
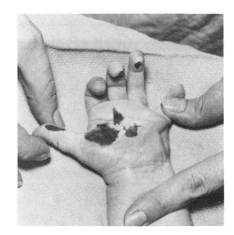
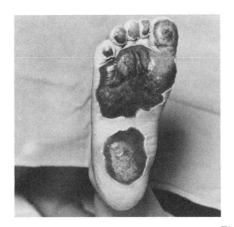
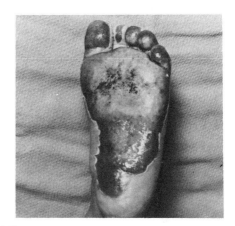

Figure 11.8

This twenty-month-old male burned only his palms and soles on a hot griddle. An injury in this pattern is unlikely to have occurred by accident.

> When a twenty-month-old boy was brought by his mother to the emergency room, she said that he had pushed a chair up to the stove, turned on the gas under the griddle, and climbed onto it. His cries woke her from her sleep, and she found him with burns of both palms and both soles only (fig. 11.8). He was said to be excessively active and to misbehave in spite of twice-daily spankings.

In addition to the specific physical criteria for abuse that accompany several modes of burning, the children may have other physical signs of neglect and abuse. Multiple, concurrent injuries or history or signs of repeated injury in the past may be present. Wilkinson noted that multiple episodes of burning occur in the same child or in several children in the same household (10). Keen et al. found that twelve of sixteen burn-abused children had multiple burns, and twelve of sixteen had other evidence of recent trauma (26). Forty-two percent of Hight et al.'s (4) and all of Ayoub and Pfeifer's (31) abusive burn victims had other physical evidence of abuse. Involvement of the buttocks or perineum should suggest abuse. Ninety-two percent of Stone et al.'s (2) and 40% of Keen et al.'s (26) burn-abused children were so injured.

Although parents may describe their children as hyperactive and impulsive, burn-abuse victims may seem withdrawn, noncommunicative, and excessively fearful of the hospital staff. They may appear malnourished, ill-kempt, and developmentally retarded. After several weeks on the burn ward, although the staff have inflicted repeated painful medical procedures, the children may become more outgoing and reponsive to attention. Apparent retardation may improve rapidly as the children begin to communicate and move in age-appropriate behaviors. As trust develops, older children may relate the circumstances of their injuries.

Different modes of burn injury imply different degrees of intent to injure. Everyone with children is familiar with drawing the bath water, checking the temperature with one's own hand, and placing an infant in the water. The child may cry or complain bitterly that the water is too hot. People are not inherently aware of the hazard of hot tap water, and adult hands sense less heat and burn less easily than children's skin. A parent who impulsively places a child in an unchecked tub of scalding water as punishment may not expect or wish injury to result. On the other hand, stove element burns, repeated cigarette burns, or caustic assaults can hardly be without abusive intent. Whether this distinction should affect therapy of the abusive situation is problematic. A rash gesture with bath water may imply a significant future risk of injury and is more often fatal than cigarette burns.

Pseudoabusive and Other Nonaccidental, Nonabusive Burns

When a health professional misses the diagnosis of an abusive burn and simply treats the child for the injury, the child returns home to a high risk of future serious injury. Perhaps equally damaging for many families is an incorrect diagnosis of abuse in accidental injury cases. Many patterns of burn are not diagnostic of abuse. Misdiagnosis of abuse sets the stage for mistrust and accusation of one parent by the other and suspicion of the health care system which falsely labeled them. Schmitt et al. described situations where over-diagnosis of abusive burning resulted in increased family stress (32). Five patients sustained contact burns from sun-heated objects. Typically, on a hot summer day in a car with dark upholstery, the seat-belt buckle is heated to damaging temperatures. The child will inexplicably scream with pain when placed in the car. Only later, when the pain may be forgotten, will a circumscribed contact burn be discovered. A high index of suspicion and careful history taking can provide the diagnosis.

Many folk-medicine treatments may result in burns. The practice of cupping (applying a heated cup to the chest to draw out congestion by cooling) may result in circular burns with central contusions (33). One Vietnamese child was treated by his family for fever by application of heated oil followed by firm rubbing with a spoon. This treatment resulted in multiple second-degree burns on his chest and upper back. This variation on the practice of *cao gao* may appear abusive unless the parent is questioned to determine the source of the burns (34). In the reported cases of *cao gao,* warm oil was placed on the chest and upper back. This area was then stroked briskly with the edge of a coin until erythema developed. When seen by physicians, linear contusions were present in the stroked region. The Asian refugee children noted above and a Saudi Arabian child we observed had cigarette-like burn injuries. The Saudi child had treatment for fever which resulted in superficial 4 mm burns spaced at ninety degrees around the umbilicus.

Although parents may intentionally expose their children to burning situations as a means of teaching burn hazard, subsequent burn injury may actually be more frequent in these families (9). This practice should be discouraged.

Nonaccidental burns may also be self-inflicted, usually in the context of a hysterical syndrome (35). These burns will exhibit all the physical characteristics of abusive burns, but tend to be located in easily reached areas of the body. Victims are likely to be school age. Teenagers who burn their forearms with cigarettes are probably most frequent.

Bullous impetigo may initially look like local second-degree burns and toxic epidermal necrolysis like a widespread second-degree burn. Generalized erythema will, however, be present, and a focus of staphylococcal infection can usually be found. Treatment with antibiotics is required.

Summary

Burn injury is a major cause of death and disability in childhood, often the consequence of disturbed home situations or abuse. The busy primary care or emergency room physician who is frequently faced with caring for childhood burn victims may become immersed in the technical aspects of the medical treatment, forgetting the basic question of how the injury occurred. Unless questioned specifically, the parent may not volunteer that information. Even if a history is given, it may be intended to mislead and to obscure the actual circumstances of injury. Careful clinical appraisal of the injury, combined with repeated attempts to obtain a history will allow the clinician to decide if the injury is likely to have been accidental, a reaction to situational stress, or frankly abusive. Effective treatment can only be planned with assessment of whether the child will receive good home care for his wound and if further injury is likely. In cases of severe injury or questionable social situations, hospitalization will be necessary for medical stabilization and to allow initial social service investigation and intervention. Not only the family of the abused child, but also many stressed and disorganized families of accidentally burned children, will need assistance to prevent additional injury.

References

1. National Safety Council. 1984. *Accident Facts.* Chicago: National Safety Council.
2. Stone, N. D.; Rinaldo, L.; Humphrey, C. R.; and Brown, R. H. 1970. Child Abuse by Burning. *Surgical Clinics of North America* 50:1419–24.
3. Phillips, P. S.; Pickrell, E.; and Morse, T. S. 1974. Intentional Burning: A Severe Form of Child Abuse. *J. Am. College of Emergency Physicians* 3:388–90.
4. Hight, D. W.; Bakalar, H. R.; and Lloyd, J. R. 1979. Inflicted Burns in Children. *JAMA* 242:517–20.

5. Feldman, K. W.; Schaller, R. T.; Feldman, J. A.; and McMillon, M. 1978. Tap-Water Scald Burns in Children. *Pediatrics* 62:1–7.

6. Lenoski, E. F., and Hunter, K. A. 1977. Specific Patterns of Inflicted Burn Injuries. *J. Trauma* 17:842–46.

7. Smith, S. M., and Hanson, R. 1974. Battered Children: A Medical and Psychologic Study. *British Med. J.* 3:666–70.

8. Gil, D. G. 1970. *Violence against Children.* Cambridge, Mass.: Harvard University Press.

9. Meyer, R. L.; Roelofs, H. A.; Bluestone, J.; and Redmond, S. 1963. Accidental Injury to the Preschool Child. *J. Pediatrics* 63:95–105.

10. Wilkinson, A. W. 1944. Burns and Scalds in Children. *British Med. J.* 1:37–40.

11. Long, R. T., and Cope, O. 1961. Emotional Problems in Burned Children. *New England J. Med.* 264:1121–27.

12. Holter, J. C., and Friedman, S. B. 1969. Etiology and Management of Severely Burned Children. *Am. J. Diseases in Children* 118:680–86.

13. Borland, B. L. 1967. Prevention of Childhood Burns: Conclusions Drawn from an Epidemiology Study. *Clinical Pediatrics* 6:693–95.

14. Feldman, K. W.; Clarren, S. K.; and McLaughlin, J. F. 1981. Tap Water Burns in Handicapped Children. *Pediatrics* 67:560–62.

15. Waller, J. A., and Manheimer, D. I. 1964. Nonfatal Burns of Children in a Well-Defined Urban Population. *J. Pediatrics* 65:863–69.

16. Bleck, E. E. 1955. Causes of Burns in Children. *JAMA* 158:100–103.

17. Jensen, G. D. 1959. Preventive Implications of a Study of 100 Children Treated for Serious Burns. *Pediatrics* 24:623–30.

18. Yanofsky, N. N., and Morain, W. D. 1984. Upper Extremity Burns from Woodstoves. *Pediatrics* 73:722–26.

19. Colebrook, L., and Colebrook, V. 1949. The Prevention of Burns and Scalds: Review of 1,000 Cases. *Lancet* 2:181–88.

20. Moyer, C. A. 1954. The Sociologic Aspects of Trauma. *Am. J. Surgery* 87:421–30.

21. MacArthur, J. D., and Moore, F. D. 1975. Epidemiology of Burns: The Burn-Prone Patient. *JAMA* 231:259–63.

22. Tempest, M. N. 1956. Survey of Domestic Burns and Scalds in Wales during 1955. *British Med. J.* 1:1387–92.

23. Moritz, A. R., and Henriques, F. C. 1947. Studies of Thermal Injury: The Relative Importance of Time and Temperature in the Causation of Cutaneous Burns. *Am. J. Pathology* 23:695–720.

24. Feldman, K. W. 1983. Help Needed on Hot Water Burns. *Pediatrics* 71:145–46.

25. Greenfield, A. D. M. 1963. *The Circulation through the Skin in Physiology, Circulation II.* American Physiologic Society. Bethesda, Md.: Williams & Wilkins.

26. Keen, J. H.; Lendrum, J.; and Wolman, B. 1975. Inflicted Burns and Scalds in Children. *British Med. J.* 4:268–69.

27. Feldman, K. W. 1984. Pseudoabusive Burns in Asian Refugees. *Am. J. Diseases in Children* 138:768–69.

28. Crikelair, G. F.; Symonds, F. C.; Ollstein, R. N.; and Kirsner, A. I. 1968. Burn Causation: Its Many Sides. *J. Trauma* 8:572–81.

29. Cohle, S. D.; Surrell, J. A.; and Alexander, R. C. 1985. Microwave Oven Burns. *J. Pediatrics,* in press.

30. Lung, R. J.; Miller, S. H.; Davis, T. S.; and Graham, W. P., III. 1977. Recognizing Burn Injuries as Abuse. *Am. Family Physician* 15:134–35.

31. Ayoub, C., and Pfeifer, D. 1979. Burns As a Manifestation of Child Abuse and Neglect. *Am. J. Diseases in Children* 133:910–14.

32. Schmitt, B. D.; Gray, J. D.; and Britton, H. L. 1978. Car Seat Burns in Infants: Avoiding Confusion with Inflicted Burns. *Pediatrics* 62:607–9.

33. Sandler, A. P., and Haynes, V. 1978. Nonaccidental Trauma and Medical Folk Belief: A Case of Cupping. *Pediatrics* 61:921–22.

34. Yeatman, G. W.; Shaw, C.; Barlow, M. J.; and Bartlett, G. 1976. Pseudobattering in Vietnamese Children. *Pediatrics* 58:616–18.

35. Curran, J. P. 1973. Hysterical Dermatitis Factitia. *Am. J. Diseases in Children* 125:564–67.

12 Radiology and Other Imaging Procedures

Frederic N. Silverman

A reexamination of the contributions of diagnostic radiology to the history of the concept of "the battered child" and a survey of its current role in diagnosis indicate the reliability of the features described in prior editions of this book, as well as areas where extension of conventional modalities of radiologic examination are useful. To this knowledge must be added new information derived from technology currently available which had not been tested previously. Although certain names customarily have been linked to the initial descriptions and popularization of the condition, the overwhelming support provided by scores of physicians caring for children must be acknowledged as securing the validity of roentgenographic examination in its various applications to the recognition of physical abuse of children.

The concept of "the battered child" and the developments in the elucidation of the condition are intimately related to the field of diagnostic radiology. Although the syndrome was recognized in practically all its manifestations and implications in 1860 by Tardieu (1), it was not until Caffey's radiologic observations eighty-six years later (2) that any significant impact upon medical, social, and legal activities was generated. Caffey's observations subsequently were confirmed and their significance supported by papers published primarily in radiologic journals and particularly by pediatric radiologists. The evidence of the radiologic signs of bone injury and repair provided the solid medical basis on which was built the social, legal, and psychopathologic aspects of the problem. The recognition of extraskeletal radiologic features has further emphasized the role of diagnostic radiology.

The patients described by West (3) in 1888 have been considered to represent some of the early instances of the battered child syndrome, but, because his report antedated the discovery of the X-ray in 1895, the diagnosis cannot be substantiated. Although great advances were made in most areas of X-ray diagnosis immediately following the introduction of X-rays, the radiographic features of injuries to bones of infants and their repair were not described in any detail until almost forty years later. At that time the bizarre

Frederic N. Silverman, M.D., is professor emeritus of clinical radiology and clinical pediatrics, Stanford University Medical Center.

radiographic manifestations of recovery from epiphyseal separation during breech extraction were reported on Snedecor and his associates (4). About the same time, articles on unusual periosteal reactions in children that were primarily to be differentiated from those of congenital syphilis began to make their appearance (5–7). Caffey (2), in 1946, was the first to call attention to multiple fractures of the long bones, of unknown origin, that accompanied a significant number of cases of subdural hematoma. Accepting the view of Ingraham and Heyl (8) that the subdural hematomas were traumatic, Caffey suggested a traumatic origin for these injuries also.

Ample support for Caffey's observations on bone lesions with subdural hematomas followed quickly (9–14). Bakwin (15, 16) reported several cases of unusual traumatic reactions in bones, among which was at least one battered child. In 1953, Silverman (17), following Caffey's lead, insisted on a traumatic basis for injuries of the type now known to occur in the battered child in a presentation of three cases of the condition without subdural hematomas. Astley (18) believed that there was a primary metaphyseal fragility of bone in affected children, but this concept was discarded by Woolley and Evans in 1955 (19). These authors reviewed material seen over an eight-year period with radiographic findings suggesting injury, with or without a history of trauma. They concluded that the radiographic manifestations of injury and its repair were identical whether a history of injury was or was not obtained and that the skeletal lesions "having the appearance of fracture—regardless of history for injury or the presence or absence of intracranial bleeding—are due to undesirable vectors of force." They also emphasized that the environmental factors surrounding the infants with the radiographic changes frequently included grossly undesirable and hazardous circumstances. Numerous subsequent reports have reinforced Woolley and Evans's conclusions, which have now become generally accepted (20–30). The radiologic aspects were dealt with in detail by Caffey in 1957 (31) and by Silverman in 1972 (32). A comprehensive report has been published in French by Rabouille (33). Cameron and Rae included a comprehensive section on radiological diagnosis in their *Atlas of the Battered Child Syndrome* (34, pp. 20–50). In 1978, Ellison et al. demonstrated computed tomography to be a useful body imaging technique in known or suspected abuse (35).

The only change in this history is the recent recognition that the cases reported by West in 1888 (3) probably did not represent patients with the battered child syndrome but rather with familial infantile cortical hyperostosis (36), another pediatric disorder whose characterization was another contribution of Dr. John Caffey (37). Consequently, the following pages will be devoted to a review of conventional radiographic features that have stood the test of time and to a description and evaluation of information provided by the availability of newer imaging modalities.

Conventional Radiographic Features

Radiologic examination has two main functions in relation to the battered child. It serves as a case-finding tool, and subsequently it can be used as a guide to the management of known cases.

In many instances the diagnostic bone lesions are noted incidental to examination for conditions other than known injury; more frequently, the examination is undertaken because of a history of injury, and then lesions are found which are much more extensive than would have been anticipated from the history or which demonstrate that the present episode was only one of several. In instances in which the battered child syndrome is suspected, the presence of radiographic changes in the skeleton can support the diagnosis; the absence of radiologic changes does not necessarily exclude it. In well-established cases of the battered child, follow-up examinations to evaluate the nature and extent of healing are helpful just as they are in the follow-up examinations of any other type of fracture.

The radiologic signs of skeletal injury and the responses to it are similar whether there is a history of injury or not. Gross fractures are obvious, and their characteristics are available in standard radiologic and orthopedic texts. The features generally considered typical of skeletal abnormalities in the battered child syndrome are predominant localization in the metaphyses of long bones, exaggerated periosteal reaction, multiplicity of lesions, and differing stages of healing and repair of the multiple lesions (2, 17, 19, 28, 32). Cameron and Rae (34) emphasized rib injuries and, particularly, the combination of any common fracture with metaphyseal or rib fractures. Surveys of abused children from several medical centers suggest that diaphyseal fractures are actually more common than metaphysical fractures (two and one-half to four times as frequent), although the latter are more "specific" (38, 39). If there is more than one injured bone regardless of the location of the injury, and the injuries are of different ages as indicated by the degree of healing or lack of it, the "specificity" is the same. The critical feature that warrants an investigation is the presence of an injury, in this context a fracture, for which an adequate explanation is not forthcoming.

Lesions of the metaphyses are a common observation and the most typical. Their occurrence is probably related to the fact that many of the injuries are incurred not so much by direct blows as by vigorous handling, as in shaking the child. The extremities are the "handles" for the mishandling. The rigidity of bone and the elasticity of ligamentous connections apparently can withstand the twisting-pulling forces of a heavy adult hand on a young extremity. In the infant under one year of age, who is the most frequent recipient of this type of maltreatment, epiphyseal separation takes place at the relatively weak cartilage-shaft junction. This may be a gross displacement, easy to recognize, a minor irregularity in the line of radiolucent cartilage between epiphyseal ossification center and shaft with slight widening (fig. 12.1), or it may be so slight as to be radiologically invisible. The lesions correspond to what are currently known as epiphyseal fractures of the Salter types I and II (see fig. 12.2). In areas where epiphyseal ossification centers are not present for their displacement to be noted, the features are initially more difficult to recognize (fig. 12.3). When a large arc of metaphyseal bone is displaced with its adjacent epiphysis, a so-called bucket-handle fracture can be observed (figs. 12.4, 12.5).

In any event, the healing process of the epiphyseal separation involves a revascularization that is reflected by subepiphyseal (metaphyseal) demineralization which can be detected radiologically approximately two weeks after an injury. If there has been no immobilization and further injury has occurred from ordinary activity, let alone further maltreatment, the destructive features are exaggerated. Rarely, epiphyseal injury is of a degree that leads to deformity and shortening.

The periosteum of young infants is relatively loosely attached to the bone in comparison with that of adults and is easily separated from it by direct physical force or by

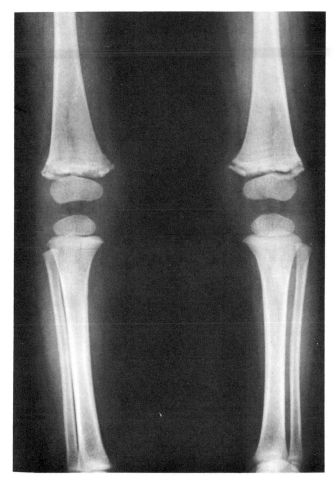

Figure 12.1

Metaphyseal fragmentation without epiphyseal displacement

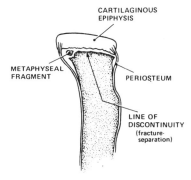

Figure 12.2

Diagram of Salter type II epiphyseal fracture (compare with fig. 12.6).

subperiosteal hemorrhage consequent to injury. In its new position, the periosteum produces new bone so that a calcified envelope (involucrum) surrounds the denuded portion of the bone (fig. 12.6). The periosteum has its strongest attachment to the epiphyseal line; as a result, most of the periosteum tends to remain attached to it even in gross epiphyseal separations. It is this feature in children that permits the newly formed bone to align itself with the displaced epiphysis, and the end result of production of new bone and resorption of old bone generally is complete reconstitution. In the interval the abundant subperiosteal new bone formation may develop an appearance suggestive of osteogenic malignancy (40). Subperiosteal ossification may be delayed if there is associated infection.

The initially elevated periosteum and its underlying blood is radiolucent. Within two to three weeks following the injury, calcium is deposited on its undersurface, which becomes

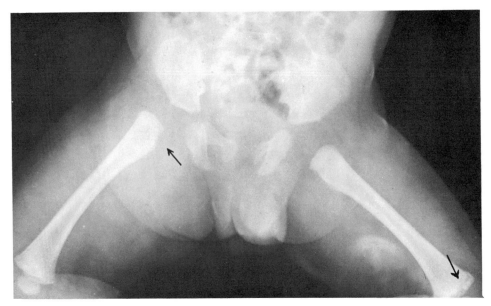

Figure 12.3

Traumatic epiphyseal separation of the right femoral head one week after vigorous pull on child's legs. Note soft tissue swelling of right thigh owing to hemorrhage. Displacement would be more obvious if ossification center for femoral head were present. Note also metaphyseal fracture at distal end of left femur.

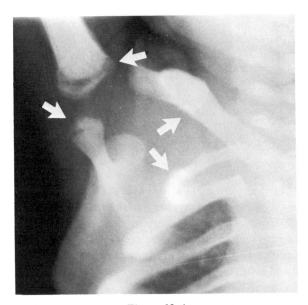

Figure 12.4

"Bucket-handle" fracture of proximal end of humerus. Same patient as in fig. 12.9. Arrows point to contemporaneous fracture of acromion process of scapula and to older, healing fractures of the clavicle and first rib.

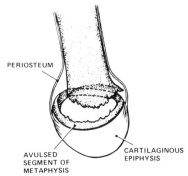

Figure 12.5

Diagram of fracture of humerus in fig. 12.4.

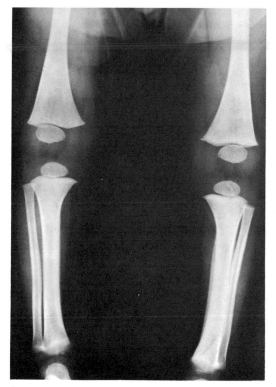

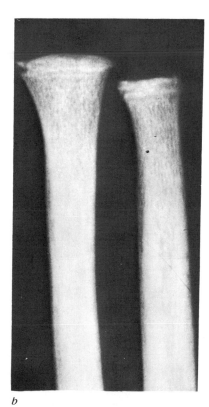

a   b

Figure 12.6

Lesions of different characters
and ages attest to the repetition of
injury. (*a*) The spiral fracture in
the left tibia is partially obscured
by the well-organized reparative
subperiosteal bone production.
There is a suggestion of a recent
metaphyseal fracture in the medial aspect of the distal metaphysis of the left femur. (*b*) Same
child, same day: recent metaphyseal injury in radius at wrist;
possible remote cortical thickening along shaft of ulna. (*c*) Same
child, same day: recent metaphyseal injury of radius at other
wrist, and remote fracture of distal humerus with exaggerated
subperiosteal new bone formation. Note density of all bones.

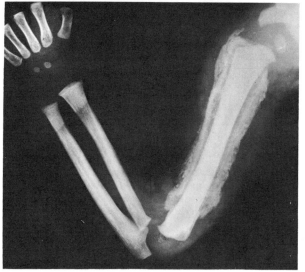

c

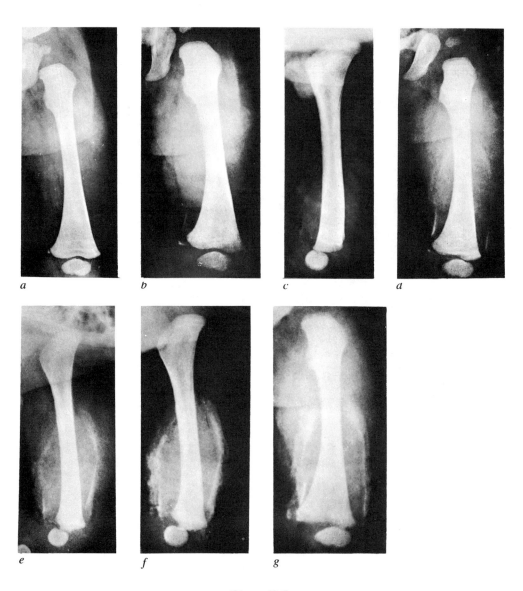

Figure 12.7

Sequence of calcification of elevated periosteum. (*a*) Four days after unexplained swelling of knee: small chip fracture, medial end of femur at knee. (*b*) Nine days after onset: chip fracture separated from bone by subperiosteal hemorrhage. (*c*) Epiphyseal separation clearly shown by posterior displacement in later projection. (*d*) Fourteen days after onset: the elevated periosteum is producing new bone, and the extent of the subperiosteal hematoma becomes visible. (*e*) Lateral projection, corresponding to *d*. (*f*) Sixteen days after onset: subperiosteal ossification has increased. (*g*) The displaced epiphysis is lined up with the center of the periosteum (involucrum) rather than the shaft from which it was separated (sequestrum). (Courtesy of *Journal of the American Medical Association*.)

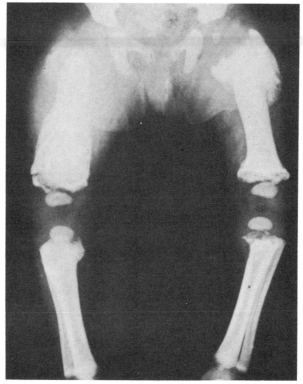

Figure 12.8

Extensive subperiosteal and metaphyseal lesions. The irregularity of the periosteal envelope suggests tears in this structure. (Courtesy of *American Journal of Roentgenology.*)

radiologically visible (fig. 12.7). If additional injury has taken place or if the initial injury was sufficient to tear the periosteum, calcifying callus may extend beyond the confines of the periosteum and develop gross irregular margins (fig. 12.8). Once the union of the fractured components of the bone has been accomplished, whether by fibrous or bony union, the periosteum responds to the usual stresses and strains, and the bone is remodeled to its original form; late residuals may merely present unusually thick cortices. Careful inspection of the tubular bones of children with the battered child syndrome frequently demonstrates periosteal elevations of varying degrees in different bones (see fig. 12.6). This variation is testimony to the repetitive nature of the injuries to which the child's skeleton has been subjected. An injury of considerable age may be indicated by a relatively thick, dense cortex; a slightly younger injury may have obvious subperiosteal new bone formation. More recent injuries may demonstrate massive calcium production with gross irregularities, and the most recent injury may show only soft tissue swelling without any bone production whatsoever. Periosteal new bone may occur in normal children and is said to be present in over 40 percent of premature and full-term babies (34),

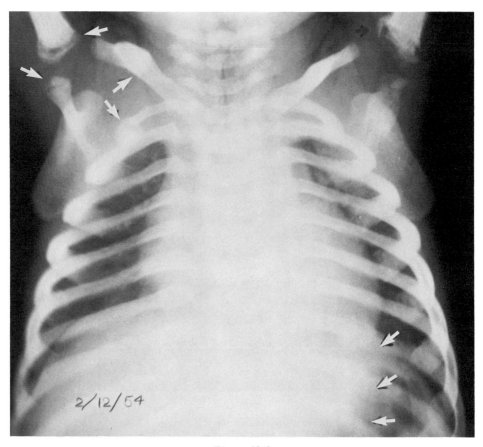

Figure 12.9

Three-month-old infant with recent "bucket handle" fractures of both humeri at the shoulders; old, healed fractures of the right clavicle and right first rib; and more recent healing fractures of the left eighth, ninth, and tenth ribs. Widening of the necks of several ribs (e.g., seventh right) may represent other healing fractures.

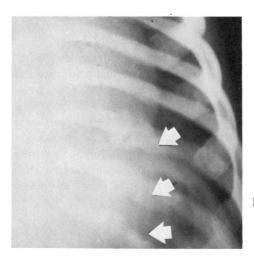

Figure 12.10

Enlargement of the left rib fractures in fig. 12.9.

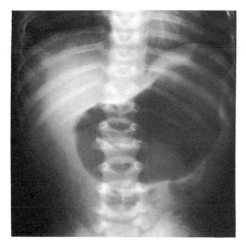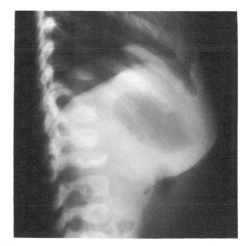

Figure 12.11

Compression fracture of vertebral body in seventeen-month-old boy with skull fracture, intramural hematoma of the duodenum, and multiple cutaneous bruises. Mother admitted punching baby in stomach.

but it may be appropriate to consider the phenomenon unexplained, rather than conclusively normal.

Fractures of the shafts (diaphyses) of tubular bones in the absence of metaphyseal lesions do not preclude the diagnosis of child abuse. In fact, as noted above, they are more common than the "typical" metaphyseal lesions and may demonstrate certain features that further support the suspicion of nonaccidental trauma. Transverse, rather than the usual oblique fractures of childhood, should be viewed with suspicion. In the absence of predisposing local bone disease, they commonly result from a direct force that is greater than a child could generate by himself, such as from a blow with a hard object.

Although the limbs are the sites of most skeletal lesions, almost any bone in the body can be affected. Rib fractures, recent or healing (figs. 12.9, 12.10), are important diagnostically and, when unexplained, should be considered manifestations of abuse until proved otherwise. In combination with other lesions elsewhere, they strengthen the case for a diagnosis of battering. They apparently do not occur as a sequel to cardiopulmonary resuscitation (CPR) but can be observed when abuse and CPR coexist (41). Fractures of the ribs in the paravertebral regions have special significance in this respect (34) as do injuries to the lateral portions of the clavicles (38) (fig. 12.9). In accidental trauma, the latter bones are affected more frequently in their lateral and middle portions respectively.

Small tubular bones of the hands and feet may demonstrate reactions to repetitive beatings (42). Compression fractures of the vertebral bodies (fig. 12.11) or fractures of spinous processes may occur following forced flexion or extension injuries (43, 44). Focal bone lesions resembling osteomyelitis or traumatic periostitis may result from medullary fat necrosis associated with pancreatitis that is secondary to child abuse (45). All these lesions and localizations are not common but when observed in association with skeletal lesions elsewhere can alert the physician to a possible case of child abuse.

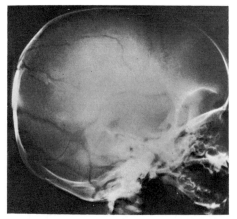

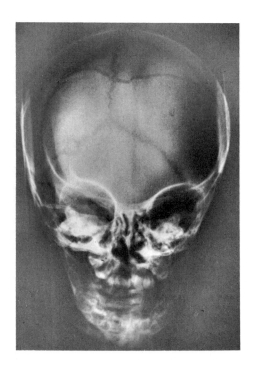

Figure 12.12

Extensive diastatic fractures of skull in child with typical limb lesions. Subdural hematomas were present bilaterally.

It is important to emphasize that it is the healing phase of the fractures that is generally recognized radiographically. Therefore, an injury that is too recent to demonstrate reparative change (less than two weeks old) may be missed entirely by conventional radiography. Radiographic evidence of soft tissue edema, of obliteration of deep and even superficial intermuscular fat septa, may provide a clue that the area in question should be reexamined after an appropriate interval.

The possibility of subdural hematoma must always be entertained when skeletal lesions are observed, and supportive evidence for subdural hematoma may be provided by the demonstration of separated cranial bones and widened sutures, other signs of increased intracranial pressure, or obvious fractures of the cranial bones themselves (fig. 12.12). Not infrequently, cranial fractures are not simple linear fractures, but are comminuted and resemble the multiple irregular fractures of an eggshell.

Computed Tomography

It is here that computed tomography (CT) of the cranium assumes paramount importance. It adds a new dimension to the imaging evaluation of suspected or obvious child abuse, particularly with respect to the intracranial complications (35). The pattern of changes in the central nervous system is distinctly different from that in the traumatized but non-abused child (46). The most frequent finding is acute interhemispheric subdural hematoma (fig. 12.13) in the parieto-occipital region with associated parenchymal injury. The interhemispheric subdural space does not communicate freely with other parts of the sub-

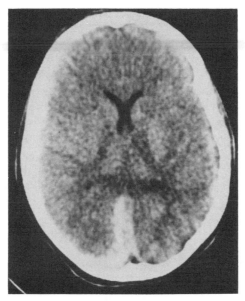

Figure 12.13

Acute bilateral interhemispheric subdural hematoma in unenhanced CT. Generalized decreased attenuation of brain suggests acute cerebral edema. (Courtesy of Dr. D. F. Merton, Duke University Medical Center.)

dural space, not even its right and left moieties (47). A hematoma in this site, therefore, is recognized as a collection of blood with a mildly curved lateral margin against the medial surface of the occipital lobe and a flat medial border formed by the falx cerebri when unilateral, and with an adjacent mirror image when bilateral. It is usually followed by permanent neurologic impairment and carries a poor prognosis. However, the recognition of even a smaller interhemispheric subdural hematoma may help identify an abused child and possibly lead to the prevention of further episodes (48).

Skull radiographs are often obtained to look for fractures and widened sutures as indications of actively increased intracranial pressure (see fig. 12.12). CT has demonstrated intracranial abnormalities in the absence of fractures or widened sutures, in the form of subdural and epidural hematomas, and cerebral hemorrhage, contusion, or edema (figs. 12.14, 12.15, 12.16) (49). These observations support the concept of vascular disruption by acceleration/deceleration movements of the brain as postulated by Caffey (50) to result from vigorous shaking of infants by adult custodians, most frequently their parents. Guthkelch (51) had suggested earlier that such movements could produce tears of the bridging veins, basing his theory on the experimental work of Ommaya et al. (52) with monkeys. Caffey emphasized that this mechanism of serious brain injury would leave no tell-tale signs such as bruising or scars to suggest physical abuse. Affected infants may show no bone lesions on skeletal surveys, but CT can clearly define the interhemispheric

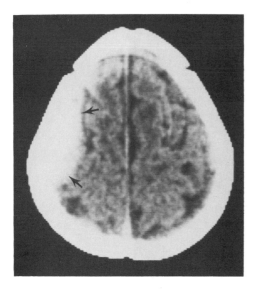

Figure 12.14

Acute convexity subdural hematoma. Unenhanced CT scan shows well-defined, lenticular, extracerebral intracranial density (*arrows*) characterized by increased attenuation in the frontoparietal region. Prominent sulci suggest atrophy resulting from previous episodes of craniocerebral trauma. (Reprinted, by permission, from D. L. Merton and D. R. S. Osborne, *Pediatric Annals* 12 (1983): 882–87.

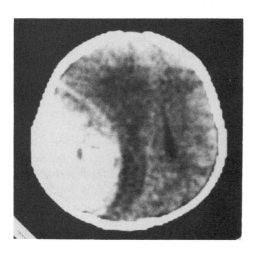

Figure 12.15

Epidural hematoma. Unenhanced CT shows an extracerebral, intracranial, dense fluid collection with rounded convex medical border. There is marked shift of the ventricular system. Acute cerebral edema indicated by reduction of grey-white attenuation. (Reprinted, by permission, from D. L. Merton and D. R. S. Osborne, *Pediatric Annals* 12 (1983): 882–87.

subdural hematomas that appear to have the same diagnostic significance as the "classical" bone stigmata of child abuse (53). On the other hand, Bennett and French (54) observed normal CT findings in an abused fifteen-month-old infant with acute but reversible increased intracranial pressure with no contusion or hematoma but with a central herniation syndrome that resolved with anticerebral edema therapy. In this context, CT showed minimal interhemispheric bleeding in three infants subjected to whiplash shaking injury in whom the diagnosis was first indicated by ophthalmoscopic examination that demonstrated extensive pale centered retinal hemorrhages (55). Obviously, CT is not infallible but it appears to be the most sensitive imaging procedure for recognition of intracranial manifestations of child abuse; moreover it is also of prognostic value permitting follow-up studies of cerebral changes (fig. 12.17) (56, 57). Cerebral contusion, with hemorrhage and

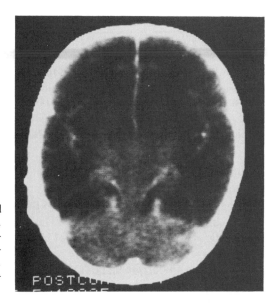

Figure 12.16

Acute cerebral infarction. Contrast enhanced CT. Normal perfusion of posterior fossa. Marked diminution in attenuation of supratentorial structures indicating bilateral occlusion of supratentorial cerebral arteries. (Courtesy of Dr. D. L. Merton, Duke University Medical Center.)

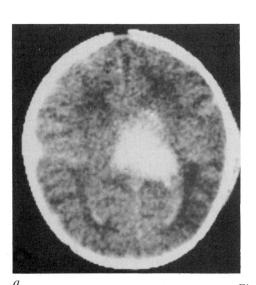

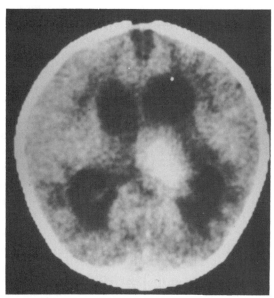

a

b

Figure 12.17

Cerebral contusion. (*a*) Unenhanced CT shows focus of increased attenuation of the corpus callosum consistent with deep, shearing cerebral hemorrhage. (*b*) Follow-up CT one month later shows deep cerebral hematoma with encephalomalacia and progressive dilatation of ventricles. (Reprinted, by permission, from D. L. Merton and D. R. S. Osborne, *Pediatric Annals* 12(1983):882–87.)

surrounding edema has been demonstrated by ultrasound and confirmed by CT (58). Thus, ultrasound may be an alternative form of examination during the first year of life, especially when there is only a slight suspicion of head injury and it is difficult to justify CT.

From the standpoint of the unreliability of history of trauma in children with craniocerebral symptoms, it is worth noting that only 3 of 246 children aged five years or less, who had fallen out of bed at home or in hospital, had identifiable skull fractures on X-ray films, and none had serious injury (59). Skull fractures, especially when multiple, invite suspicion of child abuse when an explanation on this basis is advanced.

Scintigraphy (Bone Scan)

Radionuclide scans have been advocated for initial screening for skeletal lesions in suspected child abuse victims (60–63). Their value rests on the affinity of bone-seeking radionuclides to concentrate in areas of increased blood flow and bone formation. Recent fractures appear as "hot spots" early because of increased blood flow, and late because of increased bone production (callus). Bone scans are more sensitive to the pathophysiologic changes that accompany skeletal injury than are radiograms, but they are also less specific in the identification of fracture or its progress in healing. Comparison of bone scans and radiographic skeletal surveys indicate that the two procedures are complementary, one often identifying lesions that escape the other. If multiplicity of lesions is being sought, bone scans are superb; if the anatomy or the chronology of the individual lesions is desired to indicate the nature of repetition of the injury, nothing compares with the radiographic evidence. The decision to use one or the other or both will depend on the expertise available, the requirements for medical management, and what is necessary for disposition of the social aspects of each individual case. At the present time there is not complete agreement on the relative merits of radiography and scintigraphy; contrasting points of view are available (64). Because both suffer from significant false-negative results, it has been suggested that when either is negative and blatant signs of abuse are present clinically, then the other form of examination should be performed (65).

Generally, 99m-Technicium methylene diphosphonate is injected intravenously for the bone scan and images are obtained one-and-a-half to three hours afterward. Each examination takes about fifty minutes, so that sedation is often necessary in infants and young children. Careful attention to imaging technicalities is recommended (63) to help differentiate the normally "hot" epiphyses from metaphyseal lesions. The normal epiphyseal area is ovoid in shape when the epiphyseal plate is perpendicular to the detector; if there is metaphyseal contribution to the image, it becomes globular. Attention to this feature may permit recognition of bilateral lesions that might otherwise escape detection without radiographic support. The procedure is extremely useful in the identification of rib fractures which may be difficult to detect radiographically, especially if they are recent in origin and without displacement or deformity (fig. 12.18). Scintigraphy is less valuable than radiography in the detection of skull fractures.

Scintigraphy, like conventional radiography, may provide unexpected information. A bone scan undertaken for evaluation of child abuse disclosed abnormal accumulation of 99m-Tc methylene diphosphonate in the spleen. A subsequent spleen scan with 99m-Tc sulfur colloid demonstrated a splenic defect due to a subcapsular splenic hematoma (66).

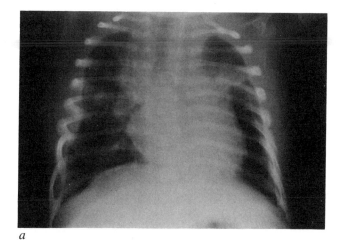

a

b

Figure 12.18

Bone scintigraphy. (*a*) In conventional radiograph, there are several undisplaced rib fractures of various ages with adjacent pleural thickening bilaterally. (*b*) Oblique and posterior bone scan shows numerous posterior fractures not apparent on radiograph in addition to those that were visible. (Reprinted, by permission, from J. R. Sty and R. J. Starshak, *Radiology* 146(1983): 369–75.

99m-Tc methylene diphosphonate has been observed also in the kidney in an abused child with myoglobinuria (67).

Other Examinations and Injuries

Injuries to tissues other than bones are occasionally recognized radiographically. McCort and Vaudagna (68) reported the findings of infants with initially unexplained visceral trauma presenting as acute abdominal crisis. The most common visceral injury was rupture of the small bowel, but lacerations of the liver and a perforation of the stomach were also noted. Laceration of the lung and subpleural hemorrhage were thoracic findings. Both multiple visceral and skeletal lesions were found. The radiographic features were pneumoperitoneum (fig. 12.19), hemoperitoneum, and/or ileus. In one patient with a perforated duodenum there was considerable delay in seeking medical care, and multiple peritoneal abscesses were found. Intramural hematoma of the duodenum (69, 70), well defined radiologically, occurs characteristically as a consequence of direct blows to the abdomen (fig. 12.20). Pancreatic pseudocysts also occur and can be diagnosed radiographically (71–74).

Focal destructive lesions in the metaphyses, shafts, and even the epiphyses of long bones may indicate areas of necrosis secondary to pancreatitis and hematogenous dissemination of proteolytic enzymes (73, 74). These findings may appear three to four weeks after the acute episode, and complete resolution usually occurs within one year. Ultrasound can be of great value in these circumstances, demonstrating the extent of the hematoma as well as its effect on contiguous structures. It is also helpful in following the course of the hematoma and to assist management.

Slovis and associates (75) favor the use of ultrasound for the diagnosis of pancreatic pseudocyst and loculated peripancreatic effusion in child abuse (fig. 12.21). They note spontaneous resolution but suggest that increasing serum amylase and size of the cyst constitute indications for surgery. Liver-spleen scintigraphy is excellent for demonstration of injuries to these organs, especially combined with radionuclear angiograms (76, 77), but the resolution is less than that obtained with CT. Kirks (76) suggests that if the patient is unstable and if the plain film demonstrates pneumoperitoneum, surgery is indicated; if the question is liver, spleen, or kidney damage, scintigraphy with multiple projections in the static and dynamic phases is good as a screening procedure; and if this is equivocal or positive, CT is desirable to assess the degree and extent of injury. In his opinion, conventional radiography is useful for identification of skeletal and pulmonary parenchymal lesions, gastric dilatation, and pneumoperitoneum; upper gastrointestinal series is best for identification of duodenal hematoma; ultrasound is appropriate for recognition of retroperitoneal hematoma, traumatic pancreatitis, and pancreatic pseudocyst; scintigraphy is limited to evaluation of the liver and spleen; and CT is the examination of choice for evaluation of nonskeletal injuries in child abuse. Some reservations for head examinations by ultrasound in infants under one year with uncertain cranial trauma may be in order (58).

Other radiographically demonstrable manifestations have included esophageal stricture following the addition of caustic alkali to a beverage given a child (78) and bilateral dense nephrograms of long duration in children with possible renal injury as well as muscle

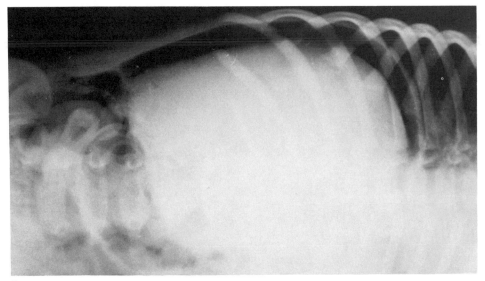

a

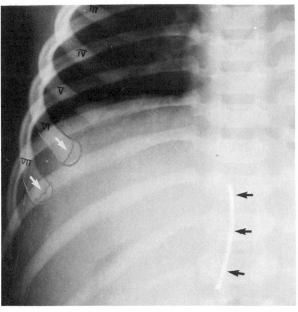

b

Figure 12.19

(*a*) Twenty-one-month-old female with pneumoperitoneum shown in horizontal beam, left lateral decubitus film. (*b*) Detail of right costochondral area and upper abdomen in antero-posterior supine film. The black arrows indicate the falciform ligament outlined by free intraperitoneal gas on both sides of the ligament. The white arrows indicate recent fractures of the anterior ends of the right sixth and seventh ribs. Mother admitted beating on baby's body as she lay in her lap.

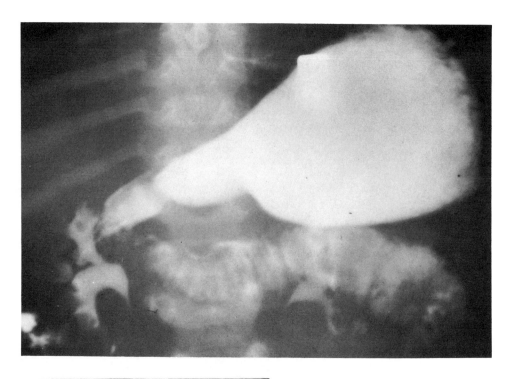

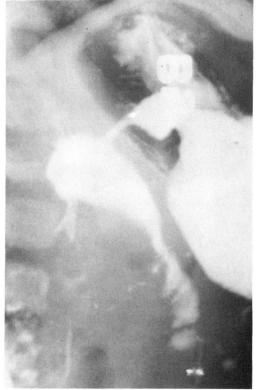

Figure 12.20

Intramural hematoma of duodenum demonstrated by barium meal in same patient as in fig. 12.11. Intravenous pyelogram had been done just before the barium examination because of microscopic hematuria. Hematoma surgically evacuated because of progressive obstruction.

Figure 12.21

On facing page. Pancreatic pseudocyst. Four-and-one-half-year-old girl with abdominal distention, vomiting, and fever; purulent ascites and left upper quadrant mass. (*a*) Ultrasound, left parasagittal scan, shows cystic mass (C) in region of pancreas, anterior to left kidney (k). (*b*) Subsequent gastrointestinal series, mass effect on pars media of stomach. (Reprinted, by permission, from P. K. Kleinman, V. D. Raptopoulos, and P. W. Brill, *Radiology* 141 (1981): 393–96.

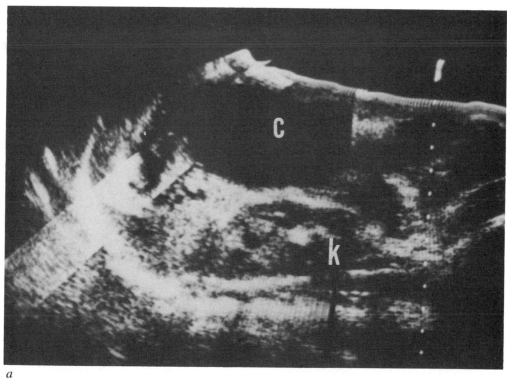

a

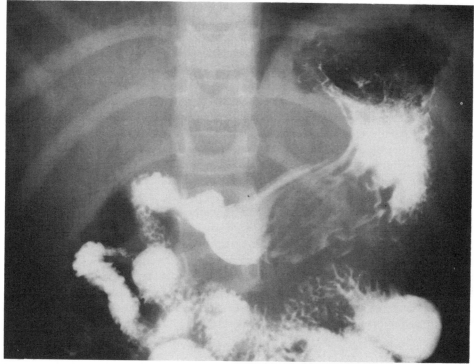

b

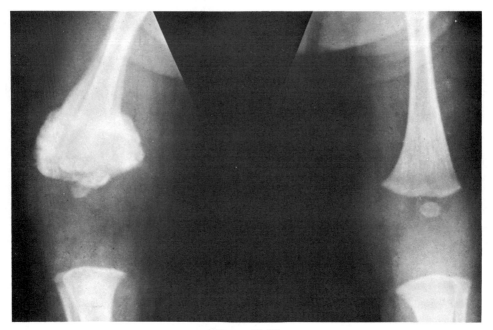

Figure 12.22

Exuberant calcified callus formation in sixteen-day-old infant who had unrecognized epiphyseal separation at knee as complication of breech extraction.

injuries and myoglobinuria (79). Caffey (50) emphasizes the mental retardation sequels which he attributes to whiplash-shaking injuries to the brain and its vessels.

In the course of management of injuries incurred by battered children, recourse occasionally is necessary to special invasive procedures such as angiography, myelography, excretory urography, cystography, etc. These are established procedures usually undertaken for evaluation of specific medical signs and symptoms and require no special consideration here.

Radiographic signs of retarded development and of malnutrition are commonly present in battered children, but they have no special diagnostic significance.

Differential Diagnosis

In general it can be said that the skeletal manifestations of the battered child syndrome are so characteristic as scarcely to be confused with anything else. Nevertheless, from time to time there is reluctance to accept the specificity of these lesions. It is felt that these manifestations of fracture are very uncommon in relation to the number of cases of fracture that are seen by radiologists in the course of their daily work. However, the circumstances of radiographic examination in instances where there is known injury and those in which there is no history of injury are quite different. Given a known epiphyseal separation, the child is treated by mechanical reduction of the deformity and immobilization, usually in plaster. Films are taken initially after reduction has been accomplished and usually at a follow-up examination about six weeks after the injury, when healing is apt to be relatively complete. If, in the intervening time, another film is taken for any reason whatsoever and subperiosteal new bone formation or metaphyseal fragmentation is noted, it occasions no concern, because it is known that an injury has taken place and these are obviously the signs of repair. Such is the situation which obtains in the newborn infant (4, 80) who has been delivered by breech extraction, has an epiphyseal separation at the knee or hip, and two-and-one-half to three weeks later shows a large calcifying hematoma (fig. 12.22). The knowledge that breech extraction is an adequate explanation for skeletal trauma is generally sufficient to allay any apprehension concerning the radiographic findings. If observed incidental to examination under any other circumstances, the same findings might be alarming.

To test this interpretation, we reviewed the films of children who had had epiphyseal separations with known cause. Among the group there were several who had films obtained more than two and less than six weeks after the injury. Almost all of them demonstrated metaphyseal irregularities and subperiosteal new bone formation which were radiologically indistinguishable from those seen in the battered child (fig. 12.23). In addition, children with acute epiphyseal separations were brought back for reexamination between two and three weeks after the known injury. Metaphyseal rarefaction and subperiosteal new bone formation of the same nature were observed regularly (fig. 12.24), although none was so severe as occurs in the battered child who does not have the benefit of immediate and effective immobilization.

There are several conditions which occasionally are confused with the battered child syndrome.

Scurvy

Naturally scurvy is one of the first to come to mind, particularly with older physicians who were familiar with the massive subperiosteal hematomas of healing scurvy in days gone by. None of the children with the battered child syndrome who have been studied this far have had scurvy, although it is quite possible for the condition to develop in the environment in which some of these children grow up. If present, scurvy would be expected to exaggerate the radiographic findings. Scurvy is a generalized disease, and although local exaggerations owing to trauma do occur, all of the bones show generalized osteoporosis. The cortices are thin, the trabecular architecture is ill defined, and the bones have a "ground glass" appearance. The epiphyseal ossification centers are sharply demarcated by the zones of provisional calcification to produce the so-called Wimberger's ring. At the ends of the shafts of all the long bones, and most prominent at the areas where growth is most rapid, there are comparable dense lines in the provisional zones of calcification. The calcification of cartilage proceeds normally; the transformation to bone (ossification) is inhibited as the osteoblasts require adequate amounts of vitamin C for their function. The decreased osteoblastic activity is reflected by a low level of alkaline phosphatase in the blood. Rarefaction of bone underneath calcified cartilaginous plates and minute incomplete fractures produce the characteristic "corner sign" of active scurvy. With subperiosteal hematomas of scorbutic origin, other manifestations of the disease, such as

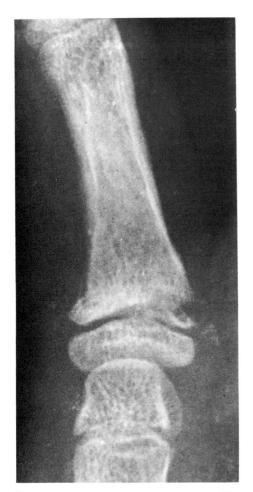
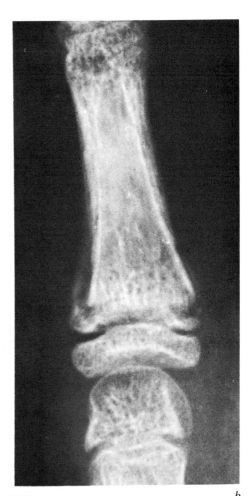

a   *Figure 12.23*   *b*

Epiphyseal separation in finger. (*a*) On day of injury. (*b*) Nineteen days later. In spite of known injury and attempt at immobilization, metaphyseal and subperiosteal reactions are present and are identical to those with unknown injury.

capillary fragility and hematuria, might also be present. It is noteworthy that ecchymoses and hematuria may also occur as the result of soft tissue injuries in the battered child. It is pertinent also that scurvy is extremely rare before the age of six months, whereas many of the infants in the battered child syndrome appear with well-developed bone lesions prior to this age. In contradistinction to scurvy, exaggerated changes may be present at one end of the bone while the opposite end or the corresponding area of the uninjured bone of the opposite extremity shows no signs whatsoever of disease.

Syphilis

Syphilis in the congenital form can result in metaphysical and periosteal lesions resembling those under discussion, especially during the first months of life. Although there is probably a traumatic factor in the distribution of the lesions of congenital syphilis, they do tend to be symmetrical, whereas those of the battered child are generally asymmetrical; and when osseous lesions as marked as those found in the battered child are produced by syphilis, other stigmata of the disease are usually present. In any questionable case, serological tests for the disease are available.

Osteogenesis Imperfecta

Osteogenesis imperfecta is also a generalized disease, and signs of the disorder should be present in bones which are not involved in the immediate productive-destructive process. In the cranium, the characteristic mosaic rarefaction (multiple sutural bones) is present in the early years of life, and in children of an age to be considered as possible battered children, the fracture-like appearance of the calvarium, much more extensive than the eggshell fractures of the battered child, should be of considerable assistance in diagnosis. In osteogenesis imperfecta the fractures are more commonly of the shafts of the bones than of the metaphyses and epiphyses. Other signs of osteogenesis imperfecta are usually present in the form of blue sclerae and obvious skeletal deformities. Usually, a family history of the condition can be elicited.

Infantile Cortical Hyperostosis

Infantile cortical hyperostosis is characterized by subperiosteal new bone formation, but there are no metaphyseal irregularities of defects. A healed lesion of the battered child might simulate a healing lesion of infantile cortical hyperostosis, but the clinical course can be helpful in differentiation. Involvement of the mandible occurs in approximately 95 percent of the children with this condition, but has been lacking thus far in the battered child in the absence of obvious mandibular fracture.

Osteoid Osteoma

Osteoid osteoma may produce swelling, pain, and periosteal reaction in a child. Metaphyseal lesions do not occur and the characteristic history of pain—worse at night, relieved by aspirin—is helpful if present. Osteoid osteoma is not a common disease in this age group. The presence of a sclerotic nidus in the center of the lesion is diagnostic.

Self-Sustained Injury

Fatigue fractures probably represent a variant of the battered child syndrome in which the child himself is responsible for the battering. More common in the metatarsal bones of adults, as in "march fractures," they do occur in the fibulas of children where they are present with pain and localized periosteal reaction (81). The remainder of the bone is normally mineralized, and there are no metaphyseal lesions.

The so-called little-league elbow (82) is another manifestation of repetitive injury where the vigorous mechanical activity of throwing a ball causes incomplete avulsions (epiphyseal separations) around the region of the elbow. The productive changes may simulate those of the battered child. The age of the patient is appreciably older than that of

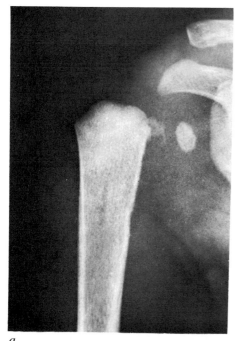

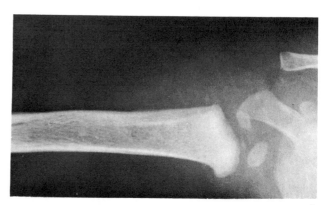

a

b

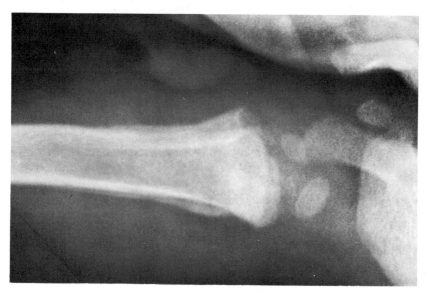

Figure 12.24   *c*

Serial films in known epiphyseal displacement. (*a*) At time of admission after motor car accident. (*b*) Twenty-four hours later; reduction is complete in abduction. (*c*) Three weeks after reduction, before application of new cast. The metaphysis, previously uninjured, now shows irregularity of mineralization, and a subperiosteal envelope of new bone cloaks the proximal end of the shaft. Had there been no immobilization, these reactions would have been more extensive.

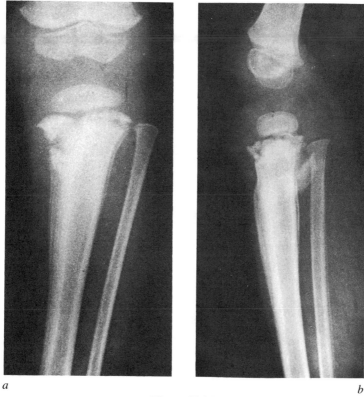

a

b

Figure 12.25

Metaphyseal fragmentation and subperiosteal new bone formation in paraplegic child with sensory defect (meningomyelocele). Swelling noted after vigorous physical therapy in attempt to correct contractures. (*a*) Anteroposterior projection. (*b*) Lateral projection.

most battered children, the remainder of the bones is in excellent condition, and a history of trauma adequate to explain the reaction is usually elicited.

Others

Multiple fractures of bones are seen in severe rickets, hypophosphatasia, leukemia, metastatic neuroblastoma, and as sequels to osteomyelitis and septic arthritis. In general, additional signs of the primary disease and a history of prior disease adequate to explain the lesions can be elicited.

The one condition which imitates the radiographic findings of the battered child is one which supports the hypothesis of a traumatic basis for the lesions—that is, neurogenic sensory deficit in relation to injury (83, 84). As has been mentioned previously, the attachment of the epiphysis to the shaft of the bone is one of the weak areas in the growing bones of the young child. If the young child also has a neurogenic sensory deficit such as that associated with paraplegia following spine injury or with meningomyelocele, separa-

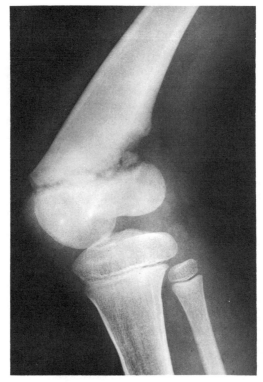

Figure 12.26

Metaphyseal irregularity, old cortical thickening, and growth disturbance in child with congenital indifference to pain. (Courtesy of *Radiology.*)

tions of epiphyses in the lower extremities as a consequence of physiotherapy, or other injury whose severity is not appreciated, can give rise to radiographic findings indistinguishable from those of the battered child (fig. 12.25).

Individuals afflicted with the so-called congenital indifference to pain (85) also fail to react normally to skeletal injuries; and metaphyseal rarefaction, excessive callus formation, and bone sclerosis develop as a consequence, just as in children with unrecognized trauma (fig. 12.26). The features of metaphyseal and physeal injuries in children with spina bifida and meningomyelocele are discussed in detail by Gyepes et al. (86). Confusion is unlikely to arise with respect to the self-mutilation lesions of the Riley-Day or the Lesch-Nyhan syndromes, but the conditions should at least enter the differential diagnosis. The question of superimposed child abuse would be difficult to resolve.

Both Menkes syndrome, a hereditary metabolic defect associated with defective copper metabolism, and acquired copper deficiency demonstrate metaphyseal changes that can be confused with the lesions of child abuse (87). In addition, innocent trauma and unrecognized osteomyelitis may result in subperiosteal new bone formation that, without adequate history, can be misinterpreted. Four infants receiving excessively vigorous manipulation to help "stretch" tight muscles showed fractures, epiphyseal separations, and periosteal reactions in addition to other bone lesions of different ages. The custodians of the infants had been instructed by nursery personnel in the attempted physiotherapy. When a serious injury was observed, the presence of the other bone changes was considered presumptive evidence of abuse (88). Even metaphyseal infractions can occur from a nonabusive accident. The evidence of different ages for the lesions is necessary for identification of child abuse; in its absence, suspicion is justified but careful investigation of the circumstances surrounding the injuries is necessary before a child and his family are exposed to the stresses that a diagnosis of child abuse subjects them. Subperiosteal new bone formation has been reported in infants on long-term prostaglandin administration (89).

Some children who have the radiographic manifestations of the battered child and whose clinical histories support this diagnosis, have certain features in their skeletal X-rays which have led competent radiologists to ask whether there is not some underlying systemic disorder. All of the features of metaphyseal fractures, subperiosteal new bone formation, healing fractures in different stages of repair, and so on, can be found in these children, but they also demonstrate a "chalkiness" (see fig. 12.6) in the skeleton, which calls to mind the fragility of bones of children with osteopetrosis (Albers-Schönberg disease). These children do not demonstrate any of the hematologic disorders of osteopetrosis and usually lose the sclerosis of bone as they become older. None has been shown to have hypercalcemia, but this aspect has not been studied adequately. The sclerotic changes may merely reflect productive changes in bone owing to multiple repetitive trauma insufficient to cause obvious fractures or the usual reparative changes which are diagnostic of the battered child. This group will merit further study, but it is almost certain that, regardless of any contributing factors, they will have in common with all the other children an episode, or repetitive episodes, of physical abuse. Support for this interpretation has been expressed by DeSmet et al. (90).

Conclusion

The radiographic signs of the battered child are surprisingly specific. They speak for the child who is unable or unwilling to speak for himself and serve to alert the physician to a hazard of considerable magnitude which threatens the life and limbs as well as the emotional and intellectual potentialities of the child. Although they may reflect the time of the injury with considerable accuracy and permit extremely accurate deductions concerning the nature of the forces producing the injury, they provide no information whatsoever concerning the circumstances surrounding the injury or the motivation of the individuals responsible. The epiphyseal separation that results from grabbing a child by a limb to prevent a serious fall is indistinguishable from the epiphyseal separation incurred while the infant is being vigorously shaken or otherwise abused by an irate, distraught adult custodian. The recognition of the radiographic changes, however, does constitute a distinct indication to investigate the circumstances surrounding the injury.

The availability of diagnostic imaging methods other than conventional radiography increases the tools that can be used to discover and evaluate physically abused children. It also introduces an element of uncertainty about which methods to use and in what sequence. For a child with clinical limb injuries, suspected of having been a victim of abuse, conventional radiography may suffice to establish the diagnosis if typical lesions are present. Further examinations would be dictated by clinical signs and symptoms. If typical lesions are not found, a radionuclide bone scan may provide objective information for proceeding further. If neither is positive, and especially if there are any neurological signs or retinal hemorrhages on physical examination, craniocerebral CT would be indicated. The sequence will be dictated by the circumstances involving equipment at hand, expertise and interest of personnel, and above all by the clinical status of the patient.

References

1. Tardieu, A. 1860. Étude médico-légale sur les sévices et mauvais traitements exercés sur des enfants. *Annales d'Hygiene Publique et Médecine Légale* 13:361–98.
2. Caffey, J. 1946. Multiple Fractures in the Long Bones of Infants Suffering from Chronic Subdural Hematoma. *Am. J. Roentgenology* 56:163–73.
3. West, S. 1888. Acute Periosteal Swellings in Several Young Infants of the Same Family, Probably Rickety in Nature. *British Med. J.* 1:856–57.
4. Snedecor, S. T.; Knapp, R. E.; and Wilson, H. B. 1935. Traumatic Ossifying Periostitis of the Newborn. *Surgery Gynecology Obstetrics* 61:385–87.
5. Epstein, B., and Klein, M. 1936. Luesähnliche Röntgenbefunde bei unspezifischen Skeletterkrankungen im Säuglingsalter. *Wiener Medizinische Wochenschrift* 86:750–53.
6. Rose, C. B. 1936. Unusual Periostitis in Children. *Radiology* 27:131–37.
7. Caffey, J. 1939. Syphilis of the Skeleton in Early Infancy: The Nonspecificity of Many of the Roentgenographic Changes. *Am. J. Roentgenology* 42:637–55.
8. Ingraham, F. D., and Heyl, H. L. 1939. Subdural Hematoma in Infancy and Childhood, *JAMA* 112:198–204.
9. Lis, E. F., and Frauenberger, G. S. 1950. Multiple Fractures Associated with Subdural Hematoma in Infancy. *Pediatrics* 6:890–92.
10. Smith, M. J. 1950. Subdural Hematoma with Multiple Fractures. *Am. J. Roentgenology* 63:342–44.
11. Meneghello, J., and Hasbun, J. 1951. Hematoma subdural y fractura de los huesos largos. *Revista Chilena Pediatrica* 22:80–83.
12. Kugelmann, J. 1952. Uber symmetrische Spontanfrakturen unbekannter Genese beim Säugling. *Annales Paediatrici (Basel)* 178:177–81.
13. Marquezy, R.-A.; Bach, Ch.; and Blondeau, M. 1952. Hématome sous-dural et fractures multiples des os longs chez un nourrisson de 9 mois. *Archives Françaises de Pédiatrie* 9:526–31.
14. Marie, J.; Apostolides, P.; Salet, J.; Eliachar, E.; and Lyon, G. 1954. Hématome sous-dural du nourrisson associé a des fractures des membres. *Annales de Pédiatric (Paris)* 30:1757–63.
15. Bakwin, H. 1952. Roentgenologic Changes in the Bones Following Trauma in Infants. *J. Newark Beth Israel Hospital* 3(1):17.
16. Bakwin, H. 1956. Multiple Skeletal Lesions in Young Children Due to Trauma. *J. Pediatrics* 49:7–15.

17. Silverman, F. N. 1953. The Roentgen Manifestations of Unrecognized Skeletal Trauma in Infants. *Am. J. Roentgenology* 69:413–26.
18. Astley, Roy. 1953. Multiple Metaphyseal Fractures in Small Children. *British J. Radiology* 26(311): 577–83.
19. Woolley, P. V., Jr., and Evans, W. A., Jr. 1955. Significance of Skeletal Lesions in Infants Resembling Those of Traumatic Origin. *JAMA* 158:539–43.
20. Jones, H. H., and Davis, J. H. 1957. Multiple Traumatic Lesions of the Infant Skeleton. *Stanford Med. Bull.* 15:259–73.
21. Weston, W. J. 1957. Metaphyseal Fractures in Infancy. J. Bone Joint Surgery 39(B): 694–700.
22. Fisher, S. H. 1958. Skeletal Manifestations of Parent-Induced Trauma in Infants and Children. *Southern Med. J.* 51:956–60.
23. Friedman, M. S. 1958. Traumatic Periostitis in Infants and Children. *JAMA* 166: 1840–45.
24. Marti, J., and Kaufmann, H. J. 1959. Multiple traumatische Knochenläsionen beim Säugling. *Deutsche Medizinische Wochenschrift* 84:984–88, 991–92.
25. Miller, D. S. 1959. Fractures among Children. I. Parental Assault as Causative Agent. *Minnesota Med.* 42:1209–13.
26. Altman, D. H., and Smith, R. L. 1960. Unrecognized Trauma in Infants and Children. *J. Bone Joint Surgery* 42(A): 407–13.
27. Gwinn, J. L.; Lewin, K. W.; and Peterson, H. G., Jr. 1961. Roentgenographic Manifestations of Unsuspected Trauma in Infancy. *JAMA* 176:926–29.
28. Kempe, C. H.; Silverman, F. N.; Steele, B. F.; Droegemueller, W.; and Silver, H. K. 1962. The Battered-Child Syndrome. *JAMA* 181:17–24.
29. McHenry, T.; Girdany, B. R.; and Elmer, Elizabeth. 1963. Unsuspected Trauma with Multiple Skeletal Injuries during Infancy and Childhood. *Pediatrics* 31:903–8.
30. Teng, C. T.; Singleton, E. B.; and Daeschner, C. W., Jr. 1964. Inflicted Skeletal Injuries in Young Children. *Pediatrics Digest,* (September), pp. 53–66.
31. Caffey, J. 1957. Some Traumatic Lesions in Growing Bones Other Than Fractures and Dislocations: Clinical and Radiological Features. *British J. Radiology* 30:225–38.
32. Silverman, F. N. 1972. Unrecognized Trauma in Infants, the Battered Child Syndrome, and the Syndrome of Amboise Tardieu. Rigler Lecture. *Radiology* 104: 337–53.
33. Rabouille, D. 1967. Les Jeunes Enfants Victimes de sévices corporels. *These. Med.* (*Nancy*).
34. Cameron, J. M., and Rae, L. J. 1975. *Atlas of the Battered Child Syndrome*. London: Churchill Livingstone.
35. Ellison, P. H.; Tsai, F. Y.; and Largent, J. A. 1978. Computed Tomography in Child Abuse and Cerebral Contusion. *Pediatrics* 62:151–54.
36. Saul, R. A.; Lee, W. H.; and Stevenson, R. E. 1982. Caffey's Disease Revisited: Further Evidence for Autosomal Dominant Inheritance with Incomplete Penetrance. *Am. J. Diseases in Children* 136:56–60.
37. Caffey, J. 1946. Infantile Cortical Hyperostosis. *J. Pediatrics* 29:541–59.
38. Kogutt, M. S.; Swischuk, L. E.; and Fagan, C. J. 1974. Patterns of Injury and Significance of Uncommon Fractures in the Battered Child Syndrome. *Am. J. Roentgenology* 121:143–49.

39. Merton, D. F.; Radkowski, M. A.; and Leonidas, J. C. 1983. The Abused Child: A Radiological Reappraisal. *Radiology* 146:377–81.

40. Brailsford, J. F. 1948. Ossifying Hematoma and Other Simple Lesions Mistaken for Sarcomata. *British J. Radiology* 21:157–70.

41. Feldman, K. W., and Brewer, D. K. 1984. Child Abuse, Cardiopulmonary Resuscitation, and Rib Fractures. *Pediatrics* 73:339–342.

42. Jaffe, A. C., and Lasser, D. H. 1977. Multiple Metatarsal Fractures in Child Abuse. *Pediatrics* 60:642–43.

43. Swischuk, L. E. 1969. Spine and Spinal Cord Trauma in the Battered Child Syndrome. *Radiology* 92:733–38.

44. Kleinman, P. K., and Zito, J. L. 1984. Avulsion of the Spinous Processes Caused by Infant Abuse. *Radiology* 151:389–91.

45. Neuer, F.; Roberts, F. F.; and McCarthy, V. 1977. Osteolytic Lesions Following Traumatic Pancreatitis. *Am. J. Diseases in Children* 131:738–40.

46. Zimmermann, R. A., et al. 1979. Computed Tomography of Craniocerebral Injury in the Abused Child. *Radiology* 140:687–90.

47. Zimmerman, R. D., et al. 1982. Falx and Interhemispheric Fissure on Axial CT: II. Recognition and Differentiation of Interhemispheric Subarachnoid and Subdural Hemorrhage. *Am. J. Nuclear Radiology* 3:635–42.

48. Merton, D. F., and Osborne, D. R. S. 1983. Craniocerebral Trauma in the Child Abuse Syndrome. *Pediatric Annals* 12:882–87.

49. Saulsbury, F. T., and Alford, B. A. 1982. Intracranial Bleeding from Child Abuse. *Pediatric Radiology* 12:175–78.

50. Caffey, J. 1972. On the Theory and Practice of Shaking Infants: Its Potential Residual Effects of Permanent Brain Damage and Mental Retardation. *Am. J. Diseases in Children* 124:161–69.

51. Guthkelch, A. N. 1971. Infantile Subdural Haematoma and Its Relationship to Whiplash Injuries. *British Med. J.* 2:430–31.

52. Ommaya, A. K.; Fass, F.; and Yarnell, P. 1968. Whiplash Injury and Brain Damage. An Experimental Study. *JAMA* 285–89.

53. Tsai, F. Y.; Zee, C. S.; Apthorp, J. S.; and Dixon, G. 1980. Computed Tomography in Child Abuse Head Trauma. *Computerized Tomography* 4:277–86.

54. Bennett, H. S., and French, J. H. 1980. Elevated Intracranial Pressure in Whiplash-Shaken Infant Syndrome Detected with Normal C.T. *Clinical Pediatrics* 19:633–34.

55. Carter, J. E., and McCormick, A. Q. 1983. Whiplash Shaking Syndrome: Retinal Hemorrhages and Computerized Axial Tomography of the Brain. *Child Abuse and Neglect: International J.* 7:279–86.

56. Roussey, M., et al. 1982. La Tomodensitometrie cranienne chez les enfants maltraites. *Annales de Radiologie* 25:237–43.

57. McClelland, C. Q.; Rekate, H.; Kaufman, B.; and Persse, L. 1980. Cerebral Injury in Child Abuse: A Changing Profile. *Child's Brain* 7:225–35.

58. Hansdorf, G., and Helmke, K. 1984. Sonographic Demonstration of Contusional White Matter Clefts in an Infant. *Neuropediatrics* 15:110–12.

59. Helfer, R. E.; Slovis, T. L.; and Black, M. 1977. Injuries Resulting When Small Children Fall out of Bed. *Pediatrics* 60:533–35.

60. Fordham, E. W., and Ramachandran, P. C. 1974. Radionuclide Scanning of Osseous Trauma. *Seminars in Nuclear Medicine* 4:411–29.

61. Haase, G. M., et al. 1980. The Value of Radionuclide Bone Scanning in the Early Recognition of Deliberate Child Abuse. *J. Trauma* 20:873–75.

62. Smith, F. W., et al. 1980. Unsuspected Costo-Vertebral Fractures Demonstrated by Bone Scanning in the Child Abuse Syndrome. *Pediatric Radiology* 10:103–6.

63. Sty, J. R., and Starshak, R. J. 1983. The Role of Scintigraphy in the Evaluation of the Suspected Abused Child. *Radiology* 146:369–75.

64. Diament, M. J.; Sty, J. R.; Starshak, R. J.; Merton, D. F.; Radkowski, M. A.; Leonidas, J. C.; Conway, J. J.; and Berdon, W. E. 1983. Letter to the Editor, and Replies. Should the Radionuclide Skeletal Survey Be Used As a Screening Procedure in Suspected Child Abuse Victims? *Radiology* 148:573–76.

65. Jaudes, P. K. 1984. Comparison of Radiography and Radionuclide Bone Scanning in the Detection of Child Abuse. *Pediatrics* 73:166–68.

66. Sty, J. R.; Starshak, R. J.; and Hubbard, A. 1982. Accumulation of Tc-99m MDP in the Spleen of a Battered Child. *Clinical Nuclear Med.* 7:292.

67. Sty, J. R., and Starshak, R. J. 1982. Abnormal Tc-99m MDP Renal Images Associated with Myoglobinuria. *Clinical Nuclear Med.* 7:476.

68. McCort, J., and Vaudagna, J. 1964. Visceral Injuries in Battered Children. *Radiology* 82:424–28.

69. Bratu, M.; Dower, J. C.; Siegel, B.; and Hozney, S. H. 1970. Jejunal Hematoma, Child Abuse and Felson's Sign. *Connecticut Medicine* 34:261–64.

70. Eisenstein, E. M.; Delta, B. G.; and Clifford, J. H. 1965. Jejunal Hematoma: An Unusual Manifestation of the Battered Child Syndrome. *Clinical Pediatrics* 4:436–40.

71. Kim, T., and Jenkins, M. E. 1967. Pseudocyst of the Pancreas as a Manifestation of the Battered-Child Syndrome. *Medical Annals of the District of Columbia* 36:664–66.

72. Bongiovi, J. J., and Logosso, R. D. 1969. Pancreatic Pseudocyst Occurring in the Battered Child Syndrome. *Pediatric Surgery* 4:220–26.

73. Cohen, H.; Haller, J. O.; and Friedman, A. P. 1981. Pancreatitis, Child Abuse, and Skeletal Lesions. *Pediatric Radiology* 10:175–77.

74. Kleinman, P. K.; Raptopoulos, V. D.; and Brill, P. W. 1981. Occult Non-Skeletal Trauma in the Battered-Child Syndrome. *Radiology* 141:393–96.

75. Slovis, T. L.; VonBerg, V. J.; and Mikelic, V. 1980. Sonography in the Diagnosis and Management of Pancreatic Pseudocysts and Effusions in Childhood. *Radiology* 135:153–55.

76. Kirks, D. R. 1984. Radiological Evaluation of Visceral Injuries in the Battered Child Syndrome. *Pediatric Annals* 12:888–93.

77. Majd, M. 1982. Hepatobiliary Scintigraphy. In *Gastrointestinal Imaging in Pediatrics,* 2d ed., ed. E. A. Franken. Philadelphia: Harper and Row.

78. Tucker, A. S., and Eloise, M. I. 1979. A Spiked Drink. Presented at Members' Miscellany, 22nd Annual Meeting, Society for Pediatric Radiology. Toronto, March.

79. Rosenberg, H., et al. 1983. Prolonged Dense Nephrograms in Battered Children. Suspect Rhabdomyelysis and Myoglobinuria. *Urology* 21:325–30.

80. Snedecor, S. T., and Wilson, H. B. 1949. Some Obstetrical Injuries to the Long Bones. *J. Bone Joint Surgery* 31(A): 378–84.

81. Griffiths, A. L. 1952. Fatigue Fracture of the Fibula in Childhood. *Archives of Disease in Childhood* 27:552–57.

82. Brogdon, B. G., and Crow, N. E. 1960. Little Leaguer's Elbow. *Am. J. Roentgenology* 83:671–75.

83. Gillies, C. L., and Hartung, W. 1938. Fracture of the Tibia in Spina Bifida Vera: Report of Two Cases. *Radiology* 31:621–23.

84. Oehme, J. 1961. Periostale Reaktionen bei Myelomeningozele. *Fortschr. Gebiete Roentgenstrahlen Nuklearmed.* 94:82–85.

85. Gilden, J., and Silverman, F. N. 1959. Congenital Insensitivity to Pain: A Neurologic Syndrome with Bizarre Skeletal Lesions. *Radiology* 72:176–89.

86. Gyepes, M. T.; Newburn, D. H., and Neuhauser, E. B. D. 1965. Metaphyseal and Physeal Injuries in Children with Spina Bifida and Meningomyelocceles. *Am. J. Roentgenology* 95:168–77.

87. Gruenebaum, M.; Horodnliceanu, C.; and Steinherz, R. 1980. The Radiographic Manifestations of Bone Changes in Copper Deficiency. *Pediatric Radiology* 9:101–4.

88. Helfer, R. E., et al. 1984. Trauma to the Bones of Small Infants from Passive Exercise: A Factor in the Etiology of Child Abuse. *J. Pediatrics* 104:47–50.

89. Ueda, K., et al. 1980. Cortical Hyperostosis Following Long-Term Administration of Prostaglandin E1 in Infants with Cyanotic Congenital Heart Disease. *J. Pediatrics* 97:834–36.

90. DeSmet, A. A.; Kuhns, L. R.; Kaufman, R. A.; and Holt, J. F. 1977. Bony Sclerosis and the Battered Child. *Skeletal Radiology* 2:39–41.

13 Pathology of Fatal Child Abuse and Neglect

Ross E. Zumwalt and Charles S. Hirsch

The absolute dependence of infants and children upon their parents or adult custodians renders them susceptible to a range of fatal maltreatment and neglect that defies the imagination of a thousand nightmares. The abuses of these nightmares run the gamut from subtly covert to shockingly obvious. Consequently, the autopsy findings in this group range from nothing at all to blatantly grotesque. However, regardless of the nature of the autopsy findings, no genus of homicide victims presents a more complex or difficult challenge to the forensic pathologist and other investigating authorities.

In this chapter we strongly emphasize the need for investigative teamwork and the imperative to interpret autopsy findings in the light of the entire case study. Narrowly focused tunnel vision, restricted exclusively to autopsy findings taken out of the context of the investigative universe, will see only part of the truth. Errors of interpretation resulting from such defective perception will leave some instances of fatal maltreatment unrecognized and, in other instances, will not provide truthful, nonsinister explanations for injuries. None of us can rest comfortably with the notion that we may have overlooked a homicide or misinterpreted homicidal injuries as an accident. However, any discomfort resulting from such false negative conclusions is luxury compared to our dread of the converse.

Our presentation of the pathology of fatal maltreatment of children begins with a discussion of types of physical abuse, emphasizing the distinction between deaths of typical battered babies and those fatalities resulting from a single episode, and then covers homicide by starvation and subtle modalities of injury and neglect. Next we discuss false accusations of child abuse. The chapter concludes with technical considerations related to the autopsy protocol and guidelines for postmortem examinations.

Ross E. Zumwalt, M.D., is deputy coroner, Hamilton County, Ohio, and associate professor of pathology, University of Cincinnati School of Medicine. Charles S. Hirsch, M.D., is chief medical examiner, Suffolk County, New York, and professor of forensic pathology, State University of New York Medical School at Stony Brook.

TABLE 13.1   Forms of Fatal Child Abuse

I. Physical Trauma
   A. Blunt trauma (beating)
      1. multiple episodes (battered baby syndrome)
      2. single episode beating
   B. Firearm injuries
   C. Stabbing and cutting
   D. Burning
   E. Asphyxia
      1. smothering and choking
      2. strangulation
      3. drowning
      4. carbon monoxide or other gases
      5. hanging
      6. chest compression
      7. exclusion of oxygen
   F. Miscellaneous (electricity, explosives, falls from height, etc.)

II. Chemical Assault
   A. Poisoning
   B. Force feeding noxious substances

III. Neglect
   A. Starvation (malnutrition)
   B. Exposure to dangerous environment
   C. Failure to provide medical care when needed
   D. Exacerbation of natural disease by neglect

IV. Munchausen Syndrome by Proxy

Terminology

Manner, Cause, and Mechanism of Death

Throughout this chapter we refer to manner, cause, and mechanism of death, and in several sections we stress the importance of distinguishing between proximate (underlying) and immediate causes of death. To insure uniformity of understanding, we begin by defining the foregoing terms.

The *manner of death* is an explanation of how the cause arose: natural or violent. Natural deaths are caused exclusively by disease. A violent death is one in which an injury either causes or contributes to the causation of the fatality. Injurious modalities include chemical agents, heat, cold, and electricity as well as mechanical trauma such as beating, shooting, and stabbing. Violence is not synonymous with foul play, because violent deaths include accidents and suicides as well as homicides. In most jurisdictions, when a violent death cannot be subclassified with reasonable certainty, it is termed either undetermined or violence of undetermined origin.

The *cause of death* is the disease or injury responsible for the fatality; a competent cause of death should be etiologically specific.

Mechanisms of death are the physiological and biochemical alterations whereby the causes exert their lethal effects. Mechanisms of death are never etiologically specific. Common examples of fatal mechanisms include cardiac arrhythmias, heart failure, asphyxia, sepsis, exsanguination, uremia, and hepatic failure. The often used term "cardio-respiratory arrest" is a description of being dead; it is neither an acceptable cause nor an illuminating mechanism of death.

Proximate and Immediate Causes of Death

The *proximate or underlying cause of death* is the disease or injury which, in a natural and continuous sequence unbroken by any efficient intervening cause, produces the fatality and without which the end result would not have occurred. *Immediate causes of death* are complications and sequelae of the underlying cause. There can be more than one immediate cause, and they can occur over a prolonged interval, but none absolves the underlying cause of its ultimate responsibility. For example, a child sustains a spinal cord injury as the result of a beating and dies two years later because of sepsis and renal failure (mechanisms) due to neurogenic bladder with chronic cystitis and bilateral pyelonephritis (immediate cause). The proximate cause of death is the spinal cord injury, and the manner of death is homicide. Even in states that have laws which preclude the prosecution of such a case because of the prolonged survival ("year and a day rule"), it is our opinion that the appropriate administrative medicolegal decision is homicide. A more common example is provided by malnourished, dehydrated infants who die with bronchopneumonia. If the malnutrition and dehydration result from deprivation of food and neglect, the cause of death is starvation and the manner of death is homicide. Bronchopneumonia, the immediate cause of death, is a predictable complication of malnutrition that fails to weaken or break the chain of causation.

Types of Fatal Abuse

The term fatal child abuse immediately brings to mind the image of an infant with multiple injuries and numerous broken bones of varying ages, a victim of repeated beatings. Actually, the minority of fatally abused children fit this image. In addition to repeated beatings, infants and children can be killed by other physical trauma, by chemicals, or by neglect. The pediatric homicide victim is conceptually similar to an adult victim when the modality of violence is shooting, stabbing, or a single beating as an isolated occurrence. However, many other forms and varieties of injury that would be nonlethal in older children and adults can kill infants. Consequently fatal child abuse can be classified in many different ways. We find it helpful to classify such homicides on the basis of modality and frequency of injury (see table 13.1).

Physical Trauma

Battered Baby Syndrome

Although many workers in the field of child abuse may refer to all fatally abused children as battered babies, the battered baby syndrome (in a strict pathologic sense) refers

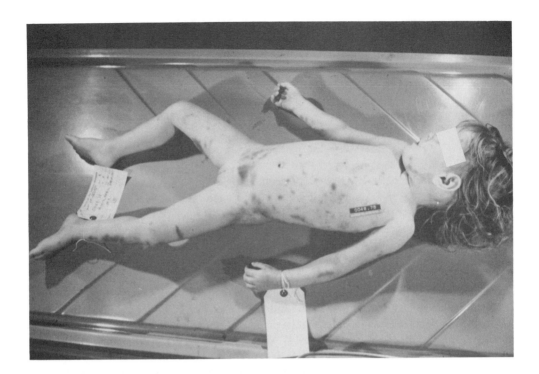

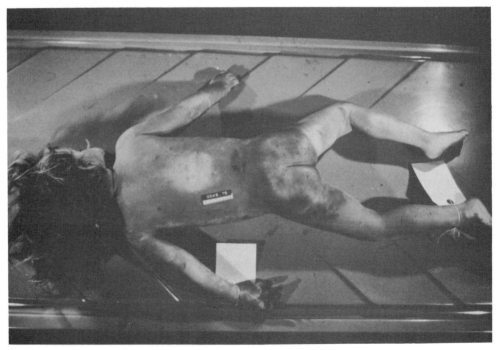

Figure 13.1

Two-year-old girl with multiple contusions of varying ages, recent and healing rib and long-bone fractures, liver and pancreas lacerations with hemoperitoneum and a recent skull fracture with subdural hemorrhage. (*a*) Front view. (*b*) Back view.

only to those infants and children who have been victims of multiple repeated abuse of one type or another as indicated by convincing objective indicia of recent, healing and healed injuries involving the skin, viscera, or skeleton. The majority of fatally abused children do not meet the above criteria for inclusion in the battered baby syndrome. For example, in our experience approximately 15–20 percent of child abuse fatalities fulfill the foregoing criteria for the battered baby syndrome.

Because of the current awareness of child abuse, particularly of the battered baby syndrome, many such fatalities are immediately recognized by law enforcement officers, social workers, and medical personnel as deaths due to willfully inflicted injuries for which an adult bears criminal responsibility. The patterns of injury and the evidence of multiple episodes of injury as documented by physical examination, X-ray, and autopsy can give irrefutable proof of repeated abuse. When battered children have severe external injuries with numerous bruises, abrasions, and lacerations and numerous old scars from lacerations, abrasions, or burns the diagnosis is usually obvious (fig. 13.1). Other battered infants, however, will have minor external injury, and the pathologist may be surprised to find multiple healing fractures or numerous internal injuries of varying ages.

Patterned injuries on the skin that are suggestive of the battered baby syndrome include parallel rows of bruises, abrasions, and hyper- or hypopigmented areas indicating blows with a belt, switch, cord, or other object (figs. 13.2, 13.3). Recent or healing burns, particularly small, round burns the size of a cigarette, should suggest abuse (figs. 13.4, 13.5). A battered baby also may have bite marks which are seen as a circular or semi-

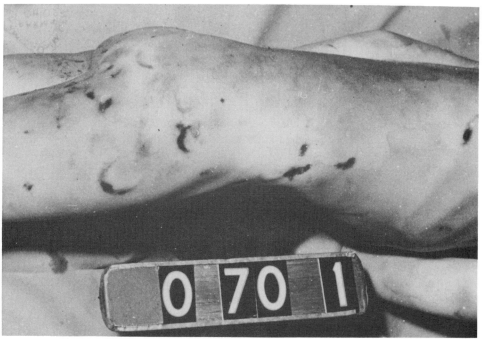

Figure 13.2

Patterned injuries recapitulating belt buckle

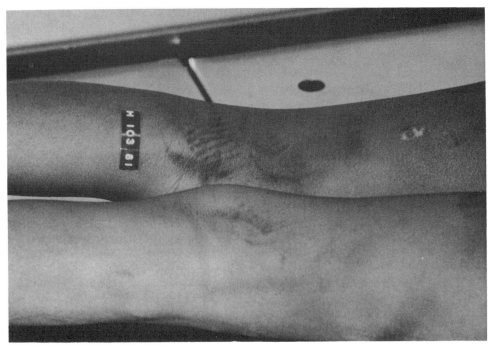

Figure 13.3

Patterned contusion of left popliteal fossa recapitulating afro comb.

circular pattern of abrasions or scars (fig. 13.6). Many children have a few scars from accidental injuries. However, multiple scars and healing injuries of varying ages in a small child or infant should always arouse suspicion of the battered baby syndrome (1, 2; also see chap. 10).

Fractures of varying ages have been well described as an integral part of the battered baby syndrome (3–9; also see chap. 12). Fractures occur when the child is struck, thrown, grabbed, or shaken or when an extremity is twisted. The long bones of the extremities are the most common site of skeletal injury in battered babies. The injuries may involve the shaft or the ends of the bones. Injuries to the epiphyseal-metaphyseal regions of the long bones in infants are nearly diagnostic of physical abuse because the forces necessary to cause such injuries generally do not occur in accidental circumstances. Fractures of the shaft or diaphysis of a long bone are more frequent than epiphyseal-metaphyseal injuries but are less diagnostic of abuse. Spiral or oblique fractures can be inflicted by willfully twisting a limb but also can occur from falls. Transverse fractures are caused by blunt impacts sustained in accidents and assaults. Since the extremities generally are not dissected during an autopsy, it is imperative that the pathologist obtain X-rays of the total body prior to autopsy in any instance of suspected abuse.

Rib fractures are common in the battered child syndrome and are uncommon in other forms of trauma in children and in cardiopulmonary resuscitation (10) (fig. 13.7). Direct blows to the chest wall result in fractures at the point of impact because a large amount of force is transmitted over a small area. Compressing the chest from front to back produces

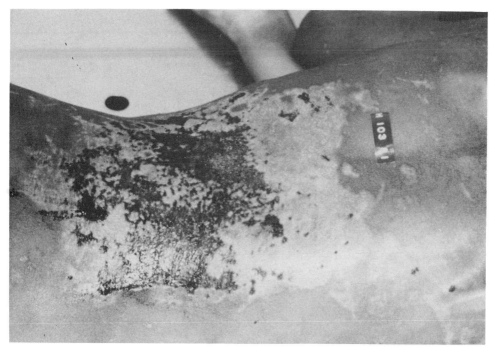

Figure 13.4

Healing untreated burn on left side of back caused by compression against hot surface
of heating appliance.

fractures laterally, and compression of the chest from side to side causes posterior fractures (7).

Most fatally battered babies have recent, healing, or old head injuries. (The subject of craniocerebral trauma is treated separately in chapter 12.) In the absence of a congenital vascular malformation or evidence of a bleeding disorder or severe natural disease, a subdural hemorrhage in an infant is the result of trauma. Occasionally, a subgaleal hematoma results from hair pulling. Traumatic alopecia may also occur when a guardian pulls out the child's hair (fig. 13.8). It may be necessary to distinguish traumatic alopecia from other forms of hair loss or from trichotillomania. Hair loss is usually more irregular and less complete with traumatic alopecia than with alopecia areata, and there is scalp tenderness (1).

The thoracic organs are rarely injured because of their protection by the ribs. However, crushing or compressing forces applied to the abdomen frequently produce injuries to the liver, spleen, pancreas, or gastrointestinal tract in battered children. A blow to the abdomen, for example, can lacerate any of these organs and commonly causes injuries of the duodenum or proximal jejunum. Punches or blows to the abdomen also can produce lacerations of the mesenteric root that often are accompanied by duodenal and pancreatic injuries and retroperitoneal hemorrhages. Such abdominal injuries often do not result in immediate death, and the children come to medical attention following the development of peritonitis.

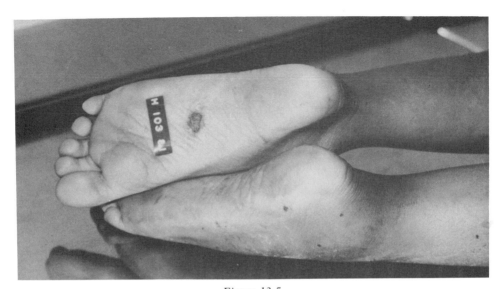

Figure 13.5

Healing untreated circumscribed burn on sole of left foot consistent with causation by cigarette.

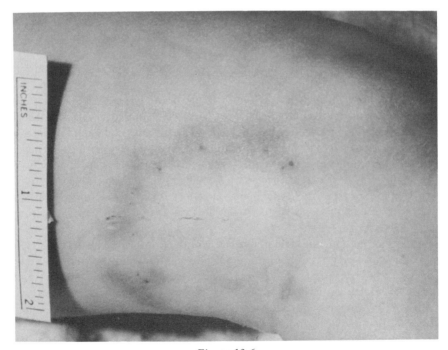

Figure 13.6

Bite mark on posterior-lateral aspect of right knee; fatal brain injury from whiplash shaking.

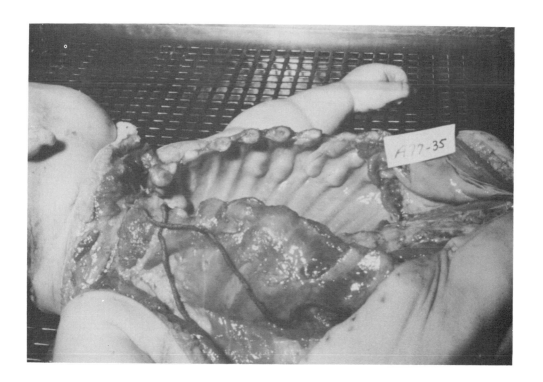

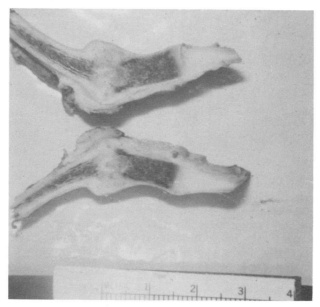

Figure 13.7

Three-month-old child who died of blows to the head. (*a*) Four healing rib fractures of lateral left chest wall. (*b*) A longitudinal section of one of the ribs reveals callus formation at the site of fracture.

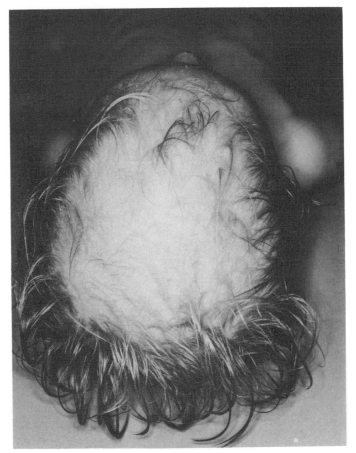

Figure 13.8

Traumatic alopecia; fatal brain injury from whiplash shaking (same case as fig. 13.6).

Case History

A two-and-a-half-month-old child was brought comatose to a hospital emergency room. The parents indicated that the child had fallen from a counter top. In spite of intensive care she died twenty-four hours after admission. At autopsy there were multiple contusions of the face, scalp, trunk, and extremities. There were multifocal, subscalpular hemorrhages indicative of multiple separate injuries. Premortem and postmortem skull films did not show fractures, but autopsy inspection of the calvarium with stripping of the periosteum and dura revealed three individual, linear fractures in areas associated with subscalpular hemorrhages. There were subdural and subarachnoid hemorrhages.

Healing rib fractures, both laterally and posteriorly were present on both sides. Numerous long-bone injuries were demonstrated by premortem and postmortem X-rays. Although the rib fractures appeared similar, each was removed, decalcified, and examined microscopically. By microscopic examination, some showed early healing while others had extensive callous formation and were clearly a different age (fig. 13.9). In this manner rib fractures of at least three different ages were identified. Likewise, histologic examination of the skull fractures revealed

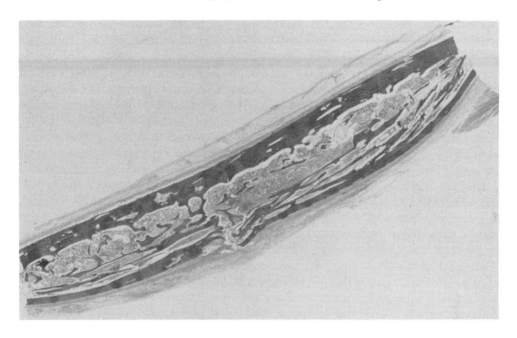

Figure 13.9

(*a*) Recent rib fracture with early organization of hemorrhage. (*b*) Healing rib fracture with callus formation.

two fresh fractures and one fracture that was healing. Histologic examination of the long-bone injuries revealed classical periosteal reaction. Histologic examination of gluteal contusions revealed fresh hemorrhage and fibrosis with hemosiderin deposition representing a healed injury.

Despite the compelling anatomic evidence of physical abuse at autopsy, it is insufficient for the prosecting pathologist to merely document and describe the extent of the injuries. In a battered baby it is important to prove the repeated nature of the assaults in a court of law. This requires documentation of injuries of different ages through photographs, X-rays, gross descriptions, or histologic techniques. Estimation of the age of fractures can be made by gross examination, radiology, and microscopic examination. Estimation of the age of bruises is less exact. Although bruises are generally initially reddish blue or purple, they can have different coloration depending on the normal pigmentation of the individual. Their color usually changes over several days from purple or blue through gray to green, to yellow with varying degrees of brown, but this will depend on many things such as the depth of the bruise (11). Likewise, determining the age of a bruise microscopically is hampered by a wide variability in the breakdown of the extravasated blood. Although it is often difficult to give a narrow range as to the age of a particular bruise, it is often possible to determine that two bruises are of different ages by microscopic examination. In order to do so it often is necessary to examine numerous skeletal, visceral, and cutaneous injuries microscopically and with different histologic stains. The appearance of macrophages containing hemosiderin or the formation of fibrosis in an injury as opposed to the lack of such changes in another injury may be more important in demonstrating the repeated assaults on a child than in pinpointing the exact time of the injury.

Any team approach to the problem of the battered baby, in particular, or child abuse in general, should consider the inclusion of an autopsy pathologist. The autopsy pathologist, particularly the trained forensic pathologist, can play an important role in the examination of nonfatal victims of abuse as well as those fatally injured. When called to see an infant or child in the emergency room or on the ward, he can focus on a careful examination and documentation of the injuries. Other members of the medical team may be too involved with diagnosis and treatment to provide this careful documentation. Nonmedical members of the team may be more concerned with family interactions or disposition or may not recognize the importance of patterns of injuries. It is important to have a careful description of injuries in the medical records if there are subsequent visits to a medical facility because of injuries and for potential use in legal proceedings.

Single Episode Abuse

In our experience, fatalities from an isolated or single beating are as common as fatalities from repeated physical assault (battered baby syndrome). These fatalities present unique problems for the pathologist or other child abuse investigator. The infant or child is usually well nourished and often appears well cared for. Without the circumstantial and anatomic evidence of repeated injuries, the distinction between inflicted and accidental injury becomes more difficult. The determination of willful injury will depend a great deal on the comparison of how the injuries were alleged to have occurred to the actual injuries found at autopsy. A frequent finding in fatally abused children is anatomic-historic disharmony. The injuries found at autopsy could not have occurred in the manner described by the adult guardians.

Case History

A two-and-a-half-year-old boy was brought comatose by his stepmother to a university hospital with a history of falling from his tricycle. On admission to the emergency room he was decerebrate with no spontaneous respirations. A laparotomy was performed because of hemoperitoneum and a lacerated liver was repaired. The child survived for five days on a respirator before being pronounced dead. The autopsy showed multiple contusions of the scalp, trunk, and extremities. Internally, there was the expected healing laceration of the liver and there was subdural hemorrhage and cerebral edema. The cutaneous injuries included discrete contusions of the front and back of the scalp, the chest, abdomen and back, the buttocks, and front and back of the extremities. A single fall could not explain the multiplicity of the injuries to the head, trunk, and extremities. Indeed, the tricycle was examined and the seat was eighteen inches high. If such severe injuries could be sustained from a fall from a tricycle seat eighteen inches high, few children would survive toddlerhood.

A fatality from a single episode of abuse may also be the result of a single injury as well as multiple injuries as described above. These fatalities are even more difficult to distinguish from accidental deaths. They require first a proper degree of suspicion and then adequate communication and cooperation among the investigating agencies to appropriately assess the circumstances and the autopsy findings.

Head Injuries

Infants and children sustain fatal brain injuries when they are struck in the head by hands, feet, or instruments; when their moving heads impact against unyielding surfaces; or when they are violently ("whiplash") shaken. Absence of a direct cranial impact in the latter situation requires separate consideration of brain trauma caused by shaking.

In blows to the head and moving head impacts, the presence or absence of externally visible scalp wounds, and the physical appearance of such wounds, are governed by the amount of force transmitted to the scalp, the rate with which such force is applied, the surface area of contact with the scalp, the nature and amount of hair or other protective scalp covering, and the specific contour and texture of the injured area. Localized or circumscribed impacts cause nonuniform displacement of tissue and are more likely to produce an external wound than forces applied over a broad area, explaining why fingertips are more likely to impart bruises than is the palm of an assailant's hand. The severity of injury and likelihood of wounding are inversely related to the duration of impact. Any prolongation of energy transfer to the head diminishes the severity of injury, explaining why it is less dangerous for an infant to fall on a carpeted than on an uncarpeted floor. Any covering of the scalp by hair or fabric can provide sufficient shielding to prevent the occurrence of external wounds. It should be emphasized, however, that absence of a scalp wound does not preclude the possibility of a skull fracture and/or brain injury.

In contrast to externally visible wounds, when children die from head injuries sustained by blows or falls, the deep surface of the scalp virtually always reveals contusions at points of impact. Therefore, it is essential for the autopsy protocol to state specifically whether or not there are foci of subscalpular hemorrhage. If present, the size, color, and location of such hemorrhages should be noted, and separately identified, appropriate samples of scalp should be retained for microscopic study. The most informative histological changes for aging injuries ordinarily are found in sections that include the transition from uninjured to injured tissue rather than the center of a contusion.

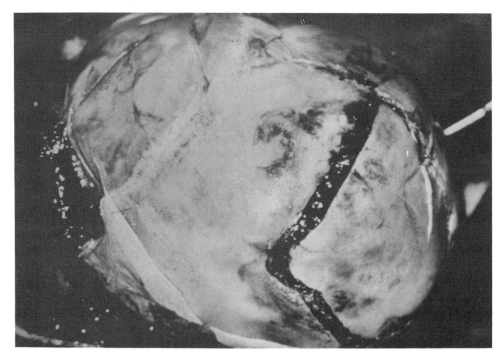

Figure 13.10

Gaping fracture of left parietal bone with subjacent hemorrhage; 6-month-old girl dropped from crib by 6-year-old brother.

Skull fractures are usual concomitants of fatal head injuries from blows and falls. A chilling testimonial to the fragility of an infant's skull and the ease with which it can be fractured is provided by Adelson's study entitled "The Battering Child" (12). He described five instances of fatal head injuries in victims ranging from seven weeks to eight months old whose assailants were two-and-a-half to eight years old. Four of the victims had extensive skull fractures, and two had such severe injuries that there were lacerations of dura mater with extracranial extrusions of grossly visible brain fragments into subscalpular hemorrhages. The injuries were inflicted by blows with blunt instruments as innocuous as toys, by being dropped to the floor, or both. Figure 13.10 shows a gaping fracture of the parietal bone with subjacent hemorrhage in a six-month-old girl who was dropped to the floor from her crib by her mentally retarded 6-year-old brother. The degree of trauma in this case appears to be much more extensive than those cases described by Helfer et al. in their "Falling out of Bed" study (13). In instances of fatal abuse it is necessary to carefully inspect the skull because linear fractures are not always apparent on X-ray and will remain undetected unless the dura is stripped from the undersurface of the skull and the periosteum is scraped from the outer surface.

Large intracranial, extracerebral hematomas are *uncommon* (sic) in fatally head-injured infants and young children. The normal firm adherence of the dura mater to the skull in this age group usually prevents the creation of an epidural space with accumulation of a large volume of blood in that traumatically created locus. Although a unilateral or bilateral thin film of subdural hemorrhage is found frequently in head-injury fatalities from falls and blows, only a small minority of such victims has a subdural hematoma sufficiently large to compress and displace the subjacent brain. The foregoing statement is not intended to denigrate the importance of the subdural hemorrhages in fatal cranio-cerebral trauma in this age group. Instead, we intend to focus attention more sharply and critically on the mechanics of brain trauma than can be derived from the pathogenetically naive assumption that blood in the subdural space is deleterious only by virtue of its inert mass effect.

Causation of subdural hemorrhages requires differential motion of the skull and brain with concomitant shearing of veins that traverse the subdural space. The initiation and termination of such brain movements also have the potential to transmit shearing stresses to the cerebral parenchyma. Our usual inability to identify localized traumatic lesions in such brains does not exclude the possibility that they have sustained traumatically induced functional derangements.

The disparity between structural change and functional derangement is exemplified most clearly by fatalities due to cardiac and cerebral injuries. Cardiac examples are conceptually simpler than brain injuries and are mentioned briefly to place in better perspective the concept of lethal trauma without demonstrable structural cause. Fatal electrocution is the least equivocal example imaginable. When the path of an electrical current is transthoracic, the lethal derangement is either ventricular fibrillation or cardiac standstill depending upon the amperage passing through the heart (14). In either instance, the heart shows no pathological change. Mechanical trauma can do the same thing. The beneficial aspect of this observation is the basis for cardioversion of arrhythmias by a precordial thump. The deleterious aspect is exemplified by deaths of otherwise healthy persons from precordial blunt trauma that fails to mark the skin, leaves the sternum and ribs intact, and produces no structurally demonstrable cardiac injury (15).

Similar disruptions of cerebral function occur from electrical injuries, and a critical evaluation of many deaths due to blunt head injuries leads us to conclude that the same principles apply to the brain. Common autopsy findings in infants and young children who die from blunt head injuries include the previously mentioned stigmas of impacts to the scalp and skull, scant unilateral or bilateral subdural hemorrhage, and a variably swollen brain with a few tiny foci of subarachnoid hemorrhage and no contusions or lacerations. In such instances, the conclusion that death resulted from a head injury rests upon an evaluation of the history, circumstances surrounding death, evidence of cranial impact(s), and the exclusion of other causes of death. Many pathologists are uncomfortable when driven to the conclusion that death resulted from head injury when there is a paucity of cerebral pathological changes. Our tradition in anatomic pathology rests upon morphology, but if we are unyieldingly anchored to morphology, we deny reality in the name of objectivity.

In this context, we should mention the possibility that infants with fatal brain trauma may have diffuse axonal injury (16). That pattern of injury is characterized by torn axones in the cerebral white matter and usually occurs in instances when the moving head impacts on the vertex of the scalp. Morphologic recognition of torn axones can be equivocal or difficult when the survival interval is insufficient to permit the formation of characteristic retraction balls and probably is an especially difficult lesion to recognize in the infant brain. Also, diffuse axonal injury frequently is associated with hemorrhages in the corpus

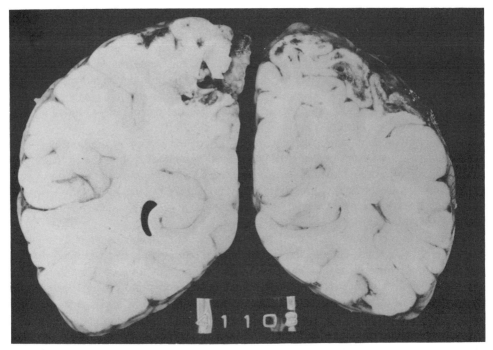

Figure 13.11

Coronal section of occipital lobes, 1-year-old child, showing adult morphology contusions (hemorrhages in cortex at crests of gyri) immediately adjacent to infant morphology trauma (lacerations of cortex and subcortical white matter).

callosum, unci opposite the edges of the tentorium cerebelli and the tegmentum of the rostral pons. None of these lesions is typically present in infants with fatal brain injuries of the sort discussed in this chapter.

When demonstrable brain injuries are present in infants, they are morphologically different than their counterparts in children and adults (17). Prior to one year of age, typical traumatic brain lesions are tears of cerebral white matter or cortex. After approximately one year of age, cerebral cortical contusions begin to have typical adult morphology and are represented by punctate and streak-like hemorrhages and necroses in the cortex chiefly distributed along the crests of gyri. Figure 13.11 is a coronal section of the occipital lobes from a one-year-old boy and exemplifies that this is the approximate transitional age from infant to older morphology brain trauma. Children beyond approximately two years of age who die from head injuries have autopsy findings similar to adults. The interval from approximately one to two years of age is a gradual transition from infant to adult traumatic neuropathology.

Autopsy findings in infants who sustain fatal brain injuries from whiplash shaking further exemplify the previously discussed disparity between structurally demonstrable damage and functional derangement. Important observations in the postmortem evaluations of shaken infants include the documentation of contusions where they are grasped by their assailants. Demonstration of injuries inflicted by grasping and shaking an infant can require incision and dissection of the upper arms (fig. 13.12). The infant victims of fatal shaking show neither scalp hemorrhages nor skull fractures (18, 19). They may or may not have subdural and/or focal subarachnoid hemorrhages, usually do not have localized brain contusions or lacerations, and develop swollen brains if they survive long enough (20–22) (fig. 13.13). The presence of retinal hemorrhages strongly supports the diagnosis, but we caution that such hemorrhages are not pathognomonic of shaking. In particular, frontal impact of the moving head can cause similar retinal hemorrhages with or without damage to the optic nerves.

We have emphasized the potential subtlety or paucity of cerebral parenchymal trauma in a variety of infant deaths from head injury. Medical treatment, particularly mechanical ventilation of infants with universal cerebral necrosis for days or weeks, greatly magnifies the difficulties of pathological interpretation. In such instances, it is essential that the pathologist acquires as much information as possible about clinical studies that may help to identify localized changes that antedate the generalized, superimposed necrosis permitted by artificial ventilation. In our experience, computer tomography scans that were done early in the hospital course are unrivaled as sources of useful information that focus the pathologist's attention on areas of the brain that otherwise might be overlooked.

Another potentially difficult medicolegal interpretation arises in instances in which children die many months or years after sustaining neurologically devastating head injuries.

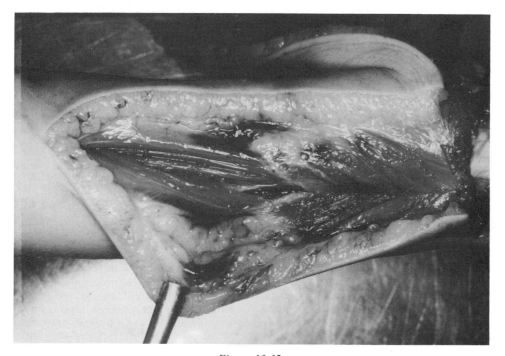

Figure 13.12

Incision of lateral aspect of left upper arm discloses hemorrhages in subcutaneous fat and muscle of infant with fatal brain injury caused by whiplash shaking.

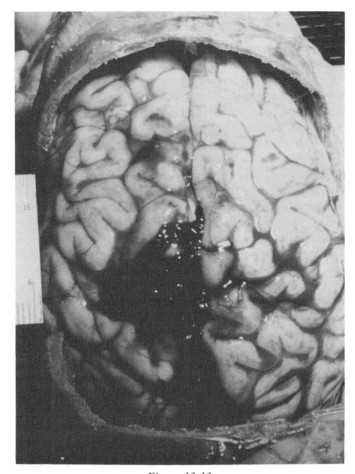

Figure 13.13

Scant subdural hemorrhage overlying swollen brain in 6-month-old whiplash shaken infant.

Case History

A thirty-month-old female infant sustained a severe head injury when struck by her mother's boy-friend. The child was comatose upon arrival at a hospital. She remained comatose and required mechanical ventilation and intensive care for several months. Eventually she was weaned from the respirator and sent home with her maternal grandmother who provided dedicated care for the next eighteen months. The child never regained meaningful neurological function, and over the span of her survival at home had developed several respiratory infections. She died at home. Autopsy disclosed marked, generalized brain atrophy (fig. 13.14) and a focus of old hemorrhagic degeneration of the cortex of the right cerebral hemisphere (fig. 13.15) that was consistent with the location of her primary head injury described in her initial clinical records and documented in an early computer tomography scan. The general autopsy showed physical retardation, multifocal, nonspecific chronic inflammation in her lungs, and acute aspiration pneumonia. It was our evaluation that the immediate cause of death was aspiration pneumonia and

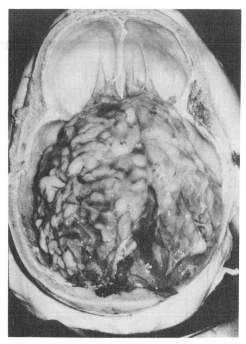

Figure 13.14

Brain in situ with enormous subdural space created by marked, post-traumatic cerebral atrophy. Same case as fig. 13.13.

that the aspiration pneumonia was the direct result of neurological impairment arising from her
post-traumatic brain atrophy. Accordingly, in spite of her out-of-hospital survival, we concluded
that the head injury was the proximate cause of death and that the manner of death was homicide. Our conclusions about the proximate cause and the manner of death would have been the
same if the immediate cause of death had been hypostatic bronchopneumonia, without aspiration
of gastric content, or any other natural complication of her debility and neurological deficit.

Thoracic and Abdominal Injuries

Although head injuries predominate in fatal beating deaths, abdominal injuries are frequent. They may be present exclusive of head injuries as the cause of death themselves, or
they may be present concurrently with head injuries. When associated with severe head
injuries causing unconsciousness or coma, they may be overlooked clinically. When associated with fatal head injury the pathologist may be surprised to find thoracic or abdominal injuries in spite of little or no cutaneous evidence of injury. With a blow to the abdomen or a severe crush or squeeze of the trunk, there may be no skin bruising even with
severe visceral injury. The liver in an infant or small child is poorly protected by the rib
cage and vulnerable to a blow to the abdomen. A lacerated liver with internal insanguina-
tion can occur with a single blow to the epigastrium that produces no external injury.

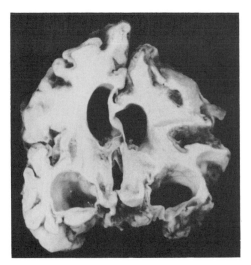

Figure 13.15

Coronal section of brain following formalin fixation. The right hemisphere, site of primary trauma, is more atrophic than the left and shows
dark discoloration of its cortex from old hemorrhage. Atrophy of left hemisphere from generalized post-traumatic swelling; no primary traumatic lesion in left hemisphere.

Other common injuries due to blows to the abdomen include mesenteric laceration with
retroperitoneal hemorrhage, pancreatic lacerations, and duodenal lacerations or hematomas (23, 24). These organs are particularly susceptible in the midline because they are
compressed against the spinal column by a blunt force. Death from delayed hemorrhage
from an intramural duodenal hematoma has been described (25).

Although these midline, upper-abdominal, visceral injuries can be sustained accidentally, their discovery clinically or at the autopsy table should suggest child abuse. The
upper abdomen is not a common site of accidental injury, and lacerations of the midline
organs require a severe blunt force concentrated over a small area. These injuries are most
consistent with a fist blow or a kick to the epigastrium.

Sexual Abuse

Although sexual abuse of children is common and underreported (see chap. 14), the
combination of sexual abuse and fatal injuries is uncommon. When it does occur, the fatal
injuries may be related or unrelated to the sexual assault itself (fig. 13.16). In small children or infants, extensive damage to the genitalia and perineum with lacerations in these
regions may lead to fatal hemorrhage. More often other injuries such as an asphyxial assault is the cause of death. Nevertheless, whether genital injuries poignantly point to sexual assault or whether there is only a suspicion of sexual assault, the pathologist must be
able to do the appropriate examinations at the autopsy table. This requires an awareness of
the proper samples to obtain and how to preserve them. In the midst of an autopsy on a

fatally abused child, it is easy to overlook one or more procedures if one relies solely on memory. To avoid omissions it is a good idea to have available a ready-made sexual assault kit complete with materials for collecting appropriate specimens. Since different crime laboratories might use different scientific techniques or have individual preferences for the way they would like specimens handled and submitted, it is a good idea to put together or use sexual assault kits approved by your consulting laboratory (26). A complete sexual assault kit might include:

    chain of custody form
    envelopes for trace evidence and hair collection
    comb for pubic hair combings (pubertal or adult)
    test tubes for blood collection
    filter paper or swabs for saliva collection
    cotton applicators for vaginal, anal, and oral swabs
    glass microscope slide labels
    checklist

Tests for sperm and acid phosphatase are most important since their presence indicates sexual activity. If semen is present, then the blood group of the assailant may possibly be determined if he is a secretor. For this determination the secretor status and blood type of

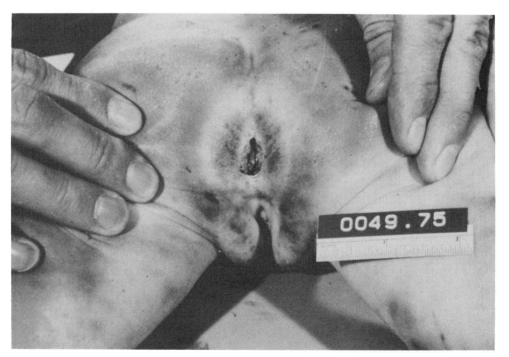

Figure 13.16

Genital and anal injuries from sexual assault in 2-year-old girl with repeated injuries (battered baby syndrome). Uncommon combination of sexual assault and battered baby syndrome. Same case as fig. 13.1.

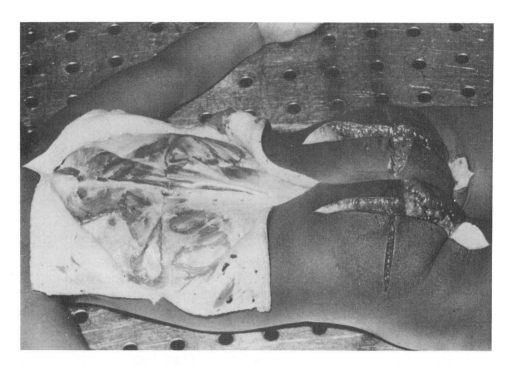

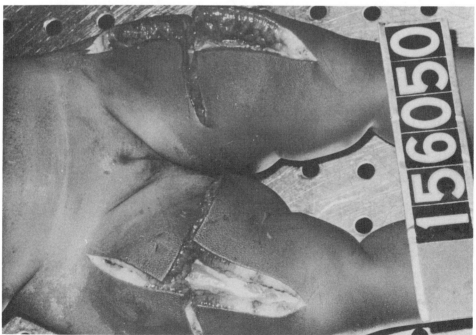

Figure 13.17
Cruciate autopsy incisions of (*a*) back, buttocks, and (*b*) thighs disclosing severe gluteal and thigh contusions.

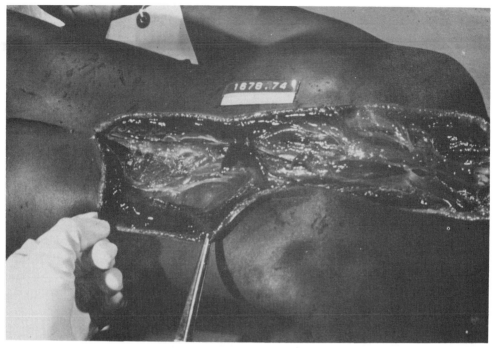

Figure 13.18

Confluent subcutaneous hemorrhage of back. Although abrasions were evident at autopsy, the confluent hemorrhage was not appreciated until the back was incised because of the dark pigmentation.

the victim must also be ascertained. A search of the body for any foreign hair or fiber is important. If there is any pubic hair it should be combed to separate foreign hair. A specimen of the victim's own pubic hair and scalp hair must be retained for possible comparison with hair found on a suspect. Fingernail clippings or scrapings may yield tissue (epidermis) which has been raked off the assailant as the victim tried to defend himself or herself.

Soft Tissue Injuries Only

Although child abuse deaths due to soft tissue injuries alone are uncommon, they can occur (27). The lethal mechanisms in such fatalities include deceptively large volumes of blood shed into soft tissues, fat embolism generated by crushing of adipose tissue, and stress induced by the cumulative effects of pain, fear, and traumatic shock. Such cases necessitate the use of multiple cutaneous incisions of the trunk, buttocks, and extremities to demonstrate the location and extent of the subcutaneous injuries (fig. 13.17).

Case History

A three-year-old, thirty-two-pound boy was found unresponsive in the backyard of his home by his stepfather who admitted to earlier striking the boy with a belt because the child urinated in his pants. At autopsy there were numerous abrasions and contusions with confluent subcutaneous hemorrhage of the back and buttocks (fig. 13.18). There were no injuries of the brain or of the organs of the abdominal and thoracic cavities.

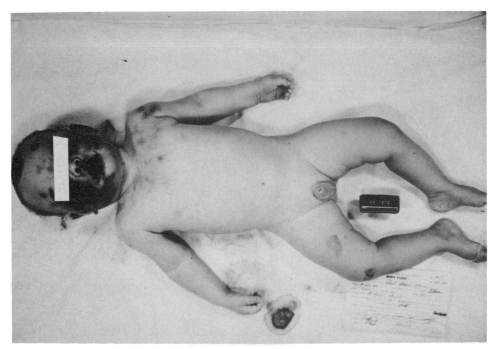

Figure 13.19

Single episode fatal beating inflicted by psychotic father.

Stress Cardiomyopathy

Potentially difficult problems of autopsy interpretation arise when injuries are restricted to the soft tissues and there is no cranial or visceral trauma that helps to explain the fatal mechanism. Such victims are virtually "beaten to death," but we ordinarily cannot provide an unequivocal, structurally demonstrable translation of the lethal pathophysiology. Slowly accumulating hemorrhage into traumatized soft tissues is usually insufficient in amount to produce exsanguination, and the slight-to-moderate pulmonary fat embolism that inevitably results from crushing adipose tissue has no important physiological effect.

We believe that the cumulative burden of painful injuries and psychological stress kills because of a responsive overproduction of catecholamines with resulting hormonally mediated myocardial injury. Support for this hypothesis is provided by morphologic evidence. A study of fifteen homicidal assault victims, four of whom were children, whose injuries were restricted to soft tissues disclosed myofibrillar degeneration consistent with "stress cardiomyopathy" in eleven (28). Animals subjected to a variety of stresses in experiments develop comparable myofibrillar degeneration and foci of myocardial necrosis (29–31). The same pathological lesions can be produced by experimental administration of catecholamines or by naturally occurring pheochromocytomas (32). Chemical evidence suggesting catecholamine-mediated myocardial injury from stress is provided by a study of the concentrations of CK, LDH, and their isoenzymes in pericardial fluid (33).

Healthy persons who died from extracardiac injuries in violent situations had higher enzyme concentrations in their pericardial fluid than either normal controls or persons who died from heart disease.

Fatal abuse or neglect of a child because of overt psychosis of a guardian occurs occasionally and usually does not take the form of the battered baby syndrome. Deaths occur either by an isolated single violent attack during psychotic behavior or by neglect (figs. 13.19, 13.20). Although psychosis is uncommon in perpetrators of fatal child abuse, the abusive parents or guardians often have emotional disturbances and sociopathic personalities. Dependency, age inappropriateness, sadomasochism, egocentricity, and narcissism may be present. They were often abused children themselves. When seen in a clinical situation, they may be impulsive, demanding, withdrawn, depressed, or angry.

Starvation

The nutritional variant of the battered child syndrome, homicide by starvation, was brought into clear focus by Dr. Lester Adelson in 1963 (34). His seminal paper on the subject described five infants who died from malnutrition and dehydration resulting from neglect and deprivation of food, and he cogently indicated that such fatalities are homicides.

Typical autopsy findings in starved infants include obvious cachexia, dehydration, atrophy of subcutaneous and deep fat, atrophy of all lymphoid organs, and an empty or nearly empty gastrointestinal tract. The victims commonly show other stigmata of neglect such

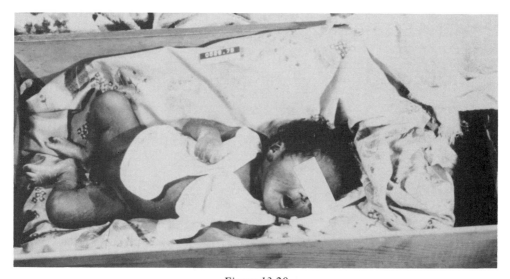

Figure 13.20
Newborn who died of dehydration after being placed in dresser drawer by psychotic mother.

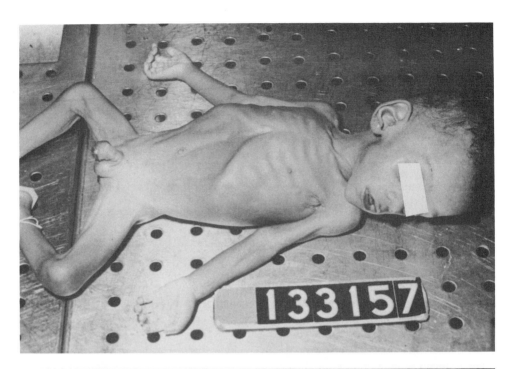

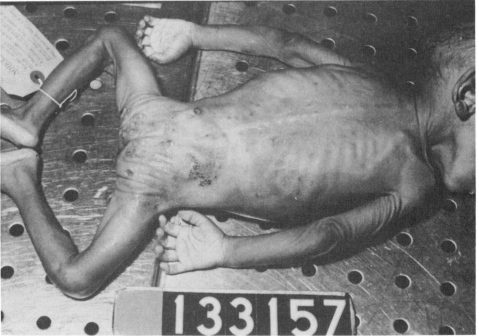

Figure 13.21

Fatal malnutrition and dehydration in an infant with chronic diaper rash. (*a*) Front view.
(*b*) Back view.

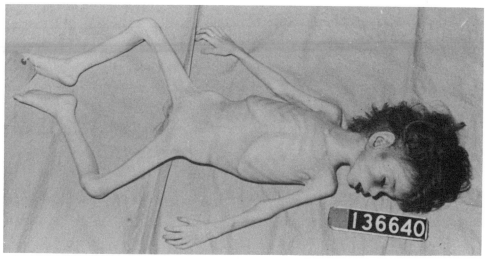

Figure 13.22
Fatal malnutrition and dehydration in 4-year-old girl.

as chronic diaper rash (fig. 13.21). Ordinarily they have not been beaten or subjected to other physical abuses.

Almost all reported instances of fatal maltreatment by starvation have been infants, reflecting their inability to acquire food for themselves and their nutritional requirements during this period of rapid growth. Figure 13.22 shows the one exception that we have encountered in our personal experience. The four-year-old girl weighed fourteen pounds at death. It was our contention that the accomplishment of her starvation required restraint to prevent her from foraging for food. Police investigation disclosed a hook-and-eye locking device on the outside of her bedroom door.

Autopsy in instances of fatal malnutrition should include total body X-ray examination; analysis of vitreous humor for electrolytes, urea nitrogen, creatinine and sugar to evaluate dehydration and diabetes; and a competent autopsy including appropriate microscopic studies to establish or exclude a natural explanation for malnutrition and dehydration. Sequelae of malnutrition, such as bronchopneumonia and stress ulcers of the stomach or duodenum, are predictable and may act as immediate causes of death. Such complications do not absolve malnutrition of its underlying responsibility.

Hypothetical situations in which natural disease produces fatal malnutrition are rarely if ever encountered in autopsies on infants who die at home or are brought moribund to an emergency room. The ghastly appearances of the children shown in figures 13.21 and 13.22 cannot develop overnight from disease in a previously healthy, adequately nourished child and are absolutely inconsistent with histories of alleged infectious diseases of a few days duration. Any parent or custodian who allows a child to wither to the depicted appearances prior to seeking medical attention has failed to provide the level of care that society has a right to expect and demand.

An essential component of the medical investigation of any fatality from malnutrition must include the study of all available medical records. A chronological log of every re-

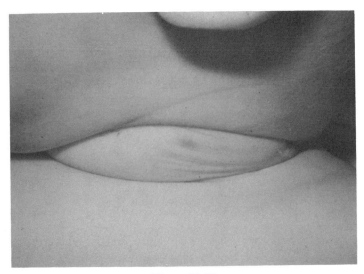

Figure 13.23

Three-month-old smothering victim. (Face to left, ear to top, hair to right of picture.) The only injury was a tiny contusion of the left side of the neck. The death was thought to be due to the Sudden Infant Death Syndrome (SIDS) until the father confessed that he held the child by the neck with one hand and placed his other hand over the child's face until the child died.

corded weight of the child can disclose fluctuations that correlate with changing custody. For example, the girl shown in figure 13.22 had a period of normal weight gain when transiently taken away from her mother.

Subtle Fatal Abuse

Subtle fatal abuse occurs when a child or infant is willfully killed in such a way that there are few or no anatomic findings that would explain the death or in such a way that the death appears to be the result of an accident or natural disease. The small size and delicacy of infants and small children render them vulnerable to death by a wide variety of such subtle mechanisms. Subtle fatal abuse can be due to either physical assault, poisoning, or negligence (35).

There are a number of ways in which physical assault in children and infants causes death without causing significant demonstrable anatomic evidence; most of them are asphyxial. A lack of suspicion in approaching unexpected childhood deaths due to asphyxia can obscure recognition of their willfully inflicted nature.

Smothering of an infant may be accomplished without anatomic injury (fig. 13.23). Placing a hand over an infant's mouth and nose until the infant dies may result in minor abrasions or contusions of the face or buccal mucosa, and evidence of such pressure should be diligently sought in every suspicious death. However, such injuries are not invariably present in smotherings. Likewise, placing a foreign object such as facial tissue down the throat may cause death with no demonstrable evidence if the obstruction is removed prior to examination. Manual or ligature strangulation can be accomplished without leaving marks, and compression of the chest (traumatic asphyxia) may also leave no marks.

Blunt impacts to the head may cause concussions in children with rapid onset of cerebral edema and death. Anatomically, cerebral edema may be the only finding. Also, as previously described, shaking an infant may cause severe cerebral damage or even death with few anatomic findings.

Physical and Chemical Agents

Hot-water scald burns are a common form of injury in infants and small children. When they are the result of abuse, they may be misinterpreted as accidental injuries. Most instances are probably accidental, but child abuse or neglect cannot be discounted. In one large series, 28 percent of such burns resulted from abuse (36–46). (These findings are discussed in chapter 11.)

A willfully inflicted minor injury that would not cause significant morbidity in a healthy infant or child, but which hastens or contributes to the death of a child severely debilitated by disease or congenital defect, could also result in a subtle fatality due to physical assault.

Chemical assault is a distinctly less common form of child abuse than physical assault. When it does occur, it is extremely difficult to detect and to prove. Few poisons or drugs produce pathognomonic or even characteristic lesions. Thus a correct diagnosis usually requires prior suspicion. The offending agent need not be a classic poison or drug because almost any substance is potentially dangerous to a child or infant if taken in sufficient quantity. The assault may be a deliberate attempt to kill the child or an attempt to quiet or discipline the child. Toxicological analyses of blood, urine, and other appropriate body fluids should prove helpful.

Fatal child abuse can result not only from an overt act, such as physical or chemical assault, but as a result of failure to act when such a duty is imposed by law. Therefore, when the law places the responsibility on parents or guardians to provide food, shelter, protection, and medical care for their children, death resulting from the willful failure to provide such care should be considered fatal child abuse. For example, placing a child in a locked, parked automobile in summertime may result in heat stroke. Any rational adult knows that a closed car parked in the sun becomes uncomfortably hot, and placing the child in that environment convincingly demonstrates a disregard for the child's well-being. Common diseases, such as sickle cell anemia and diabetes mellitus, can be exacerbated by negligent care of adults. A sickle cell crisis can be initiated by dehydration; diabetic coma by providing an improper diet. Failure to provide adequate medical care when needed may be a result of religious beliefs, reliance on unfounded methods of treatment, or simple disregard for the child. Depending on the circumstances, therefore, death resulting from improper medical care could be regarded as fatal child abuse.

Munchausen Syndrome by Proxy

A decidedly uncommon and newly described form of child abuse is the Munchausen syndrome by proxy (47). The Munchausen syndrome refers to patients who repeatedly present an elaborate and fictitious medical history in order to gain medical attention. The Munchausen syndrome by proxy occurs when a parent or guardian falsifies a child's medical history or alters a child's laboratory test or actually causes an illness or injury in a child in order to gain medical attention for the child which may result in innumerable harmful hospital procedures. Examples of the Munchausen syndrome by proxy include untruthful descriptions of symptoms (48, 49), alteration of body fluids before laboratory testing (47), or by actually causing an illness or injury by poisoning or injuring the child (50–52).

Although a death due to abuse from the Munchausen syndrome by proxy must be rare, it will never be recognized by the pathologist unless he is aware of the syndrome. Whenever there is a death following an unexplained illness or injury the potential of such subtle abuse must be considered. In these situations, the child is the unwitting victim of a serious psychiatric problem of the perpetrator. In most of the reported cases, this has been the mother. The mothers in all of these cases were described as pleasant, cooperative, intelligent, and appreciative of good medical care. It was suggested that their motives may have been similar to those of the Munchausen syndrome, a desire for the glamour of being around the emotion and pace of a hospital and the attention that was paid to them.

False Accusation of Child Abuse

Equally abhorrent as the nonrecognition of fatal child abuse is the diagnosis of abuse where none exists. It is the poor, young, unsophisticated minority parent or guardian who relates poorly to medical and law enforcement personnel who is most likely to be falsely accused. The practitioner in the emergency room and the pathologist at the autopsy table must be constantly mindful of the hazards in making the diagnosis of child abuse in order to prevent a false-positive diagnosis. Since there has been a great deal of recent public concern over abused children and the very idea of an abused child is potentially repugnant to the pathologist, there exists a potential to jump to a conclusion where injuries are suspicious and parents are hostile and uncooperative.

The pathologist must constantly keep in mind the typical injuries in child abuse and the characteristics of their guardians. The final diagnosis of child abuse rests not only on the autopsy findings and the circumstances of the death but also on an evaluation of the parents and the pathologist's experience and knowledge. Certainly some cases of fatal abuse may go unrecognized; that is inevitable. The pathologist, however, has the responsibility to avoid a dogmatic diagnosis of abuse where there is reasonable doubt about willful injury.

Clinically, chronic skin conditions are the most common misdiagnosed natural disease that leads to accusation of child abuse (fig. 13.24). Mongolian spots may mimic bruising of the back and buttocks. Bullous impetigo in infants and children may be mistaken as inflicted abrasions or burns (53). Accidental injuries such as burning by sun-heated automobile safety belts may result in a burn pattern that suggests abuse (54). There are cultural folk medicine practices that result in injuries or scars to infants that may result in inappropriate accusations of child abuse by those who do not recognize the therapeutic intent of the injuries. Included among the culturally determined injuries would be coin-

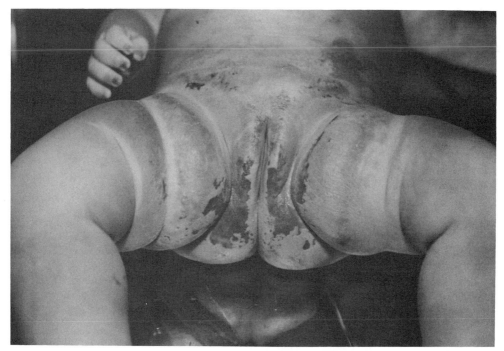

Figure 13.24
Chronic diaper rash misinterpreted as child abuse.

rolling bruises among Vietnamese refugees and superficial abdominal burns among other Southeast Asian refugees (55).

The pathologist examining the fatality where there is a possibility of abuse must not only be aware of these "pseudoabusive" practices but also possess knowledge of post-mortem artifacts that may mimic injury. Postmortem insect activity may suggest abrasions (fig. 13.25). Postmortem rodent bites and even cat or dog bites may be misinterpreted. Accentuated livor mortis or discoloration during decomposition may give the appearance of bruises. Drying of mucous membranes or skin may give a false appearance of abrasions, particularly of the lips and scrotum. Cooling of the body with the neck flexed may result in coagulation of subcutaneous fat in a pattern suggestive of injury (fig. 13.26). Because of the wide range of potential artifacts, the pathologist must constantly review his diagnosis of injury against the background of other potential causes.

Preparation of the Autopsy Protocol in Child Abuse

The autopsy protocol in a case of fatal child abuse is an important document which is the written record of the pathologist's findings. It should be prepared to facilitate an orderly description of all autopsy findings and to avoid omission of minor details. It should be objective and organized so that the major injuries or findings are completely described yet

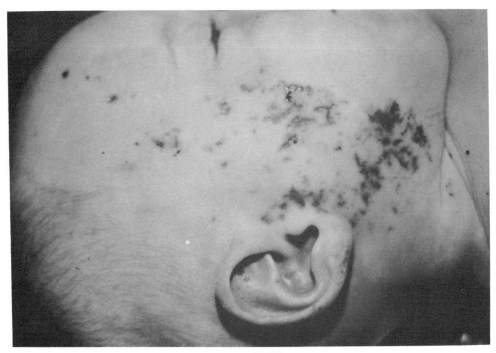

Figure 13.25

Postmortem insect activity (roach bites) in victim of the Sudden Infant Death Syndrome (SIDS).

concise so that immaterial data do not confuse the reader. Although the final form of any autopsy protocol is a personal matter and each pathologist will develop his own particular style, there are some general guidelines for organization of the protocol.

The logical way to start is with an external description of the body as first viewed and after cleaning. This section of the protocol should also include a description of the clothing, either on the body or accompanying the body.

In violent deaths, the next section should include an orderly description of the evidence of injury, both external and internal. An excellent way to arrange the injuries is to discuss the injuries by body parts, such as head, neck, trunk, and extremities. The external and internal injuries for each of the body areas are described, and the individual injuries are listed in a numerical fashion.

Following a detailed numerical description of the injuries, both external and internal, the body cavities, body organs, and organ systems can be described in the standard methods. In this description, the internal injuries previously described do not need to be repeated.

The next section should include a description of any special dissections or special autopsy examinations. Following this, a description of the examination of any of the organs, particularly the brain, that have been made after fixation or other special preparation. Next, the microscopic examination should be included, followed by the results of other special studies such as bacteriology, postmortem chemistry, serology, or trace evidence examination.

The next section should include a list of the findings or diagnoses. This list of diagnoses may eventually be incorporated into the autopsy protocol as the front page depending on the preference of the individual pathologist.

Finally, the autopsy protocol should include an opinion or conclusion by the pathologist as to the cause and manner of death. This section might also include a concise synthesis of the major features that led to the final determination of cause and manner of death. This section should be clearly labeled as the opinion or conclusion of the pathologist and should be clearly separated from the factual description of findings as expressed in the body of the autopsy protocol. The final opinion should be concise and defendable by documented anatomic and nonanatomic information. Extensive pathophysiological speculation should be avoided.

All autopsy protocols, particularly in instances of fatal child abuse, where the written description of the pathologist may be scrutinized in detail by attorneys and other interested parties, should be proofread for clarity and typographical errors. What may seem

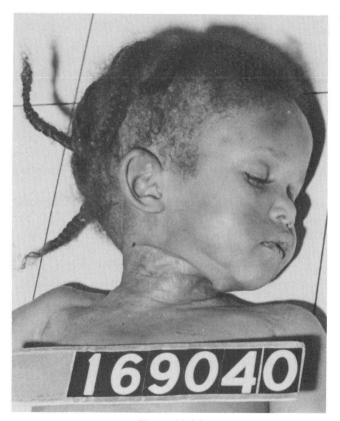

Figure 13.26

Neck creases in infant who died of natural causes are suggestive of a soft ligature mark. The child was placed in a chin to chest posture after death and cooling of subcutaneous fat in that position left the neck creases.

logical during dictation may be inaccurate or illogical on paper. The potential for typographical errors is infinite, some are humorous and some can be confusing. None will be humorous, however, if the pathologist is confronted with them on the witness stand.

Postmortem Examination Guidelines

The following is intended as a broad guideline for the pathologist for conducting a medicolegal pediatric autopsy. In many instances, the complete procedure will be neither necessary nor practical. In other cases, additional studies and/or dissections may be necessary.

I. Circumstantial Information: Obtain information regarding the circumstances of the death before starting the autopsy.
  A. Scene visit: Occasionally an infant or child is found dead and the scene is relatively undisturbed. In such situations, the position of the body, the degree of rigor and livor mortis, and the environment may provide valuable information.
  B. Police report: Communicate frequently with investigating officers to become aware of information available to the police, just as they should have expeditious access to your findings. Do not wait until all the chemical and microscopic studies are completed.
  C. Hospital and emergency room records: If the deceased survived in the hospital, a review of the hospital chart or emergency room record before starting the autopsy is valuable. If the infant is dead on arrival or dead after arrival in the emergency room, the report may be sketchy or incomplete, and more information is usually obtained by talking directly to the medical personnel involved (house officers, paramedics, emergency room nurses, etc.).
  D. Social services: If there is a suspicious death, a call to the local social services department may bring helpful information about the family background of the deceased and about previous incidents concerning the deceased.
II. External Examination
  A. Photography: Competent photography is an essential part of the medicolegal autopsy. Photographs should be taken with an identifying number and with a rule where applicable.
    1. Photographs are important to refresh your memory, particularly if there is a significant delay between autopsy and a legal proceeding.
    2. Photographs often can be entered as evidence in court.
    3. Review of photographs may illuminate an important feature that was not appreciated at the time of autopsy.
    4. Photographs provide material for consultants to review.
  B. Clothing: In many cases, clothing should be examined and retained. Undress the body yourself and examine the clothing over a clean dry surface. If you do not undress the body yourself, have someone trained in trace evidence collection do it. Each item should be dried and preserved and photographed where necessary. Do not wash or dry-clean clothing.
    1. Trace evidence may be adherent to clothing.

2. A pattern may be imprinted on the clothing.

3. Clothing may be essential for identification.

4. Clothing may be held as reference for future trace evidence recovery.

C. Trace evidence: Any adherent particle, hair, fiber, dirt, etc., may potentially link a suspect to the victim. Particularly if an infant or child is found abandoned, it is necessary to preserve any trace evidence. Remove control samples from the body, such as head hair in infants; pubic hair in adolescents.

D. X-rays: Get total body X-rays on all cases of potential abuse. X-rays are used for identifying foreign bodies as well as fractures. Look at them yourself and review them with a radiologist.

1. A trained radiologist may see something you missed.

2. He may be able to help with bone age in unidentified victims.

3. He may be able to help assess time of injury in healed fractures.

E. Sexual assault: If sexual assault is suspected, specific evidence must be obtained.

1. Swabs of oral, anal, and vaginal cavities for acid phosphatase.

2. A second swab of each cavity smeared on two glass slides and fixed: one slide for spermatozoa; the other slide can be used for ABO typing of the secretion if necessary.

3. Swab of any suspicious stain on the body.

4. Trace evidence (hairs, fibers, etc.).

5. Blood for blood type (obtained after body opened).

6. Saliva or gastric juice for secretor status.

F. General body description: Describe the general features of the body, hair color, eye color, dentition, scars, or other identifying characteristics. Be sure to describe the height, weight, degree of rigor and livor mortis, and the location of the lividity.

G. External injuries: Photograph the body as received. After collecting trace evidence and other specimens, clean the body for photographs of injuries or natural disease. It is also helpful to make a diagram of all injuries and other marks.

1. Note each injury separately.

2. Relationships of injuries to body structures and to each other.

3. Patterns of injuries.

4. Color.

5. Size.

6. Shape.

7. Foreign material.

8. Evidence of therapy.

9. Remove representative sections of skin and underlying soft tissues for histopathologic study to assist in dating or timing of injuries.

III. Internal Examination

A. Postmortem specimens

1. Blood and urine for toxicology.

2. Blood for typing.

3. Cultures.

4. Vitreous for postmortem chemistries.

5. Blood for electrophoresis, etc.

Always save specimens, even when you do not feel you will need them. It is better to discard them later than wish you had them. If blood is not available because of mutilation or putrefaction, save tissues, such as muscle, liver, kidney, spleen, and brain.

B. Head
  1. Identify injuries at each layer: scalp, skull, epidural, subdural, subarachnoid, brain.
  2. Measure or weigh amount of subdural present. Often, only a few cc's of subdural is all that is present to indicate a fatal head injury.
  3. Fix brain. Infant brains are very soft and friable. Fixation will permit better evaluation.
  4. Be sure to strip the dura from the cranial vault. Skull fractures can be missed if the dura is not stripped.
  5. Take the spinal cord when indicated.
C. Thoracic, abdominal, and neck organs
  1. Note internal injuries *in situ*.
  2. Remove all organs for dissection.
  3. Samples of organs for histology.
  4. Save appropriate gross specimen. Subtle or controversial findings should be saved for further study and for consultants.
  5. Remove and examine neck organs.
D. Special dissections: In instances of suspected child abuse, the pathologist must not be constrained by the customary Y-shaped autopsy incision. In many cases, to adequately demonstrate contusions, particularly in individuals with dark pigmentation, the pathologist must incise the back, buttocks, and extremities.
IV. Reexamination
A. Reexamine the body after the organs have been removed. Often bruises and pattern injuries will become more evident after evisceration and draining of blood. A second look at the body the next day is worthwhile if possible.
B. If the body has been released to a funeral home and more information comes to your attention, you may need to go to the funeral home to reexamine the body.
V. Consultation: Consultations with other medical specialists or other forensic scientists may be helpful in identifying unknown remains and in determining mechanism and cause of death.
A. Forensic radiologist (aging of fractures and identification).
B. Forensic anthropologist (putrefied and skeletonized remains).
C. Forensic odontologist (identification and bite-mark comparison).
D. Other medical specialists often help with metabolic disorders, drug therapy, etc.
VI. Preserve Chain of Custody: The chain of custody is a method developed to verify the actual possession of an object from the time it was first collected until it is offered into evidence in the courtroom. Each piece of trace evidence or other specimen should be labeled with the victim's name, the time and date, the nature of the specimen, an identifying number, and the pathologist's initials. The specimen should be personally transferred to the investigating officer or to the laboratory or stored in a locked desk or other container to which there is limited access. If the specimen is handled by an intermediary, that person must receipt the material and be included in the chain of custody.

VII. Contacts with News Media: The public and news media have a right to information but should not interfere with the progress of the investigation. You should have a prearranged agreement with other agencies, such as law enforcement, on who will give what information. It is best to have only one spokesman for each case.

References

1. Raimer, J. G.; Raimer, S. S.; and Hebeler, J. R. 1981. Cutaneous Signs of Child Abuse. *J. Am. Acad. Dermatologists* 5:203–12.
2. Ellerstein, N. S. 1979. The Cutaneous Manifestations of Child Abuse and Neglect. *Am. J. Diseases in Children* 133:906–9.
3. Akbarnia, B., et al. 1974. Manifestations of the Battered Child Syndrome. *J. Bone Joint Surgery* 56(A): 1159–66.
4. Beals, R. K., and Tufts, E. 1983. Fractured Femur in Infancy: The Role of Child Abuse. *J. Pediatric Orthopedics* 3:583–86.
5. Galleno, H., and Oppenheim, W. L. 1982. The Battered Child Syndrome Revisited. *Clinical Orthopedics and Related Research* 162:11–19.
6. Griffiths, D. L., and Moynihan, F. J. 1963. Multiple Epiphyseal Injuries in Babies. *British Med. J.* 2:1558–61.
7. Leonidas, J. C. 1983. Skeletal Trauma in the Child Abuse Syndrome. *Pediatric Annals* 12:875–81.
8. Swischuk, L. E. 1969. Spine and Spinal Cord Trauma in the Battered Child Syndrome. *Radiology* 92:733–38.
9. Tufts, E.; Blank, E.; and Dickerson, D. 1982. Periosteal Thickening As a Manifestation of Trauma in Infancy. *Child Abuse and Neglect: International J.* 6:359–64.
10. Feldman, K. W., and Brewer, D. K. 1984. Child Abuse, Cardiopulmonary Resuscitation and Rib Fractures. *Pediatrics* 73:339–42.
11. Wilson, E. F. 1977. Estimation of the Age of Cutaneous Contusions in Child Abuse. *Pediatrics* 60:750–52.
12. Adelson, L. 1972. The Battering Child. *JAMA* 222:159–61.
13. Helfer, R. E.; Scovis, T. L.; and Black, M. 1977. Injuries Resulting When Small Children Fall out of Bed. *Pediatrics* 60:533–35.
14. Wright, R. K., and Davis, J. H. 1980. The Investigation of Electrical Deaths: A Report of 220 Fatalities. *J. Forensic Science Soc.* 25:514–21.
15. Adelson, L., and Hirsch, C. S. 1980. Sudden and Unexpected Death from Natural Causes in Adults. In *Medicolegal Investigation of Death,* 2d ed., ed. W. U. Spitz and R. S. Fisher. Springfield, Ill.: Charles C. Thomas.
16. Adams, J. H., et al. 1981. Diffuse Axonal Injury Due to Non-missile Head Injury in Humans: An Analysis of 45 Cases. *Annals Neurology* 12:557–63.
17. Lindenberg, R., and Freytag, E. 1969. Morphology of Brain Lesions from Blunt Trauma in Early Infancy. *Archives of Pathology* 87:298–305.
18. Caffey, J. 1972. On the Theory and Practice of Shaking Infants. *Am. J. Diseases in Children* 124:161–69.
19. Caffey, J. 1974. The Whiplash Shaken Infant Syndrome: Manual Shaking by the Extremities with Whiplash-Induced Intracranial and Intraocular Bleedings, Linked with Residual Permanent Brain Damage and Mental Retardation. *Pediatrics* 54:396–403.

20. Bennett, H. S., and French, J. H. 1980. Elevated Intracranial Pressure in Whiplash-Shaken Infant Syndrome Detected with Normal Computerized Tomography. *Clinical Pediatrics* 19:633–34.

21. Carter, J. E., and McCormick, A. Q. 1983. Whiplash Shaking Syndrome: Retinal Hemorrhages and Computerized Axial Tomography of the Brain. *Child Abuse and Neglect: International J.* 7:279–86.

22. Ludwig, S. 1984. Shaken Baby Syndrome: A Review of 20 Cases. *Annals Emergency Med.* 13:104–7.

23. Kleinman, P. K.; Raptopoulos, V. D.; and Brill, P. W. 1981. Occult Nonskeletal Trauma in the Battered-Child Syndrome. *Radiology* 141:393–96.

24. McCort, J., and Vaudagna, J. 1964. Visceral Injuries in Battered Children. *Radiology* 82:424–28.

25. Norman, M. G., et al. 1984. The Postmortem Examination on the Abused Child: Pathological, Radiography and Legal Aspects. *Perspectives in Pediatric Pathology* 8:313–43.

26. Zumwalt, R. E., and Petty, C. S. 1980. Community Investigation of Rape and Sexual Assault. In *Modern Legal Medicine, Psychiatry and Forensic Science*, eds. W. J. Curran, A. L. McGary, and C. S. Petty. Philadelphia: F. A. Davis.

27. Petty, C. S. 1970. Soft Tissue Injuries, An Overview. *J. of Trauma* 10:201–19.

28. Cebelin, M. S., and Hirsch, C. S. 1980. Human Stress Cardiomyopathy: Myocardial Lesions in Victims of Homicidal Assaults without Internal Injuries. *Human Pathology* 11:123–32.

29. Corley, K. C., et al. 1973. Electrocardiographic and Cardiac Morphological Changes Associated with Environmental Stress in Squirrel Monkeys. *Psychosomatic Med.* 35:361–64.

30. Johansson, G., et al. 1974. Severe Stress-Cardiopathy in Pigs. *Am. Heart J.* 87:451–57.

31. Raab, W., et al. 1968. Isolation, Stress, Myocardial Electrolytes and Epinephrine Cardiotoxicity in Rats. *Proc. Soc. Experimental Medicine* 127:142.

32. Reichenbach, D., and Benditt, E. P. 1970. Catecholamines and Cardiomyopathy: The Pathogenesis and Potential Importance of Myofibrillar Degeneration. *Human Pathology* 1:125–50.

33. Stewart, R. V., et al. 1984. Postmortem Diagnosis of Myocardial Disease by Enzyme Analysis of Pericardial Fluid. *Am. J. Clinical Pathology* 82:411–17.

34. Adelson, L. 1963. Homicide by Starvation: The Nutritional Variant of the "Battered Child." *JAMA* 186:458–60.

35. Zumwalt, R. E., and Hirsch, C. S. 1980. Subtle Fatal Child Abuse. *Human Pathology* 11:167–74.

36. Ayoub, C., and Pfeifer, D. 1979. Burns As a Manifestation of Child Abuse and Neglect. *Am. J. Diseases in Children* 133:910–14.

37. Bakalar, H. R.; Moore, J. D.; and Hight, D. W. 1981. Psychosocial Dynamics of Pediatric Burn Abuse. *Health and Social Work* 6:27–32.

38. Baptiste, M. S., and Feck, G. 1980. Preventing Tap Water Burns. *Am. J. Public Health* 70:727–29.

39. Feldman, K. W.; Clarren, S. K.; and McLaughlin, J. F. 1981. Tap-Water Burns in Handicapped Children. *Pediatrics* 67:560–62.

40. Feldman, K. W., et al. 1978. Tap-Water Scald Burns in Children. *Pediatrics* 62:1–7.

41. Hight, D. W.; Bakalar, H. R.; and Lloyd, J. R. 1979. Inflicted Burns in Children. *JAMA* 242:517–20.

42. Katcher, M. L. 1981. Scald Burns from Hot Tap Water. *JAMA* 246:1219–22.

43. Keen, J. H.; Lendrum, J.; and Wolman, B. 1975. Inflicted Burns and Scald in Children. *British Med. J.* 1:260–69.

44. Lenoski, E. F., and Hunter, K. A. 1977. Specific Patterns of Inflicted Burn Injuries. *J. Trauma* 17:842–46.

45. Lung, R. J., et al. 1977. Recognizing Burn Injuries as Child Abuse. *Am. Family Physician* 15:134–35.

46. Mortiz, A. R., and Henriques, F. C. 1947. Studies of Thermal Injury: The Relative Importance of Time and Surface Temperature in the Causation of Cutaneous Burns. *Am. J. Pathology* 23:695–720.

47. Meadow, R. 1977. Munchausen Syndrome by Proxy: The Hinterland of Child Abuse. *Lancet* 2:343–45.

48. Meadow, R. 1984. Fictitious Epilepsy. *Lancet* 1:25–28.

49. Mitchels, B. 1982. Munchausen Syndrome by Proxy: Protecting the Child. *J. Forensic Science Soc.* 23:105–11.

50. Dine, M. S. 1965. Tranquilizer Poisoning: An Example of Child Abuse. *Pediatrics* 36:782–85.

51. Kohl, S.; Pickering, L. K.; and Dupree, E. 1978. Child Abuse Presenting as Immunodeficiency Disease. *J. Pediatrics* 93:466–68.

52. Lansky, L. L. 1974. An Unusual Case of Childhood Chloral Hydrate Poisoning. *Am. J. Diseases in Children* 127:275–76.

53. Oates, R. K. 1984. Overturning the Diagnosis of Child Abuse. *Archives of Diseases in Childhood* 59:665–77.

54. Schmitt, B. D.; Gray, J. D.; and Britton, H. L. 1978. Car Seat Burns in Infants: Avoiding Confusion with Inflicted Burns. *Pediatrics* 62:607–9.

55. Feldman, K. W. 1984. Pseudoabusive Burns in Asian Refugees. *Am. J. Diseases in Children* 138:768–69.

14 Incest and Other Forms of Sexual Abuse

Richard Krugman and David P. H. Jones

Sexual abuse is defined as the involvement of dependent, developmentally immature children in sexual activities that they do not fully comprehend and therefore to which they are unable to give informed consent and/or which violate the taboos of society. Sexual abuse includes pedophilia (an adult's preference for or addiction to sexual contact with children) and all forms of incest and rape. Sexual exploitation is another term frequently used. Indeed, these children *are* exploited because sexual abuse robs them of developmentally determined control over their own bodies. As they mature, they are further robbed of the ability to choose their sexual partners on an equal basis. This is true whether the child has to deal with a single, overt, and perhaps violent act, often committed by a stranger, or with incestuous acts continued over many years. Incest may be carried out under actual or threatened violence, or it may be nonviolent, even tender, insidious, collusive, and secretive.

From 1980 to 1986, an enormous amount of work has been done in the area of sexual abuse and incest. Yet while our knowledge is increasing at a rapid rate, there is still much to be learned. This chapter will touch on incidence studies, review some aspects of the etiology of sexual abuse, focus on the recognition of sexual abuse in all its forms and the multidisciplinary process of data gathering and assessment (including the medical, psychiatric, and social evaluations of the child and the family), and review the present status of knowledge on the reliability and validity of children's statements that they have been sexually abused.

Richard Krugman, M.D., is Director of the Kempe Center in Denver and member of the Department of Pediatrics, University of Colorado. David P. H. Jones, M.D., is consultant psychiatrist, Park Children's Hospital, Oxford, England.

This chapter is a revision of the chapter with the same title written by C. Henry Kempe for the third edition of *The Battered Child* (1980). Earlier versions of the sections of "Recognition" and "Validation of a Child's Disclosure" appeared in D. P. H. Jones and M. McQuiston, *Interviewing the Sexually Abused Child,* Kempe Center Series, vol. 6 (Denver: The C. Henry Kempe National Center for the Prevention and Treatment of Child Abuse and Neglect, 1985).

Incidence

Reliable incidence data for sexual abuse in the United States are not available. Scientific studies of incidence are even more rare in the field of sexual abuse than in the field of physical abuse. Part of the problem relates to the variability of the definition of sexual abuse, lack of coordination between criminal justice data and social services data, confusion between retrospective and concurrent approaches to gathering data, and lack of a uniform system for data collection in the United States. All these difficulties aside, sexual abuse is a problem that is at least of the same magnitude as physical abuse and therefore is among the most prevalent afflictions of children in the United States. In Colorado, one-third of all reports for abuse and neglect are now sexual abuse reports; at least half of these are "founded." Professional opinion holds that there is still a significant amount of under-reporting of sexually abused children. While the dramatically increased public awareness of sexual abuse as a problem has led to a concomitant increase in reporting, still most reports of sexual abuse come to light months or years after the occurrence, rather than immediately. This is true particularly for intrafamilial sexual abuse, as well as when the perpetrator is a friend or acquaintance of the child. Commonly used figures in 1985 are that one-third of adult American women and one-sixth of adult American men have, at some time in their childhood, been victims of sexual exploitation. Three to five percent of adult women and one to two percent of adult men were victims in their childhood of sexual abuse within the family (incest), although these figures may be too conservative (1; also see chap. 4).

Etiology

For physical abuse to take place there must be present: 1) an adult with the potential to abuse, 2) a crisis that brings this potential to the fore, and 3) a child who triggers a response from the adult through some behavior for which the adult has unrealistic expectations of the child. Similarly, a variety of factors must come together for sexual abuse to occur. Finkelhor (2) has developed what he calls the "four preconditions of sex abuse" (see figure 14.1) which provides a model for understanding how sexual abuse of children occurs. The first precondition is the presence of an individual who has the motivation to sexually abuse children. This motivation contains three components (any of which may be present but not all of which are required): emotional congruence, sexual arousal, and blockage (an individual's inability to have a normal sexual relationship). Experience as a sexually abused child is a common feature leading to emotional congruence. Numerous individual and sociocultural influences act upon each of these factors.

The second precondition is what Finkelhor calls internal inhibitors. Most individuals have internal inhibition of any intermittent desires to be sexually involved with children. When these internal inhibitors are absent, there is a greater likelihood of an abusive event. Alcohol and drugs are the two most common destroyers of normal internal inhibitors.

The third precondition for child sexual abuse is the overcoming of external inhibitors. In families the major external inhibitor is the presence of a protective parent. If the parent

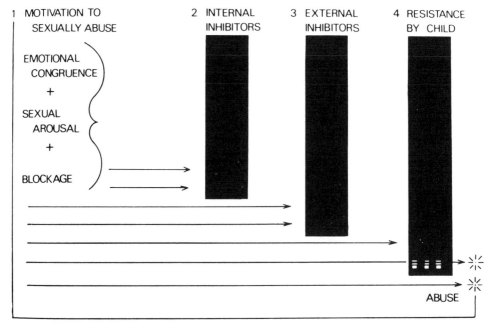

Figure 14.1

Four preconditions of sex abuse. Reprinted from D. Finkelhor, *Child Sexual Abuse: New Theory and Research* (New York: Free Press, 1979) by permission.

is not present or not protective, then an individual with a motivation to sexually abuse and no internal inhibitors finds the approach to a child easier. In cases of possible extrafamilial sexual abuse, one or both parents are generally available to protect the child, and they provide strong external inhibitors. As children are placed in other settings, such as day care, summer camps, or boarding schools, the absence of such external inhibitors makes children more susceptible.

The fourth precondition for sexual abuse is the breakdown of the child's resistance. Resistance may be taught either by parents or through sexual abuse education programs. There are other factors that increase or decrease a child's resistance, such as coercion, fear, developmental immaturity, retardation, and many that are as yet unknown. Certain children are more vulnerable and more likely to be approached by pedophiles than other children. No single factor explains sexual abuse of children, therefore no single approach will be successful in either prevention or treatment of this widespread problem.

Recognition

Children may disclose the fact that they have been sexually abused at many different points in their lives. Summit (3) has described the five stages of the "child sexual abuse accommodation syndrome." First, a child is engaged in a sexual relationship. Second, this immediately makes the child feel helpless and entrapped. Next, the enforcement of the "secret" with overt or covert threats to the child or the child's family leads to the child's accommodation to ongoing sexual abuse. Fourth, at some point the child may disclose that the sexual abuse has occurred. Finally, depending upon the responses of the parents, the child protective services, and the law enforcement systems that come into play, there may be a recantation.

The disclosure may take many forms. Many children give an *early warning* similar to Ounsted and Lynch's "open warning" in physical abuse (4), which may be a broad, ambiguous statement. For example:

> One nine-year-old boy moved to Colorado with his parents from California. Within a week he announced to the neighbors, "There's a whole lot of raping and molesting going on in California." The neighbors did not realize he was trying to tell them what his father did to him, and it was several months later before the incest secret was disclosed.

Early warning may consist of behavioral symptoms as well. For example, very young children may simulate sexual intercourse with friends or siblings; older children and adolescents may suddenly run away, hoping that someone will ask them the reason for their distress.

Children may make *direct statements* to adults or to their friends about being sexually abused. These direct statements often comprise only a small part of their sexual abuse experience. They use brief direct statements to "test the waters." Since many children have been told and threatened that they will get in trouble if they discuss the sexual abuse, they carefully gauge the response of the listener. If the response is anger or admonition not to talk of such things, they may not disclose the issue to that individual for quite some time, if ever. Direct statements from young children often occur at quiet times, such as bedtime or bathtime.

The third presentation is a *marked change in behavior.* In general, children tend to respond in a *nonspecific* way to *specific* stresses that are placed upon them. The behavioral consequences of this stress may be neurotic disorders or disturbances of conduct, both of which may be relatively nonspecific. The behaviors may include temper tantrums, fears, anxiety, inability to concentrate on school work, sleep disturbance, or appetite disturbance. Other children may show signs of withdrawal, depression, guilt, or an increased expression of anger over and above what is usual for their character. Other children may begin to lie, steal, or become aggressive with their friends. Older children and adolescents may act out their stress more dramatically. For example, they may become involved in drugs, make suicide attempts, run away, act out beyond the control of their parents or teachers, or become involved in prostitution (5).

Numerous *medical diseases or conditions* may be the first presentation of sexual abuse in children. The most obvious are venereal disease in prepubescent children and pregnancy in early adolescent children (12–15 years). Gonococcal or syphilitic infections in prepubertal children are almost pathognomonic of sexual abuse. Infections by chlamydia, trichomonas, herpes virus, or lymphogranuloma venereum (venereal warts) may have other modes of transmission to prepubertal children, and therefore it cannot be said "beyond a reasonable doubt" that these infections are associated with sexual abuse. Their presence, however, makes a report to the child protective services agency and an investigation mandatory, since they are more than "suspicious" (6). Recurrent urinary infections, symptoms of urethral irritation, and enuresis may also be medical presentations of sexual abuse. Many children have urologic evaluations for recurrent negative urinary tract infections without anyone exploring the possibility of sexual abuse as a potential etiology for their symptoms. Encopresis is also a common accompaniment to child sexual abuse, especially when the anus and rectum are sites used in the abusive acts. In comparison to the frequency of all of the presenting medical complaints, there are a few children who are brought into an emergency room immediately after an assault or rape who have acute physical signs and symptoms. Pregnancy may be another presentation in adolescence, either as a means of escape (via a boyfriend) or as a direct result of an incestuous relationship (7).

For many other children, especially boys, the first presentation of their own sexual victimization occurs when they themselves become perpetrators by sexually abusing younger children (8, 9). Finally, many sexual abuse victims do not present until adult life, when they may exhibit a wide variety of symptoms, including sexual dysfunction, suicidal behavior, drug and alcohol abuse, prostitution, and psychiatric illness (10). On occasion, the manifestations in adults do not occur until their own children begin to grow and develop.

Medical Assessment

The medical assessment and management of sexually abused children can be divided into three interrelated areas:

1. Treatment of physical and psychological trauma.
2. Collection and processing of evidence.
3. Prevention of pregnancy and venereal disease.

There is little doubt that these cases are best managed if the professional or team has been trained to deal with the issues relating to sexual abuse. If the assessment team generates a good written record, collects the appropriate evidence, and ensures that the data are indisputable, the diagnosis can be made, the treatment plan implemented, and the legal process can proceed with less difficulty.

Initial Evaluation

The child may be brought to a medical facility by a law enforcement officer, social services worker, friend, or parent. If the alleged attack or sexual molestation has not been reported, the patient, parent, or attending physician should report it immediately to the appropriate authority. In that way, the initial interview of the child can be done jointly by the law enforcement officer, the social worker, and the physician (see chaps. 5 and 6). This joint interview, which is best done under quiet conditions, preferably with two-way mirrors and video tape available. One or two individuals can conduct the interview while others observe in a nonobtrusive manner. This reduces the number of times the child needs to repeat the story of his or her victimization. The evaluation should be both supportive and documentary. The importance of obtaining a clear account of the circumstances of the alleged assault must be weighed against the importance of traumatizing the child no further. Describing an acute sexual assault may be very painful for the child.

Detailed history taking can often be deferred. When a child is evaluated for chronic sexual abuse, as is most often the case, delay in history taking is desirable and traumatization less likely to occur. The same philosophy also applies to the physical examination, although in *acute* sexual abuse cases, for legal and medical reasons, it is necessary to obtain certain historical and physical data and provide specified treatment.

Components of the Interview

The best interviews are those that use open-ended questions that the child can respond to freely, giving a detailed account of the events that have taken place. Interviews that are leading, with the interviewer asking questions to which the child responds with only "yes" or "no" or "uh huh," are far less useful and may be potentially harmful.

The evaluation of the sexually abused child cannot be done in a brief office, emergency room, or clinic visit. These evaluations, including the physical examination, may take one to two hours to do properly. For that reason, unless a child has been acutely assaulted and has specific injuries that need immediate treatment, the evaluation is best done in a quiet setting, at a scheduled time during the day. Rarely does a child who is an incest victim need to be brought to the emergency room for "a sexual abuse evaluation." Unless there is a history of intercourse or ejaculation within the preceding seventy-two hours, emergency medical assessments are unlikely to be helpful.

Whether the history is obtained from the child and parents jointly or separately depends on a number of considerations. When sexual abuse within the family is a possibility each parent and child should be interviewed separately. If the sexual abuse is extrafamilial, having the parents present with the young child during the interview may be helpful. If the parents acknowledge that incestuous behavior is occurring in the family, allowing them to express and describe their feelings is the best approach. If, on the other hand, they are denying the existence of sexual abuse, accusations are not helpful; rather a direct, supportive approach to the family is useful. The physician can point out that the child or the examination has indicated that sexual abuse has occurred, that children rarely make up such things, and that therefore an investigation of the allegation is important. Since children may be abused by any member of the family or by multiple individuals, one must not assume that a father or stepfather is the most likely perpetrator. Very often another member of the family or several other members of a family may have sexually abused the child. By assuming that there is only one perpetrator, the child may be returned to an environment where sexual abuse will continue. In general, parents who are not involved in the sexual abuse of their child will be very cooperative and will likely be terribly upset that such a thing has occurred. Parents who have sexually abused their children, on the other hand, may become defensive, feel accused, and refuse to cooperate. However, exceptions to these generalizations occur, and the question of the veracity of the child's allegations cannot depend upon the adult's response. In extrafamilial abuse similar principles apply. The interviewer must shed stereotypic notions as to who are the "typical" abusers. Separating the issue of whether abuse has occurred from the issue of the identity of the perpetrator(s) is important.

The interview with the child is a specialized task and demands specific training and skill (see chap. 9). Selected points will be made here, but the reader is referred to Jones and McQuiston (11) for a detailed account. The interview should be based upon an understanding of the child's clinical situation as well as the developmental stage of the child, particularly relating to memory and suggestibility. In addition, a variety of personal and interrelationship skills are required with children of different ages.

The interview should begin with an introductory stage which puts the child at ease before questioning begins. Then open-ended, nonjudgmental questions should be used to see if the child has been touched on "private parts of your body," even by "someone you know well." The words, timing, and sentences used by the interviewer have to be gauged according to the developmental stage of the child and that individual child's responses. Specific techniques are employed to enable younger children to express themselves, including the use of anatomically correct dolls, line drawings of the body, and other toys and play materials. The use of anatomically correct dolls should be reserved for children who cannot express themselves or relate their account of abuse through more conventional means (e.g., by indicating on line drawings of the body or through words directly). Alternatively, after having established the facts of sexual abuse through other means, anatomically correct dolls may be used to confirm the child's account by employing them as another medium of expression. At the time of writing there are no published studies comparing sexually abused with nonsexually abused children's reactions and free play with such dolls. It is not yet known whether inaccurate answers are given when, with the use of anatomically correct dolls, a nonabused child is questioned directly about possible sexual contact. Naturally much depends upon how such questions are posed and whether they contain inherent suggestion. Such research is sorely needed.

If the child discloses that sexual exploitation has occurred, then a series of specific inquiries are made. These include who, when (difficult for preschoolers), where, how violent, were threats or coercive methods used, was anyone else present, where were the other family members when the abuse occurred, did the abuse occur one time or many times? Finally, the interview must be brought to a close in such a way that the child is somewhat relieved of any sense of guilt and helped to understand what will happen next.

Physical Examination

The interview should establish a rapport with the child that will permit a physical examination to be performed without further trauma (see chap. 10). In any sexual abuse case, the child needs a general physical examination first. Examination of the pelvic and rectal areas should be deferred to the end of the exam. Since sexual abuse of children is a criminal offense in every state and most countries, the physician's physical examination is likely to be used as evidence in criminal court proceedings. If the case is intrafamilial, it is likely to be used in civil court proceedings as well. All findings must be carefully documented in the medical record, all positive physical findings photographed, if possible, and all laboratory specimens and material evidence meticulously labeled and handled. Forensic "rape kits," available in most emergency rooms, may be useful if they have been modified for pediatric use. Each "rape kit" comes with specific directions which should be observed meticulously. The collection of evidence should be witnessed and countersigned by either a nurse or a police officer present at the examination. Laboratory specimens must be given personally to the technician responsible for carrying out the laboratory tests.

The physical examination of the child should proceed as any physical examination in an age appropriate manner. The skin should be examined for the presence of injuries, especially bruises, burns, bite marks, fingernail scratches, or other impressions on the child's body. If there is dried blood or semen on the skin, it is scraped, collected, and submitted for laboratory studies. The head, ears, eyes, nose, and throat are examined for any sign of trauma. In particular, there may need to be buccal scrapings for semen, a search for signs of herpetic infection, or culturing for venereal disease, especially gonorrhea. While the examination of the chest, heart, and lungs is usually negative, this is also part of the physical assessment. The abdomen should be carefully examined for tenderness or the presence of masses. Grab marks, buckle impressions, or other bruises may be present on the abdomen. The extremities are felt carefully for signs of trauma, pain, or tenderness. The examination of the genitalia and rectum is done last. In males, signs of genital or anal trauma should be noted, and the presence or absence of urethral discharge determined. Collection of specimens from the rectum for analysis for acid phosphatase (present in semen) or semen should be done. A digital examination of the rectum may indicate the presence of tenderness or blood as well as assessing the rectal sphincter tone. Occasionally boys will have bite marks or other signs of trauma on their penis. Perianal scarring may be discovered from chronic penetration of the anus. Inspection with a Wood's lamp is often useful for finding semen or pubic hairs on children or on their clothing.

In prepubertal girls, a vaginal inspection often reveals the possibility of chronic sexual abuse. Cantwell has reported a highly significant correlation (80%) between a vaginal opening of greater than four millimeters in a prepubertal child and sexual abuse (12). Others have used magnifying colposcopy to visualize the anatomic changes seen in sexually abused children (13). Unfortunately, there are no data as yet available on control (nonsexually abused) prepubertal children to provide the reliability necessary for definite diagnosis or court action in sexual abuse cases where there is no history, no corroborating evidence, but only a magnified colposcopy finding.

Diagnostic Studies

Cultures for gonorrhea are usually indicated and should be taken from the oral cavity, vagina, and rectum in girls; from the oral cavity, rectum, and urethra (if there is a discharge present) in boys. A blood test for syphilis should be performed. If ejaculation has occurred within seventy-two hours, a vaginal or rectal aspirate should be examined for the presence of sperm. Bathing will reduce the likelihood of finding sperm. A rectal and oral swab are routinely performed since it is not always clear exactly which orifice of the child has been penetrated. Testing for acid phosphatase should also be performed on these specimens. In pubescent girls, a baseline pregnancy test is obtained. Urinalysis is performed if there has been forced penetration, since there may be urethral damage as well. The "rape kit" includes provisions for taking stained clothing, scrapings of dried blood, semen from the skin, as well as any collected material beneath the victim's fingernails. Following the completion of these laboratory procedures in pubertal children, the question arises whether to implement accepted procedures to try to prevent potential pregnancy, even though it is unlikely that the victim of an assault will become pregnant. The child can be given diethylstilbestrol (25 mg, b.i.d.) for five days, although this is unnecessary in a child who is menstruating during the time of the assault, and it is contraindicated in a child who is pregnant prior to the rape. If diethylstilbestrol is used and pregnancy still occurs, an abortion is mandatory.

Follow-up Care

If the home environment is deemed to be safe (i.e., the perpetrator has been removed from the home, or the child has been assaulted by a stranger not living in the home), then the child should be returned home. Provision should be made for follow-up, including therapy for the parents and the child. If the home setting is not safe, then the child should be placed in an alternative environment, such as a hospital, foster care, or a family crisis center. However, emphasis should be given to the fact that the very process of evaluation of child sexual abuse in itself is traumatic and requires that the child immediately begin some form of therapy. Not only is this therapy important to begin the process of healing for the child, but since many children only disclose what has happened to them when they feel safe, it may be months into their therapy before the child reveals all the details of the sexual abuse. Eight months into treatment, one of our male patients first disclosed that his mother (as well as his father) had been involved in his sexual abuse.

The Effects of Child Sexual Abuse

Children who are sexually abused within the family rarely exhibit effects that can be attributed only to sexual abuse. Intrafamilial sexual exploitation is associated with neglect, emotional abuse, deprivation, and even frank physical abuse. Each of these is likely to have an impact on the psychological and developmental state of the child, and separating these several effects from the effect of sexual abuse itself is difficult. Furthermore, some children are also involved in pornography and prostitution, which have significant influences upon their development. Children who are acutely assaulted by strangers have psychological symptoms that are similar to those observed in adults following rape. The child shows symptoms of acute anxiety and agitation, with nightmares, night terrors, specific fears or phobias, and a fear of another acute attack. Guilt feelings, depression, and a predominant feeling of helplessness are common. Gender and other sexual identity problems may develop, with boys fearing that they will now become homosexuals and girls convinced that they are "damaged goods" (14).

While the effects seen in the period immediately following disclosure of intrafamilial sexual abuse are variable, the most common reactions are nonspecific neurotic disorders or a deterioration of the child's conduct. Children may become more anxious and fearful, may be unable to concentrate and attend to their school work, and may show evidence of sleep and appetite disturbance. Approximately two-thirds of these children will show moderate or severe evidence of emotional or behavioral change like those mentioned earlier (see pp. 157–62). In the other one-third of these children, there is either no psychological disturbance immediately observable or, if there is, it is mild (15). These observations are not based on any long-term follow-up studies. The healing rate of the former group, or the deterioration rate of the latter group as the children grow older is unknown.

A significant portion of sexually abused children develop a "posttraumatic stress disorder" after exploitation. This disorder consists of recollection phenomena, numbed emotional responsiveness, and signs and symptoms of hyperawareness and anxiety with a tendency for everyday occurrences, as reminders of the old stress, resulting in an unpleasant flood of panic feelings.

The prognosis of children who have been sexually abused is clearly impacted by a variety of factors. Those studies that have been conducted indicate that the best prognosis occurs in children who are victimized once, by strangers rather than by members of their immediate family, and at an older rather than a younger age (2). A fifteen-year-old girl who encounters an exhibitionist once while jogging in the park is likely to have few psychological sequelae (although she may certainly change her route the next time she jogs). In contrast, a fifteen-year-old girl who in conversation with her peers at school discovers that it is not routine for all girls to have had a ten-year-long sexual relationship, including intercourse, with their fathers will have far more serious problems and sequelae. The effect of the intervention of the helping professions, along with the legal response, also contributes positively or negatively to the long-term outcome for these children. (These factors are discussed further in chap. 17.)

Validation of a Child's Disclosure

The mid-1980s have seen an explosion in the recognition and criminal prosecution of cases of child sexual abuse. There have been numerous, highly publicized institutional cases of child sexual abuse, where the validity of a child's statement has been brought into question. Some advocates for children have said, "Children never lie." While advocates on the other side have reiterated the suggestibility and unreliability of testimony of very young children.

Once a child's story has been elicited, using the techniques outlined previously, those involved must decide if the account is true. There is no ultimate test for truthfulness. Physiologic measures of truth (such as the polygraph examination) are not valid or reliable in children.

The many factors connected with the allegation must be pulled together in order to be able to validate whether a particular child has or has not been sexually abused. Provided here is a framework within which to consider whether a particular suspicion of sexual abuse is most likely to be true or untrue.

Sgroi et al. (5) have described their approach to validation, emphasizing that the process centers on a knowledge of the dynamics of child sexual abuse, good interviewing skills, and an ability to interpret the behavior and physical signs obtained from the investigative interviewing. They break down the process of validation into the assessment of the child's behavior, the results of the interview with the child, an assessment of credibility, the physical indicators of child sexual abuse, and, finally, the medical examination. Goodwin et al. (16) similarly have described their practice clinically, which lessens the likelihood that a false report may be adjudged true. Fuller (17) addressed the question of validation and emphasized the importance of observing an emotional response consistent with the nature of the abuse, the presence of any idiosyncratic memories surrounding the sexual incident itself, the importance of the child's viewpoint of the event, the child's statements to other children, the child's play, and the child's abnormal knowledge of sexuality itself as helpful elements in the process.

The preceding examples clarify that there is no single indicator of truthfulness. *Importance must be given to the child's statement itself as the primary source upon which to assess whether the allegation is true or not. All other information and findings may be considered as either supporting the child's statement or detracting from its worth, but it cannot substitute for the child's statement.* Future studies may reveal more concrete findings from techniques of physical examination and psychological and physiologic measures of truthfulness, but at the time of this writing these do not provide any certainty with which to make definitive statements about whether the child is telling the truth or not.

The Child's Statement

The child's statement of an alleged sexual abuse is examined for explicit detail. Younger children, particularly under the age of five, are not able to relate as much detail as are older children. However, the more detail that is recalled, the more likely the account is true, especially if it is considered unlikely that an individual child could have gained such detailed knowledge without personal experience of the event in question.

The words and sentence structure should be consistent with the age and developmental status of the child. When a four-year-old uses words such as "ejaculation" or "inappropriate," these words belie adult rather than child origins. As time passes, children may adopt their therapist's or case worker's language and so may appear unbelievable. When this is a problem, reference to the earliest statements of the child before extensive contact with therapists can help establish validity.

Idiosyncratic detail may be found both within the account of the sexual abuse or in unrelated recollections. The evaluator is struck by the unusual and unexpected memory which belies its personal poignancy for the victim. Idiosyncrasy in sexual abuse accounts is exemplified by children who can describe smells and tastes associated with rectal, vaginal, or oral sex; or when they give a "child's-eye view" of the abusive incident such as the response of one six-year-old girl when asked by the district attorney, "What did you see when you were being sexually abused?" She said, "His chest." Similarly, idiosyncratic nonsexual details may be present in the child's memory, such as an unusual feature of the room where the abuse occurred.

The child's expressed emotion during the interview is usually consistent with the abuse being described. Children may experience one part of sexual abuse as being more offensive than another. However, this differential may not coincide with the interviewer's assumption as to what was the worst experience for the child. When children describe sexual abuse, they may wrinkle their brow, become sad and cry, or become embarrassed as they describe the sexual activity. Children who give unreliable accounts are very often flat and give their account in a rehearsed manner. When children appear bland, apparently unemotive and little perturbed by serious exploitation, it raises the concern that the allegation may be false.

Clues as to the child's psychological response to the abusive incident are sought. Did the child feel sad, frightened, angry, or guilty? Do they describe a remote or removed state of mind?

The pattern of the abuse described may also help establish veracity. The clinical pattern in sexual abuse may not include intercourse and may be restricted to oral or deviate sexual practices. In abuse by persons known to the child, multiple incidents over time are common, progressing from fondling through oral sexual contact to intercourse over a period of months or years.

The element of secrecy can be found in many accounts. Children may be coerced into activity and then threatened, sometimes violently, to keep them from telling. There are other less common features which, if they are present, lend considerable credence to the account. These include descriptions of pornographic involvement, sadism, and ritualism. These elements are probably under-recognized at present, because we do not routinely inquire about them. Pornography may be present as part of the child's involvement in a sex ring or for consumption within the family only. This practice has increased with the use of home video cameras. One child described the ritual decapitation of a rabbit during her sexual abuse by a family friend, using the most graphic detail. The police were informed and searched the alleged perpetrator's basement and discovered the dead animal decapitated just as the girl had described, along with other evidence of satanic ritual. These features lend considerable credibility to a child's statement.

Secondary Factors

A number of factors need to be considered which may provide support or alternatively, if inconsistent, may raise doubts as to the veracity of the child's statement. In interfamilial sexual abuse, the biographies of other family members, combined with a detailed family history, can provide helpful supportive information. The alleged perpetrator's track record of violence, past abuse, and alcohol or substance abuse may indicate the type of individual who could be involved in the sexual abuse of a child. Similarly, the noninvolved parent's attitude and response to the allegation may be in keeping with the kind of responses often seen in child sexual abuse cases. The family may have a prior history of neglecting and abusing children and may have sexually abused other children in the past. A history of parental relationships and involvement with their children may provide further clues. The child's behavior during the period when the child was being sexually abused may also be indicative. The history of the disclosure may provide useful information. Was the disclosure similar to those of other children whose reports are confirmed or corroborated? Children often tell in the context of a crisis or change in the family or when they develop enough confidence and trust in one of their peers or an adult. Frequently the trigger precipitating disclosure is the escalation of the severity of the abuse, for example, the perpetrator attempts intercourse for the first time. Did disclosure follow a presentation of a "good touch–bad touch" sexual abuse prevention program?

The child may make statements to numerous people before the clinical interview. The question of consistency between the different statements made by a single child is complicated. There is usually in truthful accounts a consistency of the core elements of the child's exploitation, but there may be variation in the more peripheral aspects of the child's story.

Thus, the question of consistency is not an all or nothing matter; it may vary with the degree of personal poignancy of the particular experience for that child. Similarly, the more violent elements of coercion and threatening behavior by the perpetrator may be very frightening for the child and, consequently, may cause the child to suppress elements of the story for a prolonged period. In some seemingly inconsistent stories, there will be a constant thread throughout the accounts the child gives. In contrast to this situation, false statements are generally made with monotonous consistency showing no signs of variation over time.

The manner in which the child uses toys and drawing materials may also be revealing. Their drawings may contain highly sexualized themes (18–20), and their play with dolls may show similar preoccupations. If their knowledge of sexuality greatly exceeds that of children of their own developmental stage, that, too, may be corroboration for the child's statement. Children may actually observe another child being abused or may witness sexual activity among adults, either in person or on television. Differentiating this "hypersexualized" activity in a child who has not been abused from the sexual acting out behavior of a child who is being abused may be difficult, but this points to the fact that these supporting features must be considered in conjunction with the statement of the child and cannot serve as the sole explanation for the child's statement. The veracity of the child's statement becomes easier to accept when there is specific medical evidence, eyewitness accounts, corroboration, such as pornographic pictures of the child and the perpetrator, or laboratory evidence. However, the majority of cases, especially in children under five years of age, do not have this type of supportive evidence. Consequently, the question of veracity and the need for a thorough diagnostic assessment are of paramount importance.

Conclusion

Since 1980, the recognition and knowledge concerning the investigation, management, treatment, and prevention of child sexual abuse has grown exponentially in the United States, yet much more needs to be learned before we can be at ease with our knowledge. There are still a great many problems facing the individual professional and the multidisciplinary teams that are attempting to work on behalf of children. There seem to be two countervailing forces at work in our society. One is the force that has for thousands of years tried to suppress any discussion of sexual abuse within the family. For centuries, child sexual abuse was a hidden problem. Now that sexual abuse is being increasingly recognized and openly and sometimes incessantly discussed in the media, the new, second force demands quick and sure action to protect children from sexual offenders. Unfortunately the knowledge base is not sufficient and the diagnostic and treatment tools are not all that we would want them to be. The overwhelming majority of the professionals in the United States who are now dealing with the problem of child sexual abuse are doing without undergraduate or graduate training in their profession in this particular area. Therefore, the professionals' knowledge base relies either on their own experience or on the experience of others who may or may not have carefully assessed in a scientific fashion their own results with their treatment and prevention efforts. One would hope that by the next edition of *The Battered Child* we will have better follow-up data, better assessment of the long-term effects of child sexual abuse and our efforts to intervene in both treatment and preventive modes. Suffice it to say that the sexual abuse of children in intrafamilial and extrafamilial settings is a complex, heterogeneous problem that will not yield to a single solution. We must carefully evaluate what we are doing now, taking our lead from how children and families are responding to our efforts. If we are doing well, we must be prepared to evaluate these efforts over the long term. If we are doing poorly, we must be prepared to scrap our methods in favor of other approaches.

References

1. Finkelhor, D. 1979. *Sexually Victimized Children.* New York: Free Press.
2. Finkelhor, D. 1979. *Child Sexual Abuse: New Theory and Research.* New York: Free Press.
3. Summit, R. 1983. The Child Sexual Abuse Accommodation Syndrome. *Child Abuse and Neglect: International J.* 7:177–93.
4. Ounsted, C., and Lynch, M. 1976. Family Pathology As Seen in England. In *Child Abuse and Neglect: The Family and the Community,* ed. R. E. Helfer and C. H. Kempe, chap. 4. Cambridge, Mass.: Ballinger.
5. Sgroi, S. M.; Porter, F. S.; and Blick, L. C. 1982. Validation of Child Sexual Abuse. In *Handbook of Clinical Intervention in Child Sexual Abuse,* ed. S. M. Sgroi, chap. 2. Lexington, Mass.: D. C. Heath.
6. White, S. T., et al. 1983. Sexually Transmitted Diseases in Sexually Abused Children. *Pediatrics* 72:16–21.
7. Mehta, M. N., et al. 1979. Rape in Children. *Child Abuse and Neglect: International J.* 3:671–77.
8. Meiselman, K. C. 1978. *Incest: A Psychological Study of Causes and Effects with Treatment Recommendations.* San Francisco: Jossey Bass.
9. Becker, J. V., and Abel, G. G. 1984. *Methodological and Ethical Issues in Evaluating and Treating Adolescent Sexual Offenders.* Washington, D.C.: National Institute of Mental Health. Monograph.
10. Gelinas, D. J. 1983. The Persisting Negative Effects of Incest. *Psychiatry* 46:312–32.
11. Jones, D. P. H., and M. McQuiston. 1985. *Interviewing the Sexually Abused Child.* Kempe Center Series, vol. 6. Denver: The C. Henry Kempe National Center for the Prevention and Treatment of Child Abuse and Neglect.
12. Cantwell, H. 1983. Vaginal Inspection As It Relates to Young Girls. *Child Abuse and Neglect: International J.* 7:171–76.
13. Woodling, B. A., and Heger, A. 1986. The Use of the Colposcope in the Diagnosis of Sexual Abuse in the Pediatric Age Group. *Child Abuse and Neglect: International J.* 10:111–14.
14. Porter, F. S.; Blick, L. C.; and Sgroi, S. M. 1982. Treatment of the Sexually Abused Child. In *Handbook of Clinical Intervention in Child Sexual Abuse,* ed. S. M. Sgroi, chap. 4. Lexington: D. C. Heath.
15. Conte, J., and Berliner, L. In press. The Impact of Sexual Abuse on Children: Clinical Findings. In *Handbook on Sexual Abuse of Children: Assessment and Treatment Issues,* ed. L. Walker. New York: Springer.

16. Goodwin, J.; Salid, D.; and Raca, R. T. 1982. False Accusations and False Denials of Incest: Clinical Myths and Clinical Realities. In *Sexual Abuse: Incest Victims and Their Families,* ed. J. Goodwin, chap. 2. London: John Wright.

17. Fuller, K. C. 1984. Is the Child Victim of Sexual Abuse Telling the Truth? *Child Abuse and Neglect: International J.* 8:473–81.

18. Goodwin, J. 1982. The Use of Drawings in Incest Cases. In *Sexual Abuse: Incest Victims and Their Families,* ed. J. Goodwin, chap. 5. London: John Wright.

19. Naitore, C. E. 1982. Art Therapy with Sexually Abused Children. In *Handbook of Clinical Intervention in Child Sexual Abuse,* ed. S. M. Sgroi, chap. 10. Lexington, Mass.: D. C. Heath.

20. Stember, C. J. 1980. Art Therapy: A New Use in the Diagnosis and Treatment of Sexually Abused Children. In *Sexual Abuse of Children: Selected Readings.* Washington, D.C.: U.S. Department of Health and Human Services.

15 The Litany of the Smoldering Neglect of Children

Ray E. Helfer

In this discussion of the neglect of children, special emphasis will be given to family interaction and long-term follow-up. What will not be discussed are the sociological, anthropological, or physical aspects of child neglect, since these are adequately covered elsewhere in this volume (see chaps. 10 and 13). There will be a few comments about some of the political issues relating to child neglect, since decisions have been made recently (1985–86) to cut even further the funding for Medicaid, nutrition programs, and other supports for poor children in the United States. Primary emphasis will be given to how the medical care system responds over a long period of time to these neglected children and their families. Additional emphasis will be given to the personal issues that face all physicians, particularly those in family practice or pediatrics, who interact with the parents of neglected children. This chapter, however, is directed to all professionals involved with these difficult situations, including physicians for adults, social workers, psychologists, psychiatrists, public health nurses, and others. The goal is to put into perspective the process and results of the long-term neglect of children and how professionals can and should respond.

Incidence

The true incidence of child neglect is unknown, since no consensus on the definition exists (see chap. 4). The point at which a child slips from satisfactory care to neglected care is hard to define. Of course, there is little difficulty recognizing or defining severe child neglect; harder to define is low-grade, smoldering neglect, month after month, before one's very eyes in a neglected environment. Is neglect defined as something present or absent in the child, or something present or absent in the parent, or both? What *is* known about the incidence of child neglect is that approximately 65 percent of those children who are reported to social agencies throughout the United States each year as a result of child abuse

Ray E. Helfer, M.D., is professor in the Department of Pediatrics and Human Development, College of Human Medicine, Michigan State University, East Lansing.

reporting laws are categorized as neglected. This amounts to approximately 650,000 cases per year. While these reporting laws provide a definition of neglect, in reality neglect is what the schoolteacher, physician, social worker, judge, psychologist, or police officer "says it is" at the time of the report. Whether or not a protective services worker or a judge agrees with the professional making the report depends on a variety of issues, including the worker's experience, caseload, ability to document the findings, comparison group, background, and training. However, one should not get hung up on the definition of child neglect, but rather get on with helping these children who are being cared for in a manner far below our society's accepted standards.

Classification

When child neglect is listed along with physical abuse, sexual exploitation, verbal abuse, and spouse abuse under the classification of family interaction, this moves the problem into proper perspective. (Interaction between various family members and the problem of neglect are discussed in some detail in chaps. 4 and 5.) When a comprehensive evaluation of a family is undertaken, emphasis must be given to the separate categories of how parents themselves manifest the problem of neglect—what parents do or do not do, what happens or does not happen to the children—and how these children manifest the problem to various professionals.

Manifestations of Neglecting Parents

Neglecting parents manifest themselves to those who deliver health care and other professional services in a variety of ways which are not mutually exclusive. These include: 1) overt retardation, 2) psychiatric illness, 3) physical illness, 4) ecological problems, 5) development problems, 6) substance abuse, and 7) fanatical beliefs of one type or another. Harder to classify are those parents whose difficulties include several of these problem areas to a mild degree, which collectively create serious interactional problems, especially when their subculture is tolerant of inadequate child care standards.

Those who are overtly retarded may not remember to feed their babies, recall how much or when a child was fed, understand how to handle money, or know how to read or write. Some do not have the intellectual capacity to deal with the day-to-day demands of parenting. Parents who are clearly retarded are relatively easy to identify, especially if they have recently been discharged from a state institution as a result of a societal decision to encourage retarded adults to live in our communities, often within a communal setting. While this plan is commendable, our society has not considered what to do with the children that occur as a result of these communal relationships. Resolving one social problem has created another. Not uncommonly, a woman who lives in a communal setting and has a baby must leave and be on her own. These retarded parents and their babies have to fend for themselves. Few communities have considered the consequences of this outcome.

Other parents who often neglect their children are those with serious psychiatric illnesses. Adults who are psychotic or sociopathic commonly fail to interact appropriately with their children, placing these children at very high risk.

Many parents of neglected children are physically ill. They may have a variety of health-related problems, varying from gynecological issues and nutritional deficiencies to hypertension and obesity. Our medical care system has been most unresponsive to their needs. Finding physicians to care for the physical problems, many of which are chronic in nature, of neglecting parents in our current fee-for-service system is most difficult. Serious medical illnesses are so common among neglecting parents that any family care program must respond to these health care needs if comprehensive services are to be offered.

Neglecting parents often live in environments that are truly unfit, with insufficient food, shelter, heat, lights, and transportation to meet the basic needs of their families. Such devastated ecological environments may be such that no outcome for the child is possible other than neglect. These environments may occur through no fault of the parents, but rather as a result of social and political priorities.

Parents who neglect their children sometimes have development problems as a result of being neglected themselves when they were children. Their childhood environments and experiences have given them no model for positive child care. To them negative, neglectful child rearing is normal; they raise their children the way they were raised.

Substance abuse by parents may present serious problems in caring for and interacting with their children. While alcohol abuse is most common, other forms of drug abuse are also prevalent among neglecting parents. Being under the influence of drugs is not the sole reason for child neglect problems, rather the lifestyle that surrounds substance abuse and the constant drain on very severely limited financial resources to support a drug habit take their toll on child care.

Finally, some parents who neglect their children are true fanatics—religious, nutritional, or cultural. Such fanaticism may interfere with the rearing of their children. Some parents believe they should never give their children animal protein; others have bizarre religious beliefs about child discipline and training; others withhold medical care from their children and may even teach them that health care professionals are "instruments of the devil." These belief systems may result in long-term neglect of certain basic nutritional, medical, and educational needs of the children.

In spite of these separate but interrelated problems, neglecting parents often very sincerely want to do well by their children. Many parents who are retarded, psychiatrically ill, physically ill, ecologically deprived, or from neglectful families themselves are highly motivated to be better parents. This may become a most difficult personal problem confronting those who care for these children for any length of time. (This is discussed in more detail in the section on "personal issues" below.)

Manifestations of Neglected Children

Neglected children most commonly exhibit delayed development and growth in addition to varying degrees of malnutrition. Neglected children have frequent illnesses, both major and minor, in any of many physical systems, from the ears, throat, lungs, chest, and gastrointestinal tract to neurological dysfunctions. They have chronic, smoldering illnesses, many of which are not life threatening or blatantly serious. If one reviews the medical records of neglected children which list each incident, multiple visits with similar or related problems are common. As every visit or failure to show up for an appointment is tallied, as the children's heights and weights are graphed and tabulated, the litany of neglect sounds loud and clear.

Young infants who are neglected present the classic form of "failure to thrive," that is, failure over time to grow according to accepted standards for height, weight, and development (see chap. 16).

The manner in which older neglected children are recognized depends upon the professional's perception of these children. From a teacher's point of view, they may be children with learning disorders and with latchkeys around their necks. From a physician's point of view, they may be children suffering malnutrition, physical illness, or with behavioral problems.

Family Assessment

Every component of a neglectful family's interaction must be fully assessed. When the family medical history is comprehensively evaluated, many family members may be found to have some type of ongoing medical problem. This is often one of the most difficult problems confronting those in the health care system who care for neglected children. All members of the household need to be assessed to understand how health problems affect this group of individuals. Assistance from a family practitioner or internist is essential, though difficult to achieve.

The children's heights, weights, and head circumferences are measured and plotted on a regular basis. Height/weight ratios are most useful. Persistent pursuit is the rule of the day when these families "don't show." Various agencies can be used to arrange transportation for families to their appointments for medical evaluation and follow-up.

Periodic photographs and videotapes are useful to record components of the family's interactional system, physical findings, and developmental capabilities. Surprisingly, parents rarely express concerns or refuse when asked permission to take photographs and videotapes. They should have the opportunity to see them from time to time.

Numerous laboratory studies are rarely necessary in most neglected children. What is required is a comprehensive, periodic medical history and physical examination, using only those diagnostic laboratory tests necessary to follow-up on clues that are obtained in this process. Little is gained by shooting in the dark to find that rare disease. For example, one does not have to order a multiple chemistries, chest X-ray, intravenous pyelogram, blood urea nitrogen, and creatinine tests on a neglected child who is eight years old and still wetting the bed, assuming that a thorough history, physical, urinalysis, and culture failed to produce any additional leads. Very often these children are overmedicated and overstudied while their basic problem of neglect is overlooked.

Concurrently, a social worker needs to piece together the family's social history and their interactional system (see chaps. 9, 18).

Children who are chronically neglected cannot be fully evaluated without an elaborate survey of the home in which they are being reared. Often this can be the function of a well-trained public health nurse who plays an integral part in the evaluation and follow-up of these families. The presence of heat, food, lights, excessive animals, sufficient beds, and reasonably stimulating environment to meet the needs of children must be assessed. Emphasis is given to those environmental circumstances that lead to accidents, poisonings, and other catastrophes.

A logical long-term treatment plan is impossible unless the mental and psychological states of the parents and the children are understood. Because of the high incidence among neglecting families of mental retardation and psychiatric illness, a complete psychological evaluation administered by a trained child psychologist or psychiatrist is needed (see chap. 9).

Once neglect has been recognized in a child, the law clearly mandates the intervention of a protective services unit. This is easiest to achieve by telling the parents that the magnitude of their problem is beyond the capabilities of any one person. The parent should be told up front that a call to the community social worker (i.e., protective services worker) and the public health nurse is necessary. While the law does not necessitate the involvement of a public health nurse, the care of these families does. If this is done with openness and sincerity, parents rarely object. A neglect report asks professionals for their assistance. The sooner this is done, the more help they can provide.

As the family's story unfolds during the comprehensive assessment, the nature and degree of the chronicity of the problem becomes clear. If the children are school age, one cannot complete the assessment or develop a long-term plan without involving the school system and reviewing the child's educational progress. Parents usually cooperate and give permission for the school's involvement. In fact, they are often flattered by the interest shown to them and their child when the physician, clinic nurse, or social worker asks permission to visit the school and talk with the child's teacher.

Once the evaluation of *all* systems has been completed, all those involved—the public health nurse, protective services worker, school nurse, psychologist, and physician—must sit down from time to time to talk. There is no way to assess the severity and chronicity of the problem without everybody meeting in the same room at the same time. Parents are informed of the meeting and who will be in attendance, and they are asked whom they would like to give them a summary of the meeting. There should be no secrets about these meetings or their outcomes. Parents must be dealt with fairly and frequently, given as many choices as possible during this assessment and follow-up period. They will choose the person with whom they are most comfortable to give them the information that emerges from these meetings. Without such periodic meetings, the follow-up and care for children who are suffering from smoldering, chronic neglect month after month, year after year, will not be adequate. This multidisciplinary team model also works well for other chronic conditions, such as children with severe rehabilitation problems, cleft palate, learning disorders and the like. Those agencies that hesitate to share their information in these group meetings can be involved by asking the parents to sign a release for the sharing of information among professionals on the case. Again, rarely do the parents object if approached fairly and openly.

Fiscal Aspects

One of the greatest obstacles confronting physicians, psychologists, and other professionals is that there is no way to make a living caring for these chronically neglected children and their families. The fee-for-service system collapses when professionals who depend on this system for payment try to deliver services to these children. Even pre-payment plans (e.g., HMO's and others) find it most difficult to afford the number of visits and the amount of work and evaluation required. There is no resolution to this problem unless community and social service systems are geared to offer the comprehensive services that are necessary, using multidisciplinary teams. If a community or state is able and willing to supplement the salaries of the professionals needed to provide the services of a public health nurse, physician, social worker, psychologist, and protective services worker, then the comprehensive assessment and long-term follow-up that is absolutely necessary for these families will occur. Without such a community commitment, these families will not receive the care they require.

This is not dissimilar to the collapse of the fee-for-service system for the treatment of most chronic diseases that affect children. Only through supplemental service funds is one able to make a living seeing children with problems that fall in this category. Even the Crippled Children's Service in most states is not structured to provide funds for the extensive type of evaluation and follow-up required by neglecting families (except in Florida). Physicians caring for neglected children should not be viewed any differently than those caring for children with chronic renal disease or chronic pulmonary disease. Pediatric cardiologists and gastroenterologists used to receive supplemental funds, but now they are able to make their own living because the high technology of sonography and fiber optics permits a payment system for such achievements. If a "neglectoscope" were available, a flexible tube with a light on the end to move through the family system to observe and record the interactional breakdown, maybe then the health insurance systems would pay for this service. Since a "neglectoscope" does not and cannot exist, all the interdisciplinary teams must be funded externally. The cost is minimal compared to the expense of doing nothing and can be justified easily by the improved productivity of these children and the decreased cost of their education.

Determining Outcome

The determination of the type of intervention required and the likely outcome for any given family whose children are being neglected requires the utilization of all the data gathered in the comprehensive assessment described above. Without each component, incorrect decisions and plans are common.

For example, a host of community services may be made available to a given family in an effort to reverse the neglect of their children, only to find much too late that the parents are masking significant retardation, illiteracy, or severe psychiatric illness. True psychotics, certain fanatics, sociopaths, multiple personalities, and addicts have major problems rearing children. Their treatment requires more time than the children can afford. On the other hand, poverty and health problems per se may improve greatly with support and medical care, resulting in a much more positive outcome.

The bottom line: the appropriate type of intervention and the likely outcome cannot be determined without an in-depth family assessment.

Intervention

The amount of intervention necessary to help these children and their families is enormous. Some of the players on this intervention team are described above, since they are also involved in the family assessment. On the other hand, they are not sufficient. Some of the other disciplines and training that are necessary to work with these families are as follows:

1. A state-wide home extension service (formerly called the cooperative or agricultural extension service). These individuals, often available through a state university, are trained to help families who find it difficult to understand how and what to feed their children or how to make plans for day-to-day living. They may actually take the mother to a store and help her through each step of providing food for her children—shopping, preparing, and serving the food.

2. Community infant development programs, often run by mental health services. These infant development specialists work with parents of limited capacity, giving high priority to mother/father/infant interactional methods to improve the mental health of the parents as well as the overall health and development of the infants.

3. Mental health services and other psychiatric services from private agencies and community agencies. These services vary from direct one-to-one counseling to small support groups.

4. Public health nurses. Ongoing home visits are necessary to assess the physical health of the children and the environment in which they are living, and to give the parents the assistance necessary to find their way into the health care system and the community.

5. The school system can provide very valuable services to children of all ages. Recently enacted public laws mandate schools to develop an extensive evaluation service for children who are likely to require ongoing support when they are in school. Without question, children who are neglected are a major financial burden for school systems because they usually have significant learning disorders and require excessive time and effort on the part of school personnel. Early involvement is to both the school's and the family's benefit.

6. Home visitors or parent aides. These lay volunteers come from various agencies to assist mothers and fathers in the development of day-to-day living skills.

7. A medical care system in which a physician will see the children and adults consistently on an ongoing basis. Careful records must be kept. Twenty-four-hour services are necessary.

8. Financial planners from departments of social services.

9. Vocational rehabilitation services can assist some of the parents in getting retrained, relocated, and employed.

10. Protective services provide a valuable service during family assessment. Unfortunately, most protective service units are not able to stay involved over a long period of time, so their role is often intermittent and sporadic (see chap. 8). Since neglecting families often generate multiple reports to protective services, many *different* protective service workers may be involved with the same family over a period of years. This method of delivery of service is outmoded and cannot be condoned. Ongoing, long-term service by a given protective service worker with a family can be invaluable.

None of the above services is feasible unless there is someone who is the overall coordinator of services. This position is probably the single most flagrant omission in most communities. It is the hardest to sell, the hardest to fund, and often the hardest to staff. One person who calls the shots and is seen positively by the various team members and the families is critical. This individual often works for the child protection team or the multidisciplinary team within the community. This is not a role for the physician, public health nurse, psychologist, or protective services worker, but it should be seen as a separate, critically important function which must be funded independently. Those who think about the importance of this individual will immediately see that the weakest link in any long-term care of neglecting families is the unavailability of such a coordinator. Considering all the manifestations of neglecting parents, there is little wonder why such a person is so necessary to coordinate all their activities. One cannot expect the retarded, psychiatrically ill, physically ill, or poor parents to coordinate their own multidisciplinary service system. The questions of how this individual is paid and for whom he or she works have never been adequately resolved. Clearly this role cannot continue to be ignored. Equally clearly, the public sector thus far has not been willing to provide support for these individuals.

Personal Issues

When a physician, psychologist, social worker, or nurse becomes involved with a family who is caught up in the litany of smoldering neglect, the personal conflicts that arise must not be underestimated. These families, without doubt, are the most difficult cases for any professional. Trying to decide who you are, what your role is, and whether you are the advocate for the child, for the parents, or for the whole family is most difficult.

One way of handling this difficult ambivalence is to get mad at the parents and stay mad at them throughout the follow-up period; this usually results in frequent missed appointments and excessive resistance to any interventions. Another way is to establish a close rapport with the parents; this ultimately leads to empathy, frustration, and anger. The anger mounts when the parents do not follow up, give medications, or come in two or three weeks late for medical problems. The anger mounts when the community services are insufficient or are withdrawn. One becomes upset and annoyed with the parents, many of whom are truly trying but clearly do not have the capabilities to change. If while developing a close relationship with the parents, one ignores the children's lack of progress and other obvious components of neglect, this leads to a variety of external pressures from school teachers, public health nurses, and others who are saying, "Why don't you do something? You're the doctor." One's objectivity may diminish as the closeness to these families increases. Seeing them frequently is very helpful, but some of the smoldering, slowly developing problems may become less obvious.

Directing one's attention solely to the children and dealing with their problems, ignoring the parents, leads to a rapid breakdown in the rapport and increases the problems of neglect.

The personal anguish that results, the sleepless nights of trying to determine the proper approach, is inevitable. Some families are followed from the birth of their children. Over a two-to-three-year period one may get used to the problem, "accepting the way in which the kids are handled." When a new public health nurse or an extension worker arrives in the home, they may be aghast at what they find and wonder why in the world the problem has been allowed to go on for so long.

Some neglecting families barely reach acceptable standards of care even with the help of extensive intervention. All may hit the fan, as it did in the early 1980s, when our federal policies result in cutbacks of significant family services. Marginal families who were just meeting acceptable standards began to collapse. Extension workers were pulled out, protective service workers' caseloads increased, public health nurses could no longer make twice weekly visits, and school systems were losing professionals. As children's nutritional status declined, their growth became less and less acceptable.

The personal problems grow as the inevitable becomes clear. When children who are being neglected do not appear for several weeks or months at a time because of the lack of transportation and other social services available to them, and when they eventually arrive at the clinic underweight, with hollow sunken eyes, the dismay grows. At this point, one is not certain at whom the anger should be directed—At the nebulous "system"? At the retarded or psychiatrically and physically ill parents? At one's self?—but one certainly is angry. After becoming close to such a family during many years of follow-up, the next step then becomes extremely painful.

Separation of Parents and Children

As all the interactions with a family are summarized by a review of the records and the litany of the failures of these parents is documented, the gnawing feeling that the children should be taken out of the home and placed into a foster home develops. The ensuing pain that results leads one to wonder how he or she ever got into this situation in the first place. The results of saying to a family, "You just can't hack it any more. I am going to court to testify about what lousy parents you have been all these years," can only be felt and not described. Of course these are not the words actually used, but as the story unfolds, the truth of that crude message is heard over and over again. Is the professional an advocate for the children, the parents or the family? As objectivity is questioned by one's peers, nurses, the public health system, protective service workers, and oneself, the outcome is clear. Often what is right is to say, "These children deserve a better environment." Without exception, the most difficult aspect of working with these families is when the physician and other professionals find themselves in court being asked to testify about a family they have known well for several years and recommending the ultimate, a "parentectomy," the separation of children from their parents.

This should not imply, or even hint, that most or even a small segment of children who are neglected over a long-term basis are removed from their homes. The court system often does not permit this to occur; the legal rules of evidence are often contrary to the best interests of these children. If separation does occur and the children are still young and have the good fortune of being placed in a superb, warm, stimulating, "cuddly" foster home, the outcome can be truly amazing. A developmental unfolding occurs before one's eyes, as if by magic.

A brief vignette may help place these various issues into proper perspective. A family of three children with a retarded mother and father was followed for approximately two-and-one-half years. The ages of the children were six years, three-and-one-half years, and eighteen months. During this period they had visited the pediatric clinic and were seen by the same pediatrician or one of the residents on fifty-two occasions. The father consumed a good deal of alcohol but worked on a regular basis at a local bowling alley. The mother was retarded, functioning at a level of about 70 I.Q. The father's I.Q. was not much greater. While the children did not have any serious physical problems, they did have recurrent, low-grade staphylococcal infections of the skin. The baby had stool retention, beginning at the age of three months. Growth and development were slow in all of the children, each falling below the third percentile for height and weight and well below the acceptable standards in their development.

Finally, over a period of time and after great pressures from the public health nurse, extension workers, schools, and others who were working with the family, a court hearing was sought. The petition was accepted, and a request by the parents' lawyer to have a jury trial was permitted.

The long-standing, close relationship between the health care providers and the parents broke apart as a result of the testimony in court. As the presentation of the litany of neglect that was documented in the children's record unfolded, one could legitimately criticize the providers of care, particularly the physician, for waiting so long to seek court involvement. The precipitating event was a staphylococcal infection in the mother which resulted in her hospitalization. A single episode of physical abuse (the first) to one of the children by the father followed. While this was relatively minor, it created great stress for the father and for those who were following the family.

At the meeting with the parents when the physician told them of the upcoming court hearing, crying and wailing ensued as the eighteen-month-old child sat in the corner, rocking and playing with his fist. He had no language to speak, could not yet walk at that time, and still suffered from severe, ongoing stool impaction.

The jury trial resulted in the placement of the three children in two foster homes. The two youngest went to a superb home of an elderly "grandmother-type" woman who cared for them with great diligence. The children were seen in follow-up by the same physician. They began to make marked improvement, both physically and developmentally. The younger child blossomed in his development. At twenty-two months, while being measured, he insisted on standing up against the wall rather than lying on the table. When the triangle was placed on his head to check his height, he looked at it, and the first words the physician heard from this child after fifty-five outpatient visits were, "That's a triangle!" His stool impaction cleared within six weeks, his walking progressed so that within three months he was running, and he was becoming very verbal in his interactions with others. One can compare this experience only to time-lapse photography as these children developmentally unfolded before everyone's eyes.

As the emotions and guilt that mounted during the court hearing and later during the breakup of the marriage after the children were removed are compared to the elation and satisfaction of seeing each of these children improve dramatically developmentally, socially, and physically, each seems to counteract the other. As hard as it is to admit, this family structure was expendable. The children ultimately were permanently adopted. They improved dramatically. The parents' relationships collapsed, and now they are trying to find their own way in our social system that provides minimal support for retarded adults.

Epilogue

There is no good ending to the story of the smoldering neglect of at least 650,000 children each year in our country. Cutbacks in the social service system by federal, state, and local agencies, the decrease in federal funding for nutritional programs, food stamps, Women, Infants, and Children, and the Medicaid system, are all exacerbating the problem.

Without an intensive, multidisciplinary community assessment, follow-up, and treatment program, children who are neglected over long periods of time will continue to smolder and create an inordinate burden upon our societal structure, especially our school systems. The amount of time and money that it takes to educate these children is enormous. While separation from their parents is painful, it occasionally is the only resolution. Our courts and social systems must cooperate in this endeavor if it is going to be successful. Extensive and multifaceted intervention programs can be most successful if they become *ongoing, long-term* commitments. Interventions cannot be short term. For those children who remain with their families, these services must continue until they are old enough to fend for themselves. While the cost of this type of intervention, including that which is necessary for the school system, is almost prohibitive, the cost of not caring for these families is enormous. The approaches detailed in the chapter on prevention and early intervention should be seriously considered as a more viable alternative (see chapter 22).

Readings

Lolly, J. R. 1984. Three Views of Child Neglect: Expanding Visions of Preventive Intervention. *Child Abuse and Neglect: International J.* 8:243–54.

Polansky, N. A.; Chalmers, M. A.; Buttenwieser, E.; and William, D. P. 1981. *Damaged Parents*. Chicago: University of Chicago Press.

Polansky, N. A.; Gaudin, J. M., Jr.; Ammons, P. W.; and Davis, K. B. 1985. The Psychological Ecology of the Neglectful Mother. *Child Abuse and Neglect: International J.* 9:265–75.

Wolock, I., and Horowitz, B. 1979. Child Maltreatment and Maternal Deprivation among AFDC-Recipient Families. *Social Services Review* 53:175–94.

16 Malnutrition and Growth Retardation ("Failure to Thrive") in the Context of Child Abuse and Neglect

Ruth S. Kempe and Richard B. Goldbloom

Introduction: A Plea for Revised Terminology

Increased understanding and improved management of malnourished children necessitate the revision of terminology. Change is required not only in the interest of accuracy, but also to help those who treat these children and their families better understand the nature of the problem. The term "failure to thrive" should be abandoned in favor of more precise descriptions of deficits in nutrition and growth, weight and height levels, and the individual developmental and behavioral characteristics of a given child. Second, the segregation of nutritional/growth deficits into "organic" (i.e., associated with organic disease) and "non-organic" (i.e., associated with psychosocial disease) is artificial and misleading. Although failure to gain and grow may be triggered by either an organic disorder (e.g., chronic renal disease or congenital heart disease) or a psychosocial disorder (e.g., parent-child interactional difficulties), the final common pathway is the same—inadequate calorie intake. In the case of what many refer to as "non-organic failure to thrive," what begins as a psychosocial problem inevitably results in an organic disorder *and* a psychosocial problem. Certain of the organic features must be quantified, especially the deficits in height, weight, and caloric intake. Other features such as the secondary effects on digestion, absorption, hormonal secretion, and behavior must be well understood if effective treatment and follow-up are to be instituted. Likewise the difficulties in interacting with a child who is nutritionally deprived, for whatever reason, must be elucidated and a long-term treatment plan for their correction simultaneously instituted.

Inherent in the research which has attempted to clarify distinctions between "non-organic" and "disease-based" failure to thrive is the vague implication that organic and psychosocial disorders are somehow mutually exclusive. This concept has been repeatedly disproven by the realities of clinical experience. While certain behavioral characteristics

Ruth S. Kempe, M.D., is with the Department of Psychiatry, University of Colorado Health Science Center. Richard B. Goldbloom, M.D., is with the Department of Pediatrics, Dalhousie University, and the Izaak Walton Killam Hospital for Children, Halifax, Nova Scotia.

of infants and young children have been identified as hallmarks of emotional deprivation—and this knowledge is of great value in diagnosis and management—malnutrition in and of itself has effects on the emotional state and behavior of infants, children, and adults. It is also true that neglect leading to caloric deprivation may occur in the presence of an organic disease, making management more difficult or increasing the severity of the malnutrition (1).

The final reason for our recommendation for a change in terminology is that using the term "failure to thrive" as a hospital admission diagnosis often leads to the initiation of unfocused searching for hidden pathology which rarely addresses the uniquely individual features of each child's problem and rarely yields diagnostic information that is not already suspected from a comprehensive history, physical examination, and family assessment. Such investigations lead to "fishing expeditions" which may delay treatment that is obviously and urgently required. The rapid and effective correction of malnutrition is often as helpful diagnostically as it is therapeutically. The discharge diagnosis of "failure to thrive" is equally unacceptable as it tells nothing about the etiology of the case. The term "non-organic failure to thrive" has outlived its usefulness and should be discarded as a diagnostic label.

In this chapter, the medical aspects of the problem of malnutrition due to neglect, its diagnosis, initial treatment plan, and the long-term problems in parenting will be addressed. Unless all phases are adequately addressed, the child will not grow and develop appropriately.

The patients which are to be discussed are those infants up to two years of age who fail, over a period of time, to grow according to the accepted standards for the child's age. In addition to the lack of adequate caloric intake, there are often other evidences of neglect on the part of the parents which result in developmental deviations or delays. Children with growth failure disease must be considered to be receiving inadequate feeding, and the reasons for this deficiency must be addressed. Growth failure is often the first objective symptom of major parenting difficulties which, unresolved, can lead to serious physical and developmental consequences for the child.

Historical Background

The term "failure to thrive" came into use early in this century to describe the miserable state of many infants and young children living in institutions. Mortality rates for such children were appallingly high. The recognition gradually occurred that death rates could be decreased if the children were transferred to the foster care of carefully selected families and given adequate nutrition under close supervision (2).

For many years, the central role of institutional care dominated medical and sociological thinking about the etiology of this problem. This view was reinforced by Rene Spitz's observation of an association between "anaclitic" depression, malnutrition, and growth failure in hospitalized children. He labeled this syndrome "hospitalism" (3). Unquestionably, the focus on the etiological role of institutional care was appropriate in that era. Over a decade was to pass before Coleman and Provence pointed out that the same phenomenon could occur in infants and children living at home (4). Parallel with the recognition of the role of the family and home environment in determining growth, nutrition, and behavior of children came a gradual appreciation of several other key mechanisms in the manifestations of the syndrome.

The final common pathway of pathogenesis for failure of nutrition and growth is an insufficient energy intake, often compounded by secondary deficits of growth hormone or of somatomedin which improve rapidly when normal nutrition is regained. Ancel Keys's landmark studies using human adult volunteers on the biology of human starvation (5) introduced additional fundamental concepts which were critical in enhancing the understanding of this complex problem. These included:

1. Recognition that anorexia was as likely to be the result of starvation as its cause.

2. Appreciation of the impact of malnutrition on mood and behavior, particularly as a cause of apathy and depression.

3. Documentation that recovery from malnutrition requires caloric intake far in excess of that needed for maintenance under normal conditions, and the realization that psychological recovery was dependent, in part, on such supernormal intakes.

One must not assume that these studies performed with mature adults are completely applicable to immature infants who have not yet established individual eating patterns independent of their relationships to primary caretakers.

The earlier studies, particularly those of Rene Spitz, led to the widespread belief that infants and children from emotionally deprived backgrounds developed anorexia which alone was the cause of failure to gain. However, Whitten et al. (6) confirmed in 1969 that most infants from severely deprived backgrounds recovered their weight deficits rapidly in an environment devoid of almost all stimulation, providing they were assured a caloric intake 50 percent greater than normal for a healthy child of the same height. Their studies did not confirm that this weight gain continued with all children after their return home, or that developmental problems were thereby cured.

In 1963, Prader and associates (7) defined the phenomenon of "catch-up growth" by observing that children recovering from illness or malnutrition showed above-normal rates of ponderal (weight) and linear growth. A succession of advances through nutritional research have enormously improved the efficacy of managing infants and children with nutritional and growth deficits of any cause. The efficacy of oral feedings has also increased through the development of elemental feeding preparations and nutritional supplements of high caloric density and acceptable osmolality.

Initial Medical Evaluation

Three evaluative procedures are necessary to develop a diagnosis and appropriate management plan:

1. A comprehensive medical history.

2. A complete physical examination.

3. Observation of behavior and interactional analysis.

Laboratory and diagnostic imaging procedures are not included because the available evidence indicates that these rarely yield diagnostic information unless *specifically* indicated by the findings of the history and physical examination. They are not part of any *routine* assessment of these children and their families. Rather, they are used only when the above evaluation has been completed and specific studies are indicated.

Sills (8) reviewed the records of 185 infants and children admitted to a pediatric hospital with a diagnosis of "failure to thrive." Only 1.4 percent of 2047 laboratory and radiographic examinations performed on these children yielded results that supported the final diagnosis. In addition, every procedure which yielded positive results was clearly indicated by the findings of the history and physical examination.

There is an enormous number of diseases whose major presenting features may include growth failure and malnutrition. The list is too long to enumerate, but it includes various pulmonary, renal, intestinal, cardiac, and hepatic diseases, some central nervous system diseases, hereditary metabolic disorders, chronic infections, cystic fibrosis, and so on. Any condition affecting caloric intake through anorexia, impaired digestion or absorption utilization, or causing increased energy loss may lead to malnutrition and growth retardation. Thus the list of potential causes of what has been called "failure to thrive" has become so lengthy as to be of vanishing practical value. When such lists lead to prefabricated protocols of diagnostic procedures, they can be harmful, resulting in invasive interventions and distracting parents and professionals alike from the obvious need for intensive treatment of the child and family.

There is also the risk of misinterpreting abnormal studies. Secondary phenomena caused by environmental deprivation and malnutrition may be erroneously interpreted as signifying underlying organic disease. Talbot et al. (9) recognized the resemblance between some environmentally and nutritionally deprived children and those with hypopituitarism. Others have noted a physical and symptomatic resemblance to children with celiac disease (gluten enteropathy). One may be misled by laboratory investigations performed on starving children. For example, some infants and young children with undernutrition of any cause may exhibit secondary renal tubular acidosis. If the child has the misfortune of having this disturbance of renal function discovered on admission to hospital, this may lead to further uncomfortable and needless investigation of a transient disorder which, like many secondary endocrinopathies, will disappear promptly with improvement of the nutritional state.

Unless the history and physical examination reveal strong evidence of underlying disease, all investigation should be deferred until the child has had seven to ten days of uninterrupted observation coupled with a vigorous program of feeding and nurturing. Most children will require admission to hospital to permit adequate observation and effective treatment. Achievement of a caloric intake sufficient for nutritional recovery and catch-up growth may be almost impossible to accomplish in the home. On occasion, when the physician and the parents have developed an active and collaborative therapeutic approach to the problem, the home approach is possible. If a child is being examined very frequently in a clinic or private office, he or she can sometimes be kept safely at home and observed while the initial steps in diagnosis and treatment are carried out. A time limit should be set if this plan is to be used. However, if an infant is seen for the first time with a serious weight loss as judged from his birth weight or with a weight well below his age when there has been no recent medical care, hospital admission is necessary lest the parents elect not to return. Immediate admission is also indicated if signs of dehydration, other illness, abuse, or neglect are present. If there is any doubt, hospitalize.

While this recommendation is sound medically and is the only effective and economical (in the long run) way to approach this problem, the fact of the matter is that current payment policies in the United States (DRG's: Diagnostic Related Groups) may not permit this to occur. In some states (e.g., Michigan), only three hospital days are permitted for "failure to thrive." Since the diagnosis and treatment plan cannot be completed in this time frame, these children go untreated. Current hospital rates of $700 per day preclude the use of a seven-to-ten day hospitalization for feeding malnourished infants. Seeking resources outside the hospital is unlikely to be successful. Current movements to provide a varying scale of charges for hospital care, depending on the nature of services needed, may resolve this dilemma. Until then, many infants with malnutrition are not being cared for appropriately.

Medical History

In hospitals which are geared to the care of seriously ill children, medical histories obtained on admission sometimes lack important details which may impede adequate diagnosis and management. In addition to the routine medical history, detailed information is needed about the feeding, developmental, and psychosocial aspects of the family. This may be done by the physician when asking about the family's medical history and the child's nutritional history or by other staff, including nurse, social worker, psychologist, or psychiatrist. While the social worker assigned to the pediatric service may be the most likely person to take the family history, any qualified professional knowledgeable about growth failure will be able to gather these data.

The components of a comprehensive medical history, as standardized and detailed in any pediatric textbook, should be completed. In addition, three areas need more extensive review: feeding, development, and psychosocial data.

Feeding History. In growth failure due to deprivation, the history which the mother gives, and which she believes to be true, may or may not correspond to the picture seen on direct observation. The mother may not recognize the significance of the growth failure and is often unaware of obvious emaciation. She may be concerned that her child is feeding poorly, but she may perceive the difficulty to be related to vomiting, diarrhea, the wrong formula, or the child's disinterest in food. The importance of her role in the feeding process may not be appreciated. The mother may indicate that she gives her seven-week-old six ounces of formula every four hours, but in actuality one finds that she makes six bottles irregularly and skips all night bottles because the baby does not seem hungry and is not expected to feed between 10:00 P.M. and 8:00 A.M. Some mothers make bottles individually and have little idea how much the baby takes during any given time period. The same bottle may be propped up for the baby repeatedly until finished. To learn these details usually requires intermittent conversations and observations over a prolonged period of time.

Subjects to be included in a detailed feeding history are: reasons for breast feeding or bottle feeding, reasons for change from breast to bottle, method used in preparation of formula, total formula made in twenty-four hours and how much is left, formula changes, doctor's or other's feeding advice, baby's feeding pattern, schedule, appetite, length of feeding, spitting up or vomiting (how and when), diarrhea, and constipation. Other areas to be considered are: position and place for feeding, interruption by other children or duties, bottle propping, introduction of solid foods, how they are taken, self-feeding, and degree of messiness and how it is tolerated. The feeding history may be at variance with what is observed during feeding in the hospital.

Sometimes the parent will follow inappropriate advice from a friend or relative or will describe misunderstanding of medical directions. For example, an infant may have been given diluted feedings for treatment of diarrhea. The mother may not resume regular feedings in a day or two nor consult with the doctor, continuing the diluted feedings indefinitely. Other mothers describe an infant who is very hungry at first, but fussy and difficult to feed. In time, the infant may seem less irritable and may sleep for long periods; the parent may interpret this as the infant being satisfied rather than becoming apathetic. Retreat into sleep is not uncommon as a response by young infants to continued underfeeding (10).

Growth disturbances from caloric deprivation may also occur in breast-fed infants whose mothers have insufficient technical help in managing breast-feeding or inadequate support in maintaining the demanding task during the early weeks after delivery. There is, unfortunately, a lack of interest and knowledge among many physicians and nurses who are consulted about breast-feeding difficulties. This frequently results in the recommendation of a rapid change to bottle feeding, which may lead to poor acceptance of the bottle by the baby, mother and infant distress, and reluctance to accept the change followed by feeding difficulties and weight loss. If the mother refuses to accept the advice to bottle feed, but still has no adequate help in management of breast-feeding, the infant may fail to thrive because of an inadequate milk supply (11, 12). Referral to someone skilled in breast-feeding techniques may salvage the mother's milk supply, but monitoring and support are necessary.

The child over five months who is entirely breast-fed may have reached a size where the total caloric content of the breast-feedings is insufficient to maintain his size. These babies may remain apparently content, even as they fail to gain (13). Such a child needs supplementary food, in addition to continued breast-feeding, until his mother wishes to wean him.

Developmental History. The developmental component of the medical history begins with early pregnancy and continues to the present age of the child. It contains both actual occurrences as well as perceived states of the fetus's and child's development. The history of pregnancy should include initial reactions to the pregnancy, health and special symptoms or complications, preparations for the baby including reading or special classes, prenatal care, and use of coffee, tobacco, alcohol, or drugs during pregnancy. Labor, its degree and length, is an integral component of the information needed.

The history of delivery includes medications and anesthesia used, type of delivery, condition of the baby at birth (weight, Apgar, description), mother's initial thoughts or reactions on seeing her baby. The husband's, family's, and staff's reactions to the baby is important information to gather. The frequency and length of mother-infant contact after delivery up to discharge, help at home, and evidence of bonding are all necessary data. The baby's sex, temperament, and ability to interact with the parents should be explored.

Developmental topics after birth include motor functions, eye contact, social smile, activity level, vocalization, play activities, and interest in toys; how the baby is different from siblings, a typical day for mother and baby, the attention given the baby, interactions of the baby with other family members, and frequency of babysitting and day-care ar-rangements. Not only how much time the mother spends with the baby, but also the quality of the interaction, which is usually evident in the mother's affect as she describes their day, is helpful information. Asking about the mother's other daily activities will clar-ify how much time is left for the baby and herself.

Psychosocial History of Family. While discussing the baby in detail, parents are usually responsive to tactful inquiry into their own situation. The extent of the difficulties for the parents—how worrisome, frustrating, and fatiguing the problems of caring for the baby might be—is important to recognize. Parents may feel great relief and support when someone acknowledges how time-consuming and anxiety-provoking it may be to have a new baby. Recognition of how hard this may have been for the mother can be followed by a discussion of what the care of the baby has meant to the rest of the family and the kind of support the mother has had from husband, family, and friends. Other problems, such as financial, housing, and illnesses of other family members, are usually readily obtained. Discussion of whether the mother and father see the baby's problems in the same way can lead to an understanding of the parents' expectations of the child and one another, their child-rearing beliefs, and the way in which both of them were brought up. This leads natu-rally to the parents' own childhood histories, to information about abuse, neglect, or object loss in their early years, and to their perception of their relationships with their parents. Some history about their school experiences and job adjustments will give im-pressions of their coping styles, their ability to meet stress and to call on others for help. A discussion of social activities and friendships may lead to an impression of isolation, lack of resources, and depression.

Most women will talk about their husband's or boyfriend's role in the family and, if questioned with empathy, will convey the prevailing emotional tone of their relationship. If the father is present, he may contribute a great deal to an understanding of the family interactions and reveal his own influence on how care of the baby has progressed.

The psychosocial history should explore the parents' own experiences of nurturance as well as the possible difficulties they have had in attachment and in recognizing their child's needs. Only in the context of their past experiences, current stresses, and the character of the parent-child relationship as observed in the interaction does the understanding of the parents' denial of their child's nutritional and emotional needs unfold.

Physical Examination

The physical examination has three objectives: to determine whether there is any evi-dence of organic disease, to quantify the nutritional and growth states of this infant, and to determine whether the child exhibits behavioral features that are characteristic of neglect. The physical examination of the infant must be careful and comprehensive.

The child with malnutrition associated with deprivation often appears emaciated, pale, and weak with little subcutaneous fat and decreased muscle mass. Most of these children are listless, apathetic, and motionless, occasionally interspersed with states of irritability. On first glance some children may not look emaciated, but on closer examination they have poor muscle tone and weight gain. Bruises or burns are signals of abuse and should be documented photographically and in writing. A radiographic skeletal survey for evidence of trauma should follow. Such a survey should also be done if the medical history or family assessment indicates a risk of physical abuse (likely in at least one-third of these children).

In children under two years of age, recumbent length should be measured accurately and recorded on a standard growth chart. Recumbent length in this age group is significantly greater than standing height and should therefore be used preferentially. After two years of age, standing height is acceptable. If either parent is of short stature, it is wise to plot the child's length corrected for mid-parental stature (i.e., for the child's genetic endowment), using the tables published recently by Himes et al. (14), and plotting both the corrected and actual measurements. This is not a difficult exercise, requiring only a few moments and offering a much more realistic assessment of the true magnitude of any deviation from normal linear growth. It must be remembered, however, that the parents may also have suffered from neglect and growth retardation; their own genetic potential may not have been reached.

Weight should be measured on an accurate scale with the child undressed. All subsequent weighings should be performed at the same time each day on the same scale throughout the initial management period, preferably before breakfast and always with the child undressed. The height and weight are then plotted on standardized height and weight charts which compare one with the other. Significant increase of the height percentile as compared to the weight percentile results in the diagnosis of caloric deprivation.

In oral and written communications between health professionals and with the parents, it is important to use descriptive terms that clearly define the magnitude of any nutritional or growth deficit. To say that a child's length or weight is "below the third percentile" is imprecise. Three percent of the *normal* population is at or below the third percentile line for height or weight. Deficits of height and weight growth are better expressed as "height-age" or "weight-age." These can then be immediately related to each other and to the child's chronological age. The recipient of such information is given a precise and vivid picture of the child's growth status. The child's height-age or weight-age is determined by plotting the actual measurement on a standard growth chart and extrapolating a horizontal line from that point until it meets the fiftieth percentile line. The age represented by the point of intersection is the height-age or weight-age.

A useful way to express the degree of "acute" malnutrition (i.e., the extent to which the child's weight is inappropriately low in relation to actual length) is to determine the weight as a percentage of ideal ("ideal" meaning the fiftieth percentile weight for the child's actual length). McLaren and Read (15) have described an arbitrary but useful classification of the severity of protein-calorie malnutrition (PCM), as shown in table 16.1.

Behavioral and Developmental Observations

Over the past half-century certain postures and behaviors in infants and young children have been identified as characteristic of psychosocial/nutritional deprivation. Apathy and withdrawal are common, with a wide-eyed expression that suggests an element of fear. This has been aptly termed "frozen watchfulness." Smiling may be rare or absent. Often the child will silently follow the movements of people in the room with a so-called radar gaze. Some infants, especially younger ones, sleep much more than is usual for their age.

TABLE 16.1   Classification of Protein-Calorie Malnutrition (PCM)

Nutrition Level	Weight as Percentage of Ideal
Normal	90%–110%
Mild PCM	85%–90%
Moderate PCM	75%–85%
Severe PCM	75%

SOURCE: D. S. McLaren and W. C. Read, Classification of Nutritional Status in Early Childhood, *Lancet* 2(1972):146–48.

Watching the child lying in bed, one may observe postures that are distinctly abnormal for the child's age but are appropriate for newborn or very young infants. The child may lie supine with the arms flexed, the hands pronated and held near or behind the head. The legs may be flexed in the "frog" position or held with the heels off the bed. Sometimes the thumbs will be held inside the flexed fingers as seen normally in very young infants. Other malnourished and deprived children exhibit self-stimulatory rhythmic behavior, such as head-banging, body-rocking, or rumination. Typically, these behaviors are seen only when the child is in the crib and cease as soon as he or she is picked up.

Parental Behavior. The first meeting with the family offers a unique opportunity to observe how the parents treat each other and their children. Do they smile often at each other, offer verbal and nonverbal encouragement and reassurance, or are their interactions chiefly of a negative and demanding nature? Ward personnel are encouraged to observe and report significant indications of family interaction, both its presence and absence.

In a doctor's office or at the time of admission to hospital, the phenomenon of ready relinquishment should be noted if present. This is most often manifested by the parent who walks away from the examining table, leaving an infant or young child entirely to the examiner and not showing the expected protective, encouraging parental behaviors. During the hospital admission, typical situations include one in which the parent(s) can hardly wait to leave, at times demonstrating reluctance to stay long enough to have the history taken, or showing little visible emotion when taking leave of the child. Later, while visiting, parents may be more involved in watching ward activities, television, or talking to other adults than caring for or interacting with their own child. The family's response to the hospital staff is also of importance, particularly if they are reluctant to discuss their child or seem suspicious or mistrustful of the motives of hospital staff.

Infant Behavior. Deprived infants' social responses to adults or other children vary and are expressed in ways that reflect the inadequacy of their caretaking—the age of onset, severity, and duration—as well as the way in which, given their physical and temperamental endowments, they have been able to adjust to that caretaking. Some infants remain very passive, apathetic, and initially unresponsive or resistant to social overtures by adults; others seem actively distressed by early attempts to interact with them. Others may ignore the mother's overtures, yet respond with interest and even with smiling to a stranger who approaches them gently. One little boy of twelve months, hospitalized with growth failure, would turn on a brilliant smile whenever anyone came into his vicinity. As soon as they left his field of vision, his smile was turned off, leaving him looking sad and watchful. When he was seen at fifteen months, he had developed a good relationship with his foster mother and was beginning to be anxious and tearful when approached by a stranger or threatened by any separation from the foster mother. Rosenn et al. (16) have categorized the behaviors of hospitalized infants with growth failure due to deprivation as showing a definite initial preference for distance in interaction with a staff person and a preference for contact with inanimate objects, with a change to acceptance of closer contact with others as the child begins to improve in weight. Such behavior is not found in infants with an organic reason for their malnutrition, and it is assumed to be related to the environmental background of these children.

Developmental diagnosis by doing a Brazelton (17; for the newborn infant), a Bayley (18), Yale Developmental Test (19), or, at minimum, a Denver Developmental Screening Test (20) should be obtained the first or second day of admission. The most marked retardation is usually noted on gross motor behaviors and social behaviors, especially speech. The developmental assessment should be repeated before discharge if marked change in behavior is noted, thereby documenting the child's improvement in the hospital environment.

Parent-Child Interaction. The evaluation of the parent-child relationship should begin upon admission to the hospital. This can often be accomplished by recording an informal interview on videotape during a feeding and play period with parents and child. Written permission for such videotaping must be obtained from the parents, with an explanation of the reason for taping, namely, understanding better how they care for the child and what feeding problems might contribute to the growth delay. The video camera is present in the room, and the procedure is both informal and comfortable if the interviewer is skilled in putting the parent at ease. The videotape is useful in allowing for detailed review of the parent-child interaction obviating the necessity for "on the spot" judgments, and it can be a helpful teaching aid with the parents in certain circumstances. The major value lies in the ability to observe carefully what takes place between parents and child. For this no special equipment is really needed. Sensitivity on the part of the interviewer to the nuances of the interaction and recognition of their importance are needed.

The interviewer may be any professional with sufficient knowledge and experience with growth failure, infant development, and neglectful or abusive parents. During time spent with the parents and child, he or she may obtain information to supplement the medical history, particularly information which elucidates the circumstances at the onset of the feeding difficulty.

Most of the diagnostic studies done with infants who have deprivation malnutrition have observed only the mother and child together. Some research includes both parents in interactional observation and indicates that the father has considerable influence on the feeding process itself (21). Fathers should be included in the interaction evaluation. While the authors recognize the importance of observing the father, experience with mother-infant interaction is much more extensive.

The observation of the interaction between parents and child focuses upon feeding and play situations. Despite the fact that the mother knows this is a diagnostic assessment, the character of the relationship is usually clear. The attachment between mother and child, their comfort and closeness, their discomfort or comparative indifference to each other can be seen. Is the mother sensitive to the behavioral cues of her child, and does she respond? Does she time her feeding to the infant's hunger and interact positively, or does she shovel food in while the child sits motionless, hands held high? She may give the bottle to the baby while the infant reaches out to touch her and then, as soon as the child is sucking vigorously, remove the bottle to see how much has been taken. Each detail of the inter-action may individually seem insignificant, but when observed in its entirety the interaction may be diagnostic. How frequently do the mother and child have eye contact, smile at each other, speak? Are the spoken words commands ("Take your hands away from that.") or criticisms ("Aren't you ever going to eat your potatoes?")? Can they play with each other, or does the mother quickly find excuses for the baby not to be interested ("He really likes to play alone in his crib."), even though the baby can be seen eagerly reaching for a toy and smiling with great pleasure at any overture by the interviewer? At times the mother may take a toy ostensibly to show the baby how to use it and end up playing with it herself. Parallel play (using one toy while her baby plays independently with another) may be as far as she can go in stimulating her child to play. Often the baby seems to have stopped looking to the mother for social response and watches or vocalizes to a stranger instead. The mother may also focus on the interviewer for attention.

In these interactions parental behavior which reflects a mother's own experience as a vulnerable child can be seen. In the interaction the mother may fail to meet the infant's needs to such a degree that she negatively modifies that child's development. This may set up pathological defenses in the child which are integrated very early into the personality. Seen simultaneously are the parents' maltreatment of the child and the effect on the child which eventually makes that child vulnerable.

There are mothers who faithfully visit their hospitalized children, showing sincere con-cern about their babies, yet when one observes them, they rarely engage in any mean-ingful activity with their babies. They tend to stand around watching; only when there is a highly structured activity do they engage with their babies. Some mothers seem immobi-lized by their lack of skills after depression and anxiety take over. The staff may recognize their concern, but not recognize their inability to meet their children's needs.

Family Assessment

There have been many studies of parents of malnourished and deprived babies; the de-scriptions vary a great deal (22–33). Some common features do occur and can be summa-rized. In general, they do not differ from other parents in terms of age, marital status, number of children, intelligence, level of income, or source of income. Also, medical complications of pregnancy, delivery, and neonatal period did not differentiate the par-ents. Most parents in large-scale studies come from socioeconomic classes IV and V, and most suffer financial stress as well as social stress. These statistics overrepresent poor patients. While deprivation malnutrition can be present in the private pediatric office or private pediatric hospital service, it is not always so diagnosed officially, and nursing or day-care help is utilized to take care of the deficient parenting. As with many studies based on data analysis, the review of a problem area like malnutrition due to deprivation tends to emphasize the large clinic populations more readily available in a teaching hospital. Be-cause they are more often in financial stress, this may give a true idea of the malignant influence of poverty, but it deemphasizes the personality difficulties for these parents. While psychiatric studies have found no specific diagnosis, some have described mothers as depressed and deprived and most often diagnosed as having a character disorder or a borderline personality (34, 35).

In addition to financial distress, most studies describe deprivation or abuse in the parents' childhoods, social isolation, anxiety, and depression as frequently present. All of these characteristics do not necessarily distinguish the neglectful from the nurturing parents. To date, there has been no definitive study on what makes the difference. The one area where there seems to be a real difference is in the interaction between the mother and the nonthriving child, according to the studies of Egelund et al. (36) and Haynes et al. (37).

Mothers who have a comparatively good interaction with their infants but who are temporarily overwhelmed by a rapid series of events which undermine their basically good capacity to be a mother can resume the good mothering role and respond sensitively to their child, if given appropriate support during the crisis. Such mothers usually cope with fairly severe amounts of environmental stress. When the stress becomes overwhelming, they and their babies need help to bring them "back on track." This group may include those women who have suffered a severe, recent loss such as the departure of a husband or death of a mother.

Analyzing their videotaped play and feeding interactions and their complete medical histories, Haynes et al. compared fifty mother-infant pairs whose infants were hospitalized with deprivation malnutrition with twenty-five matched mother-infant pairs whose infants were growing and developing normally (37–39). The differences found suggest that the explanation for the malnutrition can usually be found in the relationship between mother and child.

In contrast to the mothers of the healthy babies, the mothers of malnourished infants either denied any childhood memories or described an unhappy, deprived childhood with a high frequency of sexual abuse, physical abuse, or neglect. Some comparison mothers also had trauma in their childhoods but they had found supportive relationships to help them.

The mothers of malnourished infants had real difficulty in recognizing the malnutrition and the need for medical help. In all cases there seemed to be a conflict between the needs of the mother and the needs of her malnourished infant, making the mother unavailable as an effective caretaker. Mothercrafting skills were not a significant problem except in the most disturbed pairs. Some mothers seemed primarily overwhelmed by current stress in the home or were depressed and therefore unable to respond. Although somewhat more aware of their previous part in the feeding difficulties, they seemed unable to recognize how to respond or unable to mobilize themselves in caring for their infants' needs. Another group of mothers seemed to be more ambivalent, seeing the weight problem as due to the babies' problems alone. They were able to respond effectively whenever their own needs and those of the infants coincided, but they misinterpreted the infants' needs when they conflicted with the mothers' wishes. These were the mothers who would suddenly feel like playing with the baby early in the feeding, ignoring the child's hunger. Some mothers were more hostile and tended to see their babies as demanding or "bad." They denied any feeding problems or need for medical help. Their approach to their babies lacked empathy, and they seemed very unskilled in relating to their babies both physically and socially. Their care occasionally became aggressive or even abusive.

Similar problems were seen in play behavior, with most mothers of the malnourished babies showing little ability to play. If not avoiding play entirely, they appeared more often like a peer (sometimes a competitive, teasing, or hostile one) of their child rather than a nurturing and facilitating adult.

The infants often showed clear evidences of changes in their behavior in response to their mothers' care. A small infant might go to sleep in response to intrusive bottle feeding; a four-month-old might become unresponsive and turn away from aggressive noisy use of a toy thrust in his face. A child who was alternately ignored or handled aggressively might become passive and withdrawn, yet by twenty months show his underlying anger in self-injurious behavior.

An important aspect of the interactional study was the evidence of a continuity in the patterns of interaction between mother and infant over six months to one year. Although the details of the activities might vary somewhat with the age and developmental advances of the child, the essential character of the relationship tended to remain much the same.

Fathers have been included in our current unpublished studies which indicate that they may play an active role in the parenting difficulties. Frequently they are simply absent and nonsupportive. In general they share deprived backgrounds and difficulties in coping with their wives (40).

The severity of parenting difficulty is underscored by the treatment outcomes for half of these families who received the services of a lay therapist in addition to the usual good quality hospital and follow-up care. The treated families showed increased stability and contact with sources of help, but there was no major difference in developmental outcome for their infants.

Treatment of Growth Failure Due to Caloric Deprivation

The initial steps in treatment of growth failure will be successful feeding of the child and demonstration of rapid weight gain on a regular diet. Simultaneously, assessment of the family and its ability to care for the child will be made through the psychological evaluation of the parents and through observation of their response to the opportunity to be involved in the treatment of the child. Nutritional treatment of the child and work with the parents must take place simultaneously so that the long-term treatment plan will be based on a knowledge of the extent of the child's needs and the parent's capabilities.

Treatment of the Nutritional State

The initial objectives of management are:

1. To correct malnutrition promptly and induce catch-up growth.

2. Simultaneously, to provide a personalized, nurturing type of care in an environment conducive to developmental stimulation.

3. To involve the parents in the treatment process as early as possible, except when it has already been decided that the child cannot be returned to the natural family.

Nutritional recovery requires a daily calorie intake that will average about 50 percent above that required by a healthy child of normal weight (fiftieth percentile) for the patient's actual length. The 50 percent caloric excess is only an average, and individual requirements for rapid nutritional recovery will vary from as little as 25 percent to as much as 100 percent above normal.

Maintenance of an accurate, daily, up-to-date record of the essential elements of hospital treatment and results is necessary. Such a record should include the child's ideal weight for length and the calculated desired daily calorie intake. The date, daily weight, calorie intake for the preceding twenty-four hours, and the calculated intake per kilogram ideal weight are recorded, plotting graphically the slope of the appropriate weight percentile for the child's actual length. On the same graph, using days of treatment as the abscissa, one can plot each day's weight. The great advantage of maintaining such a graph is that it permits everyone concerned with the child's care—nurses, nutritionists, social workers, and physicians—to appreciate whether the child's weight gain as compared to existing height is closing the gap at a sufficient rate of catch-up. Also, once catch-up growth is established at a reasonable rate, the slope of the weight recovery can be extrapolated to estimate the time required to achieve appropriate weight for length.

The formula or diet of choice offered the infant should be the same that was presumably taken at home during the growth failure period. If on this same though increased diet the child gains weight rapidly in the hospital, this is the most convincing evidence that the lack of adequate growth was due to the parents' feeding methods. Caloric intake can usually be increased to desirable levels using this method. Changing formula to soy milk or another mix may only confuse the observations.

The means of achieving satisfactory nutritional recovery is tailored to the individual infant or child. For example, a severely undernourished infant may tolerate an elemental formula better than a standard infant feeding product, especially during the first week or two of treatment, since digestive and absorptive mechanisms may be partially impaired as a result of the malnutrition. For most infants, it should be possible to achieve the designed daily calorie intake through progressive daily increments over the first week or so in hospital. For infants who demonstrate the capability to consume a reasonably large daily volume, increasing the caloric density of the feedings from the usual 20 Kcal per ounce to 24 Kcal per ounce may be sufficient to achieve a daily intake 50 percent above average for ideal weight.

Some children between one and three years of age may not begin to eat well immediately, particularly if the child has been force fed and if feeding has become a control issue between parent and child. Unless the need for calories is very urgent, the child needs to be allowed to eat entirely on his own volition, if possible in the helpful atmosphere of group meals with other children, until the child again feels in control and the emotionally charged struggle over eating is diffused.

There are some children whose serious physical condition requires a more aggressive treatment approach. For these, continuous nasogastric feeding, perhaps continued with oral feedings, may be used until weight gain is well begun. Although nasogastric feedings are not a most desirable way to treat a child whose feeding history has not included emotional nurturing, tube feeding need not be uncomfortable. The child can continue normal activities while the tube remains in place. The improved nutrition will make the child feel better physically to the point where energy and appetite improve.

A word of caution regarding nasogastric feedings. The personnel responsible for inserting the soft Silastic tubes (which have so greatly facilitated this technique) must be meticulous about measuring the length of tube insertion required to reach the stomach. They can be easy prey to the temptation to give the tube a little extra push (having already inserted the measured length) "just to make sure it is in the stomach." This extra bit of tubing inserted can be just enough to allow the tip to enter the duodenum, where the flow of nutrient may induce an osmotic diarrhea, which may be misinterpreted as intolerance of the nasogastric feeding, with resulting delays in achieving a proper caloric intake and recovery. All personnel should be warned to resist the temptation to give an extra push to the nasogastric feeding tube.

In all these efforts the advice and participation of an experienced pediatric therapeutic nutritionist is invaluable. At the same time physicians should be cautioned against completely abdicating responsibility for various elements of the child's care to allied disciplines (e.g., the nutritional problem to the nutritionist, the social problem to the social worker, and the developmental problem to the psychologist). This often results in each of the professionals "doing his or her own thing" while the physician retreats to a rather passive observer role, conducting an orchestra whose members may rarely be in the same hall at the same time. This is not a matter of professional territorialism. Everyone concerned within the family and the treatment team must be clear on the necessity for cooperative effort, as well as on whom the final responsibility for management rests. Only in this way can treatment be coordinated in the child's best interests. In the early days of management, periodic brief meetings between all concerned are of great value.

The Parents as Therapeutic Allies

When a malnourished, undergrown infant is hospitalized, a great deal of professional energy and expertise is applied to the child's physical and behavioral recovery, often with considerable success. During this initial period of management, overlooking the fact that the child may be returning to the original environment is all too easy. While at discharge the hospital treatment team might take pride in presenting parents with an infant who looks and behaves dramatically differently than the child they brought to hospital, this initial phase of treatment is no more than a beginning. The most challenging and difficult period often begins at the time of discharge. Parents of children with deprivational disorders often bring with them highly ambivalent feelings that include guilt, anger, frustration, and feelings of incompetence and helplessness. The very evident success of hospital management may convey mixed messages to them, inadvertently intensifying feelings of guilt and inadequacy, with the potential for increasing their anger toward the child or the professionals.

Planning the child's initial care so that parents feel they have played as important a role in the child's recovery as the hospital staff makes eminent sense. This requires direct parent participation in the child's hospital care. Individual variables can make such participation difficult, impossible, or even inappropriate. For families judged to have reasonable chances of long-term success, parent participation in care can be especially valuable. This can take various forms. If the hospital has a care-by-parent unit, this offers an excellent setting with the parent carrying the responsibility for most elements of care and the professional staff serving an educational and guiding role. The physical environment in such units should be more like home than like hospital, and the support and encouragement of other parents may help restore parents' confidence in their own caretaking abilities.

Lack of a care-by-parent facility does not preclude meaningful parent involvement in the child's care. A therapeutic agreement can be arranged wherein the parent undertakes to spend certain designated hours at the hospital and to take responsibility for specified caregiving activities during those hours. The explicit support and encouragement of the hospital staff is essential. All concerned need to understand the importance of helping parents feel that they are responsible to a great extent for whatever success may be achieved. Parent involvement in the child's hospital care also allows all concerned (parents and professionals) to be more certain of positive changes in parental competence, child behavior, and parent-child interaction; changes which are vital guides to prognosis after discharge.

Problem Review and Treatment Planning

Information compiled during the hospital care of the malnourished infant—demonstrating weight gain on a regular diet, observing the child's behavior, and assessing the family— usually provides clear evidence of the neglect and inadequate nurturance the child has received. The assessment should reveal the presence of neglect and how it occurred, the problem the parents have in recognizing and understanding their infant's needs for care, the difficulties they have in responding to those needs, and usually how the parents' life experiences and current stresses have led to their present problems in parenting. Sometimes as a result of psychiatric or psychological evaluation of the parents, serious psychiatric pathology or mental handicap has been identified, thereby making successful parenting impossible in the near future.

Once all these data are available, a team meeting of all the professionals involved with the family should be held well before time of discharge to work out a long-term treatment plan for the family (see chap. 18).

Reporting

When a diagnosis of growth failure due to underfeeding or neglect has been made, many state or provincial jurisdictions require a report to be made at once to the protective services division of the county welfare department. The initial telephoned report is followed by a written summary of the facts upon which the diagnosis is made. Usually this includes the absence of physical disease, the weight loss at home, and the large weight gain in the hospital with no special treatment except a regular diet. This report involves the child welfare agency in the treatment program while the child is still in hospital. Such a report, if necessary, should be made as early in the assessment process as feasible, the parents should be fully informed, and the protective service worker should be involved in the course of events. It may be necessary to file a dependency and neglect petition to ask for court supervision and a court-mandated treatment program in some cases.

The Question of Placement

On the basis of the parents' response to the diagnostic work, a decision must be made whether to send the child home or to foster care. If the child is to go home, the parents should:

1. Demonstrate understanding of how the malnutrition occurred;

2. Possess a new understanding of the child's needs for both physical and emotional nurturing;

3. Be willing to receive help via home visits to improve their care of the baby;

4. Show active cooperation with specific plans for regular medical supervision;

5. Express a willingness to make some changes in life-style, if necessary, such as no longer caring for friends' children which gave them no time to care for their own; and

6. Demonstrate the ability to make changes in the way they care for the child.

The child may need to go to a foster home if the parents:

1. Do not visit the hospital except when absolutely necessary;

2. Demonstrate an attitude toward the infant which remains negative, punitive, or indifferent;

3. Show no interest in cooperating in the treatment program or in understanding their part in the child's illness;

4. Are heavily involved in the use of drugs or alcohol and in need of a prolonged, intensive treatment program themselves before they are available to care for the baby;

5. Are suffering from severe psychiatric illness—especially depression or psychosis which makes them unavailable to their child and which requires intensive treatment;

6. Are severely retarded and unable to care for their child adequately; or

7. Have fixed, fanatical ideas which could endanger the well-being of their child, such as cultic diet restrictions.

In some cases the problems found in the parents are of such long-standing severity that there is little hope that they will respond to treatment. If the possibility of eventual termination of parental rights appears early in diagnosis, then the treatment plan should be complete and specific, practical for the parents, court ordered, and well monitored. This helps prevent the prolongation of the placement of the child in foster care for months or years, while sporadic efforts are made to document the ability of the parents to care for their child. The parents in such cases deserve all the help medical and social services can provide; only in this way can a fair judgment be made for termination in a time framework that allows the child some chance to grow and develop normally (41, 42).

Once the decision has been made that the child will go home with the family, the parents must understand the reason for the growth failure and be offered specific help to prevent recurrence. The hospital nutritionist, with a nurse or social worker, may be asked to explain a good diet and to make suggestions for cooking and feeding that will suit the patient's metabolic needs as well as the family's income and culture. Recommendations need to be concrete and specific. It is often wise to ask the mother to repeat them in her own words to be sure she understands.

If a treatment plan to aid the parents in better understanding their infant and to address their own needs has not been initiated in the hospital, this should be arranged by the time of discharge so that the parents go home with the name and telephone number of someone who will be available to help them. The doctor, nurse, and social worker must have a conference with the parents before discharge. To have the different disciplines talking together with them will reinforce for the parents the fact that all parts of the outpatient follow-up are important.

Post-Hospitalization Treatment for Deprivation Malnutrition

A well-coordinated and sustained multidisciplinary treatment program is the best hope for changing the discouraging statistics revealed in current follow-up studies. Early and frequent appointments at the hospital clinic or the physician's private office (preferably with the same physician to provide continuity) are essential. To prevent the frequent recurrence of malnutrition, medical follow-up, should extend at less frequent but regular intervals, should extend through at least the third year of life. Home visits by a visiting nurse or public health nurse are an integral part of the follow-up medical program.

Therapeutic work at home with the family may be monitored and coordinated by the nurse or the protective services caseworker who may be the major source of supportive treatment for the parents. Sometimes treatment can also be provided by a lay health visitor (or lay therapist) or by a developmental specialist who works to improve the parent-child interaction within a supportive therapeutic relationship. Occasionally in more disturbed families psychotherapy or other special treatment modalities are needed (43–46; see also chaps. 17, 19), and reinvolvement of protective services may be necessary.

Treatment Failure

When the family is unable to comply with the treatment program, or when treatment is not available and the child continues to lose weight at home, either readmission to the hospital or foster-care placement is needed. The diagnosis and treatment may need to be reevaluated and perhaps intensified or changed in the light of recent developments. Or individual professionals may need to be found who can assume responsibility for working with the family in the absence of a formal program.

Sometimes children who have been hospitalized earlier for deprivation malnutrition are later found to be seriously, even fatally, abused as well (47). Also, infants can be starved to death with no evidence of any food in their gastrointestinal tract on post-mortem (48). Therefore, every case of growth failure must be taken seriously, the parenting practices well diagnosed, and effective treatment and follow-up arranged. One aspect of the treatment program deserves special mention. If society (as represented by the hospital and protective caseworker) tells the mother initially that the child's growth failure is her fault and that she must take responsibility for better care, and if that society does little or nothing to be sure the mother has enough support for herself in caring for the child, she may become abusive or even more neglectful of the child. The outcome may be disastrous for everyone.

The immaturity, neediness, and feelings of helplessness of the neglectful mother are not transformed into empathic nurturing by one or two lectures. She herself must experience from someone the empathy and nurturing she is expected to give her baby, and she must be able to depend on this support while she learns how to be a more sensitive parent for the infant's benefit.

The Older Child with Growth Failure

Although growth failure is usually described as a problem of infants during the period of rapid growth, children between three and twelve years of age may also be found to suffer from severe growth retardation without physical disease. Some of these children are victims of early growth failure, undiagnosed or inadequately treated. Older children may manifest a syndrome called "psychosocial dwarfism" in which severe emotional problems in the family center on one child (49–51). The child may not necessarily be deprived of food but instead will have a voracious but bizarre appetite, with strange eating and drinking habits, and yet fail to grow, especially in height. There is a severely disturbed relationship between parent (often mother) and child in which food has come to have highly charged pathological meanings for them both. An occasional child between two and three years of age has been examined for growth delays in which this kind of pathological, food-centered relationship seems to be developing. Depression, apparently limited to the home or presence of the mother, plus a narcissistic personality disorder and behavioral disturbances have been noted in the children (50). Psychiatric care and usually foster-home placement are needed for these children and their families. The relationship of deprivation malnutrition and other feeding problems, psychosocial dwarfism, and anorexia nervosa or bulimia has not yet been identified, but each represents a disordered parent-child relationship with the food-related pathology progressively more focused within the child.

Follow-up Studies of Growth Failure

Thus far, studies of children hospitalized for growth failure present a bleak picture of their later progress. Chase and Martin (52) studied nineteen children who had been hospitalized under the age of one year for malnutrition; at a mean time of three and one-half years later, 68 percent were still below the third percentile in height, 53 percent in weight, and 37 percent in head circumference. Developmental scores were also depressed, to as low as 70 when the growth failure was diagnosed after four months of age.

In a retrospective study of forty children hospitalized for nonorganic growth failure by Glaser et al. (53), 42.5 percent were below the third percentile in either height or weight or both. Of the nineteen children in school, seven were experiencing school failure and several children had psychological problems. This study noted that only 20 percent of the families were referred to some kind of social agency for follow-up in addition to the referrals for follow-up medical care.

A study by Elmer et al. (54) described fifteen children at a mean time of almost five years after hospitalization for malnutrition due to deprivation. Of the fifteen, seven children were below the third percentile in both weight and height, and two were below in either weight or height. Over 50 percent of these children showed some degree of retardation intellectually. Of the seven children in school, four had major behavioral disturbances, and six were in special education.

In a study of twenty-one children reviewed a mean of six years after hospitalization, Hufton and Oates (56) found five out of twenty-one children still below the tenth percentile (their original group had a milder degree of growth delay with 50 percent below the tenth percentile). One-half of these children were found to have personality difficulties, and one-half were functioning below average in school. Finally, some children in this group had suffered subsequent physical abuse, with two deaths. Thirteen years after hospital admission, fourteen of these same twenty-one children were again evaluated along with a comparison group of schoolmates. Six of them remained small, with lower height and weight ages. As a group, they were delayed in reading ability, somewhat delayed in language development, and lower in verbal intelligence. They also had lower scores on a test of social maturity, and seven were described as behavior problems on a teacher questionnaire.

Clearly, children who have growth failure due to deprivation require more intensive and prolonged treatment of both parents and child than has been offered in the past. Continued retardation of growth on evaluation years later would indicate that medical follow-up needs to be frequent and sustained, probably for some years after hospitalization. The persistence of psychological difficulties as well implies continued deficits in the home environment and the need for developmentally oriented psychiatric treatment of the parents and child before lifelong patterns of malfunction occur (57, 58).

Summary

Growth failure without other disease is one of the early symptoms of difficulty in parenting which is often associated with other signs of neglect and abuse. Although the cause of the malnutrition is lack of adequate calories, the problem usually occurs in a context of a moderately or severely disturbed parent-child relationship and is not readily cured by simple re-education of the parents about better feeding. The inability of the parents to respond to the child's nutritional needs is often only the most obvious evidence of their inability to recognize many of his other physical, emotional, and developmental needs. This is clearly documented by these children's delays in development and often by their difficulty in relating comfortably to others.

Treatment for the child's nutritional state and for improvement of the environmental deprivation suffered within the home must be prolonged until the child is at least three years of age, because the risk of relapse is high. Treatment of the family to improve all parenting functions is a time-consuming and difficult process. This process should focus on helping the parents become more effective in coping with their own problems and on helping them become more empathic to the needs of their child. Some parents are not capable of caring for the child at first and foster care placement is needed while they are offered help in parenting. Other parents, for reasons of mental illness, mental incapacity, or the degree of specific problems in parenting, are unable to care for their child and termination of parental rights must be sought. Some parents are not only neglectful but also actively physically abusive, and the increased risk to these children's lives must be recognized.

The indication is clear that the parenting difficulties which cause inadequate feeding resulting in growth failure will continue to limit the child's future development unless prolonged and effective treatment of the family is possible. Better treatment strategies are urgently needed for these families as well as preventive measures (59, 60). The recent cutbacks in social support programs and the escalation of medical costs make efficient and creative treatment capabilities even more urgently needed.

References

1. Goldbloom, Richard B. 1982. Failure to Thrive. *Pediatric Clinics of North America* 29(1): 151–66.
2. Chapin, H. D. 1908. A Plan for Dealing with Atrophic Infants and Children. *Archives of Pediatrics* 25:491–96.
3. Spitz, R. A. 1945. Hospitalism. *Psychoanalytic Study of the Child* 1:53–74.
4. Coleman, R. W., and Provence, S. 1957. Environmental Retardation (Hospitalism) in Infants Living in Families. *Pediatrics* 19:285–92.
5. Keys, A., et al. 1950. *The Biology of Human Starvation.* Minneapolis: University of Minnesota Press.
6. Whitten, C. F.; Pettit, M. G.; and Fishoff, J. 1969. Evidence That Growth Failure from Maternal Deprivation Is Secondary to Undereating. *JAMA* 209:1675–82.
7. Prader, A.; Tanner, J. M.; and von Harnack, G. A. 1963. Catch-up Growth Following Illness or Starvation. *J. Pediatrics* 62:649–59.
8. Sills, R. H. 1978. Failure to Thrive: The Role of Clinical and Laboratory Evaluation. *Am. J. Diseases in Children* 132:967–69.
9. Talbot, N. B.; Sobel, F. H.; Burke, B. S.; Lindemann, E.; and Kaufman, S. G. 1947. Dwarfism in Healthy Children: Its Possible Relation to Emotional, Nutritional, and Endocrine Disturbance. *New England J. Med.* 236:783.
10. Cytryn, Leon. 1976. Methodological Issues in Psychiatric Evaluation of Infants. In *Infant Psychiatry: A New Synthesis,* eds. E. N. Rexford, L. W. Sander, and T. Shapiro. New Haven: Yale University Press.
11. Davies, D. P., and Evans, T. I. 1976. Failure to Thrive at the Breast (Letter). *Lancet* 2:1194–95.
12. Pfeifer, D. R., and Ayoub, C. 1978. Non-Organic Failure to Thrive in the Breast-feeding Dyad. *Keeping Abreast: J. Human Nurturing* 3/4:283–86.
13. O'Connor, P. A. 1978. Failure to Thrive with Breast-Feeding. *Clinical Pediatrics* 17:833–35.
14. Himes, J. H.; Roche, A. F.; Thissen, D.; and Moore, W. M. 1985. Parent-Specific Adjustments for Evaluation of Recumbent Length and Stature of Children. *Pediatrics* 75:304–13.
15. McLaren, D. S., and Read, W. C. 1972. Classification of Nutritional Status in Early Childhood. *Lancet* 2:146–48.
16. Rosenn, D. W.; Loeb, L. S.; and Jura, M. B. 1980. Differentiation of Organic from Non-Organic Failure to Thrive. *Pediatrics* 66:689–704.
17. Brazelton, J. B. 1974. *Neonatal Behavioral Assessment Scale.* Clinics in Developmental Medicine, no. 50. Philadelphia: Lippincott.

18. Bayley, Nancy. *Bayley Scales of Infant Development*. 1969. New York: Psychological Corporation.

19. Knobloch, H., and Pasamanick, B. 1974. *Jesell and Armatruda's Developmental Diagnosis—The Evaluation and Management of Normal and Abnormal Neuropsychologic Development in Infancy and Young Children*. New York: Harper and Row.

20. Frankenberg, W. K.; Dodds, J. B.; Foudal, A. W.; Kazuk, E.; and Cohrs, M. 1975. *Denver Developmental Screening Test: Reference Manual*. Denver: University of Colorado Medical Center.

21. Elmer, Elizabeth. 1960. Failure to Thrive: Role of the Mother. *Pediatrics* 25:717.

22. Altemeier, W. A.; O'Connor, S. M.; Sherrod, K. B.; and Vietze, P. M. 1985. Prospective Study of Antecedents for Non-Organic Failure to Thrive. *J. Pediatrics* 106(3): 360–65.

23. Evans, S. L.; Reinhart, J. B.; and Succup, R. A. 1979. Failure to Thrive: A Study of Forty-Five Children and Their Families. *J. Am. Acad. Child Psychiatry* 18:440.

24. Gaines, R.; Sandgrund, A.; Green, A. H.; and Power, E. 1978. Etiological Factors in Child Maltreatment: A Multivariate Study of Abusing, Neglecting, and Normal Mothers. *J. Abnormal Psychology* 87:531–40.

25. Green, A. H. 1976. A Psychodynamic Approach to the Study and Treatment of Child-Abusing Parents. *J. Am. Acad. Child Psychiatry* 15:414–29.

26. Jacobs, R. A., and Kent, J. T. 1977. Psychosocial Profiles of Failure to Thrive Infants: Preliminary Report. *Child Abuse and Neglect: International J.* 1:469–77.

27. Kerr, M. A. D.; Bogues, J. L.; and Kerr, D. S. 1978. Psychosocial Functioning of Mothers of Malnourished Children. *Pediatrics* 62:778–84.

28. Leonard, M. F.; Rhymers, J. P.; and Solnit, A. J. 1966. Failure to Thrive in Infants: A Family Problem. *Am. J. Diseases in Children* 111:600–612.

29. Melnick, B., and Hurley, J. R. 1969. Distinctive Personality Attributes of Child-Abusing Mothers. *J. Consulting Clinical Psychology* 33:746–49.

30. Patton, R. G., and Gardner, L. I. 1962. Influence of Family Environment on Growth: The Syndrome of Maternal Deprivation. *Pediatrics* 30:957–62.

31. Pollitt, E.; Eichler, A. W.; and Chan, G. K. 1975. Psychosocial Development and Behavior of Mothers of Failure to Thrive Children. *Am. J. Orthopsychiatry* 45:4.

32. Spinetta, J. J. 1978. Parental Personality Factors in Child Abuse. *J. Consulting Clinical Psychology* 46:1409–14.

33. Togut, M. R.; Allen, J. E.; and Lelchuk, L. A. 1969. Psychological Exploration of the Non-Organic Failure to Thrive Syndrome. *Developmental Med. Child Neurology* 11:601–7.

34. Fishoff, J.; Whitter, C.; and Pettit, M. A. 1971. Psychiatric Study of Mothers of Infants with Growth Failure Secondary to Maternal Deprivation. *J. Pediatrics* 79:209.

35. Prodgers, Alan. 1984. Psychopathology of the Physically Abusing Parent: A Comparison with the Borderline Syndrome. *Child Abuse and Neglect: International J.* 8(4): 411–24.

36. Egelund, B.; Sroufe, L. A.; and Erickson, M. 1984. The Developmental Consequence of Different Patterns of Maltreatment. *Child Abuse and Neglect: International J.* 8(4): 459–69.

37. Haynes, C.; Cutler, C.; Gray, J.; O'Keefe, K.; and Kempe, R. 1983. Non-Organic

Failure to Thrive: Decision for Placement and Videotaped Evaluations. *Child Abuse and Neglect: International J.* 7:309–19.

38. Haynes, C., et al. 1983. Non-Organic Failure to Thrive: Implications of Placement through Analysis of Videotaped Interactions. *Child Abuse and Neglect: International J.* 7:321–28.

39. Haynes, C., et al. 1984. Hospitalized Cases of Non-Organic Failure to Thrive: The Scope of the Problem and Short-Term Lay Health Visitor Intervention. *Child Abuse and Neglect: International J.* 8:229–42.

40. Green, A. H. 1979. Child-Abusing Fathers. *J. Am. Acad. Child Psychiatry* 18:270–82.

41. Schetky, D.; Augell, R.; Morrison, C.; and Sack, W. 1979. Parents Who Fail: Study of 51 Cases of Termination of Parental Rights. *J. Am. Acad. Child Psychiatry* 18:366.

42. Winick, M.; Meyer, K. K.; and Harris, R. 1975. Malnutrition and Environmental Enrichment by Early Adoption. *Science* 190:1173–75.

43. Barnard, M. U., and Wolfe, L. 1973. Psychosocial Failure to Thrive: Nursing Assessment and Intervention. *Nursing Clinics of North America* 8:557–65.

44. Fraiberg, S., ed. 1980. *Clinical Studies in Infant Mental Health: The First Year of Life.* New York: Basic Books.

45. Kempe, C. H. 1976. Approaches to Preventing Child Abuse: The Health Visitor Concept. *Am. J. Diseases in Children* 130:941–47.

46. Ramey, C. T.; Stann, R. H.; Pallas, J.; Whitten, C. F.; and Reed, V. 1975. Nutrition, Response Contingent Stimulation, and the Maternal Deprivation Syndrome: Results of an Early Intervention Program. *Merrill-Palmer Q.* 21:45–53.

47. Koel, B. S. 1969. Failure to Thrive and Fatal Injury as a Continuum. *Am. J. Diseases in Children* 118:565–67.

48. Adelson, L. 1963. Homicide by Starvation: The Nutritional Variant of the "Battered Child." *JAMA* 186:458–60.

49. Ferholt, J. B.; Rotnem, D. L.; Genel, M.; Leonard, M.; Carey, M.; and Hunter, D. A. 1985. A Psychodynamic Study of Psychosomatic Dwarfism: A Syndrome of Depression Personality Disorder and Impaired Growth. *J. Am. Acad. Child Psychiatry* 24(1): 49–57.

50. Green, W. H.; Campbell, M.; and David, R. 1984. Psychosocial Dwarfism: A Critical Review of the Evidence. *J. Am. Acad. Child Psychiatry* 23(1): 39–48.

51. Silver, H. K., and Finkelstein, M. 1967. Deprivation Dwarfism. *J. Pediatrics* 70:317–24.

52. Chase, H. P., and Martin, H. 1970. Undernutrition and Child Development. *New England J. Med.* 282:491–96.

53. Glaser, H.; Heagarty, M.; Bullard, D. M., Jr.; and Rivchik, E. C. 1968. Physical and Psychological Development of Children with Early Failure to Thrive. *J. Pediatrics* 73:690–98.

54. Elmer, E.; Gregg, G. S.; and Ellison, P. 1969. Late Results of the "Failure to Thrive" Syndrome. *Clinical Pediatrics* 8:584–89.

55. Hufton, I. W., and Oates, R. K. 1977. Nonorganic Failure to Thrive: A Long Term Follow-up. *Pediatrics* 59:73–77.

56. Oates, R. K.; Peacock, A.; and Forrest, D. 1985. Long Term Effects of Non-Organic Failure to Thrive. *Pediatrics* 75(1): 36–40.

57. Galler, J. R.; Ramsey, F.; Solimano, G.; Lowell, W. E.; and Mason, E. 1983. The Importance of Early Malnutrition on Subsequent Behavioral Development. II. Classroom Behavior. *J. Am. Acad. Child Psychiatry* 22(1): 16–22.

58. Stoch, M. B.; Smyth, P. M.; Moodie, A. D.; and Bradshaw, D. 1982. Psychosocial Outcome and Ct. Findings after Gross Undernourishment during Infancy: A 20-Year Developmental Study. *Developmental Medicine and Child Neurology* 24:419–36.

59. Kennedy, E. T., et al. 1984. The Effect of WIC Supplemental Feeding on Birth Weight: A Case-Control Analysis. *Am. J. Clinical Nutrition* 40:579–85.

60. Evans, D., et al. 1980. Intellectual Development and Nutrition. *J. Pediatrics* 97:358–63.

Intervention and Treatment

From the first call that is placed to protective services to the completion of a long-term therapeutic program, families involved in child abuse and neglect require considerable care and attention. Many very difficult decisions must be made and carried out. No one group or discipline can carry the load alone; it clearly is too heaven a burden. All of the professionals and agencies involved in a community's efforts to deal with the problem of abuse must be tied together in some type of coordinated consortium. Collectively, there is some hope for success; individually, the struggle goes on.

The authors in Part III discuss each component of the community fight against abuse, from crisis intervention to long-term therapy and the consequences of abuse on the child if our efforts fail. These consequences are not pleasant. Our efforts must not fail.

17 Treating the Abusive Family within the Family Care System

David P. H. Jones and Helen Alexander

In this chapter, treatment of the family unit will be considered from a developmental point of view. The child development field considers the child from the perspective of physical, psychosocial, emotional, and intellectual growth. In the application of the developmental framework to the family, emphasis is placed on the psychosocial and emotional development of the family as a unit. The growth of an individual child or adult within the family, the evolution of marital or parent-child relationships, and the progression of the family as a whole are all aspects of the family's overall development. This chapter incorporates all of these facets of family life and growth. The developmental orientation provides a continuing and evolving appreciation of just how a family arrives at a point where a child is being neglected or abused. Although an understanding of the family's present status is of great importance, that alone is not enough. The present has to be placed in the context of the biography of the family's development. Once the developmental level of each of the family members as well as the family as a whole is understood, then the treatment may be approached accordingly. The family's history may also be considered in a developmental context (1). What stage has been reached? Has this family separated from their family of origin? The developmental perspective can also provide a conceptual framework for the stages a family must negotiate while changing their caregiving practices.

Treatment includes all attempts to modify the family unit's way of operating, whether those attempts derive from specialized professionals, from self-help support groups such as Parents Anonymous, as well as the management of the system itself. The family to be treated consists of those individuals who care for and interact with the child. Treatment may be aimed at an isolated single parent family, or at a large extended family network which provides care for the child. On other occasions, the treatment may be directed toward a natural family in parallel with a foster family.

David P. H. Jones, MRC Psych. DCH, is with the Park Hospital for Children, Oxford, England.
Helen Alexander, M.S.W., is a clinical social worker in Modesto, California.

Child Abuse and Family Treatment

The increasing concern about the sexual abuse of children has had a positive influence upon treatment practices by forcing a more family-oriented approach. Most experts agree that child abuse in general, and sexual abuse in particular, implies family dysfunction (2). Clearly, however, much more than family dysfunction is involved in the etiology of child abuse. Finkelhor (3) has provided a useful framework for considering the variety of etiological influences which may culminate in the sexual abuse of a child. However, treatment will mean family treatment at some level, and this has led to a more systematic approach to family therapy. As society's recognition of child sexual abuse has increased, there has been a parallel growth in the family therapy movement.

The three main approaches within the field of family therapy are: that which is developed from a group analytic and object relations base; that which is rooted in a conceptualization of the family as a system; and that which is derived from an existential or experiential understanding of the behavior of the family. In practice most therapists bridge these theoretical gaps.

Furniss and colleagues (4) have discussed the use of family therapy in the treatment of child sexual abuse cases. They have developed the concepts of "depth" and "surface" structures in a family. The depth structure is derived from the family of origin (e.g., grandparents, uncles, aunts, while the surface structure comes from *this* specific nuclear family's life time. Both may be imbued with myths (5) or shared defenses which the family uses to protect its integrity in the face of perceived threats from outsiders. Perlmutter et al. (6) have described the loosened taboos against incest which exist in some remarried families. Furniss (7) has provided a systems-based analysis of how the attitudes, views, feelings, and behavior of the professionals involved in a case can often mirror the dynamics of the sexually abusing family. An understanding of this mutually reflective process can be used to educate those involved in case management. The Great Ormond Street team in London brings all the professionals involved in a case together with the family in one meeting in order to address this important difficulty (8). So often professionals merely recapitulate the views of family members unless a degree of objectivity is obtained.

Interactions and Patterns Observed in Abusive Families

What distinguishes abusive families from other families? Controlled studies of family interaction have been conducted, primarily in physically abusive and neglectful situations (9), that reveal important differences between abusive and nonabusive families. Abusive families are less verbal. When words are used, they are more likely to be negative commands: "Stop that." "Get down." "Shut up, you little . . ." (10). Abusive mothers show less maternal warmth and supportiveness when interacting with their children and they are more hesitant in initiating play than nonabusive mothers (11). Abusive mothers look at their children less often and rarely respond to the cues given by their children (12). Abusive mothers also have been observed ignoring their infants more often and teaching them less than nonabusing mothers. Infants comply less well with abusive parents' attempts to direct their play (13). Abusive and neglectful parents neither touch their children nor provide supportive comments as often as normal parents do (10). Neglectful and physically abusive mothers report a greater use of physical punishment (14); they also punish by withholding things from the child and do not often try to reason with their child (15). Abusive parents were less likely to understand the psychological complexity of their infant and showed less positive behaviors while feeding the child than did nonabusive parents (16). Further studies of abusive families have shown that by the time child abuse is discovered, the children exhibit aversive, negative behaviors and appear to adopt a negative emotional stance in relation to both their parents and other adults (17).

These findings, derived from research of the interactions in abusive families, are introduced into the clinical assessment and form the basis for a treatment plan which is then tailored to the individual family. The process of assessment should extend into the treatment phase to allow the treatment plan to change in response to newly available data.

Several authors have described the elements and constellations of dysfunction seen in the intrafamilial sexually abusing family (18–22). The original description of father-daughter incest in closed, superficially functional families does not adequately address all the situations of intrafamilial sexual abuse. The following "threads of dysfunction" have been clinically observed as the common elements in otherwise diverse family constellations (18): emotional unavailability, merging, intrusions, intergenerational abuse, indiscriminate sexuality, lack of privacy, family boundary alterations, parent-child role change, hierarchy alterations, marital dysfunction, and the presence of maladaptive family viewpoints or myths.

Emotional unavailability in one or both parents, a history of early attachment problems, and a diminished empathy expressed for the child were commonly seen together. Availability may be judged from history and direct observation of qualities such as the emotional tone of the family, the abilities to encourage independence, to allow the expression of emotion, and to show respect and regard, and the encouragement of empathy and understanding toward others. A merging between family members was observed, that is, personal boundaries, in either a literal physical sense or a psychological sense, were not respected. Individuals within the family do not see themselves as distinct, separate people, rather they express their feelings as if they were identical to those of all the other family members. Lack of individual boundaries may be accompanied by frequent intrusive statements, speaking for the other person or saying what other people are "really" feeling.

Intergenerational patterns of sexual abuse were discovered repeatedly and often emerged through use of the family geneology. Indiscriminate sexuality by adults and adolescents within a family was observed to correspond with a relative lack of privacy in the family's living situation. The family's external boundary, its relationship with the outside world, may be closed and encased in secrecy, as in the classical father-daughter incest pattern, or it may be loose and unrestricted with little or no control, as in the so-called multiproblem or chaotic family. The usual parent-child relationship is out of kilter; the normal boundary between parents and children is disturbed. This is illustrated by a mother-daughter role reversal or the absence of consistent parent role models. A disturbance in the family's hierarchy may also be seen, either with the father desperately clinging to a patriarchial, overly controlling stance, or with him being so uninvolved that he is stripped of authority and relatively ineffective. In other families, a particular child or a grandparent may hold the position of control. There is often disturbance in the marital relationship, either sexually or emotionally. However, this may not be immediately apparent because the disclosure of intrafamilial sexual abuse makes the crisis of parenting the overriding focus of concern. Throughout this whole dysfunctional pattern, the family may have weaved unusual myths or collectively shared viewpoints that have acted as a defense against change for a long time. Summit and Kryso (22) describe a range of patterns seen in child sexual abuse that involves varying degrees and combinations of these "threads of dysfunction."

Similar observations have been noted in both neglecting (23) and physically abusive families. To date there has not been a broad application of these observations and assessments to treatment, although Fraiberg (24) and Provence (25) provide some notable exceptions.

Family Aspects of Treatment Planning

The foundation for all treatment planning is a clear assessment of the family unit as well as the individuals. Early decisions will have a lasting impact on the remainder of the treatment and the ultimate outcome. Initially, of course, the protection of the child is the primary concern. However, this is not as straightforward as it may seem. For example, in the case of sexual abuse, although the identity of the perpetrator is usually revealed at the time of the child's disclosure, early decisions about visitation with relatives may prove problematic. Adequate protective steps may appear easy to take, but the noninvolved parent may be seriously shaken by the disclosure, seek to alter the child's story, and thereby return the family back to the way it used to be.

> One five-year-old child was removed to foster care following the disclosure of sexual abuse which had been perpetrated by the mother's live-in boyfriend. However, supervised visits with the natural mother continued. During one such visit, the child was taken to the bathroom by her mother for five minutes, and the child emerged saying, "John [her cousin] did it."

In addition, many sexually abused children are told that if they tell, they will be taken away to a foster home and will never see their family again. The children may also feel the need to protect their parents by recanting their original accounts (26). Therefore, the early assessment of the family has to gauge the contribution of these and similar factors when making seemingly straightforward decisions, such as allowing the children to visit their parents.

Following the initial assessment phase and the development of a safety management plan, the assessment process expands to design effective treatment. The treatment plan will include individuals as well as the family unit. Family therapists working in this area emphasize the need for parallel, individual treatment for the child (6). A case has been made for an explicitly "child's-eye view" when assessing and treating a family for abuse in order to understand and appreciate the child's predicament and the pressures bearing upon him in such a situation (18,27). A conversation that the late Professor Henry Kempe had with one of his child patients illustrates this point. When the boy announced that he was involved in family therapy, the following exchange took place:

DR. KEMPE: What is family therapy?
BOY: That's when all the adults get together and gang up on the kids.

The assessment of the adults will provide critical information about any past history of violence and aggressive outbursts, alcoholism, substance abuse, sexual problems, or psychiatric problems. History of early attachment and bonding needs to be obtained from both mother and father in relation to each of their children. Useful questions are: "Is there anything different about this child?" "In what way would you like to bring up your own children differently from the way you yourself were brought up?" The assessment will also provide information concerning the children and their present status psychologically, developmentally, and physically. The assessment of the whole family can be accomplished by learning both the history of the family and by observing the quality of their interaction—its level and style of functioning. In remarried families the role of the noncustodial parent needs to be considered.

It is not always possible to conduct a complete family assessment at an early stage either because the adults may not be able to contain their anger or rage toward the child, or because the child is simply too terrified of any contact with the perpetrator or noninvolved spouse. In these circumstances, as many family members as feasible should be gathered for evaluation. Further whole family assessment can wait for a more appropriate time.

A Composite Approach to Treatment

The concept of family treatment presented in this chapter is deliberately broad, including family psychotherapy, family case management, and management of the wider group of helping individuals. The main theoretical base is derived from object relations theory and attachment theory, with an emphasis upon maintaining a historical perspective while trying to understand a particular family. In addition, a systems approach has been useful in understanding both the family's structure and the family's relationship with the wider social system. The approach presented here, while substantially influenced by work with sexually abusive families, can be applied to abuse and neglect cases of all forms. Where differences in treatment approach are dictated by the distinctions between kinds of abuse, special mention will be made.

Phases of the Treatment Process

The treatment process is a three-stage developmental sequence: First, acknowledgment of the abuse; second, increasing parental sensitivity and emotional availability to the child; and third, resolution. While these are typical treatment phases, the actual treatment will be unique for each individual family.

The child's-eye view. The value of developing and maintaining a "child's-eye view" during all stages of treatment must be emphasized (18). This does not simply mean to adopt the position of a child advocate, rather it means consciously to develop a view of family life from the perspective of a child. A therapist needs to "walk in the child's shoes," to think about what it must have been like to grow up in this family; what it is like to live there day-by-day; what it is like to go to sleep each night and wake up each morning as a member of this particular family. This process can be very helpful to adult-oriented therapists (many family therapists do not have extensive child therapy training). Unfortunately, in child sexual abuse cases therapy is often divided between several therapists. Those who provide treatment for the adults may be unaware of the child's needs. For example, an adult therapist may state that "the patient has made substantial progress and will benefit from more contact with the child now." Adopting a child's-eye view will raise the question of whether more contact now will benefit the *child*. Keeping the child's needs in mind provides a basis for safe and logical treatment planning.

Acknowledgment of the Abuse

There are four aspects of the abuse that must be acknowledged: the abuse itself, its impact upon the child, the family's inability to provide adequate protection for the child, and the degree and extent of parental unavailability.

Is it possible to treat a family that denies the abuse? Most therapists do not think so. Some families never get beyond this initial stage and proceed, despite the best professional efforts, to relinquish their child (see the third phase of treatment below). However, it is sometimes possible to start treatment by helping the abuser acknowledge certain aspects of the abuse, for example, its impact on the child. Sometimes, after the abuser feels safer with those providing treatment, he or she will be able to face the reality of the abuse. However, this is usually unsuccessful, and the denial of the perpetrator may be unwittingly bolstered by this process. Therefore, in most cases, acknowledgment must consist of admission by the perpetrator, acceptance that the abuse occurred by the non-involved spouse and siblings, and acknowledgment of the memory of victimization by the child. Adequate time must be set aside for acknowledgment to be achieved because it forms the basis for the remainder of the treatment.

Placement decisions arise early in the first phase of treatment. Less extended out-of-home placements should be sought, if at all possible. Sometimes perpetrators will move out of the home instead of requiring their children to do so. This solution depends on the attitude and perspective of the noninvolved parent for its success. Programs which encourage early acknowledgment can often return children quickly to the home. However, some programs do not require the depth of acknowledgment outlined below. Not all the elements outlined need to be accomplished in every case before recommending return of the child. Much depends on the age and emotional strength of the child, the perspective and status of the noninvolved spouse, as well as other family dynamics. However, full acknowledgment is a prerequisite to the second phase of family treatment, that of increasing parental sensitivity and availability to the child. While the process of acknowledgment is being negotiated, the child needs considerable support. This may come from a non-abusive family member, individual therapy, or from group meetings such as Daughters and Sons United (28).

There is extreme pressure within the incestuous family to return to the old ways of interacting, often combined with denial by the perpetrator. Because of this and the complexity of the problems to be addressed in therapy, it is essential that the authority of the court be behind the treatment process (28,29). A study from Florida by Wolfe et al. (30) shows that the outcome for a group of families who were court ordered to undergo therapy was better than the outcome for those who volunteered to accept treatment. The court authority must have the protection and best interests of the child as its first priority if it exercises control over therapy and placement decisions. The question of whether the criminal prosecution of the perpetrator helps or hinders the overall family treatment is a complex one, and the answer depends largely upon how flexibly the court's authority and sentences can be applied (31).

During the first phase of treatment, problems may arise within the intervention system. Furniss (7) has drawn attention to the way the intervention process may reflect the dynamics and interaction patterns of the family being treated. Different professionals may sabotage the process in the same way that the noninvolved spouse may attempt to undermine the therapy, for example, by pressuring her daughter to recant her story. The professional may convince the perpetrator of abuse that too much is being made out of the situation. Or by colluding with the noninvolved spouse, a professional may suggest that the child is disturbed and unreliable, independent of any logically based doubt about the veracity of the child's statement. The system may simply "gaze avert" (32) from the severity and violence involved in the abusive situation, thereby thwarting the family therapist's attempts to achieve an adequate acknowledgment. Furniss (7) has emphasized how various therapists may adopt these positions in concert with the family's attempts to split into pairs, excluding the third person.

> One five-year-old girl had been sexually abused by her mother's boyfriend. He saw a therapist who said, "The child is sexually precocious, untruthful, and even if it had happened, it wasn't serious." The mother's therapist initially aligned with the boyfriend's and declared that "children have rich imaginations." The situation remained unchanged for months until the child's therapist could enable the mother's therapist to see the child's predicament. The mother-daughter relationship then became a focus of therapy and improved; however, the boyfriend and his therapist cemented their collusion, and no progress was made in that area of the child's life.

Why do therapists adopt such stances? Child abuse cases in general, and sexual abuse cases in particular, evoke strong emotions in professionals as well as in the general public. The treatment of such families is difficult and bears its toll on the providers. This effect is accentuated whenever a case resonates with experiences from the therapist's personal history. This can lead to the therapist denying the true seriousness of the situation.

The four aspects of the acknowledgement phase will now be examined.

The Abusive Incident. Acknowledgment of abuse is a process rather than a one-time cathartic admission. The aim is not to have one or the other parent dramatically confess and then to proceed with the remainder of their treatment. Rather what is needed is a more gradual unfolding of the various elements involved in the abuse. Indeed, it is not unusual for the adult to make a hasty acknowledgment and then ask, "Well, now, when do I get my kids back?" Therapy in this latter case should be aimed at expanding the abuser's awareness of the acts of commission and omission he or she needs to take responsibility for in relation to the child.

> One father, in his first session with his daughter, said, "Remember when we were in bed together, I touched your pee . . . hurt you . . . shouldn't have . . . all my fault. It is not right for daddies and little girls to touch like that, daddy wants to get better and never do that again." The daughter, in her individual therapy and when with her foster parents, said, "He said it was an accident and was sorry, but he hurt me, and he was awake . . . it happened lots of times. I shouldn't have let him."

This example illustrates the capacity of even a five-year-old child to appreciate at some level that the acknowledgment made by her father was insufficient. She perceived that he was describing an "accident." It also illustrates how subtly pressure can be applied to a young child by a parent figure. The father implied there was mutual consent when he sexually abused his daughter ("not right for daddies and little girls to touch like that"), serving to throw guilt onto the small child. She guiltily expressed the feeling that she "shouldn't have let him."

While under pressure to acknowledge the abuse, the family may well split into pairs or dyads and exclude other members. The family does this to defend itself against the overwhelming anxiety induced by the child's disclosure of the abuse. For example, the father and mother may become closer than they have been for many years and blame the child for being "seductive" or "bad." The child is perceived by the marital pair as bad for seducing the father, for telling lies and malicious "stories," or for being a "disturbed" child. On the other hand, mother and child may collude and align themselves against the father, despite the fact that they may have significant differences or deep conflicts. In this case, the father is seen as the source of all the family's ills.

This initial aspect of acknowledgment, namely admitting to the abuse itself, may be encouraged by various techniques. In selected cases, video or audio tape of the child's statement or of direct quotes made by the child may be used to facilitate the acknowledgement by playing it to the parents. The early interview with the child is most important to this process because it provides the most accurate description of what has occurred. Caution needs to be exercised in exposing the child to further pressure or risk when using his statement. The parents' therapists will need to have the child's early statement in their possession as they attempt to help the parents deal with acknowledgment.

The face-to-face admission may be rehearsed by the perpetrator, the noninvolved parent, and the child before the joint family sessions. This rehearsal can be a useful therapeutic tool in their individual therapy. Then they will be more comfortable when they bring their admissions to a family session. Often the first family appointment arranged for this purpose will be with a selected dyad: mother and daughter, or father and daughter. If this goes well, then the whole family can be involved in further sessions. The siblings are often left out of this initial process, yet they do need to be seen by the family therapist, and joint family sessions need to be arranged so that mini-alliances (collusions) rooted in secrecy do not develop anew. The family's task will be to develop an appropriate explanation for the events that is understandable to all family members. This does not mean that younger siblings must know all the specific details if they had no prior knowledge of them, but they do need to know what has happened. It is more likely that they will know much more than the therapist expects them to know, and that they have played an integral part in the cloud of secrecy pervading the family. The therapist can then model and facilitate the communication of clear messages and explanations during sessions with the whole family.

The criticism may arise, "Well, this is all staged. It doesn't stem from the heart. The players in the family merely go through their acts of openness to please the therapist, and later on they will revert to their old ways." Quite true! What can be done to insure that this does not occur? Therapists must be vigilant. The prime tool for preventing such deception is knowing that it can happen anytime throughout treatment. The family may be seductive, metaphorically as well as literally. Therapists become unwittingly engulfed in the deviant dynamic processes of the families they are treating. They then accept a superficial admission at face value and begin to advocate for family members prematurely. They may claim that the adults have changed and may advocate, both with other therapists and within the court system, that the children be returned home because they will now be quite safe. If the therapist can, at this point, adopt a child's-eye view and maintain a historical understanding of the family's evolution, then objectivity can be retained. A systems analysis can also help the therapist notice the homeostatic pressure within the family which pushes toward a return to the old pattern of functioning. This pattern is seen by the family as more comfortable and less anxiety provoking, even if it means the exploitation of one of its members. Similarly, the pressure to minimize the abuse may be substantial, for example: "He was only educating her." "I only did it one time." "She came on to me." "We wanted to be closer." A systems analysis also helps therapists to see that they do become connected to the family, and that they, too, may be drawn by the promise of an easy therapeutic process, a "quick fix" to a complicated process. The anxiety experienced by the family is infectious, and the fear of change may cause therapists to acquiesce and join the apparently easy route of minimization or, in extreme cases, total denial that the abuse occurred.

From the child's point of view, the experience of being sexually abused has several interrelated components (33). Besides the assault itself, the degree of violence employed by the perpetrator both to obtain the child's cooperation and to prevent him or her from telling anyone has to be considered. This may be the most problematic aspect of the experience for the child and the part which the other family members are the most loathe to acknowledge. In incest cases, threats of bodily harm or even death to the child should he or she disclose the abuse is not uncommon.

> One five-year could not tell the interviewer any further details about how her father had sexually abused her except that he had touched her "down here." The interviewer paused, reflected that she seemed very scared, and asked if anyone had "said anything scary to you." She replied, "He said he'd kill me if I tell."

The violence may not always be so overt. It may consist of the misuse of the authority and power bestowed upon parents and caregivers in our social structure. The abuser employs these privileges to obtain the cooperation and subsequent silence of the victim. The therapist gains knowledge about this, not from the perpetrator, but from the victim. Then the therapist works toward helping the abuser and the noninvolved parent to acknowledge both to each other and to the child that this violence has occurred. Interestingly, many parents find this process harder than the acknowledgment of the "sexual" aspect of the abuse. It is essential that the violent aspect of the abuse be adequately addressed because this misuse of power and control is not only critical to the development of the sexual abuse in the first place, it also represents an insidious pattern of interpersonal interaction which may lead to a recurrence of the sexual abuse after treatment.

The child may need vindication of his experience by confronting the perpetrator, especially if the abuser is still consistently denying the abuse. The child can be prepared and accompanied by the therapist to a session where the child tells the abuser his or her perspective of what happened. This may be hard, and few, if any, words may be uttered by the child, but the experience of the attempt plus the support of a trusted adult can be therapeutic in themselves.

Another aspect of the abusive incident, besides the trauma itself and the violence involved, is the degree to which the perpetrator was sexually aroused by the victim. There is a debate about whether there is a difference between perpetrators of incest and pedophiles (34). Do incest perpetrators have a deviant sexual arousal pattern toward the prepubescent child? Previously accepted notions that men who sexually abuse children outside the family are motivated by different forces than those who abuse within the family can no longer be considered accurate. There is, at the very least, a considerable gray area between these two extreme positions. Many incest perpetrators have also sexually abused children outside their immediate family, and many pedophiles have abused their own children. Incest perpetrators often have the same deviant views (or cognitive distortions) as pedophiles have. For example:

> One incest perpetrator explained the reason he had sodomized his son by saying, "Well, he came on to me." Another incestuous father, when trying to explain why he sexually abused his daughter, said, "I could tell she was turned on by me."

The plethysmograph responses of incest perpetrators to visual and auditory images of children may be similar to those of pedophiles in some studies (35), but other studies have thrown doubt on this latter finding (36). All that can be said, therefore, is that deviant sexual arousal may well be present in the incest perpetrator. It is unlikely that this will be voluntarily disclosed to the interviewer, even if the perpetrator recognizes it to be a problem. Consequently, therapists should be on the lookout for evidences of such arousal and address it in therapy.

> One incestuous father who had sexually abused both of his sons was observed, while waiting for an appointment, looking at other children in the therapy center with great interest. It was also noteworthy that he was still involved in boy scouting, yet he had apparently completed a "treatment program" for perpetrators. He was eventually able to discuss the fact that he thought he had fooled his therapists (with the exception of his family therapist, who, incidentally, was also treating one of his children!).

The treatment for deviant sexual arousal may include group therapy, behavioral and cognitive therapy techniques, in addition to other methods (34). In general, the child protection services or sexual assault centers do not have an adequate working liaison with those professionals managing sexual offenders. The latter group of professionals are oriented to the confrontation that is necessary in the treatment of deviant sexual arousal, and they are aware of techniques that can be used to improve the social skills of adults who perpetrate such acts. Their expertise needs to be part of the treatment of incestuous families in many instances.

In the area of physical abuse, the justifications given by parents may need to be confronted and overcome. For example, abusers may consider harsh physical punishment to be "good for kids" because that was how they were disciplined when they were children. Such justifications often represent an attempt to minimize serious inflicted injury and should not be accepted at face value.

The Impact upon the Child. The second aspect of the acknowledgment process is the impact of the abuse upon the child. The process of helping family members appreciate and then acknowledge this part of the abuse can be initiated by helping them see the behavioral consequences to the child. Sometimes these consequences are not overt, and it may be difficult for the family to grasp the reality of the ill effects from their activity. Of course, if overt neurotic or antisocial behaviors exist, then this recognition and acknowledgment process is easier. Some children show symptoms of anxiety with specific fears or phobias for people or places; others have increased general anxiety with attention problems, sleep disturbances. Other children may become withdrawn and depressed. Still others display antisocial tendencies such as lying, stealing, and fighting. Reports from third parties, such as the child's school, can be helpful in establishing a more objective view of the child's behavior than may be obtained from the family itself. The child's sexuality may have been stirred and abnormally coached by being seduced by adults. Any precocious sexual acting out behavior must be seen as a consequence of deviant parenting and not dismissed as a justification for sexual abuse. Other subtle consequences may involved the child's feeling helpless and neither in control nor responsible for anything that happens. On the other hand, the child may feel guilty and responsible for his or her parents and for everything that has happened.

Naturally such subtle effects will be difficult for the family to appreciate and understand. This process often takes a long time in individual and group psychotherapy with the adults (both abuser and noninvolved parent) in order to lead them to a sufficient understanding of the impact of the abuse for them to be able to attempt acknowledgment of what they have done to their children. At the same time, the process of helping children understand what has occurred is complex because they have frequently suffered many years of abuse which significantly distorts their view of life. For example, they may feel the need to protect their parents in contrast to being protected by them. Abused children often take on an enormous burden of responsibility for the health and welfare of the adults who are supposed to be caring for them, and may also think that something is terribly wrong with them because of being continually parented by adults who misuse and maltreat them.

The impact of sexual abuse upon a child must be placed in a developmental perspective. It is not sufficient to merely appreciate the pattern of family interaction that currently exists. The family's biography has to be placed in its proper historical context. How is this done? A useful approach is to spend time in several sessions working on the family's geneology either with the whole family or with specific dyads. During this process, details of the histories of parent-child attachments from conception to the present time can be obtained. Emphasis should be placed on the areas of child development that do not constantly remind other family members about the abuse and are thus less threatening to address. Gradually, the adult family members will come to realize some of the impact upon their maltreatment has had on their child. The geneology is also a useful method to help the family appreciate the degree of neglect and emotional unavailability that has existed in the family (see below).

The Absence of Adequate Protection. The extent to which family members have not adequately provided protection for each other is an important aspect of the acknowledgment process. The whole family unit has failed to protect one of its child members, and thus the whole family needs to understand how this came about. The process should not be a search for one family member to blame but rather a search for the understanding of how the family's structure has precluded protective steps from being taken. For example, some families are so chaotic and without controls that no one exercises care and protection for anyone. In other cases, the patriarchal family structure strips the mother and children of the ability to protest or have an adequate voice in how the family functions. A historical perspective of how such a state of affairs developed at all is necessary.

The absence of protection is often the most pertinent area of acknowledgment for the nonabusive parent. Traditional views of father-daughter incest contain the maxim that the mother colluded and tacitly encouraged the sexual contact between father and daughter. Various explanations have been put forward to explain this process, including a defense against the acknowledgment of the poverty of the relationship between the father and mother, and a defense against the mother's acknowledgment of her poor relationship with her daughter. However, these stereotypes do not accurately describe all the situations observed. There are certainly situations in which the noninvolved spouse genuinely does not know about the abuse, while there are others where they had faint suspicions but did not put them together into a coherent suspicion that the child was being abused until after the disclosure itself. There can be arguments made about whether they should have picked up on these cues sooner, but nevertheless a spectrum exists between those noninvolved parents who have no knowledge prior to the disclosure and those who actually collude and encourage the incestuous contacts.

Lack of protection is also a prominent issue in those families where neglect is the prime problem, and in the families where one parent has physically abused a child and the other has not protected the child from repeated assault.

Lack of protection by the noninvolved parent becomes even more complicated when the parent who was thought to be noninvolved turns out to have been a party to the abuse. This happens more often than has previously been acknowledged in the area of sexual abuse. For example, the disclosure is made by the child concerning the father's abuse, but there may be a period of several months before the child can acknowledge that he was abused by his mother also. In these kinds of cases, it is important to remember that the slowness of obtaining an acknowledgment from the noninvolved parents of their lack of protection may be because they have also perpetrated the maltreatment. This is even more significant in the area of physical abuse because it is often the case that both the mother and father physically abuse the child (37).

Acknowledgment of Neglect and Emotional Unavailability. The family geneology and a detailed attachment history for each child helps the family appreciate the extent to which the parents have been emotionally unavailable to their children. In many families the perpetrator of abuse may well be the one who appears more available to meet the victim's emotional needs, leaving the noninvolved caregiver in a relatively remote position as far as the child is concerned. Many professionals expect to encounter just the opposite situation. The process of uncovering and the subsequent acknowledgment by the parents of the extent of their unavailability may well extend into the next phase of treatment, serving as a foundation on which to develop the parents' sensitivity and availability toward their children.

Neglect may be evident in the quality of the home environment as well as in reports from the school or day-care center which the child attends. Neglect may be the tangible evidence of parental disinterest in the child, but the two do not always coincide. For example, it is possible to have significant emotional unavailability without overt signs of physical neglect of the children.

Emotional abuse, consisting of an absence of love, care, and affection, may be evidenced by affective coldness between specific pairs or permeating the whole family. This abuse may be displayed by carping criticism and verbal abuse directed at one member. Family evaluation sessions during the early phases of treatment will help to clarify this aspect of family life. Emotional abuse is more subtle than overt sexual exploitation or physical abuse, but its existence can be just as important. In follow-up studies of abused children, it has been noted that while the amount of physical maltreatment declines after intervention, emotional abuse continues (37). That is to say, the family life continues to provide only negative verbal interaction and even downright scapegoating of the abused child even though the physical abuse has ceased. In the case of sexual abuse, it is rare to come across a family who has exploited one or more of its children without there being significant emotional unavailability or neglect and verbal abuse. When the development of the family is traced historically, these more subtle forms of maltreatment often appear to precede the sexual exploitation of the child. This observation is supported by the findings of those who have closely observed maltreating or potentially maltreating mother-infant pairs (38).

When abuse has been perpetrated on a child by someone from outside the family, then the emphasis in family therapy is on an examination of the last three elements outlined above. In such cases questions that arise are: Was this family neglectful? Was there relative parental emotional unavailability which allowed the child to become a victim of sexual abuse from outside the family? Not all children who are abused by a nonfamily member come from neglectful families, and in the past this has been emphasized (39). However, a neglected child is a perfect target for a nonfamily member to select, and during treatment it is important to discover the relative degree to which neglect and unavailability are at issue.

A child's disclosure sometimes leads to the discovery of multiple incestuous relationships between family members both now and extending back over previous generations. Such families present special problems of acknowledgment. However, through the use of the telephone, letters, and direct sessions, the process can be facilitated and has been shown to be of benefit to some victims (40).

Developing Sensitivity and Empathy

The aim of this second stage of treatment is to increase the parents' sensitivity and emotional responsiveness to their children and to improve the degree to which they can meet their children's emotional needs. In order to undertake this phase of therapy, an adequate base of acknowledgment must have been accomplished as this must underlie any sensitivity to the child's needs and position. Further areas requiring acknowledgment may well arise during this second phase as treatment is an evolving process.

The Child's Issues. The most likely starting point for this phase grows out of the parents acknowledgment of the impact of the abuse on the child. Aspects of the impact can be used to help the parents move to a fuller appreciation and understanding of both what the child has experienced and is now experiencing. Anger is one area that can be used to explore aspects of the child's experience that may otherwise go unnoticed or even be avoided by the parents. The child's anger may be directed at the perpetrator or may be more subtly derived from feelings of being used or from the lack of protection and support from the nonabusive adults in the family. Providing a safe and supportive setting for the child to express anger as well as allowing the parents to express to the child their increased understanding of the impact of the abuse on him or her can be a very reinforcing experience for all.

The individuals involved can work through their feelings and reactions in individual therapy sessions before meeting the other family members in a group session. The family session may include all family members or a selected pair. Its aim is to allow the expression of feelings without precipitating a rapid retreat toward the previous dysfunctional style of interaction.

The "threads of dysfunction" discussed earlier are commonly problematic for abusive and neglectful families and may interfere with healthy interaction at this stage. Secrecy, particularly that occurring in sexually abusive families, is a powerful one. The family's continued pull toward old patterns may need to be challenged.

> One couple was being seen in joint marital sessions. The children, who had been sexually abused by their father, had recently returned from foster care. It emerged during a family session that the father had acquiesced to the ten-year-old boy's request for Vaseline as a masturbatory aid. The mother was unaware of this. The therapist concentrated on the secrecy of this news and supported the mother's indignation that she had not been involved in the decision. (The boy's sexual issues were dealt with at a separate, individual session.)

In this example, the momentum was geared to return to the old ways of operating, but the mother's determination enabled this family to change. The stress on the family system when pushed to change may be intolerable, and one or more family members may simply run away from therapy during this phase (19) or remove themselves from the treatment entirely (41). For other families, the stress produced by a more open style of interaction may be too much. A resolution that results in the absence of one or more family members is not uncommon. However, such an outcome should be understood by the other family members as the avoidance it represents. The therapist should not permit the victim to take responsibility when other family members decide to extricate themselves from the whole situation.

> One teenage sex abuse victim found it exceptionally hard to accept that her abusive stepfather's leaving the family was *his* choice and not a result of her "badness" for disclosing the abuse. Her mother's equivocation on the matter further fueled the girl's remorse and guilt. Therapy concentrated on understanding the stepfather's actions, and was paralleled by efforts to improve the mother/daughter relationship.

The burden of responsibility that the child victim bears, either through direct blame or from his or her own assumption of fault, is an area that must be explored and will often require intervention by the therapist.

Following the disclosure of sexual abuse, the child may feel a profound sense of loss. The origin of this feeling may be obvious, for example, he or she may miss the parental home and dislike being separated from a loved, nonabusive parent or sibling, or he or she may miss the emotional warmth that the perpetrator provided (even though abusive), or he or she may miss being with neighborhood and school friends. A more subtle sense of loss may originate from the child's realization that the parent does not meet his or her expectations. Exploration of these feelings in sessions with the parents can be rewarding.

When the child's fear of recurrent abuse is understood by the parents it can lead to their increasing awareness of the child as a separate person with his or her own perceptions and concerns. Expression of these and similar feelings by the child is easily ignored because they are painful. The family therapist can be helped by frequent feedback from the individual therapists involved as to those emotions which are being covered or blocked by individual family members.

The extent to which the victim has participated in the exploitation itself is a difficult subject, yet it is necessary to broach because the child rarely spontaneously discusses it. Guilt may derive from this participation compounded by the secrecy the victim may have maintained for a long period of time. Guilt may also originate from the child's perception that he or she has displaced the other parent in the marital relationship. These issues need to be handled with particular sensitivity by the family therapist as the perpetrator may use them to justify his or her actions if full prior acknowledgment of responsibility has not occurred. The child's prior vulnerability and subsequent participation must be understood by both family and therapist in order to move through this issue successfully.

The Adults' Issues. Inevitably the question of how the parents were parented arises. The exploration of the parents' early experiences is the natural outcome of a developmental approach to the family's history. It can also encourage the parents' appreciation of their children's needs and increase their sensitivity to their children's feelings. The capacity to see the effect of their actions on their children may be most poignantly understood if they explore their own memories and feelings about how they were parented. By analogy, the impact of their own abusive behavior on their children may become emotionally real to them.

> While describing the overwhelming pain and loss experienced in her childhood when she was "given away" to a strange family, one young mother clearly realized the anguish her own daughter was experiencing in her current placement outside the family. Following this very real understanding, she was able to allow her daughter to express her sad feelings openly.

Some adults may consciously or unconsciously use their own prior victimization as a means of excusing their abusive behavior. Traditionally the approach in treating physical abuse has been to explore the adults' own victimization and deprivation before proceeding to deal with how this has affected their present capacity to parent. Those working with sexual offenders have found that dealing with prior victimization too early appears to give the adults an escape route, preventing them from taking full responsibility for their current actions. To avoid this, emphasis can be shifted by the family therapist to the question of how their prior abuse has impacted their lives as adults. The effect of the parents' unavailability or neglect on their children can be examined similarly. This double acknowledgment of being abused and of abusing can be a very painful process, but identifying the results of such a history of abuse and understanding the impact this may have already had upon their children's development is even more difficult.

Many parents negotiate this process by concentrating on actively meeting their children's current needs, rather than focusing on what they could not provide earlier. The family members may well review the results of their unavailability or neglect during the resolution phase of the therapy process after they have achieved more positive interactions during this phase.

Many incest families are described as "enmeshed" or "merged." Such words suggest an amorphous mass that is bound together and prevents the family members from being separate individuals. Lack of privacy, both physical and emotional, as well as intrusiveness are aspects of this enmeshment. There may be no doors on bedrooms or bathrooms, or family members may constantly interrupt and speak for one another, or feelings and viewpoints are expressed as though all family members are in agreement. Nonverbal behaviors can also be observed which indicate this lack of separateness:

> During a family session, a mother was observed twisting the hair of her fifteen-year-old son whom both she and her husband had sexually abused. When the family was confronted with their behavior, the mother defended herself by saying, "It's like I'm twisting my own hair. There's really no difference."

This particular family had enthusiastically adopted the 1960s maxim that "we are all one." Active intervention by the therapist is often required in sessions with such families to allow for individual expression of differences of perception. Individual family members may also be given individualized tasks, such as listing problem areas or concerns, as a way of underlining the differences between members. Enabling the family to experience safety in individuation can be a very slow process, but success in this area eventually brings great relief to the family.

The distinction between parents and children is often unclear in incestuous families. Children may have evolved prematurely into adult roles, and adults may have relished the "freedom" of a childlike absence of adult responsibilities.

The marital relationship is also distorted and is frequently lacking in intimacy while the abuse is going on. Joint marital sessions are usually part of the treatment plan and can proceed in parallel to other therapies. A behavioral approach to any sexual dysfunction that may exist between the adults is usually the treatment of choice. Support groups for couples have also proved to be an effective means of focusing on and improving marital difficulties. Dealing with the marital relationship is a prerequisite for developing healthy parent-child roles.

The views or beliefs that the adults and children hold should be understood and clarified. One variety of belief is the collective "family myth" which can impede the family's progress. An example of one such myth is:

> Incest is bad because, if you have sex together, the welfare takes the kids away.

This view enables the family to avoid any recognition of the ill effects of sexual abuse on the children and to divert attention away from any sense of moral transgression. Furthermore, such a myth effectively projects the blame for family upset on the system, in this case the social services department. It is, therefore, a highly effective defense against the more anxiety-provoking reality. The therapist must stay alert to such viewpoints and use different means to alter them.

> In the above case, individual family members were asked to make as long a list as possible of what might be wrong with sexual abuse. They were not told the therapist's opinions on this. The process occupied several sessions. Eventually, the moral dimension that "children cannot effectively consent to being sexually abused" emerged. Additionally, the impact of childhood victimization on the father's capacity to trust and love other people was held to be another disadvantage of incest.

Maladaptive views and myths may be held by individuals too. Offender therapists have called these "cognitive distortions." They can be challenged in group therapy very effectively. They may also be altered during family therapy. For this to happen, however, the family therapist must be finely tuned to these distortions and prevent the abuser or others from presenting these views authoritatively without being challenged. Active techniques must be used to enlist the support of the less vocal family members.

A mother confidently stated that her husband would protect her son from the paternal grand-father's sexual advances. Noting the boy's discomfort, the therapist asked the boy if he could say why he looked so sad. He surprised his mother by telling her that he was not at all confident that his father would protect him. (In parallel individual therapy, the boy explored his feeling of loss that this lack of protection created in him.)

Children often hold distorted views and opinions particularly relating to their sense of responsibility and guilt for involvement in the abuse. These views need to be fully explored and worked through in individual therapy before they can be brought into the open during family sessions because the adults frequently use their children's cognitive distortions to justify their own behavior.

Placement and visitation issues arise during this stage, and the therapist's recommendations can be based on how the family has dealt with these and similar issues. Again, putting oneself in the child's shoes by adopting a child's-eye view can aid the therapist in assessing safety and progress.

There may be considerable pressure from other professionals to hasten this stage of treatment. For example, the therapist for a parent may be impressed by the progress his or her client has made in individual treatment and state that it will help the parent if the child is placed back in the home. A child's-eye view can avoid a poor or hasty decision at this stage.

One young mother, who was able to talk in individual treatment about her concern and appreciation for her daughter's distress at having been sexually abused by her stepfather, seemed ready to share her awareness with her daughter directly. During the family session, while stating that she realized how "frightening and upsetting" the sexual abuse had been, she was unable to respond to the current fears and nightmares her daughter was having while visiting her mother in the home. The mother still could not respond to the immediate reality and concerns of the child.

Resolution

The last stage in the treatment process is that of resolution. It is not the end, but rather the start of more adaptive family functioning. The treatment process takes about two years on average, which is a reasonable period of time if one considers that abuse and exploitation are the very antitheses of good or adequate parenting. Such a serious situation is unlikely to be amenable to a rapid solution. In general, there are two options during this phase: the child may be reunited with the family, or the child may leave the abusive parental home.

Reuniting the Family. Some type of reunification occurs in approximately two-thirds of sexually abusing families. Some programs report higher proportions and some lower. In many cases, the child is reunited with the nonabusive parent who divorces or terminates the relationship with the perpetrator. In other cases, the family is reunited including the perpetrator of abuse. This phase does not involve the withdrawal of therapy services, in fact, family therapy will probably need to be intensified during this stage. The child must also continue to attend group and/or individual therapy during this stage, so that if things do go wrong, there is some possibility that he or she will tell someone.

This may be a difficult stage for the foster family, as they now have to relinquish the child to whom they may have become very attached. They may have harbored hostile feelings toward the natural family, especially toward their exploitation of the child. If not involved in the reunion process, they can be extremely disruptive and unwittingly create further pressure on the child by increasing his or her sense of divided loyalty. The child's behavior may show deterioration because he or she is now placed between the foster and natural families, and partly because the postive and negative feelings toward natural parents are unleashed again. The family therapist must be prepared to work with both the natural and foster families during this phase to avoid any divisiveness which may further impede the child's progress.

Relinquishment. Relinquishment may occur in several ways. The treatment plan for the child may not be successfully completed. This may happen because the perpetrator continues to deny the abuse (approximately half maintain this position in some programs), and at the same time, the noninvolved parent be completely aligned with the perpetrator. Thus the first stage of the treatment process has not begun, and the basis for termination of parental rights proceedings is essentially the failure to comply with a treatment plan. Sometimes this pairing up of perpetrator and nonabusive parent can be avoided (see acknowledgment section above), but if it cannot be avoided, then the child cannot wait forever for the parents to become supportive, and alternative placement plans must be made. The choices are a voluntary relinquishment or a court-ordered termination of parental rights. In either case, the child may be placed with a relative or in an adoptive home. Another alternative is for the adolescent to go out on his own and effectively solve the problem independently.

Relinquishment may be viewed as a failure by the therapist, but success should be measured by the safety and best interests of the child rather than by the question of family reunification. The aim of therapy should be to reunite the family, but only if the child's safety can be assured. The outcome is frequently an imperfect one, and the therapist has to accept this and the uncertainty involved when treating these families. Difficulty can be encountered in knowing when to stop treatment. Has the family in question progressed as far as they are going to? It is not possible to place a rigid time frame on this process because it depends on the child's age and developmental status as well as other family factors. However, if a reasonable period of time has gone by and important adults are not participating in the treatment plan, then the probability of relinquishment needs to be discussed with the family. The involvement of the therapist in the court process can be extremely helpful during this phase became the therapist is likely to need outside authority to underline the best interests of the child.

The Difficult or Untreatable Family

Some families do not respond to treatment. The Kempes (42) found that physically abusing families with the following characteristics were commonly among that 10 percent who turned out to be untreatable: sadistic parents, some mentally handicapped parents, psychotic and borderline parents and alcohol and substance abusers who do not respond to treatment, violent and aggressive psychopaths, and those families where there had been prior violent deaths due to child abuse. The frequency of recurrent physical abuse is sobering. Gibbens et al. (43) report a low rate of recidivism among sexual abusers, as does Kroth (44) in his evaluation of Giarretto's program. However, it must be recognized that children will probably be reluctant to disclose sexual abuse a second time even when re-abuse does occur. For cases of sexual abuse, we must rely on children's reports and not on examinations of injuries to the child. It is of interest in this respect that one unexpected finding in Kroth's study was that the number of parents who state that they will report if sex abuse occurs again in their family *declines* from intake to a smaller percentage at the end of the treatment program. If one adds to these facts the reluctance of many treating professionals to acknowledge that they may not have been able to change individuals or a family system to the extent that they would have preferred, then one has to conclude that professionals are unlikely to hear about recurring incest. With this in mind, clinicians have found that those groups with the following characteristics tend to be the most difficult to change in the area of child sexual abuse: sadistic individuals, those who use violent force to coerce and silence their victims, recidivist sex offenders, those situations which involved both parents actively or where multiple victims were involved, those cases where the child had been exploited for a long period of time, situations where the perpetrator continues to deny the abuse and remains in contact with the child, and those families with parallel physical abuse or severe neglect. This does not mean that families with these characteristics are always untreatable, but they present more difficulties and are more commonly represented in those cases where the child is finally placed outside the family.

An approach to the treatment of abusive families has been presented in this chapter. Many questions remain to be answered, but the most logical therapeutic approach seems to be one that initially recognizes the severity of disturbance in sexually abusing families and then applies a wide range of treatment approaches in an empirical fashion. Maintaining a theoretical perspective that actively takes into consideration how the family in question has evolved to the point where its children are being abused is advocated here. If this historical context is minimized, then the severity of the situation would be easy to ignore. It is only with this historical perspective that the nature of the task facing the family, to be worked through in therapy, can be appreciated fully.

References

1. Solomon, M. A. 1973. A Developmental Conceptual Premise for Family Therapy. *Family Process* 12:179–96.
2. Rosenfeld, A. A. 1977. Sexual Misuse and the Family. *Victimology* 2:226–35.
3. Finkelhor, D. 1984. Four Preconditions of Sexual Abuse. In *Child Sexual Abuse: New Theory and Research,* ed. D. Finkelhor, pp. 53–68. New York: Free Press.
4. Furniss, T.; Bingley-Miller, L.; and Bentovim, A. 1984. Therapeutic Approach to Sexual Abuse. *Archives of Disease in Childhood* 59:865–70.
5. Byng-Hall, J. 1973. Family Myths Used As a Defence in Conjoint Family Therapy. *British J. Medical Psychology* 46:239–50.
6. Perlmutter, L. H.; Engel, T.; and Sager, C. J. 1982. The Incest Taboo: Loosened Sexual Boundaries in Remarried Families. *J. Sex and Marital Therapy* 8:83–96.
7. Furniss, T. 1983. Mutual Influence and Interlocking Professional-Family Process in the Treatment of Child Sexual Abuse and Incest. *Child Abuse and Neglect International J.* 7:207–23.

 8. Furniss, T. 1984. Organizing a Therapeutic Approach to Intra-Familial Child Sexual Abuse. *J. Adolescence* 7:309–17.
 9. Wolfe, D. A. 1985. Child Abusive Parents: An Empirical Review and Analysis. *Psychological Bull.* 97:462–82.
10. Burgess, R. L., and Conger, R. 1978. Family Interactions in Abusive, Neglectful and Normal Families. *Child Development* 49:1163–73.
11. Walker, L. M. 1978. Patterns of Affective Communication in Abusive and Non-Abusive Mothers. *Dissertation Abstracts International* 38B:5049–50.
12. Fontana, V. J., and Robison, E. 1984. Observing Child Abuse. *Pediatrics* 105: 655–60.
13. Wasserman, G. A.; Green, A. H.; and Allen, R. 1983. Going Beyond Abuse: Maladaptive Patterns of Interaction in Abusing Mother-Infant Pairs. *J. Am. Acad. Child Psychiatry* 22:245–52.
14. Loveland, R. J. 1977. Distinctive Personality and Discipline Characteristics of Child-Neglecting Mothers. *Dissertation Abstracts International* 33B:368.
15. Disbrow, M. A.; Doerr, H.; and Caulfield, C. 1982. Measures to Predict Child Abuse. Paper cited in Friedrich, W. N., and Wheeler, K. K. 1982. The Abusing Parent Revisited: A Decade of Psychological Research. *J. Nervous and Mental Diseases* 170:577–87.
16. Egeland, B., and Brunquell, D. 1979. An At-Risk Approach to the Study of Child Abuse: Some Preliminary Findings. *J. Am. Acad. Child Psychiatry* 18:219–35.
17. Reid, J. B.; Taplin, P. S.; and Lorber, R. 1981. Social Interactional Approach to the Treatment of Abusive Families. In *Violent Behaviors: Social Learning Approaches to Prediction Management and Treatment,* ed. R. B. Stuart. New York: Brunner Mazel.
18. Alexander, H., and Jones, D. P. H. 1984. Family Evaluation in Child Sexual Abuse. Paper given at the Thirteenth Annual Child Abuse and Neglect Symposium, Keystone, Colorado, May 28–31.
19. Furniss, T. 1983. Family Process in the Treatment of Intrafamilial Child Sexual Abuse. *J. Family Therapy* 5:263–78.
20. Nakashima, I. I., and Zakus, G. E. 1977. Incest: Review and Clinical Experience. *Pediatrics* 60:696–701.
21. Sgroi, S. M. 1982. Family Treatment. In *Handbook of Clinical Intervention in Child Sexual Abuse,* ed. S. M. Sgroi, pp. 241–67. Lexington, Mass.: D. C. Heath.
22. Summit, R. C., and Kryso, J. 1978. Sexual Abuse of Children: A Clinical Spectrum. *Am. J. Orthopsychiatry* 48:237–51.
23. Haynes, C. F.; Cutler, C.; Gray, J. D.; and Kempe, R. S. 1984. Hospitalized Cases of Non-Organic Failure to Thrive: The Scope of the Problem and Short Term Lay Health Visitor Intervention. *Child Abuse and Neglect: International J.* 8:229–42.
24. Fraiberg, S., ed. 1980. *Clinical Studies in Infant Mental Health.* New York: Basic Books.
25. Provence, S., ed. 1983. *Infants and Parents, Clinical Case Reports.* New York: International Universities Press, Inc.
26. Summit, R. C. 1983. The Child Sexual Abuse Accommodation Syndrome. *Child Abuse and Neglect: International J.* 7:177–93.
27. Jones, D. P. H., and McQuiston, M. 1985. The Predicament of the Child Sex Abuse Victim. In *Interviewing the Sexually Abused Child.* ed. D P. H. Jones and M. Mc-

Quiston. Denver: University of Colorado School of Medicine, Kempe Center Publications, Series no. 6.

28. Giarretto, H. 1976. Humanistic Treatment of Father-Daughter Incest. In *Child Abuse and Neglect: The Family and the Community,* eds. C. H. Kempe and R. E. Helfer. Cambridge, Mass.: Ballinger.

29. Ounsted, C.; Oppenheimer, R.; and Lindsay, J. 1974. Aspects of Bonding Failure: The Psychopathology and Psychotherapeutic Treatment of Families of Battered Children. *Developmental Medicine and Child Neurology* 16:447–56.

30. Wolfe, D. A.; Aragona, J.; Kaufman, K.; and Sandler, J. 1980. The Importance of Adjudication in the Treatment of Child Abusers: Some Preliminary Findings. *Child Abuse and Neglect: International J.* 4:127–35.

31. Will, D. 1983. Approaching the Incestuous and Sexually Abusive Family. *J. Adolescence* 6:229–46.

32. Ounsted, C. 1975. Gaze Aversion and Child Abuse. *World Medicine* 10:27.

33. Jones, D. P. H. 1985. Individual Psychotherapy for the Sexually Abused Child. Paper presented at the Fourteenth Annual Child Abuse and Neglect Symposium, Keystone, Colorado, May 28–31.

34. Quinsey, V. In press. Men Who Have Sex with Children. In *Law and Mental Health: International Perspectives,* vol. 2, ed. D. Weisstrab. New York: Pergamon.

35. Abel, G. G.; Becker, J. V.; Murphy, W. D.; and Flanagan, B. 1981. Identifying Dangerous Child Molestors. In *Violent Behaviors: Social Learning Approaches to Prediction Management and Treatment,* ed. R. B. Stuart. New York: Brunner Mazel.

36. Quinsey, F. L.; Chaplin, T. C.; and Carrigan, W. F. 1979. Sexual Preferences among Incestuous and Non-Incestuous Child Molestors. *Behavior Therapy* 10:562–65.

37. Lynch, M. A., and Roberts, J. 1982. *Consequences of Child Abuse.* London: Academic Press.

38. Haynes, C. 1985. Linking the Past, Present and Future: Observation of Parent-Child Interaction in Failure to Thrive. Paper presented at the Fourteenth Annual Child Abuse and Neglect Symposium, Keystone, Colorado, May 28–31.

39. Van Scoyck, S.; Gray, J. G.; and Jones, D. P. H. Treatment for the Victims of Child Sexual Assault Committed by a Non-Family Member. Kempe Center, Denver. Unpublished.

40. MacFarlane, K., and Korbin, J. 1983. Confronting the Incest Secret Long After the Fact: A Family Study of Multiple Victimization with Strategies for Intervention. *Child Abuse and Neglect: International J.* 7:225–37.

41. Eist, H. I., and Mandel, A. V. 1968. Family Treatment of Ongoing Incest Behavior. *Family Process* 7:216–32.

42. Kempe, R. S., and Kempe, C. H. 1978. The Untreatable Family. In *Child Abuse,* ed. R. S. Kempe and C. H. Kempe. London: Fontana, Open Books.

43. Gibbens, T. C. N.; Soothill, K. L.; and Way, C. K. 1978. Sibling and Parent-Child Incest Offenders. *British J. Criminology* 18:40–52.

44. Kroth, J. A. 1979. Family Therapy Impact on Intrafamilial Child Sexual Abuse. *Child Abuse and Neglect: International J.* 3:297–302.

18 A Developmental Approach to the Treatment of the Abused Child

Ruth S. Kempe

The classic work of Steele and Pollock (1) emphasized the intergenerational patterns of child abuse and neglect. Subsequent work by many others have confirmed these observations and verified their hypotheses about why such repetition occurs. Recent work in observation of parent-child interactions during infancy and early childhood (2) has demonstrated how significant for the child's development abusive or neglectful parenting may be; studies of young abused and neglected children amply confirm their difficulties and the remarkable similarity between pathology in the parent and pathological development in the child. Often the abusive parent has indeed seemed to be the abused child, "grown up" but relatively unchanged.

The Developmental Effects of Abuse

Any description of the effects of emotional, physical, or sexual abuse and neglect on children must emphasize the extensive deviations in personality development as well as the physical damage which can result. The forms such deviations will take and their severity varies with the age and developmental level already attained when abuse or neglect begins, and with the intermittent or continuous nature of the abuse as well as its specific form. The presence of other more positive influences in the home can prevent or help counteract some of the damage to the young child.

Neglect and abuse may begin before birth with the mother who neglects her health, or who takes drugs or alcohol regularly in such quantities as to interfere with interuterine development, resulting in the fetal alcohol syndrome (3,4), or cause symptoms of addiction at birth (5). Treatment of the addicted, pregnant mother is also treatment of her unborn child.

When severe physical abuse occurs during infancy, there often is significant risk of permanent injury to the immature central nervous system leading to mental retardation, cere-

Ruth S. Kempe, M.D., is associate professor in the Department of Psychiatry, University of Colorado Health and Science Center.

bral palsy, or blindness. Severe neglect of nutrition may result in retardation and developmental delays (see chaps. 15, 16), as well as growth failure. Neglect of medical care, in addition to poor nutrition, may mean the child has frequent illnesses which are not treated, is not immunized and therefore vulnerable to preventable diseases, and sometimes may succumb to a disease which would not have been fatal were medical care provided. Common examples of the result of medical neglect are anemia due to inadequate diet and deafness due to frequent, untreated otitis media. Several forms of abuse or neglect may occur at the same time. Malnutrition and medical neglect often accompany physical abuse. Emotional abuse is almost always an accompaniment of other maltreatment and neglect.

Even when there are no permanent physical sequelae to the body from abuse or neglect, the children still suffer significant developmental damage when there are early and sustained difficulties in parenting characterized by lack of attachment, unavailability of the parents, verbal abuse, sexual exploitation, and neglect of the child's need for attention and social response. Such abuse may result in an inconsistent primary symbiotic relationship for the infant, deterring progress through the developmental steps leading to object constancy, self-object differentiation, and establishment of a clear personal identity. For many of these children these steps are never well achieved and throughout life some remain handicapped by severe difficulties in developing relationships. For others, the inconsistent and half-hearted nurturing they receive permits only partial resolution of these developmental steps. They may retain a lack of trust in others, a poor sense of identity, and unmet dependency needs throughout life.

Any attempt to adjust to an inconsistent parent who is sometimes loving and nurturing and at other times hostile, violent, or unresponsive makes it nigh impossible to internalize an image of a parental figure who is nurturing and also sets reasonable limits. The dichotomy is too great, and the young child tends to distort the image as either all good or all bad, finally generalizing this to other relationships. If an adult meets the child's dependency needs for a time, that adult is all "good," yet at the first disappointment that same adult becomes all "bad." Such parental inconsistency is very common in abusive and neglectful parents who respond to their own internal needs rather than to the needs of the child. These parents often provide appropriate nurturance only when such behavior coincides with their own wishes. As the child grows, splitting relationships into all good and all bad can lead to the rapid formation of over-dependent relationships which invite rapid rejection.

In early infancy, the neglectful parent is often insensitive to the internal state of the infant and does not recognize the signals of need for feeding, for soothing touch and cuddling, for protection and restful sleep, or for social interchange and stimulation. An infant may be perceived alternately as a mechanical doll to be fed and changed when convenient or as a demanding, precocious tyrant, scheming how to get his own way at the parents' expense. This makes it very difficult for mother and baby to arrive at a reciprocal adjustment between the baby's comfort and the parent's enjoyment of her caretaking. When these difficulties result in physical abuse of the baby, fear of such impulses on the part of the parent, or feeding and growth problems, the child is placed in jeopardy physically and developmentally.

Sexual exploitation has various effects on the developing child, depending upon the child's age and the nature of the abuse (see chap. 14). The more profound effects occur if the sexual abuser is a parent. This parallels other forms of abuse. A child who is physically or sexually abused by someone outside his or her own family does not suffer a threat to primary relationships and is more apt to be protected and vindicated by the family, *once the abuse is known*. Effects of extrafamilial abuse may still be profound, particularly when it continues for a long period and is condoned by the social system; for example, the arbitrary and sudden movement of vulnerable children from one placement to another depending on the convenience of foster caretakers, or the parent who continues to return the child to an abusive day-care center.

While abuse and neglect have short-term effects which are visible physically, the long-term developmental effects, which may not be apparent until adolescence or adulthood, are often worse. The following are particularly significant examples:

limited ability of the victim to relate to others;
social isolation with superficial, yet dependent, and unstable relationships;
poor self-esteem;
fear of failure and unwillingness to try which all add up to problems which can lead to failure;
developmental delays and difficulties in cognitive learning; and
limited ability to cope with the ordinary problem solving needed for daily living.

The identification with parental violence as a life-style may lead to social "misfits," who are hostile and unable to get along with anyone, or to delinquency and sometimes violent criminal activity. The studies of delinquency by Dorothy Otrow Lewis and her associates (6) have shown in one small sample that abuse and violence within the family had occurred in 88 percent of the delinquents who committed murder (as opposed to 58 percent in "ordinary" delinquents). Children often do not learn how to resist maltreatment and develop a "victim" attitude which makes them prone to mistreatment as adults. Generational repetition of abuse and neglect is evidence of the long-term effects of maltreatment on many children who grow up to be abusing parents in spite of their wish to treat their own children differently. (Other developmental deficits resulting from these abnormal rearing patterns are discussed in chapter 4.)

The Context of Treatment

One of the remarkable characteristics of very young children is their great sensitivity to environmental influences which affect their development. While this is the reason children demonstrate so clearly the effects of abuse and neglect, it also makes them very responsive to treatment efforts. In contrast to this comparative adaptability of children, adults who have suffered serious neglect and abuse as children may be very resistant to treatment efforts that do not begin until their later years. They may lack motivation to participate in treatment, often because their lack of trust in authority figures is extensive. They are cautious of anyone who wishes to be of help. Even when they do participate in treatment, their lifelong problems may make tolerating the anxiety of introspection too great and the time needed to resolve them too extensive.

Recognizing the child's potential for more rapid progress in a favorable therapeutic environment and the parent's relative slowness to respond makes the temptation strong to use treatment modes which bypass the parents or accept their shortcomings as inevitable. Foster care may seem the easy answer. While the child's development may improve rapidly, the relationship with the parents often becomes more and more tenuous. This creates problems of another dimension.

Often therapists are left with the choice of foster care or the necessity of helping children learn to live in the difficult environment which meets few of their needs, gradually recognizing that they must depend on themselves and others outside the family for nurturance and guidance. Whether the child's needs and those of the family can be sufficiently met in treatment while maintaining an intact family is a major question to be answered during the assessment and treatment plan evaluation.

In this chapter emphasis will be given to specific treatment of the individual child. The child's treatment, whether at home or in foster care, must occur with simultaneous treatment of the rest of the family, foster or natural, in the context of the child's other needs at home, in day care, in school, and with peer groups.

The choice of treatment modalities will vary with the age, the developmental level, and the nature of the symptoms of a given child. The choice is often limited by the local availability of treatment programs and of appropriately trained and experienced therapists as well as by the financial resources of the family or agency. Designing a treatment plan on the basis of the child's total needs is infinitely better than fitting the child's therapeutic plan into a convenient slot of the most readily available program. The common occurrence of a child being placed in foster care, often for appropriate safety reasons, with no other therapeutic help is one reason why so many abused or neglected children continue to show their primary symptoms, and why return to their families, who will not change without direct intervention, is either impossible or unsuccessful. The recognition that parents tend to repeat with their children the abusive experiences they suffered as children led to the supposition that "re-parenting" the parents, primarily with the use of lay therapy and supportive casework, would transform them into adequate parents. While the parents may respond with improved self-esteem and less overt abuse, their underlying difficulty in empathically recognizing the child's needs tends to remain unchanged. The children also continue the behavior patterns which they learned earlier. While the child may no longer be physically battered or deprived of food, often the same verbal abuse and underlying neglect of other needs continues which originally caused so many of the symptoms. There is a block between the "re-parenting" of the parent and the application of new skills in interacting with the child. The parent is still not transformed into an effective parent because his or her own childlike needs are recognized.

There are some indications that when parents have the ability to recognize and get "in touch" affectively with their own early experiences of abuse or neglect as children, they are better able to deal with the resultant anger and sadness which had been so long repressed, and thus to recognize the effect of such experiences upon their children. Reaching for such a point in therapy is time-consuming, even with very skilled therapists. For many disturbed and abusive parents this is not possible. The work described by Selma Fraiberg, which uses the infant as a focus through which the parents get in touch with their own previously inaccessible experiences, requires very intensive, skilled therapy (7). Without such therapy, the parents' own past difficulties are often inaccessible, particularly those of the early, preverbal period which are not retrievable through memory and verbal description. Only the derivative affect related to those past experiences is apt to surface when triggered by certain situations, such as being rejected when depending on another person. Using the response to the current situation as a bridge to early experience can sometimes be helpful in treatment.

In all age groups, one of the most urgent problems to be solved in offering therapy to abused or neglected children is the approval and participation of their parents (8). Even when treatment is court ordered for both parent and child, it may be difficult to get the parents involved. Parents tend to find many ways to avoid participation unless they become convinced that treatment will be useful to them. At times the use of a lay therapist in the home or a parents' group may be an important intermediary step by which parents develop enough trust to participate. In treatment, parents may become involved in discussing their own problems and resent focusing on the problems of their children. If they do not receive what they desire for themselves during therapy, they may well sabotage the therapy of the child by preventing attendance, forbidding communication in the therapy hours, or criticizing and increasing the child's mistrust of treatment. Treatment of the child may be seen as a criticism of themselves as parents, or as a threat of the loss of the child's love. Any change in the child's behavior, which in the past has met the parents' needs, is often resisted. Treatment of the child, therefore, is limited in its effectiveness by the parents' negative attitudes. Therefore, not only the child's readiness for treatment, but also the parents' willingness to allow the child's treatment must be considered. Subsequent involvement of the parents with the treatment will change if they are able to make individual progress in accepting the child as an individual with his or her own needs.

Family therapy can help solve some of these problems, but it is seldom used in the treatment of physical abuse and neglect, perhaps because the key to making it truly successful eludes many therapists. With most children, family sessions provide a very valuable diagnostic view of how the members of the family function and may be of considerable help in treatment planning. With very young children who cannot participate well on a verbal level, family treatment is best modified by the use of games or action modes of interaction (9).

Some obstacles in family treatment are: the competition between parent and child for the attention and approval of the therapist; the difficulty for the child in defending himself against the criticism of the parents; and the problem for the therapist in encouraging the child to present his or her view without the parents seeing this as a betrayal of them. Increased experience in the use of family therapy for physically abusive families may find solutions to these problems (see chap. 17).

Behavior modification, one way in which the family group might function therapeutically for a time, may be very useful when the child's behavior is difficult for himself and his parents. However, behavior modification by itself is not sufficient when relationship problems and poor parental motivation do not allow the child's or parents' emotional needs to receive the same attention their behavior does.

Individual psychotherapy has traditionally been offered by the child or adult psychiatrist, but the psychologist or psychiatric social worker may also function as a therapist. Psychotherapy involves regular (usually weekly) individual meetings of the patient with the therapist to help that individual better understand his or her own feelings and behavior, to help the patient modify his or her outlook and behavior in order to achieve relief of anxiety or other disabling symptoms, and to help the patient achieve improved coping ability. Much of the therapeutic work takes place through the development of mutual understanding in the relationship between the empathic therapist and the patient. Communication is usually verbal, but with children play is often used in addition to talking to help the child communicate and express feelings. When the terms *therapy* and *play therapy* are used, they usually describe treatment based on the model of psychotherapy and varying chiefly (if at all) in the intensity of the relationship and in the professional sophistication of the therapist.

A combination of group and individual therapy plus behavioral modification is most effective for abused and neglected children and their parents. In general, the peer groups may work better if children near the same age developmentally are chosen who are dealing with similar problems.

Treatment of the Abused or Neglected Infant

In chapter 7, the process of assessment and the risk factors used in decision making are described and the great risk of maintaining a very young infant at home after serious abuse or neglect is discussed. Comprehensive evaluation of the relationship between parent and child should result in a description of both the specific parenting problems which may be amenable to treatment and the quality of attachment on the part of the parent. The quality of the interaction, particularly with respect to good or bad attachment (see chap. 23), seems to be a helpful prognosticator of treatment success between parent and child in families of very young abused or neglected children (10).

The Use of Foster Care in Treatment

If the child had been temporarily removed for reasons of safety, yet the prognosis for treatment of the parents seems favorable and their relationship with their child is found to be basically sound, strenuous efforts should be made to maintain frequent visiting to promote the attachment between parents and child. Separation of parents and child by foster home placement is detrimental to the attachment process at any age, including the first six months of life. While the infant may well respond positively to the more skilled alternate caregiver and the infant's developmental parameters be improved, the relationship between parents and child often suffers. Parents become increasingly uncertain about their parental abilities and commitment as separation persists, and infants become attuned to a set of expectations of parental behavior which the parents are not able to provide. Attachment to the new caretaker is often made. Some of these results can be avoided by specially training foster parents to be an arm of therapy, understanding and helping the parents, making them welcome in the foster home, modeling child care, and encouraging attachment between parents and child. The "Enriched Foster Care" program demands foster parents who are mature, nurturing people. They should be paid more than the usual minimal foster care salaries, and they should be provided with a source of professional training, consultation, and support (11). Even though a child is in foster care, treatment for the parents and child should always be part of the treatment plan.

Presumably when an infant is placed in foster care, the environmental benefits lacking in the biological home will be available in the foster home and the child will be well nurtured. Just as the child who has been inadequately fed gains weight rapidly ("catch-up growth") when provided with sufficient nurturing and calories, the child who has been given no attention or social stimulation in his own home will respond rapidly to the opportunities to interact positively with the more responsive foster care environment. The degree to which the infant's behavior changes is related to the ability of the foster home to provide the sensitive attention the child needs.

Considerable importance must be placed upon recognizing what the children have missed at home, what capacities they are ready to explore, and what behaviors they may have developed as a response to previous parenting to provide guidelines for their foster care and therapy. A five-month-old child who has been kept in her crib all day without toys or companionship of any kind needs to make up for lost social opportunities before going on. The physiological needs for food and sleep and the psychological needs for soothing, holding, and rocking must be met simultaneously. The opportunity to develop a reciprocal social interaction with a single parenting figure is mandatory. Such interaction can capitalize on the infant's readiness to engage in eye contact and smiling and cooing behavior. In the process of this affective exchange the infant learns how to take turns, an important part of social reciprocity. As this process becomes established, the infant is encouraged, by the caretaker, to begin to use motor skills by moving about on the floor, or reaching for and beginning to manipulate toys. The foster parents' regular use of speech in all their activities encourages babbling. The caretakers' encouragement of the childrens' efforts and the recognition that they have purposes in mind, help these children to strive for mastery over their own bodies and physical environment and permit them to begin to feel successful. Most foster parents will need guidance in recognizing how to facilitate these developmental steps.

The Infant at Home

Keeping the abused or neglected infant in his or her own home requires monitoring by a social service worker or a visiting nurse, plus regular medical assessments to ensure that there is no further evidence of abuse or neglect and that satisfactory developmental progress occurs. During home visits the social worker or nurse should not focus on the cleanliness of the house or on the children but rather on building a trusting relationship with the parents and showing interest in their concerns. The child's well-being and progress will become an integral part of these visits. The parents are treated as individuals who are obviously concerned about their child, not as "bad parents." Within the context of a friendly relationship, the parents may be more open to discussing their child's care. This does not mean that the social worker or nurse should only pretend to be a friend, rather he or she should always be aware of and respect the parents' feelings about what is happening, even when the parents are required to comply with a treatment plan that becomes difficult.

One way to help parents relate more comfortably with their child is to help them become more successful in eliciting desirable behavior from their baby. If they learn how to elicit a smile from the child, this can be a powerful, pleasurable stimulus to motivate them in making further efforts. Many parents find it difficult to see their infant as lovable or as loving them. This is especially true when the parents have not learned how to help the baby be socially responsive. When the parents learn how to interpret the baby's signals, how to stop its crying, and how to help the infant achieve better feedings, they will feel growing pride. Helping the parents revise unrealistic expectations is equally important. This is best done by focusing primarily on what the baby *can* accomplish and deriving pleasure from anticipated progress rather than focusing on the baby's failure to meet their unrealistic expectations. Knowing when the infant is developmental ready to begin a new behavior is very helpful in deciding what interactions to encourage between parents and baby and when to explain to the parents the importance of some behaviors they may not like. Early attempts by the infant to reach for objects, even the parents' noses and hair, must be viewed as good progress, and the parents must be shown how to facilitate these efforts rather than to discourage them.

Encouraging the parents to see their infant as an individual, emphasizing the child's good qualities, and complimenting the parents on helping the child to develop these qualities is important. One must be wary lest the parents become angered by the home visitor's admiration of a baby whom they perceive as bad and troublesome. Recognizing the importance of the parents' perceptions may help prevent difficulty for the parents in accepting their infant's accomplishment of certain developmental milestones such as locomotion.

A major problem for many abusive parents is their need to have control over their children's behavior in order to feel competent. Allowing the children to take control of some of their behavior, which is developmentally necessary, produces great anxiety in parents who feel that allowing such autonomy will produce disobedience and badness. Such adults often perceive their inability to control their child in all situations as dangerous. They need to be given support for their wishes to be good parents while being helped to revise their concepts of disobedience. Some parents may need encouragement to recognize playfulness as desirable behavior; never having learned how to play in their own childhood, they may consider the child's behavior as willful and self-indulgent, rather than as one way a child can learn by trial and error.

Another example of interpretation that may be useful during interactional therapy is helping the parents recognize and accept their child's feelings. Usually parents will need considerable help in recognizing their *own* feelings. The experience of openly expressing their own feelings and having them heard, respected, and responded to affirmatively may allow the parents to do the same for their child (see chaps. 4, 19).

If the social worker or visiting nurse is not trained or competent in these areas, an infant developmental specialist should be available to work with the parents and child on their interaction. This professional works with the parents and child together so that the parents are active participants and are involved with the infant's progress. Having an "outsider" merely tell them how to care for their child is often construed as criticism of incompetence and may result in resentment.

When the abused or neglected infant remains at home, simultaneous efforts to treat the parents and child involve, in addition to medical follow-up, any or all of the following:

1. Lay supportive therapy.
2. Parenting classes.
3. Individual therapy for the mother and father when their personal difficulties warrant it (see chaps. 17, 19).
4. Special therapy, such as an alcoholic treatment program for either parent.
5. Interactional therapy for parents and child.
6. Use of crisis nurseries or day care when the mother needs such respite.
7. Specialized therapy for major health problems, or special training for job placement.

Direct Intervention

The diagnosis of problems that may need more direct intervention depends on detailed observations of the infant's behavior and the mother-infant interaction. The crying, difficult-to-soothe baby, or the baby who ruminates, requires careful observation, perhaps in a hospital setting, in order to discover ways to help revise caretaking to better meet the child's special needs. Some babies are extremely sensitive to delays in being fed or to overstimulation by jiggling and holding. Parents need to learn how to interpret their baby's needs and how to transform an anxious, tense interaction into a more relaxed, pleasurable one. Ruminating babies, who also often show signs of deprivation growth failure, sometimes seem to respond to a more active, playful, and stimulating style of caretaking (12, 13). Parents can be shown that holding and playing quietly with the baby after feedings is apt to diminish the symptoms (see chap. 23).

Before intervention, one needs to know a good deal about the parents' own history and the reasons for their difficulty in having a comfortable relationship with their child. The parents may have never experienced a reliable, primary parenting figure in their own childhoods, or they may have had difficulty in being available to this particular child. For example, the death of a sibling near the time of the infant's birth may not have allowed the parents time to adequately mourn their loss, and may make the emotional investment in a new infant anxiety provoking, leading to depression. Clearly, the capacity of parents to respond to treatment in these two situations may be quite different. Being able to mourn their previous loss and overcome the barrier of anxiety may lead to the parents' enjoyment of their new child. Parents who have never known adequate parenting themselves have much more difficulty in being able to nurture. In this case, treatment and training for parents and the child will take longer.

Siblings

Frequently when a young infant is abused or neglected and the family is evaluated, the older siblings may receive only passing scrutiny, especially if they do not present obvious behavior disorders. A closer look often reveals that they too have suffered from abuse or neglect in the past. Although they are now apparently compliant and "getting by," they may have underlying anger, fear, poor self-esteem, and learning disabilities that cause them to perform below their potential. These older children rarely volunteer to talk about their difficulties, love their parents, accept their parents' values, and tend to feel that their problems are due to their own innate badness or inadequacies. Abused and neglected children tend to accept, without question, their parents' criticism of their inability to achieve the parents' inappropriately high expectations. This serves to lower their self-esteem even further and gives them a standard of expectations which they will try to enforce in their own parenting or even as babysitters in later childhood and adolescence. Therapy can help to reverse these expectations. This must be done in a way that will not put the child in direct conflict or confrontation with his parents, thereby avoiding the risk of renewed abuse. Many abused children recognize early in life that the rules in their home are different from the rules in the outside world. They exercise great care in adapting to each environment. For them, developing a consistent and healthy self-image is an important goal. Siblings may also provide much support and care for one another. At times one sibling may take on the major "mothering" of a younger or more vulnerable child. While this may be deleterious to the "mothering" sibling, it is helpful to the sibling being nurtured.

Treatment of the Preschool Child

By the time children have reached preschool age (three to five years), they should have accomplished several important developmental tasks. Normally reared children have progressed from dependence on their primary attachments to parents to some ability to relate comfortably with others. In doing so, they perceive themselves as having individual identities and feel the capacity to act independently in rudimentary ways. They have begun to feel competent at achieving some mastery over the use of their own bodies and the exploration of toys. They have achieved an increased ability to communicate and thereby an improved ability to influence others. These accomplishments are constantly practiced and refined by experience, helping the child develop early control over impulses. Peer relationships and socialization skills become important as normally reared children begin to see themselves as separate entities. Major learning tasks for preschoolers are the acquisition of new cognitive and motor skills, the development of speech and language, and self-help skills. Sex roles emerge as the child begins the process of identification.

Often the abused and neglected preschool-age child has not yet experienced a positive attachment with one caregiving person. Basic issues of trust have not yet been resolved, making attempts at self-assertion difficult to achieve. Deviant ways of coping begin to become solidified into behavior patterns that are handicapping. An important result is usually either withdrawn or aggressive behavior which makes it difficult for the child to get along with peers and caregivers. Abused and neglected children begin to develop serious developmental deficits at this age, resulting in unusual behaviors:

1. Difficulties in relating; relating with mistrust;
2. Hypervigilance;
3. Difficulties in emotional awareness and expression;
4. Delayed gross and fine motor development;
5. Poor language and communication skills;
6. Extremes in behavior—angry, aggressive acting out versus overly compliant or withdrawn responses;
7. Indiscriminate display of affection with adults;
8. Pseudo-adult role-reversal behavior with adults and peers, or regression to very immature behavior in a permissive environment;
9. Distractibility and hyperactivity;
10. Poor impulse control;

11. Anxiety;
12. Difficulty in integrating their chaotic experiences into any coherent framework of cause and effect; and
13. In sexually abused children, preoccupation with sexual experiences, fears, and feelings of vulnerability, and sometimes sexually provocative behavior toward others.

All of the above problems may be seen in preschool abused children but they may also be observed in older abused children. Some of these behaviors have served a survival function within their abusive or neglectful family environment, but they handicap the child in a normal environment.

While treatment of the abused preschool child will more often take place outside the home in an individual or group setting, it may also occur in the home using the services of a skilled social worker, lay therapist, nurse, or developmental specialist. The treatment plan might include speech and language therapy, physical therapy, specialized medical care, as well as play therapy, behavior modification, or an individual educational plan (14).

Day Care

Using resources outside the home is often helpful in providing abused or neglected children with safe and nurturing care and a more stimulating environment, while also providing the parents with some relief from continuous parenting tasks which may be onerous. Day care in a licensed home or in a public facility may provide these children with the opportunity to experience a safe and well-structured routine of care in the company of peers. Day-care facilities vary a good deal as to the sophistication of the caretakers, but considerable improvement of care may be achieved if consultation and explanation of the special needs of the maltreated child are provided by the protective services worker. When an effort is being made to avoid foster care and keep children within the family, day care may be tried as the child's progress is watched and the parents are provided with help in developing parenting skills. Changes in the child's behavior in response to the new environment may make the child easier to manage and more attractive to the parents. Sometimes the child may change in ways that are not pleasing to the parent, such as becoming less compliant and more self-assertive. These changes need to be identified as good signs of development growth lest the parents deem them punishable.

The Therapeutic Preschool

Placement in a therapeutic nursery school or day-care program is the treatment of choice for many children aged three to five. Some programs are able to integrate the parents into their regular schedule as active participants in child care. This requires a skilled staff with sufficient time to give extra help to the parents while also giving good care to the children. Most programs do not include the parents in the school activity, but they do offer to help parents understand their child and collaborate in joint treatment goals for the child. The parents should receive simultaneous, coordinated individual or family therapy.

Experience at the C. Henry Kempe National Center for the Prevention and Treatment of Child Abuse and Neglect in Denver has shown that many preschool-age children in the therapeutic nursery school exhibit the serious delays and disturbances in social and emotional functioning described above. The imposition of a consistent structure and a clear, daily routine offers the child the opportunity to reduce anxiety and obtain aid in the integrative process. Nonverbal communication is recognized as significant and is responded to. A simple narrative style of speaking is used to give the child words for his or her actions and feelings. At the same time, stimuli are limited and carefully introduced according to the child's capacity for integration. Developing impulse control is a major focus in treatment. The teacher intervenes to help the child tolerate delay between stimulus and response by verbalizing the child's thought process and offering alternatives for action. The same process helps children in their peer interactions and teaches them to communicate more effectively with one another. Expansion of play themes and cognitive activities is encouraged with the teacher modeling the new behavior and emphasizing verbalization.

By limiting the number of children in a group to eight to twelve, one can avoid overstimulation and provide consistency and predictability. Our experience has shown that a 1:3 staff-pupil ratio is needed when working with abused and neglected preschoolers who need much attention, nurturing, and, one-to-one relationship experience.

As they become more comfortable with the routine, the children attempt to explore the environment and try new activities. Initially, however, they are afraid to attempt anything new and need the reassurance of an adult to make the first step. Failure is often much feared and children need encouragement to try again. As in all treatment of children, a close relationship between the teacher and the child is vital for the child to use such help.

As in individual play therapy, children in a group setting repeat themes in their play that can be clarified and interpreted verbally. Preschool children often relive an abusive incident through doll play. The teacher can provide empathy for the doll victim's feelings, question the abuse, and, through role modeling, can teach alternative ways of parenting with the dolls. Consistent limits of allowable behavior and clear logical consequences (including "time out" when necessary) help children to cope in social situations with their peers and with adults.

Individual Theory

Although most abused or neglected preschool-aged children benefit considerably from the group experience in a therapeutic playschool, the therapeutic opportunities may be too fragmented or diluted by the group setting. The addition of individual therapy allows the child to develop a more intense relationship with an adult in which more individual goals can be attempted. The continuity and structure of the therapy hours allow the relationship behavior (transference), play themes, and behavior patterns to be more clearly repeated, related to specific events, and interpreted verbally or in play by the therapist. As in the preschool, themes frequently addressed are object constancy, trust, separations, verbalizing of affect and experience to validate feelings and to increase reality testing, setting limits on behavior, and encouragement of mastery.

As previously stated, in order for the child's treatment to be more effective, the parents must receive treatment as well. A goal in such coordinated treatment is for the child to become better understood and more appealing to the parent and to receive their permission to grow and develop in the therapeutic milieu. Sabotage or competition within the child's program will be lessened if the parent, too, receives support and services in addition to psychotherapy.

Extrafamilial Abuse or Neglect

Children are frequently abused or neglected by persons other than their parents; usually these perpetrators of abuse are in a position of trust as a friend or as an alternate caregiver such as a foster care parent, a babysitter, day-care provider, or school employee. Children in these situations can be very seriously abused physically or sexually, or they may be dangerously neglected. The perpetrator may not be the responsible alternate caregiver, but an employee, a friend of the caregiver, or a family member, including another child. Abuse, especially sexual abuse, may continue over a period of time without the child reporting it to anyone, either because of lack of opportunity or because of threats made by the perpetrator.

Prevention by careful investigation and monitoring of alternate caregivers, recognition of untoward symptoms in the child which might indicate maltreatment, and an active level of suspicion in any questionable situation is needed. Prompt reporting of the perpetrator and the removal of the child from such a situation is required. Full disclosure to the parents must be made by the alternate caregiver, if the abuse occurred in an officially sponsored institution, together with an explanation of the measures being taken to prevent any recurrence. If the parents chose the alternate caregiver and are reluctant to make a change, protective services may have to intercede, with court intervention if necessary, to protect the child.

Care for children abused by someone outside the family is needed, particularly if the episode was traumatic or the abuse repeated, to help them deal with their feelings of vulnerability, anger, and mistrust. The family may also need the opportunity to deal therapeutically with their own feelings of shock and anger and to learn how to help their child. The family may not be very helpful to the child if they are overwhelmed by their own reactions, or if they lack empathy with the child's plight and excuse the perpetrator. Long-term follow-up to crisis treatment may be needed. With very traumatic abuse, the child may suffer from post-traumatic stress syndrome, occasionally with a delayed appearance of symptoms. Intensive treatment may again be needed. These children may have recurrent memories of the events, dreams, sleep disturbances, hypervigilance, or a diminished interest in customary activities (15).

Therapy for the sexually abused preschool child should begin as soon as the initial diagnosis is made, for these children will often be even more acutely aware than before of their feelings of vulnerability, confusion about their own role in the abuse, and fears of the responses of all adults, especially their parents and the perpetrator who may have been very threatening or seduced them into collusion. Special problems to be addressed in individual therapy are the sexualization, or eroticization, of the child's behavior toward self, in play, and toward others. A corollary of this problem is the need to help the child recognize and seek out safe and appropriate affectionate relationships to replace those which have been sexualized. Individual therapy to clarify and validate the child's understanding of and feelings about the abuse may be alternated with family sessions, especially early in extrafamilial sexual abuse and later in intrafamilial sexual abuse. In this way the child and his or her parents may be able to learn how to talk about the abuse with one another, and the parents may able to understand the child's difficulties and become supportive of him or her. Peer group therapy may also be beneficial for some preschool children who are able to share their feelings.

The family may need support while coping with the legal system if criminal charges are filed. In such cases victims' assistance programs (16) may be available to offer support and financial help.

When the children who are removed from their own homes because of abuse or neglect are then maltreated in foster care, their original difficulties are compounded and treatment must address the feelings of betrayal and anger experienced by these children and their families.

Treatment of the School-age Child

In school-age children (six to twelve years), referrals for treatment are apt to be made only when the child has serious psychiatric symptoms (17, 18), is failing in school (19, 20), or exhibits disruptive behavior. By this time, the child's behavior is often seen as part of the child's personality, and its origin in a neglectful or abusive home environment may be missed. The child may not volunteer the information or, indeed, be aware that his home experience is unusual. The same difficulties of involving parents in therapy with children this age may be found as with younger children. Parents are sometimes more receptive to the child's having treatment when they see the problem as the child's and when the repercussions of the child's behavior are becoming more anxiety provoking. Their own involvement may still be marginal or even negative. Because many of these referrals receive little cooperation and follow-through by the parents, there have been experiments in incorporating psychotherapy in a special school program for some of those children who cannot function in a regular classroom (21). Some schools also provide individual or group therapy in the school setting for children with school-manifested behavior problems. Many abused and neglected children may fall into these categories.

Some efforts are being made to provide consulting services and special training in the dynamics and treatment of abuse and neglect for personnel in day-care centers, preschools, and schools (22). With such assistance, school counselors and social workers may be able to offer help to some of their children who would otherwise not have access to treatment because either their symptoms do not command it or their families do not want it.

Because of cognitive and social delays, lack of readiness for cognitive learning, or behavioral problems, many abused and neglected children are found in the special education classes for the learning disabled or the emotionally disturbed. On further evaluation, these children are found to be seriously handicapped by their lifelong experiences with abuse and neglect and living in an environment which is still abusive or neglectful. They may represent those situations in which treatment has been tried while allowing the child to remain in the home, perhaps with temporary episodes of foster care, but without treatment ever becoming a meaningful, effective experience for the parents. Abuse may continue, and the child, even if placed in a therapeutic school setting, responds poorly to such inadequate measures. Only with the whole family involved can optimum progress be made for such disabled children.

Group Therapy

Another treatment modality which may be helpful to school-aged children either by itself, or supplemented by individual therapy, or as part of a residential program is the use of activity and therapy groups (23, 24). Experience at the Kempe Center with such groups indicates that they may be effective with neglected or abused school-age children and also with sexually abused children. Because their parents are so seldom supportive of these activities, transportation may need to be provided. The group time can often be divided into a structured activity or a talk time, followed by free play activity, and concluded with a quiet snack time which often provides the best discussion participation. Goals for such groups vary but include development of trust in the adult therapists, improvement of peer relations, learning to verbalize and share feelings, socialization and limit setting, and experiencing the respect of the group for oneself as a person. There may be a lessened sense of conflict over loyalty to their parents and an increased ability to express their feelings when the children find that other group members share their problems. Although some children may be too disturbed for this treatment mode and may require individual therapy or special placement, there has been surprisingly good improvement, especially in academic progress, with some of these children.

Group Therapy for Sexually Abused Children

Group treatment can help sexually abused school-aged children feel less isolated and different, find a healthier way to meet their needs for closeness and companionship, and learn about more appropriate family life. Information about sex becomes part of the group's goals, because most of these children have had only inaccurate fantasies and deviant sexual behaviors as their examples of sexual expression in the past. The issues of placement and separation are major for many of these children, as well as the other concomitant problems of neglect or abuse. Boys of this age have rarely been referred for treatment of sexual abuse in the past and have therefore usually been offered individual treatment, but group therapy could be used now as boys are more often referred for sexual abuse. If the sexual abuse of a boy involved a male perpetrator, the parents and child may become very concerned about homosexuality as an outcome of the abuse and seek treatment. Treatment issues for boys are the same as for girls except there is usually more embarrassment and conflict about being unable to defend themselves against abuse.

Individual Treatment

Psychotherapy (i.e., regular individual therapy by a psychiatrist, psychologist, or social worker) or less intensive individual counseling for the school-age child should address the same issues as for other children, but the typical slow development of trust in the therapist and the testing of the therapist's reliability might take considerable time, even in a one-to-one situation. The goals in one-to-one therapy are more individual and the pace of treatment is adjusted to the child's response. The children's interpretations of their parents' behavior toward them and their feelings about their parents may be more readily recognized and interpreted in individual therapy and help for these children in dealing with these stresses can be offered over time. For sexually abused children, a combination of individual, family, and group therapy may be essential (see chap. 17).

Although they are older, many of these children still have not progressed satisfactorily through some of the earliest developmental stages. The early issues of basic trust and identity remain unsolved; sometimes they remain essentially unattached children with a poor outlook unless they and their parents become involved in effective, intensive therapy. Some of these children have already begun to exhibit the behaviors of antisocial personality disorders. When there is no treatable parent available and the famiy life is most chaotic, these children may be placed in a residential treatment setting. They may already have failed in foster home placement or be deemed too disturbed for such a placement. They represent a failure in adequate diagnosis and treatment at an earlier age, and there is little time to provide them with intensive therapy and appropriate caretaking relationships before the additional turmoil of adolescence compounds their plight.

Participation of the parents in some kind of treatment modality is very important for the school-age child in individual treatment; there is more pressure on these chidlren to reconcile their families' expectations with the different views taken by the outside world, including their therapists. This may induce conflict not just of loyalty but also of identification with parental behavior or pathology. Although mental health centers should be available as an alternative to psychiatric/psychological clinics or private psychotherapy, they rarely have trained personnel or the time to provide individual treatment for children (25). It may take special effort for the child's therapist to achieve collaboration with the therapists who undertake treatment of the parents and the family as a whole.

The problems of school-aged children which most often need to be addressed in psychotherapy are:

1. Trust-mistrust. This occurs despite the obvious pleasure the child receives from attention of an adult therapist. Difficulties persist from early relationships and are manifested by such behaviors as not perceiving the therapist as a consistent individual person. Separation after each session often seems equivalent to nonexistence for the child at first, and the therapist is tested constantly as to benevolence, reliability, consistency, and interest. Cancellations of appointments and vacations taken by the therapist are important issues; even though their significance may be denied by these children, their behavior will show the strength of their reaction. The importance of a trustworthy relationship for the abused or neglected child cannot be given too much emphasis. Being able to maintain trust even through termination of therapy may help that child seek help in the future when he needs it.

2. Need for nurturance. This is manifested in strong desires for attention, food, and possessions. For these children, the importance of the time and place set aside just for them may not be admitted; yet they react strongly to any intrusion upon it.

3. Poor self-esteem and little capacity for pleasure, related in part to a rigid, punitive super-ego. This super-ego may be poorly internalized but related to parental attitudes which are critical, allowing little self-approval and little indulgence in pleasure. The lack of pleasure often seems to be part of a chronic depression, similar to that of the parents.

4. Poor ability to express emotions verbally and nonverbally. These children often have difficulty discussing their anxiety and fears, many of which are quite reality based in their chaotic family lives. Aggression may be overtly expressed or it may be suppressed; if suppressed, it may have considerable unrecognized influence on their behavior with peers and with adults and in their transference also. Aggression may be expressed primarily in a great deal of vivid, violent fantasy. Difficulty with feelings which have not been expressed verbally may lead to problems in impulse control. Helping the child with verbal expression and with alternate ways to discharge aggressive impulses may lead to better impulse control and more socialized behavior. Behavior modification techniques may be useful in working with the family or school and the child and are incorporated into the repertoire of some psychotherapists.

5. Tendency to regress during therapy hours. Since this is more common in preschool children, its presence in school-age children may indicate how many unresolved problems they have left from earlier stages for which they still must seek solutions. For example, a very well-behaved, pseudo-adult child may spend months in water play and eventually regress to drinking from a bottle and express wishes to be babied.

6. Poor cognitive and problem-solving skills. Many of these children have difficulty performing intellectual skills on demand. They need help in acquiring confidence, in having less fear of failure, and in learning how to approach new tasks, as well as encouragement in catching up when behind in such skills as reading.

Treatment in Adolescence

Treatment of adolescents is more apt to be precipitated by their behavior, particularly school failure, delinquency, or running away. During adolescence, children's efforts at becoming independent may be jeopardized by their parents' needs to maintain a relationship in which the child continues to meet parental needs and in which the child is expected to obey a coercive authority. The long years of frustration and unexpressed anger may find expression in delinquent behavior; the lack of loving family relationships may lead to gang membership or premature sexual partnerships. Truancy and school failure become increasingly serious if early learning difficulties were not resolved. Running away may be the only way some adolescents can deal with abuse at home, including sexual abuse. Recognizing this possibility can lead to family evaluation and treatment. A few adolescents become increasingly depressed by their long-standing neglect or sexual abuse, or the underlying message expressed over the years that they are unwanted, and they attempt suicide (26).

Just as with younger children, the adolescent may not have adequately negotiated the most elementary developmental steps, particularly those involving object relations. Instead of redefining relationships from an oedipal stance, the adolescent may still be caught in unsolved preoedipal issues, with his or her primary dependency needs still unmet—a clear handicap in developing independence, trusting relationships, or any kind of mature identity.

In spite of their years, adolescents may never have learned to adequately recognize, verbally express, and cope with their own emotions. They may be prey to difficulties in impulse control. They may not have learned how to use their cognitive skills in solving life problems nor how to trust anyone enough to ask for advice.

If criticized, belittled, abused, or ignored, they may have very poor self-esteem and very little experience or motivation to use their potential abilities either academically or in learning job skills. Their lack of coping skills are both social and work handicaps and make them even more vulnerable in the adult world. Often they feel comfortable only in the counterculture fringes of society where they assume they will be accepted and valued more easily.

Many adolescents become involved in juvenile court supervision before their need for treatment becomes obvious. Both the family and the teenager may be resistant to the idea of treatment, by now, making the process slow and difficult. This is an opportunity to recognize their needs. The choice of individual psychotherapy, group therapy, or residential treatment will depend on the severity of the adolescent's pathology and the presence or absence of support for a treatment program in the home. The use of foster care or a residential group home, combined with individual or group psychotherapy, may give the adolescent a second chance and an escape from continued abuse.

Sexual Abuse

For adolescent girls involved in incest, group therapy may be suitable in much the same way as for school-aged girls, especially if this is combined with individual and family therapy at the appropriate time (27). Attitudes about the parents, resentment of separation from the family, guilt for sexual activity, and disruption of the family pattern may be shared in the group. Reevaluation of identification and sexual issues are major treatment goals as well. Boys can be involved in parent incest but are reported less often. They are sometimes found to be more disturbed and to require intensive individual or residential treatment.

Brother and sister incest occurs relatively frequently and in adolescence may lead to psychosomatic or hysterical symptoms, withdrawal, school failure, serious depression, and suicidal attempts. These children need individual psychotherapy with an evaluation of whether family therapy is also indicated. Sometimes when adolescent siblings are the same age and the relationship is nonabusive, they may request treatment without the knowledge of their parents—an ethical problem for the therapist to resolve.

Older children or adolescents sometimes sexually abuse younger children, even siblings, often with threats of violence or with bribes and seduction. Such abuse may be part of a family pattern of incest in which the older males—grandfather, father, uncles, and cousins—and sometimes females, exploit younger children. The perpetrator may be a neighbor or a trusted teenage babysitter of either sex.

Both the adolescent perpetrator and child victim need treatment in these instances, and usually their families as well. Adolescent perpetrators have usually been victimized sexually at an earlier age and often require prolonged treatment. Child victims need therapeutic help lest they fail to resolve the problem now and show symptoms (including possible abuse of others) much later.

Extrafamilial sexual abuse, including rape of boys or girls, requires not only crisis care but also prolonged therapy. The reactions of the family, concerns about being believed and being damaged, guilt about "inviting" rape by injudicious or adventurous behavior, anger, and vulnerability are all important issues to be addressed in therapy. For boys, the threat to masculine self-esteem and fear of homosexuality are major issues. Treatment of all sexually abused children is important both because of their own future development and because a certain number of them will in turn become perpetrators (see chap. 14).

Treatment Failure

When treatment fails, the removal of the child from the family is the primary alternative. The sooner this decision can be made, while safeguarding the interests of parents and children, the better the prognosis will be for the child. The list of programs already discussed in this chapter may sound impressive, but considering the number of personnel available to offer services to the many children involved, they are inadequate indeed. Treatment programs which are available and also truly effective, particularly with parents and children simultaneously, are woefully sparse.

The prediction of the probability of treatment failure early in the assessment of a family is often possible. Parents who are incapable of parenting because of severe physical or mental incapacity, who are unavailable to their children because of psychiatric illness or substance abuse which shows evidence of not being readily improved by treatment, or who are dangerous to their children and others because of fanaticism or aggressive sociopathy have a slim chance of being able to change their parenting skills in time for their children to be able to remain in the relationship without injury or developmental deterioration. In these situations, unless the clear and present danger to the child is sufficient to warrant immediate termination, the law requires that the parents must be shown to be unable to improve their parenting skills sufficiently through therapy to adequately care for their child. It is imperative that the treatment plan be carefully developed to provide maximum help, that it be practical so that the parents can follow it, and that the response of the family to treatment be very well documented. Only when society has done its best to help the family as a whole and the parents have continued to fail, will termination be likely to take place expeditiously from the point of view of the child's future placement. If treatment efforts are half-hearted, or if the parents *are* allowed to delay their involvement in treatment, time is lost and never truly made up for the child who remains in an uncertain foster care situation.

Occasionally termination of parental rights may result immediately after parental assessment without a trial of therapy. Such instances occur, albeit rarely, when the parents are severely retarded and without support, acutely psychotic, or have a history of bizarre child abuse.

Presumably, the burden to respond actively to the offer of treatment is on the parents; the burden on the protective services system is to expedite treatment for everyone, especially the child. Involvement of the court, not simply as an adversarial arena, but as a participating body in approving the treatment plan and evaluating its success on the basis of the clear and detailed evidence supplied, is usually the most successful way to direct a case toward successful treatment or toward successful termination.

One of the major reasons for treatment failure is the lack of adequate follow-up of the original treatment plans. Parents are allowed to avoid active involvement in treatment until just before the next court hearing. Placements for the child and active involvement of the child in treatment may break down because of personnel problems, and adequate substitutes are not found. This is only too easy to understand, recognizing the large number of cases and the inertia inherent in a family reluctant to change. Constant effort does have to be made to counteract delay and to persist in following the treatment plan.

Other causes of failure of treatment are usually inadeqaute initial assessment and diagnosis, particularly of parental pathology, and the use of inadequate treatment resources. These problems are partly dependent on the financial and manpower strength of a program, but they can also be solved by the implementation of good standards of professional diagnostic and therapeutic work.

Treatment may be prolonged without improvement because therapists are reluctant to admit failure. Their intense wish to help these people or their feelings of personal inadequacy if therapy is unsuccessful may cause them to remain unrealistically optimistic, to the detriment of the child.

Summary

The effective treatment of emotionally, physically, or sexually abused and neglected children is still an elementary science. The increased reporting of maltreatment has brought to light the plight of great numbers of children who are still so young that, unless physically abused, their families would not ordinarily be subjected to detailed scrutiny and they might not be recognized as maltreating families on routine well-child visits. Evidence that many young children are being subjected to development-distorting stress, while disturbing, also offers the opportunity for devising treatment programs for them long before they enter school.

Treatment for the abused and neglected child should begin whenever the diagnosis is first suspected. Ideally, it may begin before the baby is born with the prospective parents when *they* were children. If there are indications that a pregnant woman might have difficulty coping with her coming child, treatment may begin right after delivery by extra support being offered to the mother. It may begin during infancy with lay home visitors, provision of good medical care for the infant, and encouragement of better mother-child interactions through professional intervention, parenting classes, or parent groups.

Foster care should not often be required, but when it is, the foster parents must be trained and paid to promote their relationship with the natural family with the aim of returning the child to the parents as soon as possible. Good day care and continued support for the parents, through someone like a public health nurse, may be helpful. If the child's entry into treatment comes during preschool years, therapeutic day care or preschool may be required. This can be supplemented by individual play therapy and of course the involvement of the parents. An experimental program involving the use of lay people for play therapy with supervision has been suggested as one way of coping with the large numbers of children who could be involved. Another helpful measure is to increase the knowledge and therapeutic capabilties of day-care, preschool, and school personnel.

By the time the child enters the school system, more established treatment programs should be available and used, providing the child's family can be persuaded to participate. These include private or clinic psychotherapy, special school programs, group therapy, relationship programs through Big Brother and Big Sister programs, residential treatment, or hospitalization. Similar treatment programs are also available to adolescents.

Recognition that the treatment of child and parents should begin as soon as abuse and neglect is discovered helps avoid some of the heartbreaking occasions when an older child presents with very severe psychopathology after a long history of known but inadequately treated abuse or neglect. Successful and beneficial interventions for the child and family need to be explored when not enough "evidence" exists for court-ordered therapy. Earlier treatment should prevent some of the effects of abuse and neglect that cost society so much in remedial or custodial programs.

Prevention is much better than treatment. Early treatment of the child may be considered a kind of prevention of future difficulty, but it occurs only after the family is in trouble. Many prevention programs have been identified for general use as well as for at-risk populations (see chaps. 22, 24); whatever their cost they are cheaper than the expense of broken and distorted spirit, which is the price of maltreatment.

The cultural and political component of this problem is rarely given adequate recognition. Although most of us describe our children as our greatest resource and our hope for the future, we act as if they were very low on our list of priorities. We do not exert any political pressure on our leaders to vote monies for children; we do not protest to our government when programs benefiting children are cut back or eliminated; and we do not have a single outstanding active spokesman for children in our national government. Until, as a people, we insist on the activation of programs which will protect children and vote to spend our money on them, we cannot say that we really oppose the abuse, neglect, and exploitation of children.

References

1. Steele, B. F., and Pollock, C. B. 1974. A Psychiatric Study of Parents Who Abuse Infants and Small Children. In *The Battered Child,* 2d ed., ed. C. H. Kempe and R. E. Helfer, pp. 103–47. Chicago: University of Chicago Press.

2. Gordon, A. H., and Jameson, J. C. 1979. Infant-Mother Attachment in Patients with Nonorganic Failure to Thrive Syndrome. *J. Am. Acad. Child Psychiatry* 18(2): 251–59.

3. Shaywitz, S. 1984. Maternal Alcohol Ingestion Effects on the Developing Child. In *Current Pediatric Therapy,* vol. 11, ed. S. S. Gellis and B. M. Kagan, 707–11. Philadelphia: W. B. Saunders.

4. Steinhausen, H.; Nestler, V.; Huth, H. 1982. Psychopathology and Mental Functions in the Offspring of Alcoholic and Epileptic Mothers. *J. Am. Acad. Child Psychiatry* 21(3): 268–73.

5. Pildes, R. S., and Srinivasan, G. 1984. Infants of Drug Dependent Mothers. In *Current Pediatric Therapy,* vol. 11, ed. S. S. Gellis and B. M. Kagan, 705–7. Philadelphia: W. B. Saunders.

6. Lewis, D. O.; May, F.; Jackson, L. D.; Aaronson, R.; Restifo, N.; Lerro, S.; and

Simos, A. 1985. Biopsychosocial Characteristics of Children Who Later Murder: A Prospective Study. *Am. J. Psychiatry* 142:1161–67.

7. Fraiberg, S., ed. 1980. *Clinical Studies in Infant Mental Health: The First Year of Life.* New York: Basic Books.

8. Martin, H. P., and Beezley, P. 1976. Resistances and Obstacles to Therapy for the Child. In *The Abused Child,* ed. H. P. Martin. Cambridge, Mass.: Ballinger.

9. Villeneuve, C. 1979. The Specific Participation of the Child in Family Therapy. *J. Am. Acad. Child Psychiatry* 18(1): 44–53.

10. Egelund, B., and Farber, E. A. 1984. Infant-Mother Attachment: Factors Related to Its Development and Changes over Time. *Child Development* 55:753–71.

11. McBogg, P.; McQuiston, M.; and Schrant, R. 1978. Foster Care Enrichment Program. *Child Abuse and Neglect: International J.* 3:863–68.

12. Winton, A. S. W., and Singh, N. N. 1983. Rumination in Pediatric Populations: A Behavioral Analysis. *J. Am. Acad. Child Psychiatry* 22(3): 269–75.

13. Sauvage, D.; Haddet, I.; Hammery, L; Barthelemy. 1985. Infantile Rumination: Diagnosis and Follow-Up of Twenty Cases. *J. Am. Acad. Child Psychiatry* 24(2): 197–203.

14. In, P. A., and McDermott, J. F. 1976. The Treatment of Child Abuse: Play Therapy with a Four-Year-Old Child. *J. Am. Acad. Child Psychiatry* 15:430–40.

15. Terr, L. C. 1981. "Forbidden Games": Post-Traumatic Child's Play. *J. Am. Acad. Child Psychiatry* 20(4): 741–60.

16. National Organization for Victim Assistance. *The Victim Service System: A Guide to Action.* Washington, D.C.: National Organization for Victim Assistance (1757 Park Road, N.W., 20010).

17. Beezley, P.; Martin, H. P.; and Kempe, R. S. 1976. Psychotherapy. In *The Abused Child,* ed. H. P. Martin. Cambridge, Mass.: Ballinger.

18. Green, A. H. 1978. Psychiatric Treatment of Abused Children. *J. Am. Acad. Child Psychiatry* 17:356–71.

19. Sandgrund, A.; Gaines, R. W.; and Green, A. H. 1974. Child Abuse and Mental Retardation: A Problem of Cause and Effect. *Am. J. Mental Deficiency* 79:327–30.

20. Klein, D. F. 1977. Educational and Psychological Problems of Abused Children. *Child Abuse and Neglect: International J.* 1:310–7.

21. Graffignano, P. N., et al. 1970. Psychotherapy for Latency Age Children in an Inner City Therapeutic School. *Am. J. Psychiatry* 127:626–34.

22. Stein, M., and Ronald, D. 1974. Educational Psychotherapy of Preschoolers. *J. Am. Acad. Child Psychiatry* 13:618–34.

23. Gralton, N., and Pope, L. 1972. Group Diagnosis and Therapy for Young School Children. *Hospital and Community Psychiatry* 23:40–42.

24. Rose, Sheldon D. 1974. *Treating Children in Groups.* San Francisco: Jossey-Bass.

25. Cohn, A. H. 1978. An Evaluation of Three Demonstrations of Child Abuse and Neglect Treatment Programs. *J. Am. Acad. Child Psychiatry* 17:2.

26. Sabboth, J. C. 1969. The Suicidal Adolescent: The Expendable Child. *J. Am. Acad. Child Psychiatry* 8:272–86.

27. Rossman, P. G. 1985. The Aftermath of Abuse and Abandonment: A Treatment Approach for Ego Disturbance in Female Adolescence. *J. Am. Acad. Child Psychiatry* 24(3): 345–52.

19 Reflections on the Therapy of Those Who Maltreat Children

Brandt Steele

Treatment of the syndromes of abuse and neglect is never simple. The problem is one of complex interactions between caregiver and child, and both members of the dyad need help. The preceding chapter on the care of the child victim frequently refers to the necessity of treating parents. The present chapter focuses more specifically on the therapy of parents and other people who maltreat the children under their care.

Most often, those who maltreat children are the biological mothers or fathers, but the abusers may also be paramours, step-parents, and various other relatives, including older siblings, grandparents, aunts, uncles, or cousins. They may be babysitters, day-care providers, teachers, counselors, recreational directors, or any others more or less closely involved with the child's care and upbringing. In sexual molestations the perpetrator is often a stranger. The important question is not in which category the person belongs, but what the nature of his or her feelings are about the child and their interactions. One of the characteristic features of child maltreatment syndromes is the generational repetition of all varieties of abusive patterns: physical, sexual, emotional, and all kinds of neglect. Therefore, the treatment of perpetrators necessarily requires knowledge of their early life experiences and their consequences.

People tend to reenact in their child-care interactions the behavior of their parents or other early life caretakers toward themselves. We see this in simple forms, as in the case of the four-and-a-half-year-old boy who said, when asked why he had choked and shaken his baby sister, "Mommy, that's what you used to do to me." Or the case of an eleven-year-old youngster who was accustomed to being beaten for disobedience and was forced to babysit with a niece while the rest of the family went out for entertainment. He beat up the toddler when she did not obey his requests. Or a teenaged couple who said, "We don't care what the silly pediatrician says, we'll raise our baby the way we were raised." Later, their crying baby was severely injured by physical punishment. Or the child molester who repeatedly seduced latency-aged boys in much the same fashion that he was sexually abused at age nine by a "kindly" uncle. Among all the kinds of perpetrators of child abuse and

Brandt Steele, M.D., is with the Department of Psychiatry, University of Colorado Medical Center, Denver.

across the wide spectrum of maltreatment, it is necessary to know how the perpetrator's child-caring abilities have been directed or hampered by his or her own past experiences. The behavior and caregiving patterns of perpetrators are impossible to "treat" or deeply influence unless these perpetrators are understood as previously abused, neglected children rather than simply as "child abusers."

In addition to understanding the role of early life neglect and abuse as a persistent behavioral organizer in the older abuser, one needs to thoroughly explore the perpetrator's total life situation, both past and present: education, employment, religion, financial situation, marital relationship, sexual behaviors, recreational activities, ability to have pleasure, and general social relationships. In particular, an awareness of the perpetrator's psychological patterns and mental state, especially those concerning self-esteem and self-identity is necessary. In order to determine the type of treatment needed and its chances for success, one must ascertain whether or not there are signs of significant mental illness, such as serious depression, schizophrenia, paranoid personality, sociopathy, poor impulse control, sexual perversions, serious alcoholism or substance abuse, or a history of aggressivity or criminality. A successful approach to the problems of child care is difficult, if not impossible, if the more pervasive total life problems are not adequately managed. Of equal importance is to find out if the perpetrator had, in addition to all the unhappy relationships of his early life, other relationships which were good. Was there anybody—relative, neighbor, schoolteacher, or someone—whom he felt understood by and cared about, whom he felt he could love and was loved by? The presence of such a person in the perpetrator's life augers well for treatment; the complete lack of such persons indicates treatment will be difficult and improvement problematical.

Episodes of maltreatment occur in a much larger life setting. The method of treatment would vary significantly for each of the following cases:

A father who is ashamed and frustrated by just having lost his job and is now faced with the unfamiliar task of infant and child care while his wife goes out to make the family living by being a cocktail waitress.

A teenager who is saddled with excessive amounts of housework and care of younger siblings while peers are out having a good time.

A very depressed young mother, faced with the difficulty of having moved far away from her family and friends, alone with a crying baby, and coping with a husband who has become abusive and alcoholic.

Such are the extra strains and crises which can precipitate and perpetuate events of maltreatment and require immediate understanding intervention. But the discovery, recognition, and reporting of the neglect or abuse will also create a new crisis in itself. Management and treatment of the parent or other perpetrator begins at that point and must, at first, deal with the hurt feelings, denials, anger at the system, and fear of punishment instigated in the perpetrator, as well as with the disruptions, confusions, and burdens we have introduced into their lives by the interventions used to protect the victimized child.

Supportive sympathetic help in the management of crisis followed by counseling and clarification are necessary to begin treatment of perpetrators of abuse. In some relatively benign cases, caregivers can make significant change in their child-care routines and stop neglecting or physically abusing, and they will be able to maintain this change in the future. However, for the more common, more serious situations no significant, long-lasting change will occur unless deeper issues are addressed. The clear recognition and treatment of the underlying needs of the perpetrator are essential in order to change and improve his or her child-caring abilities.

A main source of child-caring behavior is the child-rearing practices seen in one's culture, accompanied by the advice and ideas gained from relatives, friends, pediatricians, magazines, and books on child rearing as well as direct observation of other caregivers' techniques. These practices, although strongly emotionally tinged, are largely acquired through cognitive learning in later childhood and adult life. They are much more easily understood and changed through simple counseling and advice. Their inadequacies can be approached with rewarding results in crisis therapy or in educational methods such as parenting classes, parent effectiveness training, and information on child development. The therapist must keep in mind that general cultural and subcultural patterns of child rearing can vary widely between cultures of different countries as well as extensively and subtly between geographic, ethnic, religious, and socioeconomic subcultures in the same country. Also there is a certain ambivalence present in most cultures relating to child abuse, for instance, the simultaneous existence of belief in gentle, loving kindness toward children along with belief in strict discipline and corporal punishment.

A second source of child-care behavior is the patterns acquired in infancy and early childhood from one's own experiences of being cared for, either well or poorly. Such patterns are more deeply embedded, unconscious, and automatic. They are harder to change. These more firmly fixed behaviors account for the generational repetition of abuse. They are less cognitively and more affectively based, acquired by internalization during early development when a child has no way of learning except by automatically absorbing into his developing psyche through imitation and identification the parental attitudes and patterns. Comparison can be made with language, religion, and politics, areas in which it is well known that children follow parental patterns, although they hardly know why. Learning a new language in later years is difficult, and the "mother tongue" is never really forgotten or relinquished. Religious belief, acquired somewhat later in more cognitive fashion, can be changed more easily, although this is usually conflictive and hard to do. Political beliefs, which are even more cognitive and learned still later in life, are often changed with greater ease. The child-caring practices related to early life learning are like language, with its special accents; they are deeply emotionally toned and cannot be modified as easily as the later cognitively learned techniques of mother crafting. This process of identifying with the caretakers of earliest life is a normal one. Those parents who are comfortable, capable, empathic caregivers were fortunate in having good parental models whose behavior and attitudes could be incorporated in infancy and automatically repeated with their own children. When one thinks of how difficult it would be to change such deeply embedded traits in a "good" parent one realizes the difficulty of changing the similarly acquired patterns of abuse.

The deleterious residues of early life experience which plague the perpetrator and hamper his caregiving are essentially the same characteristics described in the preceding chapter as the effects of neglect and abuse on the child. Most simply, the adult needs treatment for the same things the child does and, to a certain extent, the treatment of the adult is similar to that of the child. For the child a new and better experience of being cared for is needed. The failure-to-thrive baby resumes normal physical, emotional, and social development soon after appropriate feeding and empathic care is provided, either in foster care or through behavioral change of the mother. Depending on their developmental stage, older abused children, in addition to this basic empathic care, need increasingly more complex emotional and intellectual support and interventions directed toward development of cognitive awareness of what has happened to them and how their future can be improved. For both child and adult the essence of therapy is the empathic awareness of the patient's psychological state and needs and making an appropriate response to them. Added to this, the patient needs to know that he or she will be heard and understood. This therapeutic alliance is the "carrier wave" on which all other therapeutic processes must ride. Without that alliance, lasting change is unlikely.

The treatment of the child is obviously a kind of "re-parenting", and the treatment of adults has also been described as basically a "re-parenting" process. The re-parenting, in the adult case, must be carried out on a much more cognitive, symbolic level rather than the literal expressions of good parenting which can be expressed with small children. The adult patient may need to know, through our verbal response and emotional tone, that we recognize he is feeling like a lonely, frightened, three-year-old child who wants to be picked up and cuddled, even though we never actually pick him up and put him on our laps. Parental functions can be performed in this case, although in very different ways.

The parental functions with which we are concerned, in addition to the provision of elementary survival needs, are the reasonably consistent and reliable appropriate responses to the child's needs and state. Such interactions validate the child's own growing awareness of inner sensations, desires, and satisfactions. As the child grows this changes from the basic satisfaction of such needs as those for food and warmth to the more sophisticated needs of social interactions, vocal exchanges, and motor play. Later comes the parental function of interpreting reality and how to deal with it safely, then both the permission and encouragement for the child to explore the world and follow, within safe limits, his or her own initiative, plus encouragement to constantly learn and to profit from inevitable mistakes.

To a varying degree, many or all of these parental functions were diminished or distorted in the adult perpetrator's early life. This has resulted in very low self-esteem, lack of self-confidence, poor sense of identity, lack of basic trust, learning difficulties, poor ability to cope with crises, and a much diminished ability to find pleasure. The adult therapist's function is to help the adult patient recognize these problems and their origin and to reopen the channels of development so that progress can be made in developing his or her own life. In a very simple but true sense, the parents' or other caregivers' inability to be empathically sensitive and to respond appropriately to their children is a direct result of the unempathic care they received themselves in early years. Empathic awareness and understanding are the basic tools of therapists. Using them, they know what interventions can be made and when to make them; they know how to help patients gain cognitive understanding of the how and why of their own feelings and behavior and to bring some order out of the chaotic, unhappy experiences of their early years. The most valuable ingredients therapists can provide, beyond the intellectual insights that enable caregivers to grow and develop, are time, attention, tolerance, and the recognition of the immeasurable worth of the individual human beings sitting next to them.

Abusive caretakers are often described as being immature, very needy, and dependent.

These descriptive terms are essentially accurate, but too often they are used in a critical, derogatory sense rather than as valuable clues to the basic characterological difficulties which must be dealt with in treatment. The immaturity of perpetrators can best be understood as a phenomenon of developmental arrest, a blockage of normal drives toward maturation and an inhibition of normal personality growth. Having been brought up under constant admonitions to be strictly obedient to external demands and to disregard their own thoughts and feelings, their own independent maturation was inhibited. They have not been able to use their own innate abilities to develop an internal body of knowledge which would enable them to use good judgment about what to do and not to do in life. To a large extent they have remained immature and helpless, depending upon some proper authority to tell them what to do and how to do it. Most often, the "proper authority" is what they remember of the rules of their own past childhood.

Fear of criticism or punishment for independent initiative can also block maturation and lead to a kind of dependency. Rather than using his or her own ideas, the person remains at the mercy of outside admonition and advice, needing to be told what to do and needing to be reassured that he is doing it well. Many persons in treatment either wait to be told or openly ask to be told what to do and how to do it, placing their request in the context of perfectly sensible cooperation and willingness to learn. A mother can ask, for instance, "Well, what should I do when Johnny soils his pants?" If the therapist either outlines specifically what should be done or follows certain rigid therapeutic rules that prohibit giving advice, there will be repetition of the past behavior of early life parents who either ordered the patient around or disregarded his needs entirely. The therapist can avoid this dilemma by saying, "I think I might do 'a' or 'b,' but other people might look at it differently and do 'x' or 'y'; I think the important thing is for you to find out which way works best for you and Johnny." Such a statement not only lets the mother know her problems have been heard and understood, but also that the therapist is not going to give her orders or make decisions for her. Instead, the therapist has involved the patient in thinking through the problem and the process of decision making and has shown respect for the patient's own ideas, all in an atmosphere where there is no threat of punishment or criticism in case of mistakes. Counseling and therapy cannot force patients to change, but it can offer a safe environment and ideas which they can use to grow and develop their own thinking processes and self-esteem.

Another quite strong form of dependency, present in every parent who shows abusive or neglectful behavior toward his or her offspring, is sometimes expressed openly and directly very early in a therapeutic relationship, or sometimes kept covered and hidden for a long time, expressed only indirectly. This dependency is a manifestation of the patient's deep inner emptiness and a yearning for loving care and consideration. It is a persistent residue of an emotionally deprived childhood. Obviously, such intense deep needs cannot be literally satisfied in a therapeutic situation. The therapist, however, can help patients realize the extent of their need and help them face the embarrassment of feeling so little, so empty, and so helpless and afraid. The problem of dependency is tricky. Some therapists seem to be afraid of it and avoid talking about it. Many agencies have a policy of actively discouraging patients' dependency on individual therapists, almost as if it were a kind of naughtiness that must be scolded and forbidden. Actually, dependency is a core problem that must be openly dealt with sooner or later in order to help these parents to stop turning to their children as the only supply for their enormous need for love and respect. Abusive parents need to learn to trust other adults enough to establish rewarding interactions with them. Often the intertwined problems of low self-esteem and feelings of unworthiness have made them feel undeserving of love and care and reluctant to seek it. This has merely reinforced their emotional deprivation and dependent neediness. Treatment can reverse this self-perpetuating cycle and help them broaden their social contacts in order to find acceptance, pleasure, and support in relationships with other adults.

Some perpetrators' deprivation has been so great and so prolonged that their dependency needs and feelings of emptiness appear bottomless and insatiable. They often express a sense of worthlessness, hopelessness, depression and even suicidal ideation. Such persons should be given psychiatric care, and evaluated for the possible use of psychotropic medication. Matters of child care cannot be usefully approached until the more serious psychiatric problems are resolved. Therapists without special skills should not be burdened with nor attempt the care of such difficult cases.

Evidences of patient dependency on a therapist should not always be taken as signs of real trust or confidence in the therapist. Such a dependency may have some elements of trust, but it must also be considered as an automatic submission to authority and a habitual mode of adaptation in order to stay out of trouble while trying to fulfill some basic emotional needs. Real trust and confidence in the therapist can only develop after the patient has experienced the therapist's respect, trust, and consistent attempts to understand the problem and be of help without criticism and attack. Often at the very beginning of treatment it may be helpful to say, "We don't know each other, and I expect it will take a little time before you can trust me. But I must ask you for something. Since I don't know you well, I may say something that is quite wrong or that may hurt your feelings. I have to trust you to tell me if I've made such a mistake; otherwise, I won't know." This, of course, will not really be believed, but it does set the ground rule for what will inevitably happen sooner or later.

The residues of early neglect and disregard by insensitive caretakers leave the perpetrator particularly sensitive to desertion, abandonment or inattention on the part of the therapist. Therefore the patient needs to be notified as early as possible about any vacations, absences, or any necessary changes in scheduled appointments. All the appointment-related adjustments (transportation, work schedule, babysitters) to the patient's schedule should also be discussed. Although unacceptable to many agencies and practitioners, giving patients one's home telephone number may be most helpful. Rarely is this privilege abused. Usually after one or two calls in the middle of the night, they realize they will be heard at any time if necessary, and they no longer need to test the therapist's availability and will call during regular office hours. For lay therapists or homemakers, such at-home calls will be frequent and continued because they are performing the role of friend or substitute family—relationships which all healthy adults have available, but which the more socially isolated, abusive parents has been afraid to develop.

Not all perpetrators are cooperative and submissive at the beginning of a therapeutic relationship. Many are angry, rebellious, uncooperative, denying all problems and any need for help, and wish only that all the authorities would get out of their lives and leave them alone to raise their children the way they please. Ideally, the therapist should maintain some objective distance during such diatribes and attacks and not take them too personally, but rather try to understand them as expressions of long-lasting feelings that originated in their childhood toward their parents and are now transferred to all other authorities. Such angry, verbal assaults may be the adult equivalent of a childhood tantrum. They can be handled by patiently waiting until the anger subsides and then saying something like, "Now what do you suppose all that was about?" and, "What can we do to straighten things out?" Therapists, like parents, are never perfect and sometimes either say or do something, quite unintentionally, that clearly belittles or disregards the patient's feelings. In such circumstances the therapist should freely acknowledge the mistake or ineptness without being defensive or trying to blame the patient for stimulating the behavior. Such events can be quite useful in therapy, because the therapist will be modeling quite different behavior than the patient is used to, since most abusive parents never admit making a mistake or being wrong about anything. Such episodes can be useful in exploring the long-lasting residues of childhood abuse and neglect.

To a greater or lesser degree, maltreating caretakers have had difficulty in finding adequate ordinary pleasure in living throughout their lives. They do not find joy or happiness in their relationships with their spouse, their children, or even themselves. They have great difficulty in finding pleasure in social relationships. Their lives are, to a great degree, bleak and unrewarding with only superficial, shallow attempts to find pleasure. It is important to encourage and help parents work toward finding adequate pleasure in life because the lack of fulfillment of this basic human need has a direct bearing on the patterns of maltreatment. The lifelong emptiness and deprivation felt by the parent leads to the well-known phenomenon of "role reversal." Instead of being a source of love and care for the child, the parent is emotionally empty and looks to the child to supply his or her needs for love, pleasure, approval, and respect required to bolster self-esteem. No small child, of course, can possibly meet such needs. When the baby fails to meet parental expectations, the child is considered unsatisfactory and unrewarding and will either be verbally abused, emotionally neglected, or physically punished. Hence, therapy for abusive parents must be oriented toward helping them find adequate satisfactions in the world by way of other adults. This means that the abusive parents' social contacts must be enhanced, encouraged, and supported, as well as cognitively understood.

Sooner or later in one form or another, the abusive parent must be asked why he or she wanted children, what is expected of children, and what his or her feelings are about the specific child who has been abused or neglected. Nearly all abusive caregivers say they love children; nearly all say they love the child they have maltreated. But the further question is: What do they love them for? Is the child wanted and loved because of a normal and healthy desire to have and bring up children and to use one's ability to help a child grow? Or is the child loved and wanted just to fill up the emptiness left over from the caretaker's own early life? It is best not to approach the parent-to-child attitudes with a moral, punitive, or investigative attitude that appears to be trying to establish guilt. One should not ask, "Have you beaten Charlie when he was naughty?" but rather, "Has Charlie been a particularly difficult child for you to take care of?" This is more likely to reach the parent's feelings about the child, his relationship to him, and his expectations of him, and at the same time indicates that the therapist has some understanding and empathy for the parent's situation. This also opens the way for nonpunitive, noncritical discussion of what a normal child is able to do at different phases of development.

All those who work with abusive parents are familiar with two very opposing statements. The first is, "Well, I'm going to bring up my kids just the way I was brought up—that's the right way to do it." The second is, "I swore I would never bring up my children the way I was brought up, but I find I'm doing exactly what my mother and father did." Both statements stem from identification with parental care during the earliest phases of a child's attachment to primary caregivers. Both are examples of the generational repetition of maltreatment patterns, and both indicate the persistent strength of such identifications, even despite the attempt to rebel against them. While the attachments occurring in the earliest period of infancy seem to have a basic biological, obligatory quality, the characteristics of the persons to whom the attachment occurs can vary enormously. Too often, attachment is conceptualized as being only good attachment to a "good" object. What is thought of as non-attachment is maybe, in reality, attachment to a "bad" object. The behaviors related to attachment persist throughout life. Persons who were attached to kindly, good caregivers in infancy tend to seek out and relate to kindly people in adult life. Infants who have attached automatically to unempathic, cruel caregivers in earliest life tend to repeat their cruel behavior. They are deeply attached to their abusive, neglecting parents. After better experiences in foster homes they often want to return to their parents, even knowing they probably will be mistreated again. The same type of behavior occurs among many battered women, who recurrently seek out or stay with an abusive partner. Much of what we call masochistic behavior is the persistence from early life attachment to sadistic caregivers. The residues of these early attachments and the identifications with these early objects of attachment are lasting. No therapy is able to eliminate conscious and unconscious memories of what actually happened in the past. The objective of treatment is to help abusive parents become so comfortably aware of the existence of such residues that they can quickly recognize them and avoid automatically following the old patterns. In an empathic therapeutic environment, parents can learn new, more successful patterns of living and interpersonal relationships that are under their own control and that are in the best interests of themselves as well as their children. Probably the most subtle and difficult part of treatment is helping patients relinquish their automatic submission to the authoritative figures from the earliest months and years of life. In successful treatment, patients can develop and carry away a new identification with the therapist that will enable them to have empathic consideration for both themselves and others.

Often in the first weeks of treatment, especially with those who are less angry and negative to begin with, there is a sort of honeymoon during which everything seems to be going very well and relationships with spouse and children are rapidly improving. Such a happy situation should neither be attacked nor accepted at face value. It should be delicately explored to determine whether it is the real improvement which *can* happen quickly in a relatively less damaged personality, or whether it is evidence of a lifelong ability to deny the self and adapt very quickly to the expectations of the environment without any real internal change taking place. Often parents who are under the supervision of social services or the court while their children are in placement say, "I'll do anything to get my kids back." Is this a statement of a real willingness and ability to change, or of a lifelong submission to any kind of rule in order to get out of trouble? Or is it even a more specifically sociopathic tendency to outwit authority and do as one pleases? Such persons are often described as manipulative, with a very derogatory implication. Manipulation, however, is a common, relatively normal method of interpersonal relationship. Most of us were manipulated a lot in our own upbringing and we use a good deal of manipulation in rearing our own children: "You can't have any dessert until you eat your dinner first." "If you clean up your room, you can go to the movie Saturday." "You'll have to take a course in physical education before you can graduate." The task of the therapist is to make certain that the "manipulative" interaction on the part of both therapist and patient is developed as an opportunity for understanding and growth rather than exploitation.

When parents have improved in treatment during the time a child is in foster care, a determination of the nature of their improvement is very important. Has the treatment produced real change in the parents' child-caring abilities, or has the improvement been related to the fact that the problem child is no longer in the family and the parents have improved because the child is absent? There may also be a honeymoon period of good interaction after a child is first returned home from foster care. The child may have developed enough emotional strength to adapt well when first sent back to his parents before some of the old patterns show up again. Only after several weeks have passed can it be validated that therapy has produced lasting change. There is also a need to determine, gradually, whether the parents can maintain improvement only with the support of a therapist present, or whether they have absorbed and integrated enough self-esteem and self-control into their own personalities to maintain such improvement independently on their own with newly developed support systems in the community.

Recurrently during treatment, reality will intrude in the form of a variety of problems: marital strife, financial problems, illness, unemployment, broken down automobiles or household appliances, school problems, conflict with relatives; the list is endless. Early in treatment some practical help must often be given in such crises. Increasingly, more attention must be paid to the how and why of such recurring troubles. In general, maltreating families have more crises than others do. This seems more related to their poor ability to cope with events and to plan for the future than having more than the average number of troubles happen to them. Because of their early life experiences of being told to disregard their own inner feelings and thoughts and to remain completely submissive to outward admonitions, they have been deprived of the ability to take the initiative to think out what to do in case of trouble. Hence events that are easily coped with by the average person are unmanageable to them. Because of their own distrust and consequent social isolation, they cannot seek help from others and situations become increasingly out of control. Treatment needs to be directed toward encouraging the development of independent thought and ideas and instilling the courage to try independent action without fear of punishment or criticism. The pattern of learning to "do it yourself" which was inhibited or blocked in childhood can be revived in adult life with very rewarding results in both crisis-coping ability and self-esteem.

This disccusion cannot cover all the specific problems arising in different modes of treatment: group therapy, family therapy, individual psychotherapy, social case work, self-help groups, crisis therapy, behavior modification, counseling of all kinds, supportive home visiting, education in child development and parenting skills, and others. Nor can it outline all the special techniques used by social workers, psychologists, psychiatrists, mental health workers, public health nurses, lay therapists, counselors, teachers, foster parents, and residential treatment centers. There is, however, a basic underlying theme in all successful treatment. Providing a facilitating environment opens up new channels of growth, development, and maturation that were blocked and distorted in early life. Only by improving the parents' basic life patterns, can we significantly improve their child-caring potentials. Parents must be heard and cared for themselves before they are able to hear and care for their children. Jolly K., the founder of Parents Anonymous, told us during the earliest years of that organization, "It is easy to help people stop physically abusing their children; we can do it in a few weeks. What is much harder to do and takes a long time is teaching them how to love." In addition to all the cognitive enlightenment that abusive parents need to put their lives in better order, they must also experience the feelings of being safe and being loved. We learn to care by being cared for. Treating perpetrators of child abuse puts new, real meaning into the well-worn adage, "You have to love yourself before you can love anyone else." Only then will the children be in safe hands.

20 Law Enforcement's Role in the Investigation of Family Violence

Jack R. Shepherd

The Gatekeepers: A Historical Perspective

Contemporary research into the phenomenon of family violence suggests that violence in the home is a single issue regardless of whether we focus on child abuse, sibling abuse, or wife abuse. The premise is that much more importance is now being placed on the term "family" when considering family violence issues than was true in the past (1).

Researchers, such as Straus, even go so far as to suggest that in our society we learn violence from infancy. Violent tendencies are learned at home and then are modified as children begin to interact outside the home environment. Consider the following observation by Straus:

> The basic training in violence provided by the family fits a social learning theory model. It takes place through physical punishment, by observing violence, and by generalizing from the rules that are implicit in the way others react to acts of violence.

> In general the rule in the family is that if someone is doing wrong, and "will not listen to reason," it is o.k. to hit. In the case of children it is more than o.k.

> The norms within the family are far more accepting of physical violence than are the rules governing behavior outside the family (2).

Throughout the history of this country children have been punished by those responsible for their care largely on the basis of previous customs and English common law. As the focus of public attention gradually shifted toward the plight of the abused child, the role of law enforcement in dealing with family violence began to evolve.

By 1874, for example, the New York Society for the Prevention of Cruelty to Children, which was organized as a result of the famous Mary Ellen Wilson case, was given police powers still in place to this day.

Jack R. Shepherd is a detective lieutenant with the Michigan State Police, East Lansing.

The New York Society for the Prevention of Cruelty to Children, having been organized first, became the model for the law enforcement approach to child rescue, with its agents exercising police powers under legislative authority.

Other child protection groups in Massachusetts and Philadelphia did not approve of the tendency of anti-cruelty societies to become arms of the police. These early disagreements provided the seeds for the growth and development of contemporary thinking on effective methods of child protection. The modern social-work approach to protection, protective services, tends to avoid this punitive approach, but these differences in concept and philosophy have continued into the twentieth century (3).

Thus, even from the earliest attempts to deal with the issue of child maltreatment, law enforcement's role has been enmeshed in controversy. This conflict has carried well into this century and will more than likely continue as a central issue for many years to come.

The first model legislation for reporting child abuse, proposed in 1963 by the United States Children's Bureau, recommended that mandated reports be made to police agencies. While this approach would appear to signal a more favorable trend of law enforcement as a primary service provider, this was not the Bureau's intention. The reason police agencies were selected to receive the mandated reports was that they had staff available twenty-four hours a day (4).

Between 1963 and 1967 most states moved toward amending their reporting laws to reflect the public's desire for a child protective services (CPS) response to suspected incidents of child maltreatment. In a large number of states, law enforcement was clearly regarded as merely one of many agencies mandated to report incidents of suspected abuse. What was not clear to police agencies was at what point and under what conditions they were to be responsible for the investigations.

The short-term effect in many jurisdictions was ambiguity about the role of law enforcement in these cases. Police policymakers were prone to follow the philosophical intents of their state's amended reporting laws. The issue of child abuse became much less a police matter as law enforcement agencies began to turn the cases over to CPS for handling. As Besharov (4) observes: "Designating the police as recipients of reports while helping to ensure thorough investigations has the disadvantage of stressing the punitive tenor of the process and tends to discourage reporting by physicians and other professionals."

At the core of the controversy about the proper role of law enforcement in family violence is the question: To what extent does child abuse represent a violation of criminal law? If child abuse is a criminal violation, this certainly provides law enforcement with an important rationale for involvement in the cases (see chap. 21). However, this factor seemed to only add to the confusion.

In spite of a multitude of concerns that tended to place law enforcement in a secondary role, by 1970 the Los Angeles Police Department had established separate procedures for handling child abuse and neglect cases. This same agency in 1974 created the nation's first battered child unit, which was designed to handle sexual abuse cases as well as cases of physical neglect (5).

Within a relatively short period of time, most large city police departments had at least one officer assigned to the investigation of child abuse cases. Some agencies followed the lead of Los Angeles and formed specialized units. Medium-sized departments were especially affected by this trend and began to organize child abuse specialties within existing juvenile units. Renewed interest in child abuse also led to many more officers being trained in child abuse investigative techniques.

Today, most police administrators view child abuse as an important law enforcement issue. While police involvement in child abuse cases is still viewed as threatening or punitive in nature by some, it is more often being viewed as a positive step toward treatment and prevention. The nation is currently experiencing a major shift in public and professional attitudes toward law enforcement involvement. The support for this current trend comes from interagency cooperation and teamwork.

Contemporary rationales for law enforcement involvement in child abuse cases include the fact that police officers are still the most highly visible public servants within the community charged with the responsibility to help people. Police officers are also uniquely qualified in the collecting, handling, and preservation of evidence (6). Much of what we define as child abuse involves criminal violations which demand a thorough criminal justice investigation. In addition, police departments provide services twenty-four hours a day and are always open to the public (7). Law enforcement, in general, has an ethical responsibility to protect all members of society, especially its children. Finally, as an important institution within the community structure, law enforcement is bound to provide a level of service that measures up to community standards (8–9). The investigation of child abuse cases by the police department is expected by the community.

Specialized Units and Team Approaches

The commitment that law enforcement agencies have made to the battle against child abuse is best illustrated by the development of special child abuse units and multidisciplinary team strategies (see chap. 7). As mentioned earlier, most large urban police departments have instituted some type of child abuse investigative unit. Departments with over one hundred sworn officers may have a child abuse and neglect unit, a sexually exploited child unit, and a missing children's unit, all with separate staffing and administration, as well as a fully staffed juvenile unit.

Popular within medium-sized (25–100 sworn officers) departments are highly specialized juvenile units that include a full range of child abuse prevention programs, usually administered in conjunction with local school systems or related social agencies. Officers serving in a full-service juvenile unit usually have advanced degrees, are trained in instructional techniques, and are well-schooled in child abuse investigative and interviewing techniques.

However, the largest percentage of police agencies in this country are small, with less than twenty sworn officers. At this level one officer, at best, serves as an investigator for all types of child abuse. Even more common in small police agencies is the practice of making each officer responsible for investigations involving children as needed.

Forty-nine states maintain a state police force. However, in twenty-six states these forces are organized only for highway patrol functions with little or no investigative responsibilities. Seven states have highway patrols that also provide investigative services through departments of public safety.

The remaining sixteen states offer "full-service" state police departments, some of which maintain child abuse units or juvenile units that are actively involved statewide with the problem of child abuse. Other state police agencies, while not maintaining a formal unit, have investigators who work with appropriate county and local agencies on child abuse investigations (10).

The real challenge to state-level law enforcement officials is the need for leadership and coordination of an investigational unit for helping local police departments with difficult cases of child abuse and neglect. This unit could also develop educational programs for police academies as well as continuing education programs for police officers (11). State police agencies are also in the best position to secure federal grants or specially earmarked state funds for use in the area of family violence.

However, the most encouraging development in this field is the multidisciplinary team approach to managing child abuse and neglect cases. Never before have the opportunities been so great for service providers in communities to bring their talents together in an effort to assist abusing families. Although there are a variety of models for organizing and maintaining multidisciplinary teams (MDTs), they function best when they include social workers, physicians, psychologists, attorneys, developmental specialists, nurses, and police officers (12). This approach offers the best solution to addressing child abuse issues at the community level.

Undoubtedly the most important challenge to law enforcement is the ability to intervene correctly in reported incidents of child abuse. This task can better be accomplished when law enforcement practitioners, including prosecutors, are members of an MDT, through which the most appropriate type of investigation can be determined and facilitated. The decision of whether a criminal justice investigation is in the best interest of the family is made by the team in accordance with established guidelines. Decisions made about individual cases are based on a broad information base with input from a variety of perspectives.

Investigating Cases of Child Abuse and Neglect

Law enforcement can intervene in child abuse cases at several levels, beginning with basic identification and reporting. Patrol officers are excellent primary sources of information about potential child abuse situations because they interact with families in a variety of ways during the course of their normal duties. These patrol officers should be trained to take advantage of opportunities to observe children within their home environments while conducting investigations that are seemingly unrelated to family violence, such as residential burglaries, malicious destruction of property complaints, prowler complaints, and even traffic accidents. Officers need to make an effort to look for any obvious signs that a child may be living in an abusive environment, like suspicious injuries, and for the more subtle signs of neglect.

One situation where patrol officers need to check carefully for potential child abuse is the family fight call. If officers have any reason to believe that children reside in the home where they have been called to quell a family disturbance, every effort should be made to see the children. Officers may miss the fact that a child has been hurt by a parent or caretaker if they do not take the time to observe, ask questions, and determine whether a child has been involved in the disturbance.

This same responsibility extends to detectives and officers assigned to specialty units such as narcotics units. Police investigators frequently find children living with adults under very questionable conditions. When a potentially abusive situation is observed, it should be reported through normal channels for a more thorough investigation. Basic identification and reporting of child abuse should be an expected, routine function on the part of all law enforcement officers.

A professionally conducted child abuse investigation goes beyond the level of basic identification. Such in-depth investigations require a high degree of expertise and experience. The investigator needs to be familiar with the dynamics of abusive families, including a thorough knowledge of causation factors and trigger mechanisms. Child abuse investigations can be as sophisticated as any criminal justice investigation handled by a police agency.

Consider the investigator who is confronted with multiple victims of sexual exploitation under the age of five. Unique skills are required to interview young children successfully when the only evidence in the case is what can be learned through the victims' statements or actions. Similar skills are necessary when dealing with the fears and frustrations of parents who feel responsible when their child has been victimized.

Physical abuse cases require an investigator to have a working knowledge of injury patterns often produced by common household objects. Interaction and cooperation with hospital staff and MDTs require an ability to communicate intelligently about suspected causes of soft tissue injuries. Just as important is the correct handling of evidence that may have to be used in court at a later date. Officers unfamiliar with search warrant requirements in physical and sexual abuse cases may lose a valuable opportunity to establish a case. Photographic documentation is another important aspect of a thorough investigation. Knowing what to photograph and which equipment to use can make a difference in whether a case will be successfully brought to trial.

A trend within larger police agencies is the assignment of highly specialized investigative teams to the problem of sexually exploited children. This approach has been extremely beneficial in investigating incidents of child molestation. Directly related investigations include child prostitution and pornography rings. Several notable prototypes for this style of investigative team include the San Jose and Los Angeles Police Departments. Years of experience and extensive training are needed to develop investigators for these types of cases. The information that such investigative officers would need to know includes courses on pedophilia, interviewing techniques, surveillance techniques, postal and customs laws, and undercover operations.

As law enforcement becomes more heavily involved with the problem of child abuse, police administrators are beginning to look more seriously at child abuse as a separate and highly specialized area. However, most law enforcement agencies are understaffed and are not in a position to form a specialized unit. A viable option is to give all officers some training in the area of child abuse and neglect.

The Need for Training

There are many cost-effective ways to train law enforcement personnel to deal effectively with cases of child abuse and neglect. Some professionals argue that the best place to train police officers on family violence issues is at recruit school. While this would have some benefits, the drawback is that the police recruit could only be provided with the most basic information. There is so much other "basic" information given at the entry level of police work that a topic like child abuse would get lost among all the other subjects in the recruit school curriculum. Police training academies should give several hours of instruction to recruits on topics such as state child abuse reporting laws, indicators of sexual and physical abuse, and techniques for interacting with the prosecutor's office, courts, and departmental staff. This would also be an appropriate time to provide new police officers with a child abuse investigator's manual that will be used long after the basic training is over.

In-service training presents another opportunity for law enforcement personnel to obtain more information on family violence. The range of possibilities is vast. Officers can attend partial day seminars, one-day seminars, or even enroll in courses that are up to eight weeks in length. Currently there are training workshops on child abuse and neglect being offered by the federal government, colleges, universities, state and local child abuse prevention councils, and similar organizations that make such training affordable and accessible.

Officers should be highly selective when choosing an in-service training course. It is important to ask the questions: "Do I need this training?" "Will this training improve my ability to investigate child abuse cases?" "What are the qualifications of the instructors?" One should look carefully at the organization, schedule, and location of the seminars. Supervisors especially need to take note of those areas in which their investigators need more training and selectively begin to schedule training days. This is also an excellent way to encourage officers who are feeling "burned out" or unmotivated.

Another opportunity to equip the average police officer with better information and skills concerning family violence issues is roll-call training. In larger police departments before a group of police officers actually begin their shift, a briefing session is conducted by supervisors. These sessions are primarily designed to make work assignments and to discuss current department business with officers. However, this setting also serves well as a forum to conduct mini-training sessions for officers. Roll-call training, by its very nature, is limited to a relatively short time frame. However, officers can be given essential "need-to-know" information, such as amendments to child abuse reporting laws or new procedures required by the prosecutor's office, juvenile court or child protective services. Short audiovisual presentations can be very useful under these conditions. A local practitioner from another profession could also appear for a series of questions and answers.

If police officers are going to be thoroughly trained on child abuse issues, it becomes imperative for some agency or organization to take the responsibility for the facilitation of such training. State police organizations are in a unique position to assist with this task. Most states also maintain law enforcement training councils that were established to improve the professional level of law enforcement. Such councils normally set standards and policies for all police training. These councils are often charged with approving the curriculum, lesson plans, and instructors that are used in conjunction with any training the police officers in their states receive.

Professional associations are another valuable source of training, especially for supervisors and administrators. Both state and national associations provide continuing education on issues like child abuse for administrators of law enforcement agencies. Support by administrators is important. Information provided at this level will assist the administrator with the solution of management issues which are child abuse related.

Interagency Cooperation

Law enforcement practitioners can ill afford to take an isolated approach to the problem of child abuse. Beyond the obvious benefits of multidisciplinary teams, other issues related to interagency cooperation must be discussed before any major breakthroughs in cooperation will occur. The reporting process is perhaps one of the most important issues that must be resolved in order to facilitate the division of labor among agencies.

Most states now require that suspected incidents of child abuse or neglect be reported to a child protective services (CPS) agency. The next most common type of reporting law allows the reporter to choose between either law enforcement or CPS as the agency of choice (13–14). The approach that should be advocated places the responsibility for receiving all reports on the shoulders of CPS. From that point clear and specific criteria for law enforcement involvement in child abuse cases should be developed. Criteria that would mandate a joint evaluation or investigation by law enforcement and CPS might include: 1) all deaths, 2) torture, 3) severe repetitive abuse, 4) all infants, 5) acute sexual abuse, and 6) injuries that require medical treatment or hospital care.

The large number of police agencies found in most states is an inhibiting factor in interagency cooperation. Overlapping jurisdictions and confusing procedures add to the problem. While there is normally a single CPS agency found in each county, one can often find over forty police agencies within the boundaries of one county. Knowing which police agency is best suited to provide a particular service is not an easy task for CPS.

Resolution of this issue can occur if the prosecutor's office in each county will serve as the contact point for any potential law enforcement involvement. The prosecutor's office could take a leadership role in the area of child abuse and assist in the development of policy and procedures for joint investigations by CPS and local law enforcement agencies. Of course, this approach does not necessarily mean that criminal prosecution will be sought in all cases. No one course of action can be recommended. Decisions have to be made on a case-by-case basis with the best interests of the child and family as the most important variables.

Whenever interagency cooperation is attempted with law enforcement agencies, it is important to realize that most police agencies of any size are organized along paramilitary lines with two major functional components: administrative and supervisory personnel; and operational personnel, that is, patrol officers, detectives, and certain specialists. Any cooperative agreements that may be developed at the administrative level will also need to be given special attention at the "street" level of the agency. Without field support even the best of plans will not be implemented fully or correctly.

Law enforcement is in a special position within the community to coordinate interagency training and resource development. For example, training school teachers and staff in the area of child abuse and neglect is a long-term commitment that law enforcement personnel could consider in conjunction with other service agencies, such as CPS, mental health, and the local child abuse prevention council.

Service organizations offer opportunities for law enforcement practitioners to discuss the issue of child abuse with leading members of the community. Through such cooperation, community education, treatment, and prevention projects can be initiated. By carefully targeting the most active and organized groups, a police agency can gradually move an entire community in a positive direction.

Moreover, interagency cooperation is imperative if a police agency is directing a great deal of time and effort toward prevention activities. Historically, law enforcement has developed a strong image for crime prevention and has been somewhat successful in preventing property crimes and certain crimes against persons within residential and commercial settings. Similar approaches in the area of child abuse and neglect have also proven to be useful, especially when conducted in schools. Coordination with local school officials and other important segments of the prevention network, such as the local child abuse prevention council, mental health, and CPS, is necessary to develop a comprehensive approach for child maltreatment prevention efforts.

Federal standards for the law enforcement system recommend that police agencies develop programs and strategies to prevent child abuse and neglect. Prevention strategies should start with patrol officers. The ability to identify high-risk situations can be developed through in-service and roll-call training. Federal standards also recommend the implementation of formal prevention programs (15). This responsibility can only begin to be fulfilled when all segments of the community network are working together and moving in the same direction.

Summary

Law enforcement's involvement in child abuse cases has often been controversial and marked with divergent views about the need for criminal justice intervention. Police departments have slowly made the problem of child abuse a high priority. The realization that child abuse and neglect requires more attention has led to a greater degree of specialization and training throughout all levels of law enforcement. Many law enforcement agencies are learning that the multidisciplinary team approach to the problem of child abuse holds the most promise. Interagency cooperation is essential to any successful endeavor from the investigative stage to the entire realm of prevention. In the final analysis, it should be made clear that law enforcement practitioners want to be involved with the issue of child abuse because they care.

References

1. Gelles, R. 1979. Violence toward Children in the United States. In *Critical Perspectives on Child Abuse,* ed. R. Bourne and E. Newberger. Lexington, Mass.: Lexington Books.
2. Straus, M. 1978. The Social Causes of Interpersonal Violence: The Example of Family Violence and Odyssey House Non-Violence. Paper read at American Psychiatric Association meeting, August 20, Toronto.

3. Thoms, P., Jr. 1972. Child Abuse and Neglect, Part I: Historical Overview, Legal Matrix, and Social Perspectives. *North Carolina Law Review* 50.

4. Besharov, D. 1981. What Physicians Should Know about Child Abuse Reporting Laws. In *Child Abuse and Neglect: A Medical Reference,* ed. N. Ellerstein. New York: Wiley.

5. Kobetz, R. 1971. *The Police Role and Juvenile Delinquency.* Gaithersburg, Md.: International Association of Chiefs of Police.

6. Kobetz, R. 1982. *Child Abuse and Neglect: Reference Manual and Trainer's Guide.* Albany, N.Y.: New York State Police.

7. Broadhurst, D. 1979. *The Role of Law Enforcement in the Prevention and Treatment of Child Abuse and Neglect.* Washington, D.C.: U.S. Department of Health and Human Services.

8. Broadhurst, D. 1977. *The Police Perspective on Child Abuse and Neglect.* Gaithersburg, Md.: International Association of Chiefs of Police.

9. Ruddle, R., ed. 1981. *Missouri Child Abuse Investigator's Manual.* Columbia, Mo.: University of Missouri.

10. Longstreth, K. John. 1985. Michigan State Police, Executive Division. Personal communication.

11. Helfer, E. Ray. 1981. Personal communication.

12. Schmitt, B., ed. 1978. *The Child Protection Team Handbook: A Multidisciplinary Approach to Managing Child Abuse and Neglect.* New York: Garland Press.

13. Schmitt, B., ed. 1977. *A Comparative Analysis of Standards and State Practices: Abuse and Neglect,* vol. 6 of 9. Washington, D.C.: National Institute for Juvenile Justice and Delinquency Prevention.

14. U.S. Department of Health, Education, and Welfare. 1978. *Child Abuse and Neglect: State Reporting Laws.* Washington, D.C.: National Center on Child Abuse and Neglect.

15. U.S. Department of Health, Education, and Welfare. 1978. *Federal Standards for Child Abuse and Neglect Prevention and Treatment Programs and Projects.* Draft report. Washington, D.C.: National Center on Child Abuse and Neglect.

21 Liberty and Lawyers in Child Protection
Donald N. Duquette

The distinguishing feature of the juvenile or family court which sets it apart from all other elements of the child protection system is that the court acts as arbiter of personal liberty. When society at large, through child protective services, attempts to intervene in the private life of a family on behalf of a child, the court must assure that the rights of the parents, the rights of the child, and the rights of society are protected and are abridged only after full and fair and objective court process. Only the court can abridge these personal rights in other than emergencies. Only the court can compel unwilling parents (or children) to submit to the authority of the state. The court, then, controls the *coercive* elements of our society and allows those coercive elements to be unleashed only after due process of law.

If the personal freedom of parents or of children stands to be limited or infringed, then the court must hear the circumstances and decide whether or not the infringement of personal freedom is warranted. Except in emergencies, personal freedom may not be taken away without the authorization and legitimization of the court.

The personal rights at stake for both parents and children in child protection have been recognized in our law as fundamentally important constitutional rights (1). The rights of parents to the care and custody of their children and the rights of children to live with their parents without government interference can be infringed only after due process of law.

The law is an essential partner with the medical, social, and mental health professionals in coping with children who may be abused or neglected. The perspective and orientation of the lawyer and judge, however, is somewhat different from that of the other professionals. Personal rights and liberties, their protection or their abrogation in certain cases, is the unique business of the court.

Lawyers act as advocates for one side or another or for one set of interests or another. Lawyers need not pursue the solution best for all concerned and need not ascertain what is best in the circumstances, but they owe primary allegiance to their clients and must deter-

Donald N. Duquette, J.D., is clinical professor of law and director of the Child Advocacy Law Clinic at the University of Michigan Law School, Ann Arbor.

mine the client's position and advocate for that position zealously. According to our legal traditions, the adversarial presentation of competing points of view should result in a fair and just resolution (2). Attorneys who come from a background of reliance on the adversarial system are well advised to adjust their thinking in juvenile court to a less adversarial approach and to greater reliance on negotiation and mediation. Despite the movement toward more cooperation and conciliation in family and juvenile court, the legal process remains ultimately adversarial.

Physicians and social workers come from a reliance on trust and cooperation and find the adversarial court process discomforting, foreign, nonproductive, or counterproductive in terms of the "real problems" faced by the family. Even if lawyers successfully reduce the level of adversity in family and juvenile courts, the nonlawyers are likely to remain uncomfortable. Alternative ways to protect the personal liberties of parents and children are being explored (3, 4). Greater reliance on negotiation and mediation are two such alternatives to an adversarial trial. Until nonadversarial alternatives are widely used, however, all must work with the adversarial process. The advantages of the adversarial process must be appreciated and the disadvantages minimized. The following discussion is offered as a step toward interdisciplinary understanding of the court process and the legal profession's responsibilities.

All states have cruelty-to-children or assault-and-battery statutes that make it a crime to abuse or seriously neglect a child. While criminal prosecution is nearly always possible, it is not often pursued in most jurisdictions (see chap. 20). The criminal case is difficult to prove and must be proved beyond a reasonable doubt; it takes considerable time; provides no help to the family unit; and the family unit, if the prosecution is successful, may break up, rather than stabilize. If unsuccessful, the accused parent may feel vindicated and justified in his or her previous treatment of the child. The possibility of criminal prosecution may, however, have an effect on the parents by getting them to agree to a treatment program and juvenile court jurisdiction in exchange for dismissal of the criminal charges (5). Except in the most serious cases, criminal prosecution of intrafamily child abuse or neglect cases is not generally recommended (6, 7).

The Danger of Overreaching

A danger exists in child protection that the personal rights of parents and children will *not* be protected in our well-intentioned zeal to protect and help children and parents. Our good intentions do not alter the need to recognize and respect the personal integrity and autonomy of clients. Mr. Justice Brandeis warned us about the dangers to our liberty presented by the benevolently intended state:

> Experience should teach us to be most on our guard to protect liberty when the Government's purposes are beneficent. Men born to freedom are naturally alert to repel invasion of their liberty by evil-minded rulers. The greatest dangers to liberty lurk in insidious encroachment by men of zeal, well-meaning but without understanding. (8, at 479)

The U.S. Supreme Court in *In re Gault* held that benevolent state intentions do not justify any relaxation of legal safeguards or procedural protections for parents or children (9).

Monrad Paulsen addressed the risks of well-intentioned overreaching:

The "reaching out" with Protective Services, whether by a public welfare department or a voluntary agency, presents a problem which the good motives of the agency ought not to obscure. If help is offered when it is not wanted, the offer may contain an element of coercion. There is a danger of overreaching when the agency deals with the most vulnerable members of the community who may easily be cowed by apparent authority. [What is] the extent to which the offering of protective services should be reviewed by some judicial or administrative agency[?] . . . The privacy of a family ought not to be upset lightly. (6, at 158)

Child protective services is an area of state control over individuals and families rarely visible to most members of the community. Social workers and other helping professionals involved in child protection activities intend no harm to client families, but aspire instead to stabilize the family as a unit, to protect the child, and to impart skills of child rearing where they are lacking. In spite of the benevolent motives of child protective services, however, significant intrusions by government into personal and family life is possible without the safeguards of the due process of law. The extent of government intrusions in the form of child welfare services may not be warranted in some cases.

Children's services workers and supervisors should recognize that their clients often attribute considerably more power and authority to them than they may actually possess. Child welfare clients are often poor and powerless. The threat of court action is present in every child welfare case, whether expressed or implied. Clients may agree to protective services involvement out of fear of departmental authority or fear of court petition. Overestimating the power of the department, the family may believe that a petition to the court is tantamount to removal of their children, not understanding that they have rights in the legal process too. The exaggerated perception of protective services authority and the fear of the court process may intimidate clients so that they will acquiesce in "voluntary" plans for services or for placement of their children. Such "voluntary" and nonjudicial arrangements provide neither safeguards for the rights of the parents and the children nor checks on a possibly overzealous agency or social worker. A good part of any legal case brought on behalf of children (and against their parents, as the parents may see it) often comes from the parents' own statements and admissions. Parents are often "condemned out of their own mouths."

Therefore, the risk of arbitrary social work action, of agency coercion, and of overreaching in violation of personal liberty and personal integrity looms large indeed. How should personal freedoms of parents and children be preserved in child welfare? Should procedural safeguards be established within the administrative structure of children's services to protect the privacy and personal liberties of clients? Or should we rely on individual social workers to respect personal liberties and clearly advise clients of their legal rights and the limitations of social work authority whenever involuntariness and coercion may exist?

Some have suggested that all child welfare clients be given a warning upon first contact that anything they say can be used against them in court and that a warrant be required prior to any protective services investigation (10). Such warnings and warrants are not now required by law. Basic fairness and good social work practice and ethics require that clients be fully advised of the protective services role and the limits of agency authority from the very first contact.

Because child abuse and neglect cause such great societal concern and because the child protection network has been seen as benevolently motivated, society has, up to now, been willing to run the risk of occasional coerced and perhaps unwarranted invasions of family privacy in exchange for swift identification and response to child abuse and neglect and related ills. The law has not required that notice and hearing be provided before child protective services is allowed to become involved with the family. Child welfare professionals, however, ought to be aware of the personal liberty issue and be responsive to it in their every dealing with potential clients.

The Child's Advocate

Despite the fact that many commentators have attempted to prescribe the duties and responsibilities of the child's representative, there is little consensus today on what the role of the child's representative ought to be. There is little consistency of approach among courts and little or no agreement as to what constitutes good and effective representation of children (11, at 3, 11; 12–14). Representation for children in many child protective proceedings is haphazard with no consistent commitment to provide representation for the child (13, at 30; 15). Only a few jurisdictions define the duties and responsibilities of the appointed representative in their statues (14, at 862). In any case the ambitious child advocate role suggested by many commentators is sorely limited in practice by lack of training in the role and by the low fees paid in many communities to private attorneys representing children.

Some see the child's representative as an extraneous figure and argue that the interests of the child are adequately protected by the child welfare agency, by the parents, or by the judge (11, at 10; 16, at 5; 17). The child's representative may be seen as having limited value in a given case since the representative usually has no special training or background preparing him or her for this nontraditional role (12, at 51; 16, at 13; 18; 19). The influential commentators Joseph Goldstein, Anna Freud, and Albert Solnit, in deference to parental autonomy, would preserve the power to appoint a legal representative for the child to the parents, unless the parents are displaced as the legal protectors of the child by emergency out-of-home placement by formal court adjudication (20, at 111–29). Nonetheless, the prevailing view across the country today is that children should be independently represented in civil child protection proceedings (11–14).

Dissatisfaction and uncertainty about the representation and advocacy provided children in child abuse and neglect cases remain widespread. Does independent representation of the child really make any difference to the outcome of a case? Are there means other than attorney representation of the child that may be effective, perhaps at less cost? The dissatisfaction has provided an impetus for clarifying the duties and responsibilities of the child's representative and for searching out alternative means of representing children.

The search for alternatives has taken many forms. The National Center for Child Abuse and Neglect (NCCAN) has funded many demonstration projects around the country since 1981 in which children are represented by volunteer lawyers, law students, multidisciplinary child advocate offices, and lay volunteers (11). Communities have experimented with trained volunteers to either represent the child or assist a lawyer in representing the child (31). Seattle began a guardian *ad litem* program in 1977, using the title CASA (Court Appointed Special Advocate) to designate the lay volunteer who represents children in child protection cases (14). The National Council of Family and Juvenile Court Judges has encouraged CASA program development in many ways, including sponsoring a national CASA seminar.[1] The National Council of Jewish Women, having adopted CASA as a special community service project, developed an extensive manual for CASA programs and sponsored seminars around the country (21). Over 173 such programs now exist in 39 states (22). An active National Association of CASAs has been organized which provides a national newsletter, an annual meeting, and other services.[2]

The role of CASA and other lay volunteer child advocates varies greatly from community to community. The volunteer may be paired with an attorney and become the "eyes and ears" of the child's lawyer, or the volunteer may be independent of the child's legal representative and conduct an independent investigation and do independent advocacy for the child. Still other volunteer advocates function as assistants or adjuncts to the caseworkers.

The question of whether someone other than a lawyer should represent children has been raised in several quarters (17, 23). The American Bar Association (ABA) Juvenile Justice Standards Project comments:

> While independent representation for a child may be important in protective and custodial proceedings, a representative trained wholly in law may not be the appropriate choice for this function.
>
> ·
>
> Accordingly it would not seem irresponsible to suggest that a professional trained in psychology, psychiatry, social psychology or social welfare be assigned the initial responsibility for protecting children under these circumstances. There is, however, no evidence that this alternative is presently available, either in terms of numbers of competent personnel or in terms of occupational independence from official and interested agencies.
>
> ·
>
> . . .[U]ntil there are sufficient numbers of independent, competent personnel trained in other disciplines who will undertake to ascertain and guard the child's interests in these proceedings, continued reliance on legal representation for the child is necessary. (12, at 73–74)

Whether the child is represented by a lawyer or a nonlawyer or some combination, I suggest that the child advocate's role should be aggressive, ambitious, and encompass both legal and nonlegal interests of the child. This definition of the child representative's role, consistent with that of most major commentators (12, 13, 23), rejects a passive, purely procedure-oriented approach. In child protection proceedings the children need more than a technician to ensure legal precision, they need more than a passive observer and adviser to the court, they need an *advocate*. Advocacy for children includes traditional courtroom advocacy but also emphasizes out-of-court advocacy in informal meetings with the agencies and over the phone to other service deliverers. Statutes in all states require or permit the appointment of an advocate for the child in child protection cases.[3]

---

[1] For information on programs contact the Court Appointed Special Advocates Committee, National Council of Family and Juvenile Court Judges, Judicial College Building, University of Nevada, Reno, Nevada 89507.

[2] Information on current programs can be obtained from the National Association of Court Appointed Special Advocates, 909 N.E. 43rd Street, Suite 204, Seattle, Washington 98105.

[3] The Federal Child Abuse Prevention and Treatment Act of 1974 (P.L. 93-207, 42 U.S.C. §§ 5101–5106, renewed in 1984, P.L. 98-457) conditioned a state's receipt of federal funds for certain programs under the Act on the state's fulfilling certain conditions, including a requirement that the state shall "provide that in every case

That advocate is generally a lawyer and is charged with representing the "best interests" of the child and with making an independent judgment of what those "best interests" might be. The statute in Michigan is illustrative:

> The court, in every case filed under this act in which judicial proceedings are necessary, shall appoint legal counsel to represent the child. The legal counsel, in general, shall be charged with the representation of the child's best interests. To that end, the attorney shall make further investigation as he deems necessary to ascertain the facts, interview witnesses, examine witnesses in both the adjudicatory and dispositional hearings, make recommendations to the court, and participate in the proceedings to competently represent the child. (25)

But what are the child's "best interests"? What goals are child representatives obliged to pursue on behalf of the child? In most settings a lawyer has a client to articulate what he or she wants which essentially determines the position the lawyer will take. In child protection, however, the position to be taken by the advocate may be quite unclear. The child is frequently unable to express a view. Even when a very young child expresses a view, the advocate, charged with representing the child's "best interests" may disagree with the youthful client and advocate a different position (26, at 506–7).[4]

The child's best interests are not susceptible to objective definition but remain wreathed in personal values. Robert Mnookin writes:

> Deciding what is best for a child often poses a question no less ultimate than the purposes and values of life itself. Should the decision maker be primarily concerned with the child's happiness or with the child's spiritual and religious training? Is the primary goal long-term economic productivity when the child grows up? Or are the most important values of life found in warm relationships? In discipline and self-sacrifice? Are stability and security for a child more desirable than intellectual stimulation? These questions could be elaborated endlessly. And yet, where is one to look for the set of values that should guide decisions concerning what is best for the child? . . . [I]f one looks to our society at large, one finds neither a clear consensus as to the best child-rearing strategies, nor an appropriate hierarchy of ultimate values. (30, at 18)

Describing the role of the child representative as being the advocate for the best interests of the child does little to distinguish his or her role from that of the other actors in the child protection process. The child protection agency generally considers that achieving the best interests of the child is its primary goal and purpose. The parents' attorney will also argue for what his clients see as the best interests of the child (which is generally to be at home with his or her parents free of government interference). The judge makes the ultimate decision of what is in the best interests of the child, and judicial opinions consistently reinforce the paramount importance of the child's best interests in court decision making.

If the child's representative is to decide what is in the child's best interests, certainly nothing in law school training has equipped him or her to assess parental conduct, to ap-

---

involving an abused or neglected child which results in a judicial proceeding a guardian *ad litem* shall be appointed to represent the child in such proceedings" [42 U.S.C. § 5103(b)(2)(G)]. Neither the Act nor the implementing regulations required that the guardian *ad litem* be an attorney. See also the report from the National Center on Child Abuse and Neglect (11) and Kelly and Ramsey (24, at 408).

[4] Most recent commentators have urged, however, that advocates for the child take the position identified by the youthful client when the young person is considered capable of judgment. See ABA Standards (12, at 1–5 and § 3.1(b)), Ramsey (27), Long (28, at 611), and Horowitz and Davidson (29, at 296–99).

praise the harms to a child presented by a particular environment, to recognize strengths in the parent-child relationship, or to evaluate the soundness of an intervention strategy proposed by the social agency. The child's representative must synthesize: the results of the protective services investigation; the child's psychological, developmental, and physical needs; the child's articulated wishes; the represenative's own assessment of the facts and of the treatment resources available. Many of the child's best interests are ordinarily addressed by other actors in the child protection process, but others may be easily overlooked by all but the child's representative.

Certainly the child is to be protected from physical and emotional harm and provided with minimally adequate food, clothing, shelter, guidance, and supervision. The social worker and the court generally address such serious and obvious deficiencies in the child's care. But other interests are more subtle. The state intervention itself presents additional risks to the child of which the child advocate must be wary. The interests of an individual child are not always consistent with those of the state agency. Because of high caseloads the agency may not be willing or able to meet each child's individual needs (e.g., for frequent visitation). An overburdened caseworker may not be as sensitive, as careful, as skilled in judgment as she or he should be. The child runs the risk of being inappropriately separated from familiar surroundings. The child runs the risk of an inadequate assessment of the home situation so that remedies prescribed are inappropriate, inadequate, or too late. The child runs the risk of being placed in multiple foster homes, of being placed in inappropriate places, of being abused in foster care, of not having frequent enough visits with his parents and family. Reasonable case plans may be developed by social agencies but not implemented properly or implemented too slowly, thus adding to the length of time the child is out of his or her home and lessening the child's chances of ever returning home.

In coming to a position for the child, the child's advocate must ascertain the facts of the case as clearly as possible by relying on the protective services investigation in some cases and by interviewing family members, neighbors, and others as necessary. The child advocate should meet the child client in every case, even if it is only for the purpose of getting a "feel" for the child as a real person facing a serious personal dilemma. The advocate should always keep the child in mind in the midst of all the paperwork of court petitions and social work reports.

The child's representative ought not to agree with social work recommendations without question. While maintaining a cooperative spirit, he or she should question the social worker closely and extract the underlying basis for the caseworker's positions and recommendations. The advocate's conclusions should be reached independently.

The advocate should strive to identify what the determinants of the problem are. Once the underlying determinants are identified, the advocate can help discover ways to ease them. Thus, a child advocate is encouraged to take a broad view of the child's interests, to avoid a piecemeal approach to the child's and the family's problems, and to see the child in the context of his or her family.

Having identified the needs and interests of the child, the representative should advocate vigorously for those interests. The advocacy for the child ought to begin with the social agency which filed the petition. The child's representative should advocate for a careful assessment of the family situation, for adequate and specific case plans, and for timely implementation of case plans. The child's interests include preserving his or her placement with a parent or parents, if at all possible, when consistent with his or her own well-being and safety. The child generally has an interest in maintaining contact with the family through regular visits. If removal from the family is necessary, it should be for the shortest time possible, and placement should generally be to a familiar setting (the least restrictive, most family-like setting).[5] If services to the child or the family are needed before he or she can return home, those services should be identified accurately and provided promptly.

The child's advocate can play a significant role in facilitating negotiation and mediation. Swift resolution of the legal dispute which is as cooperative and as nonadversarial as possible and which provides the needed protection and services to the child is nearly always in the child's best interests. Child's representatives should be trained to encourage negotiation and to play the role of mediator and conciliator between the social agency and the parents.

In the court hearing the child's representative ensures that all the relevant facts are brought before the judge and advocates for a resolution of the case most likely to achieve the identified interests of the child.

The role of the child's representative after adjudication should remain vigorous and active. The child advocate can press and persuade the responsible social agencies for services and attention which the child client (and perhaps the family) needs. Preferably such nudging can be done in a collegial, nonaccusatory manner, but if social workers or agencies are not fulfilling their responsibilities to a particular child (or to the parents) the child's representative may insist on a higher standard of service either by a direct request to supervisors in the agency or by formally raising the issue before the court.

Thus the child advocate's role includes not only the traditional legal representation of the case, but also strongly emphasizes the social, psychological, and service delivery aspects of the case so important to the child. In an empirical study, advocates trained to represent children in the manner described here provided improved representation for children and achieved better care outcomes for their young clients (31).

Protective Services Attorney

Traditionally in child protection cases no attorney appeared in most court actions on behalf of the social agency or the individual who filed the petition alleging child abuse or neglect. In the recent past, if an attorney did appear, he or she was likely to be a young assistant prosecutor or assistant county corporation counsel with little preparation time, limited experience in such cases, and little familiarity with either the juvenile court or child protection law. The child neglect attorney was often the one most recently hired by the county prosecutor's office. Attorneys complained about the lack of specificity with which their social worker clients presented their cases and about the "murkiness" and lack of legal standards in the juvenile court generally. Juvenile court, and especially child abuse and neglect cases, often received low priority among members of the bar.

---

[5]Other authorities advocate for the "least intrusive form of intervention" (12, at 82); the "least detrimental alternative" (32, at 53–64); and the Federal Adoption Assistance and Child Welfare Act of 1980, P.L. 96-272, 42 U.S.C.A. § 675(5)(A) requires the use of the least restrictive (or family like) setting available in close proximity to the parents' home, consistent with the best interest and special needs of the child.

In recent years, concurrent with the due process revolution in juvenile court, the role and functioning of all attorneys in juvenile court has gained importance and more precise definition. The need for competent legal advice for petitioning agencies in child protection has been increasingly recognized. Proving child abuse or neglect in child protection cases is often very difficult. The parents are generally represented by an attorney. The child may be independently represented. A petitioning protective services worker is at a distinct disadvantage if he or she is charged with the burden of proof in an adversarial court without legal counsel. In fulfilling their responsibilities to children and to families, child protection agencies need consistent and reliable legal assistance.

The role of the petitioner's attorney in child protection cases includes conventional attorney duties, but differs from the traditional lawyer tasks in several respects.

Lawyers who represent banks learn the banking business very well. Lawyers who represent labor learn labor unions and labor organizing from top to bottom. Likewise, lawyers who represent child welfare agencies should get to know and understand social work as a profession and the child welfare system. The child welfare lawyer must understand and appreciate the emphasis on nonjudicial (yet fair) handling of child protection cases. In addition to traditional legal skills, understanding juvenile court and family law and philosophy is essential. The attorney should know and respect the functions, the capabilities, and the limitations of social workers and other behavioral scientists. The foster care system—its limitations and strengths, its advantages and disadvantages, the benefits and risks to children—must also be appreciated.

What is the nature of the attorney-client relationship between the child protection agency and its lawyer? The legal agency which assumes responsibility for legal representation of the child protection petitioners in the juvenile or famiy court vary from state to state or sometimes even from county to county. The duties may be assumed by the local prosecuting attorney, the state attorney general's office, the county corporation (civil) counsel, or sometimes by lawyers who are actually employees of the child protection agency. Some legal agencies representing protective services assume a quasi-judicial role and will initiate legal action as requested by the social agency only if in their judgment such action is warranted. Such lawyers exercise a sort of prosecutorial discretion about which child protection cases are brought to court.

In contrast, a recommended position is that the legal representatives of the agency see themselves in a traditional attorney-client relationship. In invoking the court system, child protection service workers should have access to a lawyer whom they can trust and who will act as the advocate of their point of view as necessary.

Points of view and judgments about strategy may differ between the lawyer and the agency personnel, but such differences are certainly not unusual between lawyer and client and are rather common in both personal and corporate practice. When such disagreements occur the lawyer should rely on the traditional counselor function of the lawyer in which the matters are discussed in-house and recommendations for actions are negotiated. If some differences cannot be resolved in this manner, the lawyer should defer to his or her social agency clients in matters within the scope of their expertise (i.e., in social, psychological judgments and assessments of the needs of the child and family), while the agency should defer to the lawyer in matters of trial strategy and legal judgment. Unfortunately the boundaries between legal and social spheres of expertise are often not clear and distinct in this context. Almost every judgment in child abuse and neglect cases reflects a value judgment that certain parental behavior constitutes legal neglect. Normative fact judgments are made at every step of the child protection process: by the reporting person, by the social worker, by the social work supervisor, by the lawyers, and finally, and most importantly, by the judge. What is the minimum community standard of child care to which every child is entitled? What is the threshold of child care below which the state may and should intervene, even coercively, on behalf of the child (and for the good of the family unit, or so goes the theory)? These questions, addressed in every child protection case consciously or not, blur the distinctions between legal and social spheres of expertise.

With the understanding that the spheres of competence are not always clear and distinct, the attorney and the client agency ought to arrive at in-house positions, each deferring to the other's expertise where appropriate, with the lawyer acting as advocate for their joint position.

The interface between the child protection agency and the court system must be explored and understood by the attorney representing the agency. The role of the court must be placed in context for the agency by their lawyer. The court acts as arbiter between the individual citizens and the social agency as to the agency's right to intervene in the privacy of the family. When the family does not voluntarily agree to the agency intervention, the court must decide whether or not the circumstances justify coercive, authoritative state intervention on behalf of the child.

Delivery of services to the dysfunctional family remains the duty of the child protection agency whether or not court action is taken. The social workers have the charge and the skills and the expertise to actually provide assistance to the children and their families. The court's role is to authorize the agency to act in cases in which parents will not voluntarily accept services. The court's authorization facilitates the agency intervention. The court itself, however, has no treatment expertise, nor should it be relied upon to develop a treatment plan. The social worker may not recognize the limited role of the court as a judicial body and that the social agency bears the responsibility to develop and implement a treatment plan for the children and family. The agency lawyer must make clear to the social worker clients that the court itself can do no treatment or social planning for a family. The court's role is to prevent unwarranted interferences with their private lives and to monitor the agency intervention.

The agency lawyer must understand the role and functioning of protective services well enough to identify the long-term social objectives of the agency as separate and distinct from the generally shorter term, more immediate legal objectives. If the lawyer understands the agency goals, he or she can be more creative in the use of the court process. The agency lawyer should not define the client's goals only in terms of legal objectives— for instance, to acquire temporary jurisdiction, to prove probable cause, or to obtain emergency detention. With the help of the social worker, the attorney must identify the *social goals* of the agency as specifically as possible. Thereafter, by creative use of the court process, the lawyer may be able to help accomplish the social goals, whether or not the specific legal goals prove to be attainable.

The legal process itself may add to the family dysfunction. Sometimes the trauma of adversary litigation cannot be avoided. But often, when the social objectives of the agency are clearly in mind, an attorney can accomplish the goals of the agency without trial, through strategies of negotiation, mediation, and pacing the litigation.

The attorney should work closely with the protective services agency. In the initial interview with an agency social worker the lawyer must ask: "What do you want to result from the legal action?" "What are your professional (i.e., social work) goals for the client family?" The lawyer should test the social work strategy in a collegial but "devil's advocate" way: "Will court action facilitate the social work intervention strategy?" "How will it do so?" "Can each of the elements of the intervention plan be justified by facts presentable to the court?"

The social worker, with his or her experts and team members, must be able to articulate the social objectives of court action. The lawyer may wish to attend multidisciplinary treatment team meetings regarding cases on which he or she is or may be active. The lawyer needs to know the behavioral science reasoning behind a particular intervention strategy, and he or she may be able to contribute knowledge to the team about the legal process available to facilitate the strategy (see chap. 7). Knowing the plan and its basis, the lawyer is better able to support it in court through expert and material witnesses.

A further challenge for the lawyer is to achieve the social results in an efficient, effective, and direct way which avoids or minimizes the negative effects of the adversary process. A process of mediation or negotiation may avoid the adversary system in which family members must testify against family members and helpers, such as social workers and physicians, must testify against the parents they are trying to help. Skills and tactics in negotiation and mediation are especially important to the child protection attorney.

We have identified two separate aspects of the protective services attorney's role: first, to prove and present the client's case in the most persuasive fashion possible; second, to understand and embrace the social goals of the client agency and to further those goals by nonadversarial means if possible.

We now come to a third aspect of the agency attorney's role: preparing the client agency for on-going court review of a treatment plan ordered by the court. Certainly preparation of the treatment plan remains in the sphere of the social worker. However, the lawyer understands the degree of specificity and prompt action required by the court for such plans and serves the client well by prompting the client to efficiently and clearly state what the goals of a plan are and what the specific details of a plan are. The lawyer understands the legal importance of the treatment plan and the ramifications that noncompliance by the agency or the parents may have in subsequent court proceedings.

The court retains ultimate responsibility for the well-being of children under its jurisdiction. It cannot abrogate that responsibility. New legislation and several recommended model statutes contain procedures for formalizing legal standards for the review of continued intervention in a family under court authority (33, 34).

At a review hearing the child protection agency is in a position of giving account of its stewardship. Before such a hearing, the court will have taken jurisdiction over a child and ordered certain interventions which may have included placement of the child and counseling or other treatment for the family. At a review the agency must give account to the court of what services have been provided and what progress has been made by the family. The agency attorney can aid his or her client by not letting matters drift between the initial court order and the review hearing. Correlatively, the parents must give account of themselves and show what progress they have made in correcting the problems that brought their child to the attention of the court.

The agency, in essence, is asking that the court continue its authorization to intervene in the family, perhaps including continued placement or termination of parental rights. Agencies must show that a treatment plan has been followed and that the legal and social intervention is justified by correlative benefits, either realized or nearing realization, to the child and the family.

If the agency cannot justify its continued involvement with the family by demonstrating good faith efforts to rehabilitate the family, the court may revoke the agency's authority to act, that is, terminate the court's jurisdiction, place the child with another agency, or return a child home in spite of agency requests to the contrary. Admittedly, a return home against the agency recommendation is a rare and probably risky thing for a judge to do without some expert opinion to counter the agency recommendation or without additional resources to deal with a particular family. A court whose orders are not followed may also use its contempt power and levy fines or even jail time.

The agency attorney's role demands well-developed traditional legal skills. However, the attorney must also know the "business" of his or her clients very well. Ultimately, a successful intervention in a family requires close collegial cooperation between the lawyer, the child protection agency, and the psychiatric, psychological, and medical consultants to the agency.

Attorney for the Parents

The attorney for the parents is charged with representing the interests of his or her clients zealously within the bounds of the law (2). Advocacy for the parent usually takes the form of minimizing the effects of state intervention on the family and may include diplomatic attempts to get petitions dismissed, in-court advocacy for dismissal, insistence that the charges brought by the state be legally proven in court, and negotiation for dispositions that are most acceptable to the parents.

The attorney should know the applicable law and the local court procedures and practices. He or she should understand the particular family and thoroughly investigate the facts of this particular case (35). He or she should also be familiar with the common dynamics of child abuse and neglect and with the treatment programs in the local community that deal with such problems. Considerable information can be obtained from reading, but the lawyer should also understand and be familiar with the local scene. One of the best ways to do this is to spend time with local social workers, physicians, psychologists, and other lawyers with experience in child abuse and neglect cases.

Representation of parents in cases of alleged child abuse and neglect requires unique skills and resources in addition to traditional lawyer advocacy. Lawyers must first deal with their negative feelings toward the client parent accused of child abuse or neglect. The feelings toward a client parent, unless dealt with properly from the beginning, can sabotage a lawyer's advocacy either consciously or unconsciously. One means of dealing with personal feelings toward allegedly abusive or neglectful parents is to understand the dynamics behind child abuse and neglect. Accused parents often have difficulty trusting others, forming relationships (including relationships with their lawyers), and deferring gratification. The lawyer must understand and cope with these and other characteristics of many such parents.

Lawyers are counselors at-law as well as advocates. In the agency attorney's role, the lawyer may advise a client social worker to pursue nonlegal avenues in a case before taking legal action or to consult other professionals about treatment strategy before initiating court action. Similar advice may be given to parents.

The lawyer as counselor to parents must feel comfortable engaging the parent as a person, must evaluate the parents' difficulties and their legal and social situation, and then provide legal counsel as to how to accomplish their goals. The lawyer may explore the parents' perspective on whether or not personal and family problems exist with which the social agencies may assist. He or she may counsel parents to accept certain services, seeking postponement of the court process in the interim. As a result, the parents may be willing to accept some limited assistance from an agency voluntarily. The parents may even be advised to forego immediate legal advantage in order to benefit from a social intervention that is calculated to prevent recurrence of abuse or neglect.

The parents' attorney can sometimes perform valuable functions for the parents by encouraging nonjudicial resolutions of the case. A voluntary plan of treatment may avoid formal court jurisdiction and still protect the child and address the problems which may have been identified by protective services. Nonjudicial resolutions with legal representation of the parents avoids the danger of improper invasion of personal liberties without due process. A lawyer representing parents should be assured that whatever agreement the parents enter into is done voluntarily and knowingly, that is, with full awareness of possible consequences.

Where the parents are willing to accept some services under the shadow of court action, the parent's lawyer should obtain from the social worker a detailed treatment plan for the family. The social worker should also make a contract with the parents defining in concrete terms the problems that are to be worked on, the obligations of the parents and of the agency, and what is expected to be achieved by the parents prior to the return of the child or the termination of intervention by the agency.[6]

The counselor's role is quite consistent with traditional lawyer functioning and is based on trust and dealing with clients as important individuals. However, these nonadversarial tasks of the lawyer may be even more important in child protection than in other areas of the law. In exercising the counselor function, the lawyer must be careful to establish whatever trust he or she can with the clients. When recommendations of cooperation with social agencies are made, they should be made carefully so that the clients understand that if the suggestions of the lawyer are not accepted, the lawyer will stand by them as advocate of their position in subsequent proceedings.

After exercising the counselor function, the lawyer may decide that vigorous advocacy of his or her client's goals is necessary. This decision may be based on an appraisal that the case against the parents is weak or unfounded, or the agency response may seem unduly harsh or drastic in light of the problems identified by the agency. The agency may offer no better alternative for the child. The tenuousness of foster care may be less desirable than attempting to protect the child in his own home and providing necessary family services. Federal law requires that a child be placed in the "least restrictive alternative placement" (33) and that "reasonable efforts" be taken to prevent or eliminate the need for out-of-home placement of the child (33, 42 U.S.C.A. §§671 (a)(15), 672(a)(11)). The client may also firmly deny the allegations in the petition and instruct the lawyer to contest the case.

---

[6] See elements of case plan required by P.L. 96-272, 42 U.S.C.A. § 675(5)(A).

The lawyer is then duty bound to advocate zealously for his or her client. As one commentator notes:

> It is imperative that the attorney *not* be concerned with the best interests of the child. That is the initial task of the caseworkers and the ultimate task of the court. (35, at 229)

Certainly the lawyer begins his advocacy for the client through negotiation and conciliation efforts with the protection agency itself. Some discussion and negotiation may lead to a resolution of the conflict between parents and agency. Lawyers must learn the important art of persuading a large bureaucracy convinced of the inherent rightness of its position to modify that very position. In spite of the desirability of nonjudicial resolutions of disputes between the parents and the social agency, it is often necessary to proceed to trial.

The responsibility of a parent for injuries to or possible neglect of a child may be a contested issue. The lawyer has a duty to vigorously and resourcefully stand as the ardent protector of his or her client's constitutional and personal rights. The lawyer must bring to the task the usual tools of the advocate—familiarity with the applicable law, the ability to logically present the pertinent facts, and the facility for forceful and persuasive exposition of parents' cause. Many professionals often find the lawyer's role as the zealous advocate for the parent in serious child abuse cases disquieting and difficult to understand. This issue is one raised regularly in interdisciplinary groups concerned with child abuse and neglect.

In the dispositional phase of a case, the parents' lawyer may serve several different functions: a) The lawyer can ensure impartiality by acting as a counterbalance to pressure exerted on the court by the very nature of the issues. b) He or she can assure that the basic elements of due process are preserved, such as the right to be heard and the right to test the facts upon which the disposition is to be made. c) He or she can make certain that the disposition is based upon complete and accurate facts and that all the circumstances which shed light upon the conduct of his or her client are fully developed. d) The lawyer can test expert opinion to make certain that it is not based on mistakes arising from either erroneous factual premises or limited expertise. e) He or she can give the frequently inarticulate parents a voice in the proceeding by acting as their spokesperson. f) The attorney's relationship with the parents may even enable him or her to give the protective services or court staff new and meaningful insights into the family situation. g) Finally, the parents' attorney can interpret the court and its processes to the clients and thus assist the parents in genuinely accepting the actions of the court (36).

Attorneys in child protection, whether representing the child, the parents, or the state, face unique challenges for which traditional law school education has probably not prepared them. To function effectively in any of the lawyer roles, the attorney needs advice and consultation from social work and mental health professionals. Nonlawyers in child protection services need to have some idea of what to expect of the lawyers they meet in the court system. Interdisciplinary knowledge is as important to effective legal proceedings as it is to other aspects of state intervention on behalf of children.

The Child as Witness

Unfortunately, child abuse, neglect, and sexual exploitation cases sometimes result in a child being called to give testimony. Widespread dissatsifaction exists with the way children are dealt with in the justice system, particularly when they are called as witnesses. Michigan Court of Appeals Judge John H. Shepard reflected that dissatisfaction when he wrote:

> This case demonstrates the unsatisfactory methods available for establishing guilt or innocence in parent-child incest cases. The child is frequently so traumatized by the events and by the adversary nature of trial procedure that evidence produced at trial is often of questionable reliability. The psychological damage done to a child by requiring in-court testimony can be permanently devastating. (37)

Some studies have found that child sexual abuse victims who participate in judicial proceedings suffer more harm than children who do not go to court (38), although there is little direct evidence of exactly which aspect of the court experience causes the trauma (39). Children are traumatized by the court process in both civil and criminal court actions and often by the lack of coordination among courts and social agencies (40, 41). Children are often subjected to repeated interviews by social workers, police officers, and lawyers before a case is actually presented in court. A child may be subjected to prolonged direct and cross-examination over several days, particularly in criminal prosecutions.

Each community should develop a coordinated policy covering child abuse prosecutions which involves both criminal and civil court, the prosecutor or district attorney, the child protective services, law enforcement, and mental health services. The psychological harm to a child witness can be reduced by careful coordination of the many aspects of the case. Several national groups have advocated reforms in the way children are dealt with in the court process.[7] Among the reforms suggested are: joint interviews between child protection and law enforcement agencies which are recorded on videotape and viewed by all other professionals who have a need to know; "vertical prosecution," where the same prosecutor or district attorney handles a child abuse case from the beginning to the end and in all courts; using the power of the criminal law or family court to protect the child victim in his or her own home, perhaps by ordering the perpetrator out of the home, rather than routinely placing the victim into foster care; limiting the spectators at a hearing in which a child is testifying; streamlining court proceedings in cases of child abuse or where there is a major child witness by giving them docket priority over all other criminal matters and by making adjournments and postponements very difficult to obtain; enacting new legislation allowing broader hearsay exceptions for the child witness; and expanding the use of videotaped depositions so that the child would not have to testify in open court so often, if at all, and not have to face the accused parents. Each of these reforms is discussed below.

Legal Capacity to Testify

What is the general capacity of a child as a witness? Children are commonly perceived to have difficulty distinguishing between fact and fantasy and to be considerably less reliable as witnesses than adults. Recent psychological research does not support that conven-

---

[7] American Bar Association, "Guidelines for the Fair Treatment of Child Witnesses in Cases Where Child Abuse Is Alleged," May 1985. Attorney General's Task Force on Family Violence, September 1984. National Conference of the Judiciary, 1983. ABA National Legal Resource Center on Child Advocacy and Protection, 1982.

tional view. There are many myths about child witnesses that recent psychological research addresses. Our intuitive beliefs about children's abilities need to be replaced with solid evidence and greater understanding (42).

Understanding the difference between a truth and a lie is often the first requirement for testifying in court. For adults, taking the oath is itself sufficient evidence that the witness knows the difference between a truth and a falsehood. Child witnesses are asked questions to determine their capacity for truthfulness in most jurisdictions. The questioning often refers to the religious upbringing of the child and whether he or she fears punishment for not telling the truth (43): "Do you know the difference between the truth and a lie?" "What is the difference?" "What happens if you do not tell the truth?" If a child does not answer these questions to the satisfaction of the judge the child is not permitted to give testimony.

Yet in children as well as in adults, comprehending the oath and the difference between a truth and a lie does not guarantee honesty. Several researchers have shown that moral behavior or telling the truth does not necessarily follow from an understanding of the difference between a truth and a falsehood (44).

Twenty states have followed the federal rules of evidence by presuming competence of all persons to testify, including children (45). The Attorney General's Task Force on Family Violence urges that "children, regardless of their age, should be presumed to be competent to testify in court. A child's testimony should be allowed into evidence with credibility being determined by the jury" (46, at 39).

Accuracy and Reliability of Child Witnesses

What is the child's ability to accurately perceive events, remember them, and communicate them accurately? Johnson and Foley have reviewed current studies and conclude that children's memory is not necessarily worse than that of adults. "Children often report more limited information than do adults, but what they report can be just as accurate" (47, 48). There seems to be little justification for disqualifying children based on memory recall as research shows no difference between children and adults in short-term or long-term retention of memory (48). Addressing the common perception that children confuse fact and fantasy more than adults do, Johnson and Foley report that "based on current laboratory studies, children do not seem more likely than adults to make such confusions" (47, at 39).

Are children able to communicate the facts of a case accurately? Researchers are able to tell us that certain measures will improve the performance of a child. Anatomically correct dolls may facilitate a child's testimony by allowing the child to act out the incidents in question. The lawyer's questions should be tailored to the child's level of language development (49). Rapport with the questioner and familiarity with the proceedings and the courtroom will result in less anxiety and the child will perform better on the witness stand. On the other hand, anxiety will detract from a child's performance as a witness. Several researchers have found that the accuracy and efficiency of recall abilities are reduced when the situation is perceived as being hostile (50). "If a child appears incompetent on the stand, chances are that it is anxiety about the trial situation or the inappropriate nature of the competency exam that is rendering the child incompetent" (51).

Preparing the Child to Testify

Careful and sensitive preparation of the child is critically important to both lessening the psychological trauma to the child and improving the child's performance on the stand. The person who will ask questions of the child at trial should first learn the child's story through viewing the videotaped statements, talking with social workers, counselors, police officers, and others who have already spoken with the child, and then finally talking with the child. The child should meet with the person doing the questioning several times, not merely to go over the testimony but primarily to help the child feel comfortable with the questioner. The child should be taken to the courtroom in advance of the trial date and the courtroom and court procedures should be explained. The child should be allowed to sit in the witness box and to move about the courtroom rather freely to get comfortable with the surroundings. Some practice preliminary questions, such as, "What is your name?" "What is your address?" "Where do you go to school?" will help the child get familiar with the process. The child is told who will be sitting where and what to do in the case of objections or other legal activity. If the child wants a recess during the testimony, he or she can ask the lawyer, another support person, or the judge. The child should also be told to stay cool and to tell the truth as clearly and fully as possible.

Assisting the Child Witness

In addition to the careful and full preparation of the child for testimony and the use of anatomically correct dolls, many jurisdictions are adopting other measures to assist the child witness. Although trial judges have the power to do so without legislation, various states have passed statutes allowing and encouraging the use of a support person at the trial for the child witness. This support person can be a relative or a friend or a witness assistance person hired by the court who will stay with the child through all the phases of the court process. The child can have such a person near during the testimony and may even sit on the person's lap if desired.

Various states have also reduced the number of spectators allowed in the courtroom during a child's testimony in an effort to reduce the pressures on the child witness. Judges may simply request that all the public except members of the press leave the court. Family and juvenile courts have traditionally been closed to the public.[8] Blanket closures of the courts in criminal matters may run afoul of the defendant's constitutional right to a public trial and must meet the tests the U.S. Supreme Court set forth in *Globe* and *Richmond News* which require a specific case by case finding of harm to the child before closure is possible (53).

Many authorities have recommended streamlining court proceedings in cases of child sexual abuse or when there is a major child witness in a case (see footnote 7 above). Far too often legal proceedings drag on for months and months during which the child has to remain ready to provide testimony to the court. Not only do the number of court appearances cause trauma to the child, but also the weeks and months over which the case ex-

---

[8]There is considerable doubt whether a blanket closure of juvenile and family court will withstand constitutional challenge based on the first Amendment protections for freedom of the press and Sixth Amendment guarantees of public trial which could be extended to youth (52).

tends. The time factor is very important to young children. Courts control their own dockets and have the power to give priority to these kinds of cases if they will.

Alternatives to Child Testimony

Settlement of the case without the child having to testify is usually the optimum resolution from the child's perspective, but if a matter goes to trial it may be possible to proceed without having to call the child as a witness in court. Several exceptions to the hearsay rule may be applicable. The most common ones are excited utterance (Federal Rules of Evidence 803(2)) and statements made in the course of medical examination (Federal Rule of Evidence 803(4)). A number of states have created special exceptions to the hearsay rule for child sexual abuse victims.[9] The state of Washington allows admission of a reported statement by a child under ten which would otherwise be inadmissible if the statement provides sufficient indicia of reliability *and* either the child testifies at the proceedings *or* the child is unavailable and there is corroborative evidence of the fact (Wash. Rev. Code §9A.44.120). This statute and a similar statute in Kansas were upheld against a challenge that it denied the defendant his right of confrontation (54).

America's fascination with technology has led to a greater use of videotape to preserve the statements of child witnesses and victims. Videotape has become a helpful investigative tool that allows a professional especially trained and skilled in the fine art of interviewing children to take a statement from a child soon after the abuse incident has been reported. All other agencies in need of that information can get it from the video rather than re-interviewing the child. Besides saving the child repeated interviews, this system promotes settlement of cases. Once the defendant views the videotape of the child telling his or her story, perhaps with the use of anatomically correct dolls, he or she very often enters a plea rather than taking the matter to trial (51, at 47).

An innovation that has received a great deal of attention is the use of a videotaped statement of a child in lieu of direct testimony at trial (55, 56). A large number of states have passed or are considering measures that allow such videotaped evidence in court. The many critics of these measures argue that such a system violates the defendant's right of confrontation:

> Radical alternations such as permitting ex parte videotaped statements of a child witness, provided the child is available to be called by the defendant, are neither necessary nor constitutional. (57, at 48)

Several states have allowed the use of videotape in place of live testimony *only if* the court finds that testifying will be traumatizing to the child or if the child witness is medically or otherwise unavailable (51). The U.S. Supreme Court has yet to deal with the issue of videotaped depositions of child witnesses directly, but their rulings on cases dealing with the defendant's confrontation right indicate that it is not an absolute right and that evidence may be admitted without an opportunity for eye-to-eye confrontation under certain circumstances (58). In the case of *Ohio v Roberts,* Justice Blackmun wrote for the U.S. Supreme Court:

[9] At least nine states have done so: Arizona, Colorado, Delaware, Indiana, Kansas, Minnesota, South Dakota, Utah, and Washington (51).

. . . [W]hen a hearsay declarant is not present for cross-examination at trial, the Confrontation Clause normally requires a showing that he is unavailable. Even then, his statement is admissible only if it bears adequate "indicia of reliability." Reliability can be inferred without more in a case where the evidence falls within a firmly rooted hearsay exception. In other cases, the evidence must be excluded, at least absent a showing of particularized guarantees of trustworthiness.

Thus upon a showing that the child is somehow unavailable to testify and that his or her videotaped statements possess indicia of reliability or guarantees of trustworthiness, admission of videotapes in lieu of live testimony at trial would probably pass constitutional scrutiny.

Although a great deal of attention has been paid to the use of videotape as an alternative to live testimony, it may be that our energy is misplaced and may be better spent on behalf of the child witness. Gary Melton discusses reforms that would make the present system more responsive to the special needs of children without challenging the prevailing criminal procedure (39). A consultant to the U.S. Justice Department says:

Our research leads us to conclude that too much attention is presently directed to legislative reforms permitting innovative practices that benefit only a handful of the growing number of children enmeshed in the criminal justice system. A large portion of the effort now devoted to statutory reform might be more productively focused toward alternative techniques that are less dramatic, yet equally—or even more—effective. In other words, creative exploitation of resources that are already available might achieve the same goals without threatening the structural premises of American law. (51, at 84)

Conclusion

At long last considerable national attention is being directed toward the problems facing children who take the witness stand. Some of the reforms proposed, such as limited eye-to-eye contact between the child and the accused, are dramatic with profound constitutional implications. But other devices are within the reach of a great many of us. Community coordination of court and social agency responses to child sexual assault, sensitive preparation of children for testimony, eliminating unnecessary court appearances, and streamlining the court process can all be done at a local level without significant law changes. We all have some power to improve the way children are treated in the court system. ABA President John C. Shepherd pointed the way when he pledged "to put the needs of the children of America, which have long been overlooked, high on the agenda of the American Bar Association. . . . The need is urgent. The mission is one of our most important" (59).

References

1. Meyer v. Nebraska, 262 U.S. 390 (1963); Pierce v. Society of Sisters, 268 U.S. 510 (1925); Griswold v. Connecticut, 381 U.S. 479 (1965); Stanley v. Illinois, 405 U.S. 645 (1972); Roe v. Wade, 410 U.S. 113 (1973); Moore v. City of East Cleveland, 431 U.S. 494 (1977); Smith v. Organization of Foster Families for Equality and Reform, 431 U.S. 816 (1977); Lassiter v. Dept. of Social Services, 452 U.S. 18 (1981); Santosky v. Kramer, 455 U.S. 745 (1980).

2. American Bar Association (ABA). 1971. ABA Code of Professional Responsibility. Canon 7. Chicago: ABA.

3. National Institute for Dispute Resolution, 1901 L Street, N.W., Suite 600, Washington, D.C. 20036

4. Vorenberg, E. W. 1982. *A State of the Art Survey of Dispute Resolution Programs Involving Juveniles.* Monograph of ABA Special Committee on Alternative Means of Dispute Resolution. Washington, D.C.: ABA.

5. Buckley, J. 1982. *Innovations in the Prosecution of Child Sexual Abuse Cases.* Monograph of ABA National Legal Resource Center on Child Advocacy and Protection. Washington, D.C.: ABA.

6. Paulsen, Monrad G. 1974. The Law and Abused Children. In *The Battered Child,* 2d ed., ed. C. H. Kempe and R. E. Helfer. Chicago: University of Chicago Press.

7. Delaney, James J. 1972. The Battered Child and the Law. In *Helping the Battered Child and His Family,* ed. C. H. Kempe and R. E. Helfer. Philadelphia: Lippincott.

8. Olmstead v. United States, 277 U.S. 438 (1928) [Mr. Justice Brandeis dissenting].

9. In re Gault, 387 U.S. 1 (1967).

10. Levine, R. S. 1973. Caveat Parens: A Demystification of the Child Protection System. *Univ. Pittsburgh Law Rev.* 35:1.

11. U.S. Dept. of Health and Human Services (DHHS). 1980. *Representation for the Abused and Neglected Child: The Guardian Ad Litem and Legal Counsel.* Special report from the National Center on Child Abuse and Neglect (August). DHHS Pub. No. (OHDS) 80-30272.

12. American Bar Association. Institute of Judicial Administration. 1977. *Juvenile Justice Standards Project: Standards Relating to Counsel for Private Parties.* Cambridge, Mass.: Ballinger.

13. Fraser, B. 1976. Independent Representation for the Abused and Neglected Child: The Guardian ad Litem. *California Western Law Rev.* 13:16.

14. Note. 1983. The Non-Lawyer Guardian ad Litem in Child Abuse and Neglect Proceedings: The King County, Washington, Experience. *Washington Law Rev.* 58:853.

15. Ray-Bettineski, C. 1978. Court Appointed Special Advocate: The Guardian ad Litem for Abused and Neglected Children. *Juvenile and Family Court J.* 29:65.

16. Davidson, H. A. 1980. *Representing Children and Parents in Abuse and Neglect Cases.* Monograph of ABA National Legal Resource Center on Child Advocacy and Protection. Washington, D.C.: ABA.

17. Johnson, C. L. 1979. *Much More To Do about Something: The Guardian ad Litem in Child Abuse and Neglect Judicial Proceedings.* Athens, Ga.: Regional Institute of Social Welfare Research, Inc.

18. Berstein, B. E. 1980. The Attorney ad Litem: Guardian of the Rights of Children and Incompetents. In *Who's Watching the Children? A Collection of Readings on the Legal Aspects of Child Welfare Services for Neglected Children,* ed. Clara Simmons, pp. 40–45. Cleveland, Ohio: Case Western Reserve University, School of Applied Social Sciences.

19. Knitzer, J., and Sobie, M. 1984. *Law Guardians in New York State: A Study of the Legal Representation of Children.* Monograph. Albany, N.Y.: New York State Bar Association.

20. Goldstein, J.; Freud, A.; and Solnit, A. 1979. *Before the Best Interests of the Child.* New York: Free Press.

21. Blady, M. 1982. *Children at Risk: Making a Difference through the CASA Project.* (Available from the National Council of Jewish Women, 15 East 26th Street, New York, NY 10010.)

22. National Association of Court Appointed Special Advocates, Seattle, Washington. Personal communication, March 1986.

23. Johnson, C. L.; Thomas, G.; and Turem, E. 1980. Implementing the Guardian ad Litem Mandate: Toward the Development of a Feasible Model. *Juvenile and Family Court J.* 3 (November).

24. Kelly, R., and Ramsey, S. 1983. Do Attorneys for Children Protection Proceedings Make a Difference? A Study of the Impact of Representation under Conditions of High Judicial Intervention. *J. Family Law* 21:405.

25. Michigan Compiled Laws Annotated 722, 630.

26. Isaacs, J. L. 1963. The Role of Counsel in Representing Minors in the New Family Court. *Buffalo Law Rev.* 12:501.

27. Ramsey, S. 1983. Representation of the Child in Protection Proceedings: The Determination of Decision Making Capacity. *Family Law Q.* 17:287.

28. Long, L. 1983. When the Client is a Child: Dilemmas in the Lawyer's Role. *J. Family Law* 21:607.

29. Horowitz, R. M., and Davidson, H. A. 1984. *Legal Rights of Children.* Colorado Springs: Shepards/McGraw-Hill.

30. Mnookin, R. 1985. *In the Interest of Children.* New York: W. H. Freeman.

31. Duquette, D., and S. Ramsey. 1986. Using Lay Volunteers to Represent Children in Child Protection Court Proceedings. *Child Abuse and Neglect: The International Journal* 10:293; D. Duquette and S. Ramsey. 1987. Representation of Children in Child Abuse and Neglect Cases: An Empirical Look at What Constitutes Effective Representation. *Michigan Journal of Law Reform* 22 (forthcoming).

32. Goldstein, J., Freud, A., and Solnit, A. 1973. *Beyond the Best Interests of the Child.* New York: Free Press.

33. Federal Adoption Assistance and Child Welfare Act of 1980. P.L. 96–272, 42 U.S.C.A. §671(a)(15), 672(a)(11).

34. American Bar Association. 1981. *Juvenile Justice Standards Project: Standards Relating to Abuse and Neglect.* Cambridge, Mass.: Ballinger.

35. Hewitt, C. 1983. Defending a Termination of Parental Rights Case. In *Foster Children in the Courts,* ed. Hardin. Boston: Butterworth Legal Publishers.

36. Isaacs, J. L. 1972. The Role of the Lawyer in Child Abuse Cases. In *Helping the Battered Child and His Family,* ed. C. H. Kempe and R. E. Helfer. Philadelphia: Lippincott.

37. People v. Wilkins 134 Mich App 39 (1984), concurring opinion.

38. Katz, S., and Mazur, M. 1979. *Understanding the Rape Victim.* New York: Wiley.

39. Melton, G. W. 1984. Child Witnesses and the First Amendment: A Psycho-Legal Dilemma. *J. Social Issues* 40(2): 109–23.

40. American Bar Association. National Legal Resource Center on Child Advocacy and Protection. 1981. *Innovations in the Prosecution of Child Sexual Abuse Cases,* ed. J. Bulkley. Washington, D.C.: ABA.

41. American Bar Association. National Legal Resource Center on Child Advocacy and Protection. 1982. *Recommendations for Improving Legal Intervention in Intrafamily Child Sexual Abuse Cases*. Washington, D.C.: ABA.
42. Goodman, Gail S., ed. 1984. The Child Witness. *J. Social Issues* 40(2).
43. McCormick, Charles T. 1972. *Handbook of the Law of Evidence,* § 63. St. Paul, Minn.: West.
44. Goodman, Gail S. 1984. Children's Testimony in Historical Perspective. *J. Social Issues* 40:12.
45. Federal Rules of Evidence 601.
46. Attorney General's Task Force on Family Violence. Report of September 1984.
47. Johnson, M. K., and Foley, M. A. 1984. Differentiating Fact from Fantasy: The Reliability of Children's Memory. *J. Social Issues* 40:33–50.
48. Goodman, G. S. 1984. The Child Witness: An Introduction. *J. Social Issues* 40:4.
49. Berliner, L. and Barbieri, M. K. 1984. The Testimony of the Child Victim of Sexual Assault. *J. Social Issues* 40:125.
50. Dent, H. E., and Stephenson, G. M. 1979. An Experimental Study of the Effectiveness of Different Techniques of Questioning Child Witnesses. *British J. Social and Clinical Psychology* (1979): 41.
51. Whitcomb, D.; Shapiro, E. R.; and Stellwagov, L. D. 1985. *When the Victim is a Child: Issues for Judges and Prosecutors*. Washington, D.C.: U.S. Dept. of Justice, National Institute of Justice.
52. Note. 1983. The Public Right of Access to Juvenile Delinquency Hearings. *Michigan Law Rev*. 81:1540.
53. Globe Newspaper Co. v. Superior Court, 457 U.S. 596 (1982); Richmond Newspapers v. Virginia, 448 U.S. 555 (1980).
54. K.S.A. 60–460 (dd); State v. Slider, 688 P. 2d 538, 38 Wash. App. 689 (1984), and State v. Rodriquez, 657 P. 2d 79, 88 (Kan. App. 2d 353 (1984)).
55. Ordway, D. 1981. Parent-Child Incest: Proof at Trial without Testimony in Court by the Victim. *Univ. Michigan J. Law Reform* 15:131.
56. Note. 1985. The Testimony of Child Victims in Sex Abuse Prosecution: Two Legislative Proposals. *Harvard Law Rev*. 98:806–27.
57. Graham, M. 1985. Child Sex Abuse Prosecutions: Hearsay and Confrontation Clause Issues. University of Miami. Unpublished monograph.
58. Ohio v. Roberts, 448 U.S. 56 (1980); California v. Green, 399 U.S. 149 (1970); U.S. v. Benfield, 593 F.2d 815 (8th Cir. 1979).
59. Shepherd, J. C. 1984. Child Advocacy and Protection Is a Key to the Future. *ABAJ* (October): 6.

PART

IV

Prevention

22 An Overview of Prevention
Ray E. Helfer

The goal of any individual or group working in as difficult a field as child abuse and neglect is prevention. While this goal is truly admirable, the very thought is overwhelming. Preventing a phenomenon that occurs at least a million times each year, that adversely affects children's physical growth and emotional development, and that eats away at the very foundation of our society—the family—is a goal that must always be before us.

What Is Being Prevented?

In the narrow sense, the answer to this question of what is being prevented is very clear: physical abuse. Broadening this answer only slightly would add overt severe neglect. Limiting the goal to these two manifestations makes the studies and research in this field rather simple. Expansion of the answer to include the prevention of adverse forms of parent-child interactions complicates the research picture considerably, yet both extremes have been studied.

O'Connor et al. demonstrated that rooming-in after the delivery of a newborn decreases risk of physical abuse, abandonment, and failure to thrive (1). Burgess demonstrated that mother-child interactions are more negative and less frequent in abusive families than in nonabusive families (2). Both extremes of this interactional continuum can be measured and the preventive intervention assessed. Combining both extremes of this continuum into one definition is difficult, but feasible (see chap. 4).

With very few exceptions, if one wishes to prevent something bad from happening, the development of something good must come first. Eliminating cholera and dysentery from our society required the development of sewers and clean water systems. Preventing polio required building polio antibody levels in the bodies of our children through vaccination. Fire prevention necessitates cleaning up our closets and installing sprinkler systems. Likewise, to prevent child abuse and the other adverse outcomes of the breakdown in the inter-

Ray E. Helfer, M.D., is professor in the Department of Pediatrics and Human Development, College of Human Medicine, Michigan State University, East Lansing.

actional systems within our families (see chap. 4) we must *enhance* interpersonal skills in those very folks who like each other the most, those who will make up our future families, the mothers and fathers to be.

This raises two critical questions: 1) What programs must be implemented to enhance interpersonal interactions? 2) How does one gain access to individuals before they become parents to implement these programs?

Before considering these two issues, an important though obvious consequence of this approach must be acknowledged. Child abuse prevention programs should *not* be expected to result in an immediate decrease in the incidence of child abuse. While this is desirable, the ramifications of family dysfunctions and the manifestations of abuse are too massive and our ability to identify and measure their incidence is too inaccurate for such to be identified within a short period of time. What can be expected of prevention programs, on the other hand, is *improvement* of interactional skills between those individuals to which the programs are aimed. Their interactional skills can improve as demonstrated by Bristor et al. (3) and Lutzker et al. (4).

What Programs Enhance Interactional Skills

In a 1982 review of the literature on the prevention of abuse (5), the following components of primary prevention programs were identified as necessary:

1. A community consortium committed to the dictum that family violence in their community is unacceptable;

2. A never-ending mass media campaign to educate the public on this dictum;

3. A major change in our health services to include some form of training for *all* new parents in the art of communicating with one's baby;

4. A home health visitor program for *all* new parents for the one to two years after the birth of their firstborn child;

5. An early child development program for all preschool children run by churches, schools, community colleges, or whomever;

6. An interpersonal skills program (how-to-get-along curriculum) in the public schools (K–12) built upon interpersonal skills in grade school, advancing to courses in sexuality and parenting in high school; and

7. An adult education program for two levels of young adults—those who had a positive childhood experience themselves and want a refresher course on childhood before they become parents, and those whose childhood experiences were negative who need a "crash course in childhood" before parenting is undertaken.

Figure 22.1 diagrams chronological age in cyclical fashion, listed inside the circle. Outside the circle various intervention programs are identified. These programs are lettered, with a brief discussion for each given below. Appropriate references are given where they are available. With this diagram the reader should be able to place the programs discussed in this part of the book and in the literature in some perspective.

A. Perinatal coaching. New parents are provided training in the interactional skills necessary to communicate with their newborn (6–8; see also chap. 23).

B. Home care training. New parents are provided home visitors to assist them in resolv-

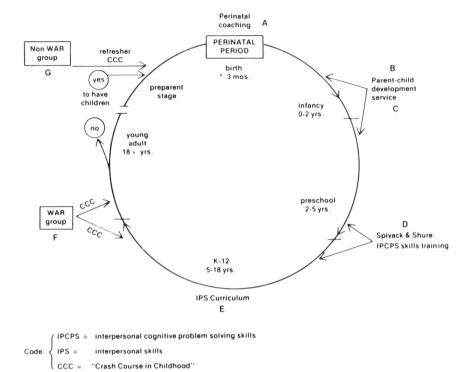

Figure 22.1

A paradigm for prevention. (See text for discussion and references.)

ing day-to-day issues and health problems, and in increasing interpersonal communication skills with their infants (9, 10).

C. Expanded well-baby care. The proposal here is that physicians and nurses must better meet the needs of young parents when they bring their new babies in for traditional well-child care. No longer is it appropriate to limit the service provided to that which simply demonstrates that the child is physically well (11).

D. Interpersonal cognitive problem-solving skills. Techniques have been developed by Spivack and Shure to teach small children (ages four to ten years) how to solve everyday problems. These can be taught by preschool and primary school teachers (12, 13).

E. Interpersonal skills (IPS) teaching for middle (junior high) school and high school. This program, at this time, is a fantasy, but an achievable one. Schools should be teaching "how to get along" skills—getting along with peers, teachers, parents, girls, boys, dates, mates, and one's children. They should *not* isolate one or two of these issues (e.g., sex education and parenting). The IPS curriculum should be continuous throughout this six-to-eight-year period. No good study of this concept has yet been found by this author. All of the above are proposed for everyone.

F. Crash course in childhood for adults. Some young people have arrived at adulthood by way of a childhood which, to say the least, was less than optimal. These young adults need a second chance to learn the skills of interaction, skills which should have been learned during their childhoods (see chap. 4). This relearning and retraining is best done before one arrives at the pre-parent stage of life (14).

G. Pre-parent refresher. Many of the young adults, both men and women, who had a positive childhood experience and those graduates of the "crash course in childhood" will decide to enter the pre-parent stage (getting ready for pregnancy and parenthood). Some will have placed many years of work and/or cognitive learning (college and graduate school) between their childhood and their parenthood. These soon-to-be parents need a refresher course in the concepts of interacting with children and mates (14).

The most encouraging programs of those listed are the new parent-newborn communication training, the lay health visitor programs, and the school-age-child training by Spivack and Shure.

In their discussion of the lay health visitor (LHV), Gray and Kaplan (9) summarize this service training program as follows: The coordinator and the pediatrician develop the initial relationship with the mother on the postpartum ward. All new mothers are approached in a nonthreatening, nonjudgmental manner. The major focus of the interview is to evaluate the mother's attitudes, perceptions, and feelings for the baby in order to assess her ability to care for the infant. The pediatrician and the coordinator contact the mothers frequently during their postpartum hospitalization to obtain as much information as possible about the family and facilitate the home follow-up by the LHV. Another important responsibility of the coordinator and pediatrician is the communication of information to hospital staff, community agencies, and the LHV so that discharge plans and follow-up services can be arranged.

The utilization of a hospital-based pediatrician and coordinator who interview *all* mothers has several advantages. First of all, it enables the interviewer to observe a wide range of mothers, infants, and family situations. Thereby, expertise in assessing the potential for parenting problems is developed. The pediatrician and coordinator are also able to gather more information from a new mother when they can sit down and talk to the mother and do not have to perform a task (i.e., take blood pressure or temperature). In informal conversation they can gather information that is more subtle than that revealed to the hospital staff.

The pediatrician and the RN coordinator see all the mothers on a daily basis and, on occasion, some are seen more than once daily in order to build trust, answer questions, and help resolve any current problems. During their contacts with the mother, information is gathered in eight general areas:

1. the prenatal, labor, and delivery experience
2. the family's support system
3. attachment behaviors of the parents
4. the mother's relationship to significant others (her parents, husband, and older children)
5. the mother's background
6. the father's background
7. the parents' financial status and source of health care
8. the parents' expectations for the baby

After information is gathered in the categories listed above, the LHV program is explained to the mother as a service which is offered to all mothers in order to provide extra support, answer questions about care of a newborn, and to serve as liaison for medical care and community agencies. If the mother accepts the program (the majority do), her

LHV meets her on the postpartum ward, and they arrange a home visit during the first week after hospital discharge. This affords immediate continuity of care, which is generally unavailable in other agencies.

The subsequent LHV service involves a minimum of contact of two home visits during the first month. At that point, the LHV and her supervisor (pediatrician, coordinator, or research associate) assess the family's strengths and needs and determine the focus for subsequent intervention. The intervention may take any one of many directions but is primarily geared to reducing family stresses in ways that would be beneficial for the entire family. This can mean that medical care for the family is arranged, that a public health nurse referral is appropriate, or that some other community agency (e.g., department of social services, ADC, food stamps) is necessary. The mother and the LHV work together on problem solving. This shared problem solving gives the mothers increased self-confidence and raises their self-esteem.

Classification

The question of the appropriate goal for prevention programs is usually resolved by inserting the word *primary* in front of prevention, thereby indicating prevention before the fact. While this should help, the fact that child abuse is a cyclical event, from one generation to another, adds complexity to this terminology. Treatment of parents after a child has been abused (see chap. 17) would be considered secondary prevention as far as the child is concerned (preventing recurrences). Treatment of the child, on the other hand, would be primary prevention as far as the child's children are concerned (see chap. 18). Providing a new mother, formerly abused, with special training in how to interact with her baby (see chap. 23) is primary prevention for the baby and secondary for the mother.

All this can be summarized as follows:

Primary prevention: providing training and services to enhance those skills necessary to keep abuse and its many ramifications from ever occurring (e.g., perinatal coaching programs).

Secondary prevention: providing training and services to enhance those skills necessary to keep abuse and its many ramifications from occurring in the next generation and services (e.g., programs for the child or adolescent who is treated after being the victim of abuse).

Tertiary prevention: providing training and services to enhance those skills necessary to keep abuse and its many ramifications from recurring once it has been identified (e.g., all those programs currently underway and discussed in parts II and III of this book; after-the-fact interventions).

At Whom Are Prevention Programs Directed?

Early Identification and Selection[1]

The ability to initiate any program that enhances parent-child interaction and has the potential to prevent outcomes of serious breakdown in these interactions, such as failure to thrive, abuse, and neglect, inevitably raises the question of preselection or screening. Who should receive such a program? How should they be chosen?

[1] This section was published originally in W. B. Bristor, A. L. Wilson, and R. E. Helfer, "Perinatal Coaching: Program Development," *Clinics in Perinatology* 12:367–79, and is reprinted here by permission.

The simplest, and safest, answer is that all mothers and fathers should have the benefit of perinatal coaching. If not all, then certainly all new mothers and their infants. While this may be the goal, realistically many new programs cannot service such a large number at the outset. How then would those who receive perinatal coaching be selected? Some have narrowed the population by age, serving only those below 18 years. Others have offered the training only to those delivering on Tuesdays or on alternate days or months. These plans have the distinct advantage of not adversely labeling the recipients. This also protects the program from receiving a label that may be inappropriate—for example, "only mixed-up or high-risk parents and babies are helped." Both these labels must be avoided.

But this begs the question somewhat. What are the methods available to screen or identify those who really need these extra services? Five such techniques have been tested and reported. Others will surely appear in the literature and may already have been published but are unknown to the author. These five fall into three distinct categories: the self-administered questionnaire, the standardized interview, and the observational checklist.

The self-administered questionnaires are useful in that they take little time and personnel and are inexpensive. The Adult-Adolescent Parenting Inventory (AAPI) and the Michigan Screening Profile of Parenting (MSPP) have been developed and tested for several years (15, 16). They are both short (32 and 50 questions respectively) and utilize a forced choice-response scale. Both are relatively easy to score, but the MSPP requires a special computerized scoring program (17). Neither have been used in long-term follow-up studies to determine predictive validity, sensitivity or specificity. Both have yielded acceptable validity in known sample comparisons.

The standardized interview has been studied extensively (18). This method of screening has the distinct advantage of using a one-to-one, face-to-face technique, which in turn carries the distinct disadvantage of extensive training for the interviewers, cost, and time. This also has acceptable validity and reliability.

Two observational checklists have been studied and reported (19, 20). One was used by emergency room personnel and the second by clinic (health center) staff. The former was assessed in a long-term evaluation. Both show encouraging results.

Each of these tools is useful in research studies, especially when one wishes to determine the presence or absence of high-risk parenting dysfunction in both the study and control group. The utilization of instruments with so-called predictive capability on a "routine" basis carries a considerable burden. At best, these have an 80–85 percent sensitivity and specificity. One must use great care not to adversely label or make invasive intervention decisions solely on the results of these tests. Their use in clinical decision-making mandates that services be available for referral and follow-up for those in need of them. Great care must be taken to avoid adverse or inappropriate labeling. At the current level of validity, these instruments should be reserved for well-designed studies approved by human research committees.

Access to the Population

Any prevention endeavor must gain access to a *large* number of individuals *before* whatever one is trying to prevent occurs. Programs in the child abuse field are no exception. However, gaining access prior to the onset of abuse may be difficult if one pursues the theme which advocates "preventing something bad." On the other hand, marketing programs which enhance interpersonal skills is much easier and more acceptable. Such programs are nonthreatening, nonlabeling, and eliminate any concerns about cultural or religious bias. They even override the concerns of those who feel "parenting should be taught in the home," since interpersonal skill training programs teach *how* to interact, not what form the interaction should take or on what belief system it should be based.

An additional advantage to giving emphasis to the enhancement of interactional skills rather than the prevention of abuse is that gaining access is much easier. The key places in our society where access to a *large* number of people *before* abuse has occurred is feasible are hospital newborn centers (primary prevention) and schools at every level, from preschool through community colleges and universities (secondary prevention). Initiation of programs to improve interpersonal interaction is more acceptable to the boards and committees who "guard the entrance gates" to those institutions, and the populations involved are attracted to these "self-help" programs. To date, for example, very few new parents turn away the perinatal coach when asked if they wish to learn how to interact better with their infant.

Emphasis on enhancement rather than prevention decreases the need to screen for the "high-risk population." All new parents, for example, need improved skills of interacting with their baby; some, of course, need them much more than others. Involvement in the program does not, in itself, adversely label the parent or the child.

Knowledge and its Relationship to Prevention

Any discussion of prevention would not be complete without consideration of the question, "Does knowledge, per se, lead to prevention?" If this could be answered in the affirmative, our task would be much simpler. Teaching facts is indeed much easier and cheaper than teaching skills and influencing one's affective domain.

Certainly, using the media to tell the population that child abuse exists and what to do about it has increased awareness and reporting. Telling the masses that smoking is related to cancer and speeding to fatal auto accidents seems to curtail, to some degree, these behaviors. However, most campaigns to teach parents to keep aspirin out of the reach of children did little to prevent aspirin poisoning. It was not until the tops were made hard to remove that aspirin poisoning was almost eliminated.

Does telling and showing elementary school chidlren about "good touching" and "bad touching," as is done in many traveling shows and videotapes, decrease sexual abuse? It does seem to increase reports, but data are not in, and may never be in, on the preventive effects of these important educational endeavors.

One would hope that the mere knowledge of the devastating effects of sexual abuse on the development of a small child would dissuade a father from sexually exploiting his children. But these data are not in either.

The answer to the question, "Does knowledge, per se, lead to prevention?" seems to be, "To some extent, if the behavior change required is not too complex and the attitude change is not too fundamental."

For example, telling drivers to buckle their seat belts will result in a behavioral change in a certain segment of the population. Making it a law will add more to that group, but not all. In the child abuse area, one would expect that baby shaking would decrease significantly if we put as much money into the TV message "Don't Shake the Baby" as we do in teaching the public "Don't Squeeze the Charmin."

Knowledge, per se, is not sufficient when the behavior change is complex and/or if the attitudes are based on a fundamental belief system. Reading a book or seeing a television demonstration on "how to parent" or "how to play golf" will not, in itself, be sufficient. One must learn these skills by modeling, coaching, one-to-one interaction, and PRAC-TICE. That, after all, is what childhood, in a reasonably normal environment, is all about.

References

1. O'Connor, S.; Vietze, P. M.; Sherrod, K. B.; and Altemeier, W. A. 1980. Reduced Incidence of Parenting Inadequacy Following Rooming-In. *Pediatrics* 66:176–82.
2. Burgess, Robert. 1979. Private communication.
3. Bristor, M. W.; Helfer, R. E.; Coy, K. B. 1984. Effects of Perinatal Coaching on Mother-Infant Interaction. *Am. J. Diseases in Children* 138:254–57.
4. Lutzker, J. R.; Megson, D. A.; Webb, M. E.; and Darkman, R. S. 1985. Validating and Training Adult-Child Interaction Skills to Professionals and Parents Indicated for Child Abuse and Neglect. *J. Child and Adolescent Psychotherapy* 2:91–104.
5. Helfer, R. E. 1982. Preventing the Abuse and Neglect of Children: The Physician's Role. *Pediatric Basics* 23:4–7.
6. Helfer, R. E. 1980. Perinatal Coaching Guide. *Pediatric Basics* 26:10–14.
7. Helfer, R. E., and Wilson, A. L. 1982. The Parent-Infant Relationship. *Pediatric Clinics of North America* 29:249–60.
8. Bristor, W. B.; Wilson, A. L.; and Helfer, R. E. 1985. Perinatal Coaching: Program Development. *Clinics in Perinatology* 12:367–79.
9. Gray, J., and Kaplan, B. 1980. The Lay Health Visitor Program: An Eighteen-Month Experience. In *The Battered Child*, 3d ed., ed. C. H. Kempe and R. E. Helfer, 373–78. Chicago: University of Chicago Press.
10. Kempe, C. H. 1976. Approaches to Preventing Child Abuse: The Health Visitor Concept. *Am. J. Diseases in Children* 130:940–47.
11. American Academy of Pediatrics. 1986. The Well Child.
12. Spivack, G., and Shure, M. 1974. *Social Adjustment of Young Children*. San Francisco: Jossey-Bass.
13. Spivack, G., Pratt, J., and Shure, M. 1976. *The Problem Solving Approach to Adjustment*. San Francisco: Jossey-Bass.
14. Helfer, R. E. 1984. *Childhood Comes First: A Crash Course in Childhood for Adults*, 2d ed. Lansing, Mich.: Helfer Publications.
15. Bavolek, S. J. *Adult-Adolescent Parenting Inventory*. Family Development Associates, Inc., Box 94365, Schaumburg, Illinois 60194.
16. Schneider, C.; Helfer, R. E.; and Hoffmeister, J. K. 1980. Screening for the Potential

to Abuse: A Review. In *The Battered Child,* 3d ed., ed. C. H. Kempe and R. E. Helfer, 420–30. Chicago: University of Chicago Press.

17. Hoffmeister, J. *Michigan Screening Profile of Parenting.* Test Analysis and Development, Inc., 2400 Park Lake Drive, Boulder, Colorado 80301.

18. Altemeier, W., et al. 1982. Antecedents of Child Abuse. *J. Pediatrics* 100:823.

19. Murphy, L. S., and Orkow, B. 1985. Prenatal Prediction of Child Abuse and Neglect: A Predictive Study. *Child Abuse and Neglect: International J.* 9:3.

20. Rosenberg, N. M.; Meyers, S.; and Shackleton, N. 1982. Prediction of Child Abuse in an Ambulatory Setting. *Pediatrics* 70:879.

23 Promoting a Positive Parent-Infant Relationship

Ann L. Wilson

Over the past ten years a growing enthusiasm has surrounded the development of what have become dubbed "early intervention programs" for young families. Noting the changing demographic trends toward increasing numbers of single, young, and working mothers and toward greater separation of parents from traditional supportive resources, communities are searching for ways to assist families with parenting responsibilities.

A perusal of the professional literature and materials available to the service provider uncovers ample evidence of interest in the development of programs to support families. The Family Resource Coalition is a national grassroots network of individuals and organizations that promotes the development of prevention-oriented, community-based programs. This organization has compiled over 1500 files of programs available in communities across the nation. At a national conference convened in May 1983 in conjunction with the Yale Bush Center in Child Development and Social Policy, eighty of these programs were reviewed as models of community-based efforts to reach families with assistance (1).

The National Center for Clinical Infant Programs was created in 1976 by mental health, pediatric, and child development professionals "to achieve a long sought after goal of primary prevention in the earliest years of life" (2). This group recognizes a new clinical science and its application in the form of comprehensive clinical infant development programs. Focusing on the mental health of parents and infants, this group has developed publications and educational conferences to reach clinicians who work with young families.

Infant stimulation programs, originally developed for handicapped babies or those considered to be at risk for disabilities, have also become popular among parents of "normal" infants who want to do "everything for their babies." Emphasizing exercises and structured activities, these programs aim to optimize the developmental potential of babies.

The Systematic Training for Effective Parenting (STEP) program is an example of a packaged parenting course for community support programs that assist families with the development of communication and other parenting skills (3). The Minnesota Early

Ann L. Wilson, Ph.D., is with the Department of Pediatrics, University of South Dakota, Sioux Falls.

Learning Design (MELD), another such model program that utilizes peer support and education for parents, is being implemented in many communities nationwide (4).

Historical Foundations

Along with turbulent times, the 1960s brought an enthusiasm for how early education for disadvantaged children could increase their IQ's and subsequently improve their future social and economic status. The notions of the malleability of intelligence and "the earlier the help, the better" produced and pervaded the Head Start movement, the vanguard of early intervention programs. The very early evaluations of Head Start fuel an overestimation of its effectiveness in increasing children's intelligence. Today the long-term effects of Head Start are known, and they are manifest not so much in higher IQ scores as in a child's being able to enroll in an age-appropriate grade level rather than having to be placed in Special Education (5).

Along with the concept of "the earlier the better" came the notion that parental involvement enhanced the outcome of children involved in Head Start programs. Family involvement seems an obvious determinant of child outcome, but apparently this was not fully appreciated at the onset of Head Start. Ecological approaches which account for the family and community impact on child growth and development are fundamental today.

In the 1970s, there was an enthusiastic response to the concept of "bonding" which emerged primarily from the pediatric literature. No clearer synthesis of the 1960s concepts of "the earlier the better" and "parental involvement" can be imagined than the early claims of a sensitive period following birth during which it is necessary for parents to have contact with their newborn for "later development to be optimal" (6). To some extent the findings from early studies were seized upon and applied to clinical settings with inappropriate zeal. Since that time, the authors of the original studies have toned down the implications of their research (7). However, there is no doubt that the recognition of the bonding phenomenon has positively affected the development of more humane hospital care for the delivering mother, her newborn baby, and the entire family (8). Coupled with the widespread recognition of bonding and the role of early parental contact was an increased awareness of the newborn's sensory capabilities enabling communication from the time of birth.

Efforts to Enhance Parent-Infant Relationships

There are four different kinds of family support programs: those which provide information to families, those which help parents develop specific skills, those which offer social support to new families, and those which offer psychotherapeutic assistance to deal with any emotional barriers affecting the new parents' emerging relationship with their baby.

Several tenets about families have been identified as family support services have developed (1). These are:

1. Parenting is not completely instinctive;
2. Parenting is a tough and demanding job;

3. Parents desire and try to do the best for their children;
4. Parents want and need support, information, and reinforcement in their parenting role;
5. Parents are also people with their own needs as adults;
6. Programs should focus on and work with family strengths, not deficits; and
7. Programs should empower families, not create dependence on professionals.

Especially important for those who are developing programs to assist parents during their child's infancy are the facts that the skills of caring for a baby are not instinctive and that caring for an infant is a difficult, demanding responsibility.

Many who provide care to new families see bonding as an important first step in the beginning of this new relationship. Early findings prompted the belief that the extra time mothers and babies spend together in the early days of life can positively alter their future relationship. While the specific early claims have been modified, the identification of this time as unique is still accepted.

Knowing that caregiving skills do not come naturally implies that these skills can be taught. However, these necessary skills go beyond the mere mechanics of caregiving and include the interactional skills that the parents need to communicate with their infants. Babies clearly have social skills which need to be appreciated and understood by those who care for them.

Social Behavior of Newborns

A shallow, unenlightened view of newborns includes only the perceptions that they weigh six to eight pounds, are warm, and spend their time either sleeping, eating, or crying. Reflected in this description is the image of self-centered human beings who occupy all their time and energy satisfying their own physiological needs. Even for a tiny preterm baby such a description fails to recognize a very important part of the baby's behavioral repertoire—alert attentiveness. All babies experience episodes of very alert behavior when they visually explore the world around them and respond to the sounds of their environment. During these periods babies are amazingly responsive to those caring for them.

To capture these moments of wonderful attentiveness, parents need to become aware of when their baby will be most responsive to them. The different states of consciousness that can be observed in a newborn's behavior have been examined carefully (9). With an understanding of these states, parents can better perceive their babies' level of consciousness and how they will respond to the attention received.

Brazelton identifies six states of consciousness which can be easily observed in a newborn's behavior (10). They are:

1. Deep sleep—eyes closed, regular breathing, no activity except startles, no eye movement.
2. Light sleep—eyes closed with rapid eye movement observed, low activity level with random movements and startles.
3. Drowsy—semidozing with open or closed eyes, variable activity level.
4. Alert—bright look, attention on source of stimulation, minimum motor activity.
5. Active—considerable motor activity, thrusting movements of extremities, fussing may or may not be present.
6. Crying—intense cry which is difficult to break through with stimulation.

During the alert state, babies are best able to respond to the attention caretakers give them. When crying, babies are in need of stimulation that can calm them. With the appropriate amount of stimulation, a crying baby can be calmed so that he or she can again become alert or drift into a sleep state. By holding babies and providing them with movement and soft talking, one can often calm them. The warning is often offered by well-intentioned bearers of wisdom that picking up a crying baby will spoil him. Actually the movement provided by handling a baby clearly helps to calm a crying baby (11). Tending to a crying baby during the first six months of life in the manner described will *decrease* the amount of irritability demonstrated during the second half of the first year (12).

Babies have ways of calming themselves when they are in a crying state. Crying infants when brought to caretakers' shoulders, often calmed by the movement they receive, will then hold up their heads and continue to calm themselves by scanning their surroundings. New babies are also often able to calm themselves by sucking on their fists or fingers. Both of these self-initiated actions provide them with calming self-stimulation. Parents do not have an innate understanding of these facts, but they can be shown how to calm their baby and given guidance as they learn.

When in an alert state, newborns see and respond to visual stimuli. Interestingly, they can best focus upon a target as close as six to twelve inches away, the usual distance between them and the person who is caring for them. A newborn baby is able to both visually fixate and follow a moving target. Though at first visual following may be jerky and the baby may lose sight of the visual target, this capability becomes increasingly refined within a few days or weeks. By six months of age, a baby's vision is as mature as it will ever be. This area of development obviously far exceeds many other capabilities which require years to reach maturity.

Newborns can perceive high contrast edges and angles (13). When presented with the choice of a bull's eye or stripes, the curved lines of the bull's eye attract greater attention from newborns (14). When looking at human faces, newborns tend to scan external features such as the eyes, chin, and hair line (13).

Along with well-developed visual capabilities, a newborn baby is able to hear well and visually locate the source of auditory stimulation. Evidence has accumulated which indicates that babies exhibit heightened sensitivity to human-like auditory stimuli (15). In particular, they prefer high-pitched sounds, especially those made by female voices, and they may even recognize the sound of their mother's voice (16). These findings provide further evidence that babies are born ready to respond to those who care for them. They are able to discriminate and preferentially respond to those sounds which have social significance for them.

Observations in newborn nurseries show that adult women and men speak to newborns from the first day of the babies' lives. Their observed speech is extensive, grammatically well formed, and almost entirely limited to comments on the infant's behavior and characteristics and on the care being provided. From these findings, Rheingold and Adams (17) concluded that newborns are powerful evokers of speech; research findings discussed above indicate the newborn's capability to respond visually to the person speaking to them.

Sights and sounds are powerful sensory stimuli available to newborns. How they use their vision and hearing to entice and sustain parental attention may well be at least partially related to parental awareness of these capabilities. That social interaction begins from the moment of birth is an indisputable fact. Recent data have shown that thirty-six-hour-old newborns, in an alert state, can imitate at least three different facial expressions (18). When a baby was held in a face-to-face position with an adult who alternately exhibited sad, surprised, and happy facial expressions, an observer standing behind the adult was able to correctly guess (at better than chance accuracy) the emotion being demonstrated by the baby's facial expressions. Such findings lead to speculation about how the animation of the parents affects the baby's responses and the ongoing cycle of interaction.

The newborn's ability to demonstrate olfactory capabilities also contributes to their early interaction with parents. Within six days following birth, breast-fed babies can differentiate the smell of their mothers' breast pads from those of other women (19). When presented with the breast pad of another woman and one of the mother, a baby clearly preferred to smell the mother's breast pad. Mothers, too, have been reported to detect a particular scent of each of their babies. By allowing close contact between a mother and baby, they can begin identification of each other's individual odor and learning to know each other through the use of this sensory mechanism (20).

In 1890 William James wrote that the baby experiences life "all as one great blooming, buzzing confusion" (21). Today, almost one hundred years later, we know this to be inaccurate. Babies are able to regulate the input from their environment so that it is not experienced as a "great blooming, buzzing confusion." Most certainly, James's comment has been disproven as observations of newborns clearly demonstrate that babies attend to the salient features of their environment and can "tune out" stimuli to avoid disorganization in their processing of stimuli.

Habituation is the term used to describe how an individual decreases his response to repeated stimulation and thus avoids bombardment by environmental stimuli. Newborns can clearly habituate immediately after birth and probably *in utero*. If babies used their sensory apparatus indiscriminately, their world would be perceived as one of confusion and chaos. In response to a repetitious stimulus, babies will "shut down" their response or habituate to this stimulus. This can be observed with a sleeping newborn. While the baby is in the light sleep state a bell may be rung over the infant's ear; the baby usually responds to the sound. If fifteen seconds later the bell is rung again, the baby more than likely will again respond to this auditory stimulus. With repeated presentations of the same stimulus, the infant is likely to show less and less response to it. This decrement in response is considered to indicate that the baby has habituated to the sound (10).

This principle also functions when the baby is awake and alert, interacting with a caretaker. When the infant's level of arousal becomes too high, the infant will attempt to avoid increased stimuli. The child may do this by averting his or her gaze, changing body position, or by altering his or her state of consciousness. When excessively stimulated, the response is often crying or irritability. The infant may then need the help of soothing care to bring his or her state to a level where he or she can again attend to the environment (22).

To interact effectively with a baby requires a degree of sensitivity to help identify *how much* as well as *what kind* of stimuli a baby will be optimally responsive to. This sensitivity develops with experience. Mothers often say "he's too tired to sleep," or "the company has her too excited." These are extreme examples of situations where the baby has become overstimulated. By closely examining behavior while babies and caretakers are interacting, one can watch babies determine how much stimulation they will tolerate. The babies may momentarily turn away, close their eyes, stare unresponsively, or change their state in response to the stimulation. These are ways babies can control input from the environment. New parents must be shown how to gauge their interaction with the baby and the baby's level of tolerance for such stimulation. Demonstrations can be provided to new parents to help them observe and interpret what the baby is indicating by his or her behavior. A new mother and father can easily feel rejected by their baby if attempts made to play with the baby do not become pleasurable episodes of mutual exchange.

Newborns have behavioral capabilities which facilitate how they respond to and interact with those who care for them. What must also be highlighted is the fact that each newborn has behavioral characteristics that represent his or her individuality and will contribute to the quality of that infant's interactions with others.

The notion that a child's temperament can be identified early in infancy and has long-lasting effects on the child's future development was carefully described in the work of Thomas and Chess (23). Three constellations of temperament were identified: the "easy child," the "slow-to-warm-up child," and the "difficult child." The nine behavioral characteristics used to form these categories were: activity level, rhythmicity, approach-withdrawal, adaptability, threshold of responsiveness, intensity of reaction, quality of mood, distractibility and attention span, and persistence. Their work, begun in the 1950s, has made an important contribution by focusing on how innate characteristics of babies will affect how they will interact with others in the future. Progress in this area has gone beyond this early work. The original research on infant temperament began with observations and parent interviews when the babies were two to three months of age. Today studies are looking at the behavior of infants in the neonatal period to identify behavioral characteristics which affect how they begin interacting with their parents.

The nature of a new baby's care affects the expression of his or her unique behavioral traits. Newborns more easily develop patterns in their rhythms of hunger, sleep, and waking behavior when they are cared for by one as opposed to multiple caretakers (24, 25). Newborns who receive care by a single caretaker, either a nurse or mother, also show less restlessness, distress, and irritability in their behavior than do new babies cared for by multiple caregivers. By responding to the style of interaction provided by one caregiver, as opposed to many, babies are able to regulate their unique behavioral patterns to the one caring for them. This illustrates evidence of a very early synchrony in interaction which develops as a newborn uses his or her sensorium to differentially respond to the care provided and to initiate interaction with a unique style and rhythm of behavior. Of recent special interest is research that shows that a baby's cycling of behavioral states can be monitored prenatally. One can wonder whether the synchrony of interaction between mother and baby may begin long before birth (26).

Helping New Parents Communicate with Their Newly Born Infants

With an understanding of the capabilities of newborn babies, parents can be shown how to respond to their babies and to develop greater sensitivity to their babies' communication (see chap. 18). Various studies using the Brazelton Neonatal Behavioral Assessment Scale (10), a standardized instrument used to provide descriptive data about a newborn's behavioral capabilities, have been conducted to examine the effects of demonstrating this assessment with parents observing their newborn's examination. For the most part follow-up studies of the effects of this observation have been very short term, but findings reveal that mothers who have had this experience demonstrate greater synchrony with their newborns during the first month. In a series of studies reviewed by Liptak et al. (27), two investigations involved the parents actually participating in the Brazelton test and one involved teenage mothers administering the Brazelton themselves for four weeks. This research demonstrated that by twelve months the babies whose mothers received this intervention scored higher on the Bayley Scales of Infant Development.

Bristor and colleagues (28) have demonstrated that "coaching" or helping new parents acquire skills essential for communicating with their newborns enhances parent-infant interactions. This program is introduced to new parents in the first days following the birth of their baby (29, 30). Parents are given a picture book illustrating parent-baby communication and are then shown how their new baby can use sensory capabilities to respond to caregiving. The Direct demonstration and feedback given to the new parents by the volunteer "coach" are important aspects of this program.

Nationally, numerous projects are being conducted to provide parents with an early awareness of their babies' capabilities. Data evaluating the effectiveness of these programs are minimal, but general enthusiasm exists regarding parents' positive reception to this kind of assistance and to their increased knowledge about their babies.

Supportive Assistance for New Parents

Being a parent can be lonely. The tough and demanding work of parenthood is made easier when parents have the understanding support of other parents, volunteers, or professionals. Various approaches to providing this kind of assistance have been attempted from home visitor programs to group sessions where parents gather to share experiences and learn from one another.

The findings of Cochran and Brassard (31) assert that personal support networks influence parental attitudes and behaviors which have direct and indirect effects on children's development. Crinic and co-workers (32) have shown that stress and support significantly predicted mothers' attitudes at one month and their interactive behavior with their babies at four months. The relationship of a mother's social support system to the nature of infant-mother interaction has been demonstrated by Crockenberg (33) and Pascoe and Earp (34). Crockenberg's research demonstrates a consistent association between the adequacy of maternal social support when the family is under stress and the security of the infant-mother attachment at one year.

In European communities, support for new families has been an available and expected health service in the form of home visitor programs, an outreach service to parents of infants and young children. Programs using lay home visitors have been initiated in this country to reach parents with support and information about child development, behavior, and safety. Initial findings from these programs show that they are well received and are helpful to families (35).

Tieing these findings to those of long-term follow-up studies of the early intervention programs of the 1960s helps demonstrate the likely effectiveness of these programs. Bronfenbrenner, in his 1974 report "Is Early Intervention Effective?" (36), has indicated that unless there is parental involvement in an early intervention program which affects parental attitudes, behavior, and interactions, the effects of a program geared to children are likely to be short term. Bromwich (37) has developed guidelines which are useful in establishing a framework for any infant-parent program. Specifically, her guidelines are:

Enable a parent to remain in control;
Avoid the authority-layman gap;
Deal with parents' priorities and concerns;
Build on parents' strengths;
Respect parents' goals for their infants;
Involve parents in planning;
Respect individual styles of parent-infant interaction;
Use of reinforcement is not enough, describe how and why behaviors are helpful;
Give parents an out, parents should not sense failure; and
Share how it feels to get no response.

Each of these reveals respect for the uniqueness of any one parent-baby dyad and the need to support parents through their own perceptions of their child.

Summary

Creating programs for new parents that will provide information, guidance in developing new skills, and support for the difficulty of caring for infants is a challenging task. Reaching those families who could most benefit from this assistance is even more challenging (29). Evaluations of how these programs are affecting families demonstrate, to date, that parent-infant interaction can be enhanced.

By the next edition of *The Battered Child,* perhaps more statistical data can be reported as these programs are further developed and evaluated. In the meantime, efforts to develop helpful programs for parents and their infants must continue. Parental receptiveness is enthusiastic and the programs are inexpensive and nonintrusive. This indicates that these programs are addressing parents' perceived and real needs.

References

1. Payne, C., ed. 1983. *Programs to Strengthen Families: A Resource Guide.* Report of May 1983 National Conference. New Haven: Yale Bush Center in Child Development and Social Policy.
2. Lourie, R. S. 1980. The National Center: Primary Prevention in the Earliest Years. *Zero to Three* 1:1.
3. Dinkmeyer, D., and McKay, G. D. 1976. *Parents' Handbook—Systematic Training for Effective Parenting.* Circle Pines, Minn.: American Guidance Service, Inc.
4. M.E.L.D. (Minnesota Early Learning Design), 123 East Grant Street, Minneapolis, Minnesota 55403.
5. Burrueta-Clement, J. R.; Schweinhart, L. J.; Barnett, W. S.; Epstein, A. S.; and Weikert, D. P. 1984. *Changed Lives: The Effects of the Perry Preschool Program on Youths through Age 19.* Monograph no. 8. Ypsilanti, Mich.: High Scope Press.
6. Klaus, M. H., and Kennell, J. H. 1976. *Maternal-Infant Bonding.* St. Louis: C. V. Mosby Company.

7. Klaus, M. H., and Kennell, J. H. 1982. *Parent-Infant Bonding.* St. Louis: C. V. Mosby Company.

8. Korsch, B. M. 1983. More on Parent-Infant Bonding. *J. Pediatrics* 102:249–50.

9. Prectle, H., and Beintema, D. 1964. The Neurological Examination of the Full-Term Newborn Infant. *Clinics in Developmental Medicine* (London), no. 12.

10. Brazelton, T. B. 1984. Neonatal Behavioral Assessment Scale, Second Edition. *Clinics in Developmental Medicine* (Philadelphia: Lippincott), no. 88.

11. Korner, A., and Grobstein, R. 1966. Visual Alertness As Related to Soothing in Neonates: Implications for Maternal Stimulation and Early Deprivation. *Child Development* 37:867–76.

12. Bell, S., and Ainsworth, M. 1972. Infant Crying and Maternal Responsiveness. *Child Development* 43:1171–90.

13. Maurer, D., and Salapatek, P. 1976. Developmental Changes in the Scanning of Faces by Young Infants. *Child Development* 47:523–27.

14. Fantz, R., and Miranda, S. 1975. Newborn Infant Attention to Form of Contour. *Child Development* 46:224–28.

15. Muir, D., and Field, J. 1979. Newborn Infants Orient to Sounds. *Child Development* 50:431–36.

16. DeCasper, A. J., and Fifer, W. B. 1980. Of Human Bonding: Newborns Prefer Their Mothers' Voices. *Science* 208:1174–76.

17. Rheingold, H. L., and Adams, J. L. 1980. The Significance of Speech to Newborns. *Developmental Psychology* 16:397–403.

18. Field, T. M., et al. 1982. Discrimination and Imitation of Facial Expressions by Neonates. *Science* 218:179–81.

19. MacFarlane, J. A. 1975. Parent-Infant Interaction. In *Ciba Foundation Symposium 33.* Amsterdam: Elsevier Publishing Company.

20. Porter, R. H.; Cernoch, J. M.; and McLaughlin, F. J. 1970. Maternal Recognition of Neonates through Olfactory Cues. *Physiological Behavior* 30:67–78.

21. James, W. 1980. *Principles of Psychology.* New York: Holt, Rinehart, and Winston.

22. Kearsley, R. B. 1973. The Newborn's Response to Auditory Stimulation: A Demonstration of Orienting and Defensive Behavior. *Child Development* 40:582–90.

23. Thomas, A., and Chess, S. 1977. *Temperament and Development.* New York: Brunner Mazel.

24. Burns, P., et al. 1972. Distress and Feeding: Short Term Effects of Caregiver Environment on the First Ten Days of Life. *J. Am. Acad. Child Psychiatry* 11:427–35.

25. Sanders, L. W., and Julia, H. L. 1966. Continuous Interactional Monitoring in the Neonate. *Psychosomatic Medicine* 28:822–35.

26. Rosen, M. G., et al. 1979. Fetal Behavioral States and Fetal Evaluation. *Clinics in Obstetrics and Gynecology* 22:605–16.

27. Liptak, G. S.; Keller, B. B.; Feldman, A. W.; and Chamberlain, R. W. 1983. Enhancing Infant Development and Parent-Practitioner Interaction with the Brazelton Neonatal Assessment Scale. *Pediatrics* 72:71–78.

28. Bristor, M. W.; Helfer, R. E.; and Coy, K. B. 1984. Effects of Perinatal Coaching on Mother-Infant Interaction. *Am. J. Diseases in Children* 38:254–57.

29. Bristor, M. W.; Wilson, A. L.; and Helfer, R. E. 1985. Perinatal Coaching: Program Development. *Clinics in Perinatology* 12:367–80.

30. Helfer, R. E., and Wilson, A. L. 1982. The Parent-Infant Relationship: Promoting a Positive Beginning through Perinatal Coaching. *Pediatric Clinics in North America* 29:249–60.

31. Cochran, M., and Brassard, J. 1979. Child Development and Personal Social Networks. *Child Development* 50:601–16.

32. Crinic, K., et al. 1983. Effects of Stress and Social Support Influences on Mothers and Premature and Full-Term Infants. *Child Development* 54:209–17.

33. Crockenberg, S. 1981. Infant Irritability, Mother Responsiveness, and Social Support Influences on the Security of Infant-Mother Attachment. *Child Development* 52:857–65.

34. Pascoe, J. M., and Earp, J. A. 1984. The Effect of Mothers' Social Support and Life Changes on the Stimulation of Their Children in the Home. *Am. J. Public Health* 74:358–60.

35. Gray, J., and Kaplan, B. 1980. The Lay Health Visitor Program: An Eighteen-Month Experience. *The Battered Child,* 3d ed., ed. C. H. Kempe and R. E. Helfer, 373–78. Chicago: University of Chicago Press.

36. Bronfenbrenner, U. 1974. *A Report on Longitudinal Evaluations of Preschool Programs: Is Early Intervention Effective?* Washington, D.C.: Department of Health, Education, and Welfare Publication no. OHD 74-25, vol. 2.

37. Bromwich, R. 1978. *Working with Parents and Infants.* Baltimore: University Park Press.

24 Our National Priorities for Prevention

Anne H. Cohn

The Battered Child was first published in 1968. Much progress has been made since then. This chapter traces that progress, characterizes this nation's response to child abuse in the mid-1980s, and maps out priorities for the future.

In the preface to the first edition of *The Battered Child,* the editors refer to the "tens of thousands of children . . . severely battered or killed in the United States in 1967." In the preface to the second edition, a mere six years later, the editors acknowledged that since 1968 "understanding has deepened, many more people have become involved, some courts have improved, treatment programs are being developed all over the country, and . . . in 1972 almost ten thousand cases of suspected abuse and neglect were reported in New York City alone." And in 1980, in the third edition's preface, the editors acknowledge "one and one-half percent of the children in the United States [over 600,000] are reported annually to protective service units as victims of suspected abuse and neglect. . . .Every year another one and one-half percent is added to the toll." And, "Together we are turning the corner and moving toward prevention." In 1986, just prior to the publication of the fourth edition, over two million suspected cases of child abuse were reported to the authorities.

Less than two decades have passed since *The Battered Child* was first published and in that time our knowledge of the incidence of the problem has grown dramatically. Cases— literally by the hundreds of thousands—have come out of the closet and have been reported to the authorities. Our investigative and treatment systems have grown in response, as has our interest in prevention—stemming the tide, stopping the problem before it occurs. And something else has happened. Child abuse, slowly at first and recently quite rapidly, has risen to a higher level on the nation's agenda of social concerns. No longer conceived of as someone else's problem, the nation—not just social workers or doctors or lawmakers—has embraced the child abuse issue. How did it happen? Why did it happen? A quick review of the events of the last two decades is revealing.

Anne H. Cohn, D.P.H., is the executive director of the National Committee for Prevention of Child Abuse, Chicago.

The Last Two Decades

In the early 1960s, with help from the medical profession, the modern-day public got its first introduction to child abuse. Dr. C. Henry Kempe coined the term "the battered child syndrome" and spoke out about the atrocities he and his colleagues were seeing in their emergency rooms and private practices. The media picked up on the story; pictures of severely neglected or battered children made the front pages. The immediate public reaction seemed to be one of horror; the public recoiled. Some professionals and lawmakers did not, and through the 1960s and into the early 1970s states across the country passed or improved upon their child abuse reporting laws, and they developed or expanded their capacities to investigate and treat reports of child abuse. By the early 1970s the rudiments of a nationwide response system were in place, but knowledge about the nature and extent of the problem was still scant.

Public Action

In 1973 the first congressional hearing on the topic of child abuse was held. Chaired by then Senator Walter Mondale, the hearing record points up how scant our knowledge was at that time. One witness testified that there may be as many as 60,000 children nationwide who are abused each year. But the hearings did establish the gravity of the problem and the need for federal leadership. As a result, the Federal Child Abuse Act (Public Law 934-247) was passed and signed into law early in 1974. The Act established a National Center on Child Abuse and Neglect (NCCAN) within the federal Department of Health and Human Services (at the time, Department of Health, Education, and Welfare); up to $24 million a year was appropriated to NCCAN to be spent on research, demonstrations, training projects, and grants to states.

Since 1974, NCCAN has had between $16 and $24 million a year to spend on child-abuse-related activities. In general, grants have been small and multiple; over four hundred have been given out to national, state, and local public and private groups. Over one hundred demonstration programs were funded, and evaluation studies were funded to assess the relative effectiveness of the programs. Numerous research projects to analyze the causes of abuse were supported. So too were efforts to establish a count of the number of abuse cases reported nationally to help establish a better measure of the incidence of the problem. Our knowledge base grew considerably. Training grants and conferences were supported; a cadre of trained professionals emerged. States were eligible for grants only if their state child abuse reporting laws complied with federal guidelines. Consequently, during the 1970s many states improved their child abuse laws. As a result of this small federal program, state and local professional organizations across the country became involved in the problem, and our understanding of the magnitude of the problem grew. National groups working in the field were pulled together.

Throughout the 1970s the atmosphere of child abuse field might have been best characterized as "everyone for himself." Although our knowledge suggested that collaborative efforts, team approaches, and coordinated activities were essential in responding to individual cases of abuse, agencies and organizations rarely operated in concert with each other except on individual cases. For example, periodically during the 1970s the Federal

Child Abuse Act was up for reauthorization; each organization interested in this legislation sent a representative to Washington, D.C., to tell the lawmakers how they felt the law
should be rewritten or rearranged. Congress was bombarded with a variety of ideas from a
large number of individual special interest groups. Threats to the whole federal program
have since changed this scattershot approach.

In 1981 the Reagan Administration proposed eliminating the federal child abuse program entirely. Deeply concerned, a number of organizations met together and formed the
National Child Abuse Coalition so that they would have a single, strong voice in Washington. National organizations with a singular interest in child abuse (e.g., the National
Committee for Prevention of Child Abuse, National Parents Anonymous, and the American Humane Association's Children's Division) joined with other groups which had taken
on child abuse as a major concern (e.g., the National Association of Junior Leagues and
the National Association of Social Workers). As a result of the collective and coordinated
advocacy efforts of these groups, the Federal Child Abuse Act was reauthorized in 1981.
The coalition has remained intact, has grown to include more than twenty organizations,
and retains a half-time lobbyist in Washington. Not only has the coalition continued to
advocate successfully for the continuation of the federal child abuse program at increasing
funding levels, it has also diversified the collective activities of the member organizations.
The list of legislative concerns has grown to cover an array of concerns (e.g., Title XX
funding, day care regulations, maternal and child health funding). As political interests
have drawn unrelated or marginally related issues into the child abuse arena—ranging
from spouse abuse to Baby Doe—the coalition has responded, with an emphasis on keeping the NCCAN program focused on child abuse and neglect as originally defined.

All this professional interest and new knowledge would not have been sufficient for
child abuse to climb to the top of the nation's social action agenda. Certain private sector
activities were important.

Private Sector Initiatives

In the early 1970s a number of private citizens became concerned about the child abuse
problem and sought to do something about it. A social worker in Southern California, Len
Lieber, and one of his clients, Jolly K., established Parents Anonymous (originally called
Mothers Anonymous) to give abusive parents a place to meet and help each other. Today,
Parents Anonymous boasts over 1500 self-help groups in the United States and across the
world. A counselor in Northern California, Henry Giaretto, and his wife Anna expressed
concern about the sexual abuse problem and the inadequacy of existing treatment approaches by founding Parents United, a set of treatment services for families dealing with
sexual abuse. As with Parents Anonymous, Parents United, with over 150 centers, has
been adopted in communities across the country. Other organizations, such as SCAN,
Incorporated, a lay therapy program, were also established in the early 1970s and have
spread across the country.

In 1972, Donna J. Stone, a Chicago philanthropist, became concerned about the apparently increasing incidence of infant deaths due to inflicted injury. She described her concern with an analogy to a washbasin. She said, "Picture a washbasin with the stopper
down and both the hot and cold water on full blast. The sink fills up and the water runs

over the edge. And we have been running around getting buckets to catch the dripping water. I think we need to try to turn the water off." She felt the public needed to be alerted to the problem so something could be done about it, so she founded the National Committee for Prevention of Child Abuse (NCPCA).

In 1976 NCPCA launched a nationwide media campaign with the Advertising Council geared to alert the public to the problem of abuse. The campaign has continued ever since. Although a small cost to NCPCA, the campaign generated between $20 to $40 million worth of free public service advertising each year through television, radio, newspapers, magazines, billboards, and transit posters. The campaign's messages through 1982 were: "Child abuse is a big problem. There are many different kinds of abuse. Child abuse hurts us all, because it is linked to so many other social problems. We must prevent child abuse." In addition to the extensive national media exposure of this campaign, various state and local groups developed their own campaigns to advertise reporting hotlines, helplines, or other local resources.

For example, in 1982 a group of citizens in Kansas City, Kansas, formed a coalition to educate the community about how to stop child abuse and family violence. And the "No Hitter Day" concept was born. No Hitter Day, patterned after the American Cancer Society's Smokeout Campaign, was intended to:

- raise people's awareness about child abuse and family violence in their own communities;
- help people acknowledge their own capacity to be violent;
- offer people alternatives to deal with their rage;
- acquaint people with helpful resources in their own community for dealing with violence; and
- help individuals become less violent.

No Hitter Day was linked to baseball, because baseball is a national pastime and a respected nonviolent sport. The first No Hitter Day was planned for the last Saturday in April 1983 as part of Child Abuse Prevention Month. Television and radio spots, articles in the print media, and other local activities promoted the day and offered alternatives to violence. At the game itself the stop violence theme was apparent, rather than a seventh-inning stretch, there was a seventh-inning hug!

Since 1983, the No Hitter Day idea has taken hold from coast to coast with a number of major league and minor league teams. In 1986 over twenty-five communities observed the day.

All these public service efforts were supplemented by periodic news coverage of specific cases of child abuse. The impact is measurable.

In the early 1970s, based on an informal study conducted by executives of the 3M Company, fewer than one in ten adults in this country were aware of the battered child syndrome or the child abuse problem. In the early 1980s Louis Harris and Associates conducted two studies on the topic. They found that over 90 percent of the American public were aware of child abuse as a serious social problem, understood the connections between economic stress, unemployment, and child abuse, and recognized linkages between child abuse, juvenile delinquency, and adult criminal behavior. Another finding of the Louis Harris surveys, which was later confirmed by some focused group research conducted by NCPCA, was that the the public was deeply concerned about the problem but did not know what to do to help; the public saw the problem as belonging to someone other than themselves and their own families.

With all this expanded public awareness and knowledge, the necessary elements were present for child abuse to rise to a higher level on the nation's social action agenda.

A Rude Awakening in 1984

And then in 1984 the issue of child abuse quite literally shook the entire nation and demanded a response. How did it happen?

In early January 1984, ABC, a major national TV network, courageously aired a two-hour, made-for-television movie entitled "Something about Amelia." The movie presented a story of child sexual abuse. Its broadcast was the first time American viewers were exposed directly to the issue of incest, a topic previously considered taboo. The effect was notable. As a result of seeing the film, thousands of individuals across the country began to talk about child sexual abuse, about how it had happened to them. For example, the NCPCA received over 3000 letters from men and women in their 30s and 40s, and in their 50s and 60s—letters that described experiences with sexual abuse never told before. People told of incest and of rape as children by uncles, family friends, and teachers. Many of the letters were ten and twenty pages long and chronicled the hurt:

> I need help. I was an incest victim from the ages of 3 to 19 with my stepfather . . . I tried to get help, but no one would believe me. I ran away from home several times and tried to kill myself.

> As a child of age 5 to 11 or 12 I was a victim of sexual abuse by my father. I told my mother not to leave me with him (she would go out shopping sometimes two or three times a week) because he would hurt me. She did not listen to me and told me I would be alright and would go out anyway. I felt I could not tell anyone else after that . . . Although I am 28 years of age . . . I feel someone should tell these kids that it's ok to say *no* to people that want to touch them in the wrong way, and to not give up when someone does not listen the first time. To keep telling until someone does listen and hears.

The movie "Something about Amelia" clearly did a lot more than describe incest. It telegraphed the messages: "If you have been sexually abused, you're not alone." "It's ok to talk about it."

"Amelia" opened up the conversation about sexual abuse; that conversation became animated after reports of sexual abuse in a day care center in Southern California. In March 1984, allegations were made of sexual abuse of nearly three hundred children at Manhattan Beach, California's prestigious Virginia McMartin Pre-School by members of the McMartin family and their employees. While the accused persons are still awaiting trial in mid-1986, the story permeated the media. From coast-to-coast, national and local newspapers, magazines, television, and radio revealed the atrocious stories of sexual abuse against young children which had allegedly been going on for years. The public response was tremendous. How could this have happened? Why didn't the parents know? Most important, the public identified with the McMartin Pre-School parents—"It could have been my child, my grandchild, or my nieces and nephews." For the first time, it seemed that the public understood just how directly they could be touched by child abuse. To reinforce that understanding, news stories broke of alleged sexual abuse in day-care centers and other child serving agencies in other parts of the country—a day-care center in New York, a day-care center in Chicago, a Children's Theater in Minneapolis, a babysitting service in Miami.

Then on 26 April 1984, a nationally known and respected politician announced at a U.S. Senate hearing that she had been a victim of abuse. Senator Paula Hawkins (R-Fla.) testified that she had been a victim of sexual abuse, and that although her mother believed her, the judge did not and the molester was never convicted. Senator Hawkins's story seemed to communicate to the public that "child abuse can—and does—happen to anybody." What followed that April 1984 hearing was a spate of additional stories of abuse in city after city across the country. By the fall of 1984, television specials and talk shows on the topic were regular fare. (The extensive media coverage should, in a way, not be surprising. Child sexual abuse is a topic which the media would find most appealing since it deals with three of the big issues which attract audiences—sex, violence, and children.)

Although the media's handling of the issue has been criticized, much of the coverage has gone beyond the sensational and sought to explain the problem's causes, magnitude, and effects. For example, James Squires, editor of the *Chicago Tribune,* assigned two reporters to a "child abuse beat"; for twelve months the newspaper featured regular front-page stories on child abuse. Squires, along with a dozen other major city newspaper editors, also ran a special "The Amazing Spider-Man" comic book about sexual abuse prevention in his paper's Sunday comics section. Squires stated in an interview on the *Today Show* (13 February 1985) that newspapers have a responsibility to contribute to the solution of the problem in addition to covering the story.

A Backlash Appears

Inevitably, the extensive coverage of the child abuse issue brought a backlash in its wake. This seems to have started with the events in Jordan, Minnesota. There it was alleged that more than twenty children had been sexually abused by their parents and their parent's friends in various group activities. During the spring and summer of 1985 the public became very familiar with the story as the media relentlessly covered it. In the fall of 1985 the case went to trial. Investigatory problems coupled with other legal and logistical problems appeared to get in the way of a full hearing of the case. For example, one child on the witness stand under intense interrogation seemed to change or drop the allegations, and soon thereafter charges against all the parents were dropped.

The media stepped up its coverage of the possibilities of false accusations in cases of child sexual abuse. Several other cases came to light shortly after the Jordan, Minnesota, story in which a California schoolteacher, a Texas babysitter, and a few others were possibly falsely accused of abusing a child. The realization that some children do lie about this problem was the basis for the backlash. Some segments of the public became concerned that children were being unnecessarily terrified about the possibilities of sexual abuse; they were becoming afraid of touching and essentially paranoid about adults. Some became concerned that reporting—that is *false* reporting—was being used increasingly in child custody and visitation battles between divorced couples. Professionals recognized the need for quality diagnostic assessments to decrease this risk as well as the paucity of trained professionals to conduct them.

Others became vocally critical of the existing child abuse laws. One Minnesota-based group, VOCAL (Victims of Child Abuse Laws), believes that existing laws violate the civil liberties of adults in this country. Even Ann Landers, the syndicated newspaper advice columnist, called for a narrowing of child abuse reporting laws.

Professionals in the field poised themselves to fight the so-called backlash, ready to reestablish public awareness and understanding of the magnitude and seriousness of the child abuse problem. To date, that fight has not been necessary. Despite the play in the media, the backlash has not dulled the nation's concern about the problem of child abuse.

Positive Responses to Public Concern

In fact, the response from all sectors has been considerable. Numerous private sector organizations have identified child abuse prevention as a priority: the National Parent-Teacher Association, the General Federation of Women's Clubs, the American Contract Bridge League, the Boys Clubs and the Girls Clubs, the YMCA and YWCA, Big Brothers and Big Sisters, among others. Each of these national organizations identified child abuse prevention activities for its member groups across the country. Professional associations expressed greater interest in the child abuse issue, from the American Medical Association and its auxiliaries to the American Public Health Association, the American Academy of Pediatrics, and the American Association of Funeral Home Directors.

Corporate America took note of the problem and volunteered involvement. In addition to expanding employee assistance programs to help parents under stress, corporations got involved in special prevention projects. For example, Marvel Comics donated a creative team to develop a special "The Amazing Spider-Man" comic book on the issue of child sexual abuse; the International Paper Company and the Manistique Company contributed the paper for the first printing; and over a dozen major city newspapers carried the comic book in their Sunday editions. In the first six months of 1985, over nine million copies were distributed. The Southland Corporation, in conjunction with local PTA's and various child abuse prevention programs, developed and implemented media campaigns across the country.

In addition, the federal government expressed greater interest in the issues of child abuse and neglect. The U.S. Surgeon General planned a conference of leading health professionals to examine child abuse and family violence. The U.S. Attorney General, through the Justice Department's National Center on Missing and Exploited Children, launched a number of child abuse prevention programs. And, President Ronald Reagan established a Presidential Commission called the National Public/Private Sector Partnership on Child Safety to address the issues of child abuse and exploitation and what the relative roles of the public and private sectors should be.

Legislative Activity

Legislative activity at the federal and state level has been considerable. As the 98th Congress came to a close in the fall of 1984, numerous bills were introduced in both the House of Representatives and the Senate. Most could be characterized as "quick fixes." Rather than looking at authorizing legislation which would result in more funding for child abuse service delivery, the bills focused on regulation and on training. Most popular were bills dealing with the federally funded day-care program, such as those requiring fingerprinting of all day-care employees, presumably because sexual abuse cases involving day-care centers had been so much in the news. The facts that: (a) few molesters have criminal records, and (b) statistically few day-care children are victims of sexual abuse compared to other sexually abused children, did not seem to sway the legislators. With a major election on their heels (in 1984 the presidential election was coupled with the congressional) it seemed most important just to pass *something* in response to the problem. (It is interesting to note that the 98th Congress did pass a law requiring the fingerprinting of all employees in federally funded day-care centers, and the 99th Congress sought to drop it.) The 98th Congress also reauthorized the Federal Child Abuse Act, which supports the U.S. National Center on Child Abuse and Neglect, and appropriated funds comparable to the pre-1981 period. State legislatures and city councils also frantically responded to the problem. By the spring of 1985, no fewer than one hundred different child-abuse-related bills had been introduced to the California Assembly.

Some more thoughtful or planned legislation was acted upon during this period in response to a growing movement at the state level for something called the Children's Trust Fund. First thought of by Dr. Ray E. Helfer, the Children's Trust Fund is to establish a fund to be generated in a given state through means other than annual legislative appropriations and to be distributed to local community groups for child abuse prevention activities. The fund is to be administered by a citizens' advisory group so that it can remain at arm's length from the political process. The first Children's Trust Fund was established in Kansas in 1980; the state bill called for an added surcharge of $7.00 on marriage licenses. Those funds, amounting to close to $200,000 a year, have gone directly into the Trust Fund. In 1982, four additional states sought to establish a separate source of income to support community-based child abuse prevention programs and developed their own Children's Trust Funds. Some diversity with the design of the bill evolved; in one state the surcharge was added to birth certificates; in another, taxpayers were given the option of designating a portion of their state income tax refund to the Children's Trust Fund. By mid-1986, more than two-thirds of the states had passed Children's Trust Fund bills. In response, members of the 99th Congress passed a supplemental appropriations bill to allow for federal matching funds for states' Children's Trust Funds.

A Return to Criminal Justice Concerns

Certain legislative activities suggest some movement back toward criminal justice solutions to the problem. Well before the 1970s, when efforts to respond to child abuse first became apparent across the country, the common response to child abuse was a criminal justice one: police intervened and jail for the perpetrator or foster care for the child were the solutions. Concerns for the therapeutic needs of the perpetrator as well as for those of the victim were not usual. As states began to establish and strengthen children's protective service agencies, and as our knowledge about the problem and its causes grew, interest in the well-being of all involved in abuse also grew. After all, it was argued, people who abuse children are people who typically love their children and who need help. Treatment programs flourished; the prevailing concern appeared to be keeping the family intact and helping adults stop abusive behavior. By the mid-1980s, our knowledge of the causes of abuse had grown considerably, as had our knowledge about the effectiveness of treatment. In general, treatment programs had not proven to be very effective; reincidence rates of 30 percent while families were in treatment and success rates of only 40–50 percent by the end of treatment were the norm. Some professionals turned their attention to prevention activities, believing that waiting until abuse had occurred and trying to treat it was futile. Others sought better after-the-fact responses. One recurrent theme in 1984 when the U.S. Attorney General's Task Force on Family Violence held hearings across the country was the need for criminal justice. As one witness said in relation to sexual molesters:

> I didn't say that they can't be treated, but I know of no treatment program for pedophiles . . . we may have to incarcerate them until we find a way of dealing with them. (Final Report, Attorney General's Task Force on Family Violence, p. 93)

The Attorney General's Task Force heard about a variety of interesting and promising preventive and treatment programs, but they also heard repeatedly, "child abuse is a crime; we should respond accordingly." This sentiment appeared to be shared by the general public. The pendulum had indeed swung back toward where it had been before 1970. An examination of the more than one hundred bills pending in the California legislature in 1985 supports this; most deal with changes in criminal justice procedures (e.g., how cases are handled in the courtroom when children are witnesses) rather than treatment or prevention issues. Because criminal justice responses do not affect the incidence of a problem, only how it is handled once it occurs, this author does not believe that criminal justice issues will dominate the agenda for the next five years. Rather they will be blended with concerns for reducing the incidence of abuse.

Despite the surge of interest in the problem from the general public, private organizations, and legislative and government agencies, and despite the dramatic increase in reported cases of abuse and neglect, funding for child abuse research, treatment, and prevention programs did not grow measurably during the early to mid-1980s due to a variety of economic and political factors, chiefly the federal administration's interest in controlling and curtailing federal spending for social programs. Some states were exceptions. For example, $15 million were made available in California for prevention activities, and the number of children's protective service workers in Rhode Island has doubled. But in general, dollars for child abuse activities did not increase. The federal child abuse program was at essentially the same funding level in 1986 that it was at in 1975.

Public Misimpression

The public still does not have a complete grasp of the nature of this problem which has finally come out of the closet. In fact, there appears to be some serious misunderstandings about certain facets of the problem.

For example, the general public has heard so much about child sexual abuse in day-care centers—to the point that such abuses dominated the news, including cover stories in *Time* and *Newsweek,* and interviews on talk shows—that there now appears to be a widely held belief that most sexual abuse of children occurs in day-care settings and that it usually only happens to the very young child. Efforts to make day-care centers safe for children heads the list of many citizen groups' activities. Yet the facts are that children of all ages are sexually abused and most of them are sexually abused in their own homes.

The issue of missing children gained public awareness during the early to mid-1980s and became entwined with the child abuse and child sexual abuse issues. Considerable attention was given to instances of child abduction as a result of the repeated broadcasts of the NBC TV-movie "Adam," which was based on a true story about a young boy of the same name from Florida who had been abducted, presumably by a stranger, and murdered. Television stations, milk distributors, and grocery bag manufacturers began displaying photos of missing children in the hopes of finding some. The number "over one million" was used frequently in connection with the problem, rather than the actual suspected 1,000 or so abductions by strangers and 40,000–50,000 abductions by children's own parents. The public response, in addition to linking all forms of child abuse with child abductions, has been an enormous, albeit not centrally organized, campaign to develop and distribute materials which teach children to be wary of strangers. "Stranger danger" films, story books, puppet shows, and games were produced by most every children's book and toy entertainment company in the country. Perhaps some parents and child care workers feel relief (not unlike the relief some legislators felt when they passed the bill requiring fingerprinting of employees in day-care centers) by fingerprinting their children or tatooing their teeth for identification or educating them not to take rides with strangers. But all of this is being done at a time when statistics suggest that strangers have not been menacing nearly as many children as family members have.

It is quite reasonable to assume that the general public in 1986 still perceived the child abuse problem as "something which does not happen in my home;" yet they may clearly have gained an appreciation for the fact that it could happen to their children. It is also quite reasonable to assume that the general public still felt tremendous anger and hostility toward those who abuse children.

The Mid-1980s: A Unique Moment

By the mid-1980s the nation had awakened to the child abuse problem; the citizenry had accepted the problem as one which they were concerned about and wanted to do something about. They were not looking solely to government to solve the problem, nor were they looking just to social workers or law enforcement personnel. While public opinion seemed to support the notion that molesters and child abusers in general deserved criminal prosecutions, there also appeared to be a groundswell of interest in prevention, in activities which would keep abuse from happening in the first place. If ever there was a moment when this nation appeared interested in substantially altering the way it treats its children, that moment was in the year 1985.

How can a nation best take advantage of prevailing interst in a major social problem and turn that interest into activities which would dramatically reduce or end that social problem? The National Committee for Prevention of Child Abuse dedicated 1985 to the development of a rational answer to that question. The NCPCA wanted to develop a long-range plan for the nation which would assure a significant reduction in the size of the child abuse problem within the next five years. Their guiding principle was the notion that the prevention of child abuse in all its forms was dependent upon a nationwide commitment to and involvement toward a common goal. Despite the risks inherent in articulating numbers with such a goal, particularly numbers which will be exceedingly difficult to measure, the NCPCA set a goal to reduce the actual incidence of child abuse by at least 20 percent by 1990. In order to meet this goal, the following five objectives need to be accomplished:

1. To have a public that is fully aware of the child abuse problem, its implications, its prevention, and what individuals can do to make a difference.

2. To have a more complete body of knowledge about how best to prevent abuse, and to make that new knowledge available in a format that can be used by the public.

3. To have Children's Trust Funds or other funding methods (public or private sector) to assure the availability of prevention activities in all states.

4. To have comprehensive preventive services: all new parents get parenting education and support; all children get preventive education; all adolescent and young adults get preventive education; all parents under stress have access to self-help groups and other supportive services; and all victims and survivors of abuse have access to self-help groups and other supportive services.

5. To have a nationwide network of concerned citizens that involves all interested individuals, groups, and organizations.

Goals and objectives such as these are bold but not unrealistic. Each can be accomplished if there is a *nationwide* commitment to preventing child abuse in all its forms. The incidence of child abuse can be reduced by at least 20 percent by 1990. The idea is to identify a few preventive activities which can make a difference and do them repeatedly, everywhere, and well. The challenge is to make a *long-term* commitment now while the public is so concerned with child abuse. Special initiatives and quick fixes will not do. Child abuse prevention activities need to become embedded in our other regular activities, be it in the hospital maternity ward or the elementary school classroom. We must not let other issues divert us from emphasizing prevention and the goal of reducing and eventually *ending* child abuse. Great pioneers like Dr. C. Henry Kempe and Donna J. Stone taught us how to move forward with commitment. It is time to follow.

Readings

American Humane Association. 1984. *Trends in Child Abuse and Neglect: A National Perspective*. Denver: American Humane Association.

Attorney General's Task Force on Family Violence. 1984. *Final Report*. Washington, D.C.: U.S. Department of Justice.

Burgdorf, K. 1980. Recognition and Reporting of Child Maltreatment: Findings from the National Study of the Incidence and Severity of Child Abuse and Neglect. Report prepared for the National Center on Child Abuse and Neglect, Washington, D.C., December.

Cohen, S.; Gray, E.; and Wald, M. 1984. *Preventing Child Maltreatment: A Review of What We Know*. NCPCA, Working Paper no. 24. Chicago: National Committee for Prevention of Child Abuse.

Cohn, A. H. 1975. Assessing the Impact of Health Programs Responding to New Problems: The Case of Child Abuse and Neglect. Ph.D. diss., University of California, Berkeley.

———. 1979. Essential Elements of Successful Child Abuse and Neglect Treatment. *Child Abuse and Neglect: International J.* 3:491–96.

———. 1983. *An Approach to Preventing Child Abuse*. Chicago: National Committee for Prevention of Child Abuse.

Daro, Deborah, and Cohn, A. H. 1984. A Decade of Child Maltreatment Evaluation

Efforts: What We Have Learned. Paper presented at the Second National Conference for Family Violence Researchers, Durham, New Hampshire, August 7–10.

Gelles, R. 1984. Applying Our Knowledge of Family Violence to Prevention and Treatment: What Difference Might it Make? Paper presented at the Second National Conference for Family Violence Researchers, Durham, New Hampshire, August 7–10.

Gerbner, George; Ross, Catherine J.; and Zigler, Edward, eds. 1980. *Child Abuse: An Agenda for Action.* New York: Oxford University Press.

Gil, D. G. 1970. *Violence against Children: Physical Child Abuse in the United States.* Cambridge, Mass.: Harvard University Press.

Gray, J.; Cutler, C.; Dean, J.; and Kempe, C. H. 1977. Prediction and Prevention of Child Abuse and Neglect. *Child Abuse and Neglect: International J.* 1:45–58.

Gray, J., and Kaplan, B. 1980. The Lay Health Visitor Program: An Eighteen-Month Experience. In *The Battered Child,* 3d ed., ed. C. H. Kempe and R. Helfer, pp. 373–78. Chicago: University of Chicago Press.

Kennell, J.; Voss, D.; and Klaus, M. 1976. Parent-Infant Bonding. In *Child Abuse and Neglect: The Family and the Community,* ed. R. Helfer and C. H. Kempe. Cambridge, Mass.: Ballinger.

Louis Harris and Associates, Inc. 1982. Study no. 823002. Conducted in May for NCPCA. Working Paper no. 003. Chicago: National Committee for Prevention of Child Abuse.

NCPCA. 1984. *The Size of the Child Abuse Problem.* Working Paper no. 008. Chicago: National Committee for Prevention of Child Abuse.

Nelson, Barbara J. 1984. *Making an Issue of Child Abuse: Political Agenda Setting for Social Problems.* Chicago: University of Chicago Press.

O'Connor, S.; Vietze, P.; Sherrod, K.; Sandler, H.; and Altemeier, W. 1980. Reduced Incidence of Parenting Inadequacy Following Rooming In. *Pediatrics* 66:176–90.

Olds, D. 1980. Improving Formal Services for Mothers and Children. In *Protecting Children from Abuse and Neglect,* ed. J. Garbarino, S. H. Stocking, and Associates. San Francisco: Jossey-Bass.

Olds, D.; Chamberlin, R.; Henderson, C.; and Tatelbaum, R. 1985. The Prevention of Child Abuse and Neglect: A Randomized Trial of Nurse Home Visitation. Rochester, N.Y.: University of Rochester, School of Medicine. Unpublished paper.

Pelton, L., ed. 1981. *The Social Context of Child Abuse and Neglect.* New York: Human Sciences Press.

Straus, M.; Gelles, R.; and Steinmetz, S. 1980. *Behind Closed Doors.* New York: Doubleday.

U.S. Surgeon General. 1980. *Promoting Health/Preventing Disease.* Washington, D.C.: Department of Health and Human Services.

Final Thoughts
and Future Directions

The late 1970s brought considerable optimism to those working in the area of child abuse, neglect, and sexual exploitation. Our knowledge base grew rapidly, treatment programs were increasing in numbers, national and international societies were developing, community and service groups and agencies began to work together, and state and federal priorities clearly showed concern for families and children. This positive atmosphere is depicted in the "Final Thoughts and Future Directions" which appeared at the end of the third edition:

> The six years that have passed since the second edition of *The Battered Child* have seen enormous progress in the study of child abuse and neglect. In every area of our society there is some understanding and involvement. The National Committee for the Prevention of Child Abuse has been formed and many states have developed chapters.[1] Awareness is increasing. Even the children in less-developed countries are being given attention, and their plight from the effects of abuse and neglect is finally being recognized.
>
> Truly, children in many Third World countries face the eminent threats of starvation, chronic malnutrition, and death or disability from a variety of infectious diseases. Priorities in the allocation of national and world resources are such that child abuse must take a secondary role. Surprisingly, there is increasing interest and discussion even in these countries about the problems resulting from abuse and neglect. The International Society for the Prevention of Child Abuse was formed within the past six years, with some 1,000 participants attending the 1978 international meetings in London.[2] Over twenty-five countries were represented. National societies have sprung up in many of these countries since the advent of the international organization. *The International Journal of Child Abuse and Neglect* is now in its third year of publication.
>
> The worldwide movement on the behalf of children has begun. The rights of children are slowly being recognized.
>
> The future looks less bleak than it did in 1974. We hope a fourth edition of *The Battered Child* can be devoted almost entirely to the area of prevention.

During the seven years that have passed since the third edition was published, those working in this field have witnessed considerable setbacks. Federal, and in turn state, pri-

[1] NCPCA, 322 S. Michigan Avenue, Suite 950, Chicago, Illinois 60604.
[2] ISPCA, 1205 Oneida Avenue, Denver, Colorado 80220.

orities have shifted away from families and children. This change has resulted in enormous tangible cuts in support for mental health, protective services, public health, aid to families with dependent chidlren (AFDC), and nutritional programs.

The loss of two dynamic leaders, Henry Kempe and Donna Stone, both of whom had considerable influence at every level, from an individual child who suffered abuse to the Senate Appropriations Committee, has had considerable impact.

These factors have caused many to pause, reflect, and look objectively at the future. What is in store for the million children in the United States, and surely millions more throughout the world, who experience abuse *each year*? In a December 1985 commentary based on these reflections, entitled "Where To Now, Henry?" (4), I identified eight priorities for the future:

1. National and international professional societies must make child abuse, neglect, and sexual exploitation a major priority and demonstrate such with both philosophical and financial commitment.
2. Medical specialties, such as psychiatry, family practice, pediatrics, and medical examiners, must require training experiences in child abuse cases for residents and practitioners in their respective disciplines.
3. A thorough review and reassessment of our protective service programs is mandatory, giving high priority to the dismantling of the unidisciplinary system of service and the building of multidisciplinary assessment and long-term follow-up teams.
4. The political walls which surround service programs and prevent the dissemination of good ideas must be eliminated.
5. Research—truly a re-search—of scores of unanswered questions must be expanded. These include such issues as: an in-depth study of survivors of apparent abuse; the true relationship between family violence of all types and future antisocial and antifamily behavior; the long-term effect of sexual exploitation during a child's developmental years; the rather simple, but unfunded, study of how normally reared children respond to anatomically correct dolls; and the improvement of research techniques to measure interpersonal skills in order to study the effects of prevention programs.
6. The ineffectiveness of the court system for handling child abuse, neglect, sexual exploitation, custody, adoption, and spouse abuse must be faced. Radical change is mandatory if *all* the members of these families are to be treated fairly and adequately.
7. Currently no existing bureaucratic agency has the responsibility to develop, fund, and implement prevention programs. This void must be recognized and eliminated at the federal level. Great debate will ensue when the question is asked, "Who should be so mandated?" Compelling reasons exist to argue against giving this charge to any of the existing state or federal agencies. I have a prevailing fantasy that children's trusts will be developed at the state and federal level with the funds being used *solely* for prevention (3). These trusts would be administered by boards *outside* the existing bureaucratic system with an overall federal board setting basic policy and direction.
8. The education of our professions and the public about child abuse and its outcomes has only begun. Were we to spend a fraction of our advertising dollars on these educational efforts, our country would be well informed about the problem and surely solutions would soon follow.

At least 20% of our young adult population are experiencing the effects of having been reared in adverse environments. Their ability to develop and maintain close personal relationships has been jeopardized. Our society is slow, even dormant, in recognizing the connection between these negative early childhood experiences and future adult behaviors. Each year another million of our children have their developmental "tape" imprinted in a similar fashion.

Recent developments in this field help predict the directions which are likely during the next several years. The emphasis on fetal abuse through the maternal use of drugs, alcohol, and tobacco during pregnancy is becoming a major concern. While the study by Black and Mayer clearly demonstrated the special problems exhibited by parents with alcohol and opiate addiction (1), the adverse effects of these substances upon the fetus is now a matter of record. Chessan and Pascoe recently reported the alarming statistic that women who failed to stop smoking during pregnancy had a significantly higher child abuse reporting rate in the eighteen months following delivery than did women who quit smoking while pregnant (2).

On the other hand, there are some encouraging directions. While poor single mothers are the most likely group to be reported for abuse (table 4.1), a massive social support program for adolescent mothers in Traverse City, Michigan, has demonstrated a dramatic decrease in the second pregnancy rate (5) in this young group. Also on the encouraging side are the recently published results of two national family violence surveys by Straus and Gelles (6). Severe parent-to-child violence decreased between 1975 and 1985, from 140/1,000 children aged three through seventeen to 107/1,000. However, overall family violence, in all forms, has remained the same, that is, 620/1,000. Both figures remain concerning, even with the decrease.

Finally, recent events reveal another distressing trend, that is, the use of the child abuse reporting statute to carry out a vendetta against another person. These occurrences, while infrequent, are on the increase, especially between estranged or divorced parents, one of whom may report the other as abusive, using the child as a pawn. Vindictive reports are also being made by some angry neighbors and abusive parents. The amount of media attention given this issue far exceeds the frequency, often leading to the public obtaining an incorrect picture of this problem. Great caution is needed by protective services in evaluating cases when an abuse report is made by one spouse against the other or an abusive parent against a professional or neighbor. Unfortunately, "great caution" means a thorough diagnostic, multidisciplinary assessment which is not feasible for most protective service units until priority 3 (above) has been accomplished.

The question, "Where to now, Henry?" is not difficult to answer. Are we, collectively and individually, willing to take the bold steps necessary to create a future where children are protected? Millions of children throughout the world await our answer.

R.E.H.

References

1. Black, R., and Mayer, J. 1980. Parents with Special Problems: Alcoholism and Opiate addiction. In *The Battered Child*, 3d ed., ed. C. H. Kempe and R. E. Helfer, ch. 6, Chicago: University of Chicago Press.
2. Chessan, J., and Pascoe, J. 1986. Smoking during Pregnancy and Child Maltreatment. *Int. J. of Biosocial Research*, 8:1–6.
3. Helfer, Ray E. 1978. *Child Abuse: A Plan for Prevention*. National Committee for the Prevention of Child Abuse.

4. ———. 1985. Where To Now, Henry? A Commentary on the Battered Child Syndrome. *Pediatrics* 76:6.

5. ———. 1987. The Perinatal Period: A Window of Opportunity for Enhancing Parent-Infant Communication. *Child Abuse and Neglect, the International Journal* 11:2.

6. Straus, M., and Gelles, R. 1986. Societal Change and Change in Family Violence from 1975 to 1985. *Journal of Marriage and the Family* 48:465–79.

Contributors

Helen Alexander, M.S.W.
2800 Braden
Modesto, California 95356

Claudia A. Carroll, Psy.D.
601 Emerson Street
Denver, Colorado 80218

Anne H. Cohn, D.H.P.
National Committee for the
    Prevention of Child
    Abuse
332 South Michigan
    Avenue
Suite 950
Chicago, Illinois 60604

Donald N. Duquette, J.D.
Child Advocacy Law Clinic
University of Michigan
    Law School
371 Legal Research
    Building
801 Monroe Street
Ann Arbor, Michigan
    48109

Kenneth W. Feldman, M.D.
Department of Pediatrics
University of Washington
2101 East Yester Way
Seattle, Washington 98122

Richard B. Goldbloom,
    M.D.
Department of Pediatrics
I. Walton Killam Hospital
5850 University Avenue
Halifax, Nova Scotia
B3J 3G9 Canada

Carol C. Haase, M.S.W.
Kempe Center
1205 Oneida
Denver, Colorado 80220

Mary Edna Helfer, M.A.
Continuing Medical
    Education
A-112 East Fee Hall
Michigan State University
East Lansing, Michigan
    48824

Ray E. Helfer, M.D.
College of Human
    Medicine
A-254 Life Sciences
Michigan State University
East Lansing, Michigan
    48824

Charles S. Hirsch, M.D.
Department of Forensic
    Pathology

State University of New
    York Medical School
Stony Brook, New York
    11790

David P. H. Jones, M.D.
Park Hospital for Children
Old Road
Oxford OX37LQ England

Glenda Kaufman Kantor,
    Ph.D.
Department of Sociology
Horton Social Science
    Center
University of New
    Hampshire
Durham, New Hampshire
    03824

Ruth S. Kempe, M.D.
Department of Psychiatry
Kempe Center
1205 Oneida
Denver, Colorado 80220

Jill E. Korbin, Ph.D.
Department of
    Anthropology
Case Western Reserve
    University
Cleveland, Ohio 44106

Richard Krugman, M.D.
Department of Pediatrics
Kempe Center
1205 Oneida
Denver, Colorado 80220

Samuel X Radbill, M.D.
River Park House,
  Apt. 1513
3600 Conshohocken
  Avenue
Philadelphia, Pennsylvania
  19131

Barton D. Schmitt, M.D.
Department of Pediatrics
University of Colorado
  School of Medicine
4200 E. Ninth Avenue
Denver, Colorado 80262

Elizabeth A. W. Seagull,
  Ph.D.

Department of Pediatrics
  and Human Development
B-240 Life Sciences
Michigan State University
East Lansing, Michigan
  48824

Det./Lt. Jack R. Shepherd
Michigan State Police
714 South Harrison
East Lansing, Michigan
  48823

Frederic N. Silverman,
  M.D.
Department of Radiology
Stanford University
  Medical Center
Stanford, California 94305

Brandt Steele, M.D.
Department of Psychiatry
Kempe Center

1205 Oneida
Denver, Colorado 80220

Murray A. Straus, Ph.D.
Department of Sociology
Horton Social Science
  Center
University of New
  Hampshire
Durham, New Hampshire
  03824

Ann L. Wilson, Ph.D.
Perinatal Center
Sioux Valley Hospital
Sioux Falls, South Dakota
  57101

Ross E. Zumwalt, M.D.
Department of Pathology
University of Cincinnati
  School of Medicine
231 Bethesda Avenue
Cincinnati, Ohio 45267

Index